JOSS WHEDON

Zack **Whedon** • Chris **Roberson** • Georges **Jeanty** • Karl **Story** • Laura **Martin** • Wes **Dzioba**

firefly™

LEGACY EDITION BOOK TWO

Collection Designer
Scott Newman

Original Series Editors
Scott Allie, **Sierra Hahn**,
Freddye Miller, **Jim Gibbons**

Legacy Edition Assistant Editor
Gavin Gronenthal

Legacy Edition Editors
Jeanine Schaefer and **Sierra Hahn**

Special Thanks to
Nicole Speigel and **Carol Roeder**
at **Twentieth Century Fox**,
Becca J. Sadowsky, **Chris Harbert**.

Originally published by
Dark Horse Comics

Ross Richie CEO & Founder
Joy Huffman CFO
Matt Gagnon Editor-in-Chief
Filip Sablik President, Publishing & Marketing
Stephen Christy President, Development
Lance Kreiter Vice President, Licensing & Merchandising
Arune Singh Vice President, Marketing
Bryce Carlson Vice President, Editorial & Creative Strategy
Scott Newman Manager, Production Design
Kate Henning Manager, Operations
Spencer Simpson Manager, Sales
Elyse Strandberg Manager, Finance
Sierra Hahn Executive Editor
Jeanine Schaefer Executive Editor
Dafna Pleban Senior Editor
Shannon Watters Senior Editor
Eric Harburn Senior Editor
Chris Rosa Editor
Matthew Levine Editor
Sophie Philips-Roberts Associate Editor
Amanda LaFranco Associate Editor
Jonathan Manning Associate Editor
Gavin Gronenthal Assistant Editor
Gwen Waller Assistant Editor
Allyson Gronowitz Assistant Editor
Jillian Crab Design Coordinator
Michelle Ankley Design Coordinator
Kara Leopard Production Designer
Marie Krupina Production Designer
Grace Park Production Designer
Chelsea Roberts Production Design Assistant
Samantha Knapp Production Design Assistant
José Meza Live Events Lead
Stephanie Hocutt Digital Marketing Lead
Esther Kim Marketing Coordinator
Cat O'Grady Digital Marketing Coordinator
Amanda Lawson Marketing Assistant
Holly Aitchison Digital Sales Coordinator
Morgan Perry Retail Sales Coordinator
Megan Christopher Operations Coordinator
Rodrigo Hernandez Mailroom Assistant
Zipporah Smith Operations Assistant
Sabrina Lesin Accounting Assistant
Breanna Sarpy Executive Assistant

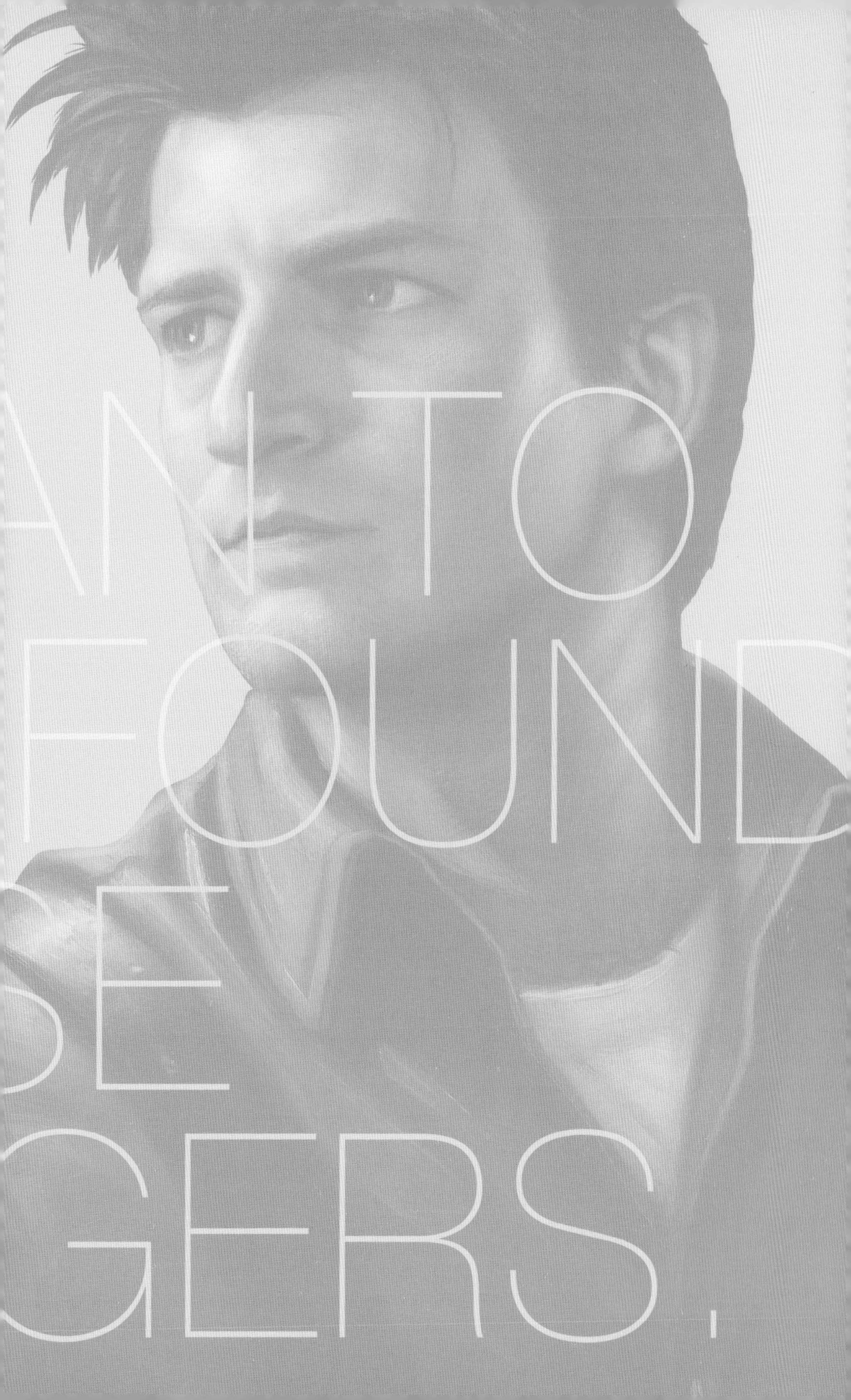
N TO
OUND
E
GERS.

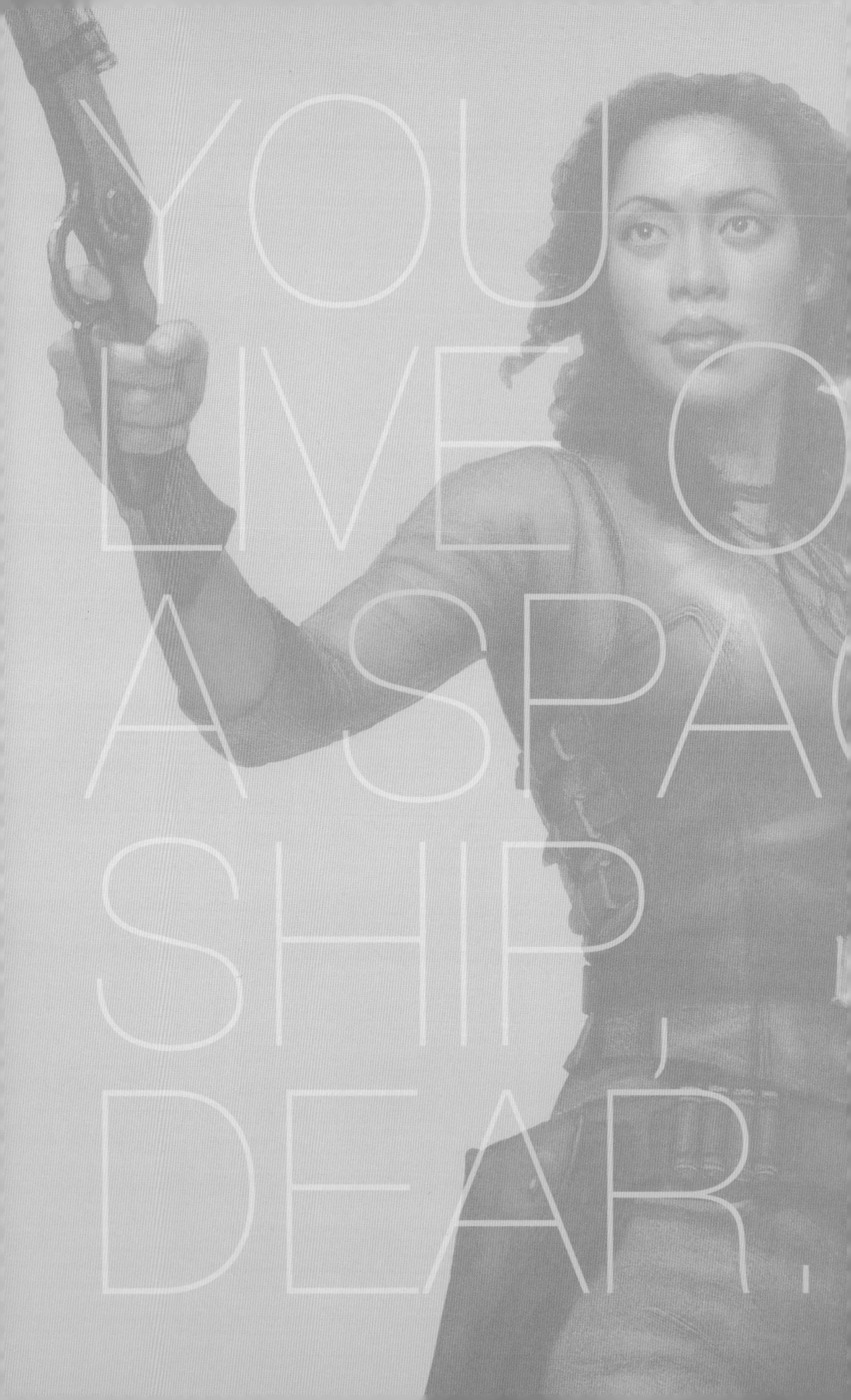
YOU
LIVE O
A SPA
SHIP,
DEAR.

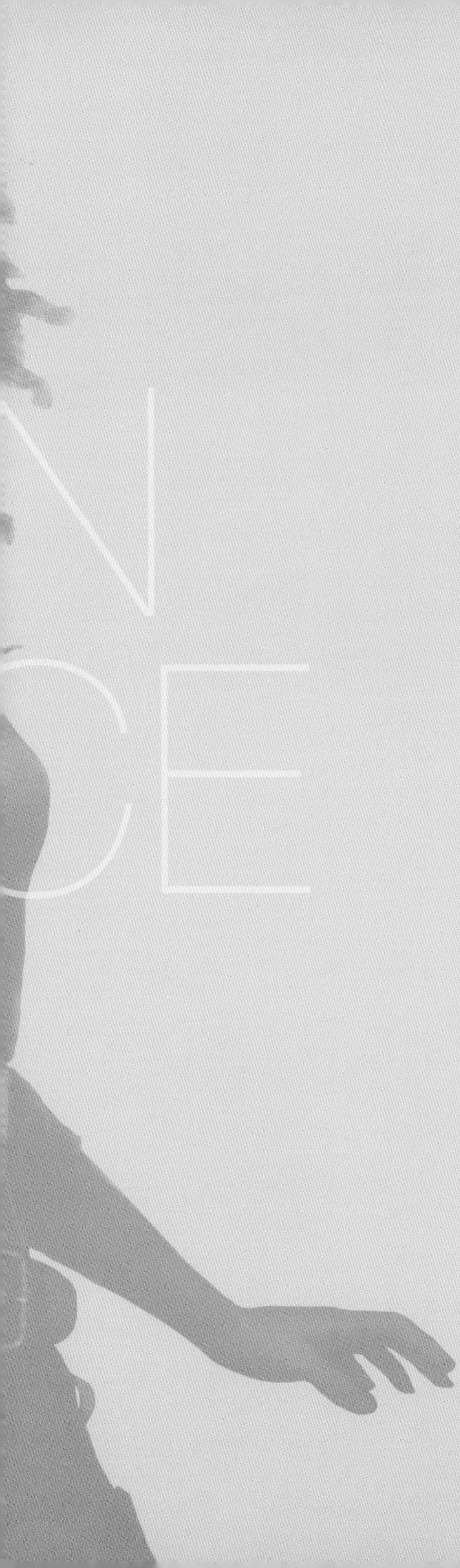

Created By
Joss Whedon

LEAVES ON THE WIND
Written by
Zack Whedon
Pencils by
Georges Jeanty
Inks by
Karl Story
Colored by
Laura Martin
with **Lovern Kindzierski** (Chapter Six)
Lettered by
Michael Heisler

THE WARRIOR AND THE WIND
Written by
Chris Roberson
Illustrated by
Stephen Byrne
Lettered by
Michael Heisler

NO POWER IN THE 'VERSE
Written by
Chris Roberson
Pencils by
Georges Jeanty
Inks by
Karl Story
Colored by
Wes Dzioba
Lettered by
Michael Heisler

Cover by
Nimit Malavia

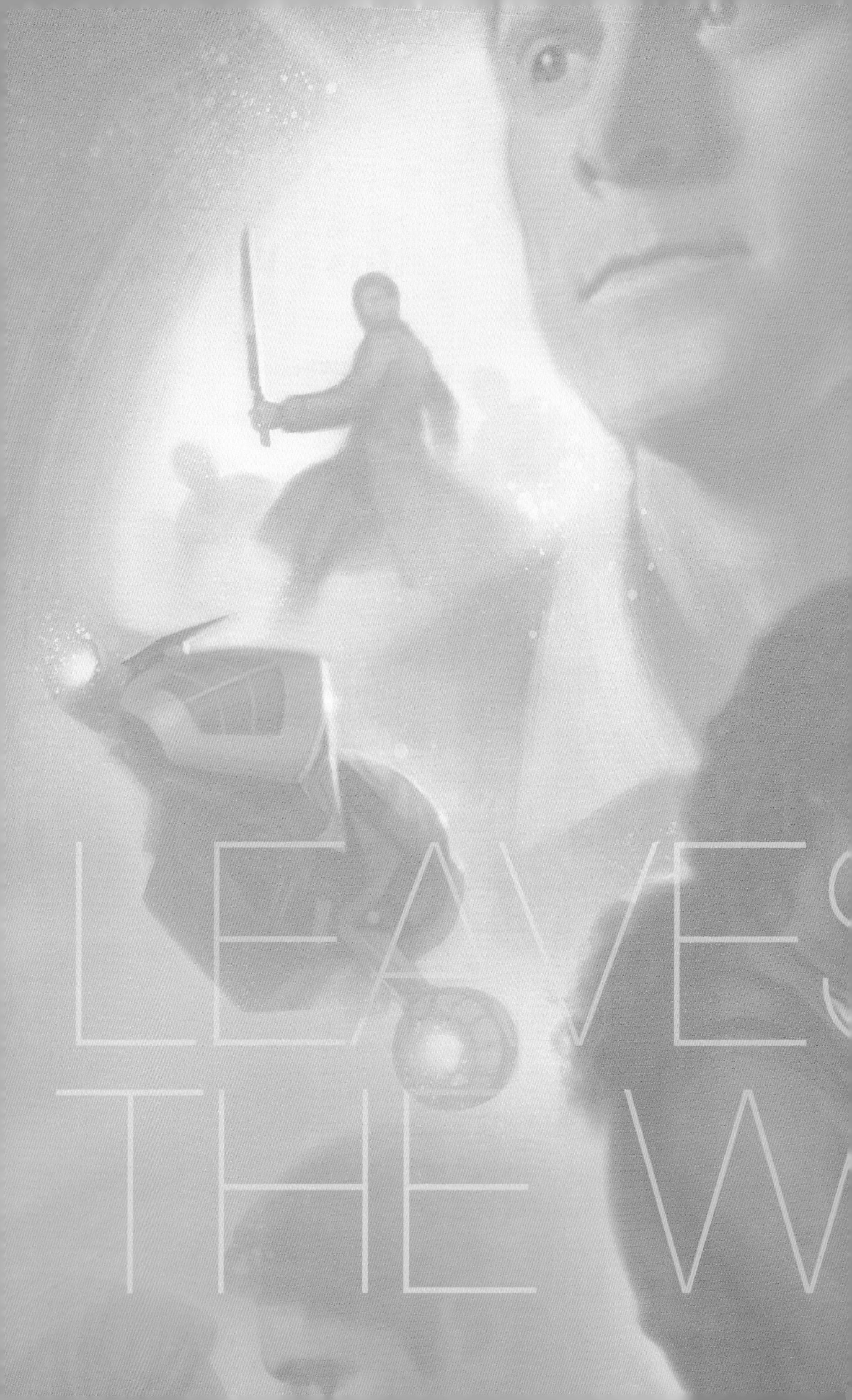
LEAVES
THE

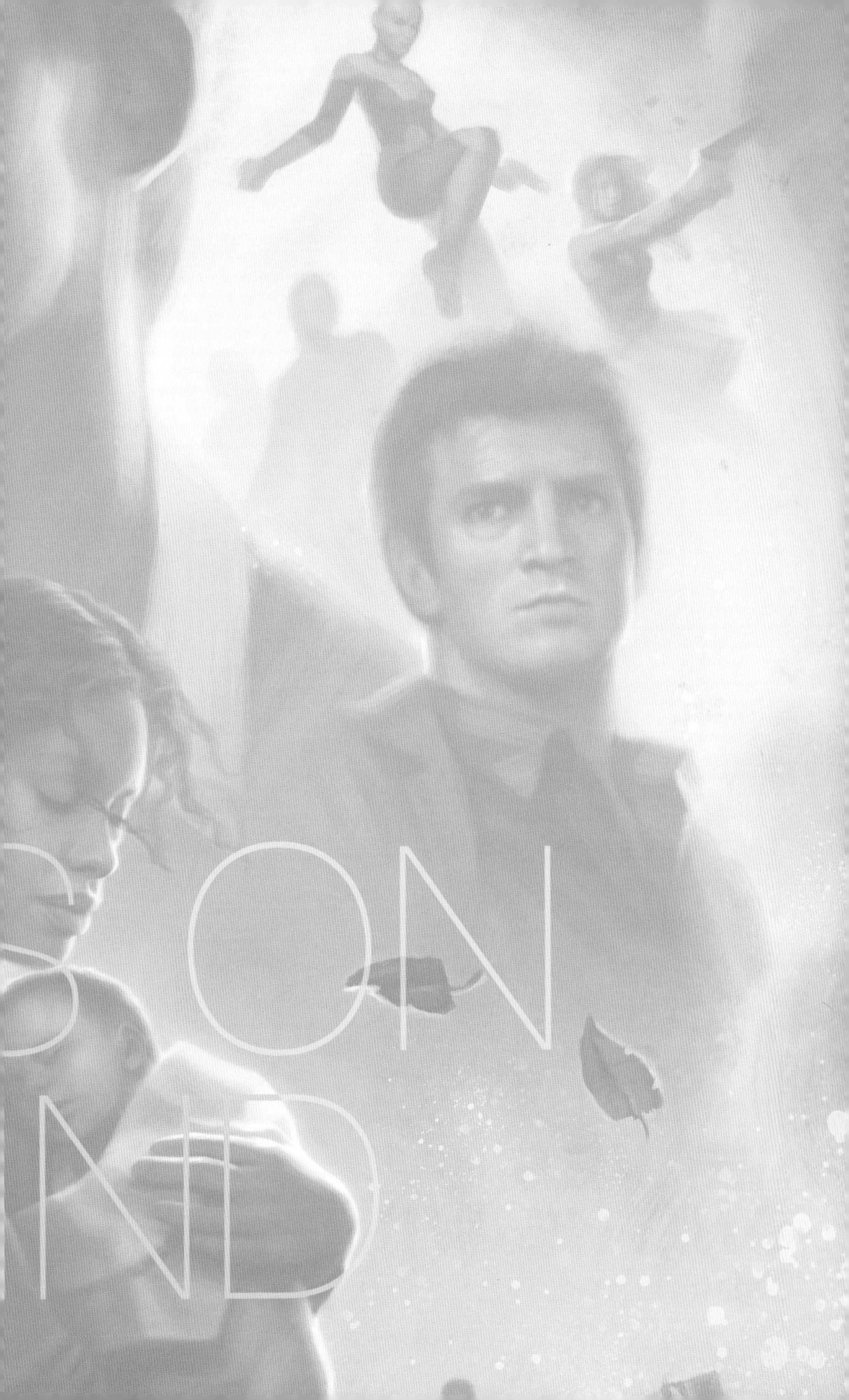
ON
ND

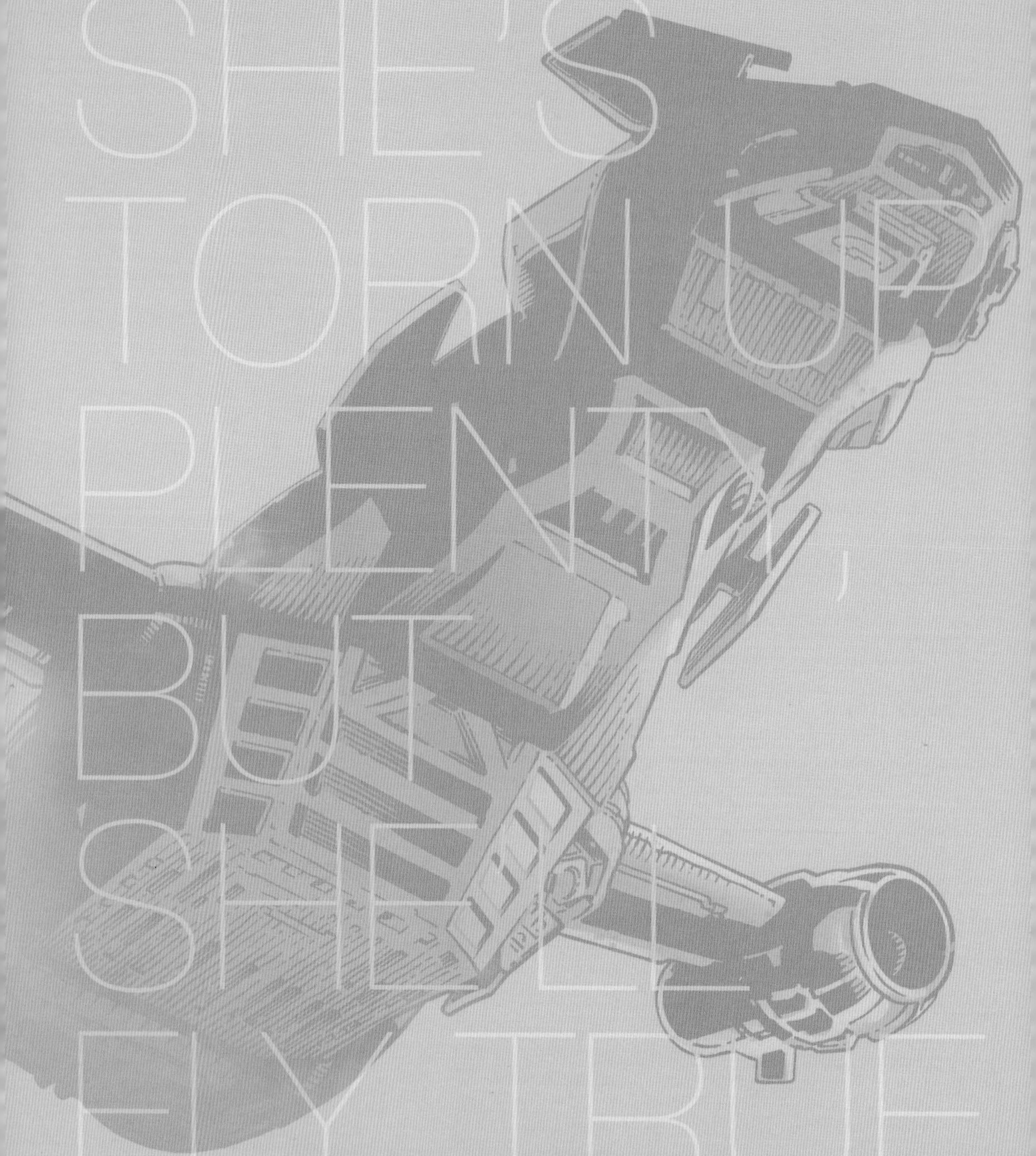
SHE'S
TORN UP
PLENTY,
BUT
SHE'LL
FLY TRUE.

LEAVES ON THE WIND

CHAPTER ONE

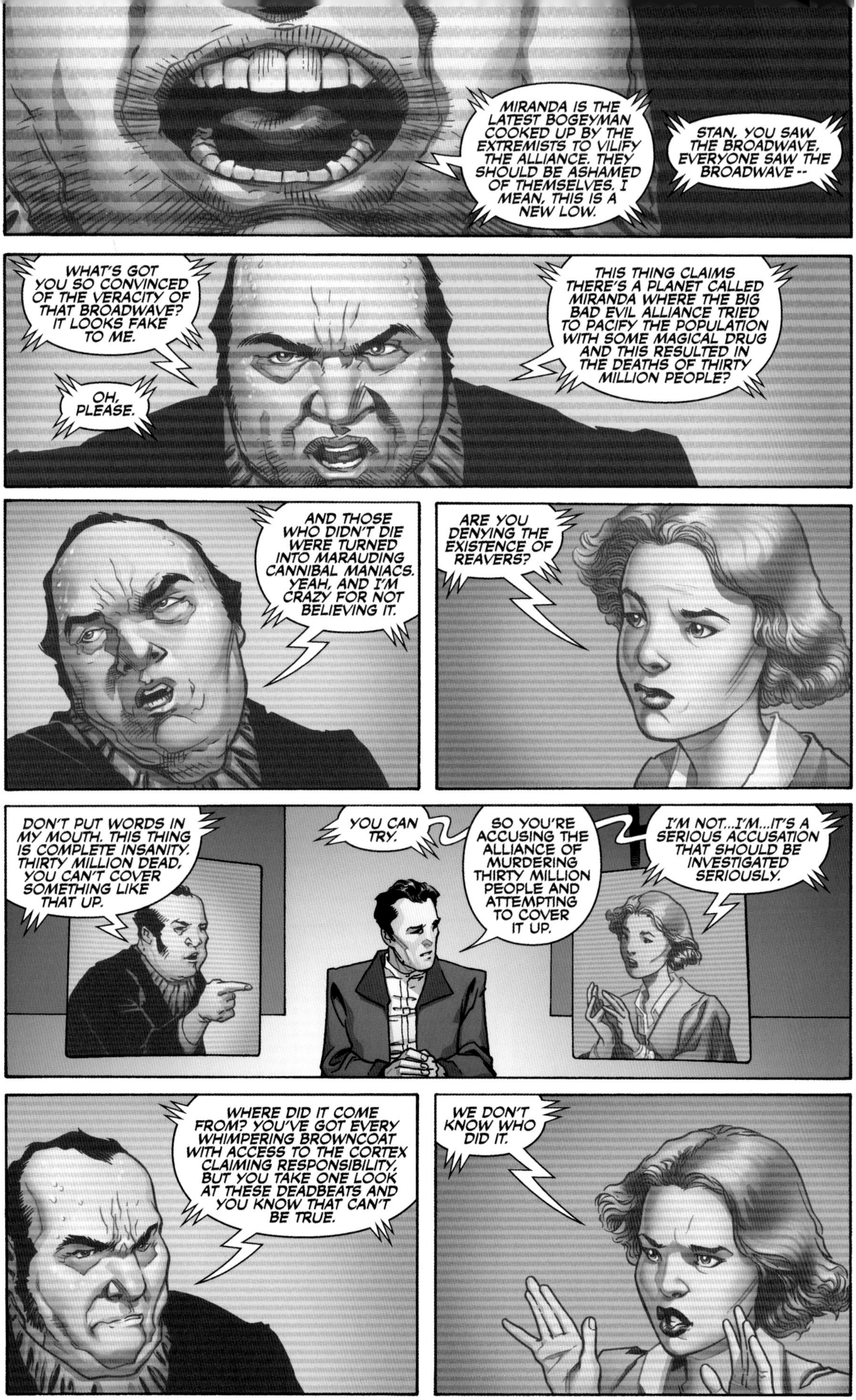
MIRANDA IS THE LATEST BOGEYMAN COOKED UP BY THE EXTREMISTS TO VILIFY THE ALLIANCE. THEY SHOULD BE ASHAMED OF THEMSELVES. I MEAN, THIS IS A NEW LOW.
STAN, YOU SAW THE BROADWAVE, EVERYONE SAW THE BROADWAVE --
WHAT'S GOT YOU SO CONVINCED OF THE VERACITY OF THAT BROADWAVE? IT LOOKS FAKE TO ME.
OH, PLEASE.
THIS THING CLAIMS THERE'S A PLANET CALLED MIRANDA WHERE THE BIG BAD EVIL ALLIANCE TRIED TO PACIFY THE POPULATION WITH SOME MAGICAL DRUG AND THIS RESULTED IN THE DEATHS OF THIRTY MILLION PEOPLE?
AND THOSE WHO DIDN'T DIE WERE TURNED INTO MARAUDING CANNIBAL MANIACS. YEAH, AND I'M CRAZY FOR NOT BELIEVING IT.
ARE YOU DENYING THE EXISTENCE OF REAVERS?
DON'T PUT WORDS IN MY MOUTH. THIS THING IS COMPLETE INSANITY. THIRTY MILLION DEAD, YOU CAN'T COVER SOMETHING LIKE THAT UP.
YOU CAN TRY.
SO YOU'RE ACCUSING THE ALLIANCE OF MURDERING THIRTY MILLION PEOPLE AND ATTEMPTING TO COVER IT UP.
I'M NOT...I'M...IT'S A SERIOUS ACCUSATION THAT SHOULD BE INVESTIGATED SERIOUSLY.
WHERE DID IT COME FROM? YOU'VE GOT EVERY WHIMPERING BROWNCOAT WITH ACCESS TO THE CORTEX CLAIMING RESPONSIBILITY, BUT YOU TAKE ONE LOOK AT THESE DEADBEATS AND YOU KNOW THAT CAN'T BE TRUE.
WE DON'T KNOW WHO DID IT.

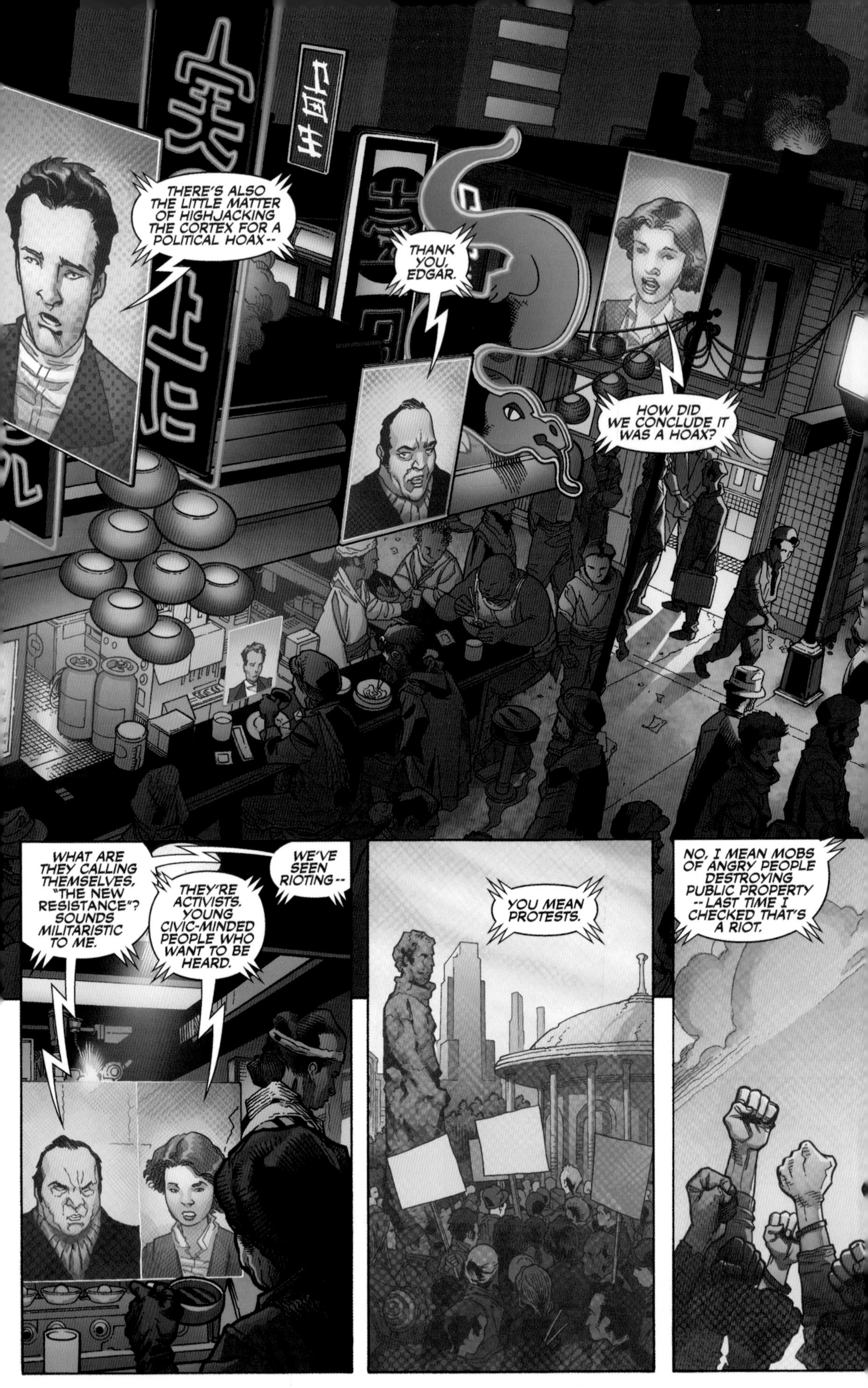
THERE'S ALSO THE LITTLE MATTER OF HIGHJACKING THE CORTEX FOR A POLITICAL HOAX--
THANK YOU, EDGAR.
HOW DID WE CONCLUDE IT WAS A HOAX?
WHAT ARE THEY CALLING THEMSELVES, "THE NEW RESISTANCE"? SOUNDS MILITARISTIC TO ME.
THEY'RE ACTIVISTS. YOUNG CIVIC-MINDED PEOPLE WHO WANT TO BE HEARD.
WE'VE SEEN RIOTING--
YOU MEAN PROTESTS.
NO, I MEAN MOBS OF ANGRY PEOPLE DESTROYING PUBLIC PROPERTY --LAST TIME I CHECKED THAT'S A RIOT.

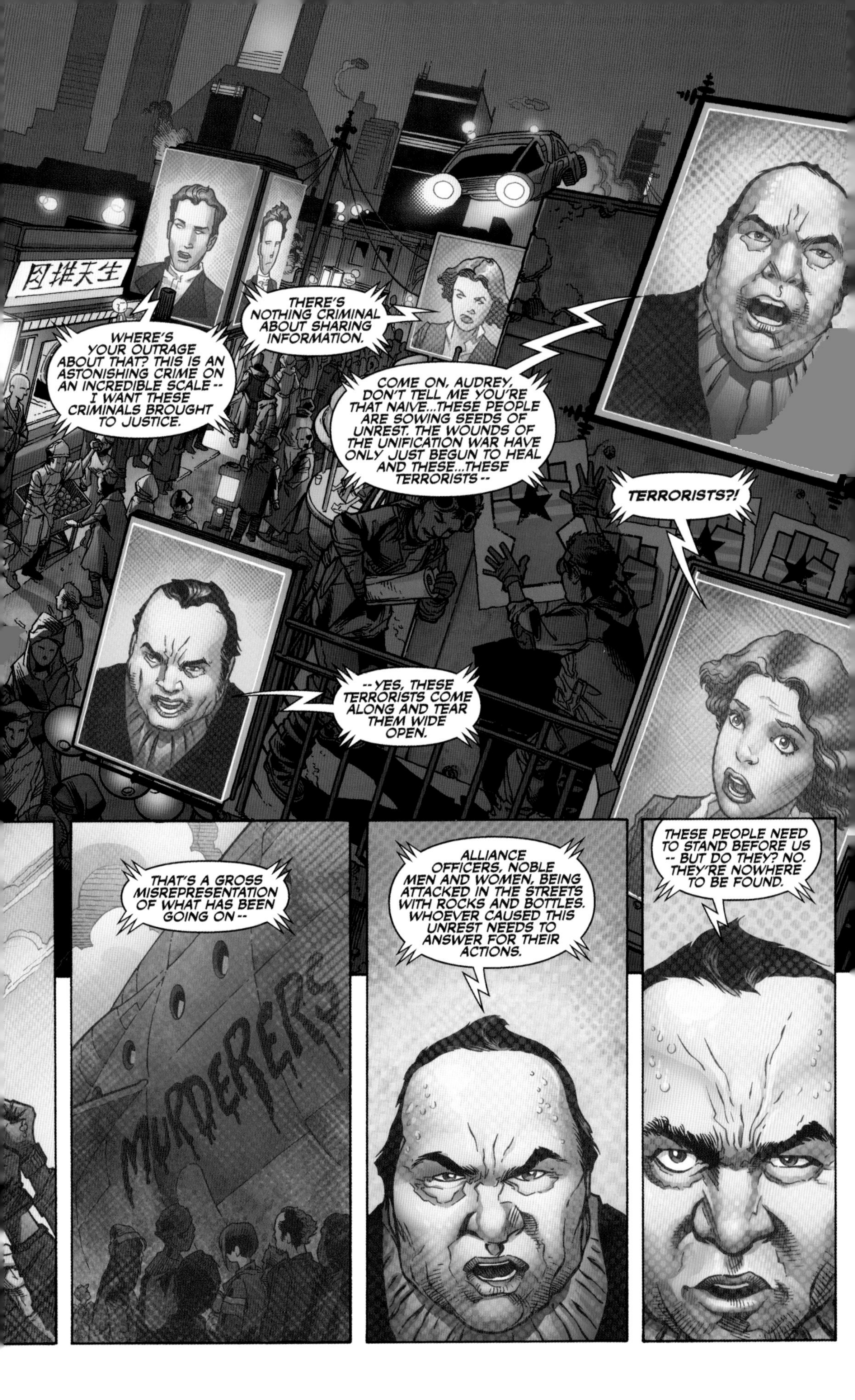
WHERE'S YOUR OUTRAGE ABOUT THAT? THIS IS AN ASTONISHING CRIME ON AN INCREDIBLE SCALE -- I WANT THESE CRIMINALS BROUGHT TO JUSTICE.
THERE'S NOTHING CRIMINAL ABOUT SHARING INFORMATION.
COME ON, AUDREY, DON'T TELL ME YOU'RE THAT NAIVE...THESE PEOPLE ARE SOWING SEEDS OF UNREST. THE WOUNDS OF THE UNIFICATION WAR HAVE ONLY JUST BEGUN TO HEAL AND THESE...THESE TERRORISTS --
TERRORISTS?!
--YES, THESE TERRORISTS COME ALONG AND TEAR THEM WIDE OPEN.
THAT'S A GROSS MISREPRESENTATION OF WHAT HAS BEEN GOING ON --
MURDERERS
ALLIANCE OFFICERS, NOBLE MEN AND WOMEN, BEING ATTACKED IN THE STREETS WITH ROCKS AND BOTTLES. WHOEVER CAUSED THIS UNREST NEEDS TO ANSWER FOR THEIR ACTIONS.
THESE PEOPLE NEED TO STAND BEFORE US -- BUT DO THEY? NO. THEY'RE NOWHERE TO BE FOUND.

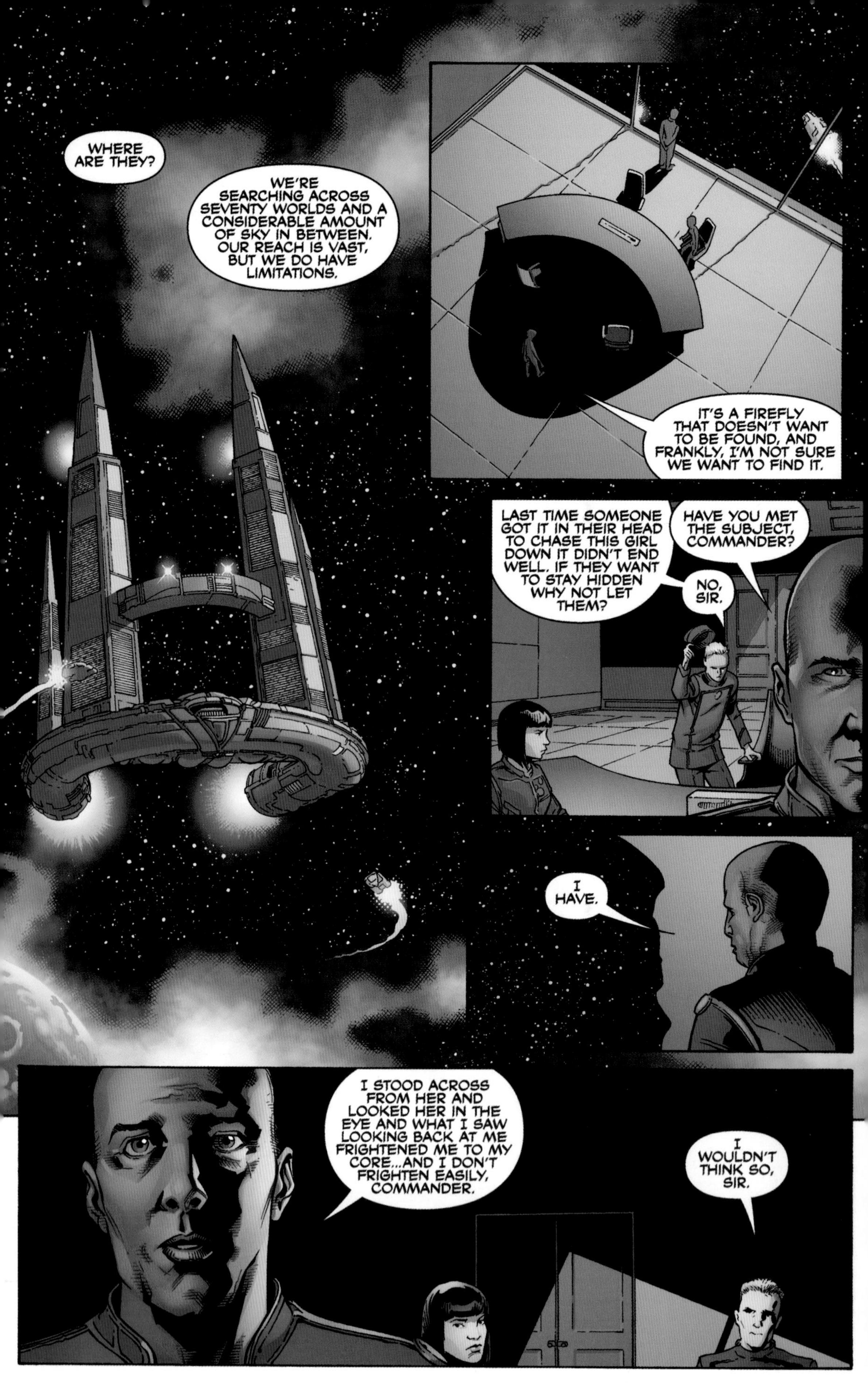
WHERE ARE THEY?
WE'RE SEARCHING ACROSS SEVENTY WORLDS AND A CONSIDERABLE AMOUNT OF SKY IN BETWEEN. OUR REACH IS VAST, BUT WE DO HAVE LIMITATIONS.
IT'S A FIREFLY THAT DOESN'T WANT TO BE FOUND, AND FRANKLY, I'M NOT SURE WE WANT TO FIND IT.
LAST TIME SOMEONE GOT IT IN THEIR HEAD TO CHASE THIS GIRL DOWN IT DIDN'T END WELL. IF THEY WANT TO STAY HIDDEN WHY NOT LET THEM?
HAVE YOU MET THE SUBJECT, COMMANDER?
NO, SIR.
I HAVE.
I STOOD ACROSS FROM HER AND LOOKED HER IN THE EYE AND WHAT I SAW LOOKING BACK AT ME FRIGHTENED ME TO MY CORE...AND I DON'T FRIGHTEN EASILY, COMMANDER.
I WOULDN'T THINK SO, SIR.

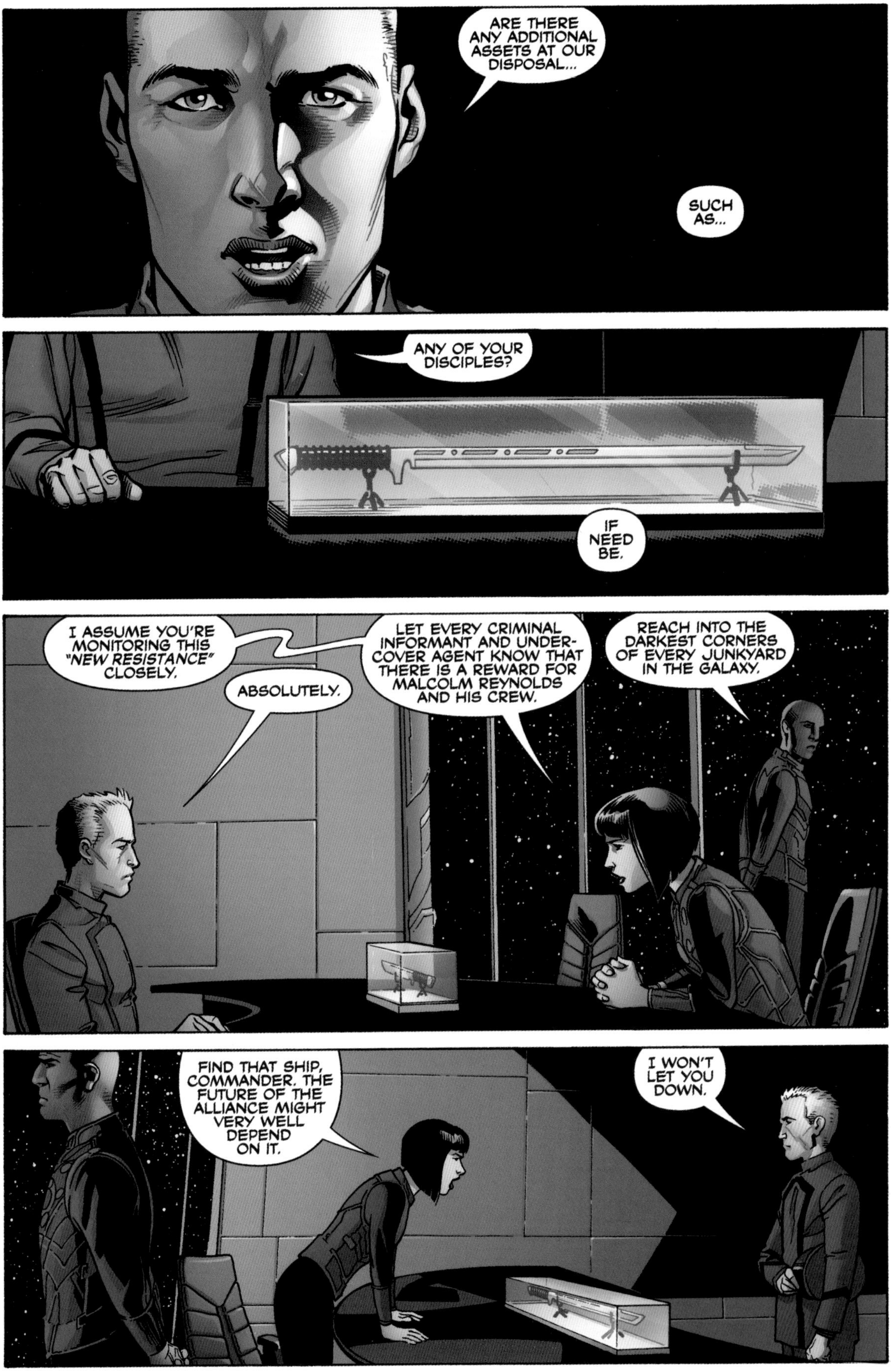
ARE THERE ANY ADDITIONAL ASSETS AT OUR DISPOSAL...
SUCH AS...
ANY OF YOUR DISCIPLES?
IF NEED BE.
I ASSUME YOU'RE MONITORING THIS *"NEW RESISTANCE"* CLOSELY.
ABSOLUTELY.
LET EVERY CRIMINAL INFORMANT AND UNDER-COVER AGENT KNOW THAT THERE IS A REWARD FOR MALCOLM REYNOLDS AND HIS CREW.
REACH INTO THE DARKEST CORNERS OF EVERY JUNKYARD IN THE GALAXY.
FIND THAT SHIP, COMMANDER. THE FUTURE OF THE ALLIANCE MIGHT VERY WELL DEPEND ON IT.
I WON'T LET YOU DOWN.

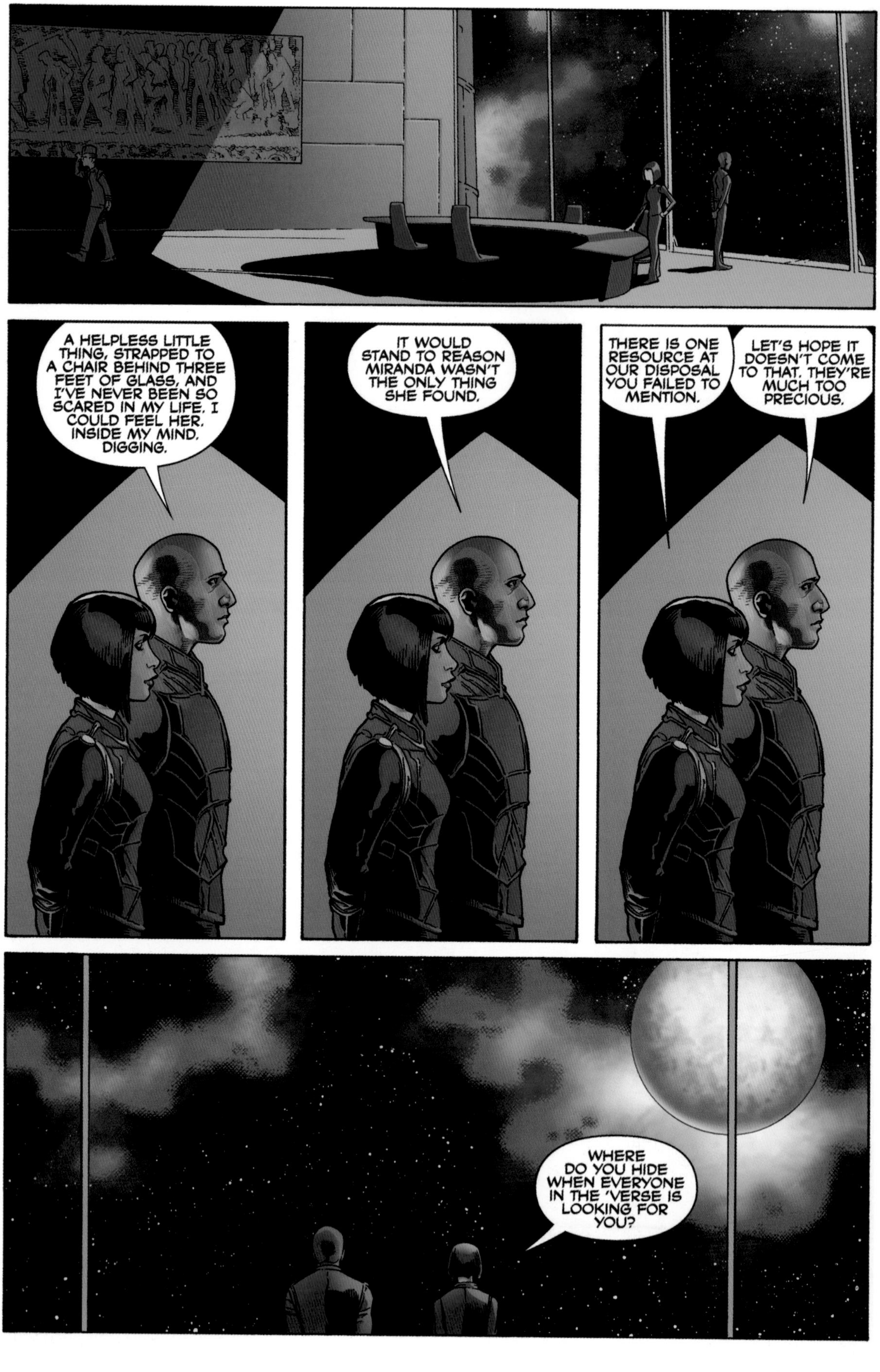
A HELPLESS LITTLE THING, STRAPPED TO A CHAIR BEHIND THREE FEET OF GLASS, AND I'VE NEVER BEEN SO SCARED IN MY LIFE. I COULD FEEL HER. INSIDE MY MIND. DIGGING.
IT WOULD STAND TO REASON MIRANDA WASN'T THE ONLY THING SHE FOUND.
THERE IS ONE RESOURCE AT OUR DISPOSAL YOU FAILED TO MENTION.
LET'S HOPE IT DOESN'T COME TO THAT. THEY'RE MUCH TOO PRECIOUS.
WHERE DO YOU HIDE WHEN EVERYONE IN THE 'VERSE IS LOOKING FOR YOU?

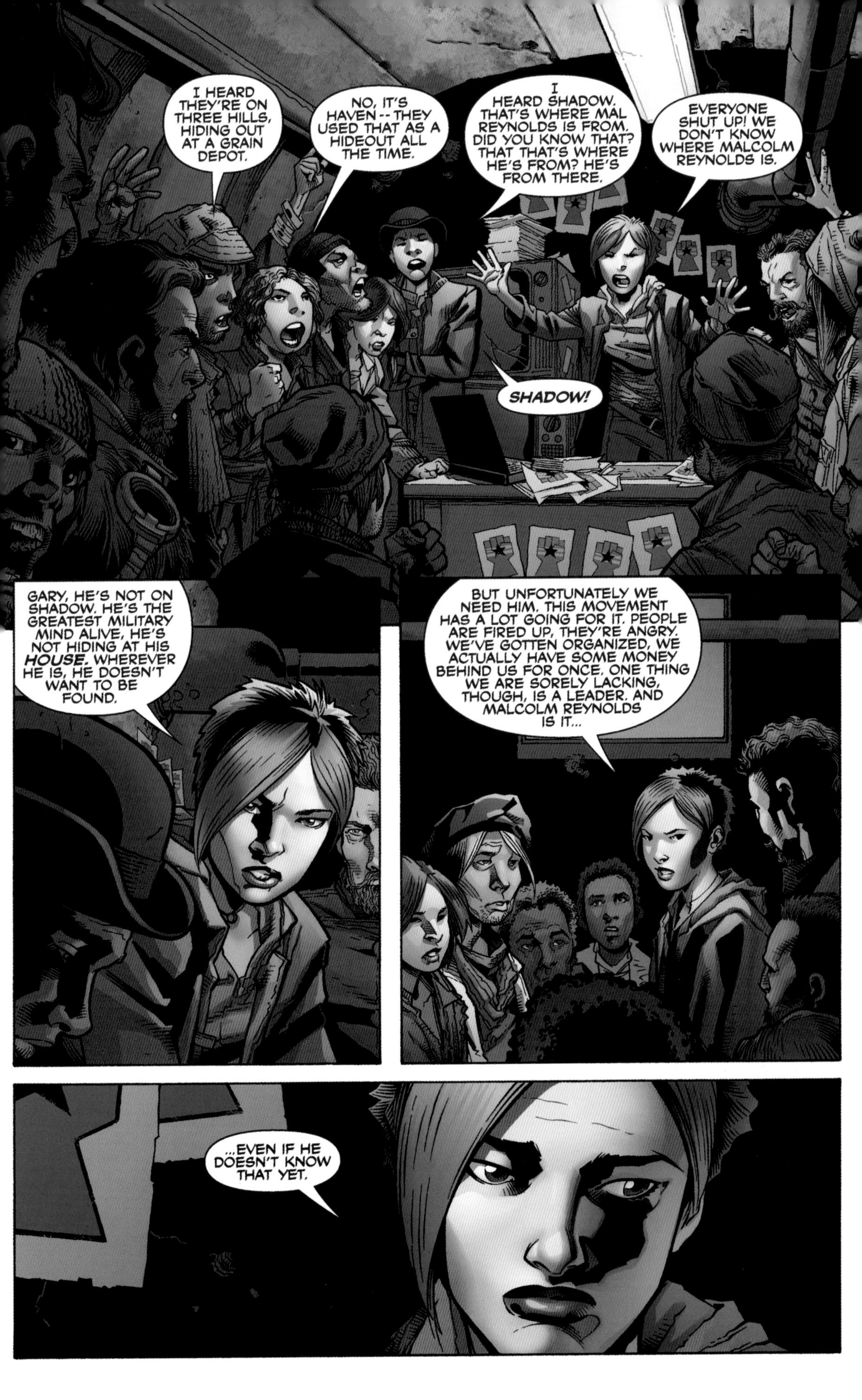
I HEARD THEY'RE ON THREE HILLS, HIDING OUT AT A GRAIN DEPOT.
NO, IT'S HAVEN -- THEY USED THAT AS A HIDEOUT ALL THE TIME.
I HEARD SHADOW. THAT'S WHERE MAL REYNOLDS IS FROM. DID YOU KNOW THAT? THAT THAT'S WHERE HE'S FROM? HE'S FROM THERE.
EVERYONE SHUT UP! WE DON'T KNOW WHERE MALCOLM REYNOLDS IS.
SHADOW!
GARY, HE'S NOT ON SHADOW. HE'S THE GREATEST MILITARY MIND ALIVE, HE'S NOT HIDING AT HIS *HOUSE.* WHEREVER HE IS, HE DOESN'T WANT TO BE FOUND.
BUT UNFORTUNATELY WE NEED HIM. THIS MOVEMENT HAS A LOT GOING FOR IT. PEOPLE ARE FIRED UP, THEY'RE ANGRY. WE'VE GOTTEN ORGANIZED, WE ACTUALLY HAVE SOME MONEY BEHIND US FOR ONCE. ONE THING WE ARE SORELY LACKING, THOUGH, IS A LEADER. AND MALCOLM REYNOLDS IS IT...
...EVEN IF HE DOESN'T KNOW THAT YET.

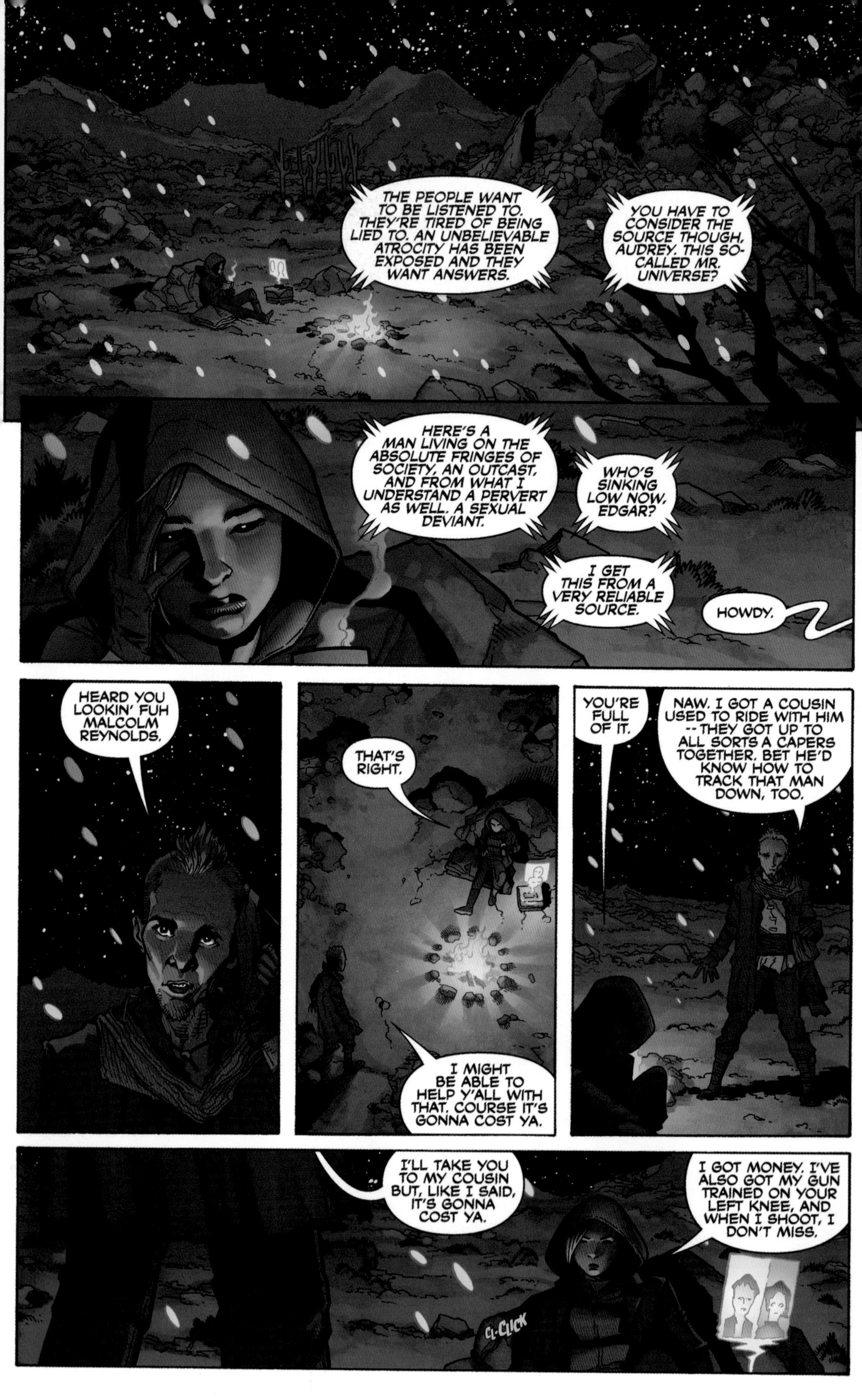
THE PEOPLE WANT TO BE LISTENED TO. THEY'RE TIRED OF BEING LIED TO. AN UNBELIEVABLE ATROCITY HAS BEEN EXPOSED AND THEY WANT ANSWERS.
YOU HAVE TO CONSIDER THE SOURCE THOUGH, AUDREY. THIS SO-CALLED MR. UNIVERSE?
HERE'S A MAN LIVING ON THE ABSOLUTE FRINGES OF SOCIETY, AN OUTCAST, AND FROM WHAT I UNDERSTAND A PERVERT AS WELL. A SEXUAL DEVIANT.
WHO'S SINKING LOW NOW, EDGAR?
I GET THIS FROM A VERY RELIABLE SOURCE.
HOWDY.
HEARD YOU LOOKIN' FUH MALCOLM REYNOLDS.
THAT'S RIGHT.
I MIGHT BE ABLE TO HELP Y'ALL WITH THAT. COURSE IT'S GONNA COST YA.
YOU'RE FULL OF IT.
NAW. I GOT A COUSIN USED TO RIDE WITH HIM -- THEY GOT UP TO ALL SORTS A CAPERS TOGETHER. BET HE'D KNOW HOW TO TRACK THAT MAN DOWN, TOO.
I'LL TAKE YOU TO MY COUSIN BUT, LIKE I SAID, IT'S GONNA COST YA.
I GOT MONEY. I'VE ALSO GOT MY GUN TRAINED ON YOUR LEFT KNEE, AND WHEN I SHOOT, I DON'T MISS.
CL-CLICK

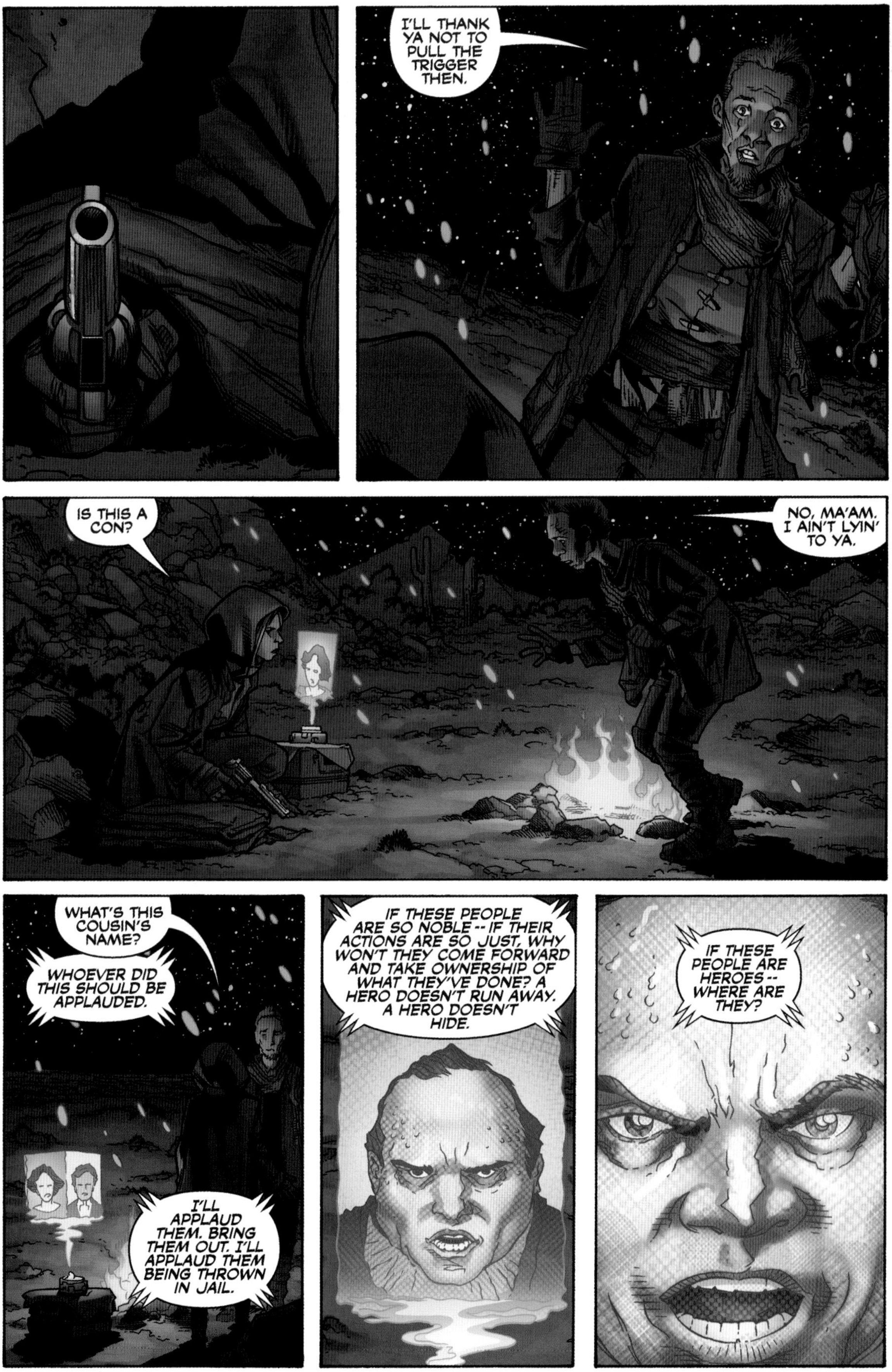
I'LL THANK YA NOT TO PULL THE TRIGGER THEN.
IS THIS A CON?
NO, MA'AM. I AIN'T LYIN' TO YA.
WHAT'S THIS COUSIN'S NAME?
WHOEVER DID THIS SHOULD BE APPLAUDED.
I'LL APPLAUD THEM. BRING THEM OUT. I'LL APPLAUD THEM BEING THROWN IN JAIL.
IF THESE PEOPLE ARE SO NOBLE -- IF THEIR ACTIONS ARE SO JUST, WHY WON'T THEY COME FORWARD AND TAKE OWNERSHIP OF WHAT THEY'VE DONE? A HERO DOESN'T RUN AWAY. A HERO DOESN'T HIDE.
IF THESE PEOPLE ARE HEROES -- WHERE ARE THEY?

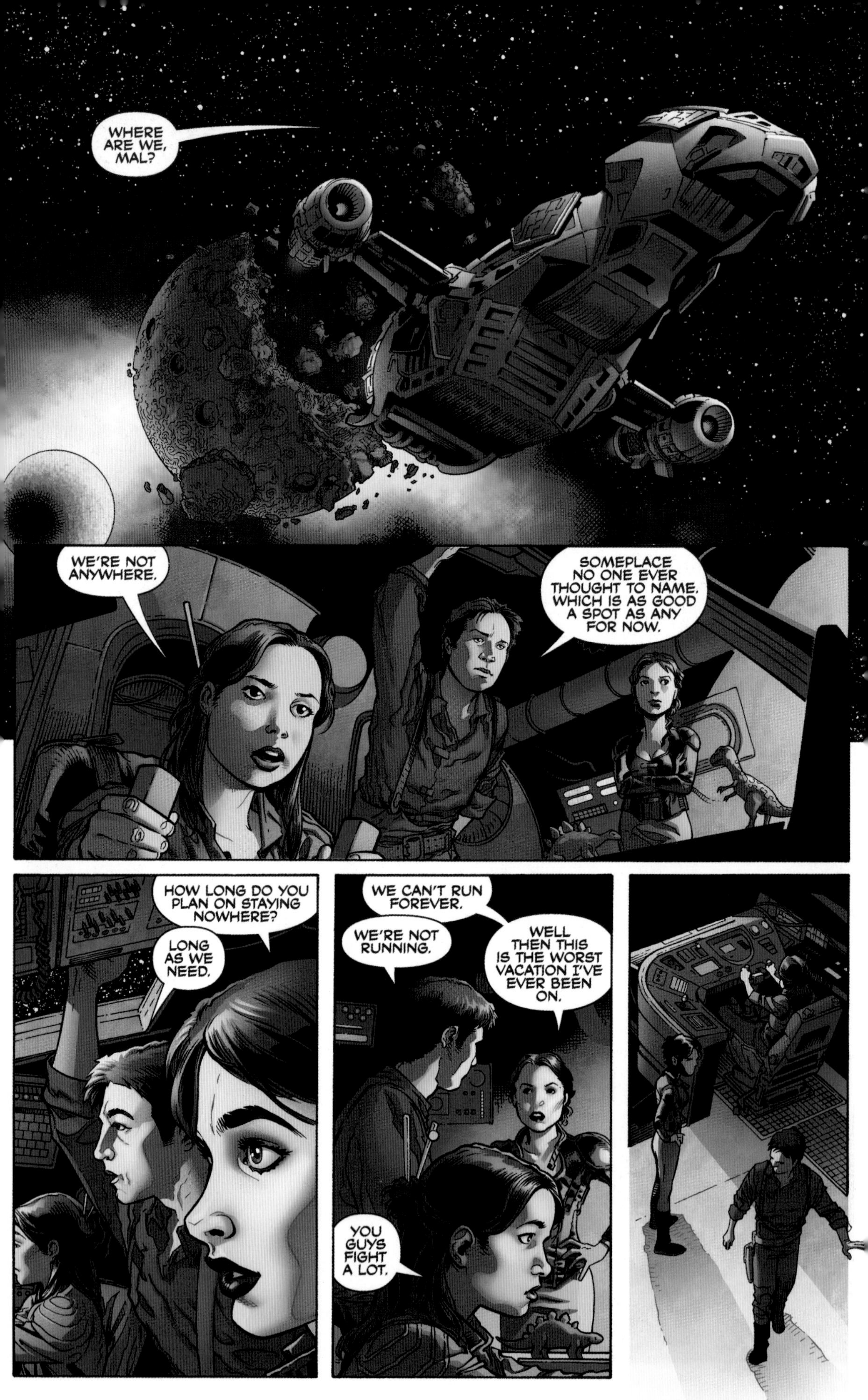
WHERE ARE WE, MAL?
WE'RE NOT ANYWHERE.
SOMEPLACE NO ONE EVER THOUGHT TO NAME. WHICH IS AS GOOD A SPOT AS ANY FOR NOW.
HOW LONG DO YOU PLAN ON STAYING NOWHERE?
LONG AS WE NEED.
WE CAN'T RUN FOREVER.
WE'RE NOT RUNNING.
WELL THEN THIS IS THE WORST VACATION I'VE EVER BEEN ON.
YOU GUYS FIGHT A LOT.

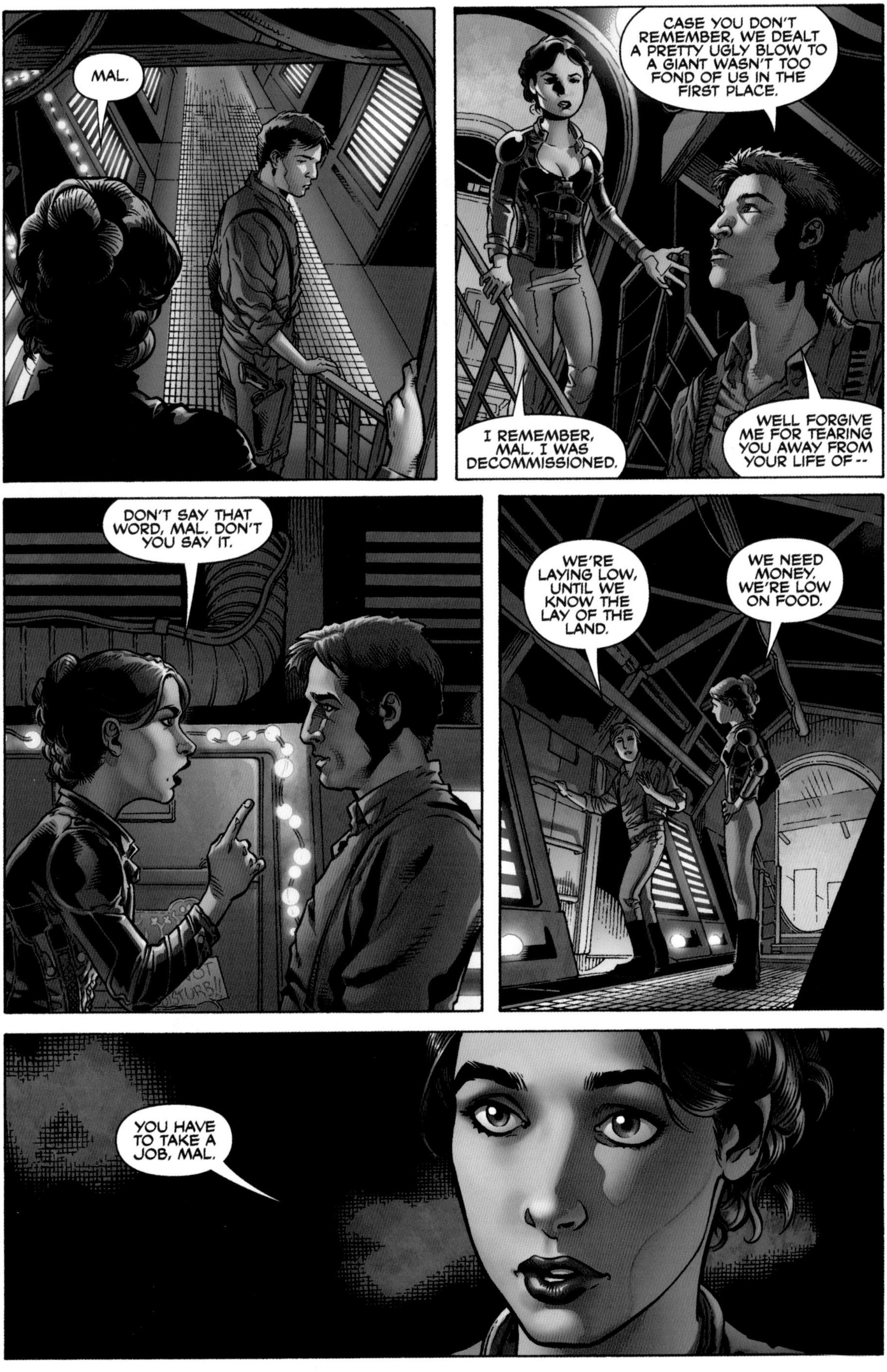
MAL.
CASE YOU DON'T REMEMBER, WE DEALT A PRETTY UGLY BLOW TO A GIANT WASN'T TOO FOND OF US IN THE FIRST PLACE.
I REMEMBER, MAL. I WAS DECOMMISSIONED.
WELL FORGIVE ME FOR TEARING YOU AWAY FROM YOUR LIFE OF --
DON'T SAY THAT WORD, MAL. DON'T YOU SAY IT.
WE'RE LAYING LOW, UNTIL WE KNOW THE LAY OF THE LAND.
WE NEED MONEY. WE'RE LOW ON FOOD.
YOU HAVE TO TAKE A JOB, MAL.

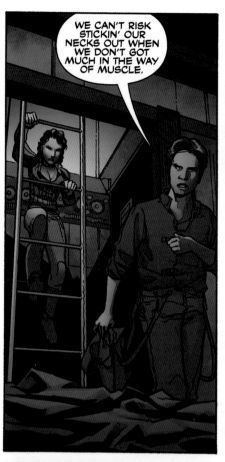

WE CAN'T RISK STICKIN' OUR NECKS OUT WHEN WE DON'T GOT MUCH IN THE WAY OF MUSCLE.

ZOE'S OUT, OBVIOUSLY.

WHAT ABOUT RIVER.

THAT GIRL'S HEAD IS A MINEFIELD. WE'RE GOING ON EIGHT MONTHS NOW THAT SHE HASN'T SPOKEN IN A GORRAM RIDDLE AND I AIM TO KEEP THAT STREAK ALIVE...

...ESPECIALLY WHEN SHE'S GOT HER HANDS ON THE YOKE OF MY BOAT.

I CAN'T BELIEVE I'M SAYING THIS, BUT I ACTUALLY MISS JAYNE.

JAYNE DID WHAT'S RIGHT FOR HIM. WE'D BE SMART TO DO THE SAME.

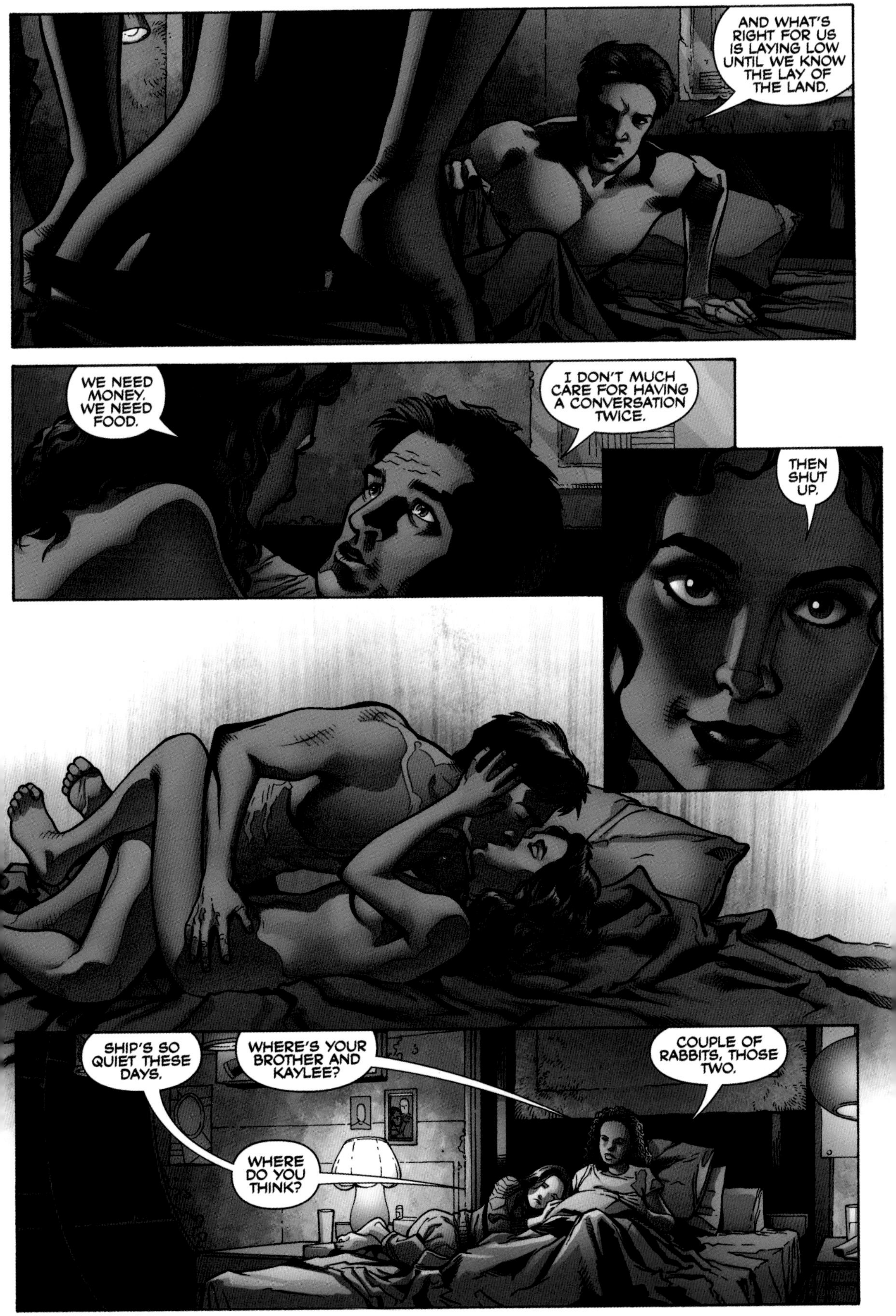
AND WHAT'S RIGHT FOR US IS LAYING LOW UNTIL WE KNOW THE LAY OF THE LAND.
WE NEED MONEY. WE NEED FOOD.
I DON'T MUCH CARE FOR HAVING A CONVERSATION TWICE.
THEN SHUT UP.
SHIP'S SO QUIET THESE DAYS.
WHERE'S YOUR BROTHER AND KAYLEE?
WHERE DO YOU THINK?
COUPLE OF RABBITS, THOSE TWO.

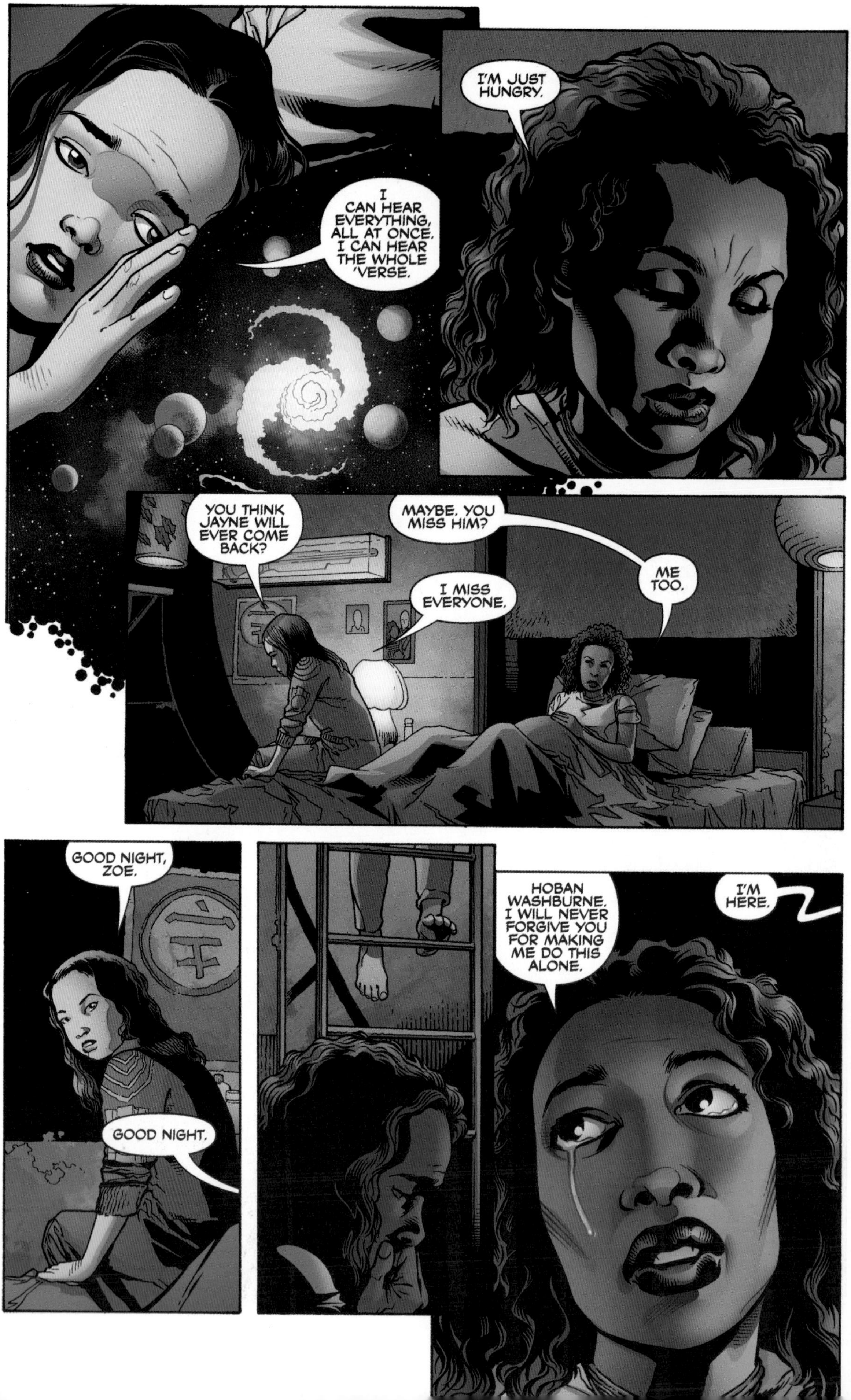
I CAN HEAR EVERYTHING, ALL AT ONCE. I CAN HEAR THE WHOLE 'VERSE.
I'M JUST HUNGRY.
YOU THINK JAYNE WILL EVER COME BACK?
MAYBE. YOU MISS HIM?
I MISS EVERYONE.
ME TOO.
GOOD NIGHT, ZOE.
GOOD NIGHT.
HOBAN WASHBURNE. I WILL NEVER FORGIVE YOU FOR MAKING ME DO THIS ALONE.
I'M HERE.

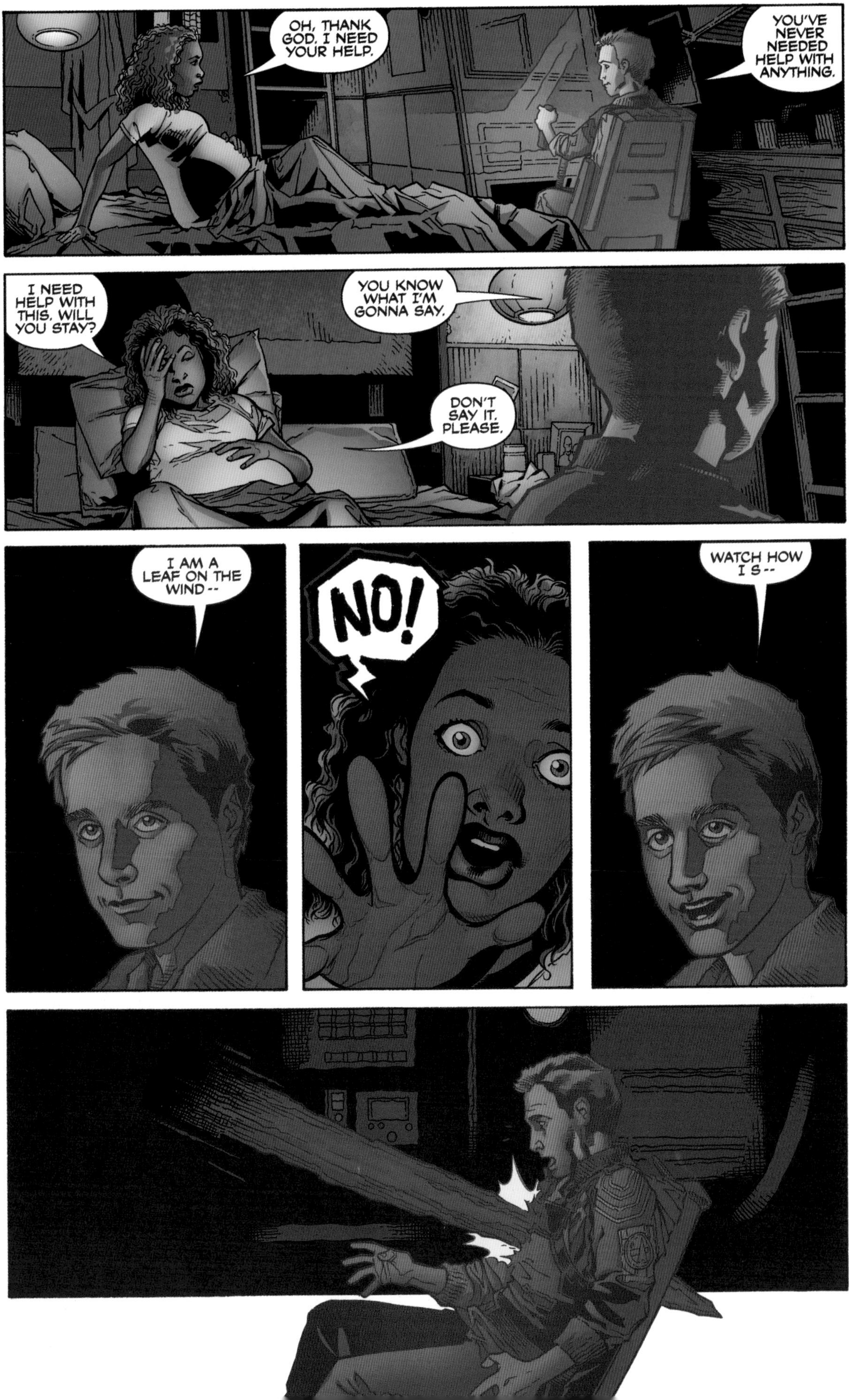
OH, THANK GOD. I NEED YOUR HELP.
YOU'VE NEVER NEEDED HELP WITH ANYTHING.
I NEED HELP WITH THIS. WILL YOU STAY?
YOU KNOW WHAT I'M GONNA SAY.
DON'T SAY IT. PLEASE.
I AM A LEAF ON THE WIND --
NO!
WATCH HOW I S --

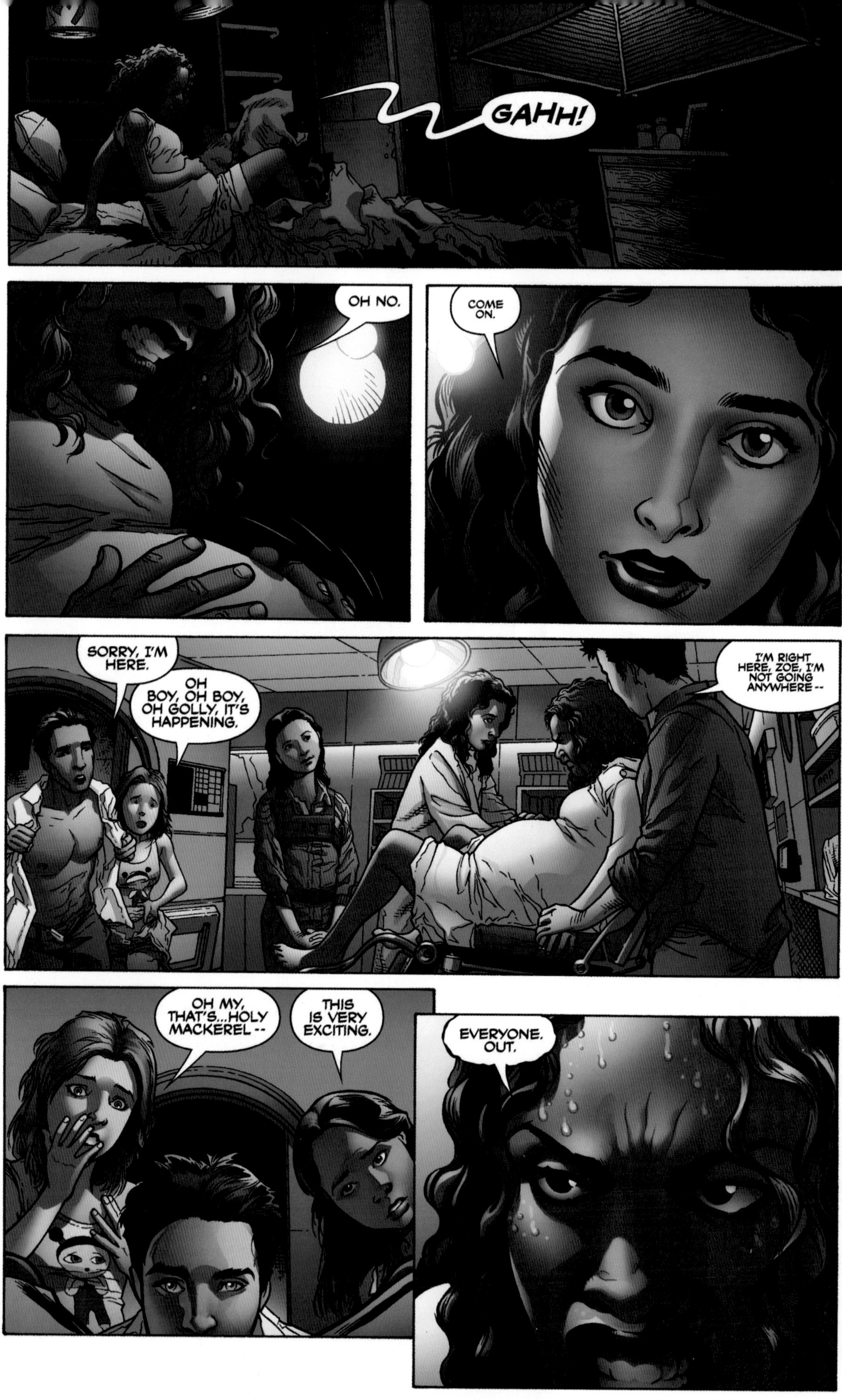
GAHH!
OH NO.
COME ON.
SORRY, I'M HERE.
OH BOY, OH BOY, OH GOLLY, IT'S HAPPENING.
I'M RIGHT HERE, ZOE, I'M NOT GOING ANYWHERE --
OH MY, THAT'S...HOLY MACKEREL --
THIS IS VERY EXCITING.
EVERYONE. OUT.

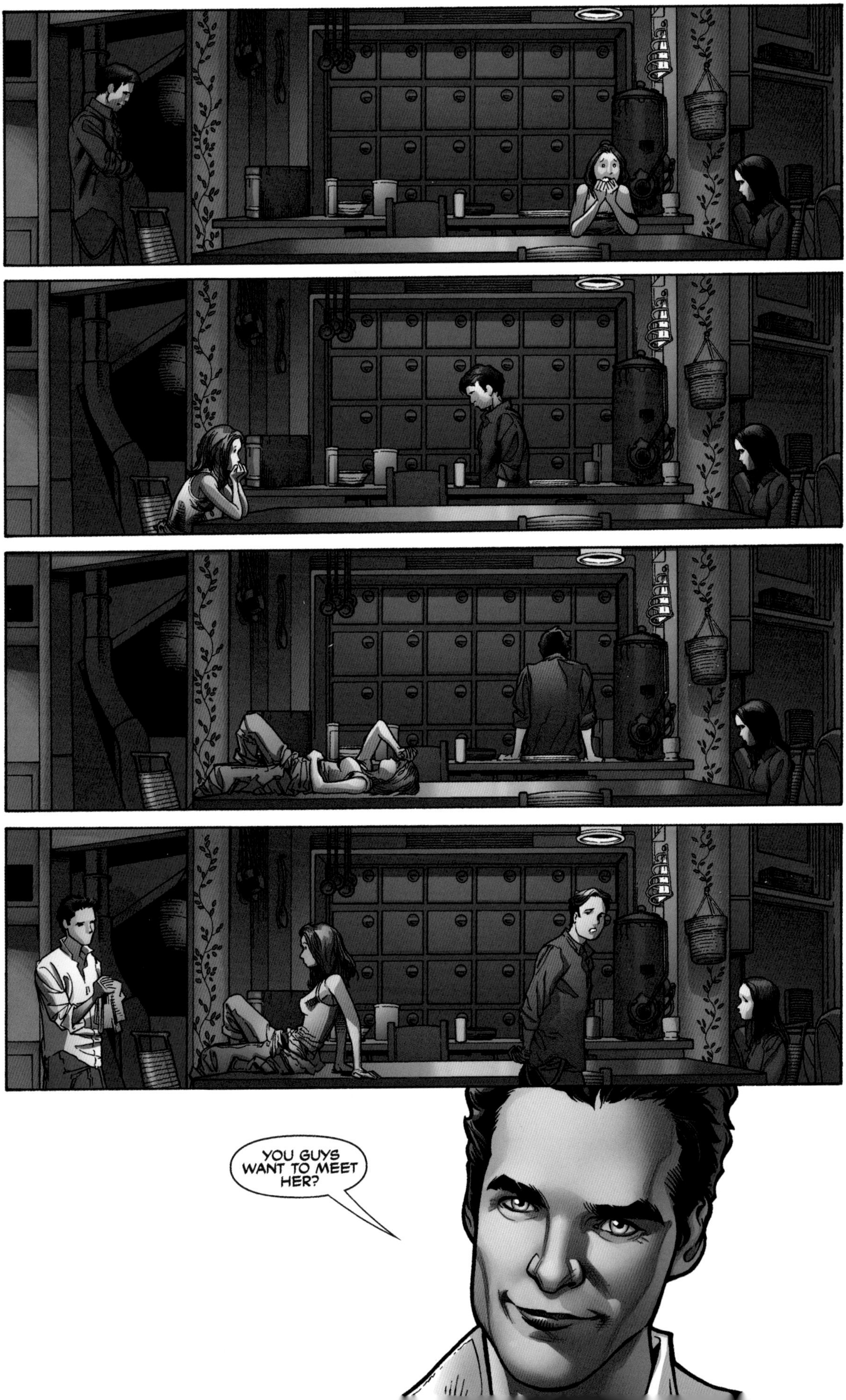
YOU GUYS WANT TO MEET HER?

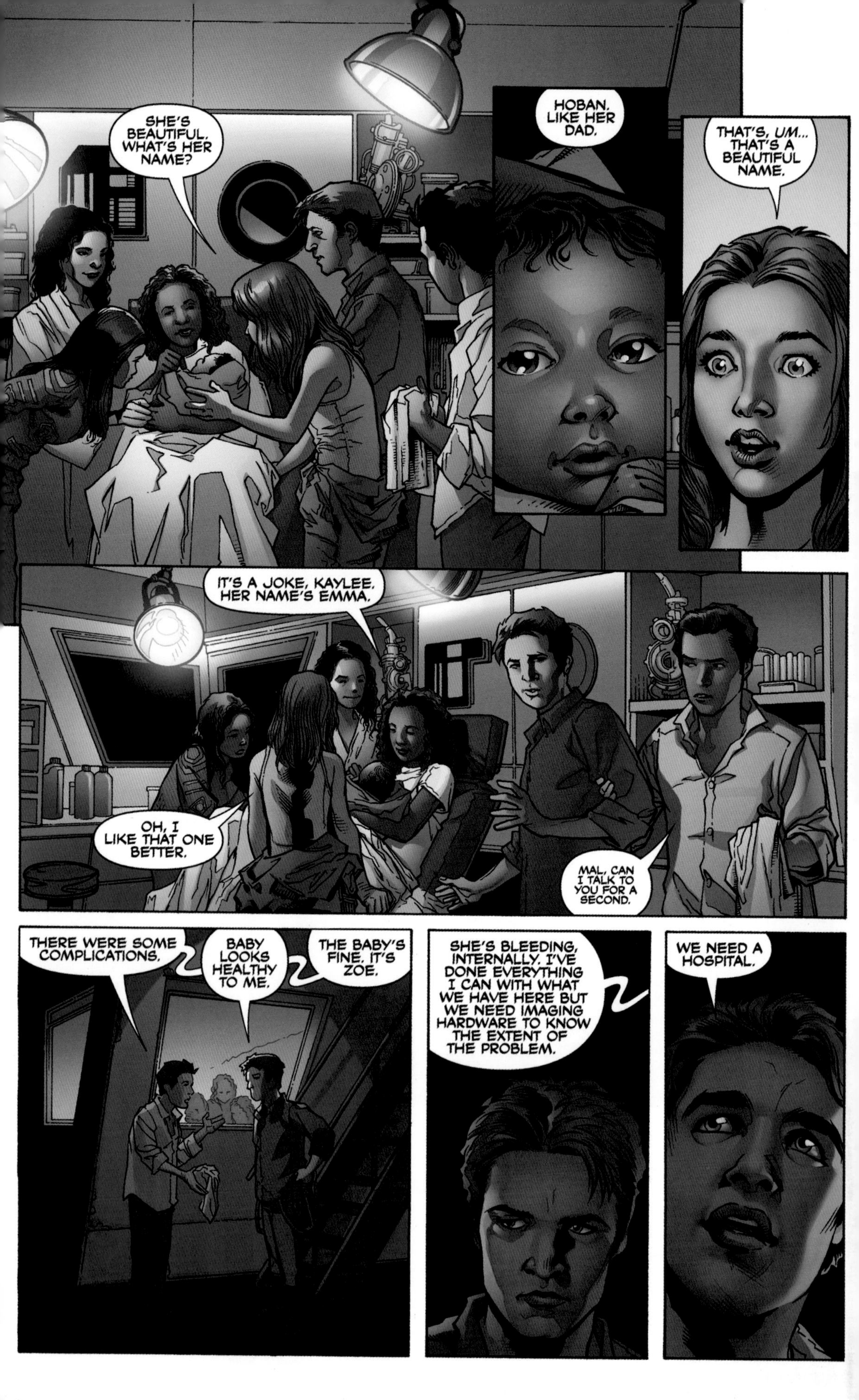
SHE'S BEAUTIFUL. WHAT'S HER NAME?
HOBAN, LIKE HER DAD.
THAT'S, UM... THAT'S A BEAUTIFUL NAME.
IT'S A JOKE, KAYLEE. HER NAME'S EMMA.
OH, I LIKE THAT ONE BETTER.
MAL, CAN I TALK TO YOU FOR A SECOND.
THERE WERE SOME COMPLICATIONS.
BABY LOOKS HEALTHY TO ME.
THE BABY'S FINE. IT'S ZOE.
SHE'S BLEEDING, INTERNALLY. I'VE DONE EVERYTHING I CAN WITH WHAT WE HAVE HERE BUT WE NEED IMAGING HARDWARE TO KNOW THE EXTENT OF THE PROBLEM.
WE NEED A HOSPITAL.

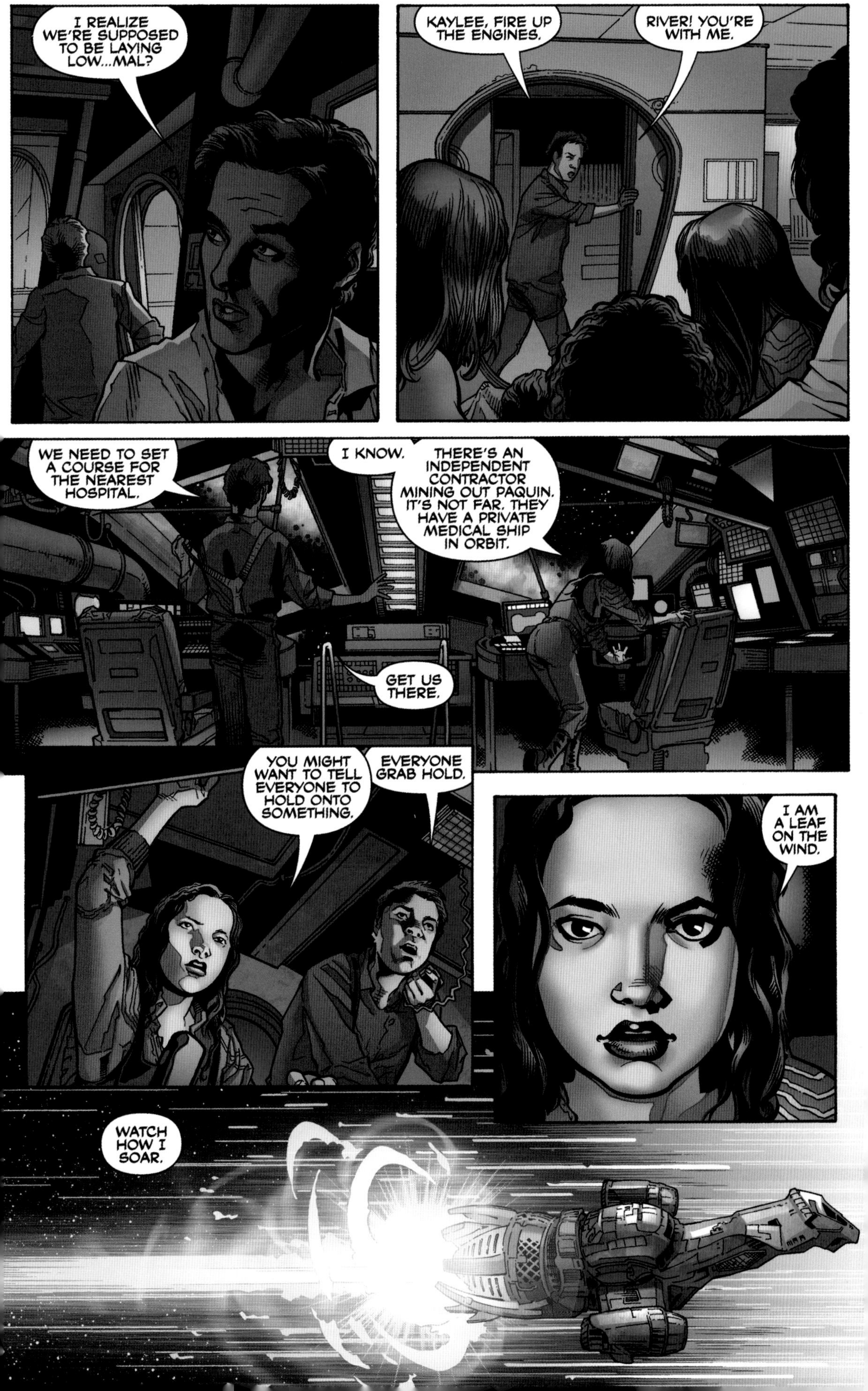
I REALIZE WE'RE SUPPOSED TO BE LAYING LOW...MAL?
KAYLEE, FIRE UP THE ENGINES.
RIVER! YOU'RE WITH ME.
WE NEED TO SET A COURSE FOR THE NEAREST HOSPITAL.
I KNOW.
THERE'S AN INDEPENDENT CONTRACTOR MINING OUT PAQUIN. IT'S NOT FAR. THEY HAVE A PRIVATE MEDICAL SHIP IN ORBIT.
GET US THERE.
YOU MIGHT WANT TO TELL EVERYONE TO HOLD ONTO SOMETHING.
EVERYONE GRAB HOLD.
I AM A LEAF ON THE WIND.
WATCH HOW I SOAR.

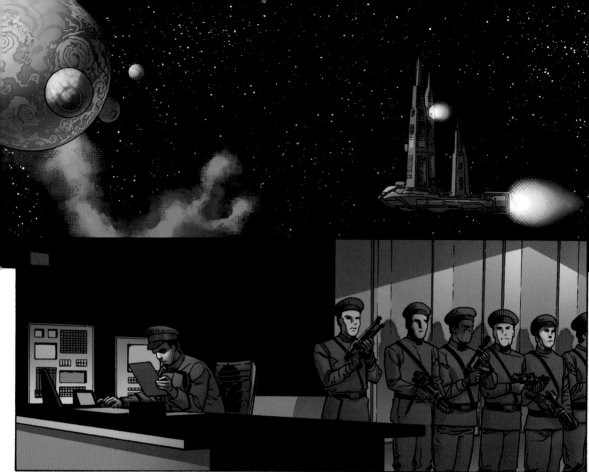

WHO ARE YOU.

YOU CAN'T BE IN HERE.

HMM.

I CAN'T BE...AND YET...HERE I AM.

CLINK

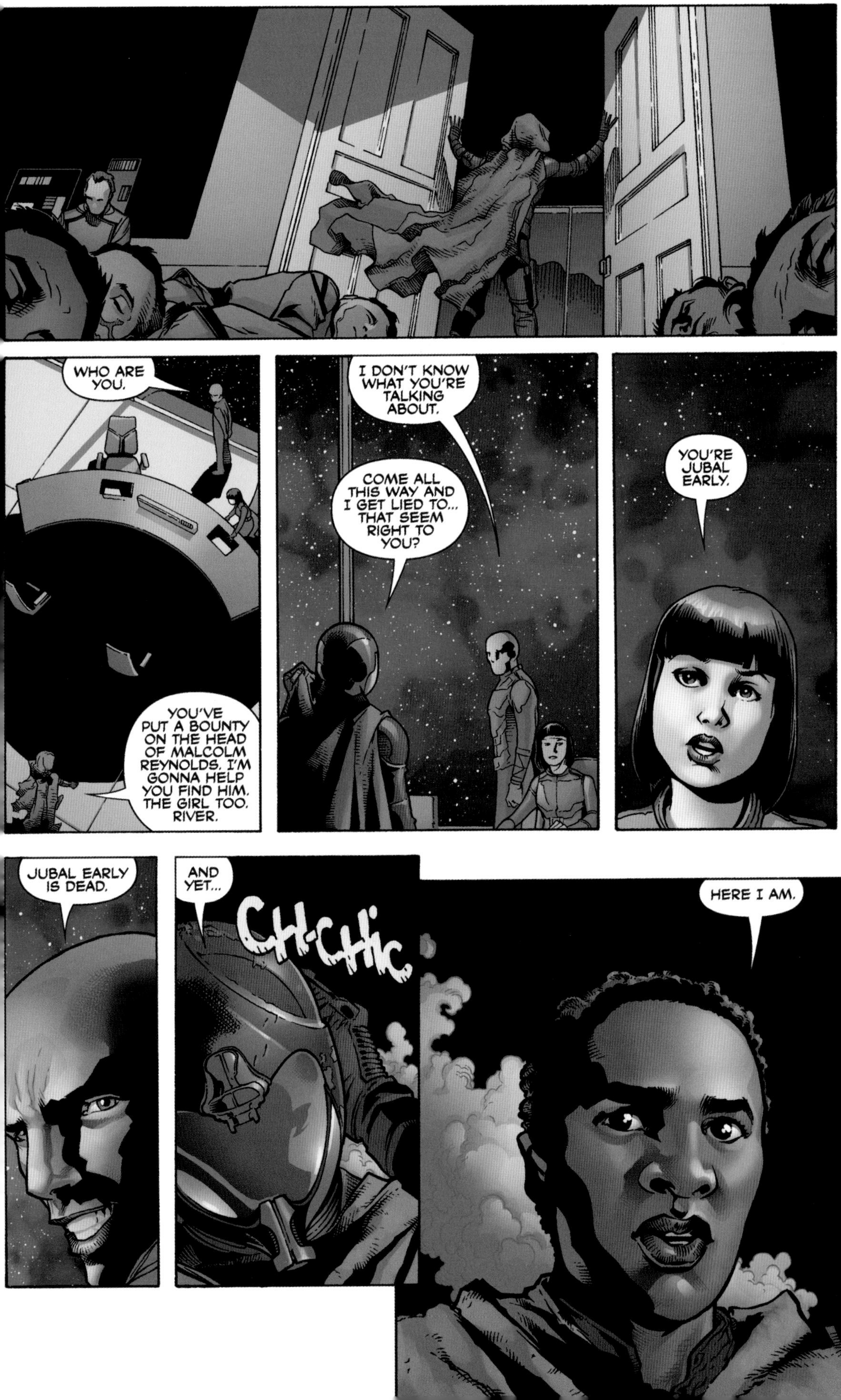
WHO ARE YOU.
YOU'VE PUT A BOUNTY ON THE HEAD OF MALCOLM REYNOLDS. I'M GONNA HELP YOU FIND HIM. THE GIRL TOO. RIVER.
I DON'T KNOW WHAT YOU'RE TALKING ABOUT.
COME ALL THIS WAY AND I GET LIED TO... THAT SEEM RIGHT TO YOU?
YOU'RE JUBAL EARLY.
JUBAL EARLY IS DEAD.
AND YET...
CH-CHIC
HERE I AM.

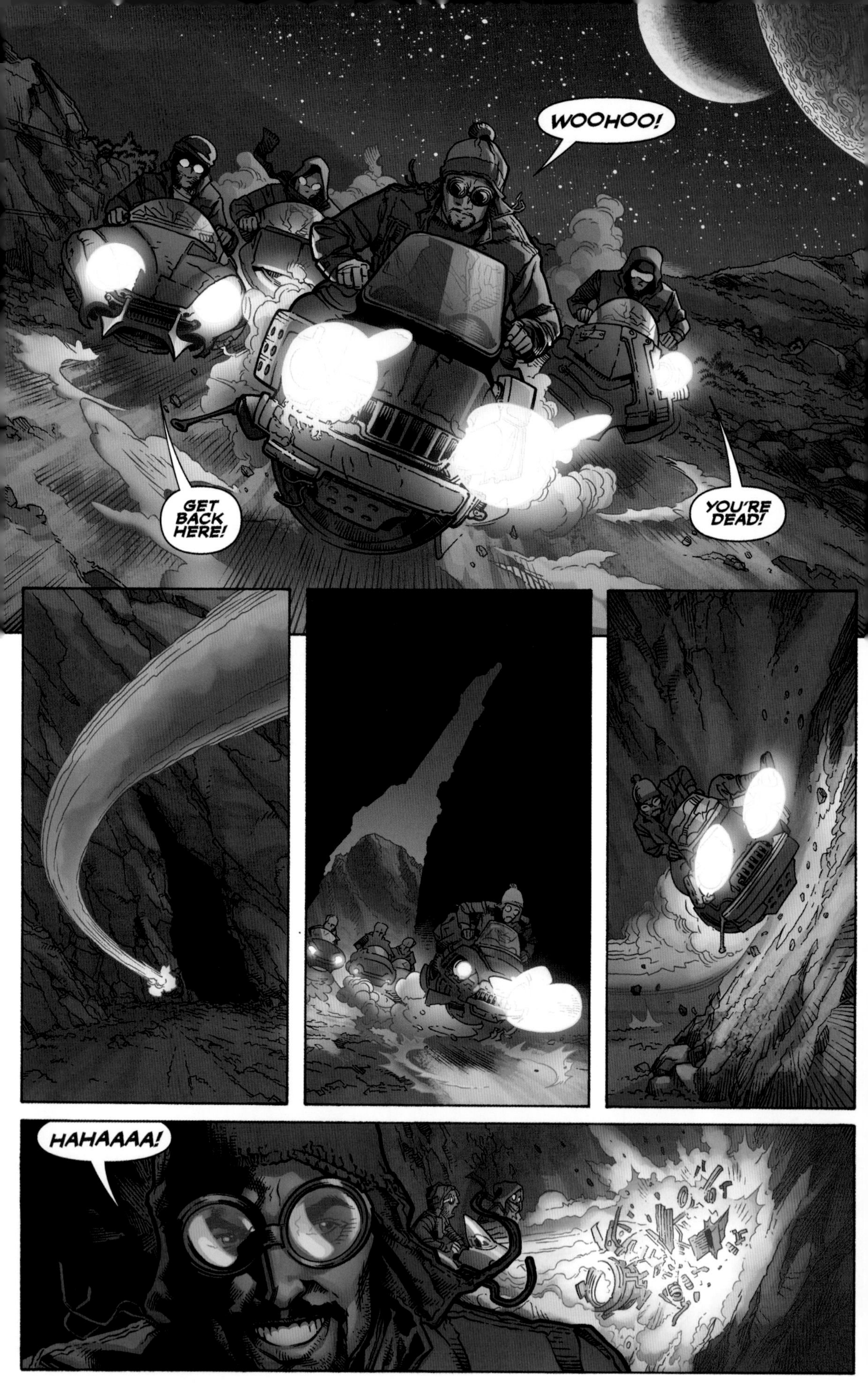
WOOHOO!
GET BACK HERE!
YOU'RE DEAD!
HAHAAAA!

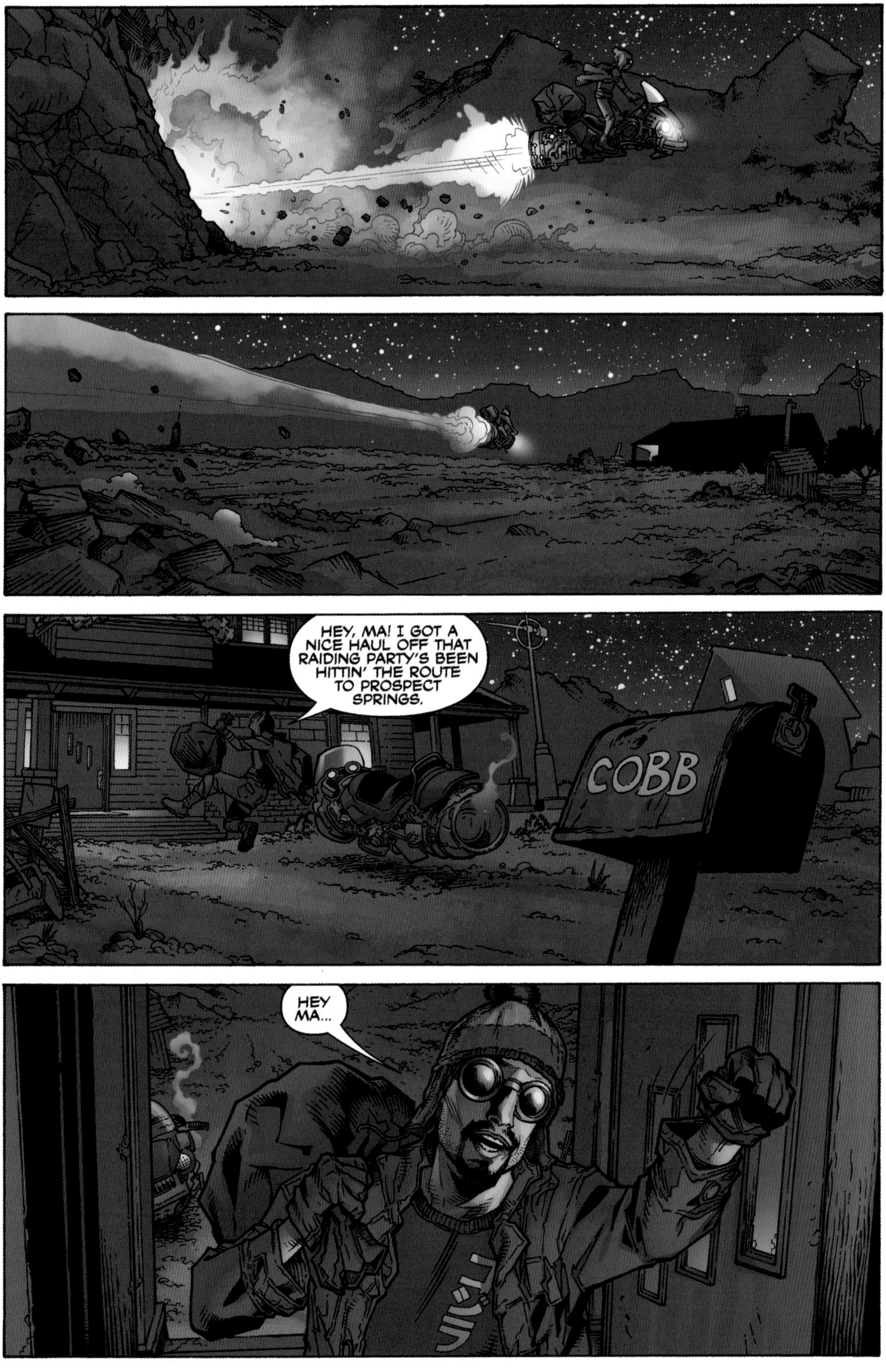
HEY, MA! I GOT A NICE HAUL OFF THAT RAIDING PARTY'S BEEN HITTIN' THE ROUTE TO PROSPECT SPRINGS.
COBB
HEY MA...

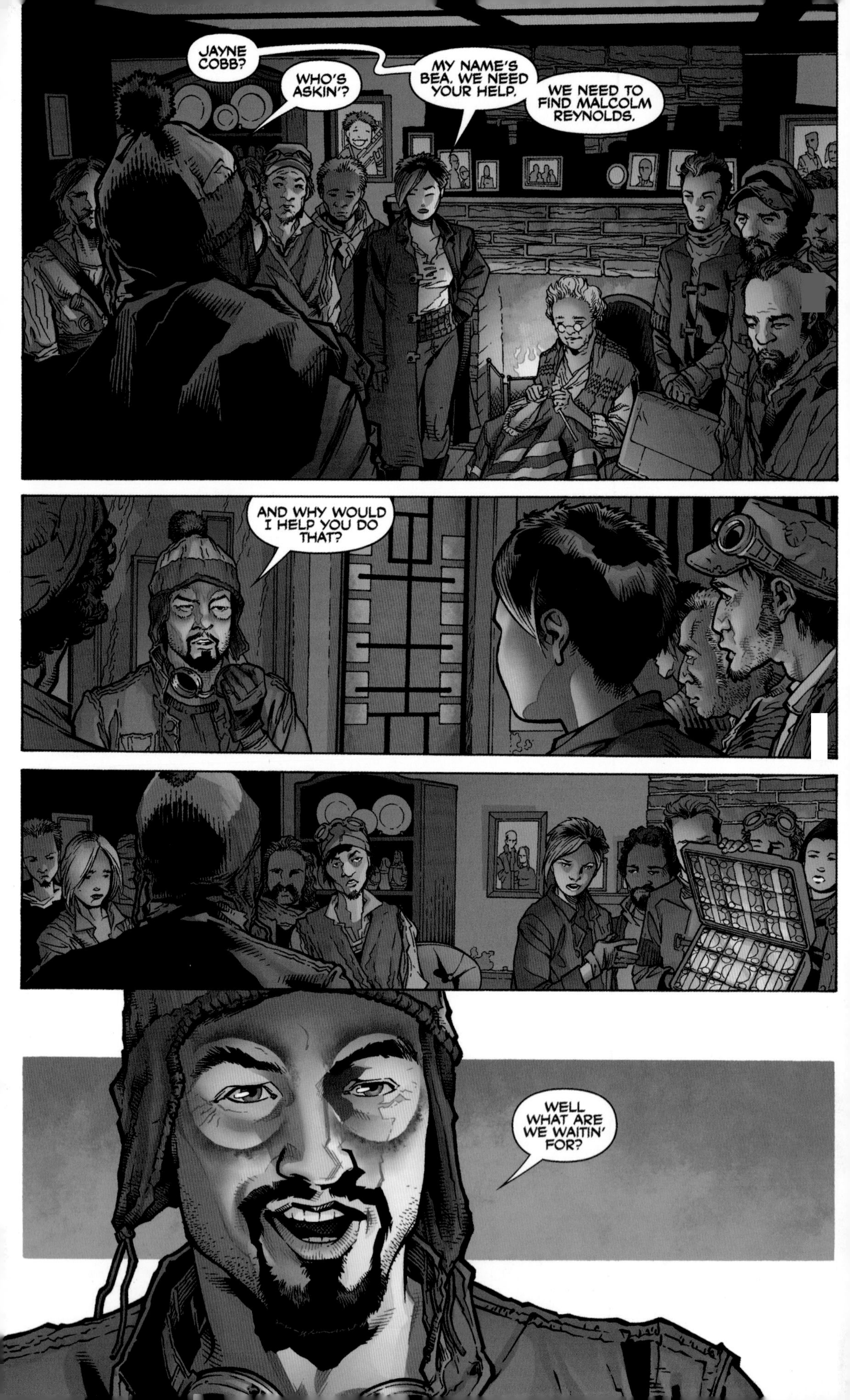
JAYNE COBB?
WHO'S ASKIN'?
MY NAME'S BEA, WE NEED YOUR HELP.
WE NEED TO FIND MALCOLM REYNOLDS.
AND WHY WOULD I HELP YOU DO THAT?
WELL WHAT ARE WE WAITIN' FOR?

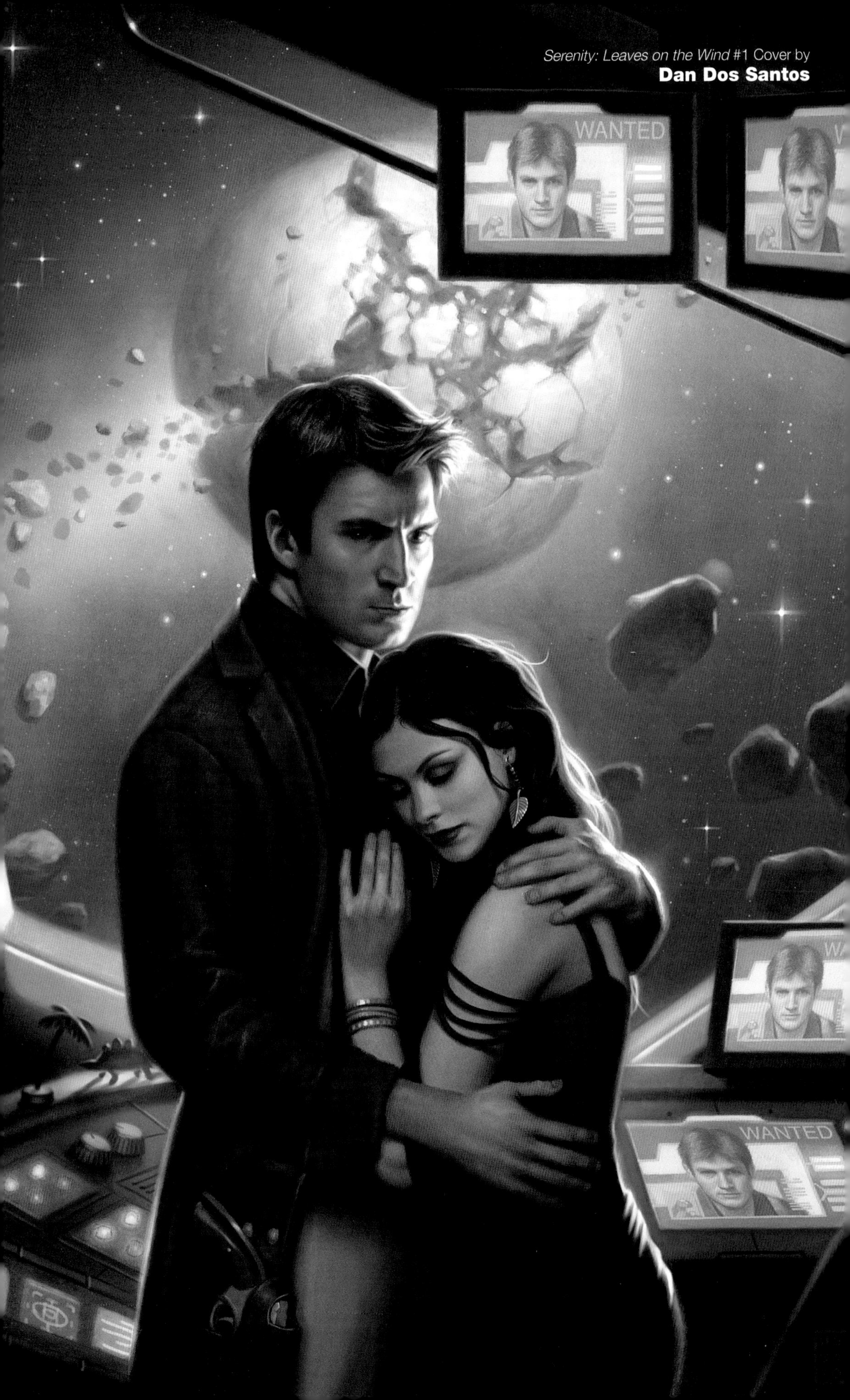
WANTED
WANTED

Serenity: Leaves on the Wind #1 Cover by
Dan Dos Santos

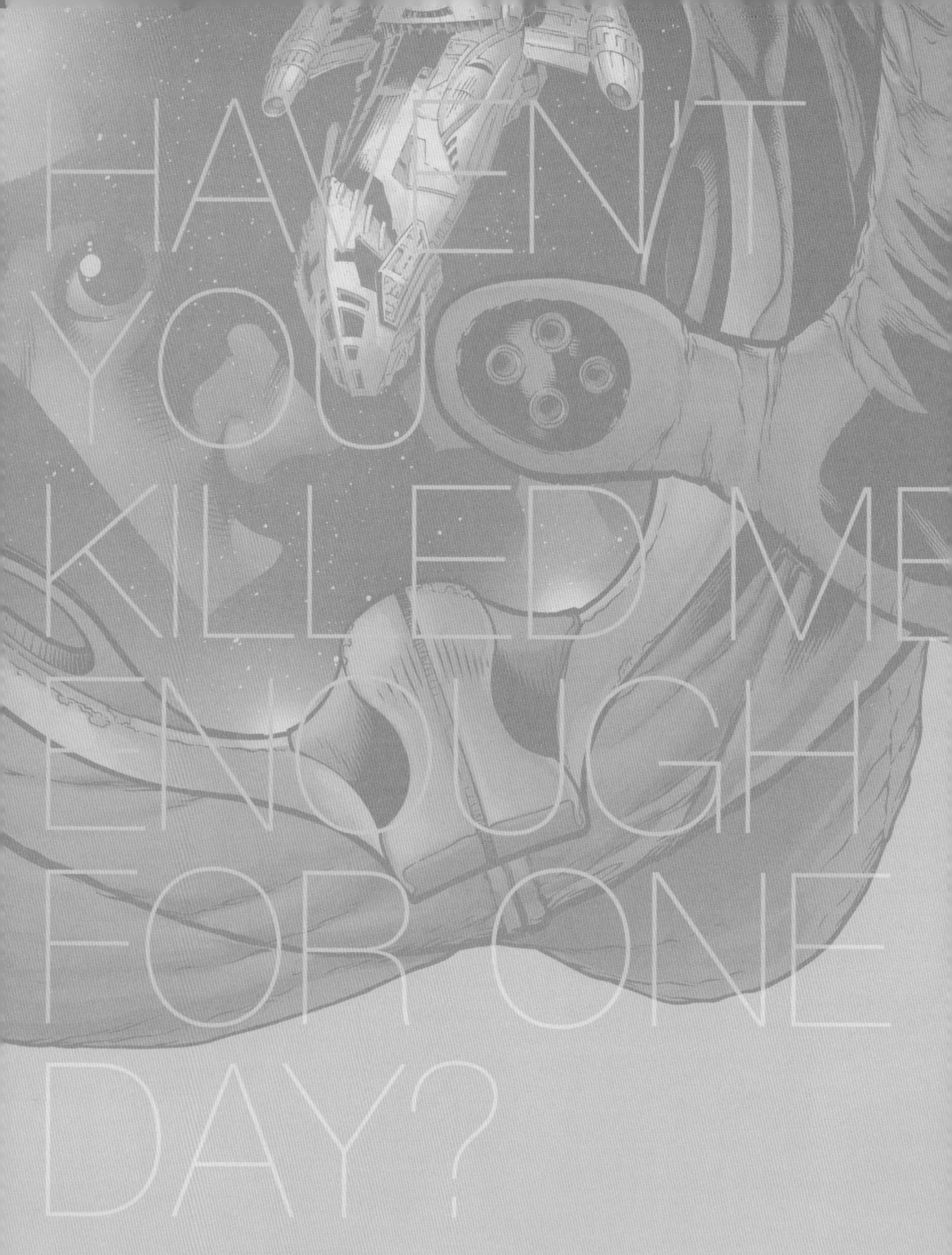
HAVEN'T
YOU
KILLED ME
ENOUGH
FOR ONE
DAY?

LEAVES ON THE WIND

CHAPTER TWO

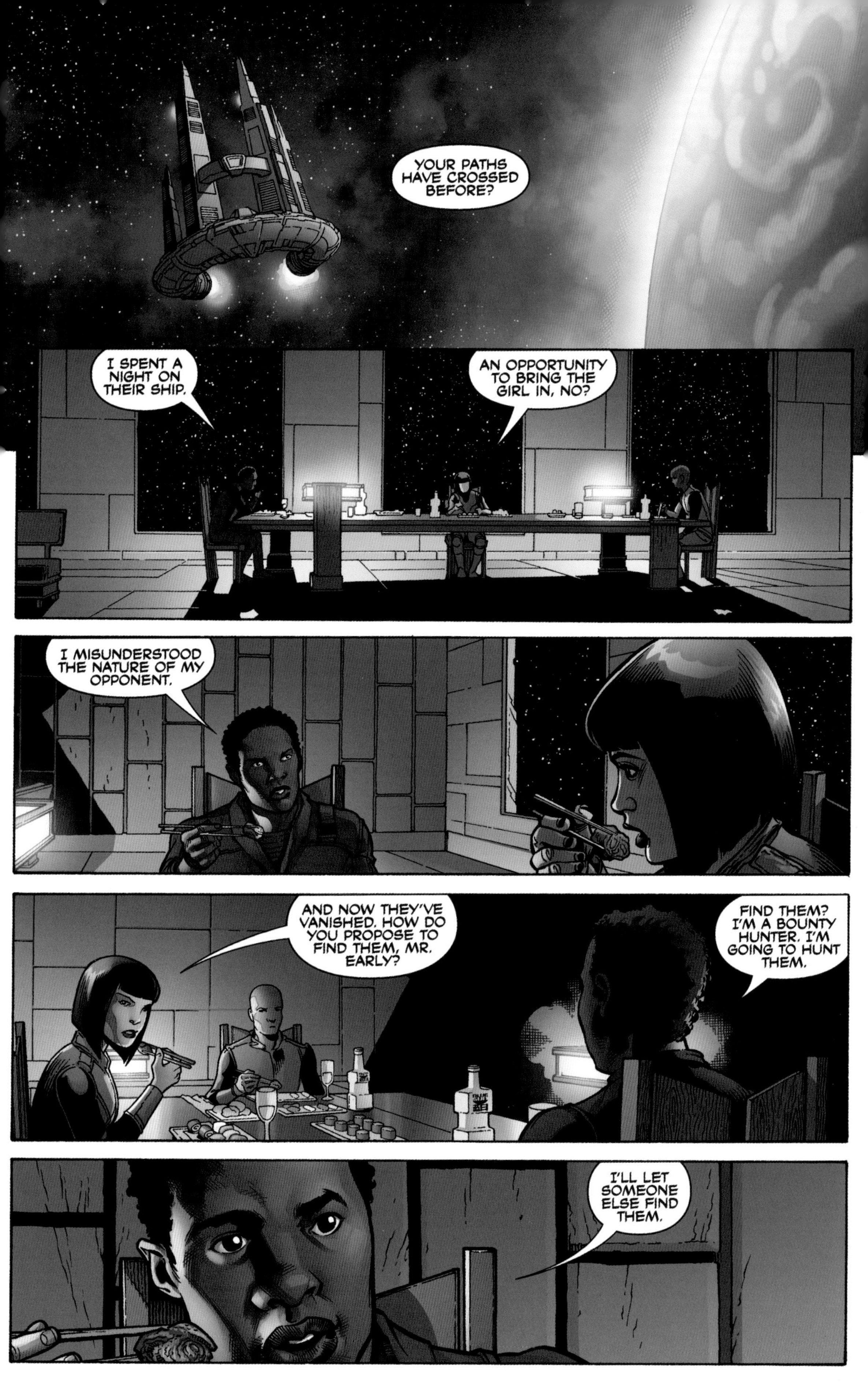

YOUR PATHS HAVE CROSSED BEFORE?
I SPENT A NIGHT ON THEIR SHIP.
AN OPPORTUNITY TO BRING THE GIRL IN, NO?
I MISUNDERSTOOD THE NATURE OF MY OPPONENT.
AND NOW THEY'VE VANISHED. HOW DO YOU PROPOSE TO FIND THEM, MR. EARLY?
FIND THEM? I'M A BOUNTY HUNTER. I'M GOING TO HUNT THEM.
I'LL LET SOMEONE ELSE FIND THEM.

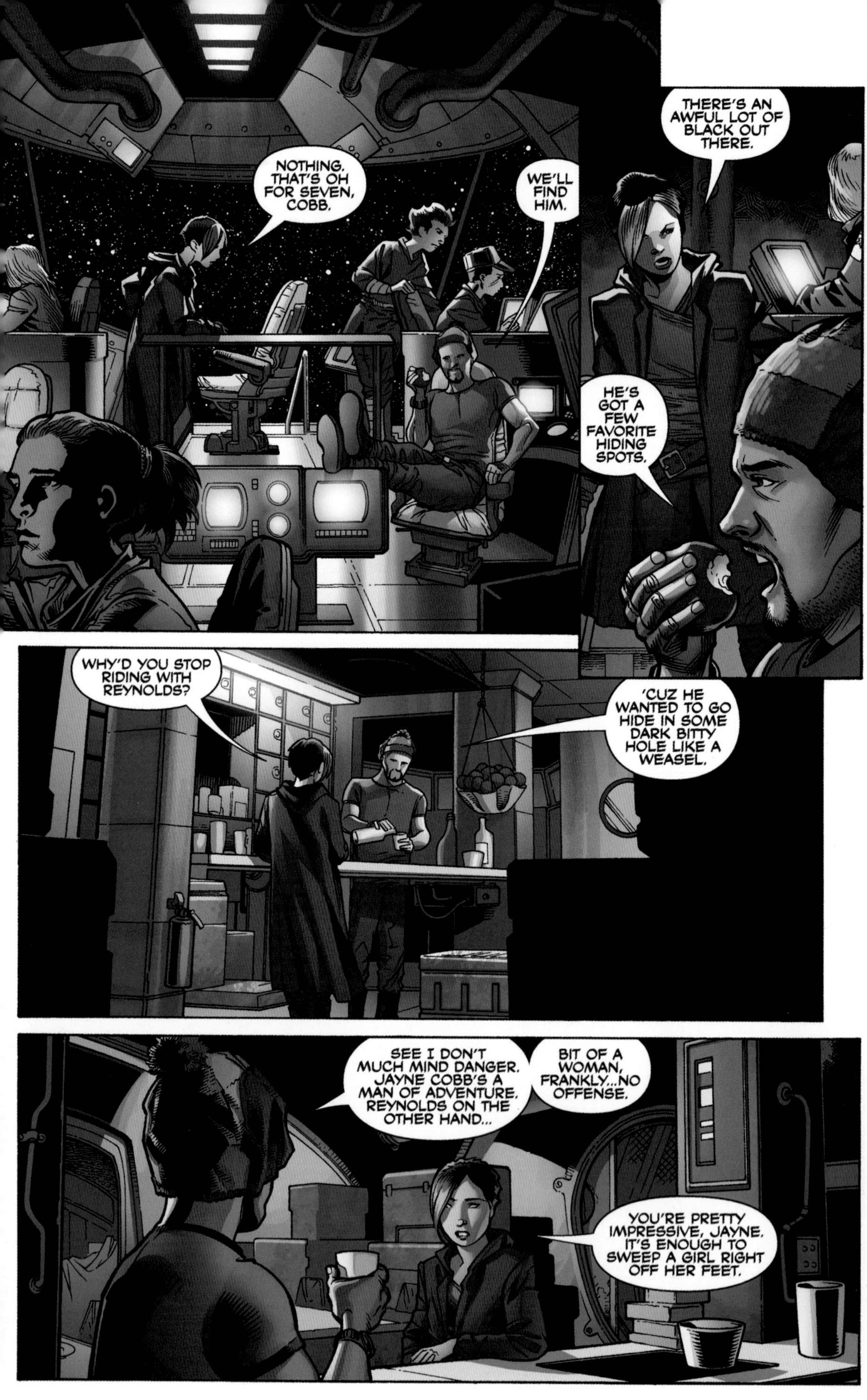
NOTHING. THAT'S OH FOR SEVEN, COBB.
WE'LL FIND HIM.
THERE'S AN AWFUL LOT OF BLACK OUT THERE.
HE'S GOT A FEW FAVORITE HIDING SPOTS.
WHY'D YOU STOP RIDING WITH REYNOLDS?
'CUZ HE WANTED TO GO HIDE IN SOME DARK BITTY HOLE LIKE A WEASEL.
SEE I DON'T MUCH MIND DANGER. JAYNE COBB'S A MAN OF ADVENTURE. REYNOLDS ON THE OTHER HAND...
BIT OF A WOMAN, FRANKLY...NO OFFENSE.
YOU'RE PRETTY IMPRESSIVE, JAYNE. IT'S ENOUGH TO SWEEP A GIRL RIGHT OFF HER FEET.

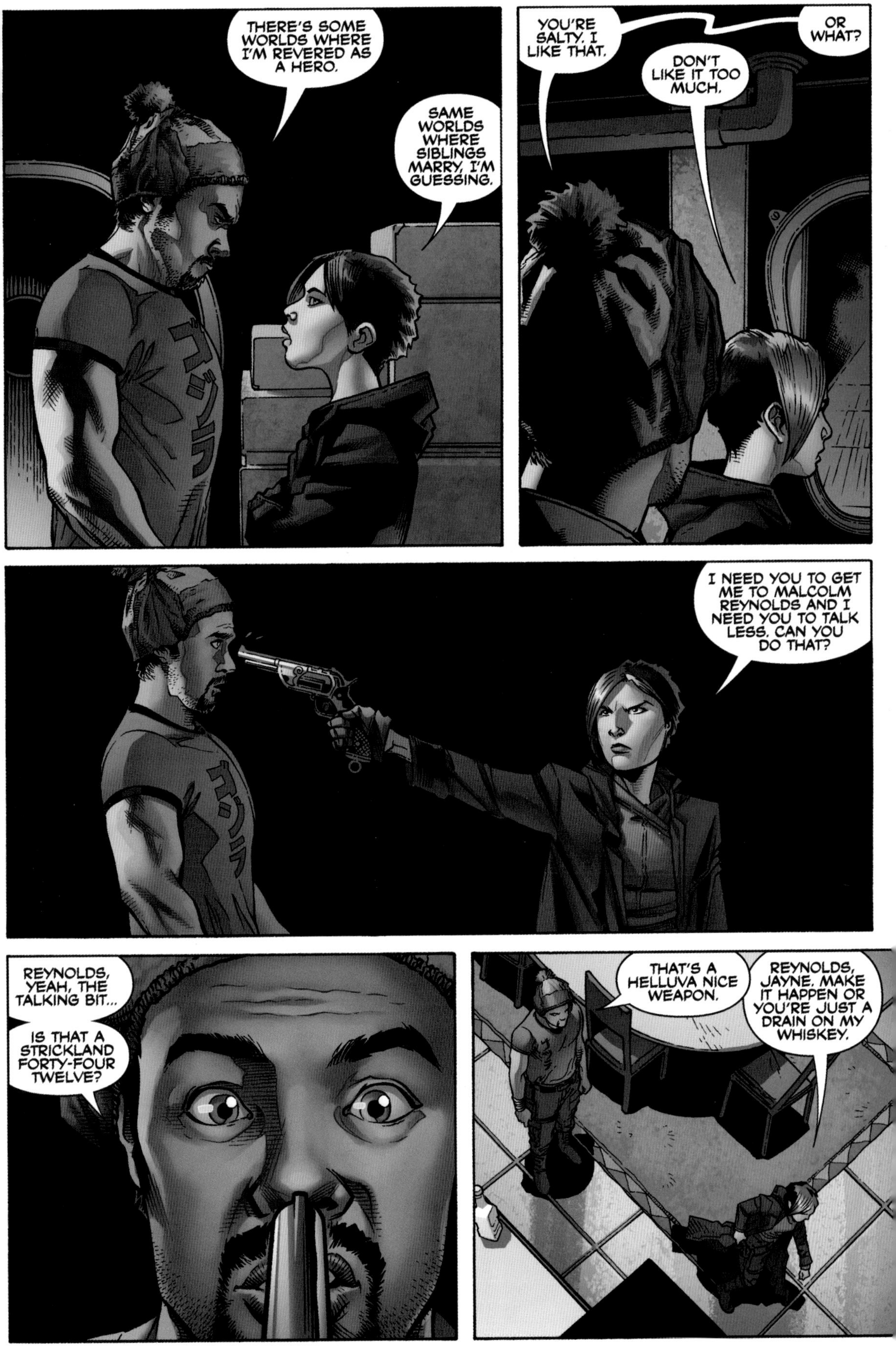
THERE'S SOME WORLDS WHERE I'M REVERED AS A HERO.
SAME WORLDS WHERE SIBLINGS MARRY, I'M GUESSING.
YOU'RE SALTY. I LIKE THAT.
OR WHAT?
DON'T LIKE IT TOO MUCH.
I NEED YOU TO GET ME TO MALCOLM REYNOLDS AND I NEED YOU TO TALK LESS. CAN YOU DO THAT?
REYNOLDS, YEAH, THE TALKING BIT...
IS THAT A STRICKLAND FORTY-FOUR TWELVE?
THAT'S A HELLUVA NICE WEAPON.
REYNOLDS, JAYNE. MAKE IT HAPPEN OR YOU'RE JUST A DRAIN ON MY WHISKEY.

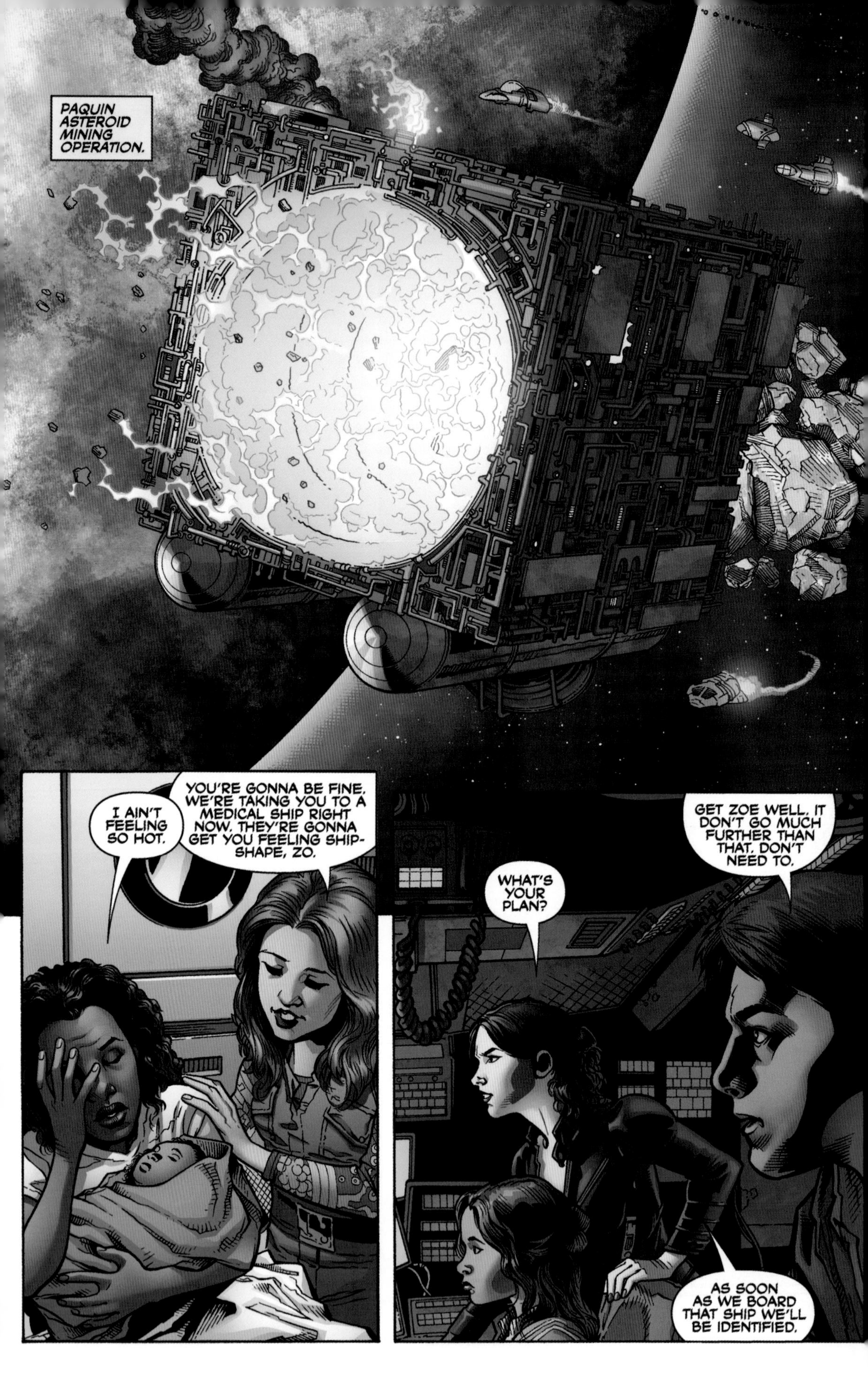
PAQUIN ASTEROID MINING OPERATION.
I AIN'T FEELING SO HOT.
YOU'RE GONNA BE FINE. WE'RE TAKING YOU TO A MEDICAL SHIP RIGHT NOW. THEY'RE GONNA GET YOU FEELING SHIP-SHAPE, ZO.
WHAT'S YOUR PLAN?
GET ZOE WELL. IT DON'T GO MUCH FURTHER THAN THAT. DON'T NEED TO.
AS SOON AS WE BOARD THAT SHIP WE'LL BE IDENTIFIED.

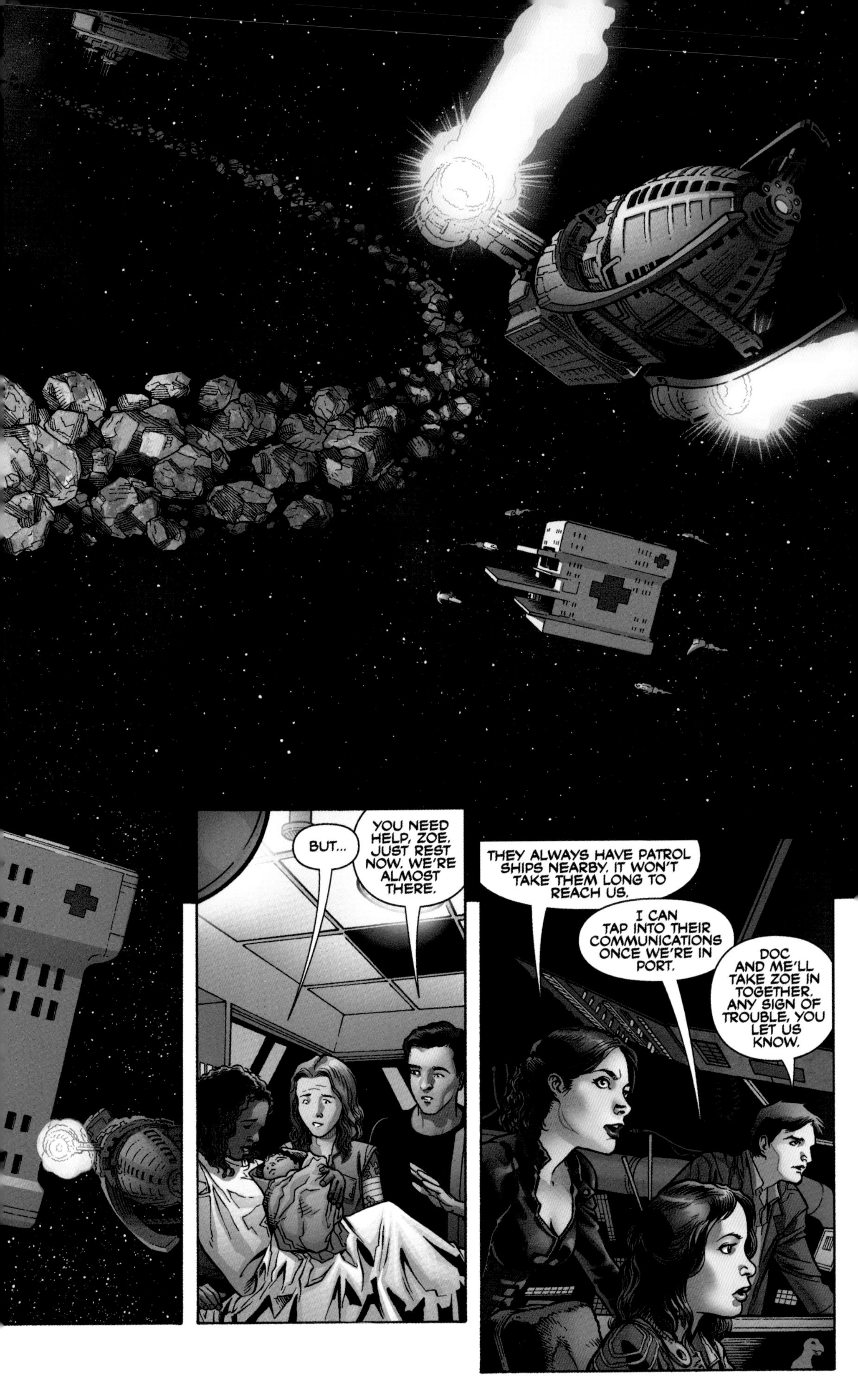
BUT...
YOU NEED HELP, ZOE. JUST REST NOW. WE'RE ALMOST THERE.
THEY ALWAYS HAVE PATROL SHIPS NEARBY. IT WON'T TAKE THEM LONG TO REACH US.
I CAN TAP INTO THEIR COMMUNICATIONS ONCE WE'RE IN PORT.
DOC AND ME'LL TAKE ZOE IN TOGETHER. ANY SIGN OF TROUBLE, YOU LET US KNOW.

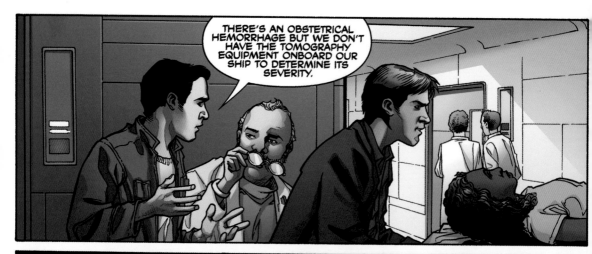

THERE'S AN OBSTETRICAL HEMORRHAGE BUT WE DON'T HAVE THE TOMOGRAPHY EQUIPMENT ONBOARD OUR SHIP TO DETERMINE ITS SEVERITY.

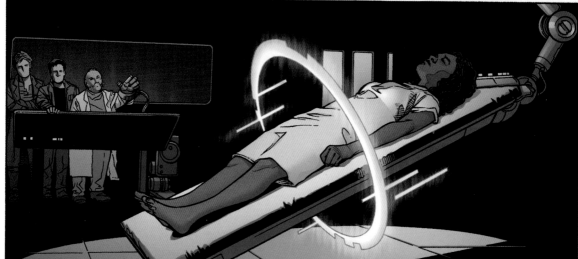

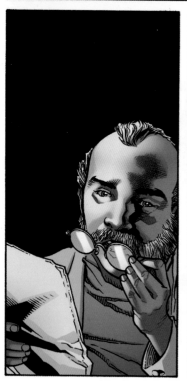

GOOD NEWS IS WE'RE GOING TO BE ABLE TO SAVE HER. BUT WE NEED TO OPERATE RIGHT AWAY.

HOW LONG TILL SHE'S BACK ON THE SHIP?

NOT TOO LONG, MAYBE FIVE DAYS?

WE DO NEED TO ACT FAST THOUGH. A TRAUMA TEAM IS ON THEIR WAY UP NOW.

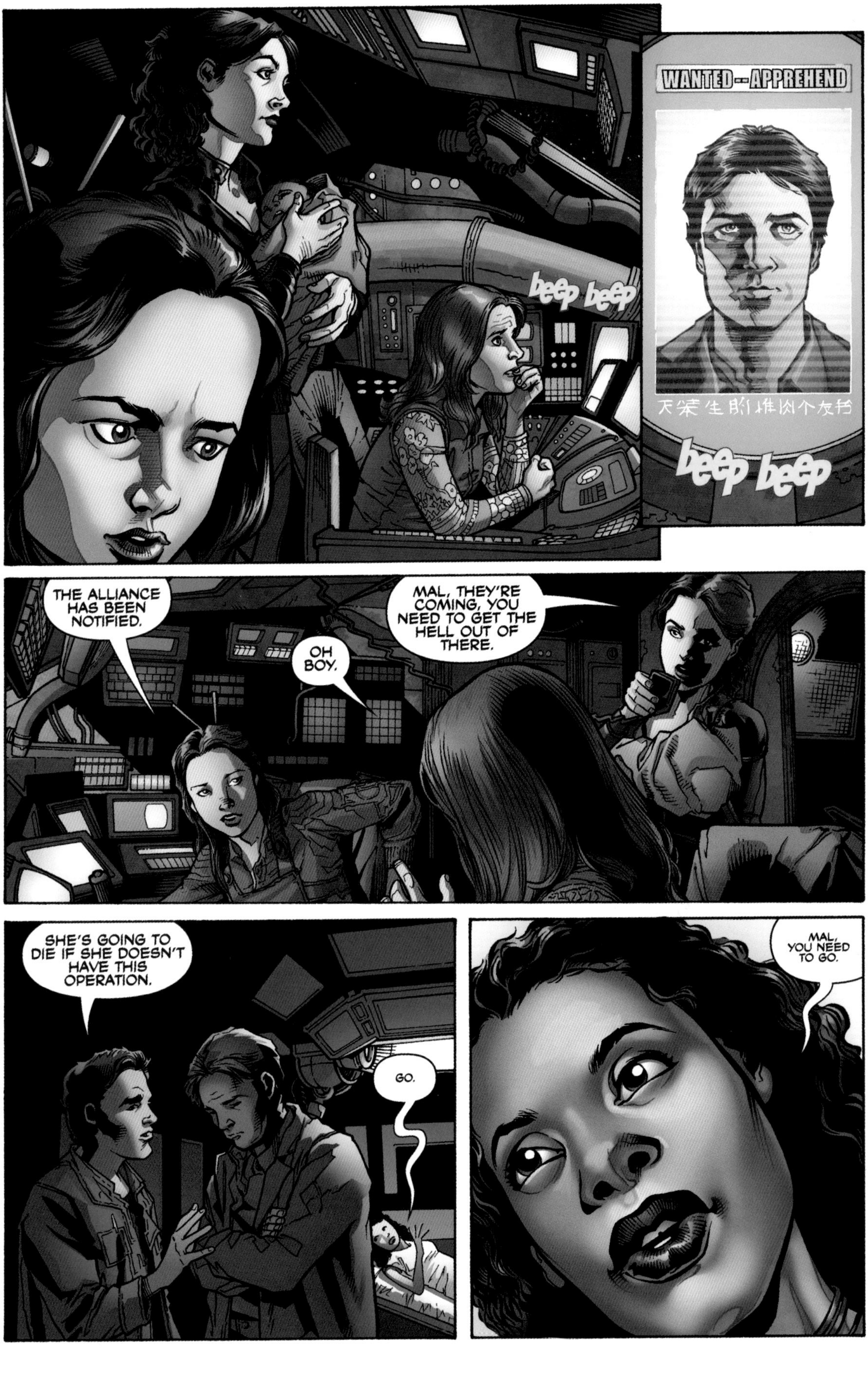
beep beep
WANTED--APPREHEND
beep beep
THE ALLIANCE HAS BEEN NOTIFIED.
OH BOY.
MAL, THEY'RE COMING, YOU NEED TO GET THE HELL OUT OF THERE.
SHE'S GOING TO DIE IF SHE DOESN'T HAVE THIS OPERATION.
GO.
MAL, YOU NEED TO GO.

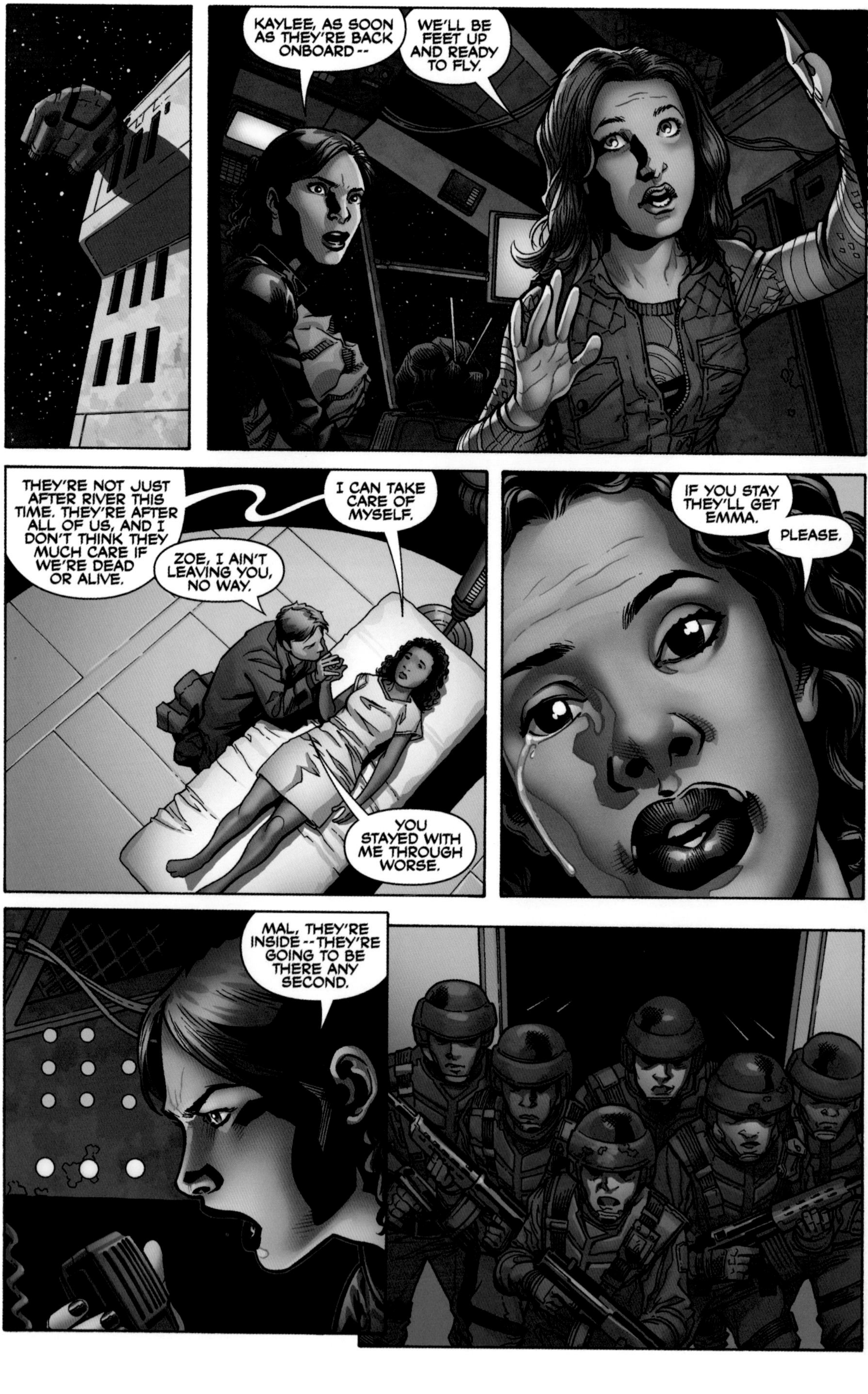
KAYLEE, AS SOON AS THEY'RE BACK ONBOARD--
WE'LL BE FEET UP AND READY TO FLY.
THEY'RE NOT JUST AFTER RIVER THIS TIME. THEY'RE AFTER ALL OF US, AND I DON'T THINK THEY MUCH CARE IF WE'RE DEAD OR ALIVE.
I CAN TAKE CARE OF MYSELF.
ZOE, I AIN'T LEAVING YOU, NO WAY.
YOU STAYED WITH ME THROUGH WORSE.
IF YOU STAY THEY'LL GET EMMA.
PLEASE.
MAL, THEY'RE INSIDE--THEY'RE GOING TO BE THERE ANY SECOND.

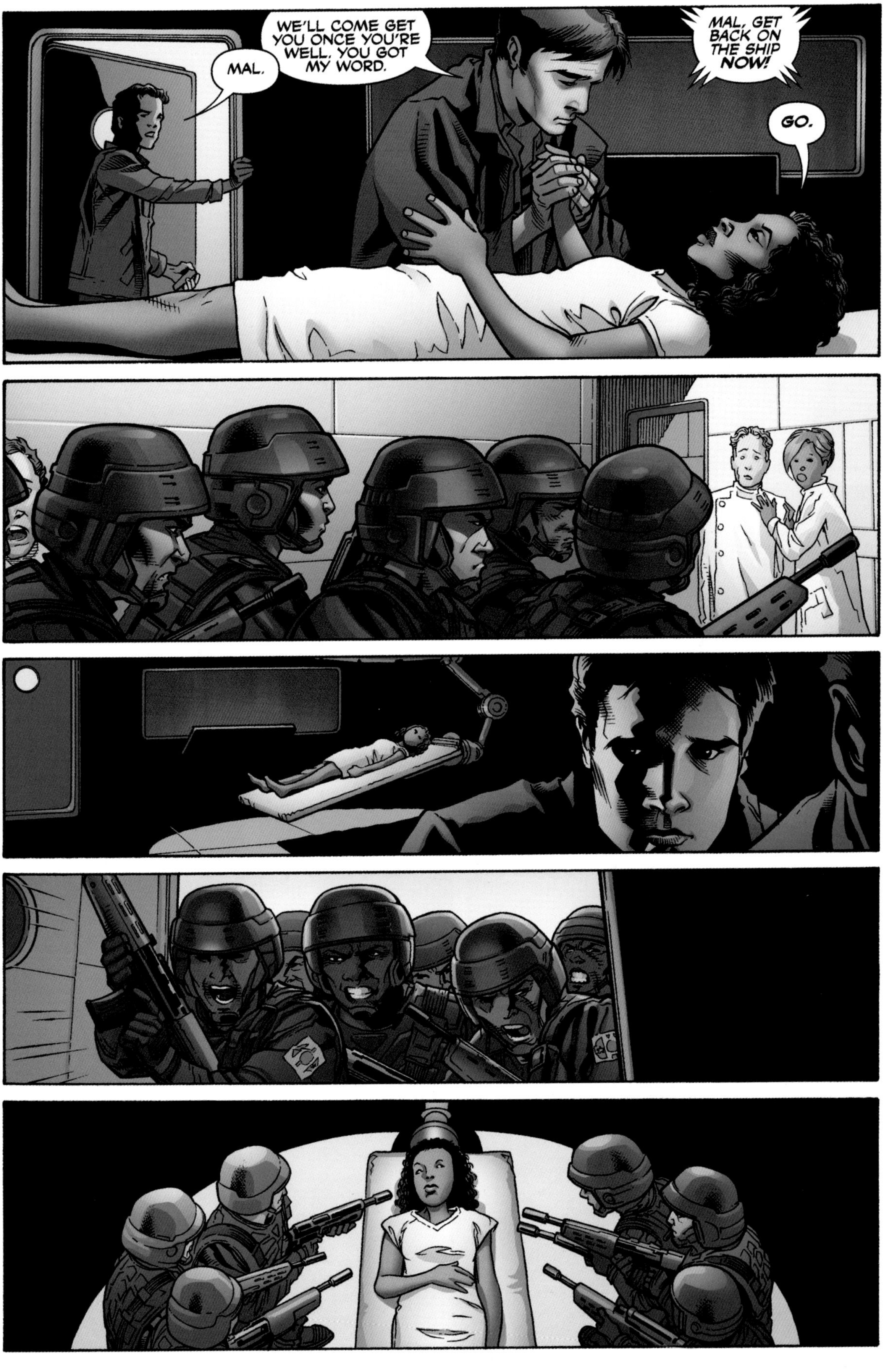
MAL.
WE'LL COME GET YOU ONCE YOU'RE WELL. YOU GOT MY WORD.
MAL, GET BACK ON THE SHIP NOW!
GO.

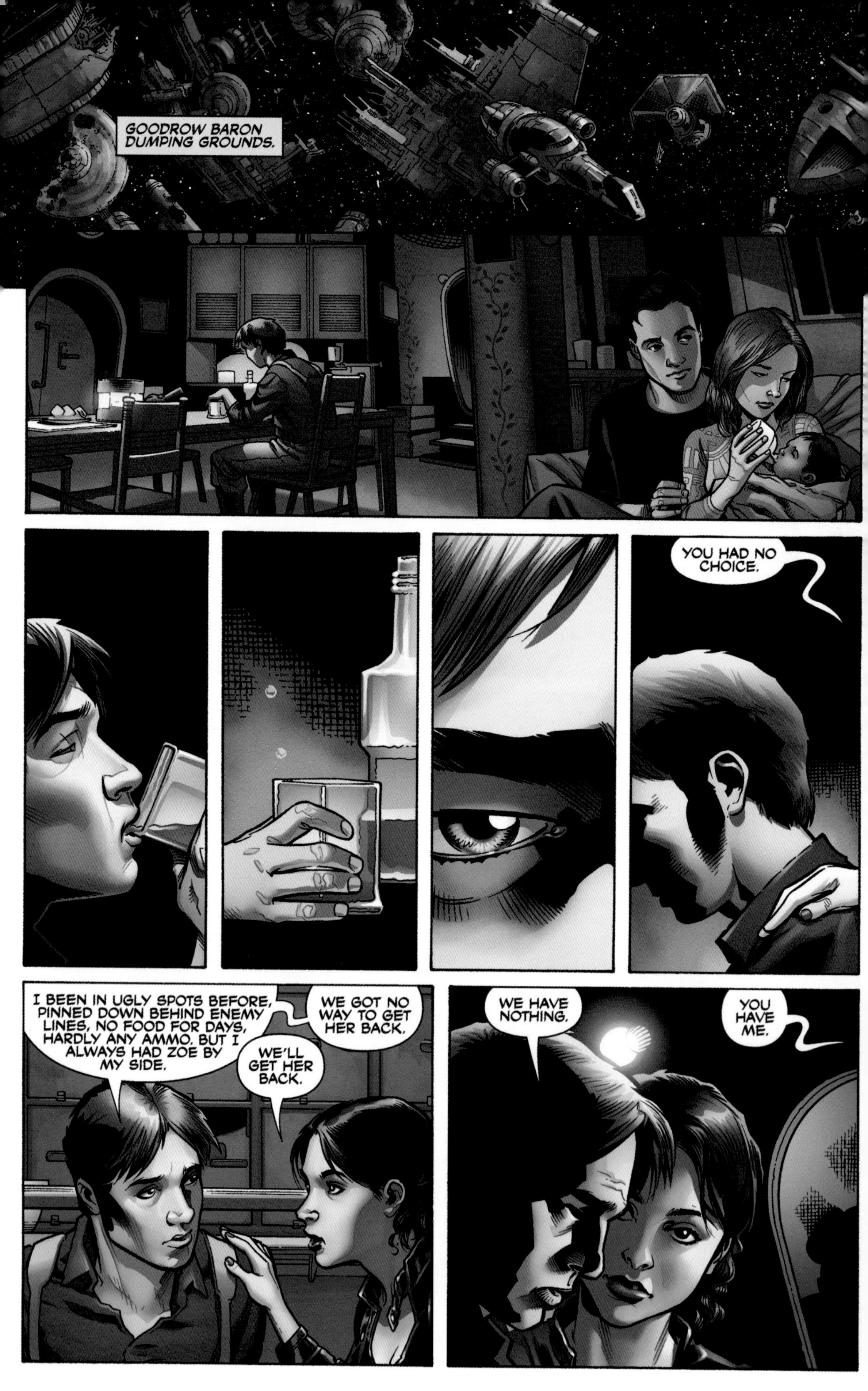
GOODROW BARON DUMPING GROUNDS.
YOU HAD NO CHOICE.
I BEEN IN UGLY SPOTS BEFORE, PINNED DOWN BEHIND ENEMY LINES, NO FOOD FOR DAYS, HARDLY ANY AMMO. BUT I ALWAYS HAD ZOE BY MY SIDE.
WE'LL GET HER BACK.
WE GOT NO WAY TO GET HER BACK.
WE HAVE NOTHING.
YOU HAVE ME.

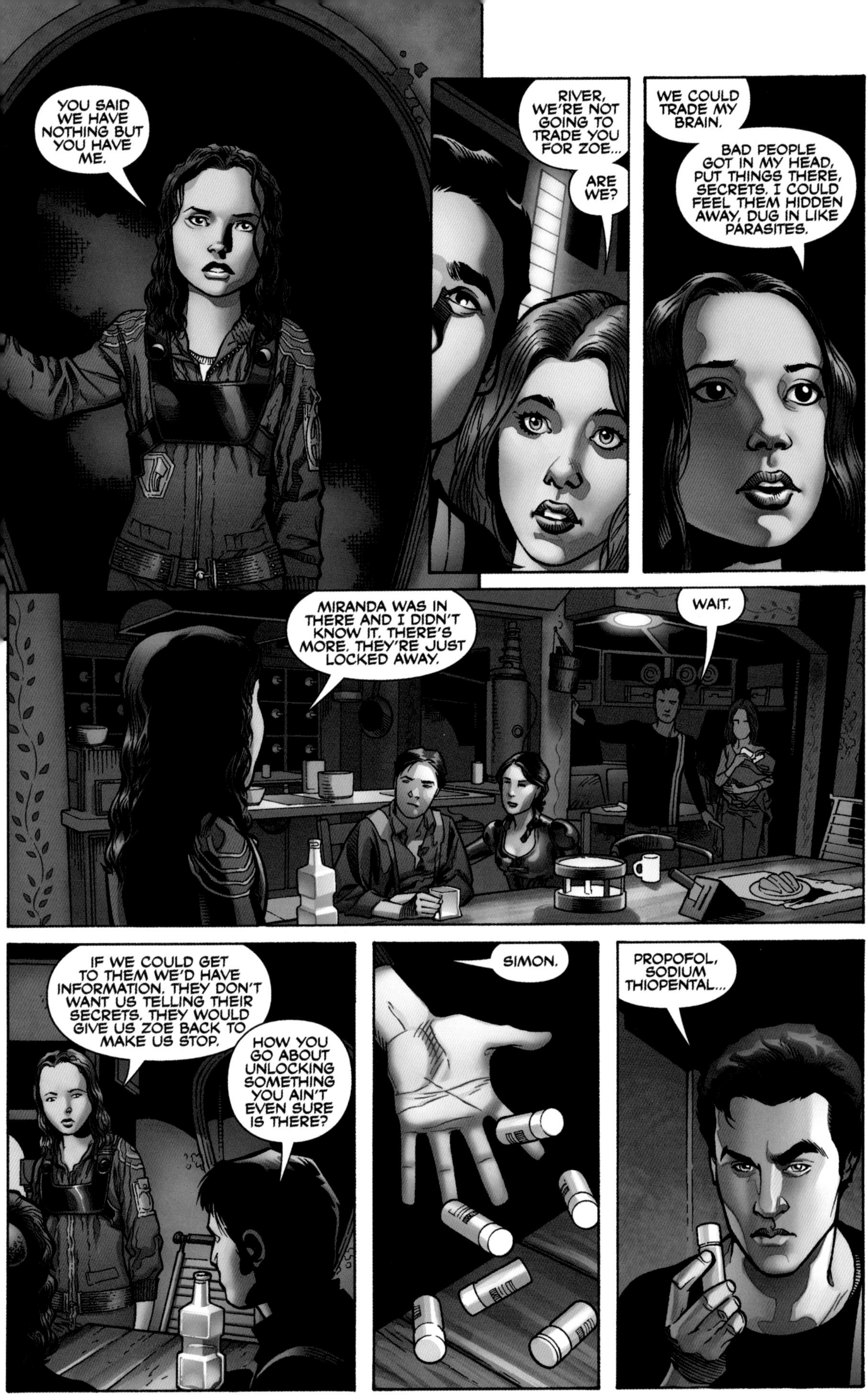

YOU SAID WE HAVE NOTHING BUT YOU HAVE ME.
RIVER, WE'RE NOT GOING TO TRADE YOU FOR ZOE...
ARE WE?
WE COULD TRADE MY BRAIN.
BAD PEOPLE GOT IN MY HEAD, PUT THINGS THERE, SECRETS. I COULD FEEL THEM HIDDEN AWAY, DUG IN LIKE PARASITES.
MIRANDA WAS IN THERE AND I DIDN'T KNOW IT. THERE'S MORE. THEY'RE JUST LOCKED AWAY.
WAIT.
IF WE COULD GET TO THEM WE'D HAVE INFORMATION. THEY DON'T WANT US TELLING THEIR SECRETS. THEY WOULD GIVE US ZOE BACK TO MAKE US STOP.
HOW YOU GO ABOUT UNLOCKING SOMETHING YOU AIN'T EVEN SURE IS THERE?
SIMON.
PROPOFOL, SODIUM THIOPENTAL...

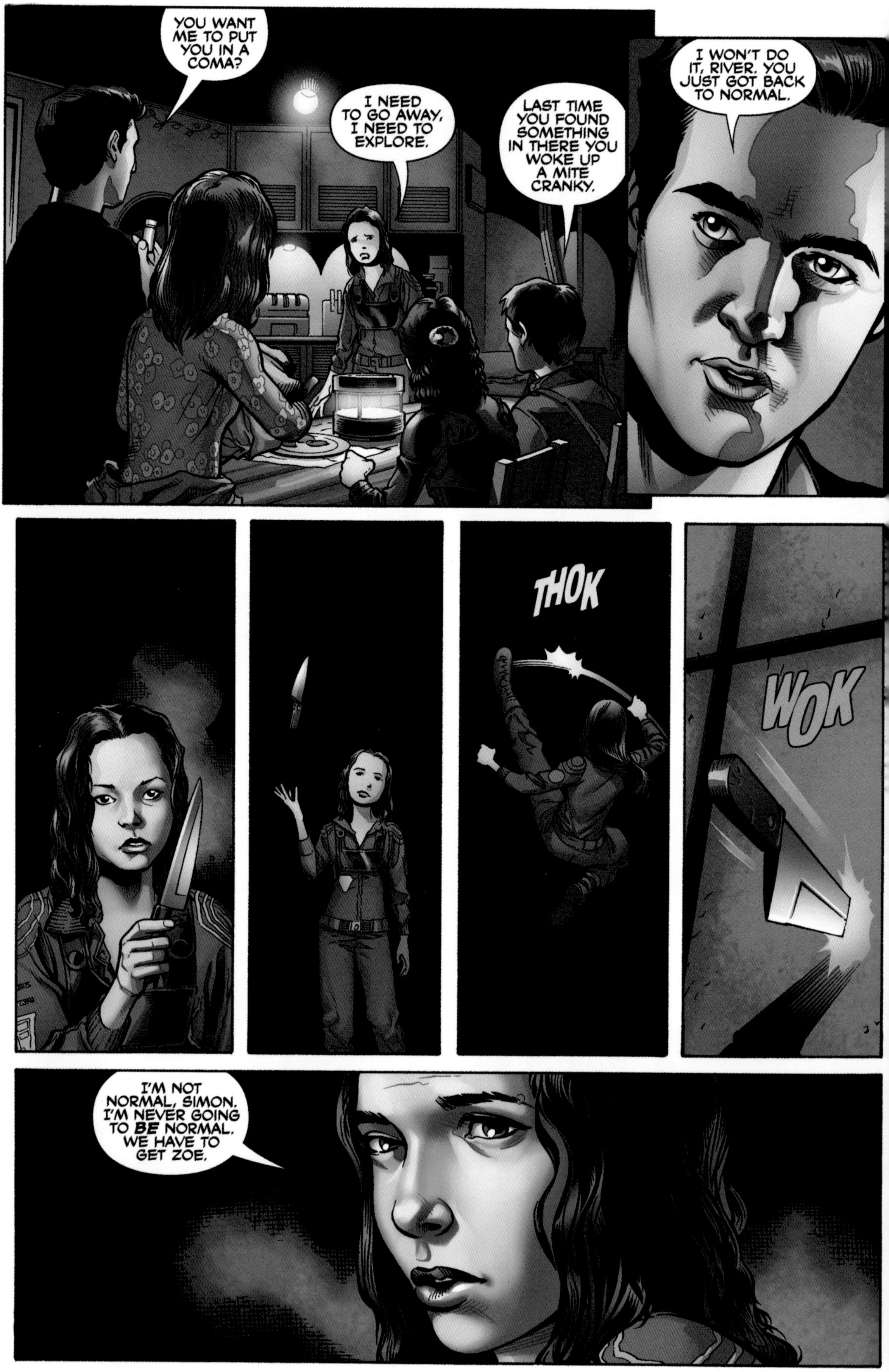
YOU WANT ME TO PUT YOU IN A COMA?
I NEED TO GO AWAY, I NEED TO EXPLORE.
LAST TIME YOU FOUND SOMETHING IN THERE YOU WOKE UP A MITE CRANKY.
I WON'T DO IT, RIVER. YOU JUST GOT BACK TO NORMAL.
THOK
WOK
I'M NOT NORMAL, SIMON. I'M NEVER GOING TO *BE* NORMAL. WE HAVE TO GET ZOE.

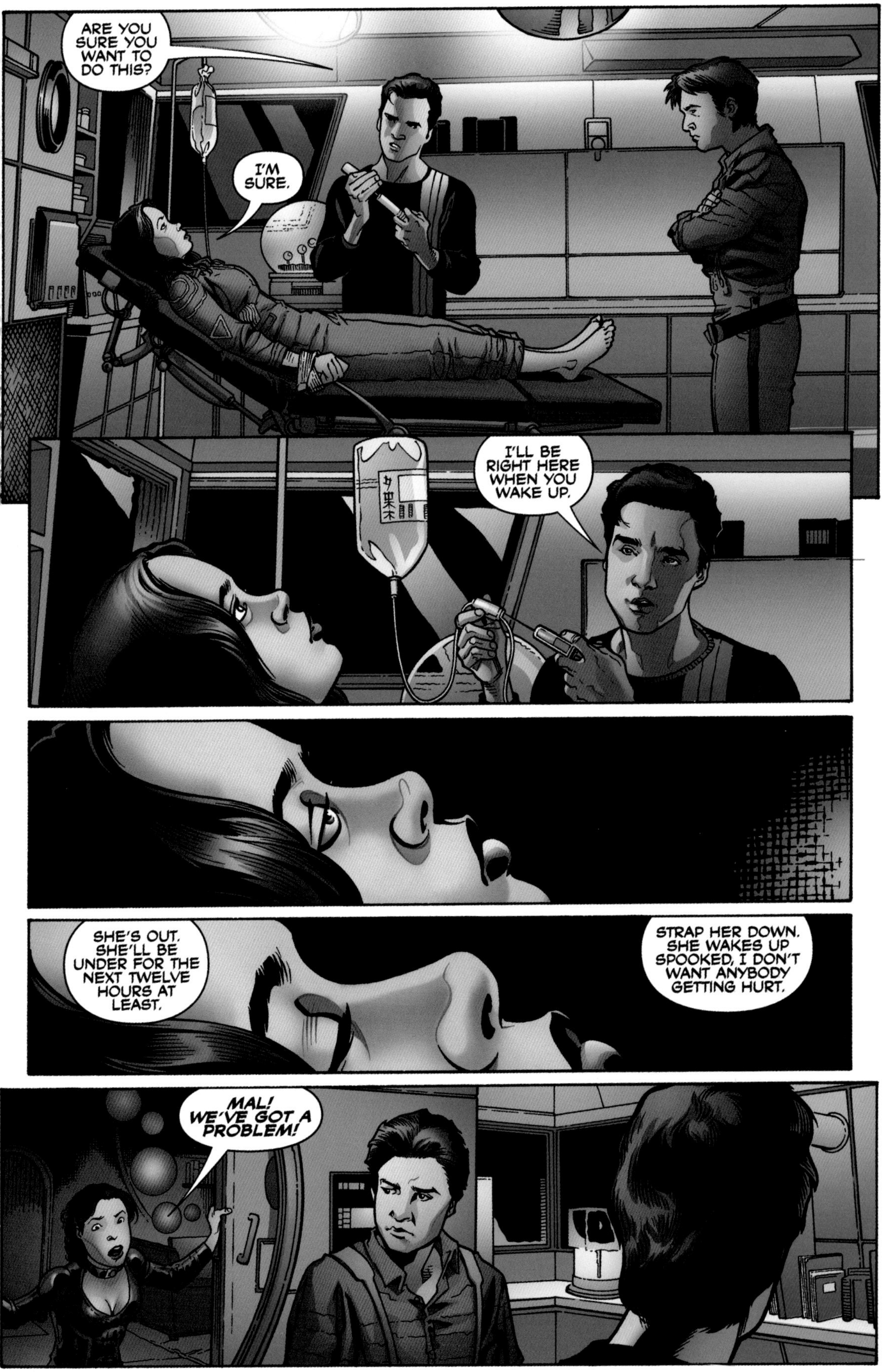
ARE YOU SURE YOU WANT TO DO THIS?
I'M SURE.
I'LL BE RIGHT HERE WHEN YOU WAKE UP.
SHE'S OUT. SHE'LL BE UNDER FOR THE NEXT TWELVE HOURS AT LEAST.
STRAP HER DOWN. SHE WAKES UP SPOOKED, I DON'T WANT ANYBODY GETTING HURT.
MAL! WE'VE GOT A PROBLEM!

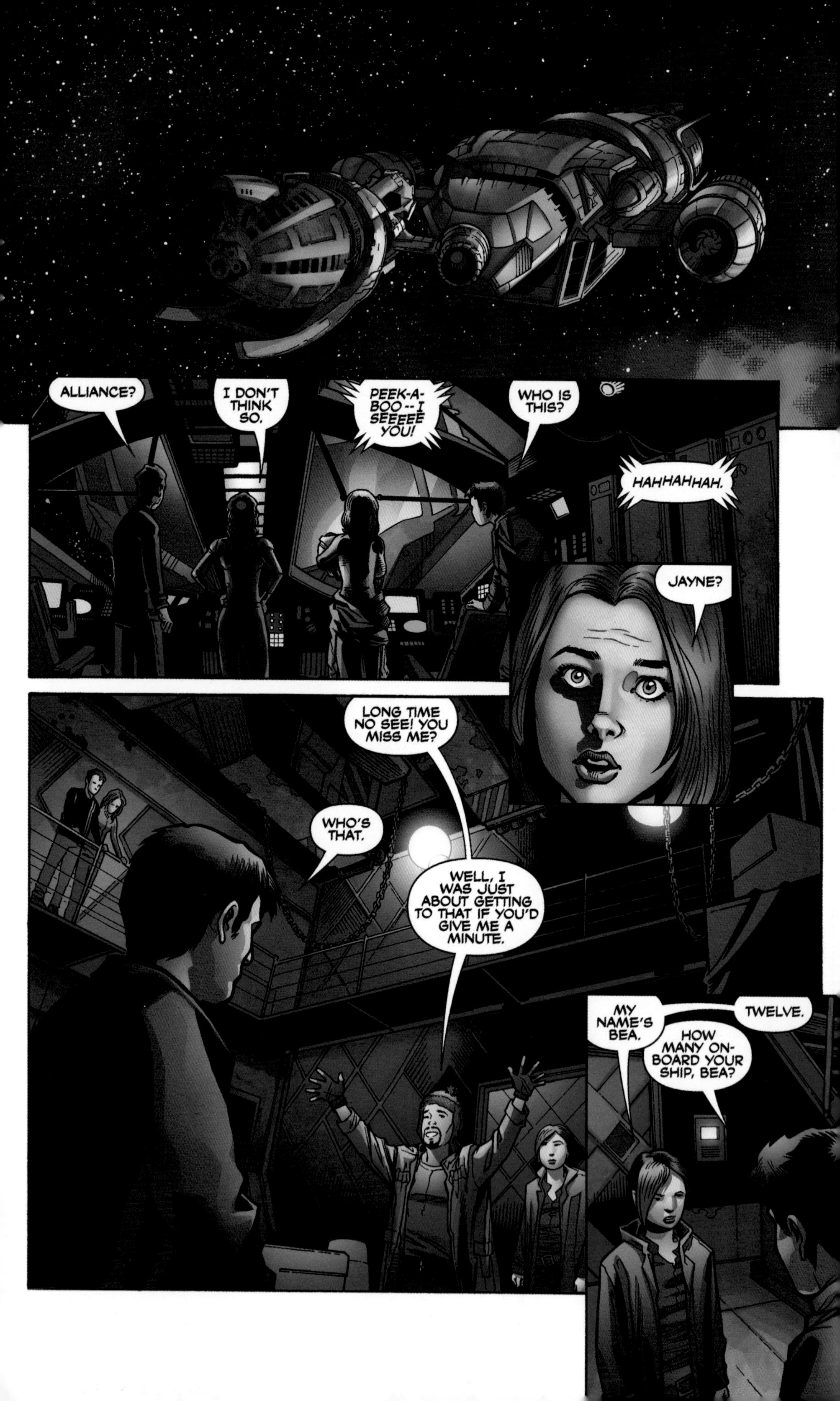
ALLIANCE?
I DON'T THINK SO.
PEEK-A-BOO -- I SEEEEE YOU!
WHO IS THIS?
HAHHAHHAH.
JAYNE?
LONG TIME NO SEE! YOU MISS ME?
WHO'S THAT.
WELL, I WAS JUST ABOUT GETTING TO THAT IF YOU'D GIVE ME A MINUTE.
MY NAME'S BEA.
HOW MANY ON-BOARD YOUR SHIP, BEA?
TWELVE.

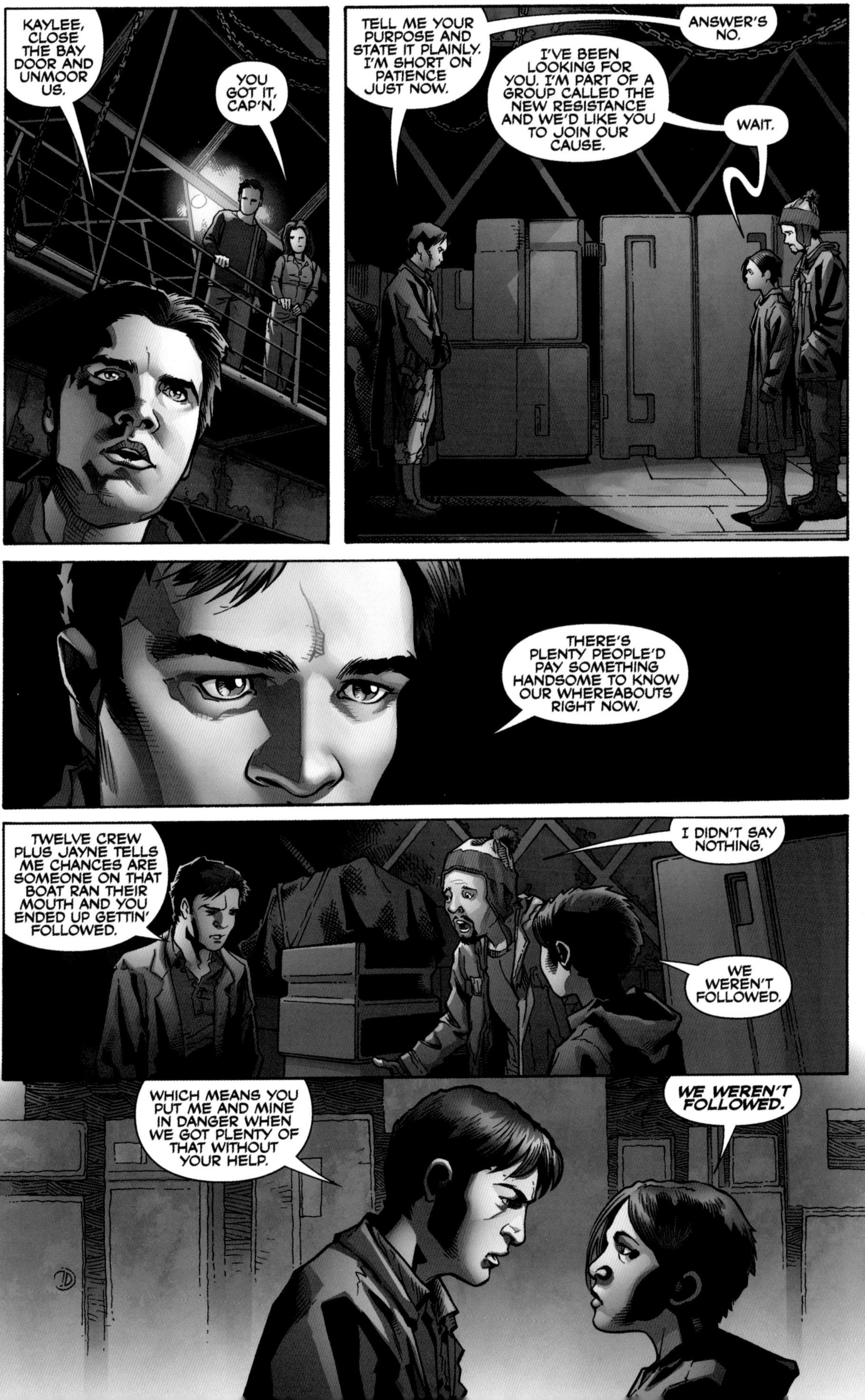
KAYLEE, CLOSE THE BAY DOOR AND UNMOOR US.
YOU GOT IT, CAP'N.
TELL ME YOUR PURPOSE AND STATE IT PLAINLY. I'M SHORT ON PATIENCE JUST NOW.
I'VE BEEN LOOKING FOR YOU. I'M PART OF A GROUP CALLED THE NEW RESISTANCE AND WE'D LIKE YOU TO JOIN OUR CAUSE.
ANSWER'S NO.
WAIT.
THERE'S PLENTY PEOPLE'D PAY SOMETHING HANDSOME TO KNOW OUR WHEREABOUTS RIGHT NOW.
TWELVE CREW PLUS JAYNE TELLS ME CHANCES ARE SOMEONE ON THAT BOAT RAN THEIR MOUTH AND YOU ENDED UP GETTIN' FOLLOWED.
I DIDN'T SAY NOTHING.
WE WEREN'T FOLLOWED.
WHICH MEANS YOU PUT ME AND MINE IN DANGER WHEN WE GOT PLENTY OF THAT WITHOUT YOUR HELP.
WE WEREN'T FOLLOWED.

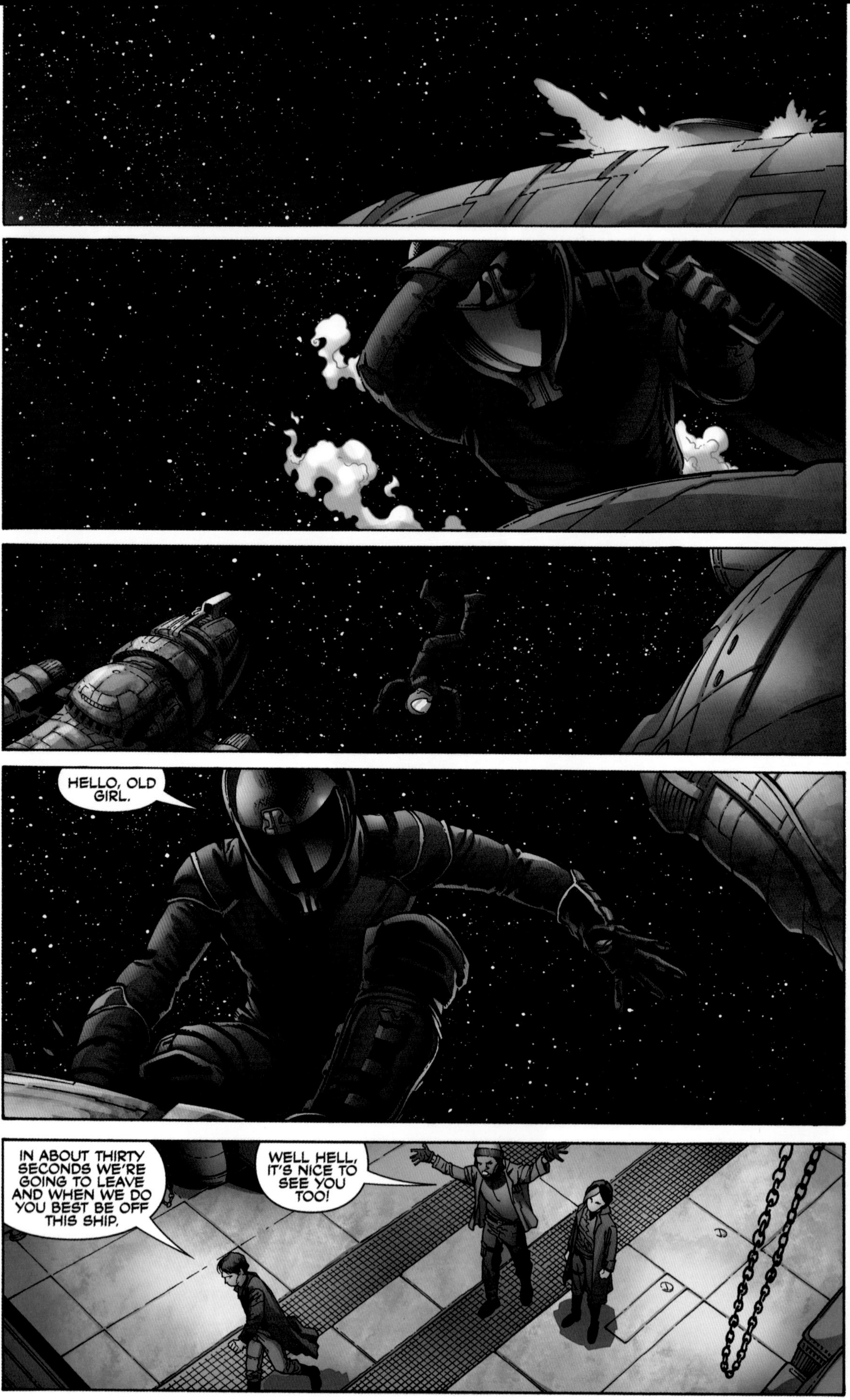
HELLO, OLD GIRL.
IN ABOUT THIRTY SECONDS WE'RE GOING TO LEAVE AND WHEN WE DO YOU BEST BE OFF THIS SHIP.
WELL HELL, IT'S NICE TO SEE YOU TOO!

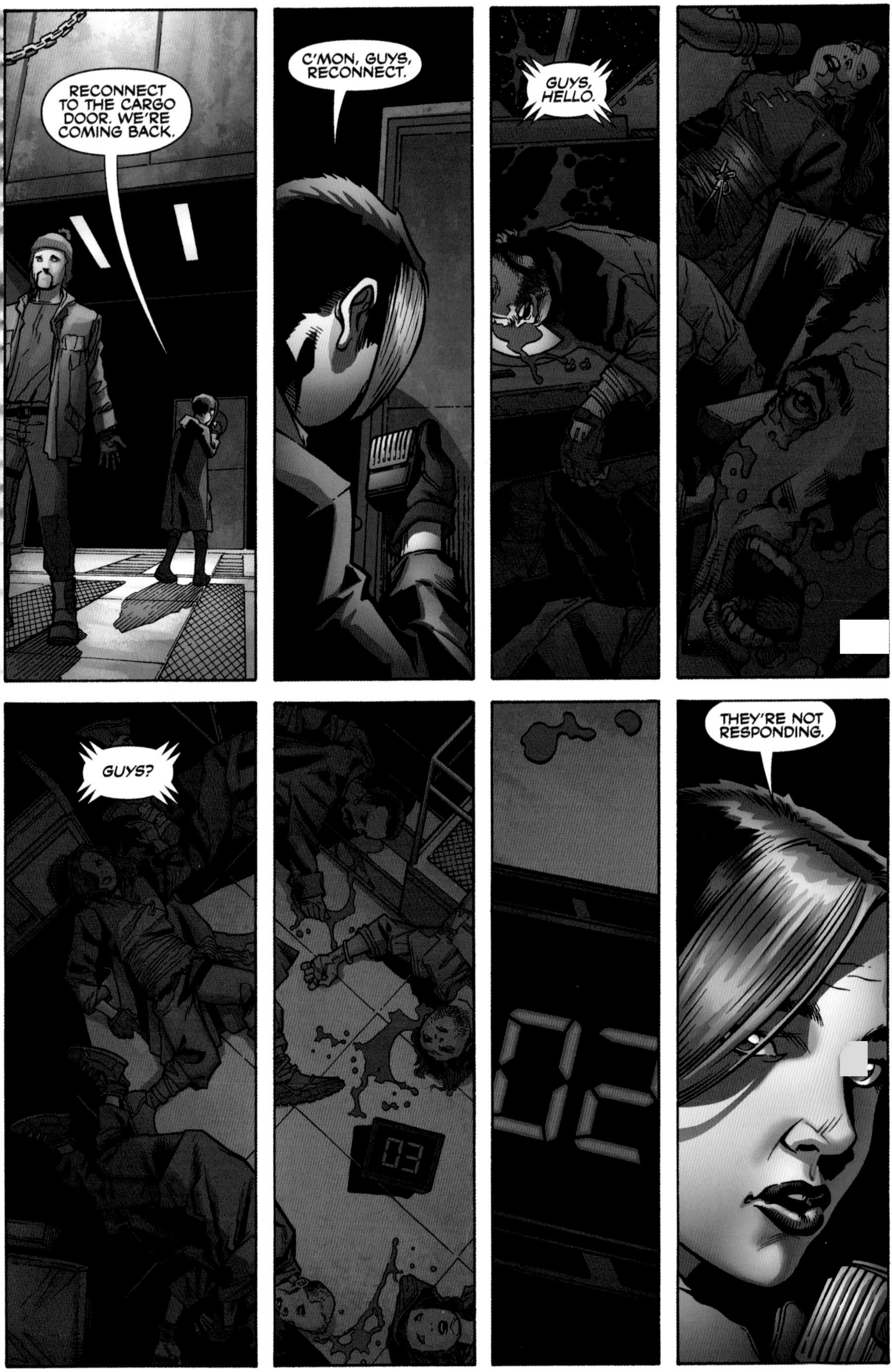
RECONNECT TO THE CARGO DOOR. WE'RE COMING BACK.
C'MON, GUYS, RECONNECT.
GUYS, HELLO.
GUYS?
THEY'RE NOT RESPONDING.

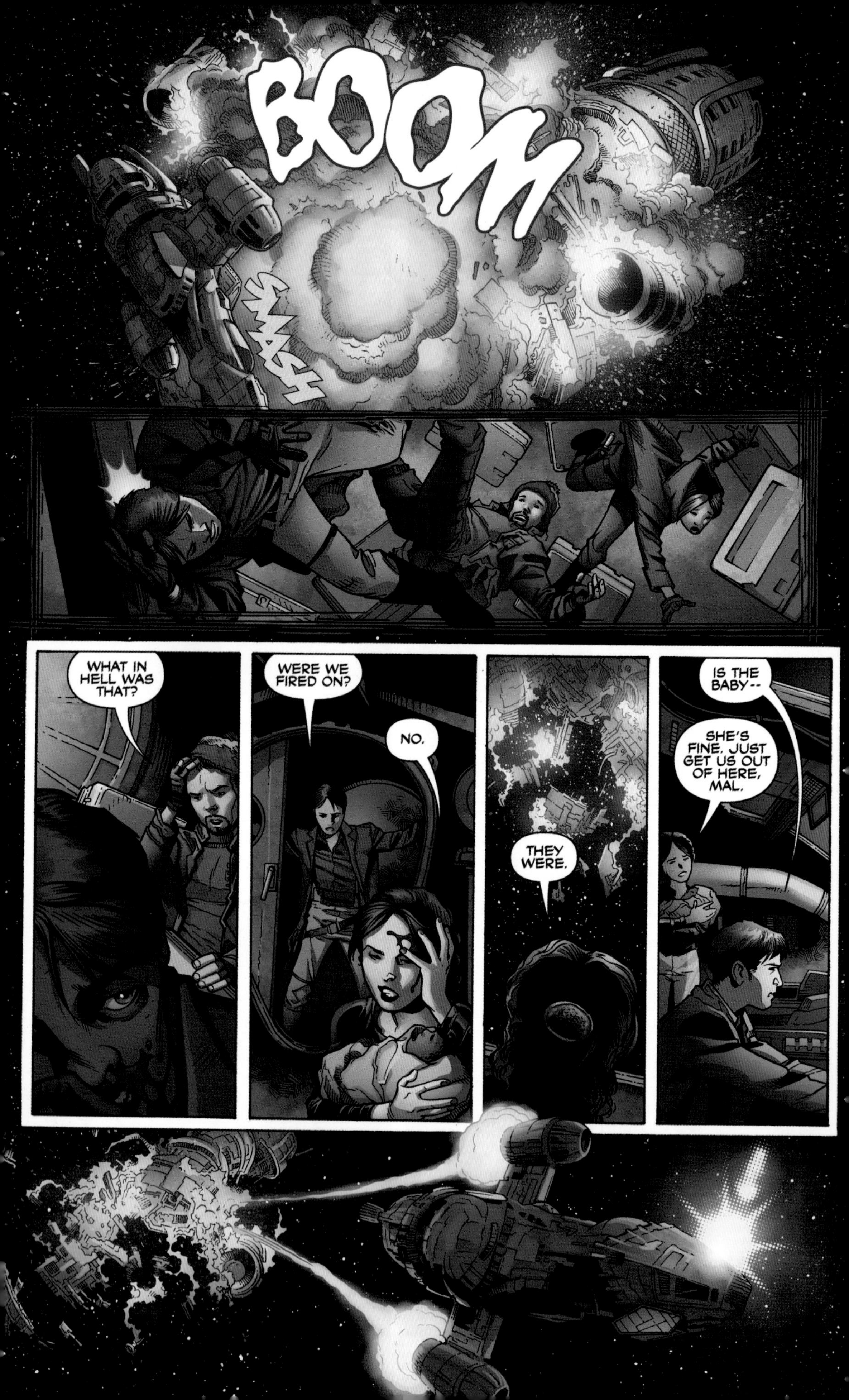
BOOM
SMASH
WHAT IN HELL WAS THAT?
WERE WE FIRED ON?
NO.
THEY WERE.
IS THE BABY--
SHE'S FINE. JUST GET US OUT OF HERE, MAL.

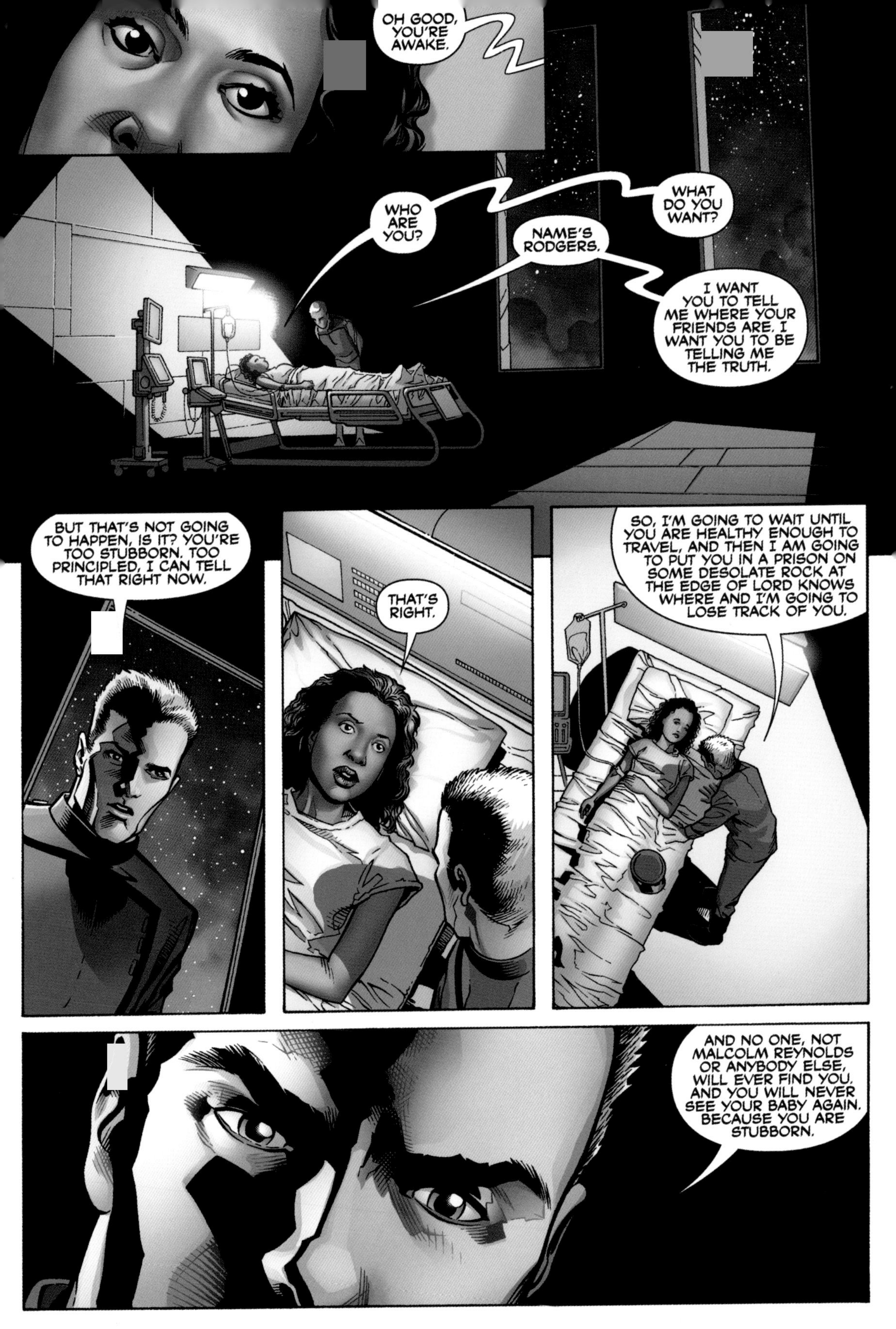
OH GOOD, YOU'RE AWAKE.
WHO ARE YOU?
WHAT DO YOU WANT?
NAME'S RODGERS.
I WANT YOU TO TELL ME WHERE YOUR FRIENDS ARE. I WANT YOU TO BE TELLING ME THE TRUTH.
BUT THAT'S NOT GOING TO HAPPEN, IS IT? YOU'RE TOO STUBBORN. TOO PRINCIPLED, I CAN TELL THAT RIGHT NOW.
THAT'S RIGHT.
SO, I'M GOING TO WAIT UNTIL YOU ARE HEALTHY ENOUGH TO TRAVEL, AND THEN I AM GOING TO PUT YOU IN A PRISON ON SOME DESOLATE ROCK AT THE EDGE OF LORD KNOWS WHERE AND I'M GOING TO LOSE TRACK OF YOU.
AND NO ONE, NOT MALCOLM REYNOLDS OR ANYBODY ELSE, WILL EVER FIND YOU. AND YOU WILL NEVER SEE YOUR BABY AGAIN. BECAUSE YOU ARE STUBBORN.

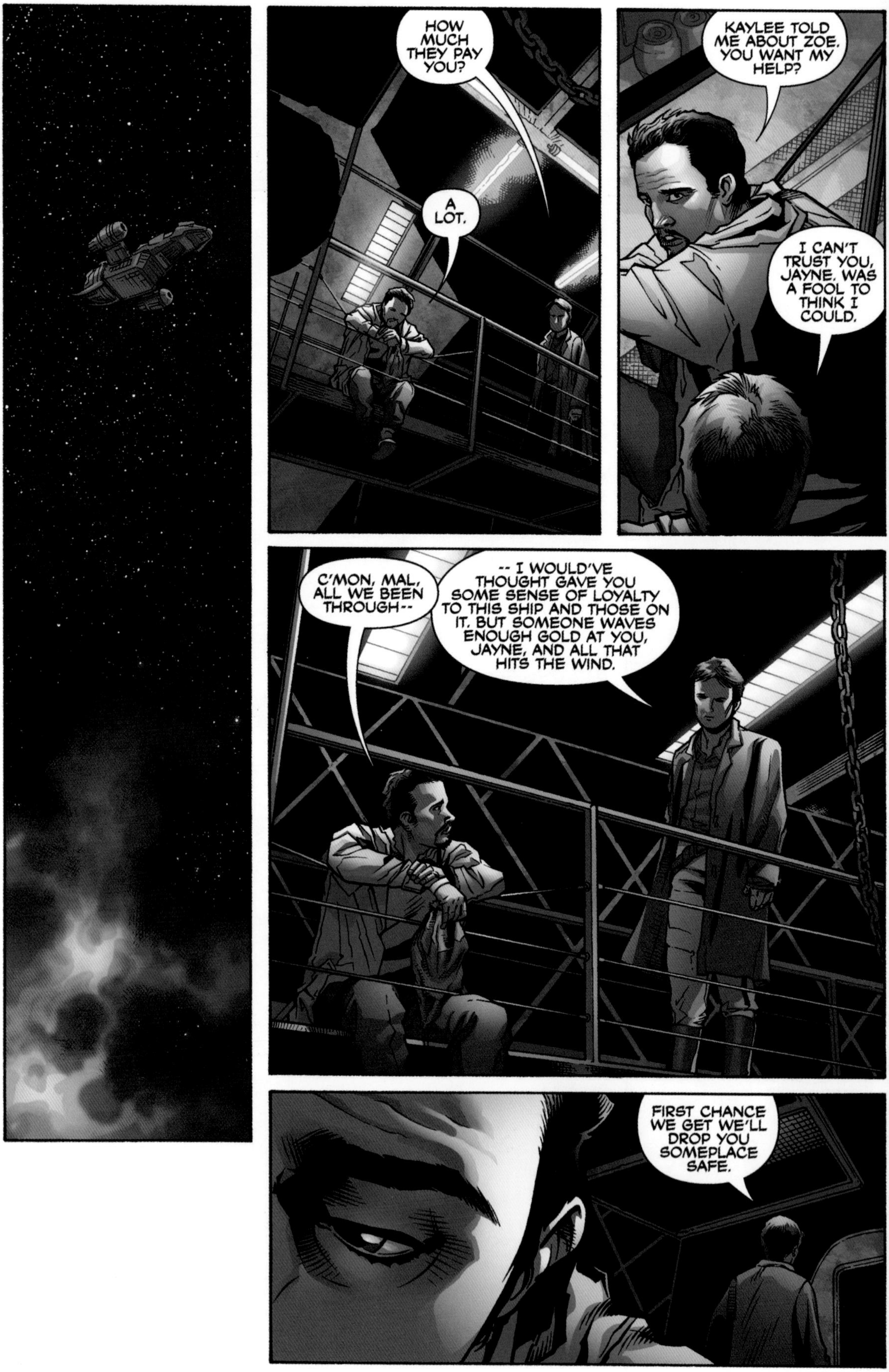
HOW MUCH THEY PAY YOU?
A LOT.
KAYLEE TOLD ME ABOUT ZOE. YOU WANT MY HELP?
I CAN'T TRUST YOU, JAYNE. WAS A FOOL TO THINK I COULD.
C'MON, MAL, ALL WE BEEN THROUGH--
-- I WOULD'VE THOUGHT GAVE YOU SOME SENSE OF LOYALTY TO THIS SHIP AND THOSE ON IT. BUT SOMEONE WAVES ENOUGH GOLD AT YOU, JAYNE, AND ALL THAT HITS THE WIND.
FIRST CHANCE WE GET WE'LL DROP YOU SOMEPLACE SAFE.

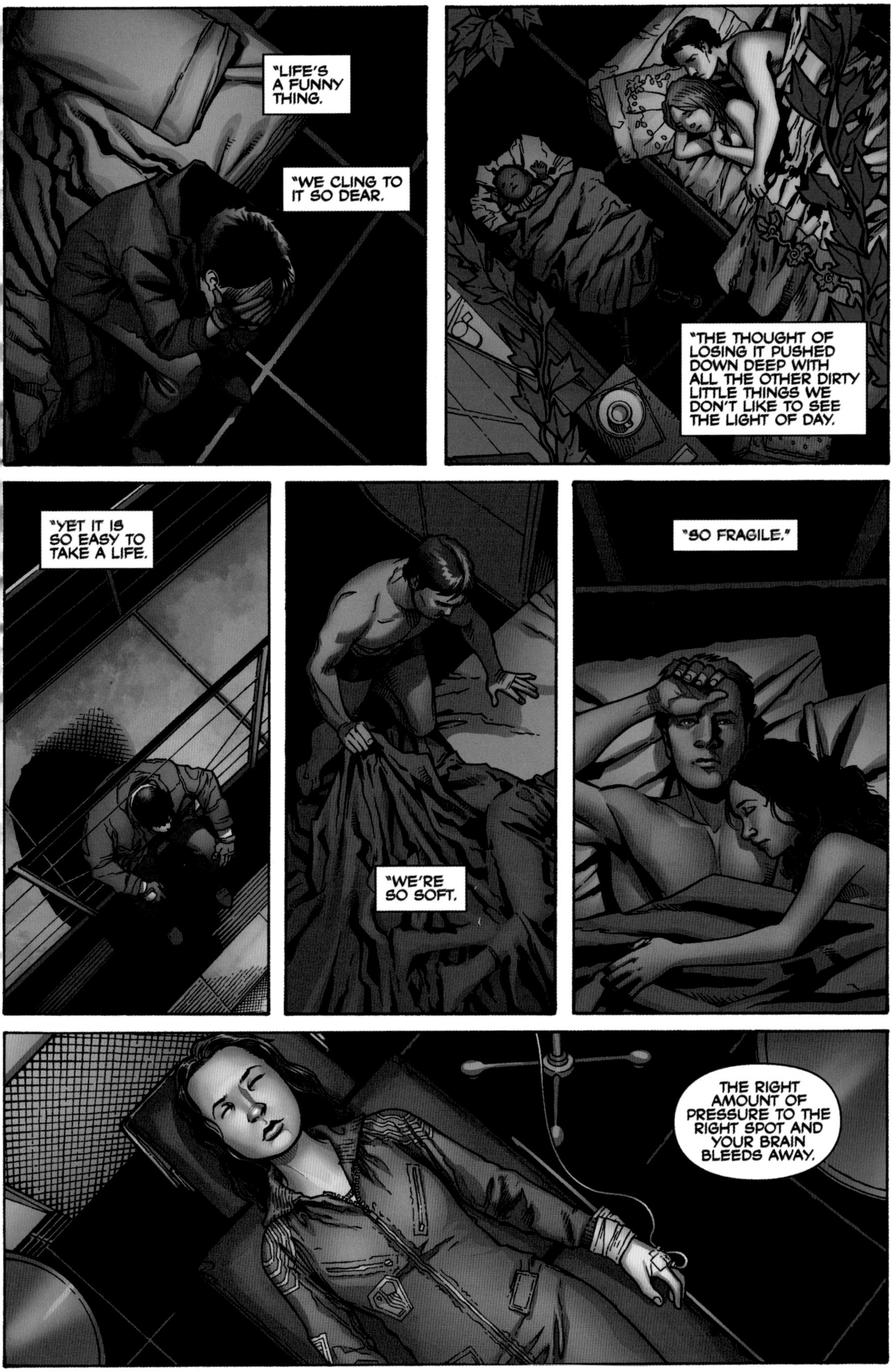

"LIFE'S A FUNNY THING.
"WE CLING TO IT SO DEAR.
"THE THOUGHT OF LOSING IT PUSHED DOWN DEEP WITH ALL THE OTHER DIRTY LITTLE THINGS WE DON'T LIKE TO SEE THE LIGHT OF DAY.
"YET IT IS SO EASY TO TAKE A LIFE.
"WE'RE SO SOFT.
"SO FRAGILE."
THE RIGHT AMOUNT OF PRESSURE TO THE RIGHT SPOT AND YOUR BRAIN BLEEDS AWAY.

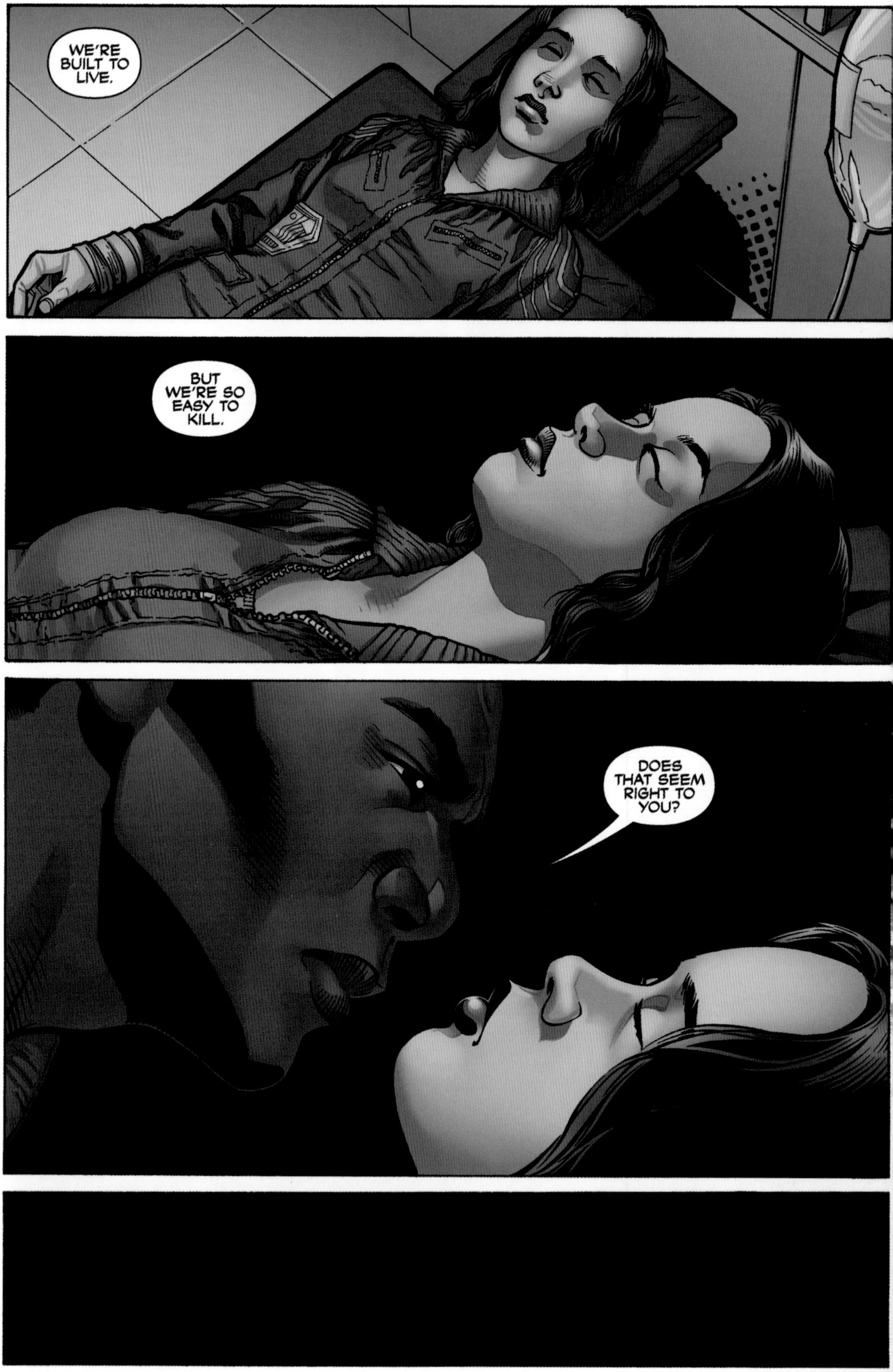
WE'RE BUILT TO LIVE.
BUT WE'RE SO EASY TO KILL.
DOES THAT SEEM RIGHT TO YOU?

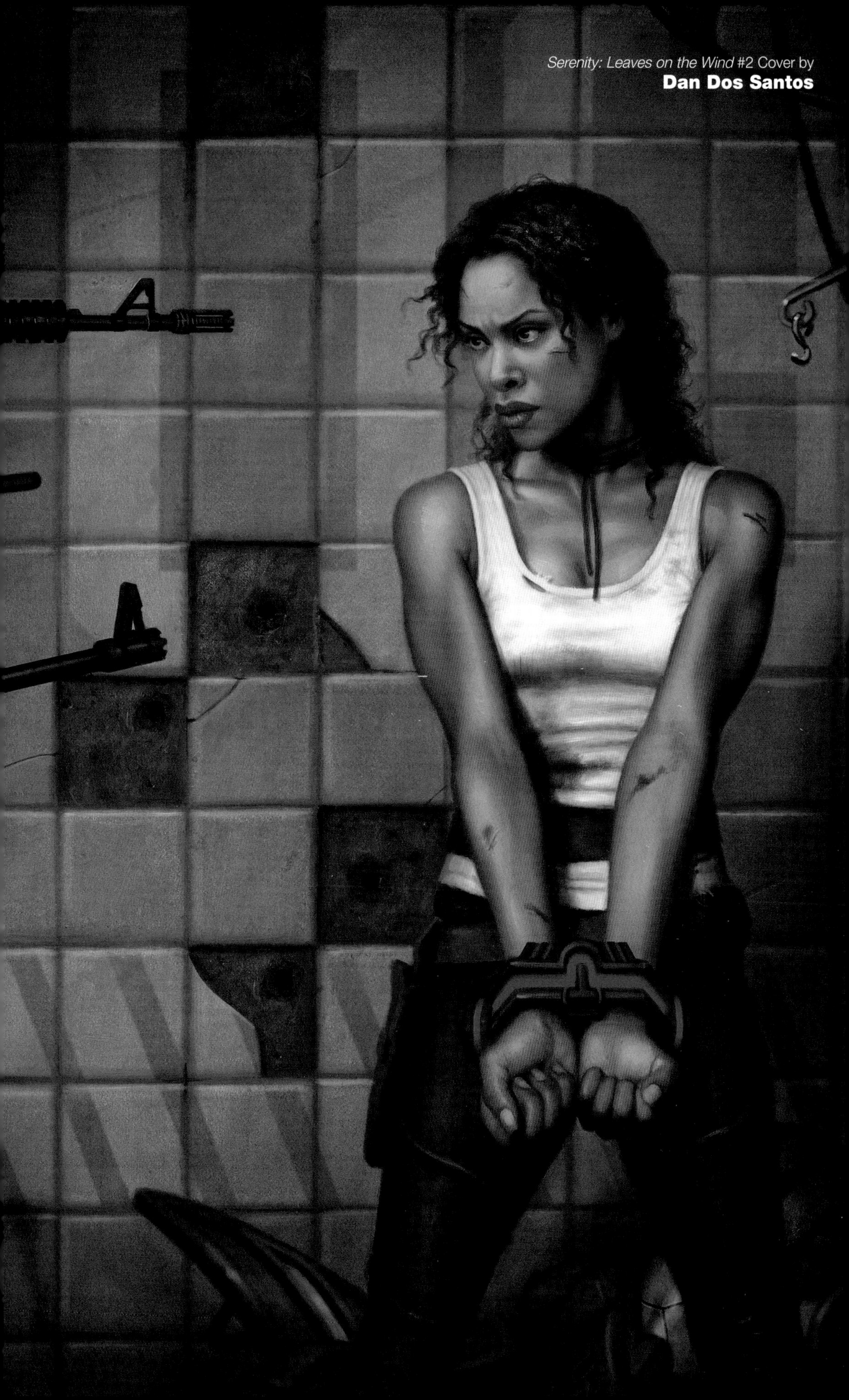

Serenity: Leaves on the Wind #2 Cover by
Dan Dos Santos

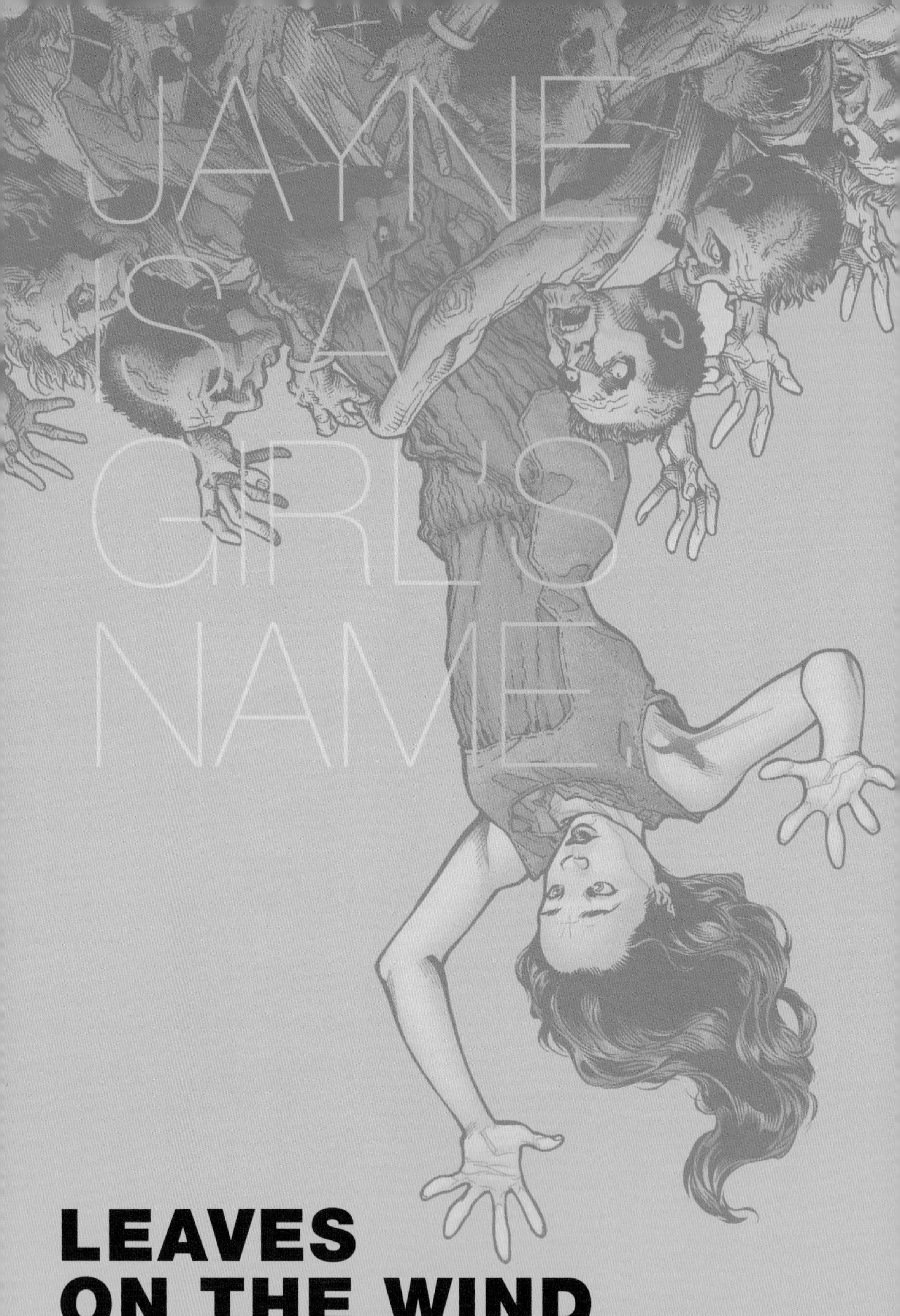
JAYNE IS A GIRL'S NAME.

LEAVES ON THE WIND
CHAPTER THREE

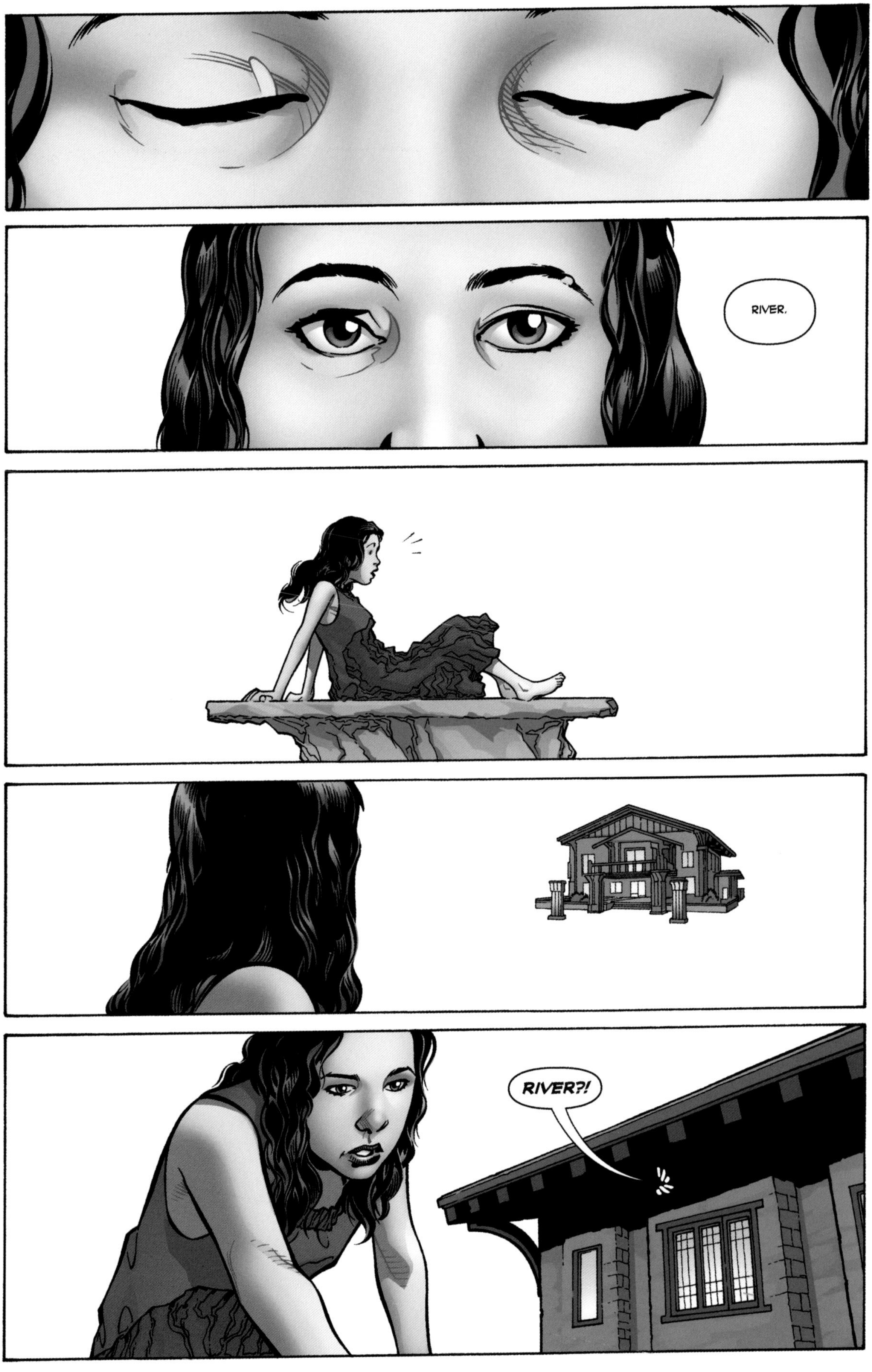
RIVER.
RIVER?!

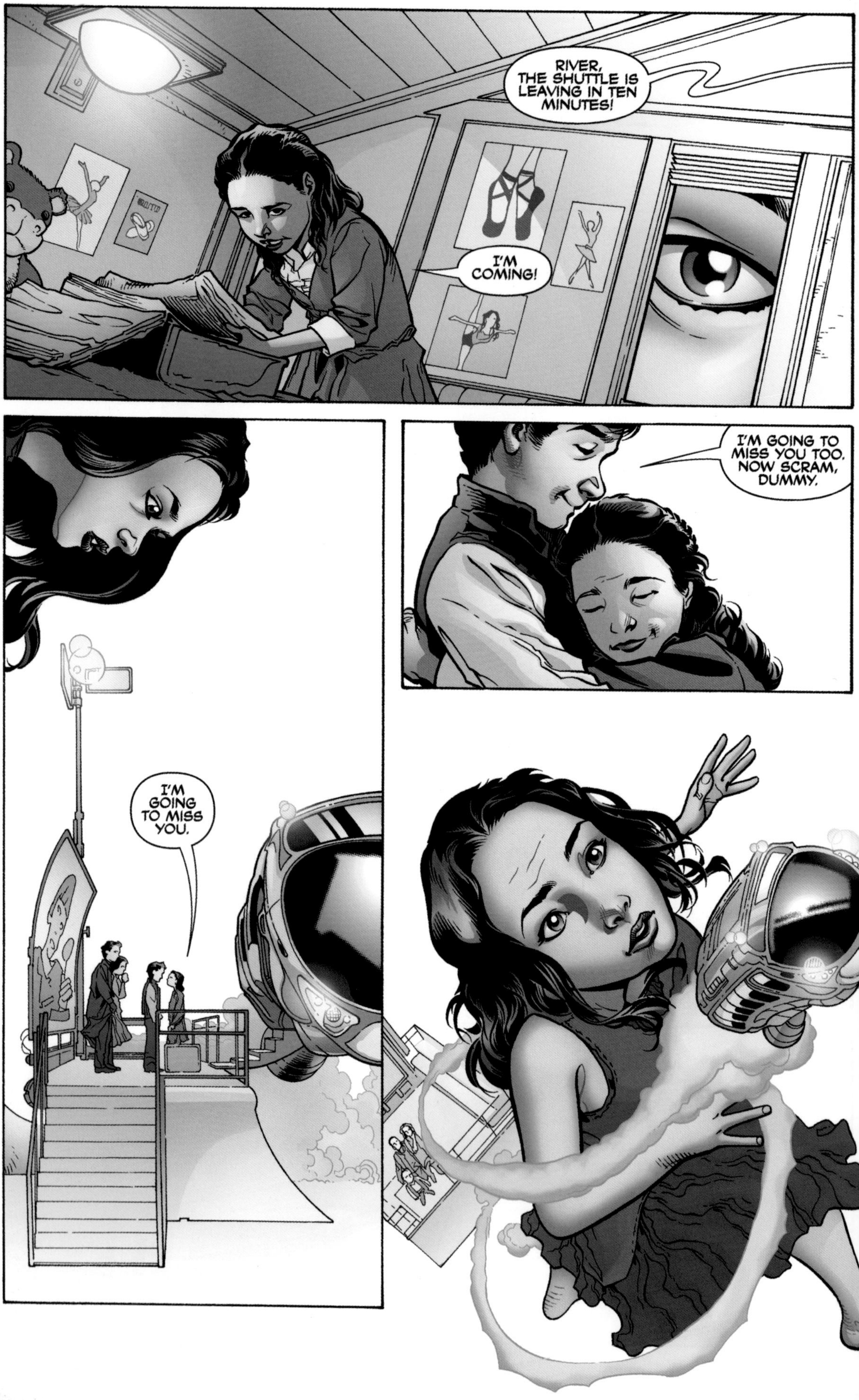
RIVER, THE SHUTTLE IS LEAVING IN TEN MINUTES!
I'M COMING!
I'M GOING TO MISS YOU TOO. NOW SCRAM, DUMMY.
I'M GOING TO MISS YOU.

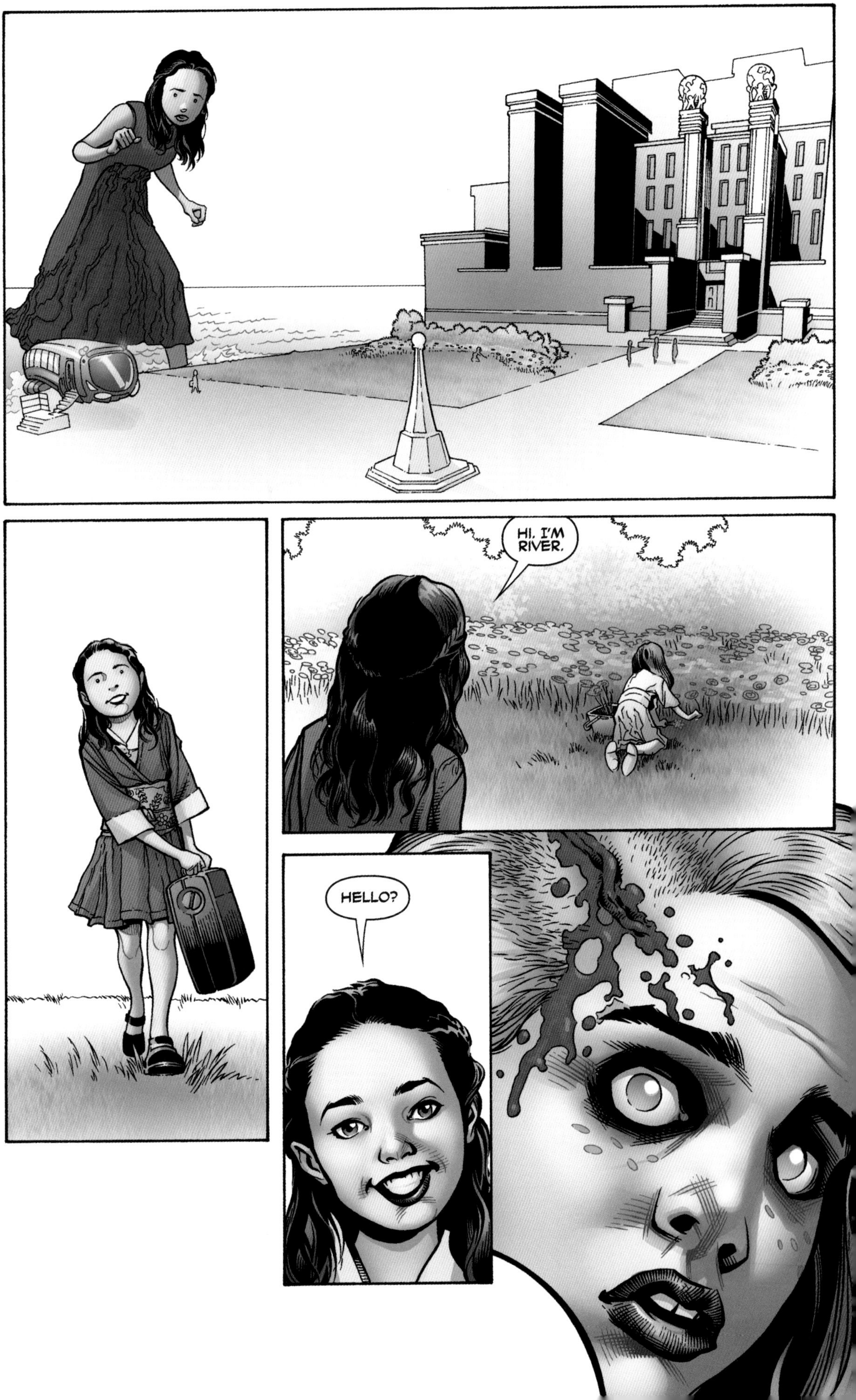
HI. I'M RIVER.
HELLO?

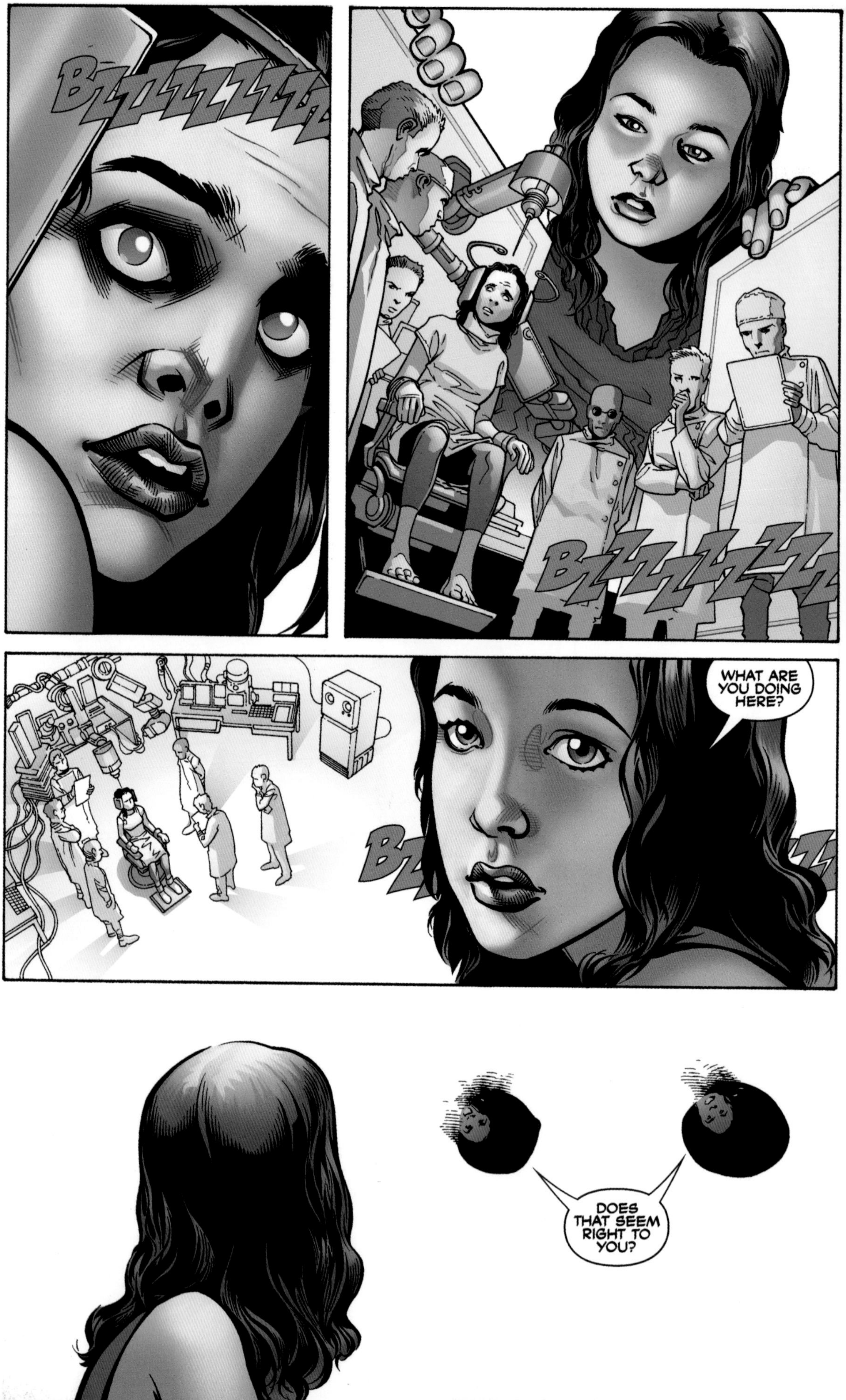
BZZZZZZZ
BZZZZZZZ
WHAT ARE YOU DOING HERE?
DOES THAT SEEM RIGHT TO YOU?

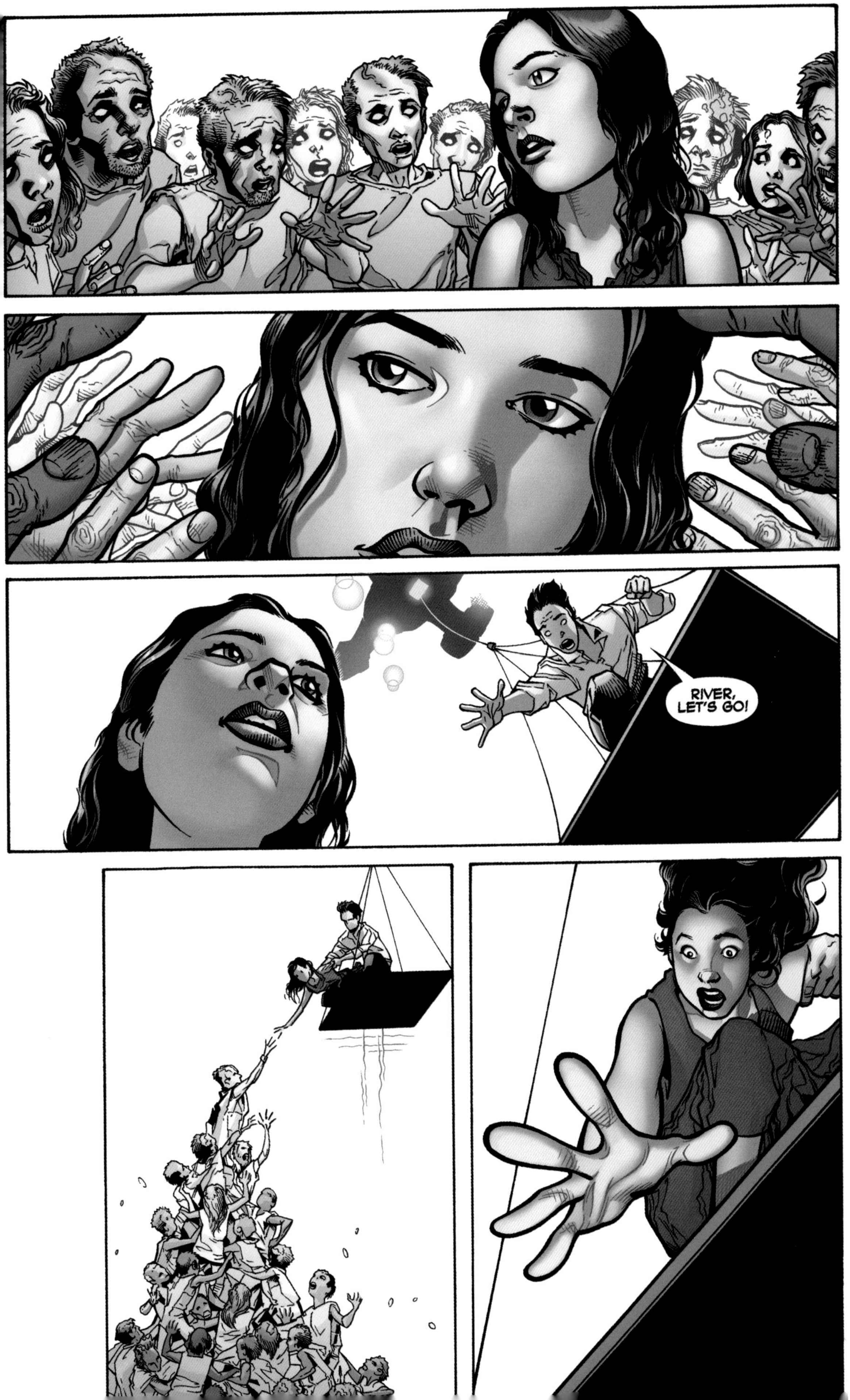
RIVER,
LET'S GO!

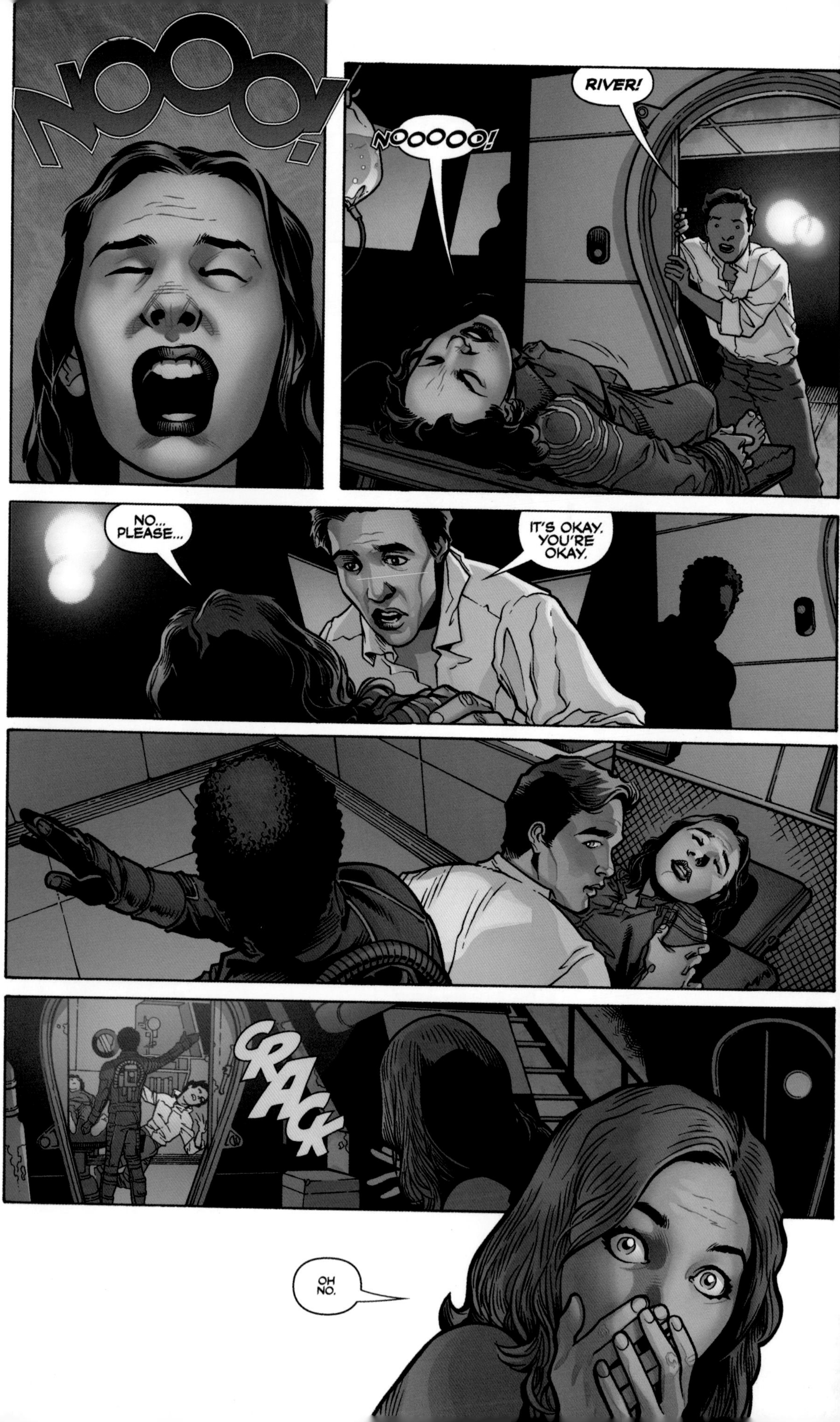
NOOOO!
NOOOOO!
RIVER!
NO... PLEASE...
IT'S OKAY. YOU'RE OKAY.
CRACK
OH NO.

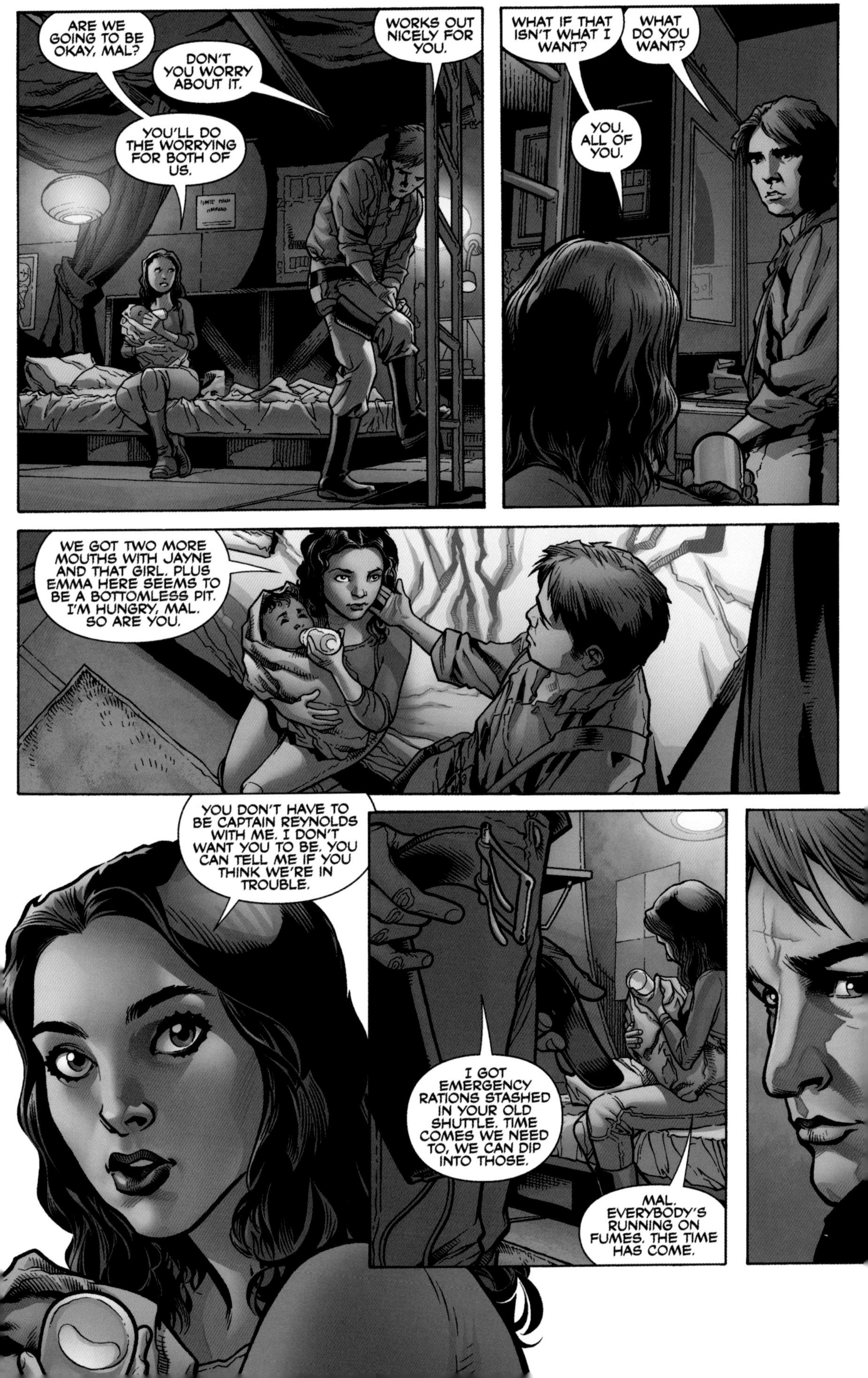
ARE WE GOING TO BE OKAY, MAL?
DON'T YOU WORRY ABOUT IT.
YOU'LL DO THE WORRYING FOR BOTH OF US.
WORKS OUT NICELY FOR YOU.
WHAT IF THAT ISN'T WHAT I WANT?
WHAT DO YOU WANT?
YOU. ALL OF YOU.
WE GOT TWO MORE MOUTHS WITH JAYNE AND THAT GIRL. PLUS EMMA HERE SEEMS TO BE A BOTTOMLESS PIT. I'M HUNGRY, MAL. SO ARE YOU.
YOU DON'T HAVE TO BE CAPTAIN REYNOLDS WITH ME. I DON'T WANT YOU TO BE. YOU CAN TELL ME IF YOU THINK WE'RE IN TROUBLE.
I GOT EMERGENCY RATIONS STASHED IN YOUR OLD SHUTTLE. TIME COMES WE NEED TO, WE CAN DIP INTO THOSE.
MAL. EVERYBODY'S RUNNING ON FUMES. THE TIME HAS COME.

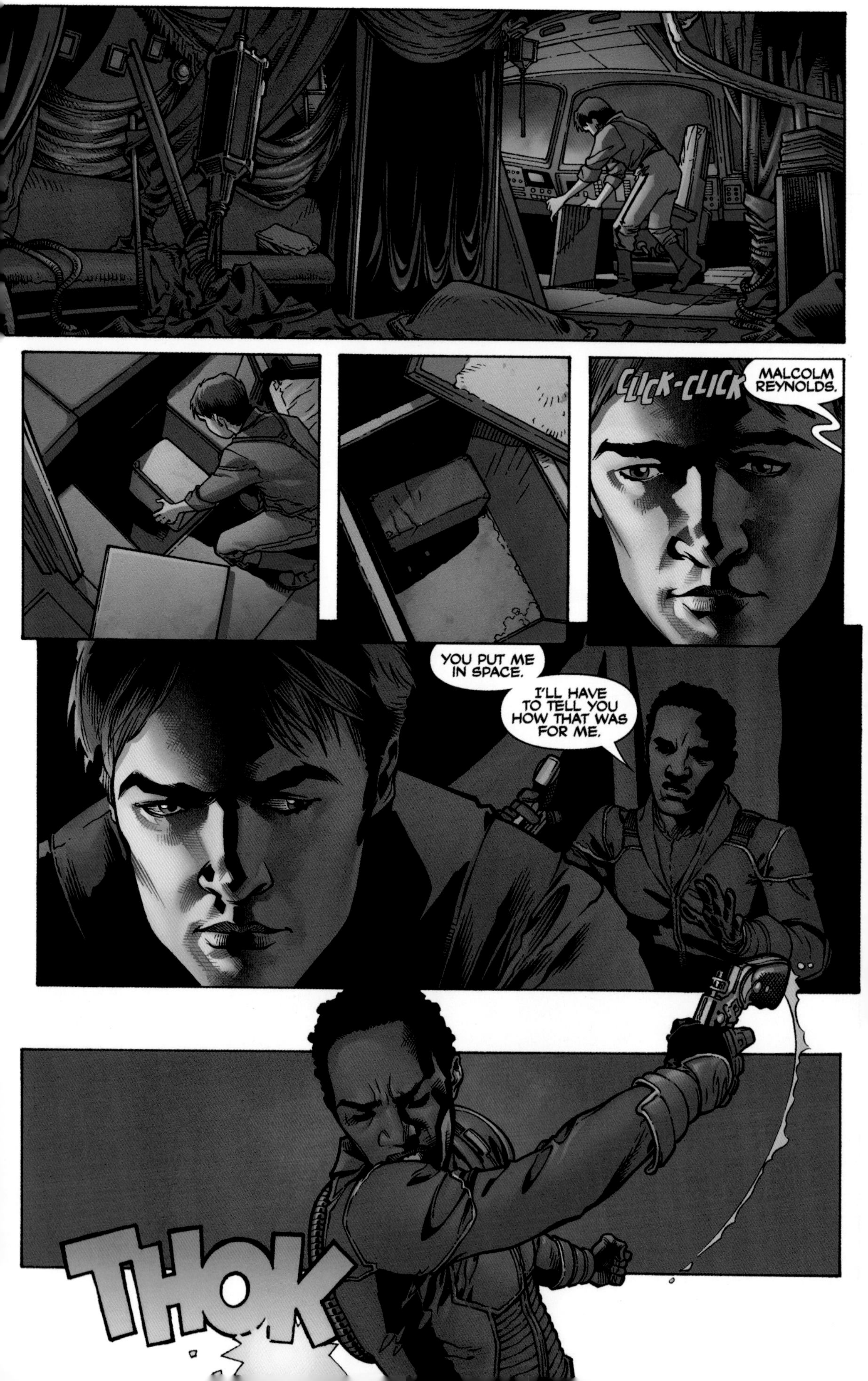
CLICK-CLICK
MALCOLM REYNOLDS.
YOU PUT ME IN SPACE.
I'LL HAVE TO TELL YOU HOW THAT WAS FOR ME.
THOK

LOT OF TIME, MONEY, AND LIVES TO GET ME HERE. FOR NOTHING. SHOULDN'T'VE BELIEVED THE LEGENDS.

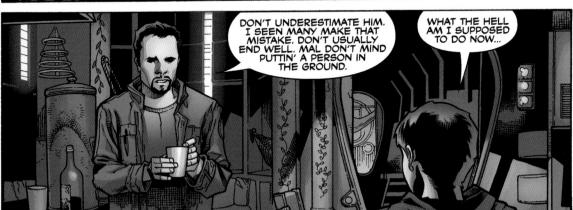

DON'T UNDERESTIMATE HIM. I SEEN MANY MAKE THAT MISTAKE. DON'T USUALLY END WELL. MAL DON'T MIND PUTTIN' A PERSON IN THE GROUND.

WHAT THE HELL AM I SUPPOSED TO DO NOW...

WELL, THE POOR BASTARD'S GOT PRINCIPLES. I DON'T KNOW, PREY ON THOSE YOU MAYBE GOT A SHOT.

PLUS ALSO YOU GOT ME ON YOUR SIDE. I'M SURE YOU MET SMARTER BUT I KNOW YOU NEVER MET NO ONE CAN SHOOT LIKE ME. THAT AIN'T NOTHING.

I'M SORRY AS HELL ABOUT YOUR SHIP. SEEMED LIKE GOOD FOLK.

THANKS.

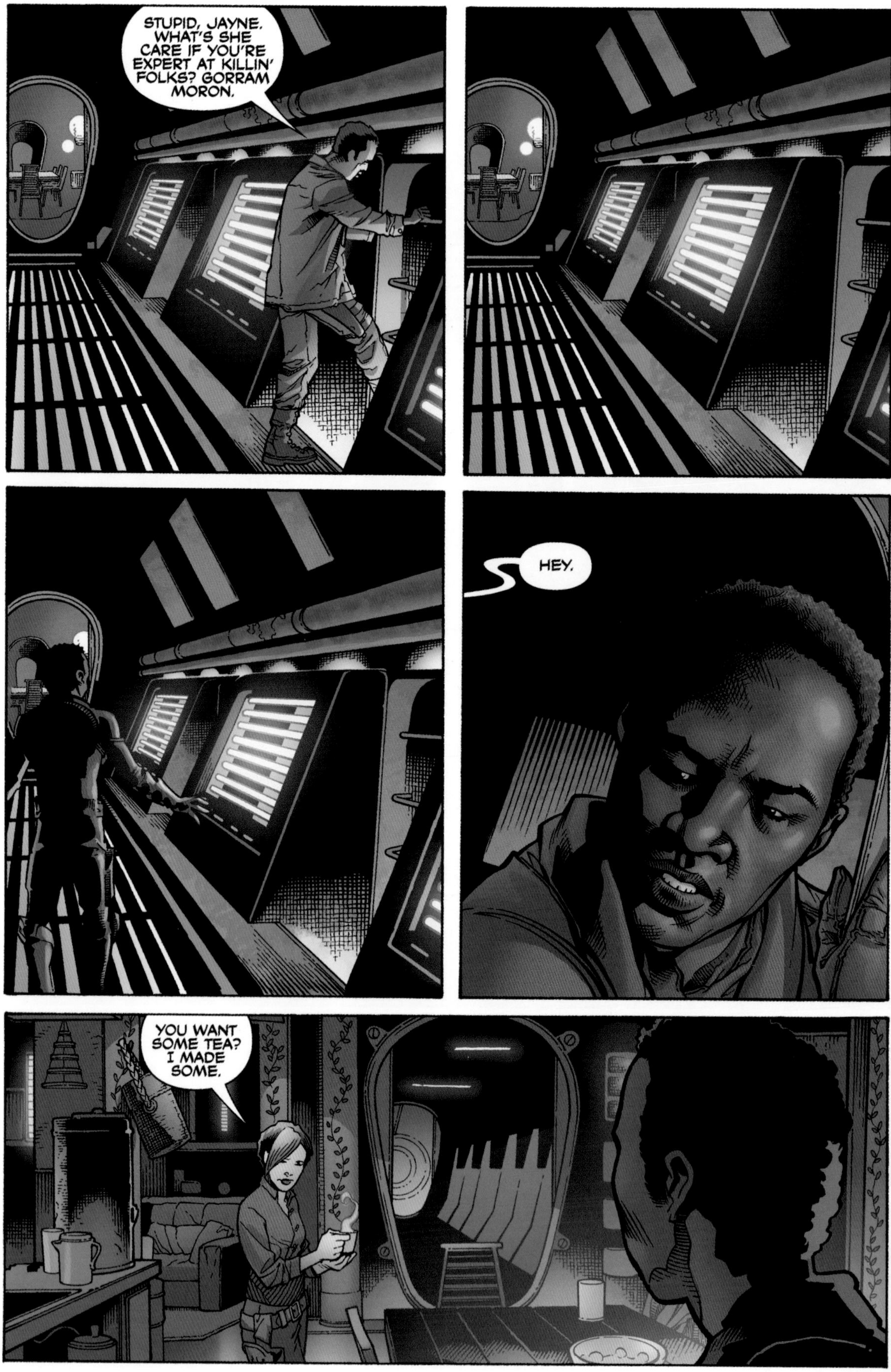
STUPID, JAYNE. WHAT'S SHE CARE IF YOU'RE EXPERT AT KILLIN' FOLKS? GORRAM MORON.
HEY.
YOU WANT SOME TEA? I MADE SOME.

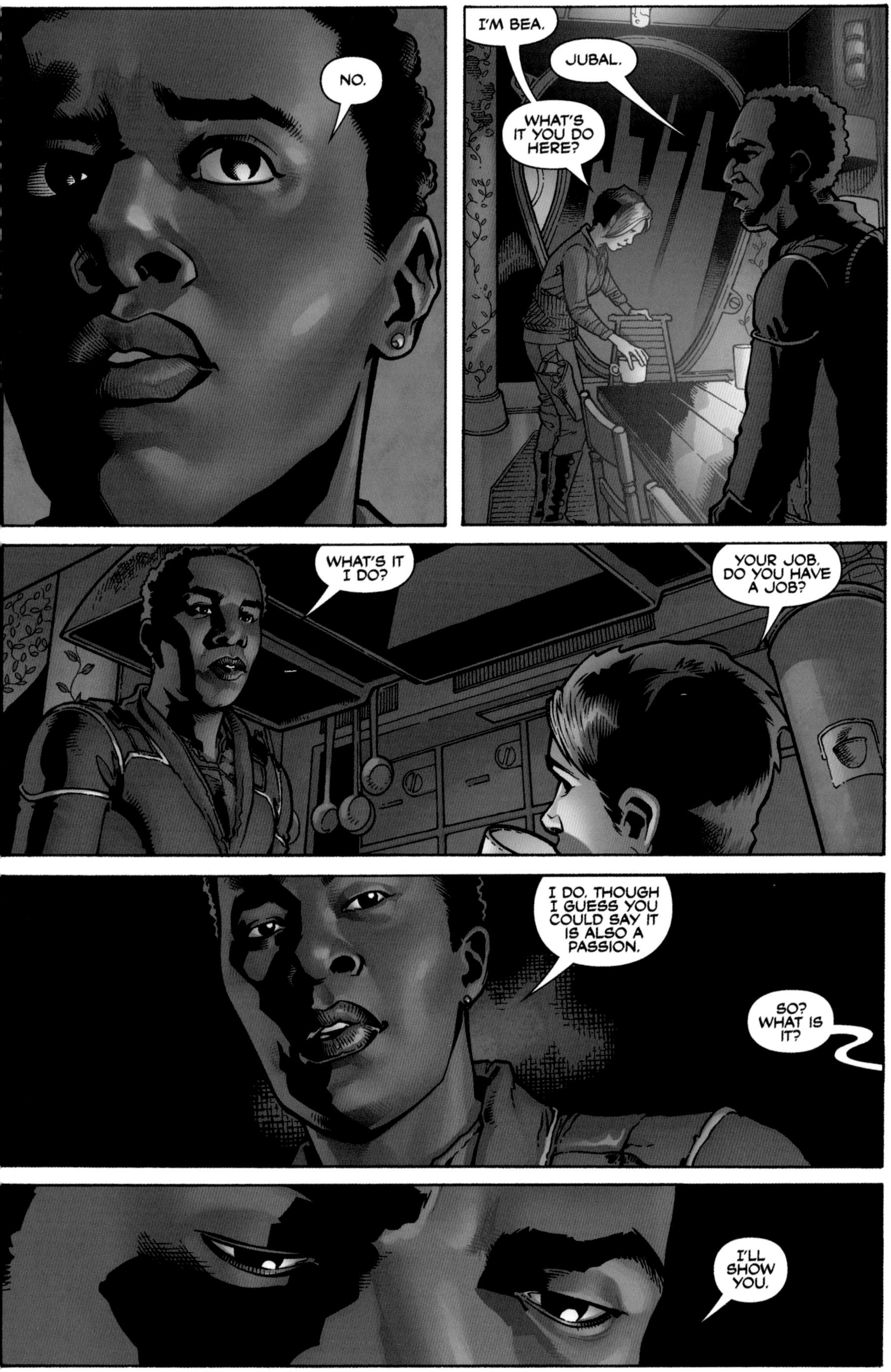
NO.
I'M BEA.
JUBAL.
WHAT'S IT YOU DO HERE?
WHAT'S IT I DO?
YOUR JOB. DO YOU HAVE A JOB?
I DO. THOUGH I GUESS YOU COULD SAY IT IS ALSO A PASSION.
SO? WHAT IS IT?
I'LL SHOW YOU.

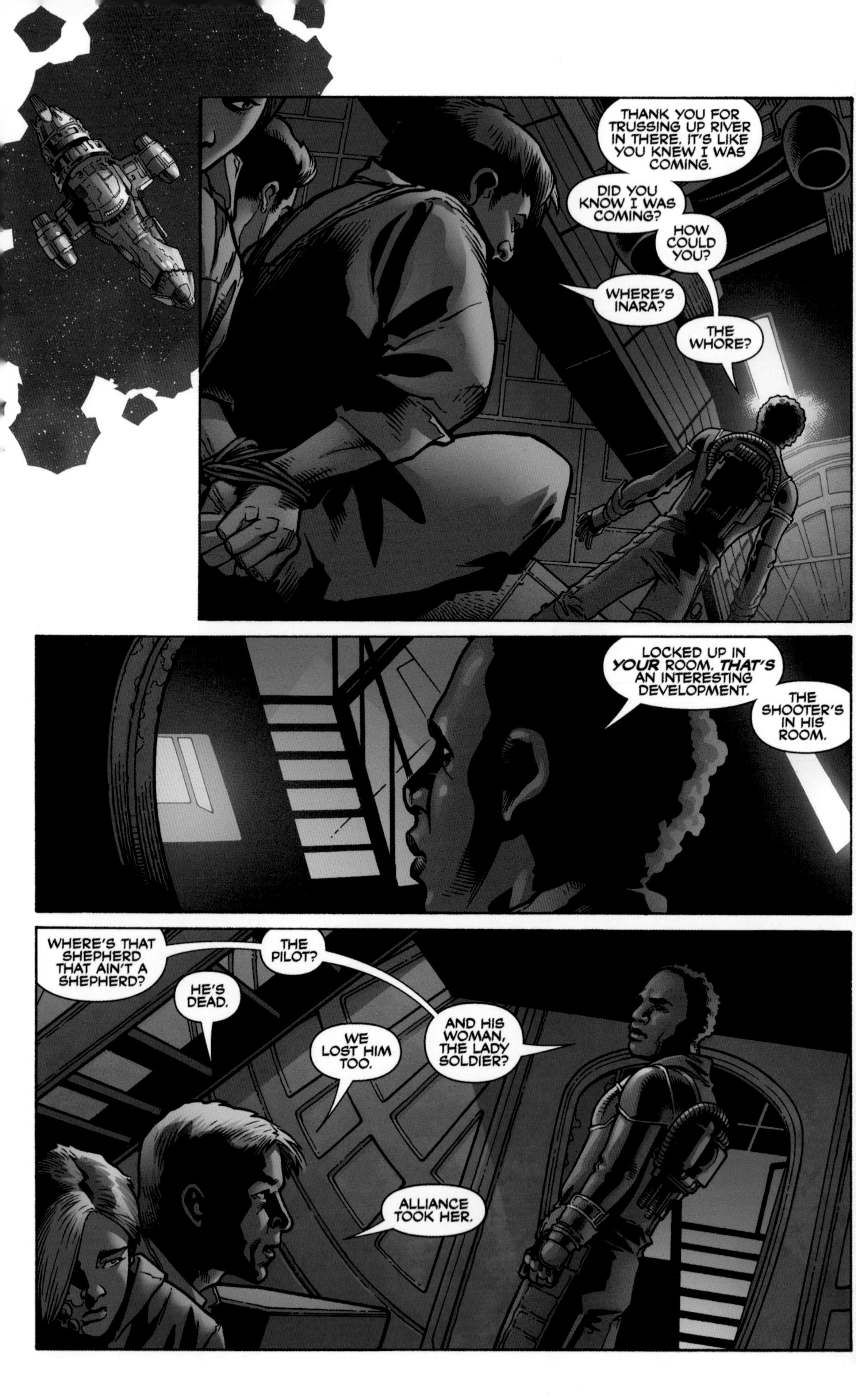
THANK YOU FOR TRUSSING UP RIVER IN THERE. IT'S LIKE YOU KNEW I WAS COMING.
DID YOU KNOW I WAS COMING?
HOW COULD YOU?
WHERE'S INARA?
THE WHORE?
LOCKED UP IN *YOUR* ROOM. *THAT'S* AN INTERESTING DEVELOPMENT.
THE SHOOTER'S IN HIS ROOM.
WHERE'S THAT SHEPHERD THAT AIN'T A SHEPHERD?
HE'S DEAD.
THE PILOT?
WE LOST HIM TOO.
AND HIS WOMAN, THE LADY SOLDIER?
ALLIANCE TOOK HER.

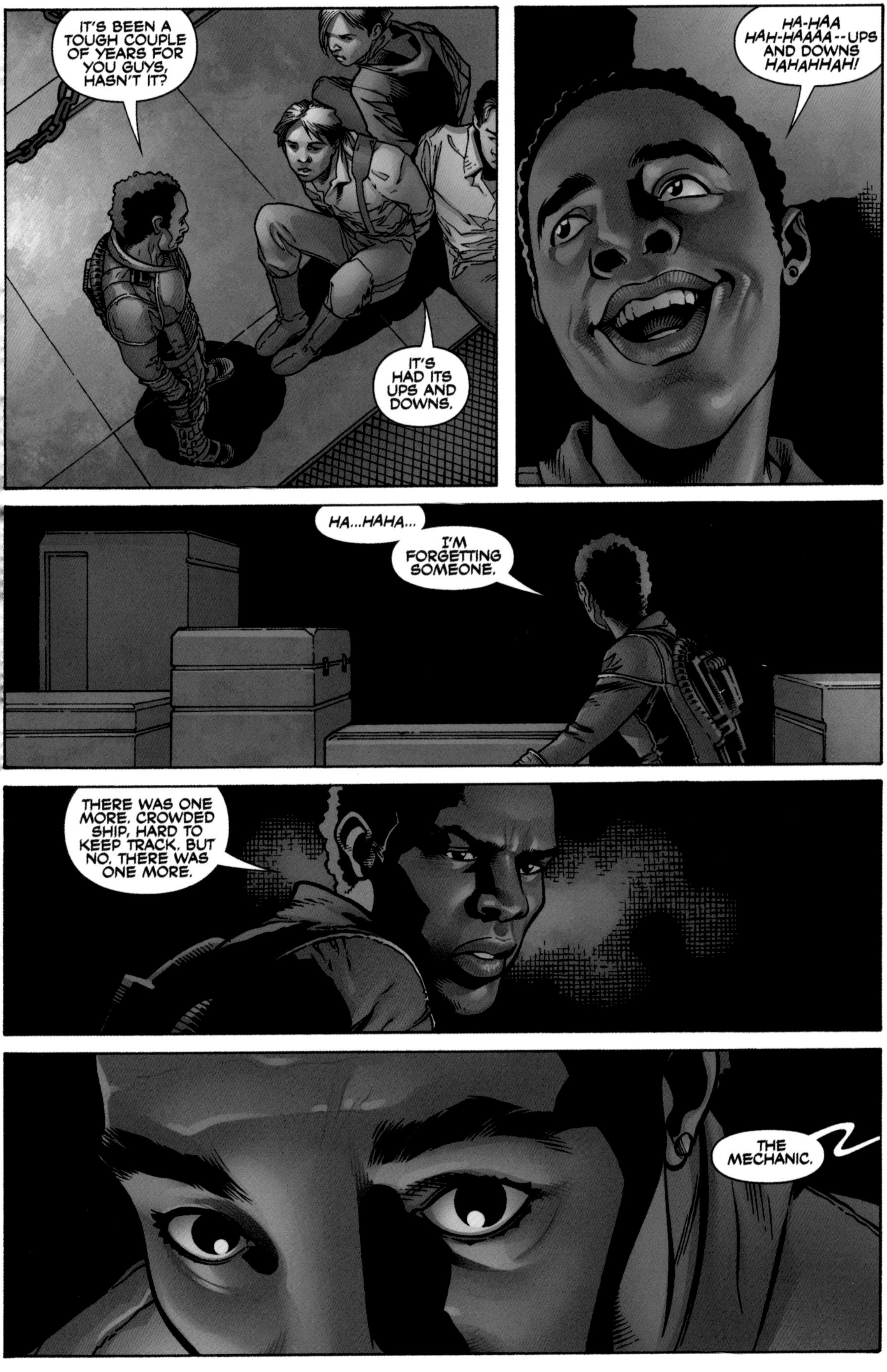
IT'S BEEN A TOUGH COUPLE OF YEARS FOR YOU GUYS, HASN'T IT?
IT'S HAD ITS UPS AND DOWNS.
HA-HAA HAH-HAAAA--UPS AND DOWNS HAHAHHAH!
HA...HAHA...
I'M FORGETTING SOMEONE.
THERE WAS ONE MORE. CROWDED SHIP, HARD TO KEEP TRACK. BUT NO. THERE WAS ONE MORE.
THE MECHANIC.

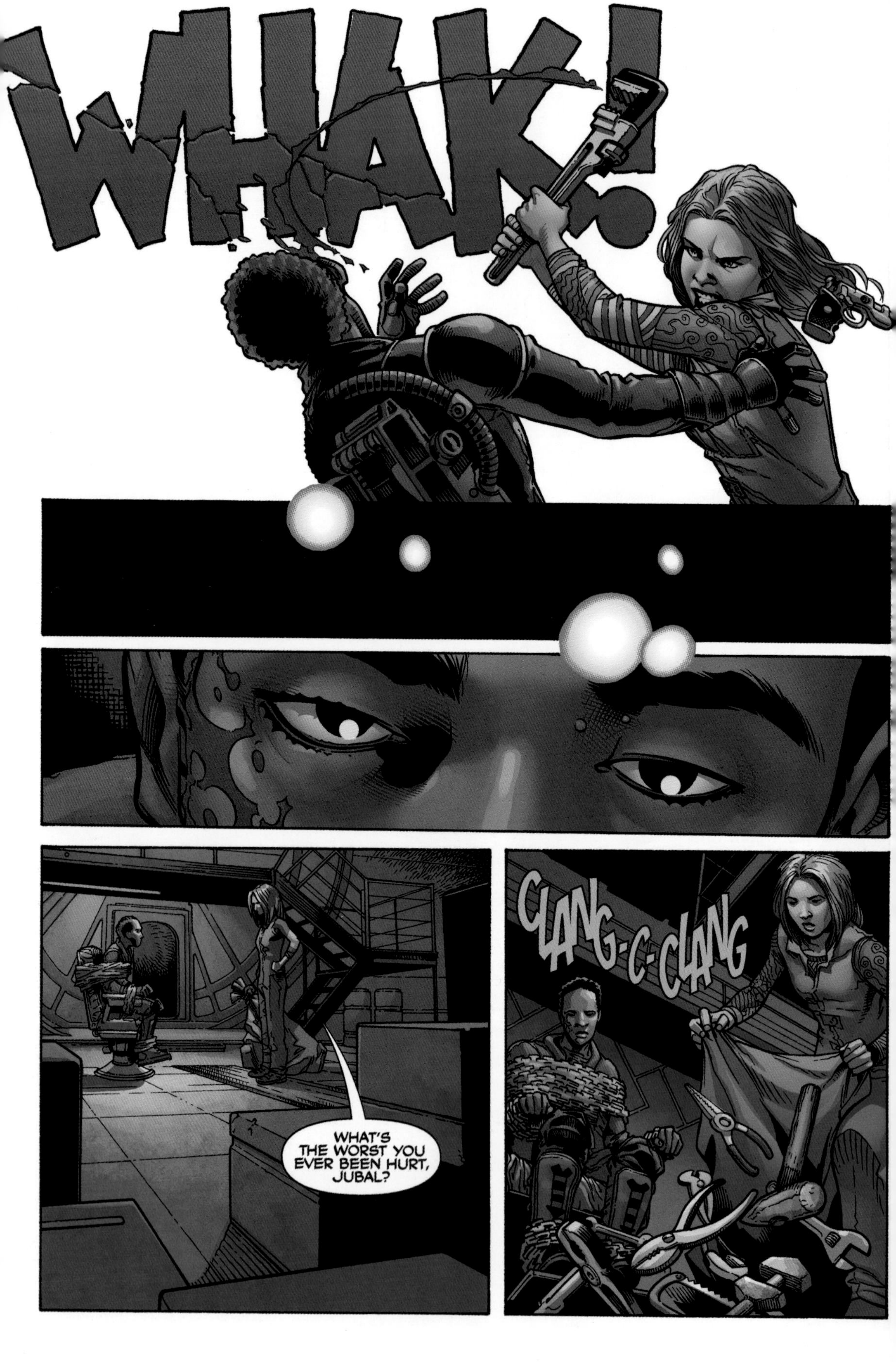
WHAK!
WHAT'S THE WORST YOU EVER BEEN HURT, JUBAL?
CLANG-C-CLANG

I AIN'T SPECIAL LIKE RIVER. BUT I AM GOOD WITH TOOLS.

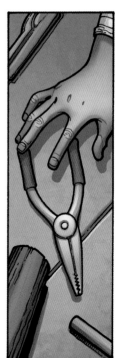

YOU MESS WITH US, YOUR BODY IS FORFEIT. IT'S JUST A BODY TO ME, JUBAL. AND I CAN FIND ALL UNSEEMLY MANNER OF USE FOR IT.

JUST GIMME A GORRAM REASON.

HOPE YOU BROUGHT A CHANGE OF SHORTS, BIG GUY.

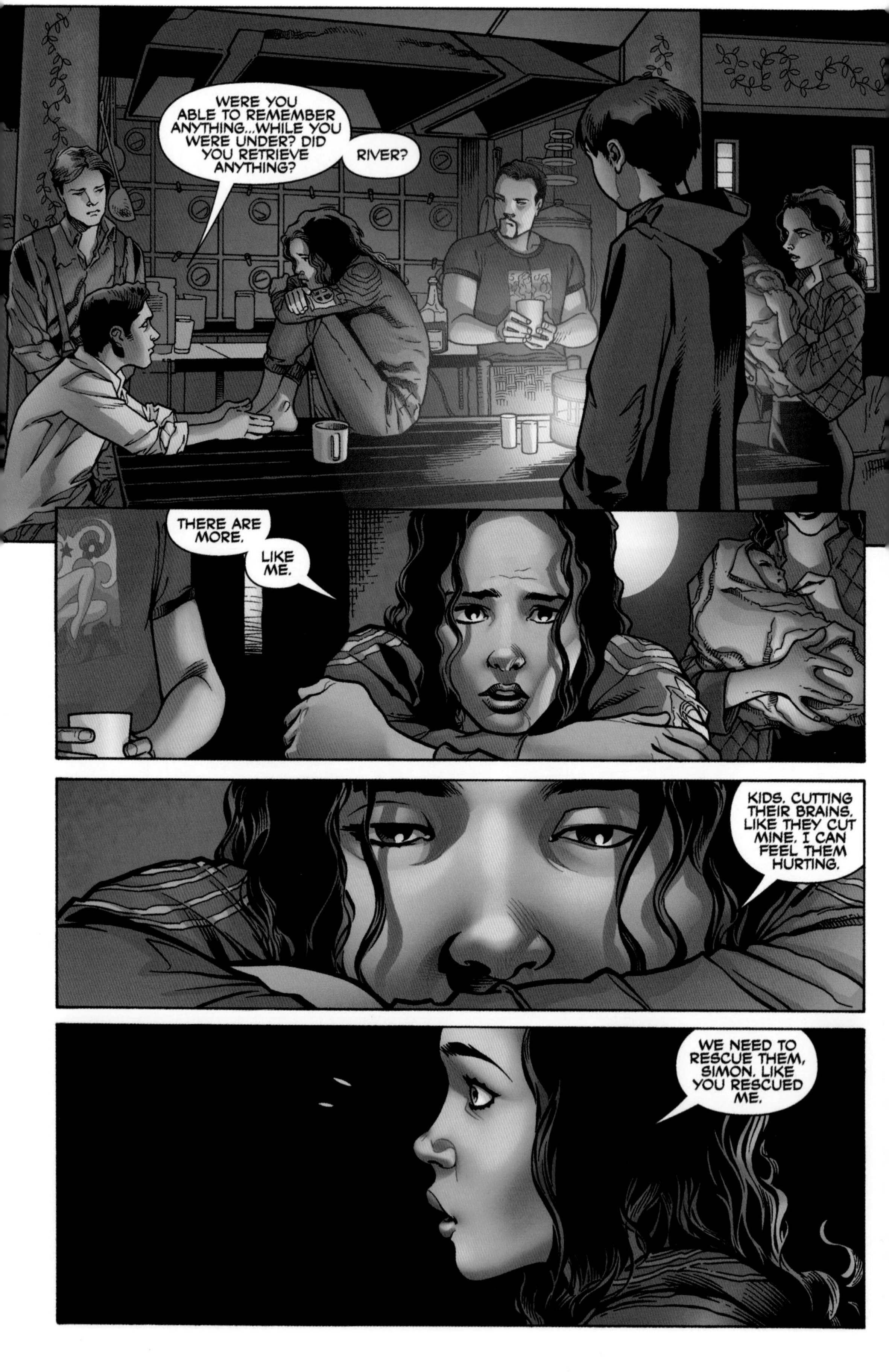
WERE YOU ABLE TO REMEMBER ANYTHING...WHILE YOU WERE UNDER? DID YOU RETRIEVE ANYTHING?
RIVER?
THERE ARE MORE.
LIKE ME.
KIDS. CUTTING THEIR BRAINS. LIKE THEY CUT MINE. I CAN FEEL THEM HURTING.
WE NEED TO RESCUE THEM, SIMON. LIKE YOU RESCUED ME.

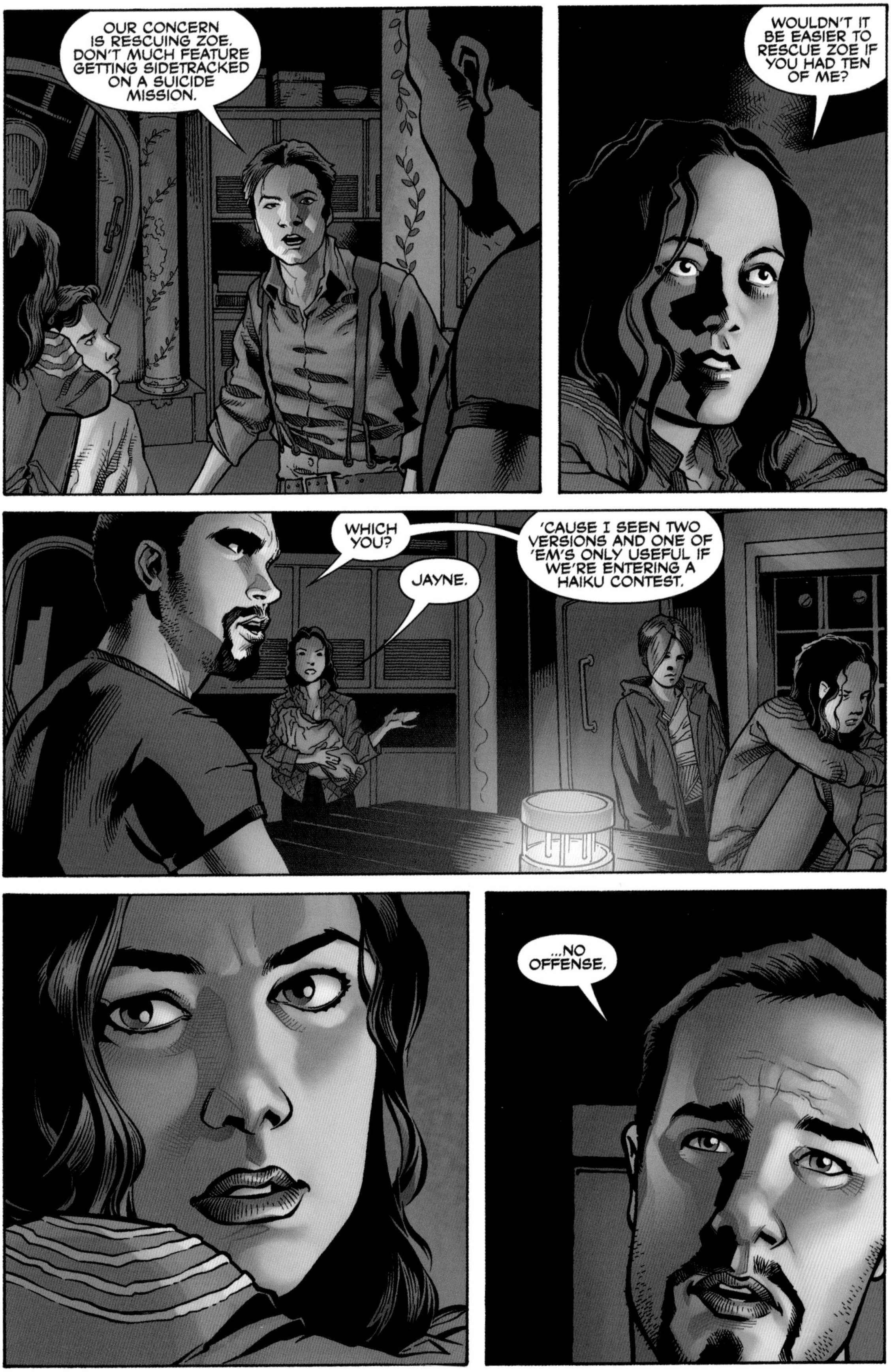
OUR CONCERN IS RESCUING ZOE. DON'T MUCH FEATURE GETTING SIDETRACKED ON A SUICIDE MISSION.
WOULDN'T IT BE EASIER TO RESCUE ZOE IF YOU HAD TEN OF ME?
WHICH YOU?
JAYNE.
'CAUSE I SEEN TWO VERSIONS AND ONE OF 'EM'S ONLY USEFUL IF WE'RE ENTERING A HAIKU CONTEST.
...NO OFFENSE.

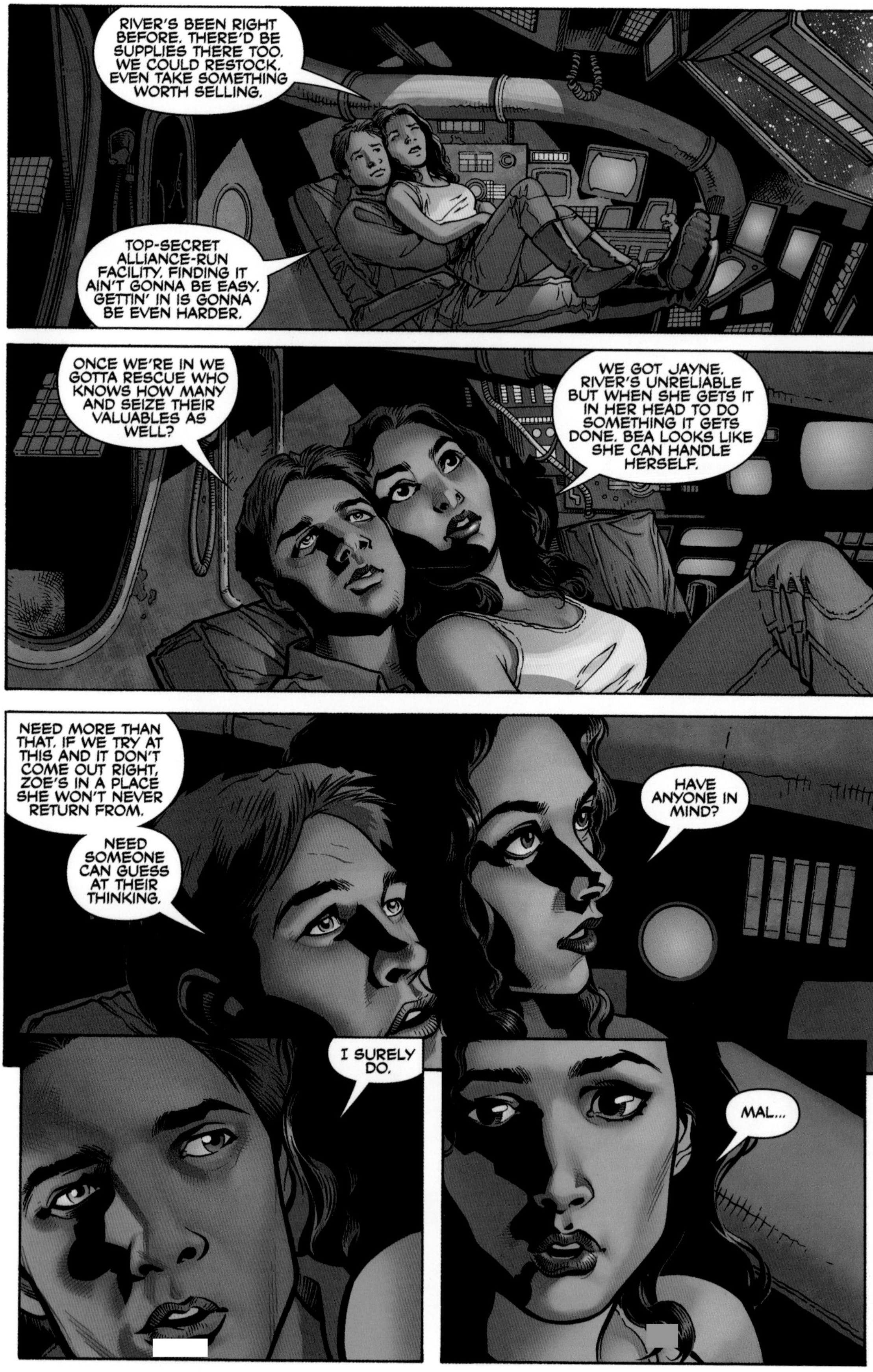

RIVER'S BEEN RIGHT BEFORE. THERE'D BE SUPPLIES THERE TOO. WE COULD RESTOCK. EVEN TAKE SOMETHING WORTH SELLING.
TOP-SECRET ALLIANCE-RUN FACILITY. FINDING IT AIN'T GONNA BE EASY. GETTIN' IN IS GONNA BE EVEN HARDER.
ONCE WE'RE IN WE GOTTA RESCUE WHO KNOWS HOW MANY AND SEIZE THEIR VALUABLES AS WELL?
WE GOT JAYNE. RIVER'S UNRELIABLE BUT WHEN SHE GETS IT IN HER HEAD TO DO SOMETHING IT GETS DONE. BEA LOOKS LIKE SHE CAN HANDLE HERSELF.
NEED MORE THAN THAT. IF WE TRY AT THIS AND IT DON'T COME OUT RIGHT, ZOE'S IN A PLACE SHE WON'T NEVER RETURN FROM.
NEED SOMEONE CAN GUESS AT THEIR THINKING.
HAVE ANYONE IN MIND?
I SURELY DO.
MAL...

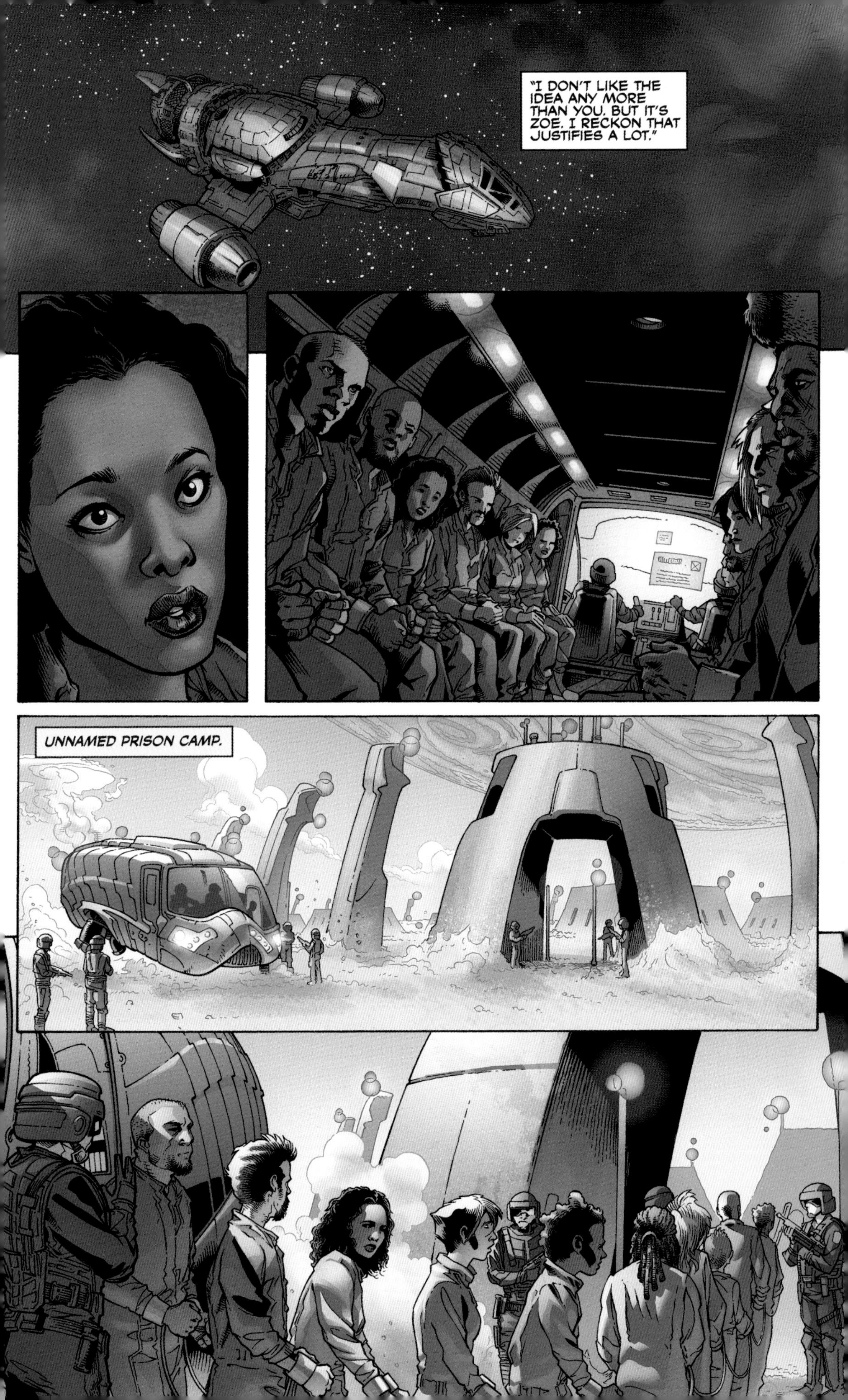
"I DON'T LIKE THE IDEA ANY MORE THAN YOU. BUT IT'S ZOE. I RECKON THAT JUSTIFIES A LOT."
UNNAMED PRISON CAMP.

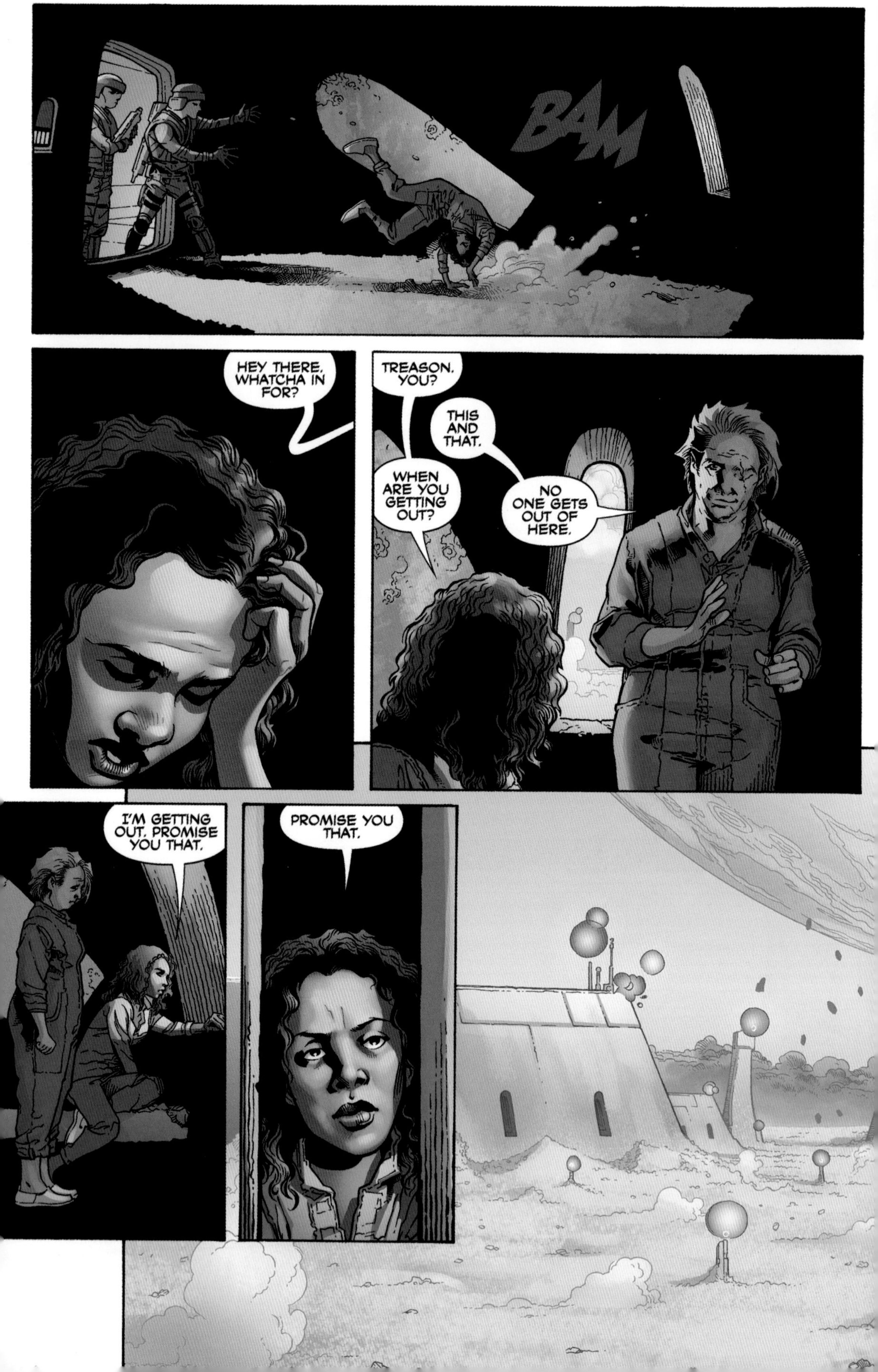
BAM
HEY THERE. WHATCHA IN FOR?
TREASON. YOU?
THIS AND THAT.
WHEN ARE YOU GETTING OUT?
NO ONE GETS OUT OF HERE.
I'M GETTING OUT. PROMISE YOU THAT.
PROMISE YOU THAT.

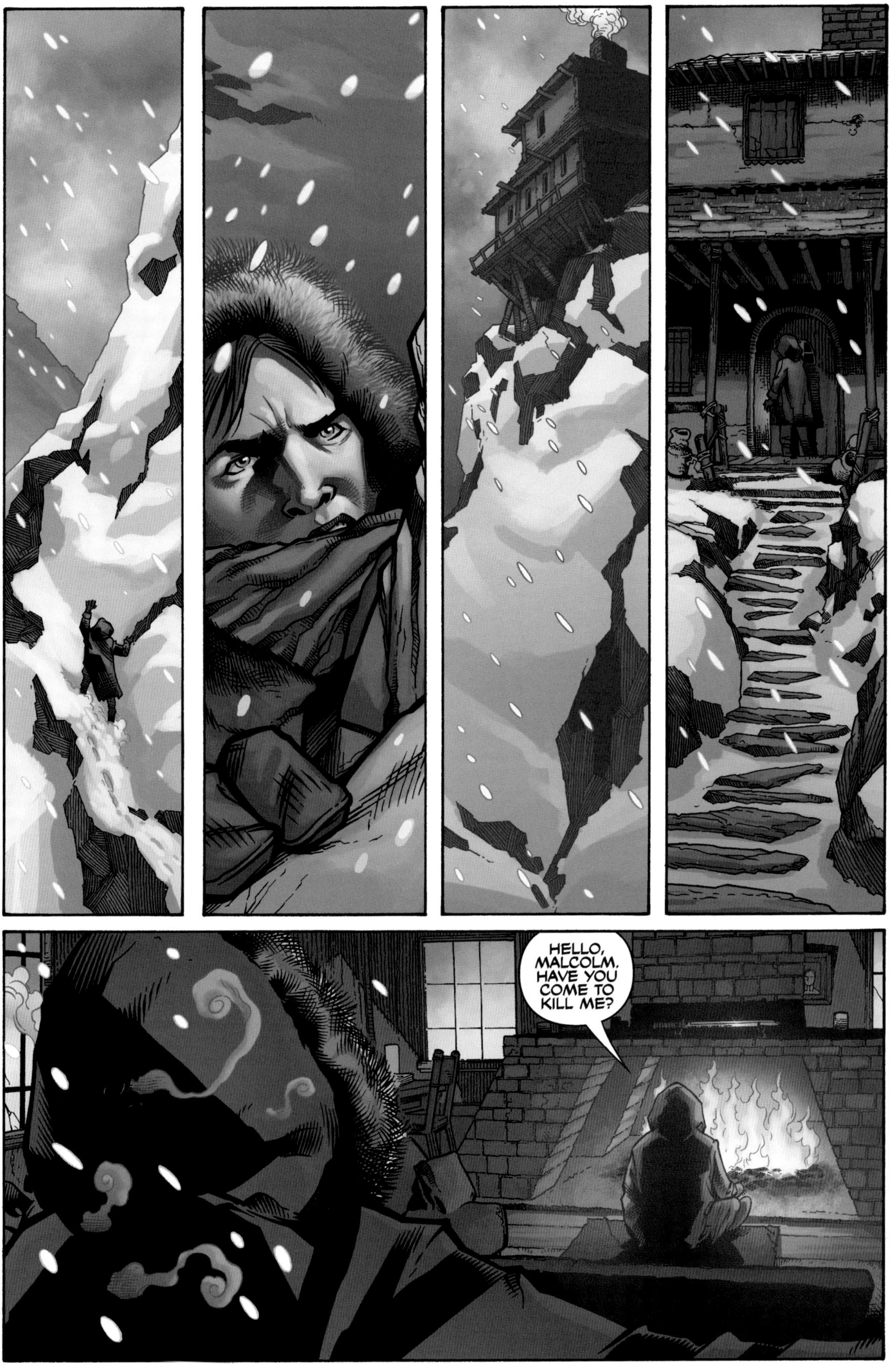
HELLO, MALCOLM. HAVE YOU COME TO KILL ME?

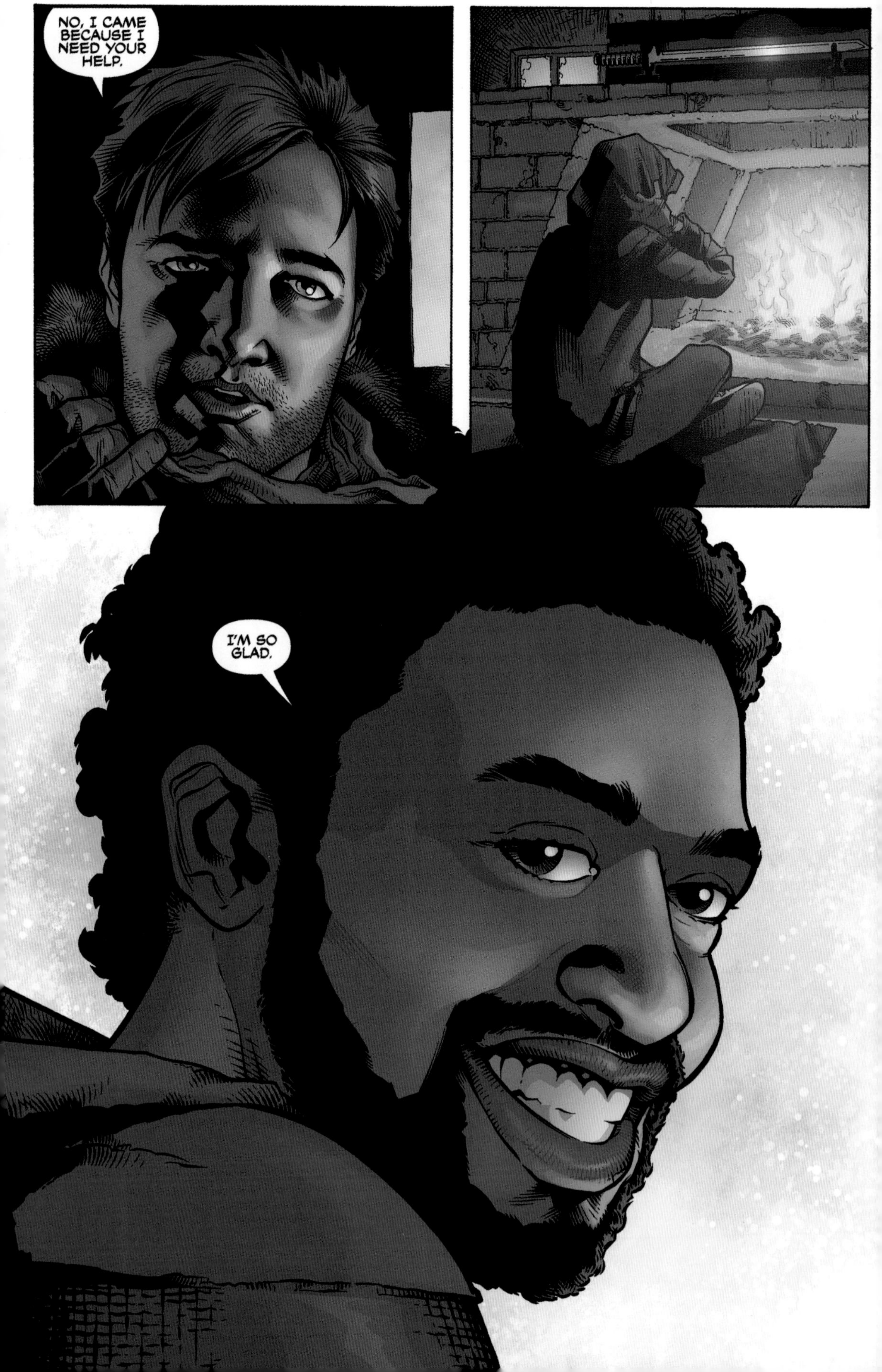
NO, I CAME BECAUSE I NEED YOUR HELP.
I'M SO GLAD.

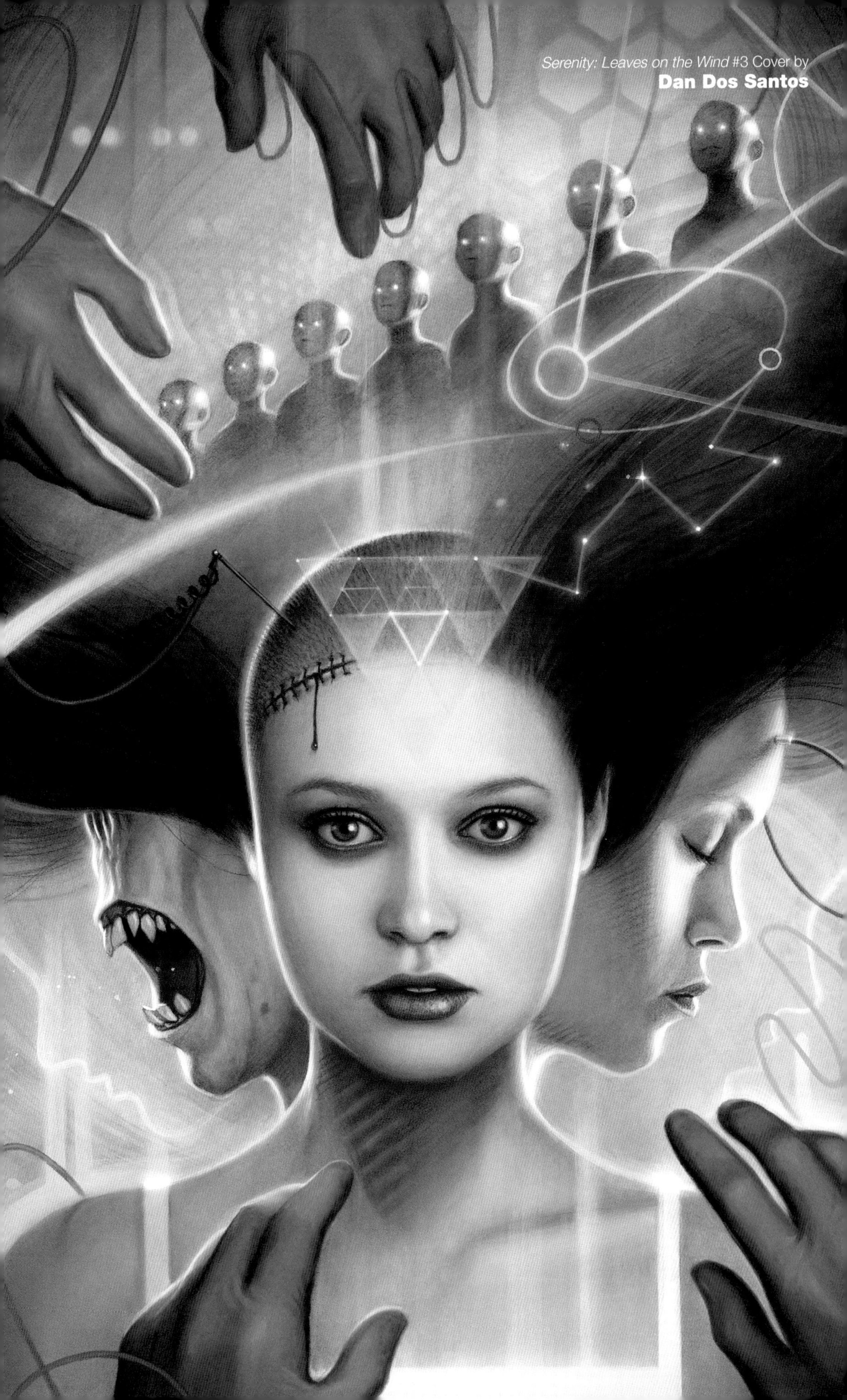

Serenity: Leaves on the Wind #3 Cover by
Dan Dos Santos

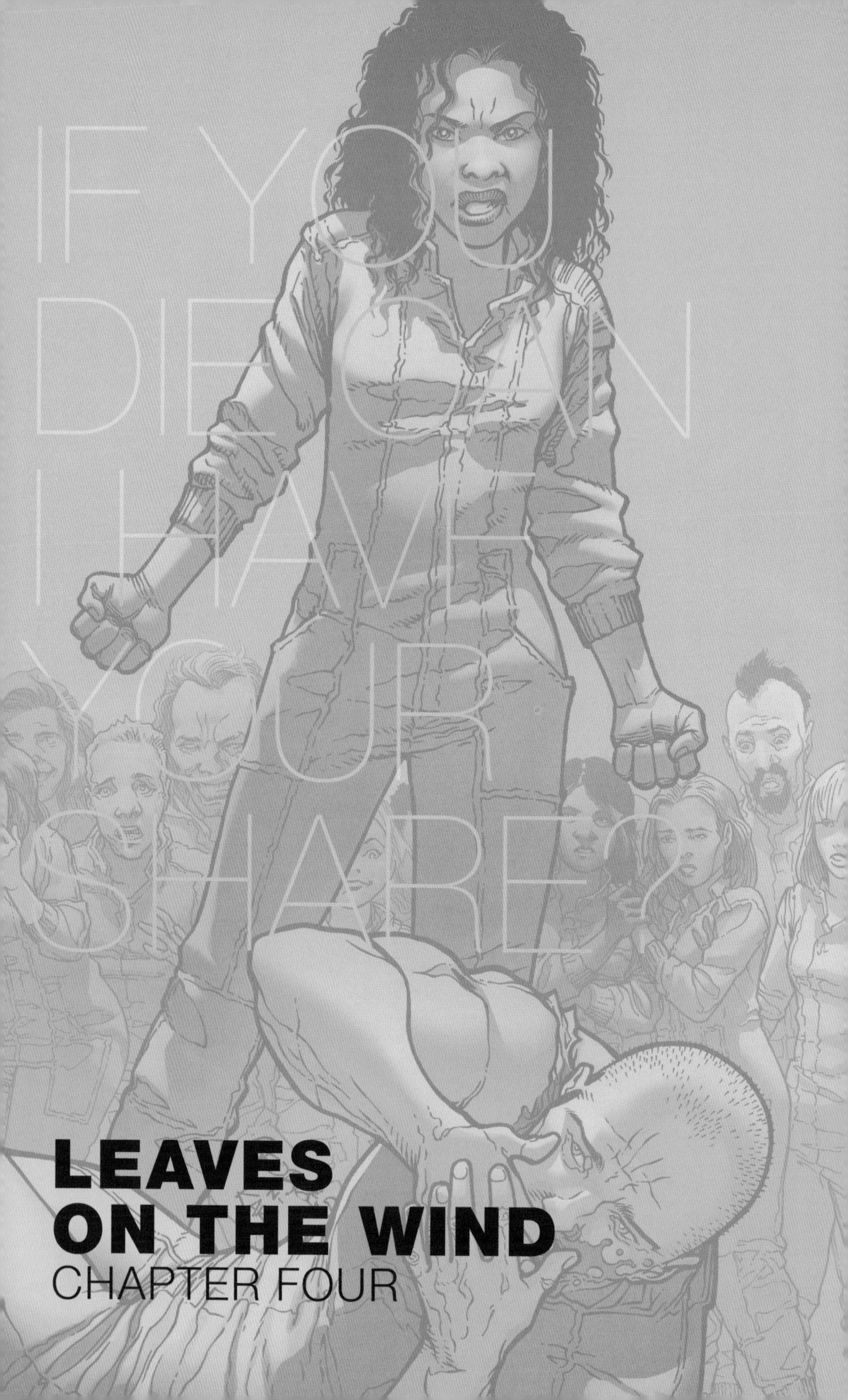
IF YOU
DIE CAN
I HAVE
YOUR
SHARE?

LEAVES ON THE WIND

CHAPTER FOUR

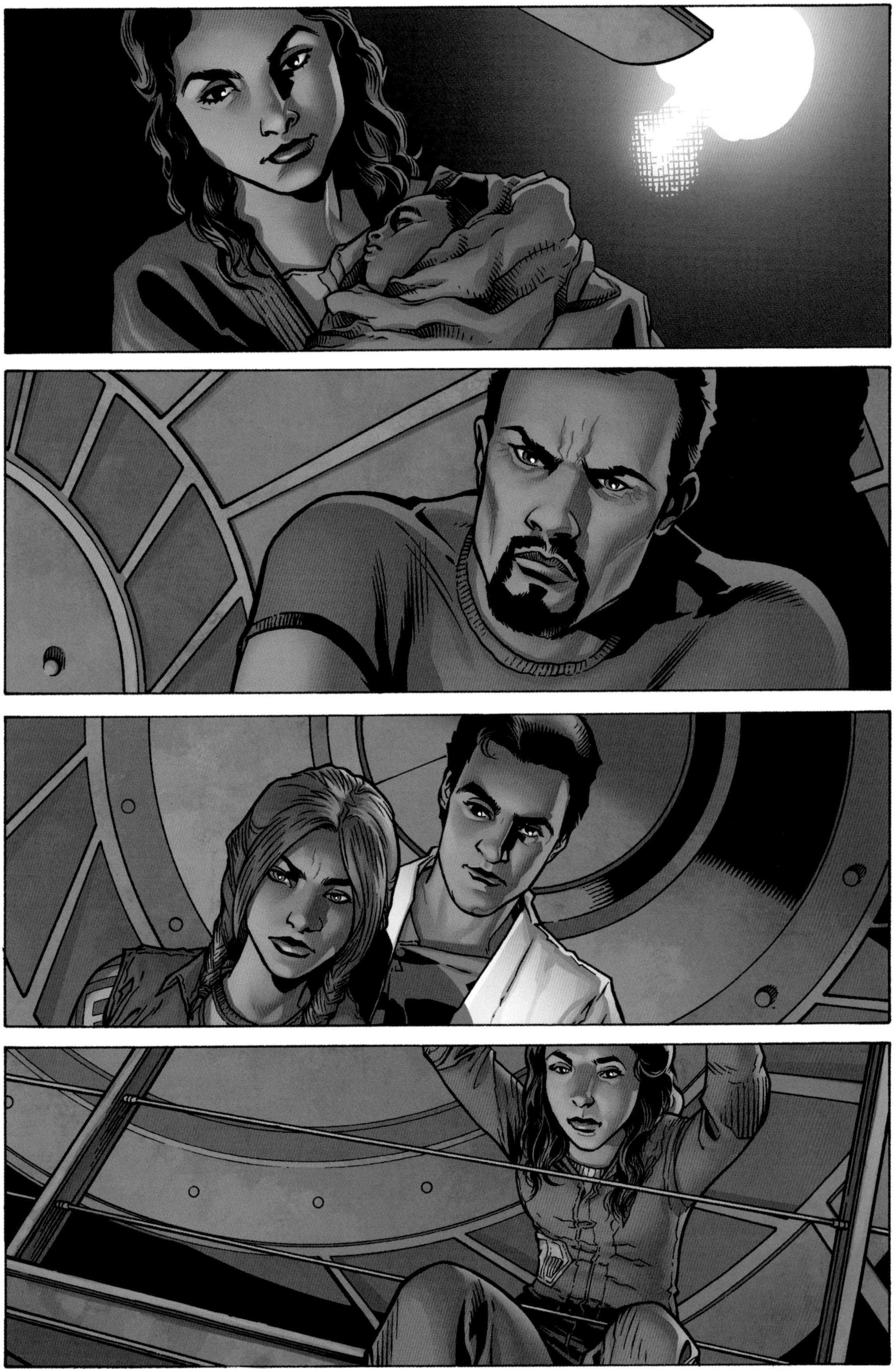

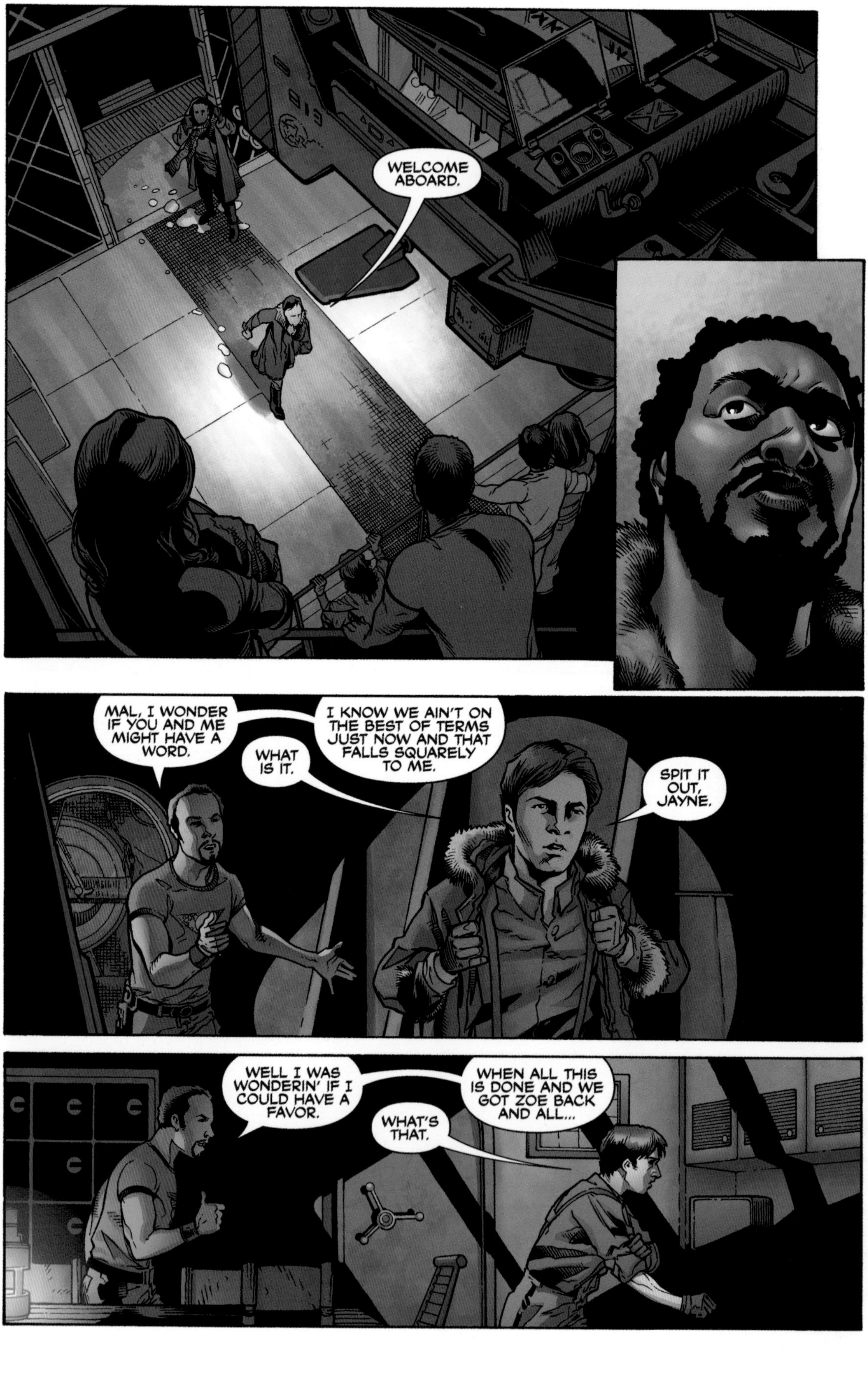
WELCOME ABOARD.
MAL, I WONDER IF YOU AND ME MIGHT HAVE A WORD.
WHAT IS IT.
I KNOW WE AIN'T ON THE BEST OF TERMS JUST NOW AND THAT FALLS SQUARELY TO ME.
SPIT IT OUT, JAYNE.
WELL I WAS WONDERIN' IF I COULD HAVE A FAVOR.
WHAT'S THAT.
WHEN ALL THIS IS DONE AND WE GOT ZOE BACK AND ALL...

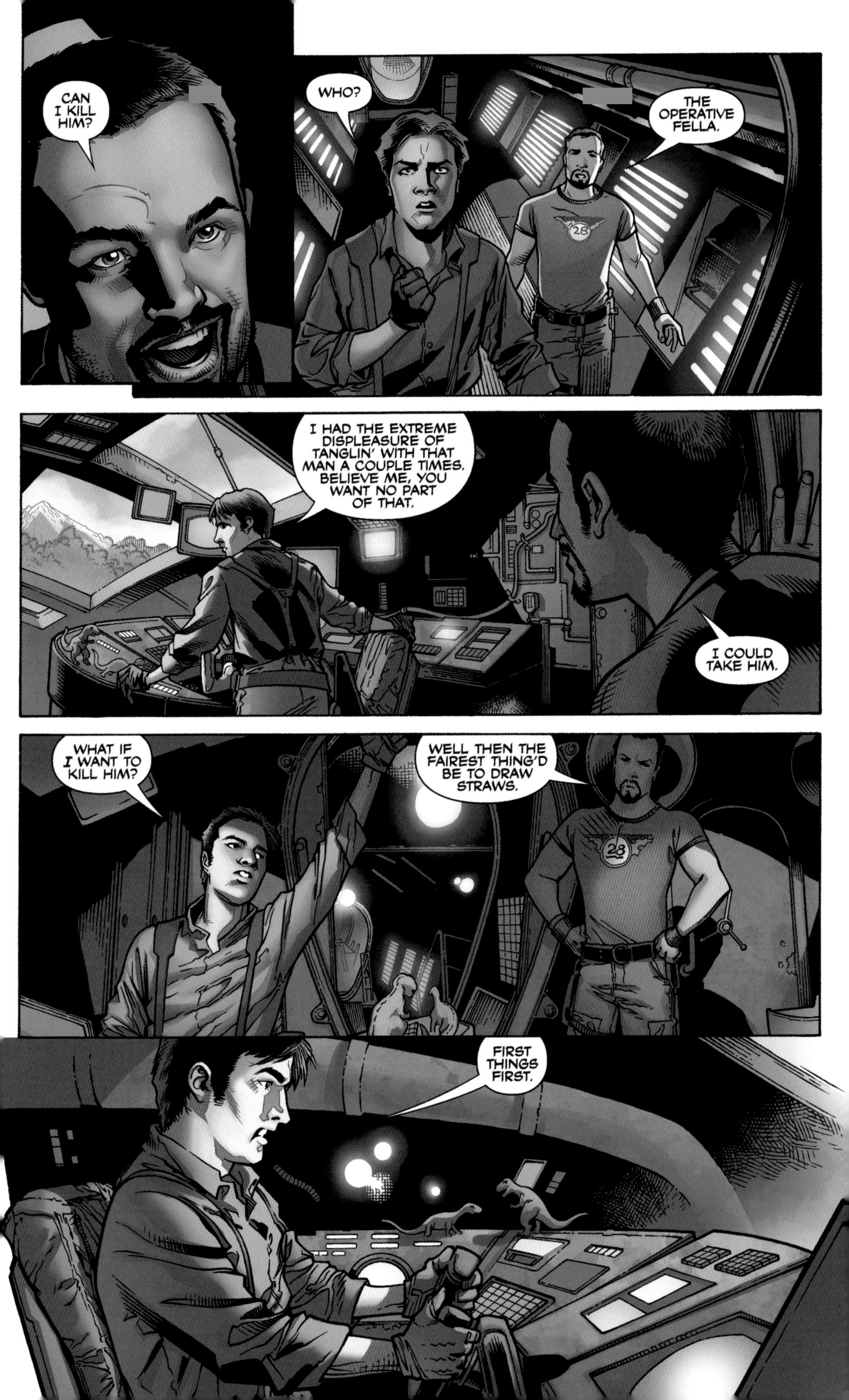
CAN I KILL HIM?
WHO?
THE OPERATIVE FELLA.
I HAD THE EXTREME DISPLEASURE OF TANGLIN' WITH THAT MAN A COUPLE TIMES. BELIEVE ME, YOU WANT NO PART OF THAT.
I COULD TAKE HIM.
WHAT IF *I* WANT TO KILL HIM?
WELL THEN THE FAIREST THING'D BE TO DRAW STRAWS.
FIRST THINGS FIRST.

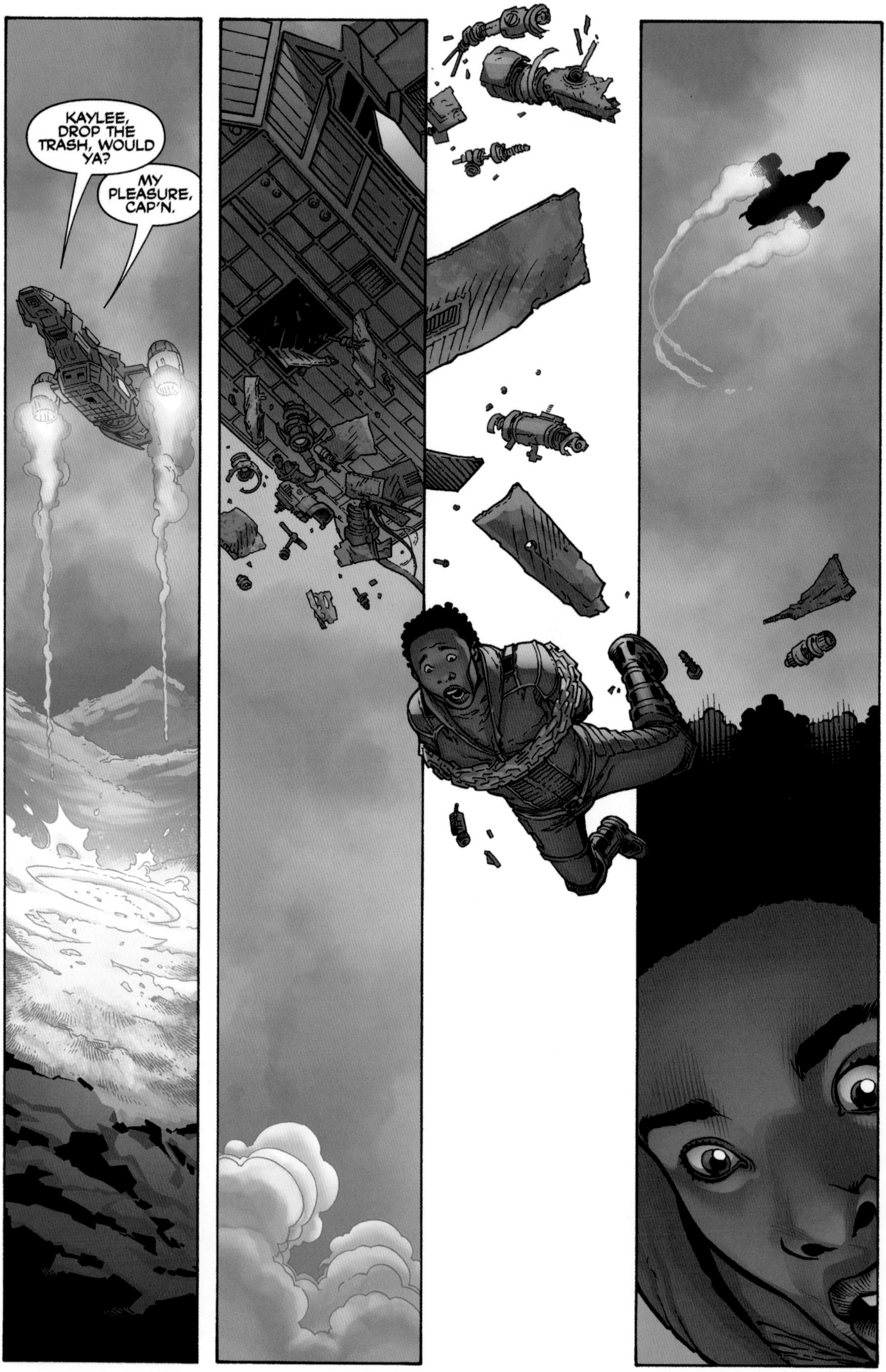
KAYLEE, DROP THE TRASH, WOULD YA?
MY PLEASURE, CAP'N.

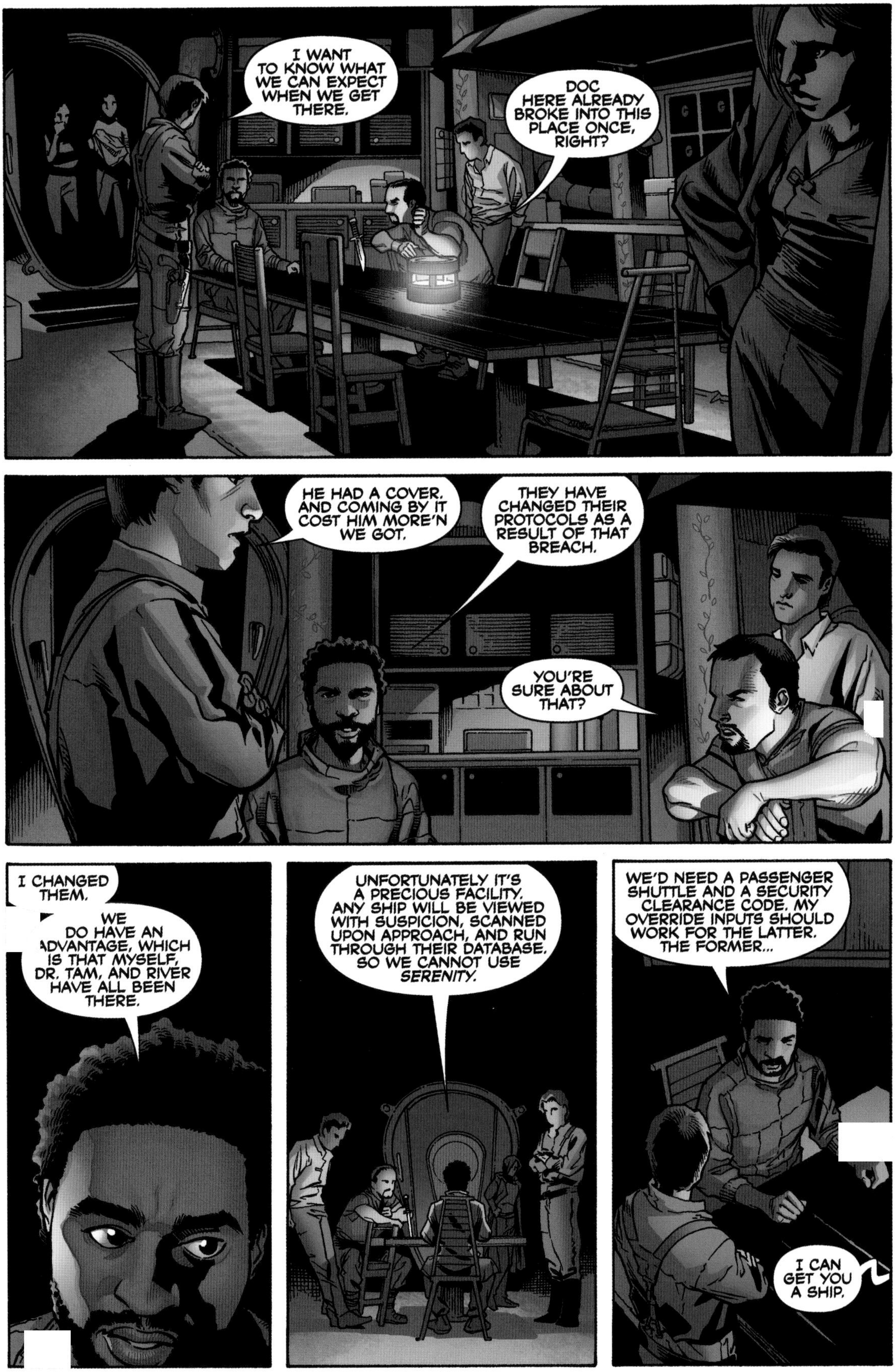
I WANT TO KNOW WHAT WE CAN EXPECT WHEN WE GET THERE.
DOC HERE ALREADY BROKE INTO THIS PLACE ONCE, RIGHT?
HE HAD A COVER. AND COMING BY IT COST HIM MORE'N WE GOT.
THEY HAVE CHANGED THEIR PROTOCOLS AS A RESULT OF THAT BREACH.
YOU'RE SURE ABOUT THAT?
I CHANGED THEM.
WE DO HAVE AN ADVANTAGE, WHICH IS THAT MYSELF, DR. TAM, AND RIVER HAVE ALL BEEN THERE.
UNFORTUNATELY IT'S A PRECIOUS FACILITY. ANY SHIP WILL BE VIEWED WITH SUSPICION, SCANNED UPON APPROACH, AND RUN THROUGH THEIR DATABASE, SO WE CANNOT USE *SERENITY.*
WE'D NEED A PASSENGER SHUTTLE AND A SECURITY CLEARANCE CODE. MY OVERRIDE INPUTS SHOULD WORK FOR THE LATTER. THE FORMER...
I CAN GET YOU A SHIP.

YOU GOT MY EAR. SPEAK YOUR PIECE.

THE NEW RESISTANCE. OUTFITS ARE POPPING UP ALL OVER THE 'VERSE. WE'RE ORGANIZED, WE'VE GOT MONEY.

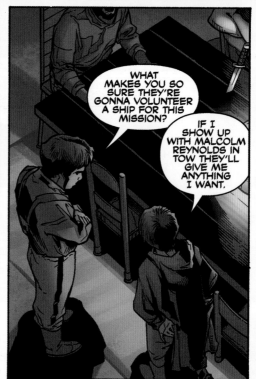

WHAT MAKES YOU SO SURE THEY'RE GONNA VOLUNTEER A SHIP FOR THIS MISSION?

IF I SHOW UP WITH MALCOLM REYNOLDS IN TOW THEY'LL GIVE ME ANYTHING I WANT.

THEY'RE STILL UNDER THE IMPRESSION YOU'RE SOME KIND OF HERO.

THIS AIN'T RIGHT, HAVIN' THAT MAN ON OUR SHIP.

I KNOW, KAYLEE, BUT MAL THINKS WE NEED HIM, AND WHEN IT COMES TO ZOE HE DOESN'T WANT TO TAKE ANY CHANCES.

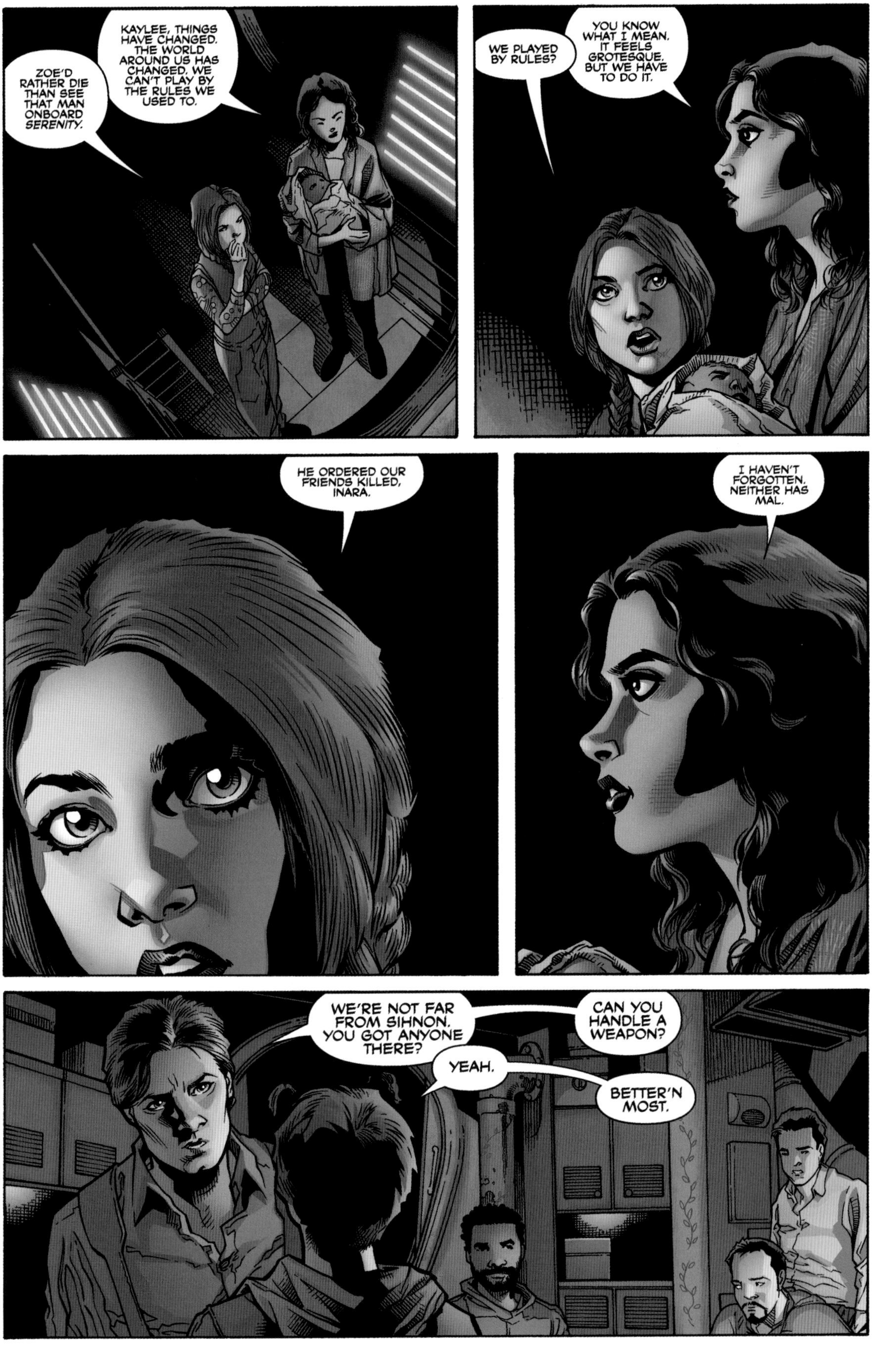
KAYLEE, THINGS HAVE CHANGED. THE WORLD AROUND US HAS CHANGED. WE CAN'T PLAY BY THE RULES WE USED TO.
ZOE'D RATHER DIE THAN SEE THAT MAN ONBOARD *SERENITY.*
WE PLAYED BY RULES?
YOU KNOW WHAT I MEAN. IT FEELS GROTESQUE. BUT WE HAVE TO DO IT.
HE ORDERED OUR FRIENDS KILLED, INARA.
I HAVEN'T FORGOTTEN. NEITHER HAS MAL.
WE'RE NOT FAR FROM SIHNON. YOU GOT ANYONE THERE?
YEAH.
CAN YOU HANDLE A WEAPON?
BETTER'N MOST.

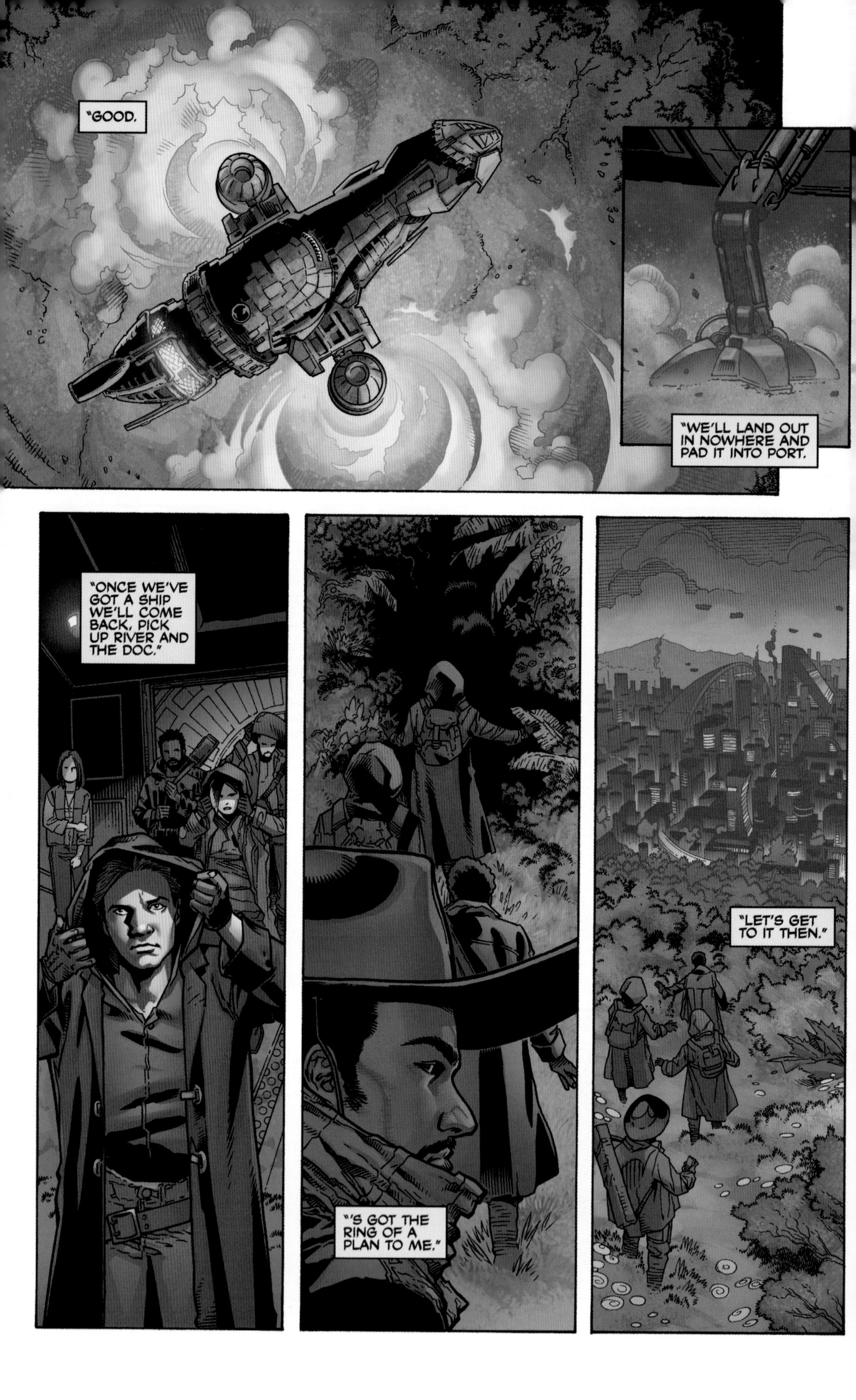
"GOOD.
"WE'LL LAND OUT IN NOWHERE AND PAD IT INTO PORT.
"ONCE WE'VE GOT A SHIP WE'LL COME BACK, PICK UP RIVER AND THE DOC."
"'S GOT THE RING OF A PLAN TO ME."
"LET'S GET TO IT THEN."

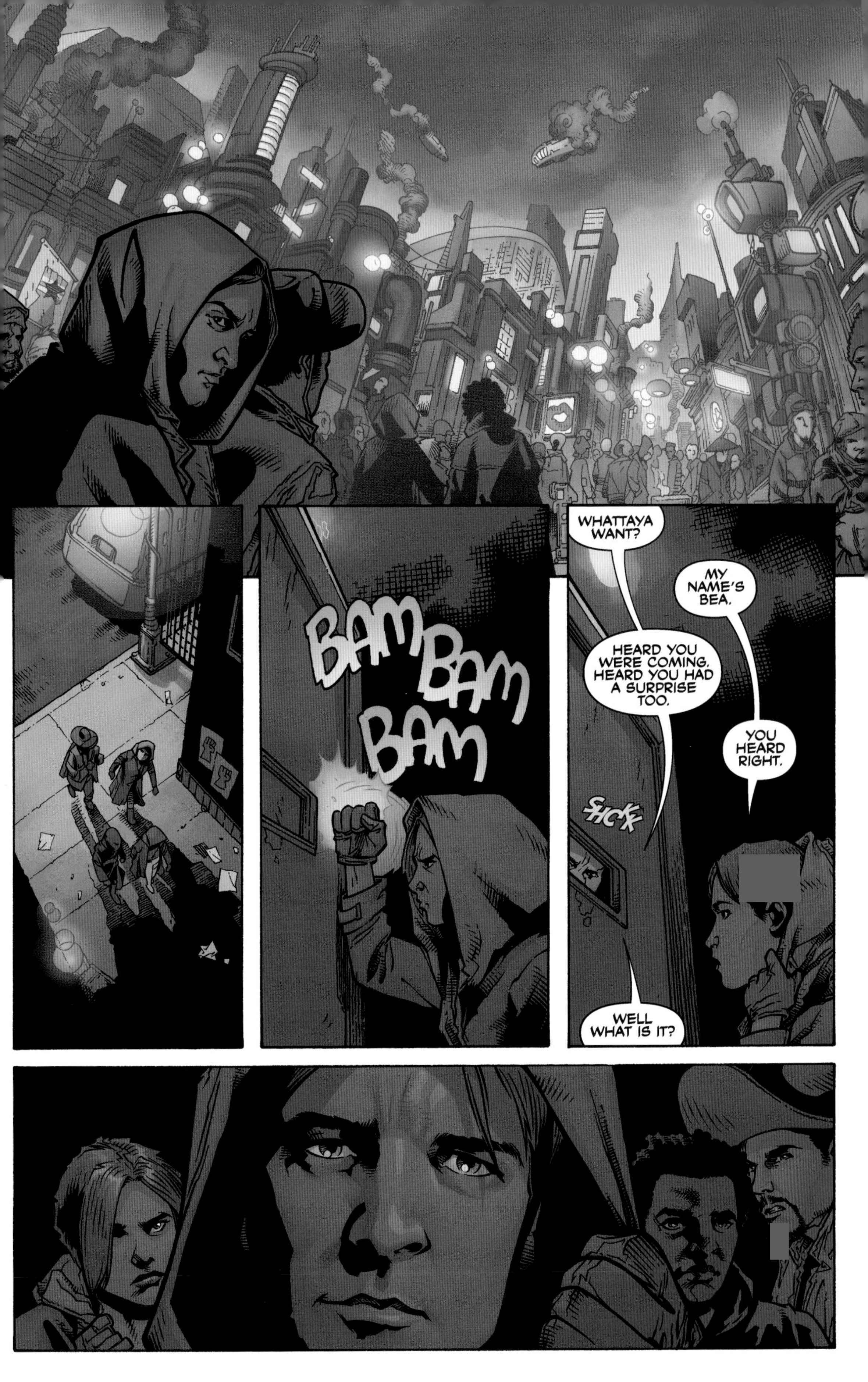
BAM
BAM
BAM
SHCKK
WHATTAYA WANT?
MY NAME'S BEA.
HEARD YOU WERE COMING. HEARD YOU HAD A SURPRISE TOO.
YOU HEARD RIGHT.
WELL WHAT IS IT?

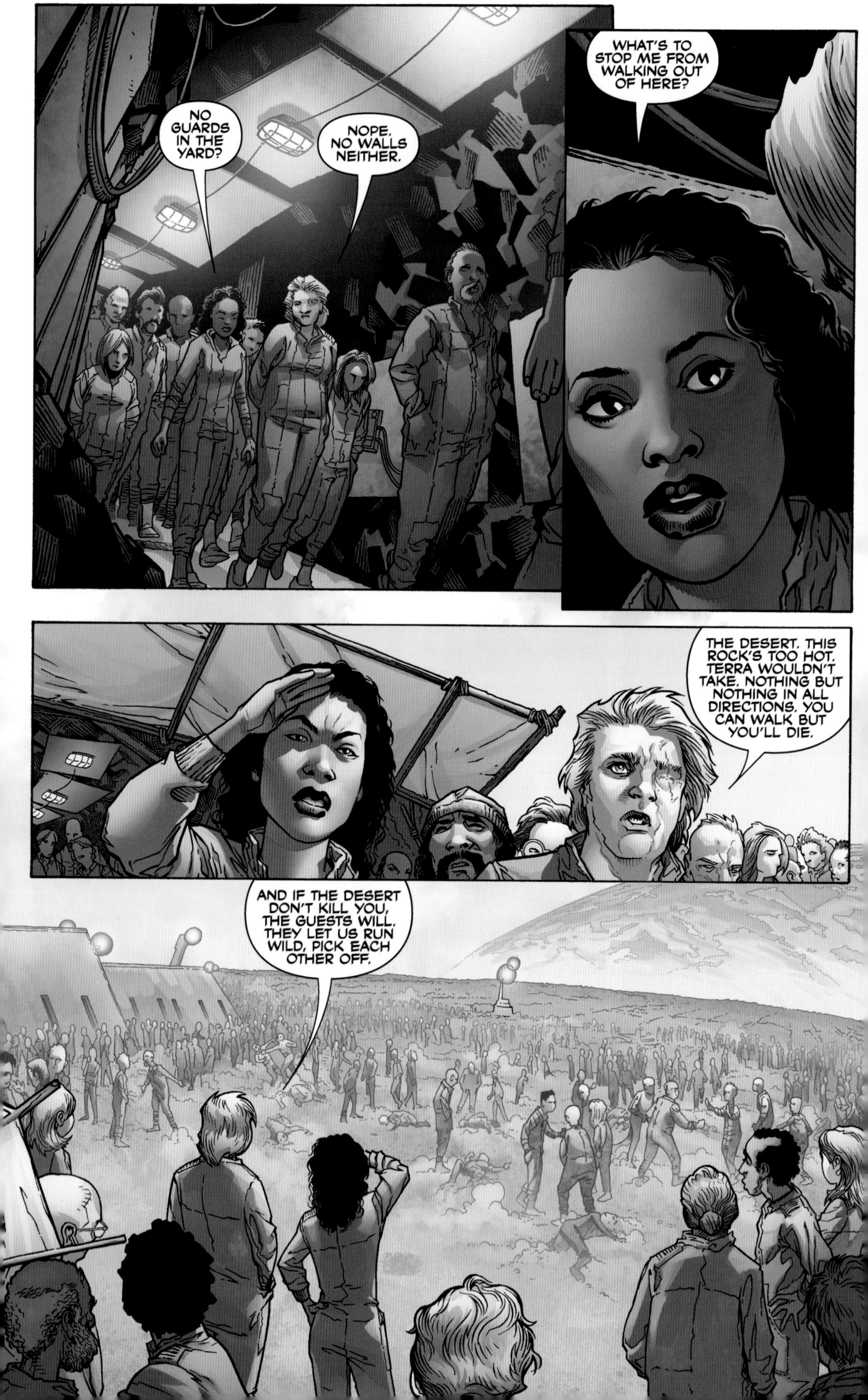
NO GUARDS IN THE YARD?
NOPE, NO WALLS NEITHER.
WHAT'S TO STOP ME FROM WALKING OUT OF HERE?
THE DESERT. THIS ROCK'S TOO HOT, TERRA WOULDN'T TAKE. NOTHING BUT NOTHING IN ALL DIRECTIONS. YOU CAN WALK BUT YOU'LL DIE.
AND IF THE DESERT DON'T KILL YOU, THE GUESTS WILL. THEY LET US RUN WILD, PICK EACH OTHER OFF.

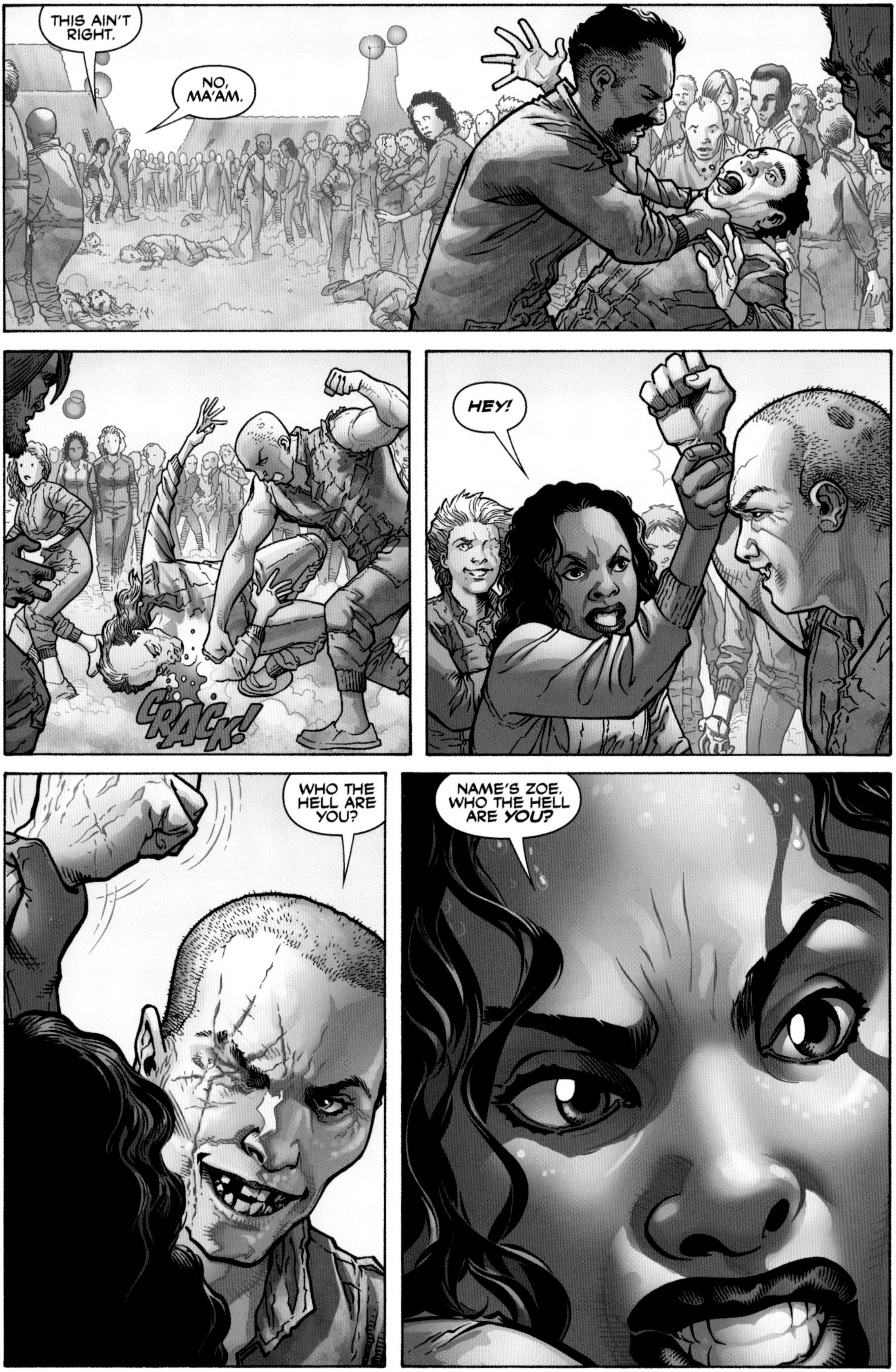
THIS AIN'T RIGHT.
NO, MA'AM.
CRACK!
HEY!
WHO THE HELL ARE YOU?
NAME'S ZOE. WHO THE HELL ARE YOU?

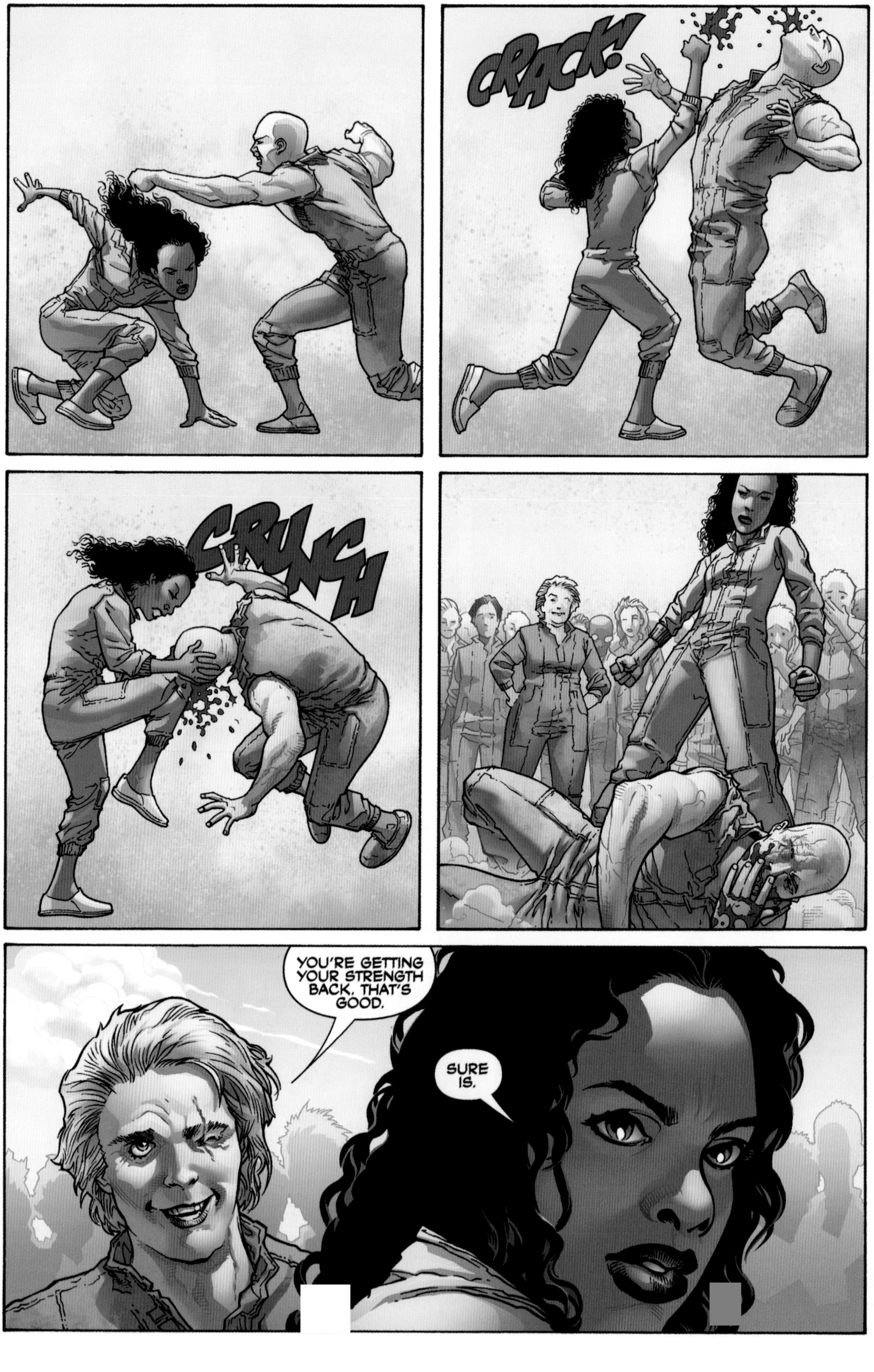
CRACK!
CRUNCH
YOU'RE GETTING YOUR STRENGTH BACK. THAT'S GOOD.
SURE IS.

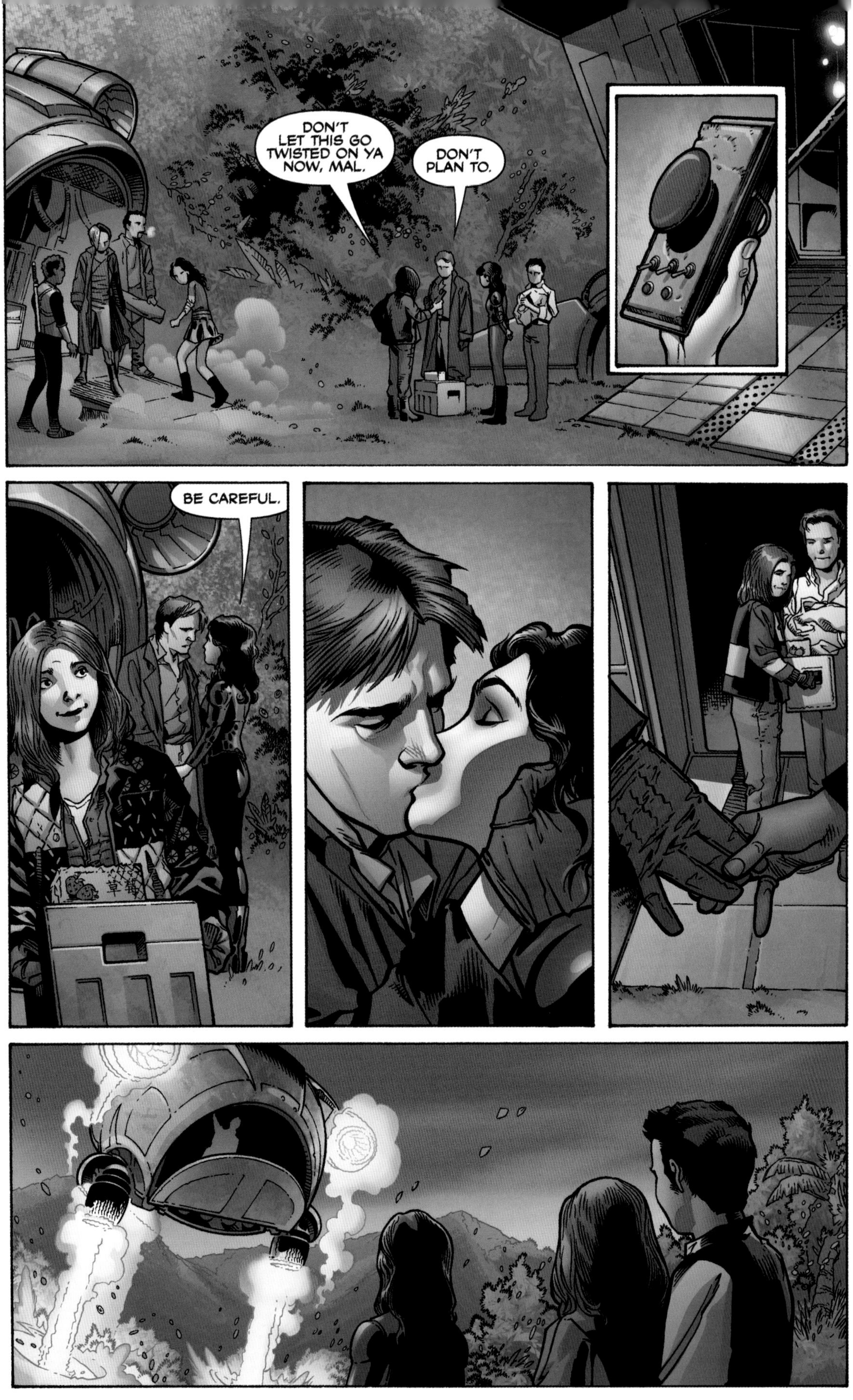
DON'T LET THIS GO TWISTED ON YA NOW, MAL.
DON'T PLAN TO.
BE CAREFUL.
草莓

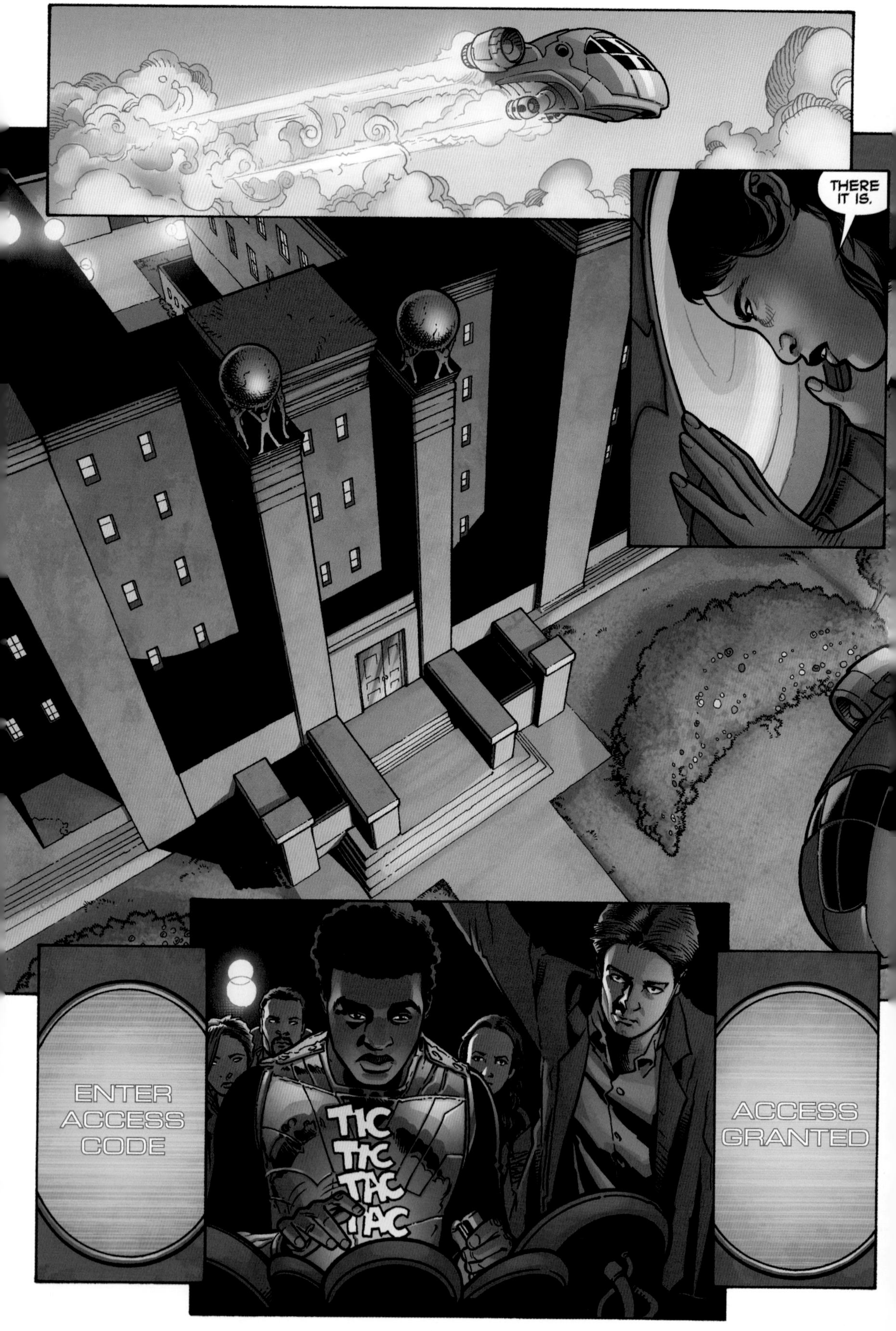
THERE IT IS.
ENTER ACCESS CODE
TIC TIC TAC TAC
ACCESS GRANTED

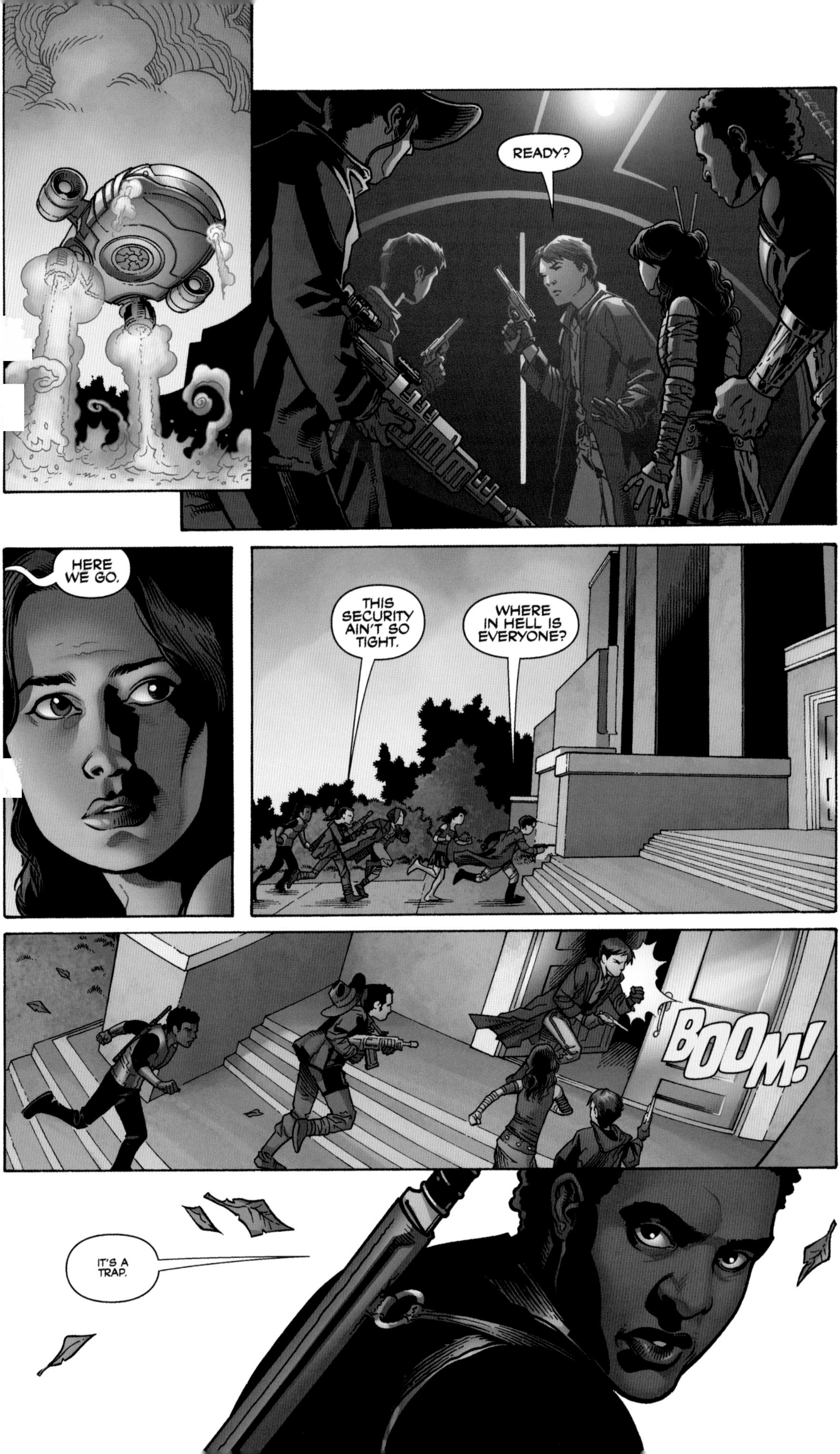
READY?
HERE WE GO.
THIS SECURITY AIN'T SO TIGHT.
WHERE IN HELL IS EVERYONE?
BOOM!
IT'S A TRAP.

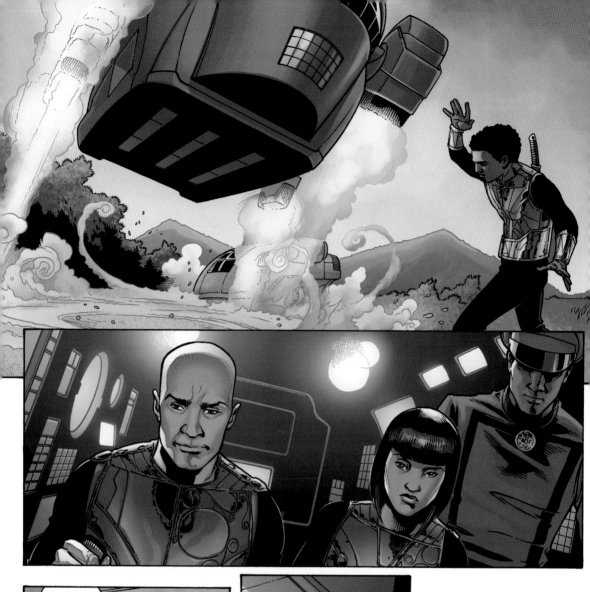

YOU GO, I'LL HOLD THEM.

THERE.

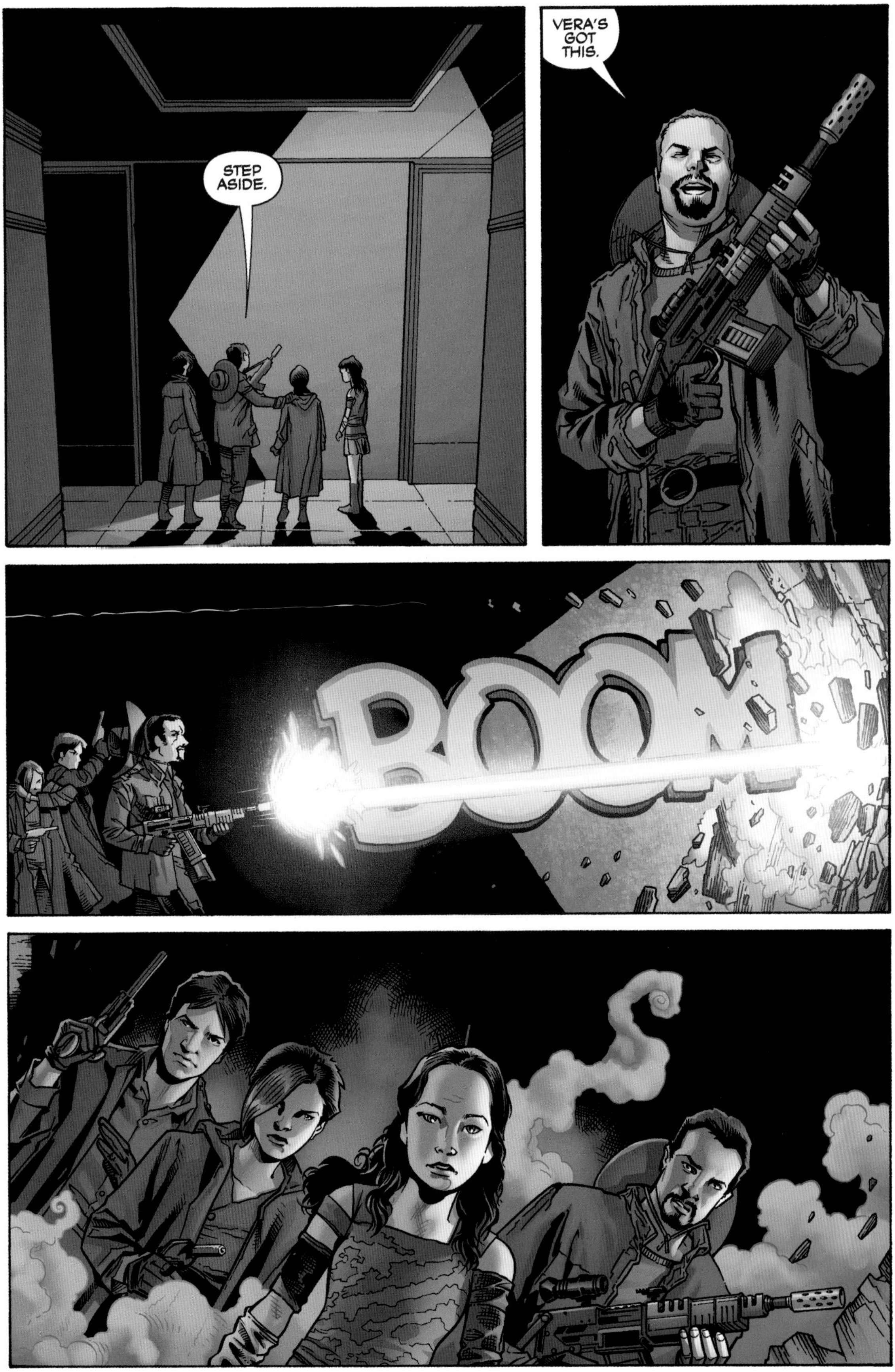
STEP ASIDE.
VERA'S GOT THIS.
BOOM

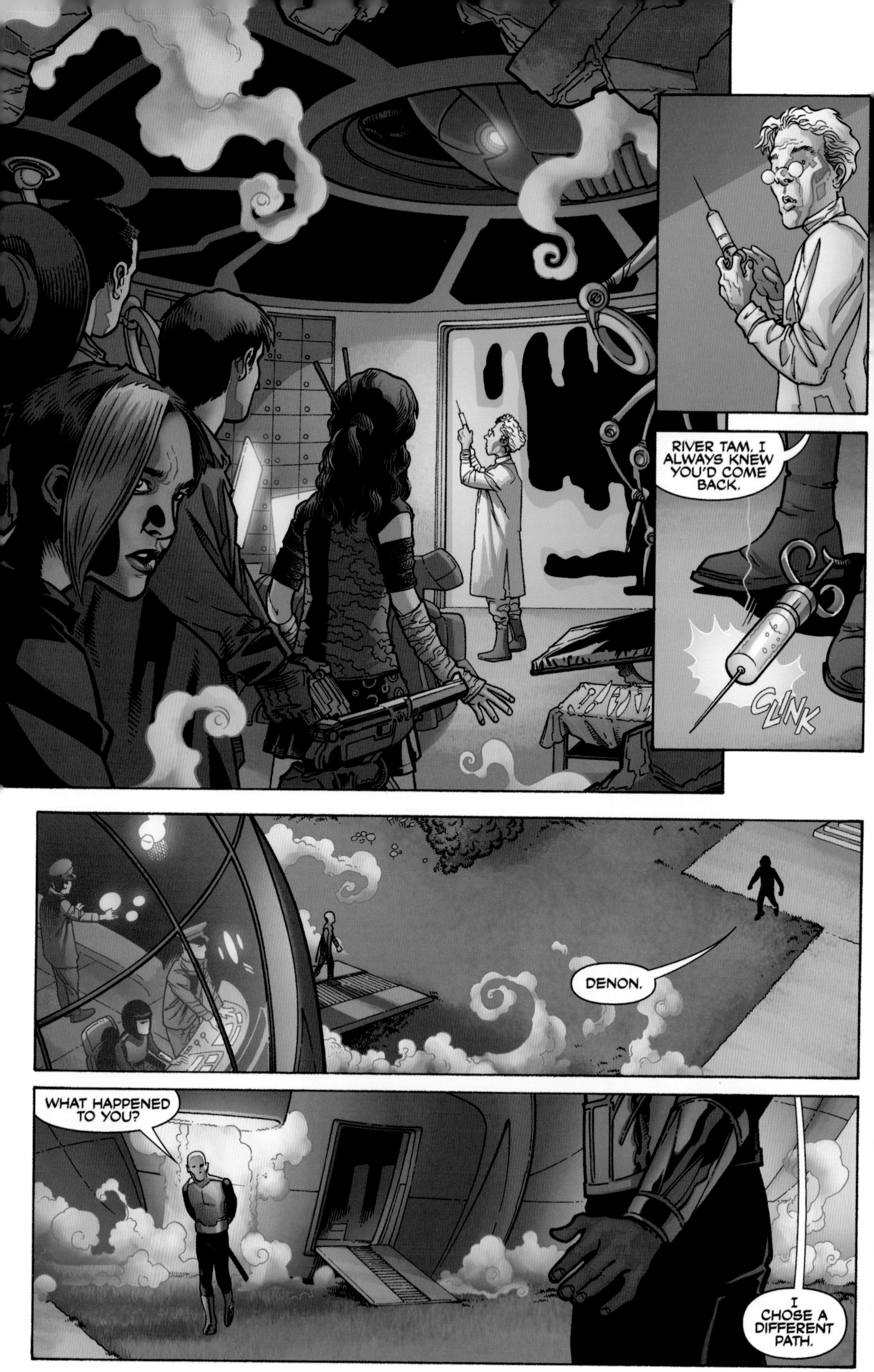
RIVER TAM. I ALWAYS KNEW YOU'D COME BACK.
CLINK
DENON.
WHAT HAPPENED TO YOU?
I CHOSE A DIFFERENT PATH.

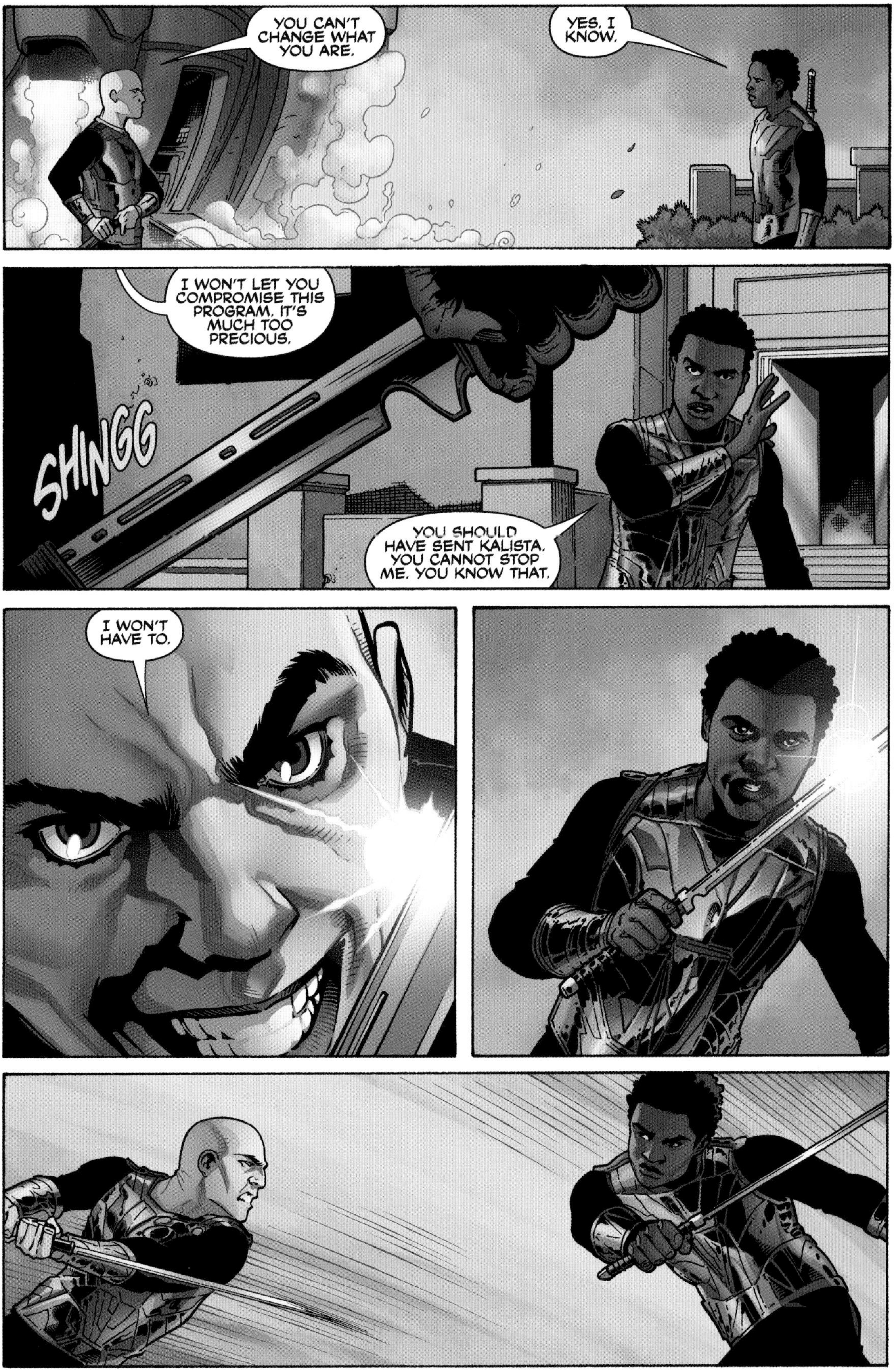
YOU CAN'T CHANGE WHAT YOU ARE.
YES, I KNOW.
I WON'T LET YOU COMPROMISE THIS PROGRAM. IT'S MUCH TOO PRECIOUS.
SHINGG
YOU SHOULD HAVE SENT KALISTA. YOU CANNOT STOP ME. YOU KNOW THAT.
I WON'T HAVE TO.

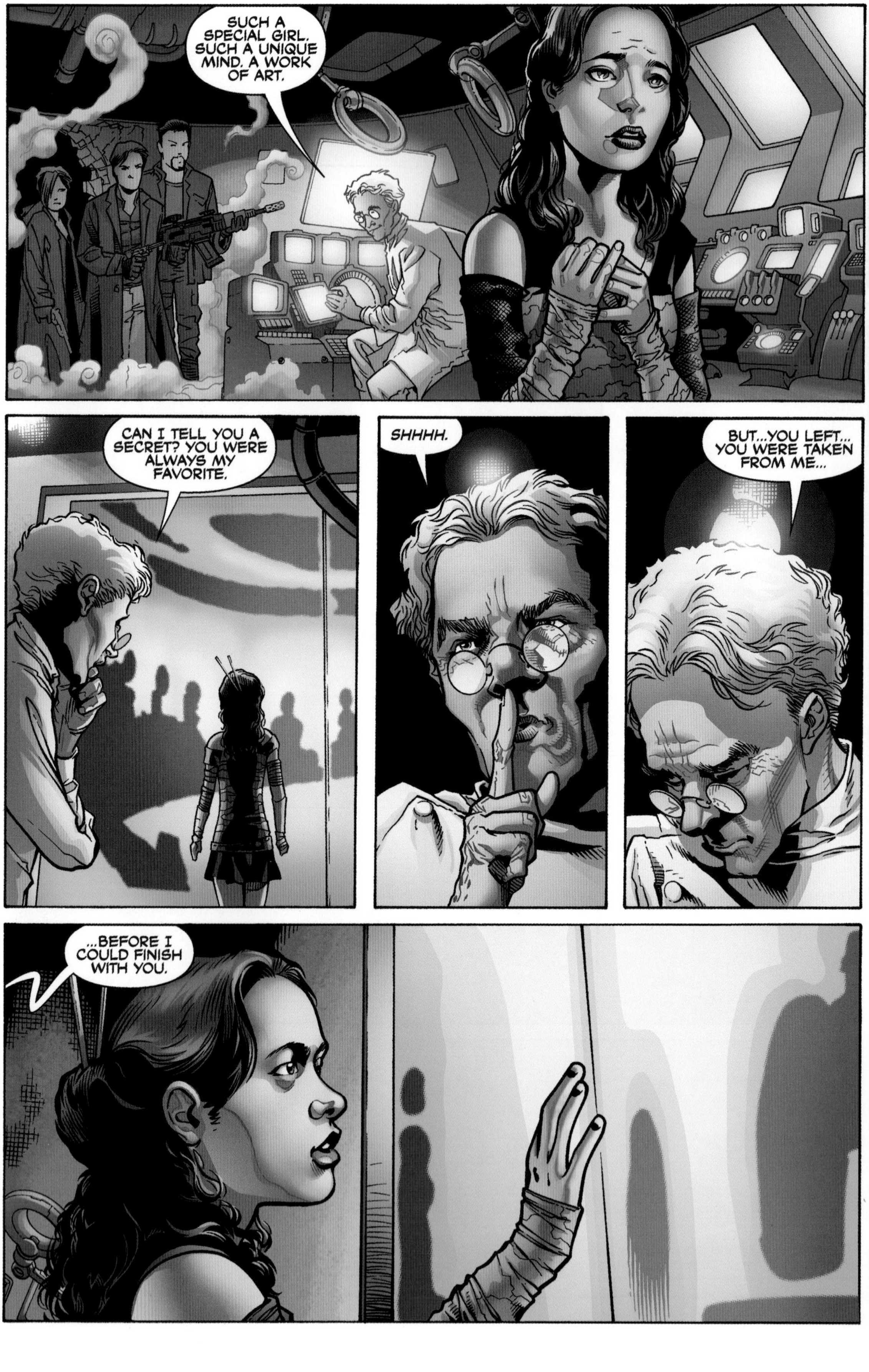
SUCH A SPECIAL GIRL. SUCH A UNIQUE MIND. A WORK OF ART.
CAN I TELL YOU A SECRET? YOU WERE ALWAYS MY FAVORITE.
SHHHH.
BUT...YOU LEFT... YOU WERE TAKEN FROM ME...
...BEFORE I COULD FINISH WITH YOU.

TSSSSS

THE GIRLS WHO STAYED...THEY WERE SPECIAL TOO...

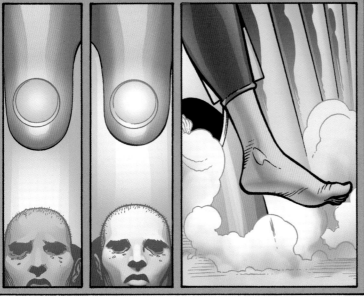

ACTUALLY, THEY'RE SOMETHING YOU NEVER WERE...

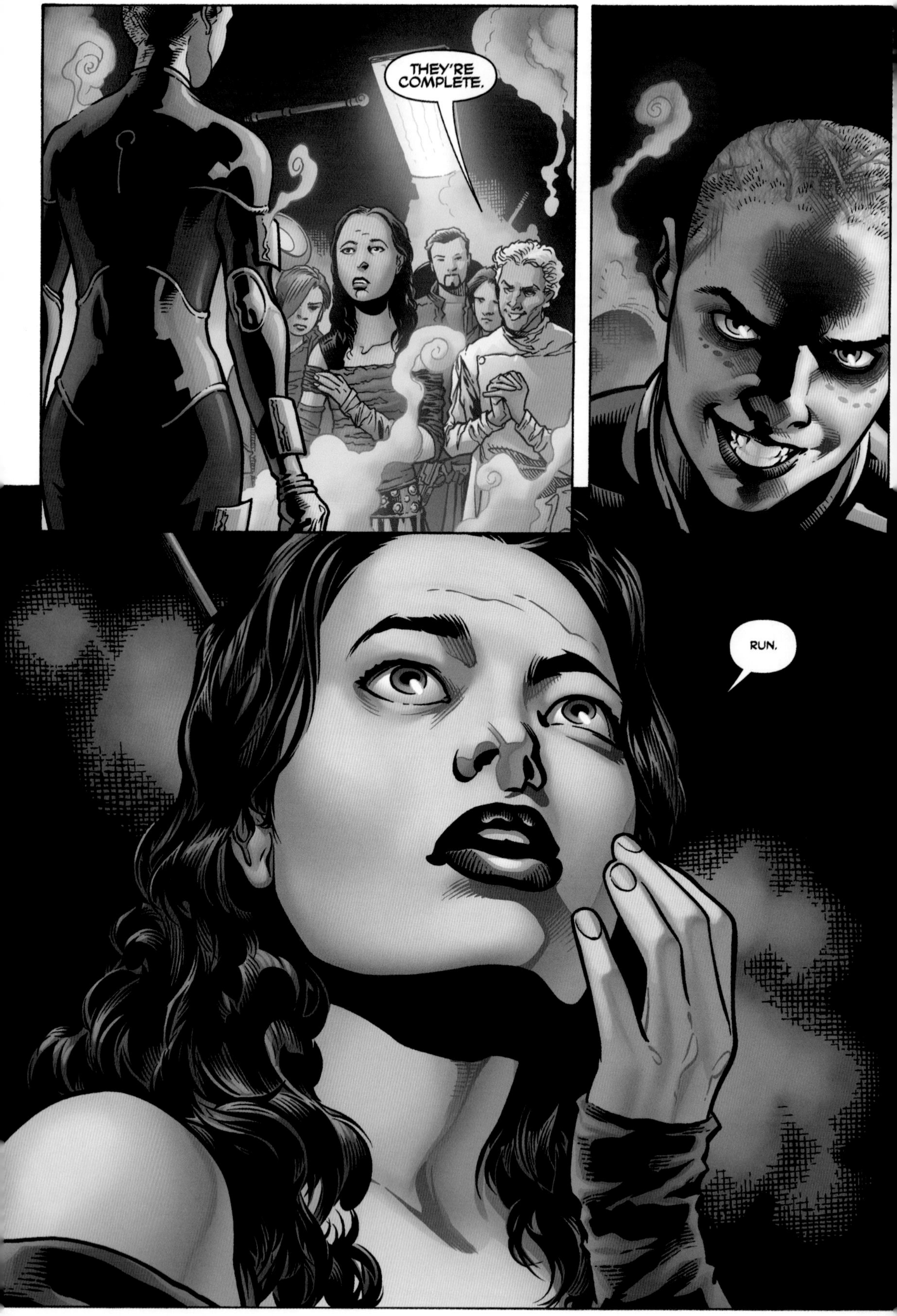
THEY'RE COMPLETE.
RUN.

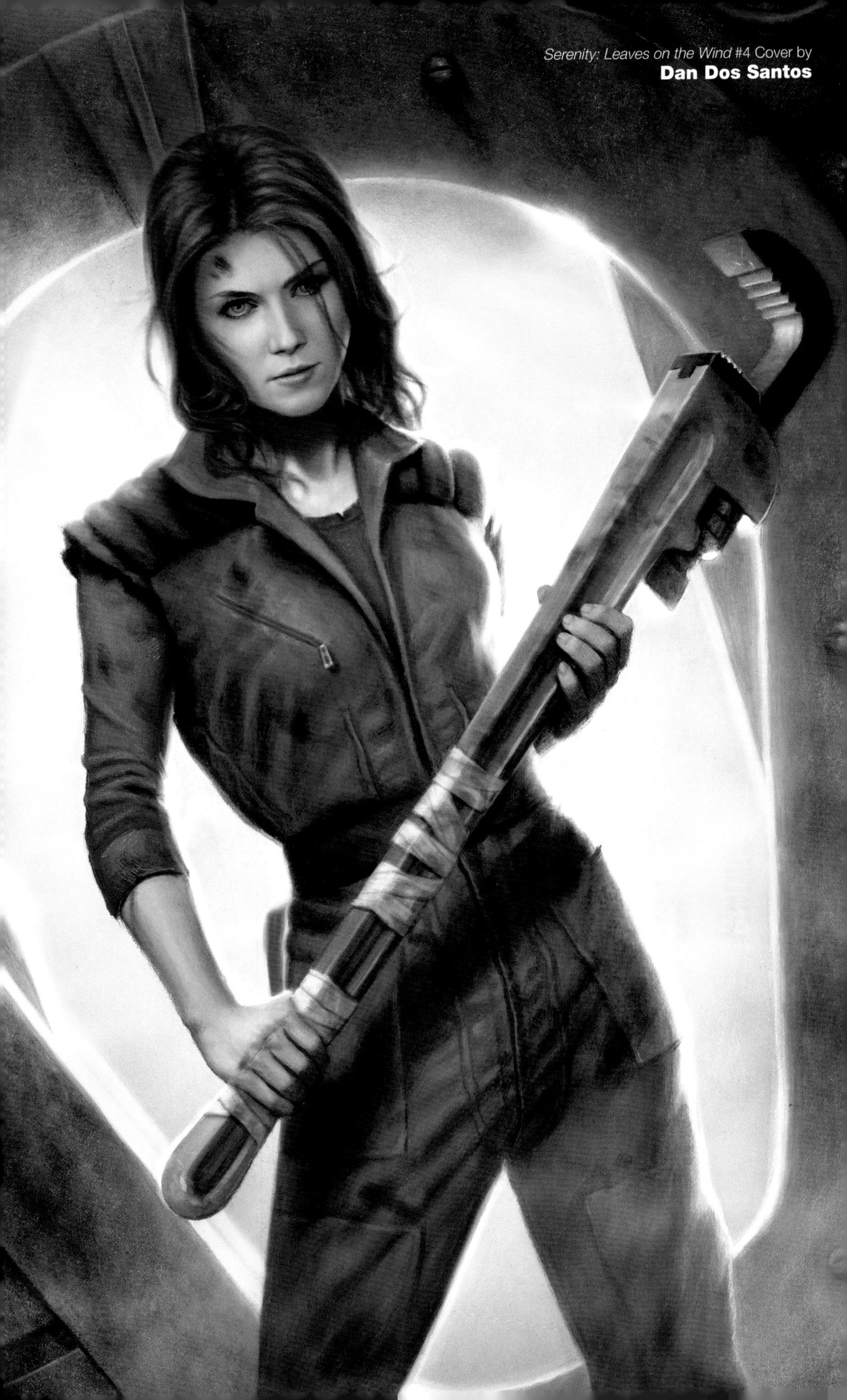

Serenity: Leaves on the Wind #4 Cover by
Dan Dos Santos

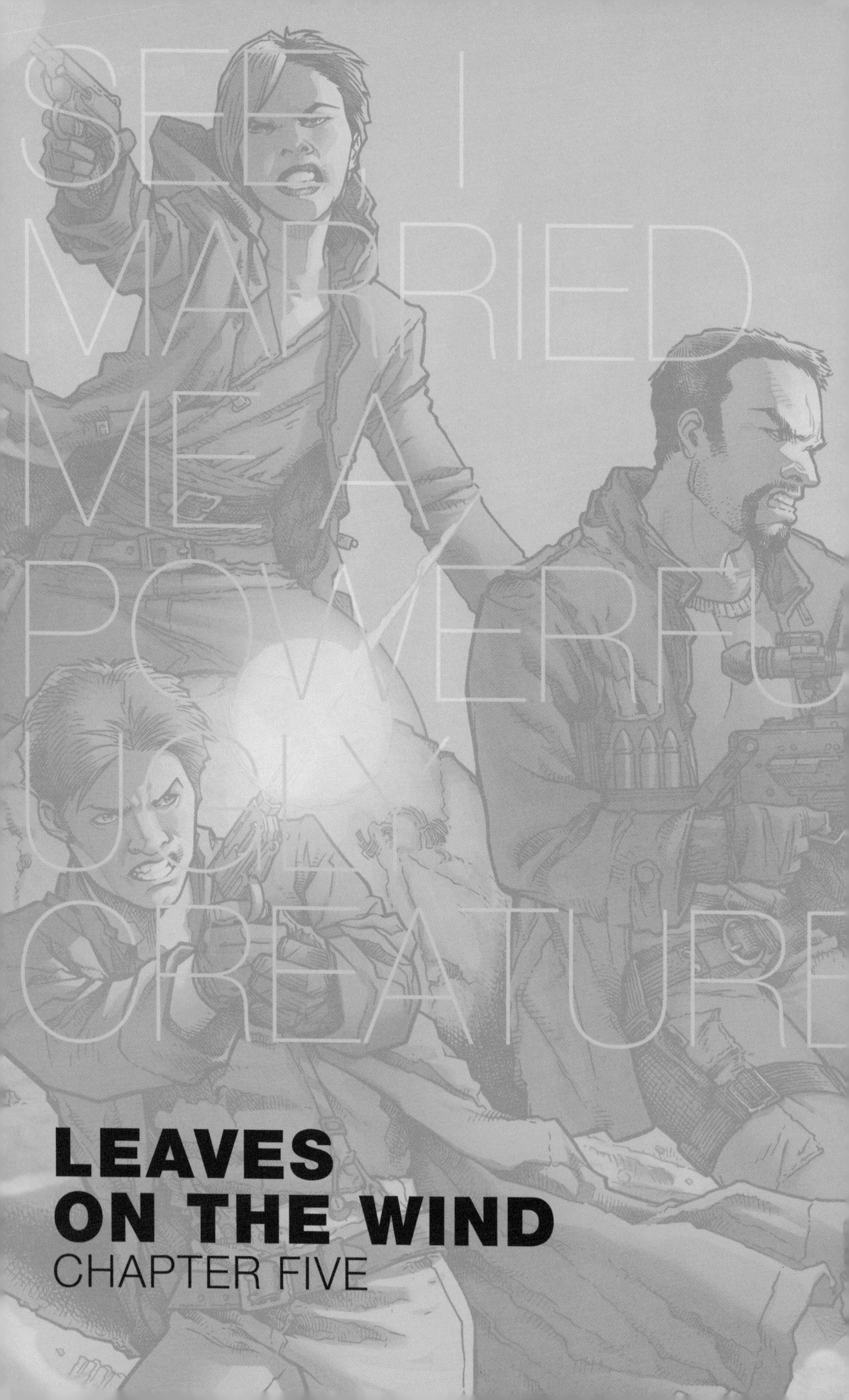
SEE I
MARRIED
ME A
POWERFU
L
CREATURE

LEAVES ON THE WIND

CHAPTER FIVE

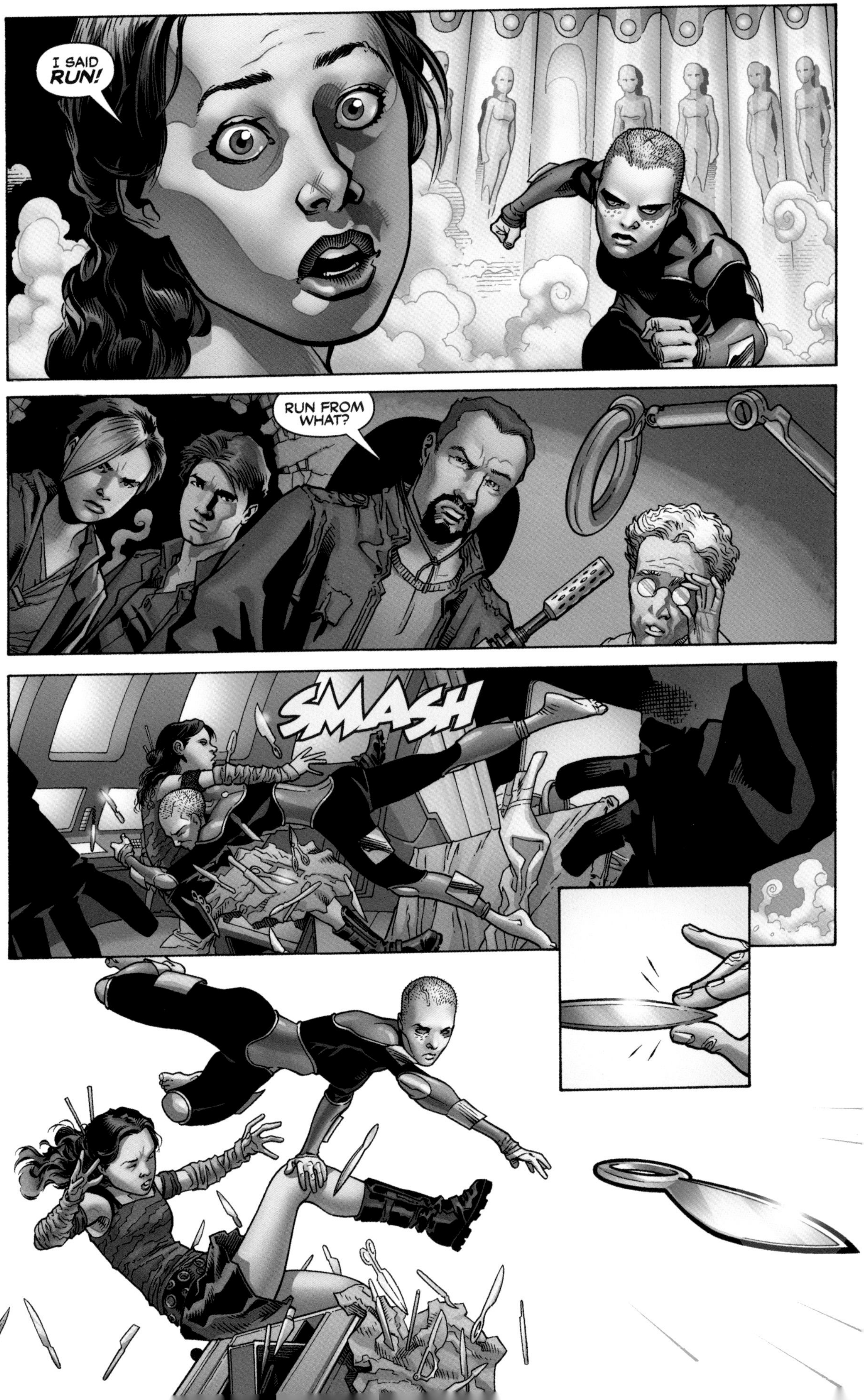
I SAID RUN!
RUN FROM WHAT?
SMASH

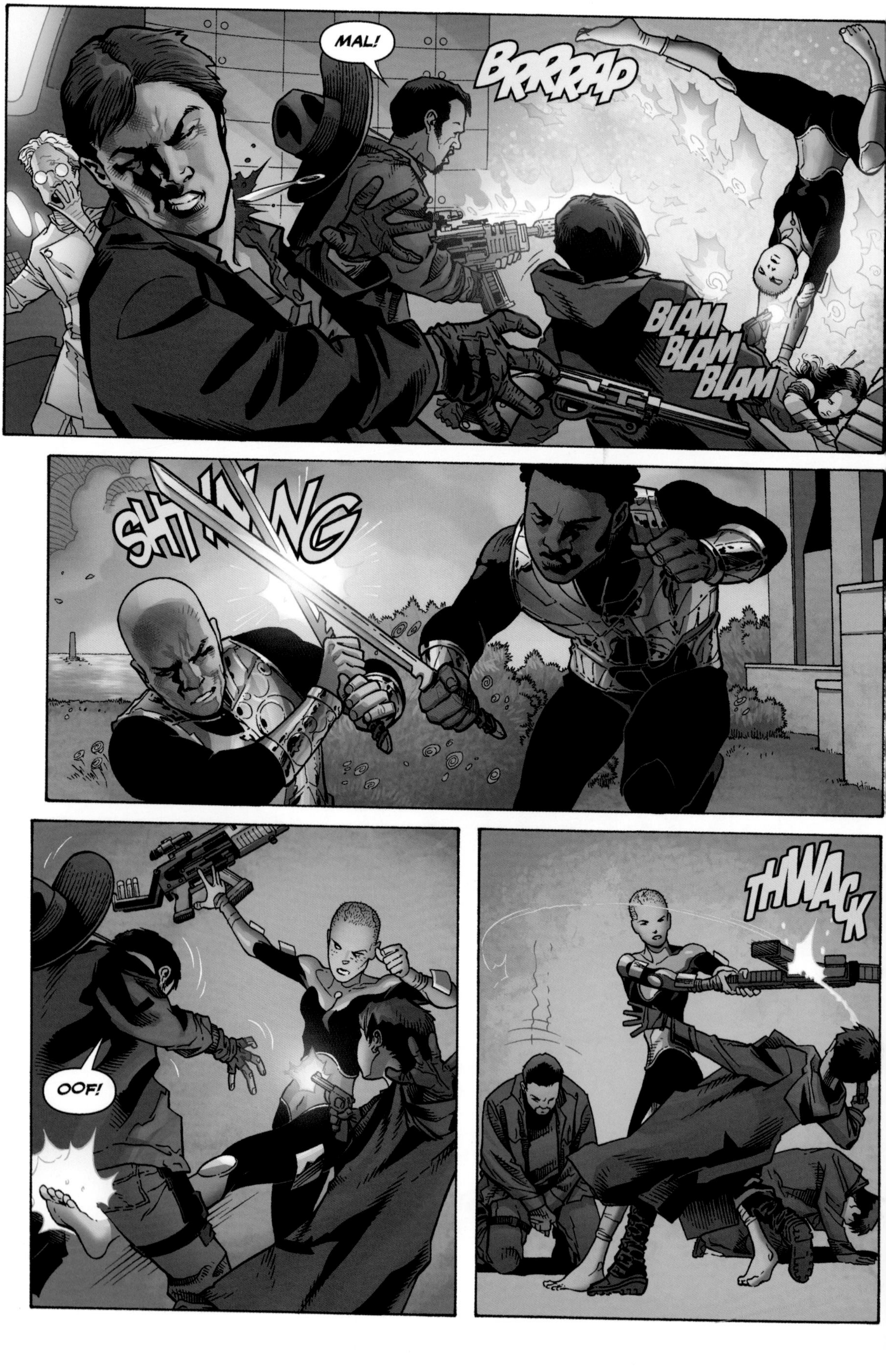
MAL!
BRRRAP
BLAM BLAM BLAM
SHING
OOF!
THWACK

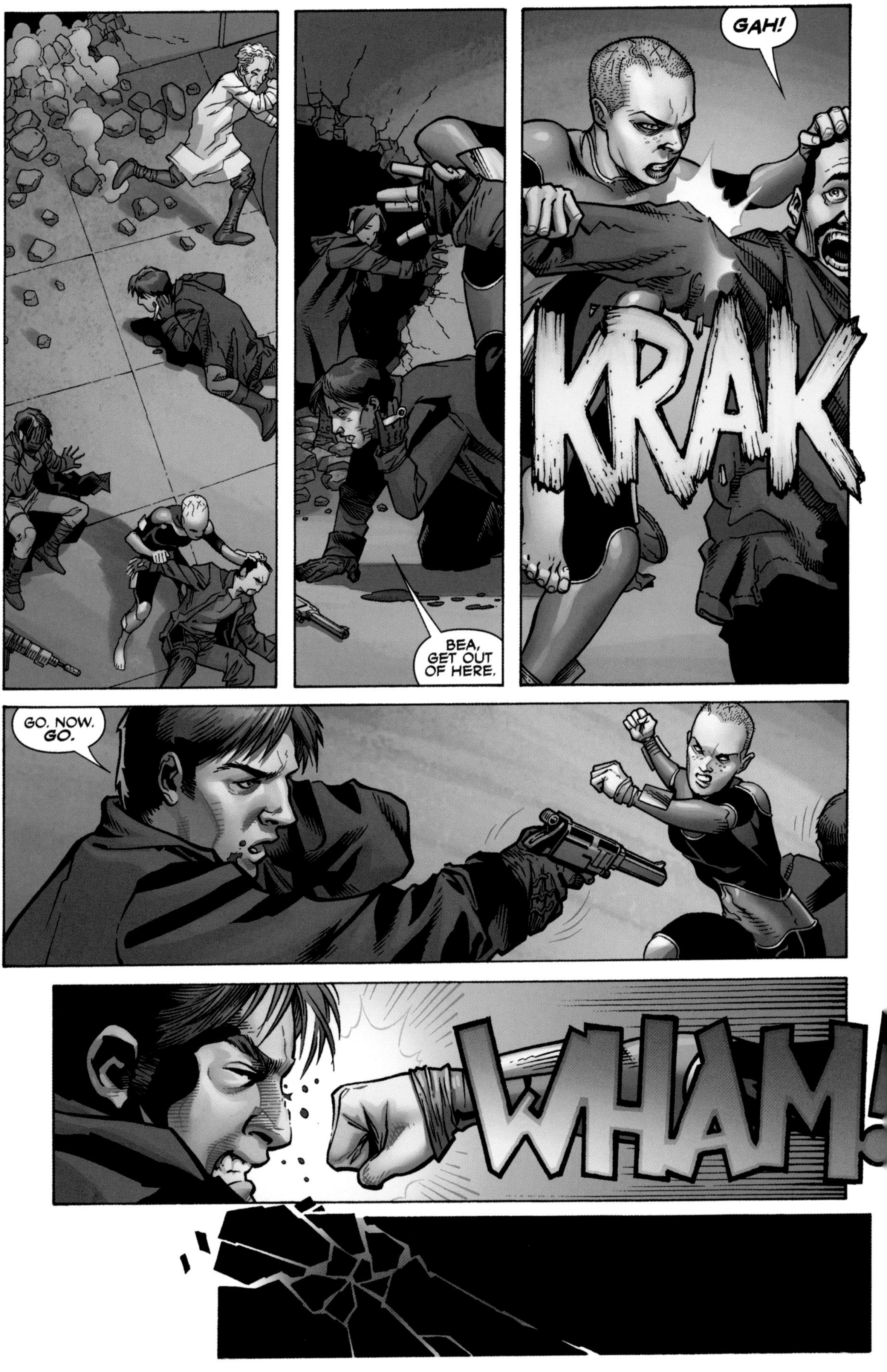
BEA, GET OUT OF HERE.
GAH!
KRAK
GO. NOW. GO.
WHAM!

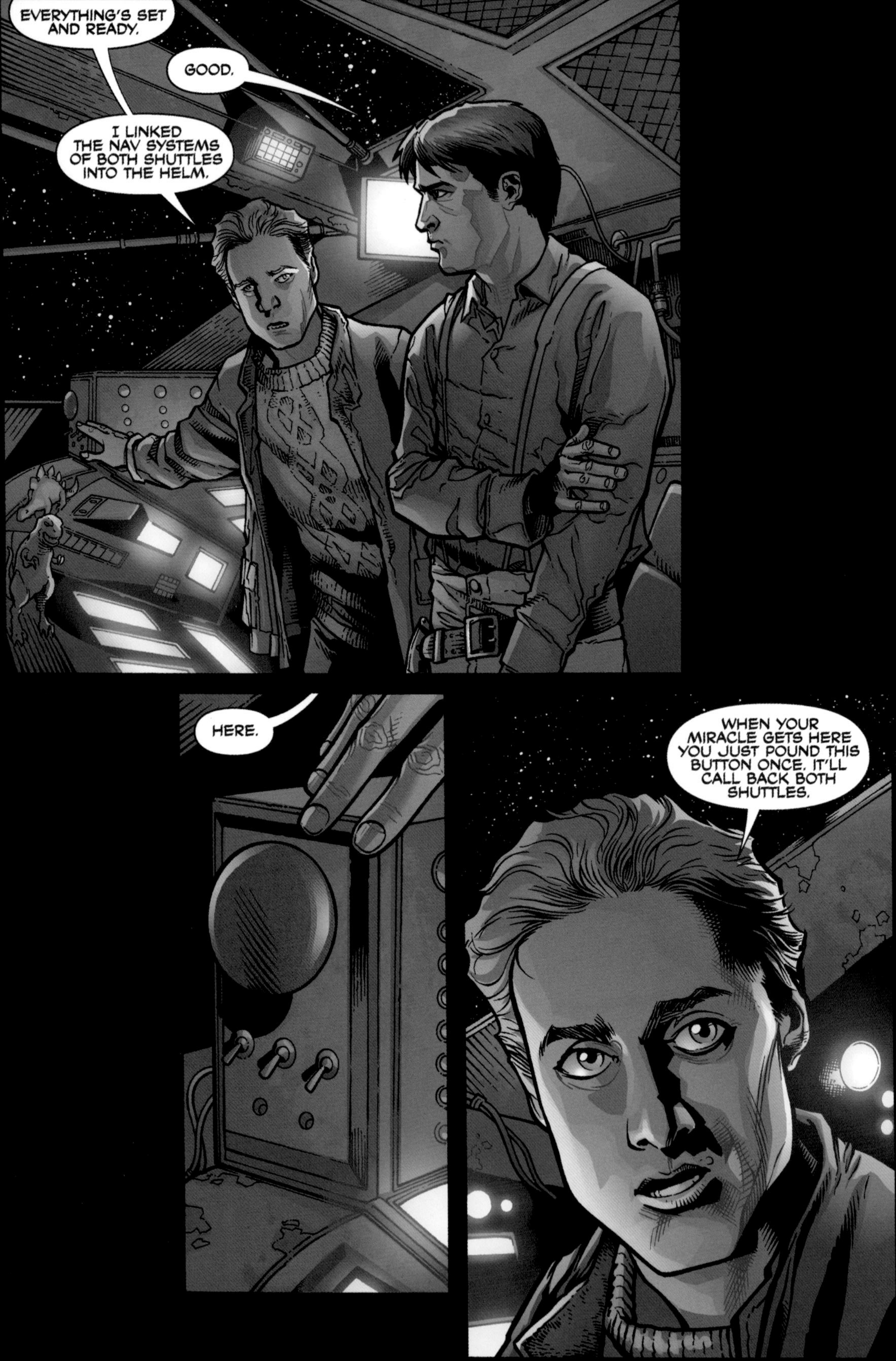
EVERYTHING'S SET AND READY.
GOOD.
I LINKED THE NAV SYSTEMS OF BOTH SHUTTLES INTO THE HELM.
HERE.
WHEN YOUR MIRACLE GETS HERE YOU JUST POUND THIS BUTTON ONCE. IT'LL CALL BACK BOTH SHUTTLES.

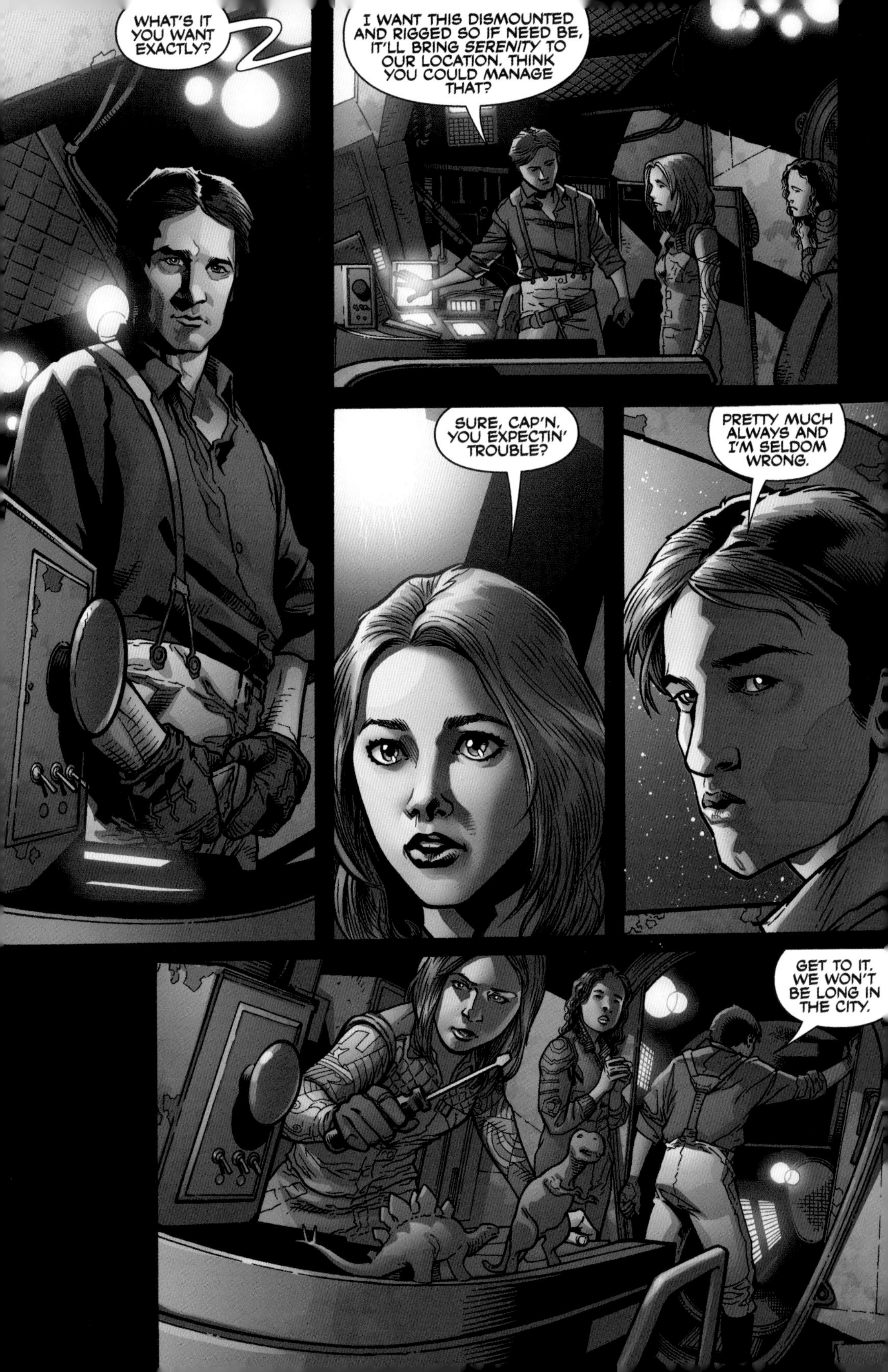
WHAT'S IT YOU WANT EXACTLY?
I WANT THIS DISMOUNTED AND RIGGED SO IF NEED BE, IT'LL BRING *SERENITY* TO OUR LOCATION. THINK YOU COULD MANAGE THAT?
SURE, CAP'N. YOU EXPECTIN' TROUBLE?
PRETTY MUCH ALWAYS AND I'M SELDOM WRONG.
GET TO IT. WE WON'T BE LONG IN THE CITY.

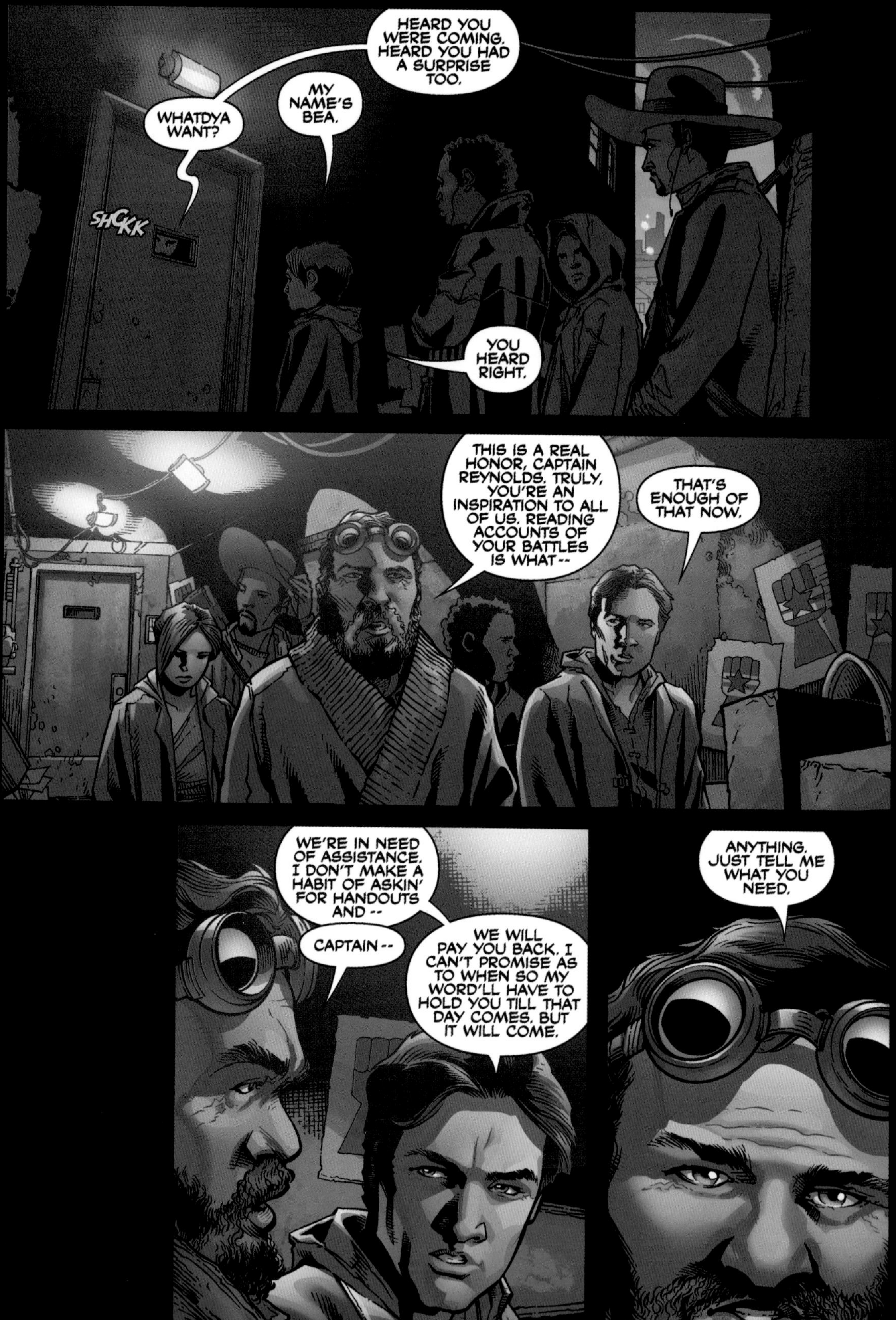
SHCKK
WHATDYA WANT?
MY NAME'S BEA.
HEARD YOU WERE COMING. HEARD YOU HAD A SURPRISE TOO.
YOU HEARD RIGHT.
THIS IS A REAL HONOR, CAPTAIN REYNOLDS. TRULY, YOU'RE AN INSPIRATION TO ALL OF US. READING ACCOUNTS OF YOUR BATTLES IS WHAT--
THAT'S ENOUGH OF THAT NOW.
WE'RE IN NEED OF ASSISTANCE. I DON'T MAKE A HABIT OF ASKIN' FOR HANDOUTS AND --
CAPTAIN --
WE WILL PAY YOU BACK. I CAN'T PROMISE AS TO WHEN SO MY WORD'LL HAVE TO HOLD YOU TILL THAT DAY COMES, BUT IT WILL COME.
ANYTHING. JUST TELL ME WHAT YOU NEED.

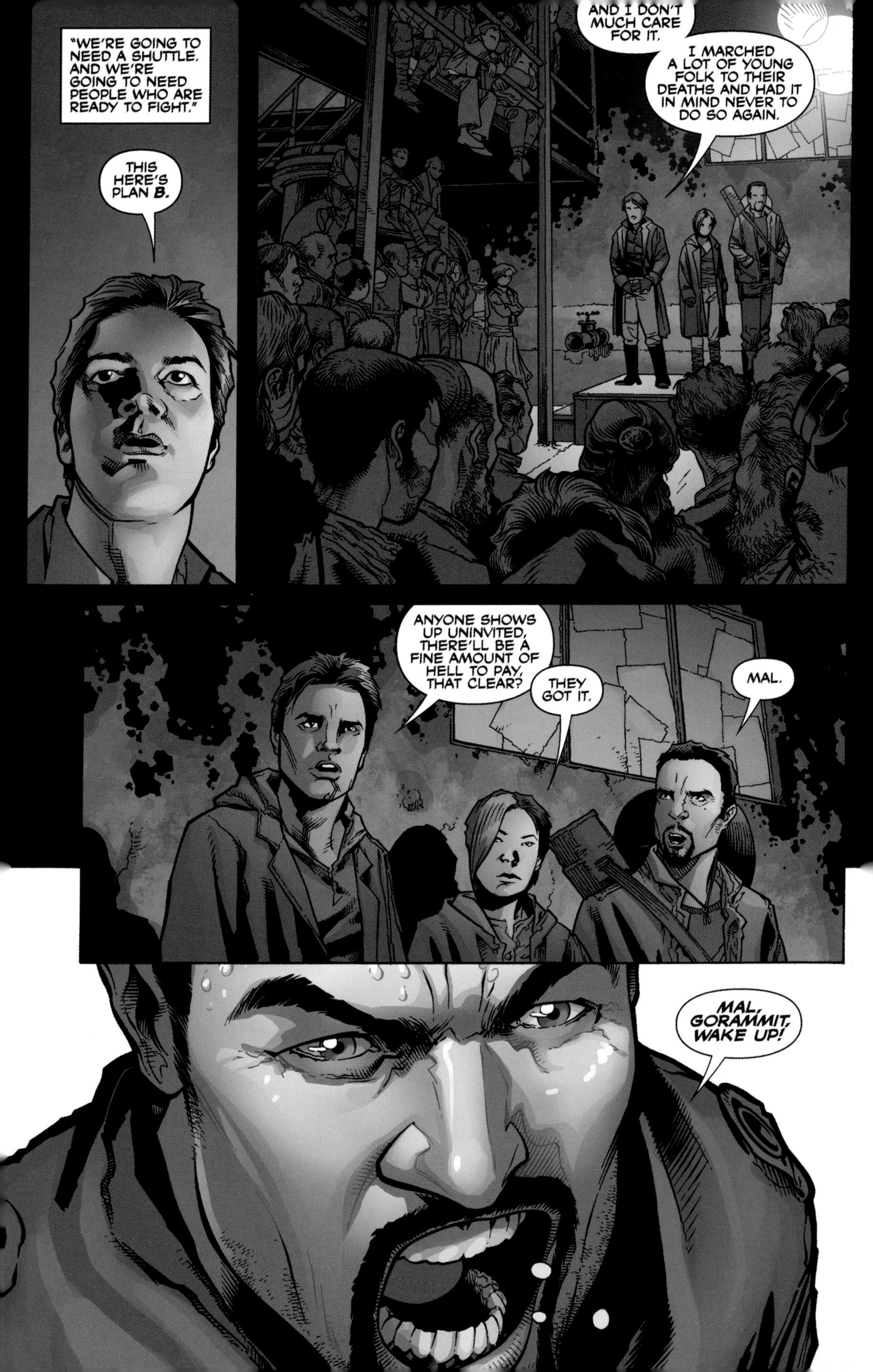
"WE'RE GOING TO NEED A SHUTTLE. AND WE'RE GOING TO NEED PEOPLE WHO ARE READY TO FIGHT."
THIS HERE'S PLAN B.
AND I DON'T MUCH CARE FOR IT.
I MARCHED A LOT OF YOUNG FOLK TO THEIR DEATHS AND HAD IT IN MIND NEVER TO DO SO AGAIN.
ANYONE SHOWS UP UNINVITED, THERE'LL BE A FINE AMOUNT OF HELL TO PAY, THAT CLEAR?
THEY GOT IT.
MAL.
MAL, GORAMMIT, WAKE UP!

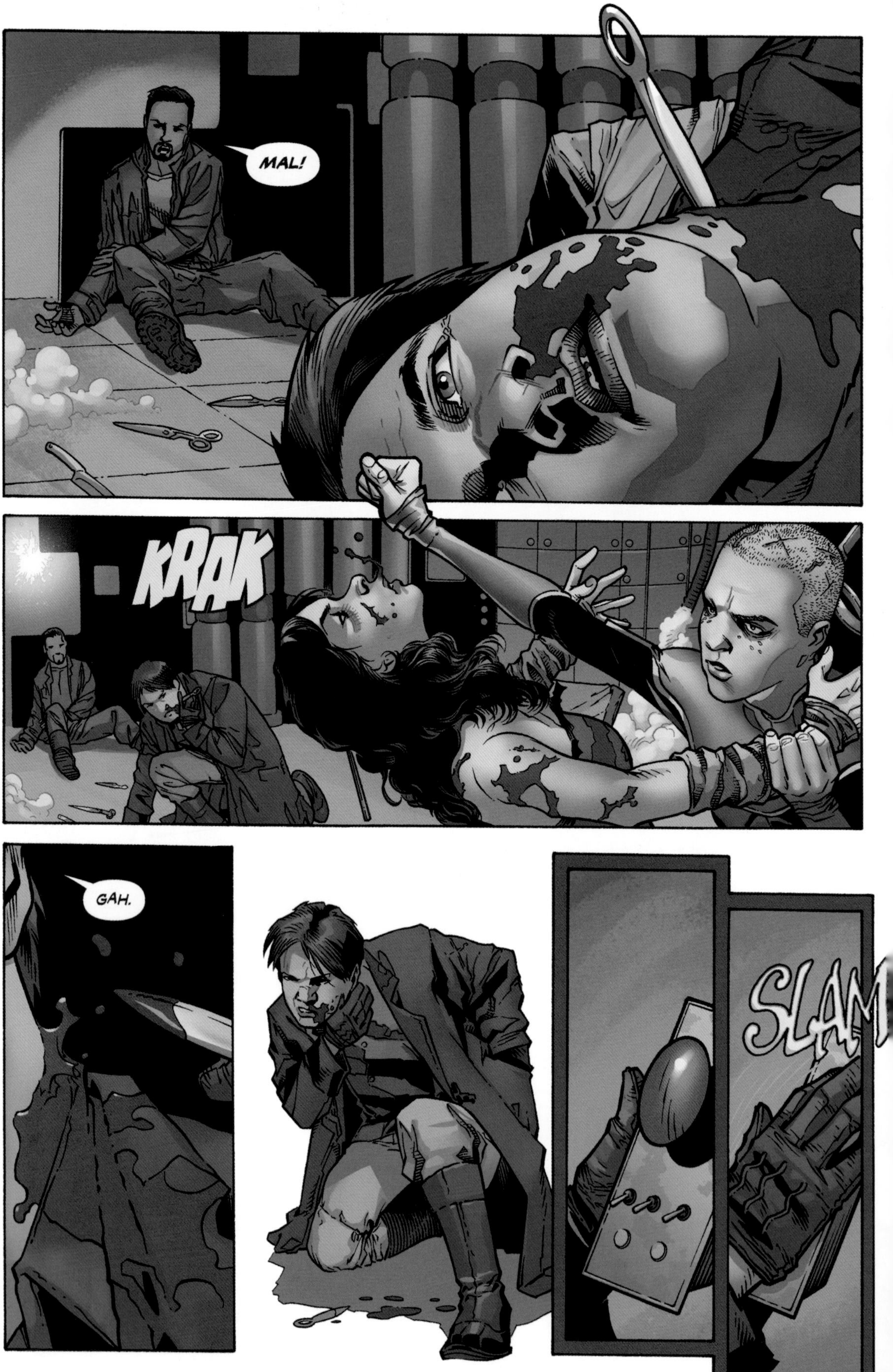
MAL!
KRAK
GAH.
SLAM

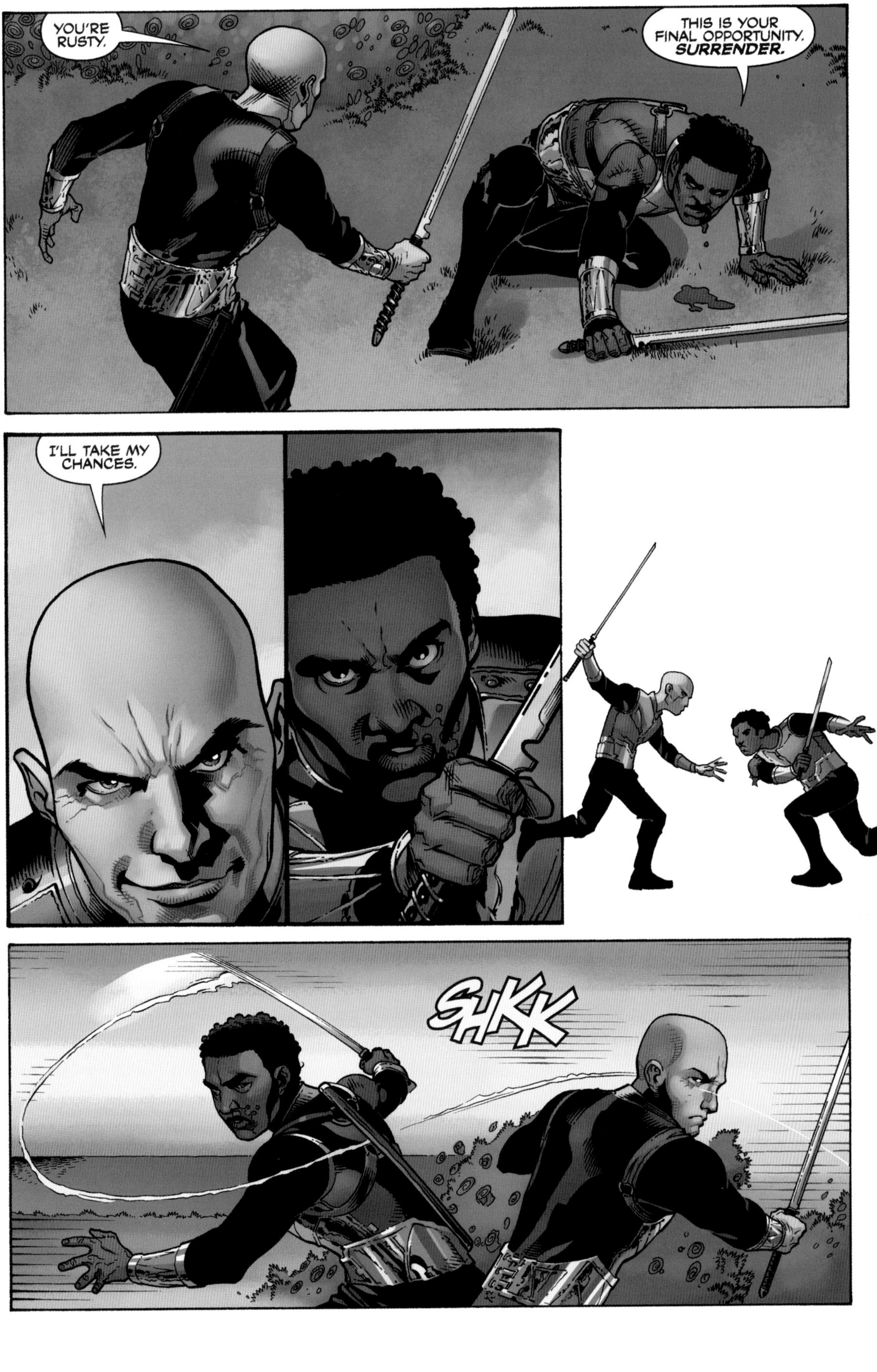
YOU'RE RUSTY.
THIS IS YOUR FINAL OPPORTUNITY. SURRENDER.
I'LL TAKE MY CHANCES.
SHKK

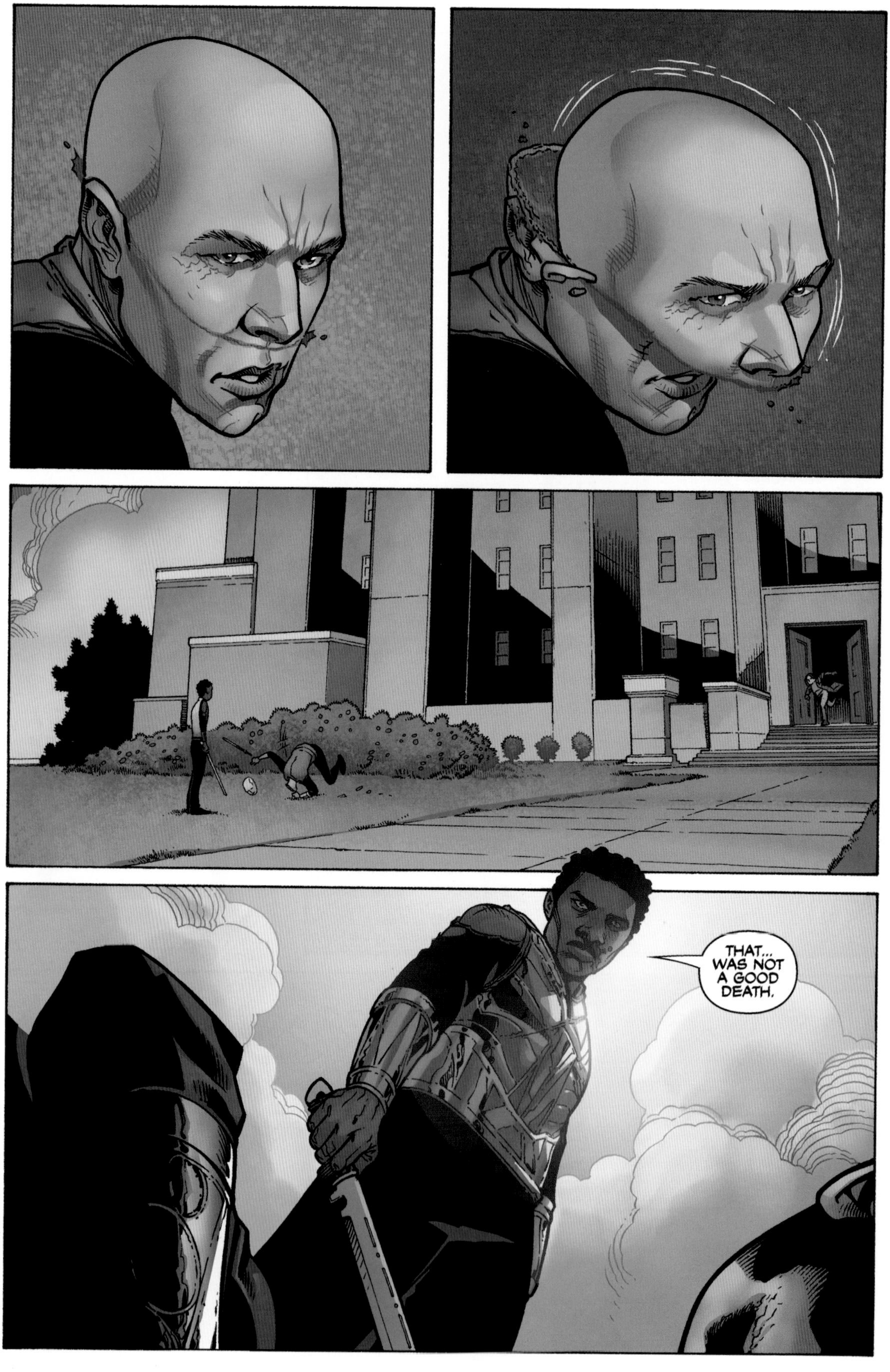
THAT... WAS NOT A GOOD DEATH.

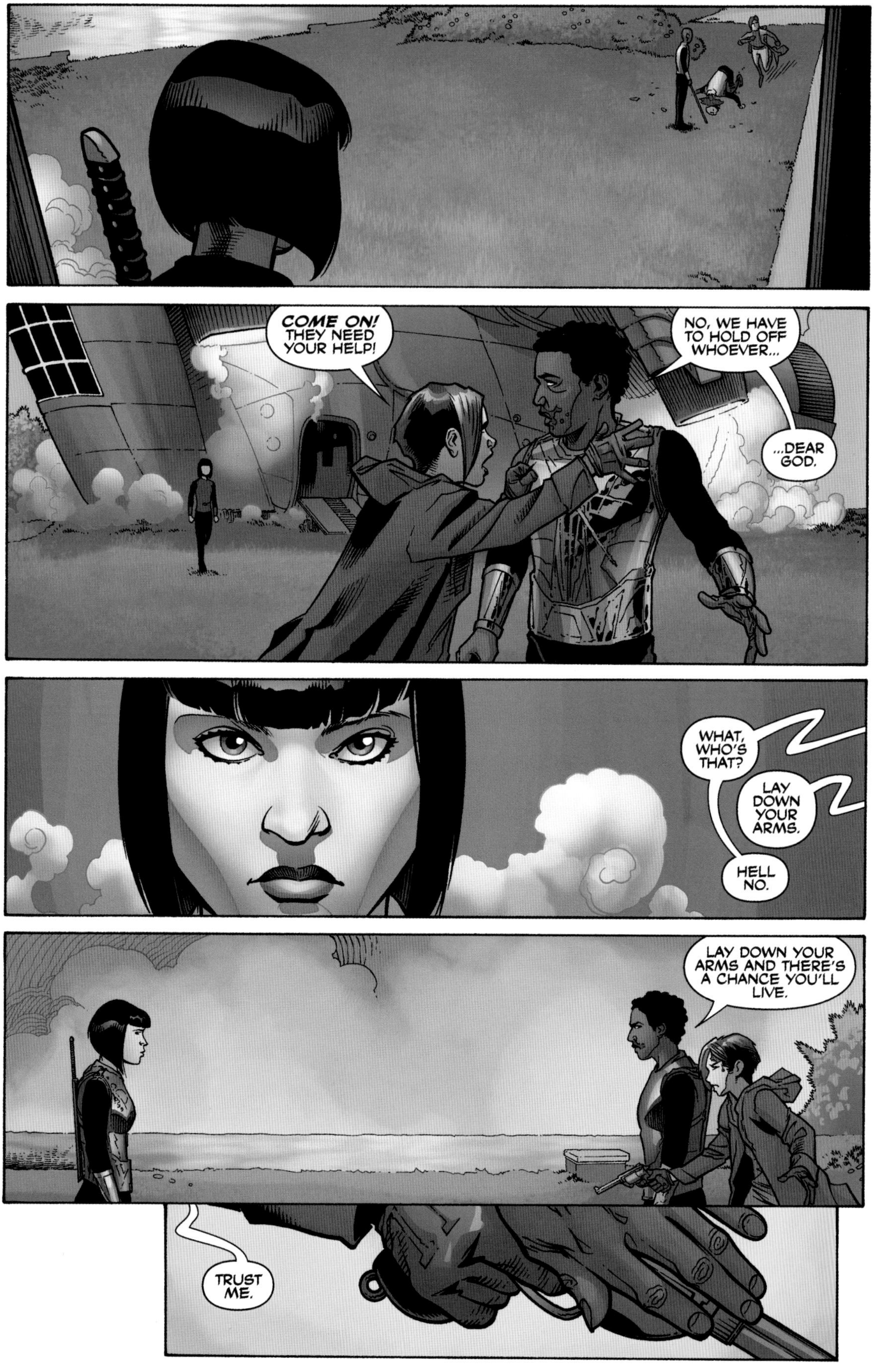
COME ON! THEY NEED YOUR HELP!
NO, WE HAVE TO HOLD OFF WHOEVER...
...DEAR GOD.
WHAT, WHO'S THAT?
LAY DOWN YOUR ARMS.
HELL NO.
LAY DOWN YOUR ARMS AND THERE'S A CHANCE YOU'LL LIVE.
TRUST ME.

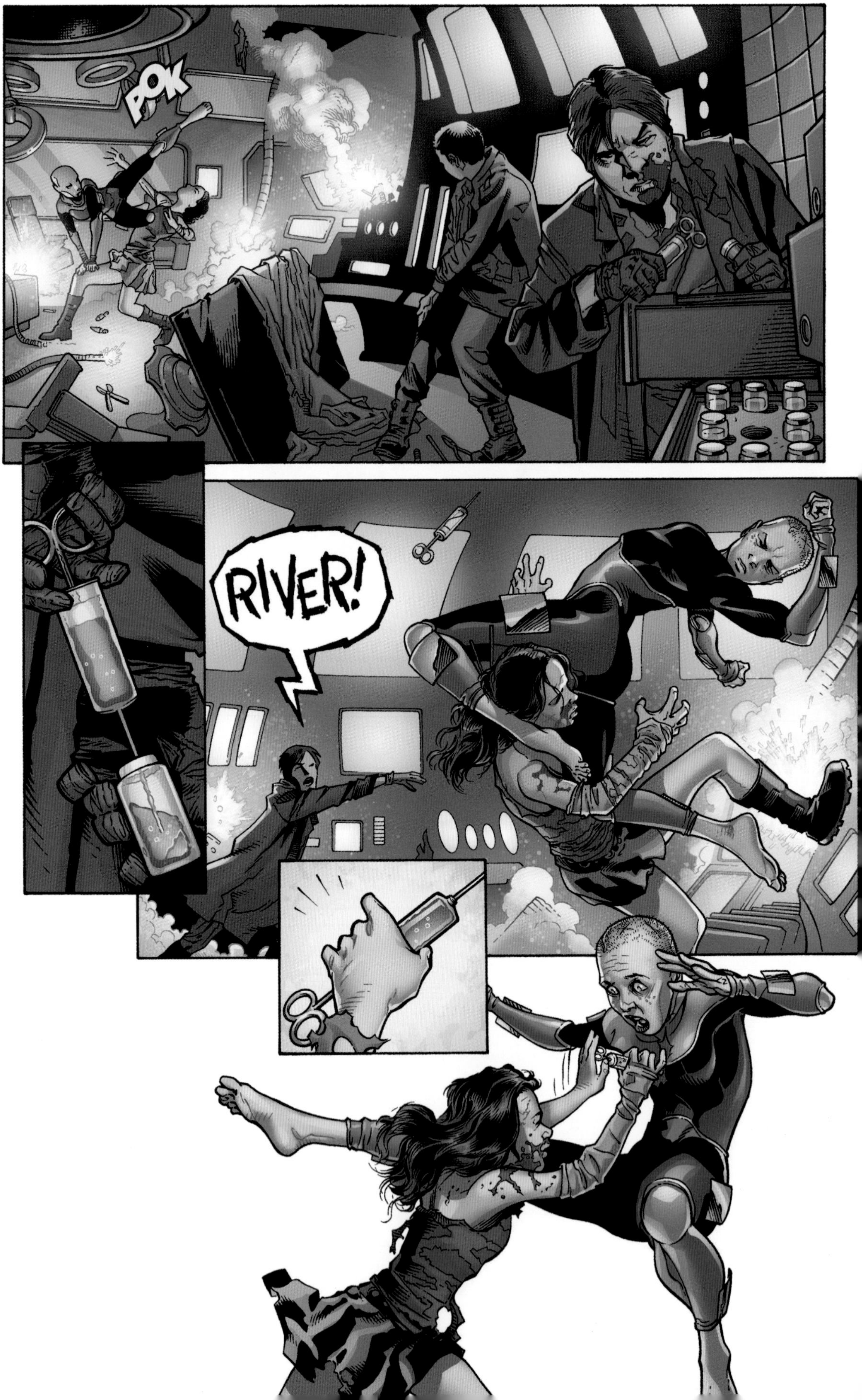
POK
RIVER!

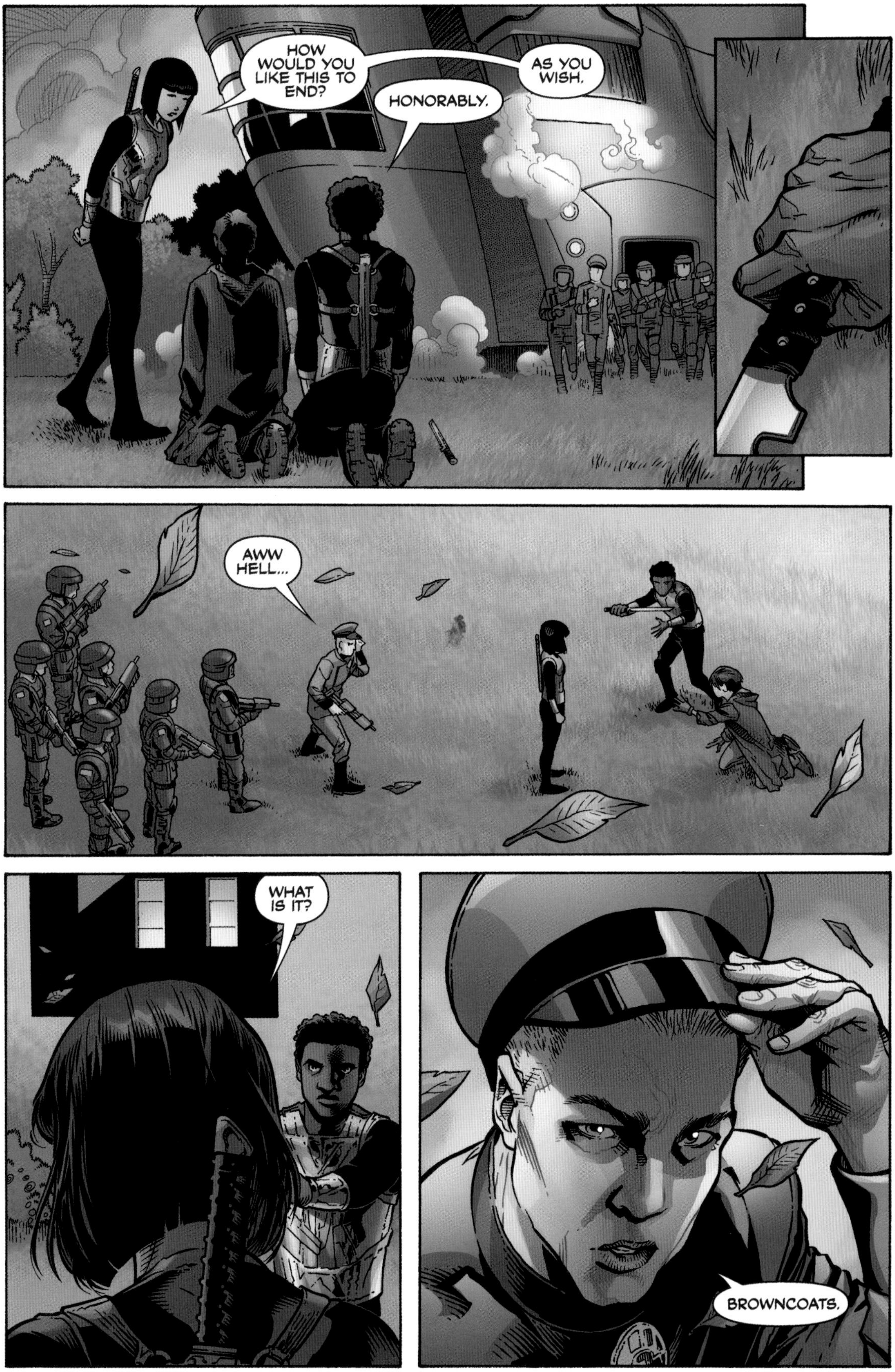
HOW WOULD YOU LIKE THIS TO END?
HONORABLY.
AS YOU WISH.
AWW HELL...
WHAT IS IT?
BROWNCOATS.

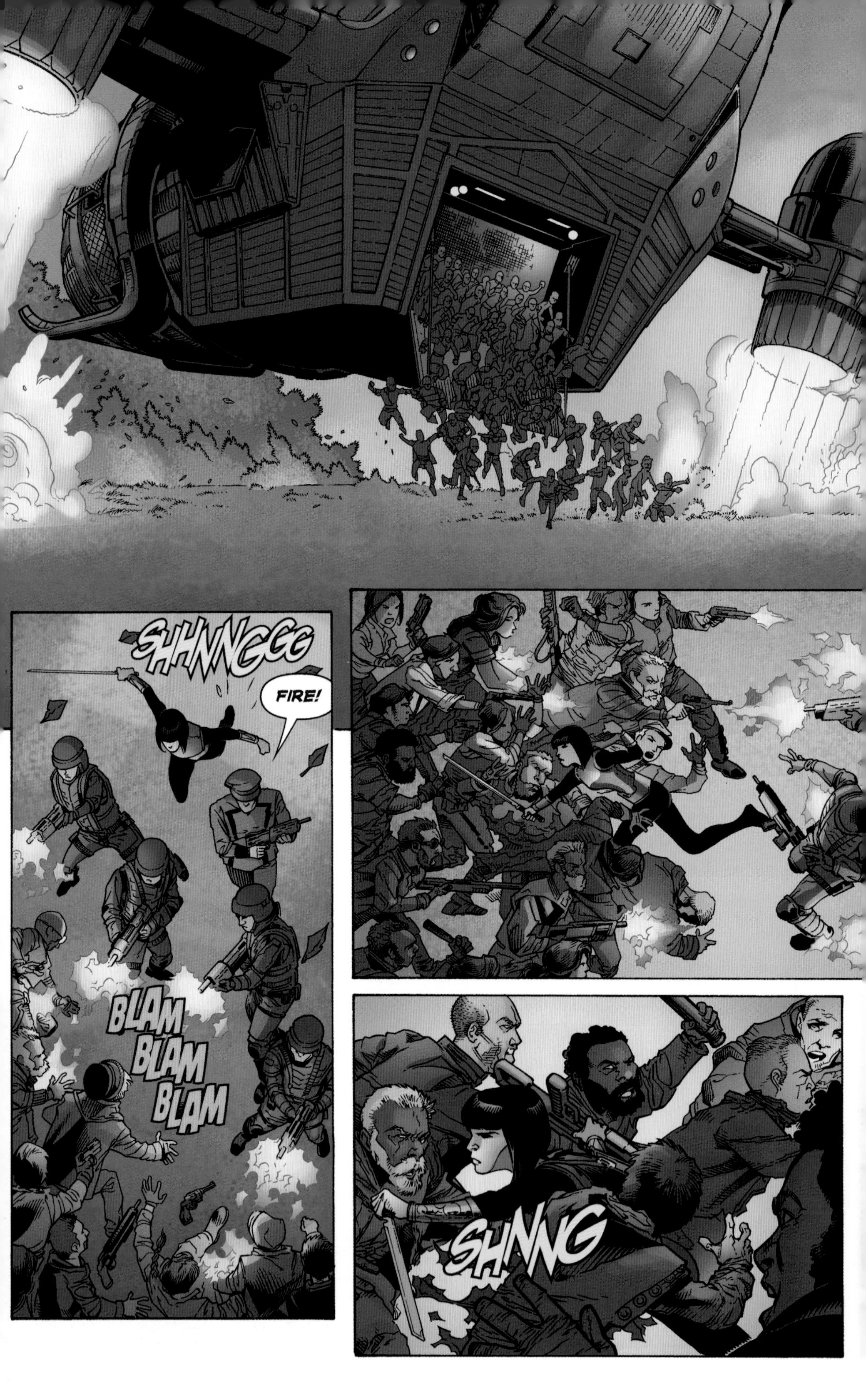
SHHNNGGG
FIRE!
BLAM
BLAM
BLAM
SHNNG

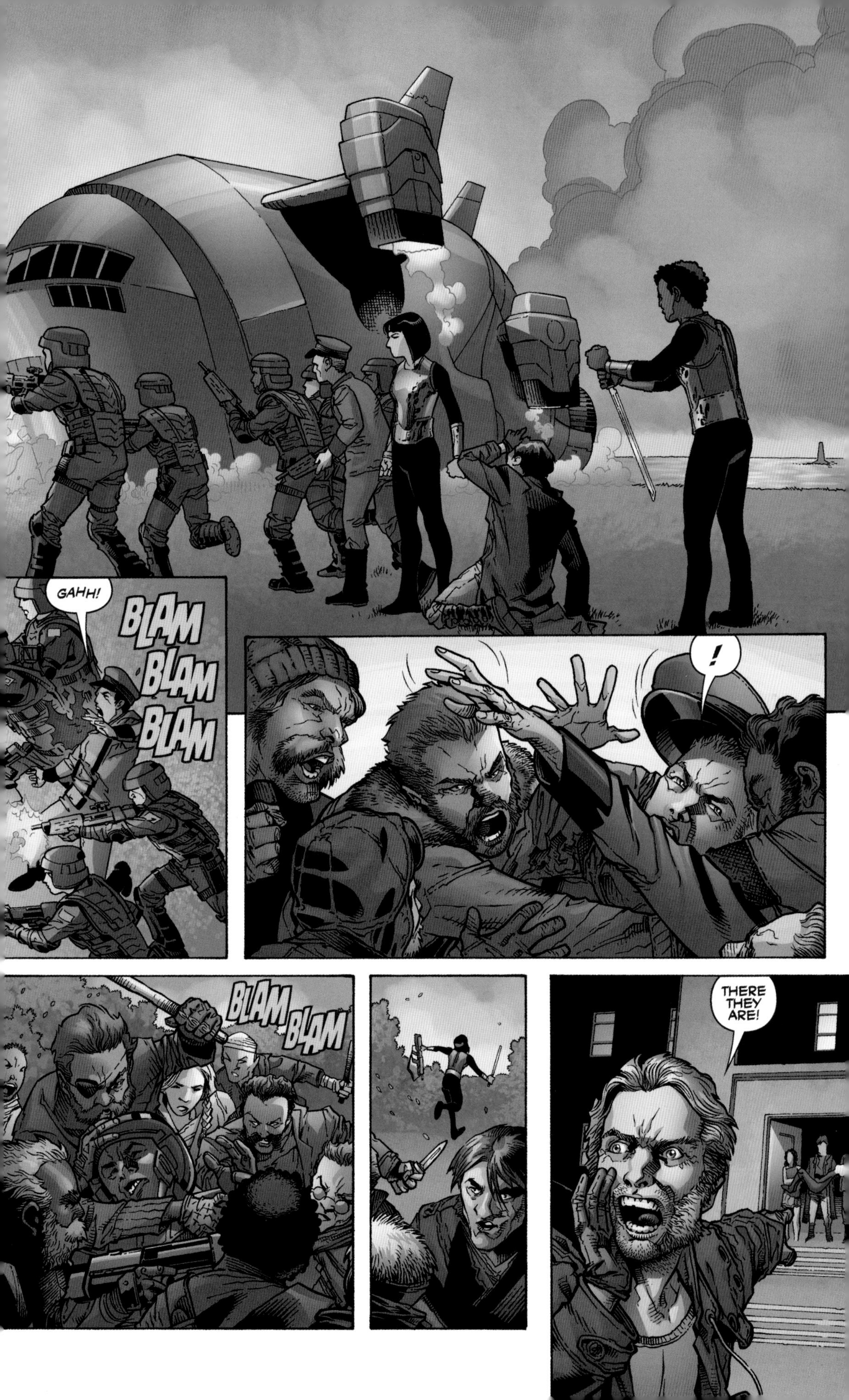
GAHH!
BLAM BLAM BLAM
!
BLAM BLAM
THERE THEY ARE!

RIG THEIR SHIP WITH EXPLOSIVES AND GRAB HIM.

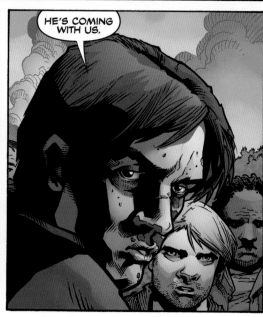

HE'S COMING WITH US.

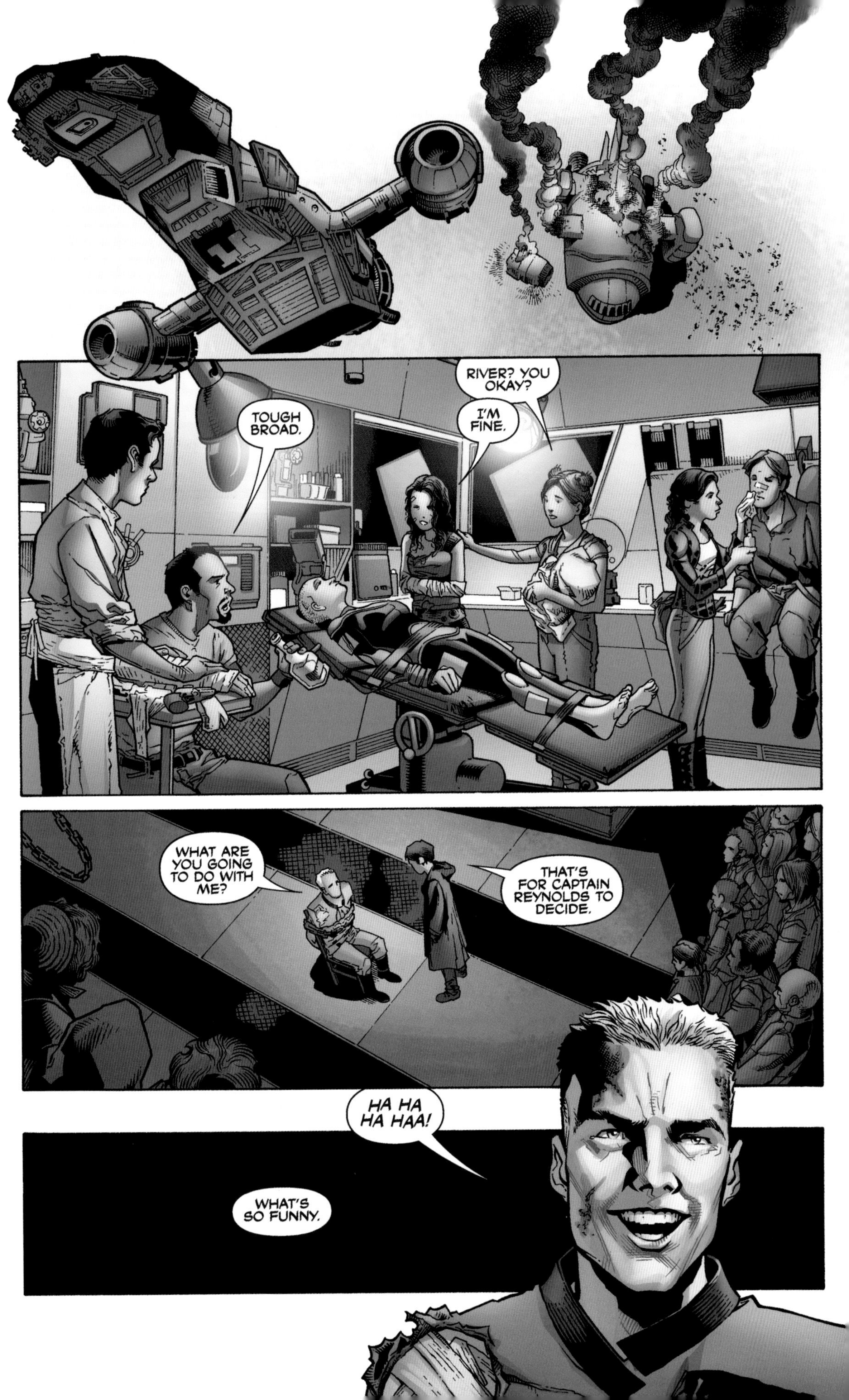
RIVER? YOU OKAY?
TOUGH BROAD.
I'M FINE.
WHAT ARE YOU GOING TO DO WITH ME?
THAT'S FOR CAPTAIN REYNOLDS TO DECIDE.
HA HA HA HAA!
WHAT'S SO FUNNY.

MALCOLM REYNOLDS ISN'T YOUR LEADER. I AM.

WHAT ARE YOU TALKING ABOUT?

YOU KNOW WHAT THE BIGGEST ADVANTAGE IS FOR ENEMIES OF THE ALLIANCE?

THE ALLIANCE WEARS UNIFORMS, WE OPERATE IN CONCERT. IF YOU WANT TO HURT US YOU KNOW WHERE TO STRIKE.

YOU CAN'T DO MUCH DAMAGE, HAPHAZARD AND WEAK AS YOU GENERALLY GORRAM ARE, BUT AT LEAST YOU KNOW WHERE TO AIM YOUR ATTACK.

NOT LIKE THAT FOR US. YOU'RE ALL SCATTERED, SCURRYIN' AROUND, NO RHYME OR REASON...TOUGH TO PREDICT.

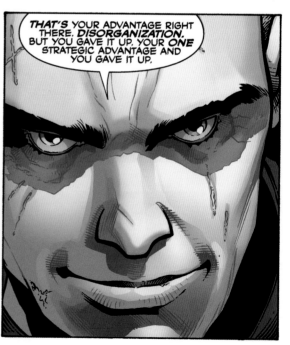

THAT'S YOUR ADVANTAGE RIGHT THERE. *DISORGANIZATION.* BUT YOU GAVE IT UP. YOUR *ONE* STRATEGIC ADVANTAGE AND YOU GAVE IT UP.

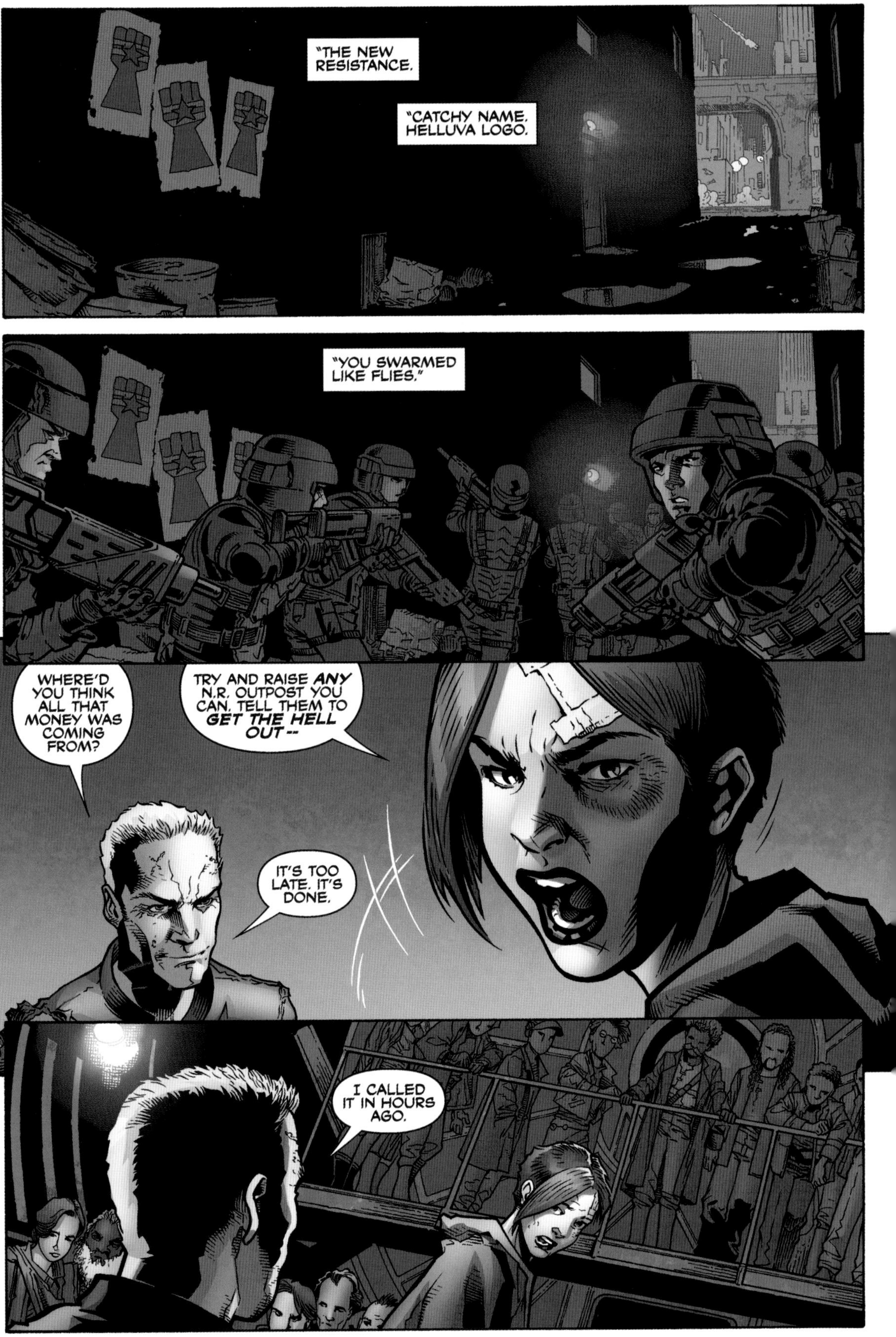
"THE NEW RESISTANCE.
"CATCHY NAME. HELLUVA LOGO.
"YOU SWARMED LIKE FLIES."
WHERE'D YOU THINK ALL THAT MONEY WAS COMING FROM?
TRY AND RAISE ***ANY*** N.R. OUTPOST YOU CAN. TELL THEM TO ***GET THE HELL OUT --***
IT'S TOO LATE. IT'S DONE.
I CALLED IT IN HOURS AGO.

I ASSURE YOU THAT *THIS* IS ALL THAT'S LEFT OF THE *"NEW RESISTANCE."*

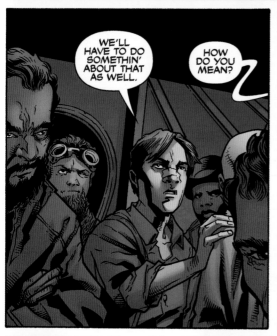

WE'LL HAVE TO DO SOMETHIN' ABOUT THAT AS WELL.

HOW DO YOU MEAN?

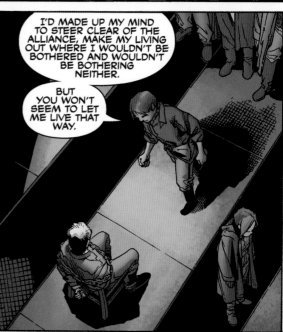

I'D MADE UP MY MIND TO STEER CLEAR OF THE ALLIANCE, MAKE MY LIVING OUT WHERE I WOULDN'T BE BOTHERED AND WOULDN'T BE BOTHERING NEITHER.

BUT YOU WON'T SEEM TO LET ME LIVE THAT WAY.

EVERY TIME I TRY TO WALK AWAY, YOU COME FOLLOWIN'. WELL, FROM NOW ON, YOU CHOOSE TO CHASE ME, I'M GONNA TURN AND MEET YOU HEAD ON. BE HONEST, I'M DEVELOPIN' A TASTE FOR IT.

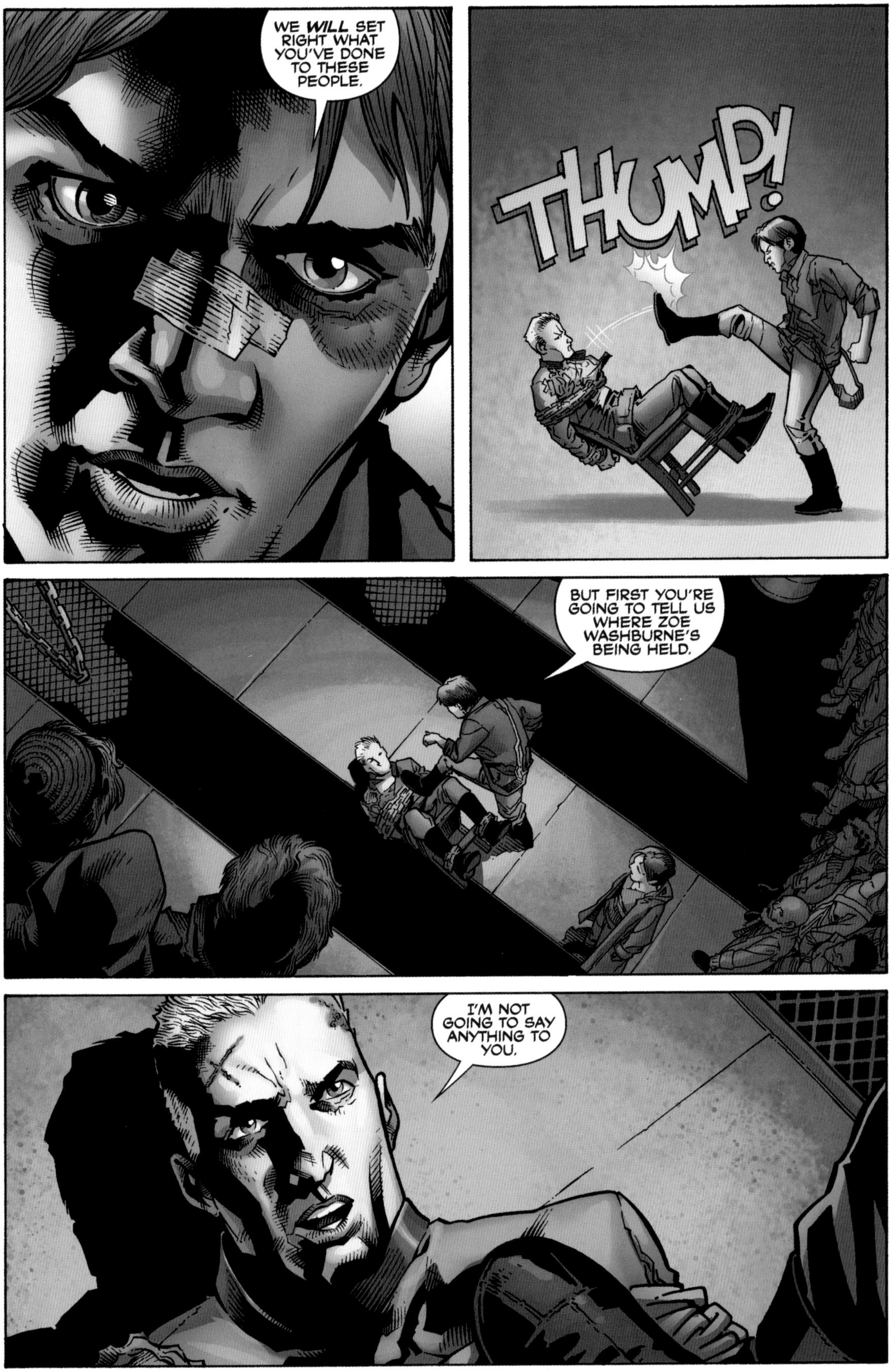
WE WILL SET RIGHT WHAT YOU'VE DONE TO THESE PEOPLE.
THUMP!
BUT FIRST YOU'RE GOING TO TELL US WHERE ZOE WASHBURNE'S BEING HELD.
I'M NOT GOING TO SAY ANYTHING TO YOU.

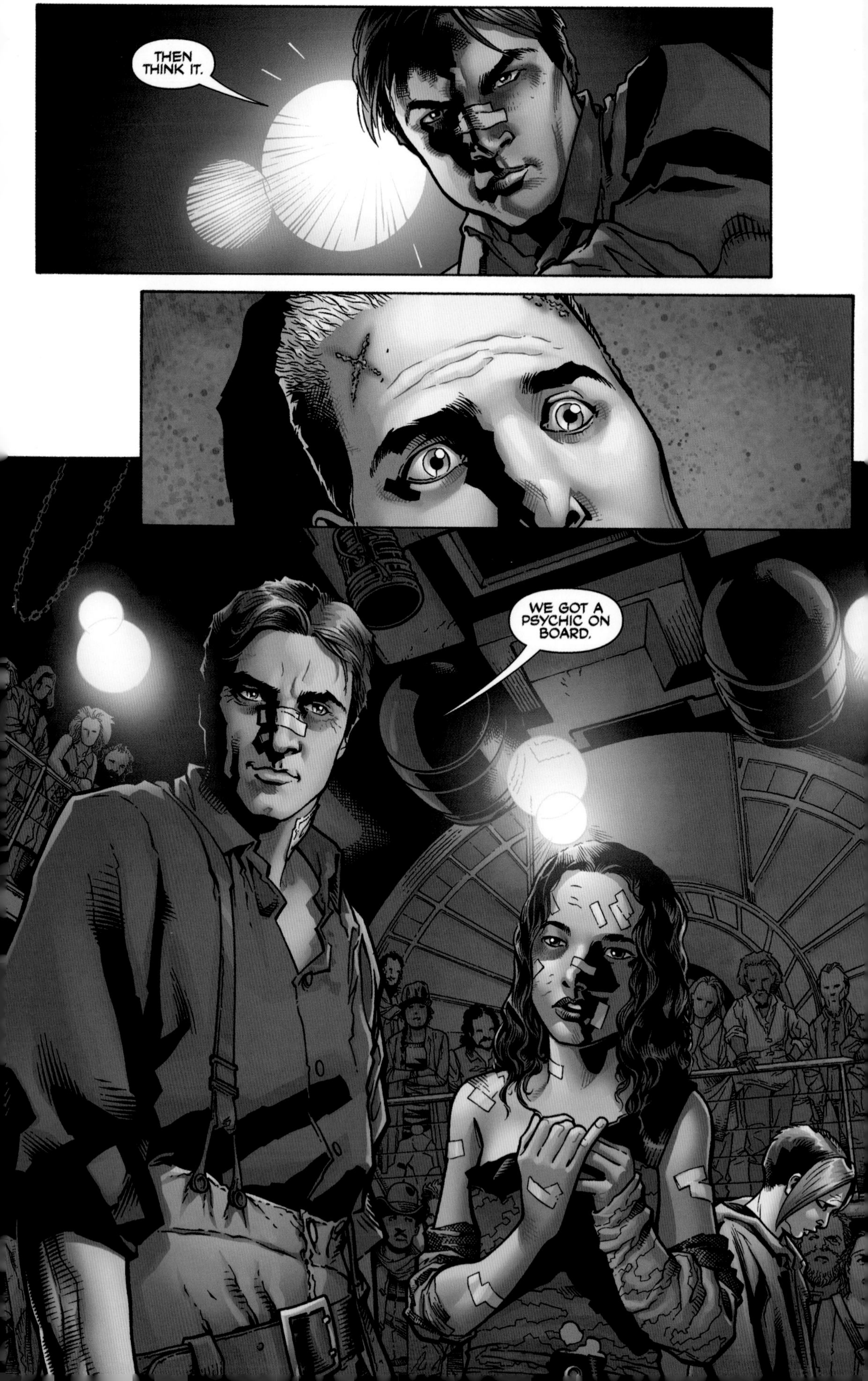
THEN THINK IT.
WE GOT A PSYCHIC ON BOARD.

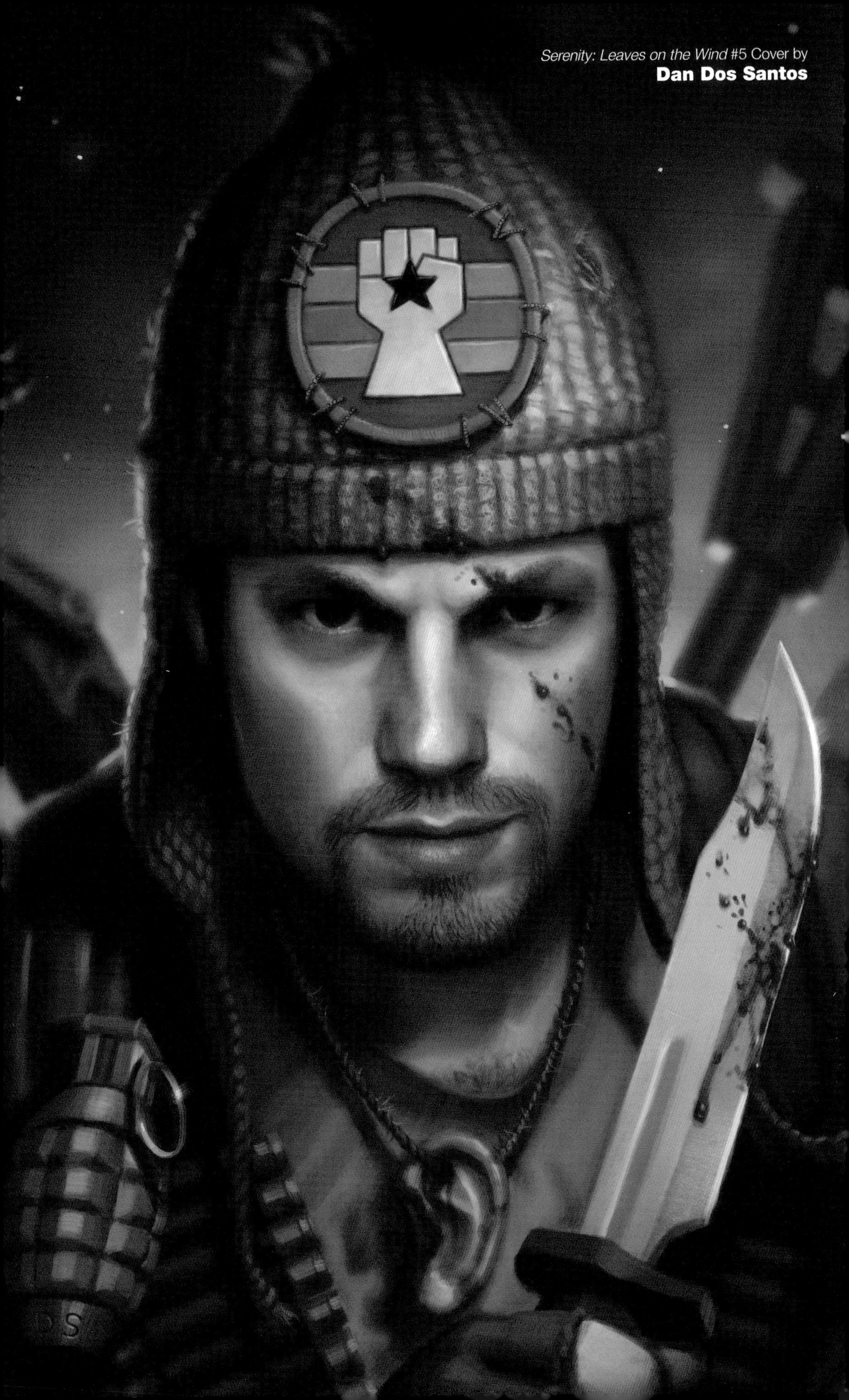

Serenity: Leaves on the Wind #5 Cover by
Dan Dos Santos

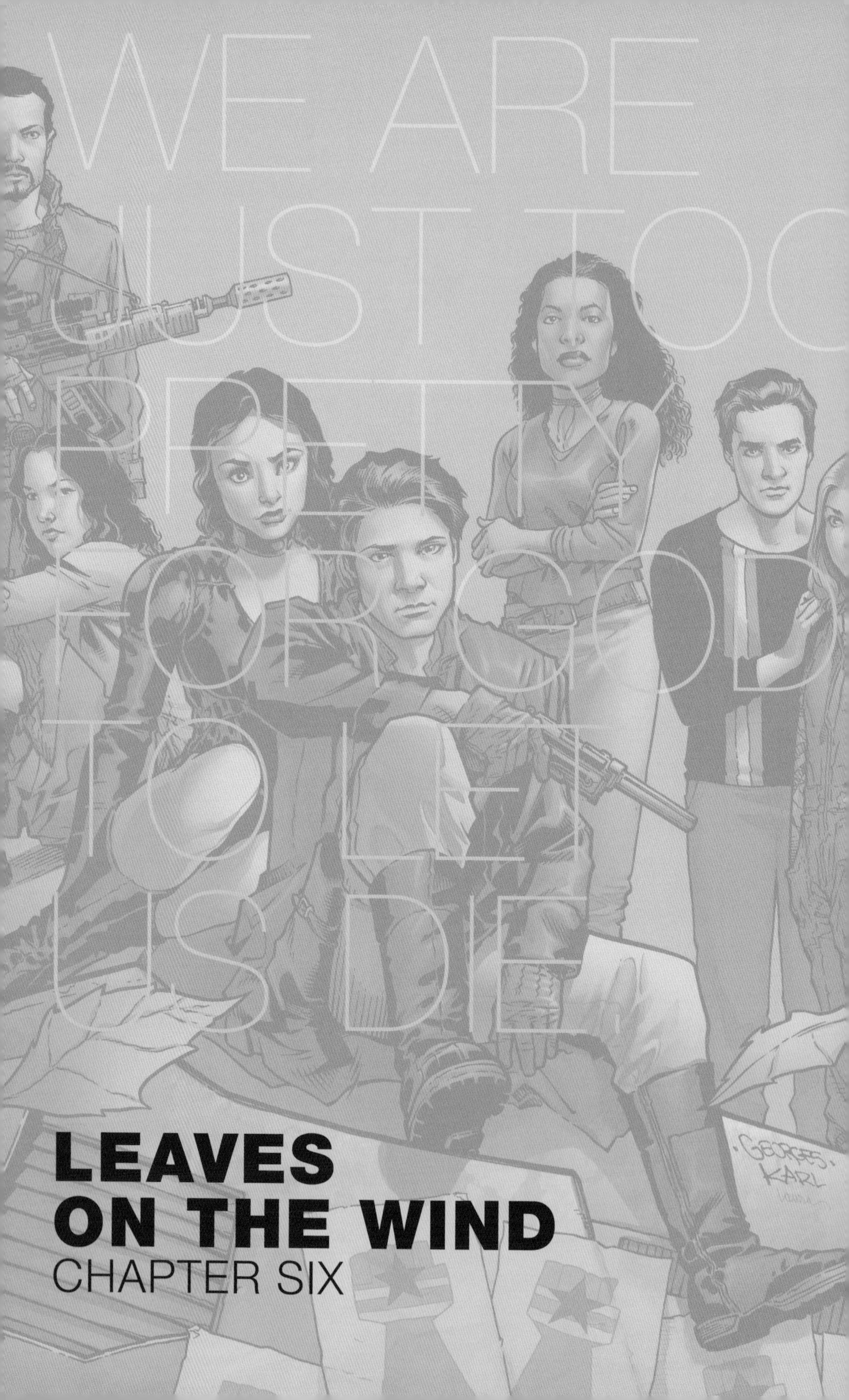
WE ARE JUST TOO PRETTY FOR GOD TO LET US DIE
GEORGES
KARL

LEAVES ON THE WIND
CHAPTER SIX

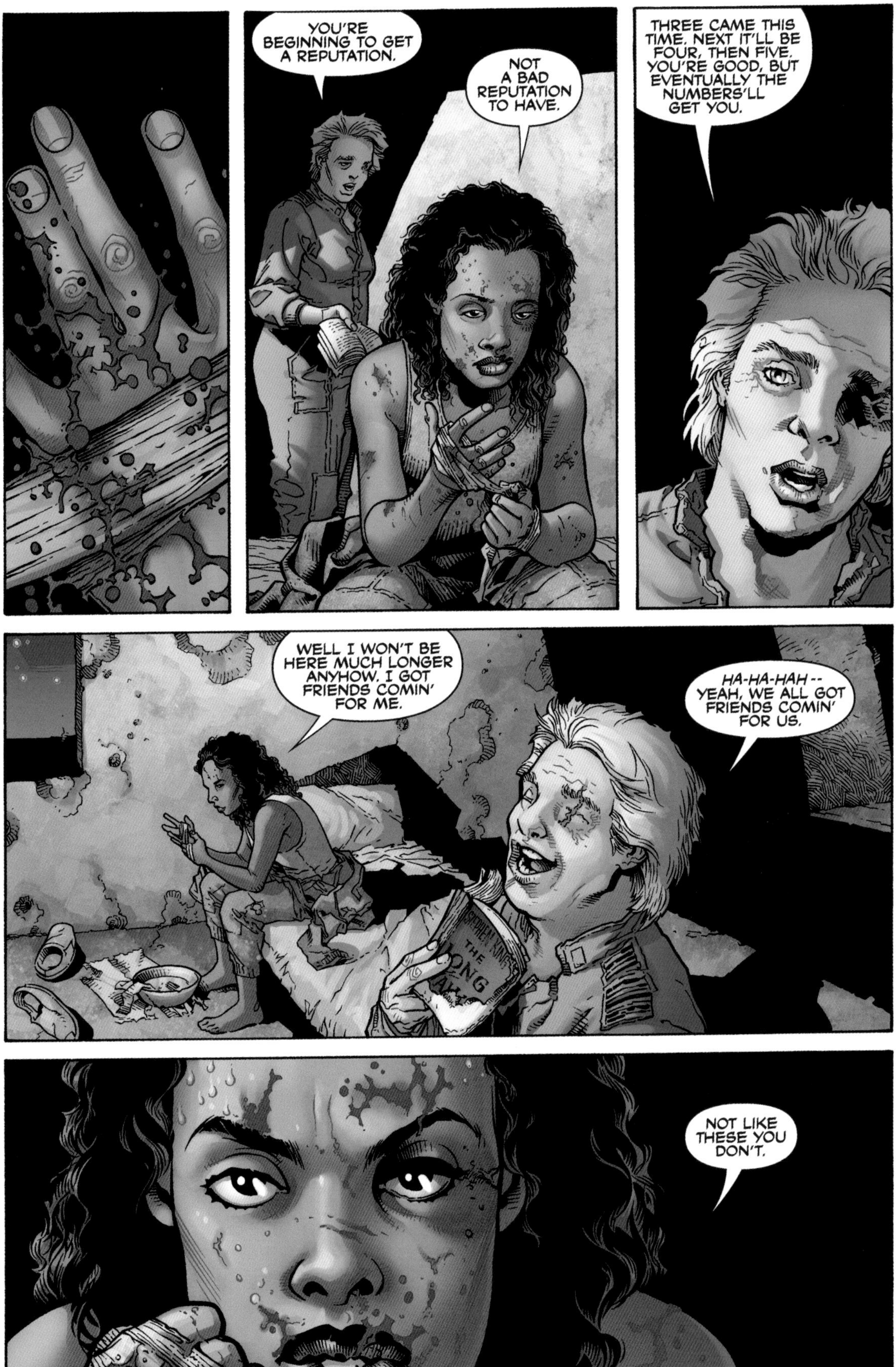
YOU'RE BEGINNING TO GET A REPUTATION.
NOT A BAD REPUTATION TO HAVE.
THREE CAME THIS TIME. NEXT IT'LL BE FOUR, THEN FIVE. YOU'RE GOOD, BUT EVENTUALLY THE NUMBERS'LL GET YOU.
WELL I WON'T BE HERE MUCH LONGER ANYHOW. I GOT FRIENDS COMIN' FOR ME.
HA-HA-HAH -- YEAH, WE ALL GOT FRIENDS COMIN' FOR US.
NOT LIKE THESE YOU DON'T.

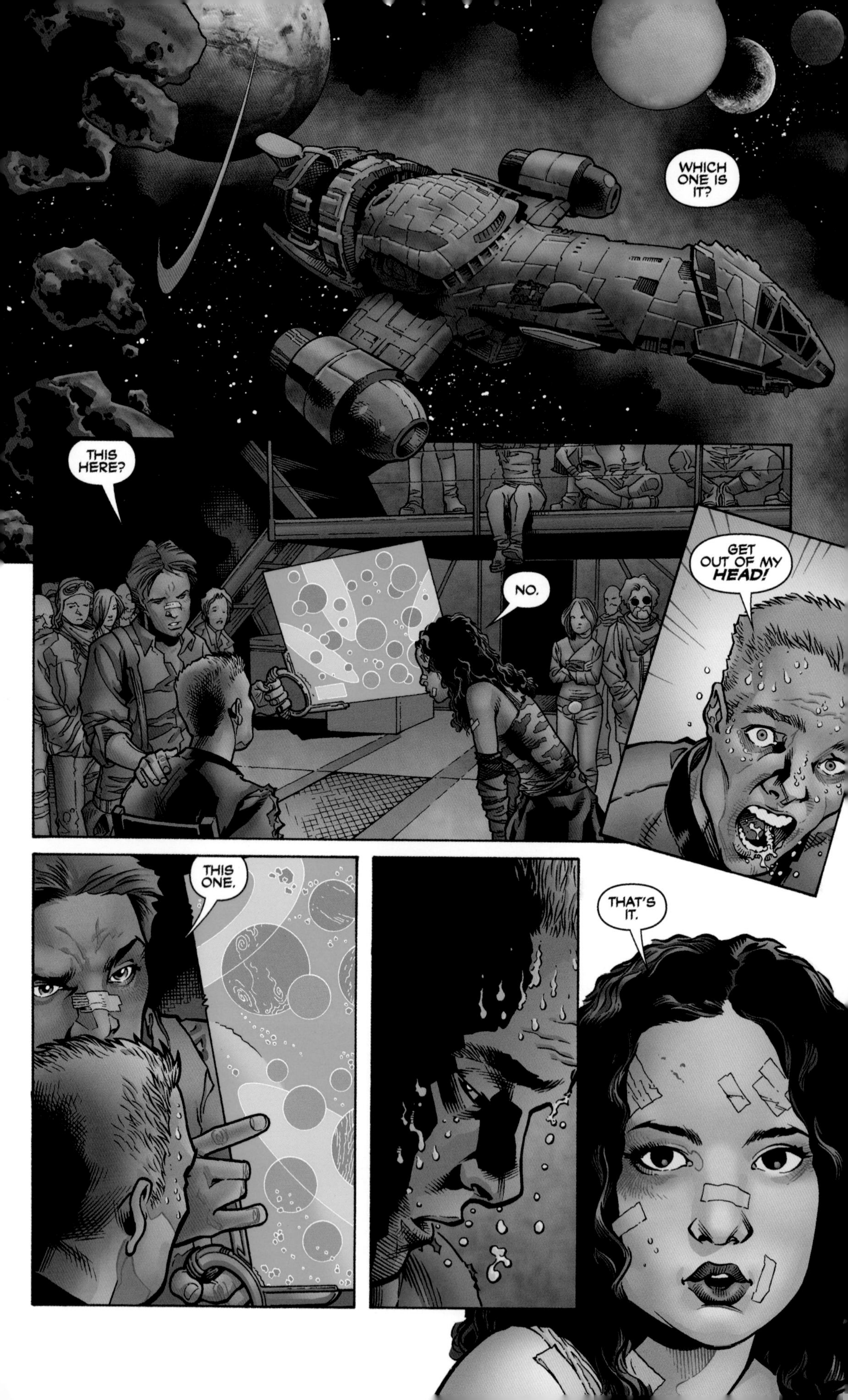
WHICH ONE IS IT?
THIS HERE?
NO.
GET OUT OF MY HEAD!
THIS ONE.
THAT'S IT.

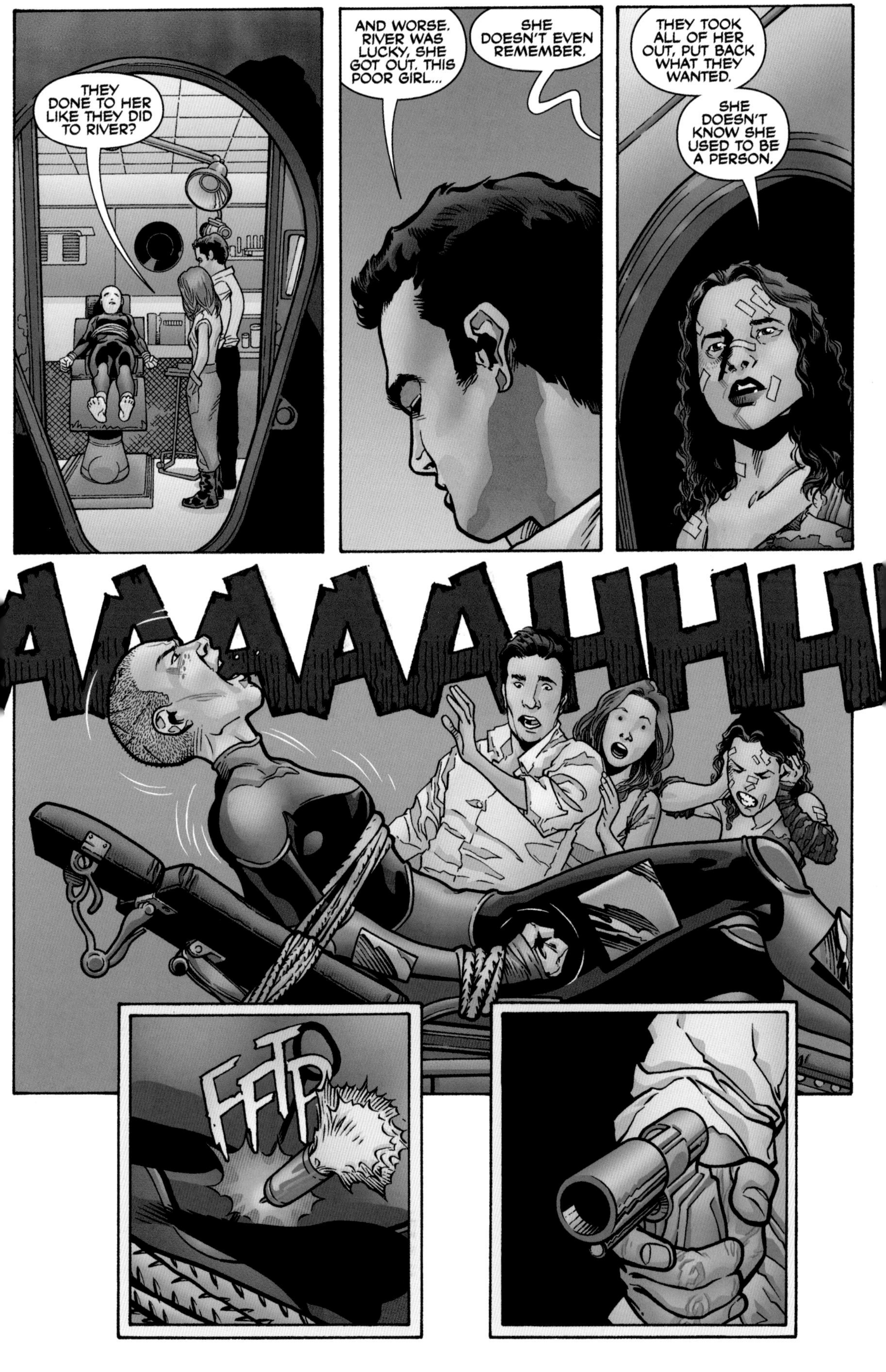
THEY DONE TO HER LIKE THEY DID TO RIVER?
AND WORSE. RIVER WAS LUCKY, SHE GOT OUT. THIS POOR GIRL...
SHE DOESN'T EVEN REMEMBER.
THEY TOOK ALL OF HER OUT, PUT BACK WHAT THEY WANTED.
SHE DOESN'T KNOW SHE USED TO BE A PERSON.
AAAAAHHHH
FFTP

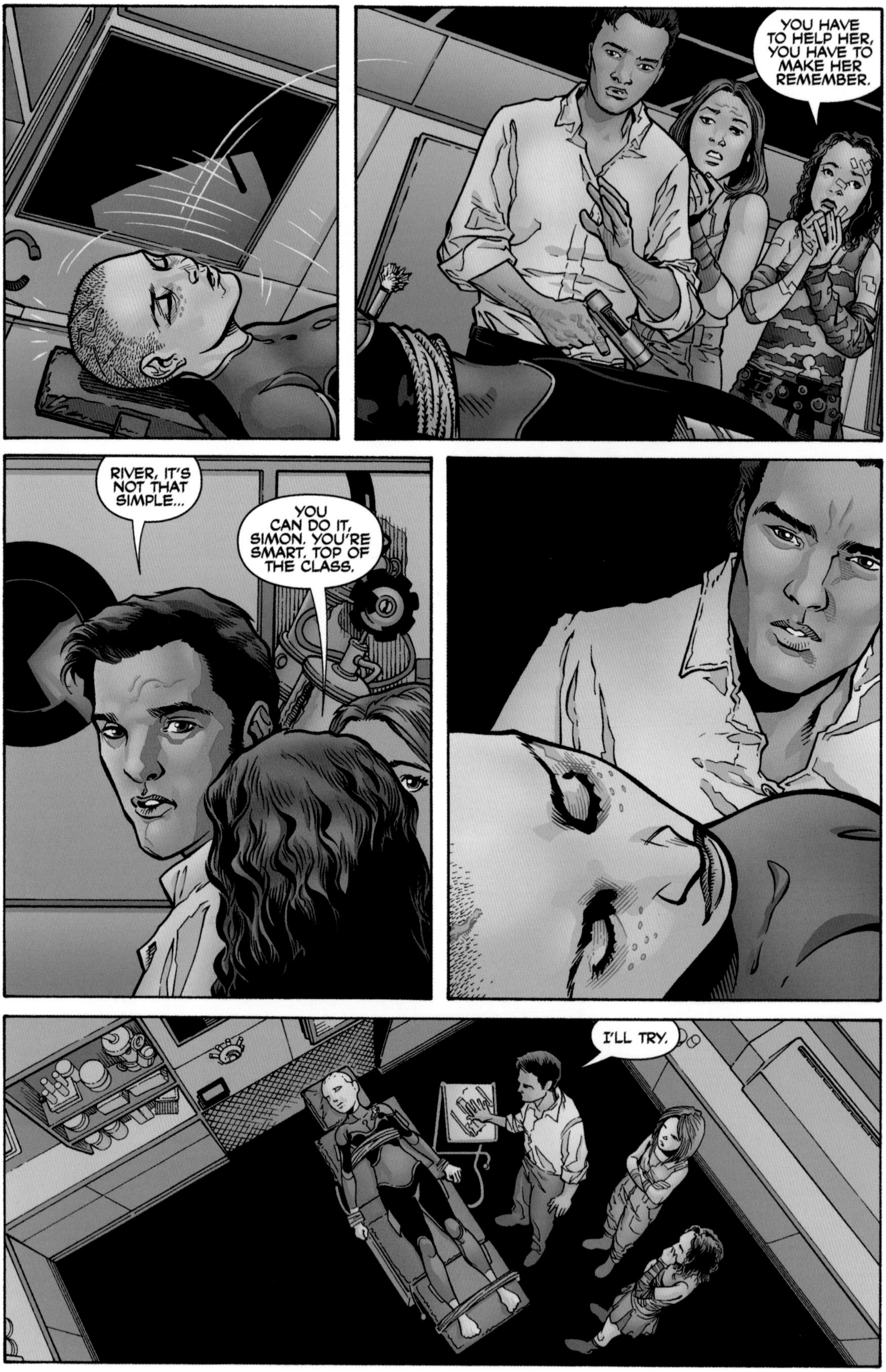
YOU HAVE TO HELP HER, YOU HAVE TO MAKE HER REMEMBER.
RIVER, IT'S NOT THAT SIMPLE...
YOU CAN DO IT, SIMON. YOU'RE SMART. TOP OF THE CLASS.
I'LL TRY.

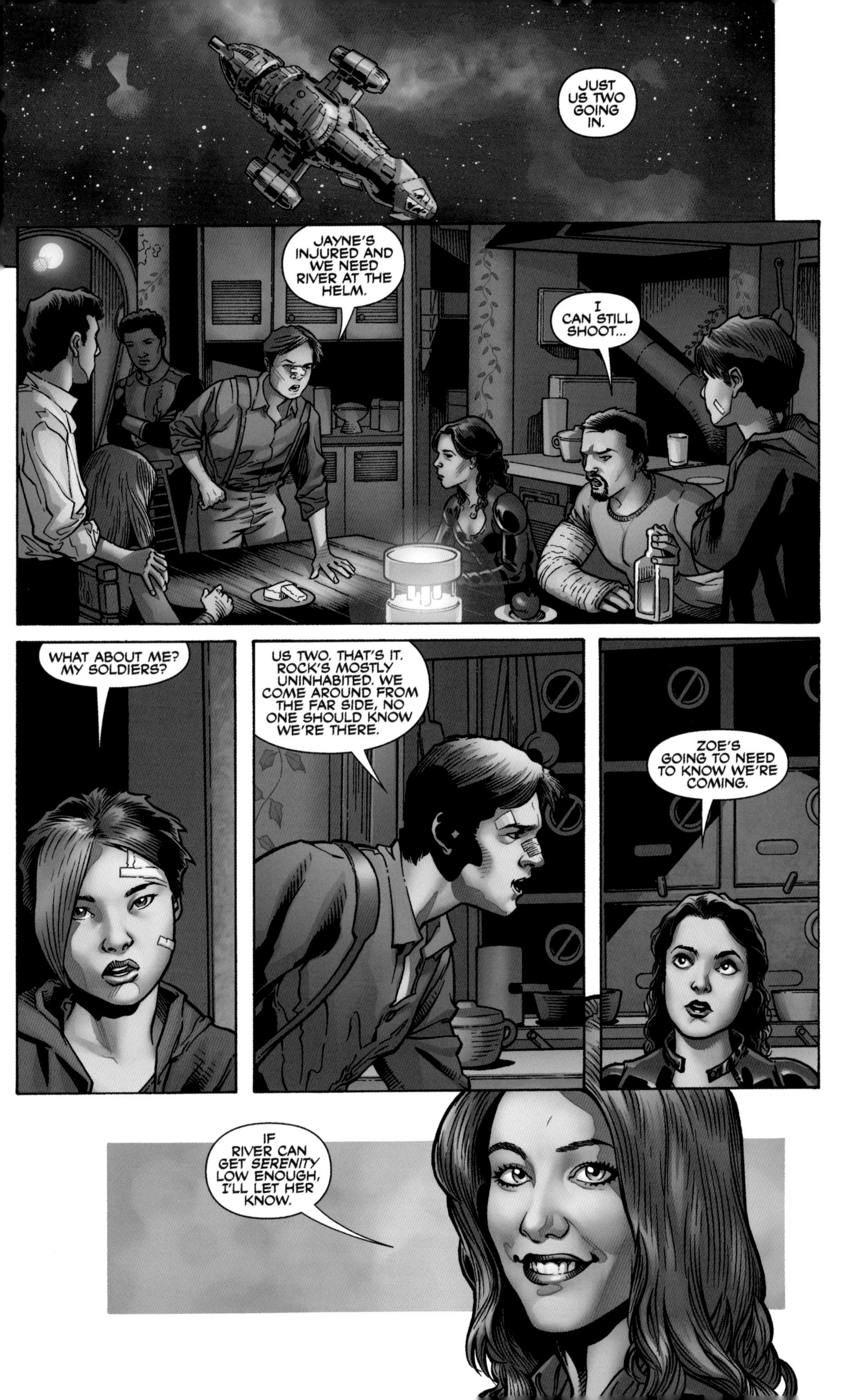
JUST US TWO GOING IN.
JAYNE'S INJURED AND WE NEED RIVER AT THE HELM.
I CAN STILL SHOOT...
WHAT ABOUT ME? MY SOLDIERS?
US TWO. THAT'S IT. ROCK'S MOSTLY UNINHABITED. WE COME AROUND FROM THE FAR SIDE, NO ONE SHOULD KNOW WE'RE THERE.
ZOE'S GOING TO NEED TO KNOW WE'RE COMING.
IF RIVER CAN GET *SERENITY* LOW ENOUGH, I'LL LET HER KNOW.

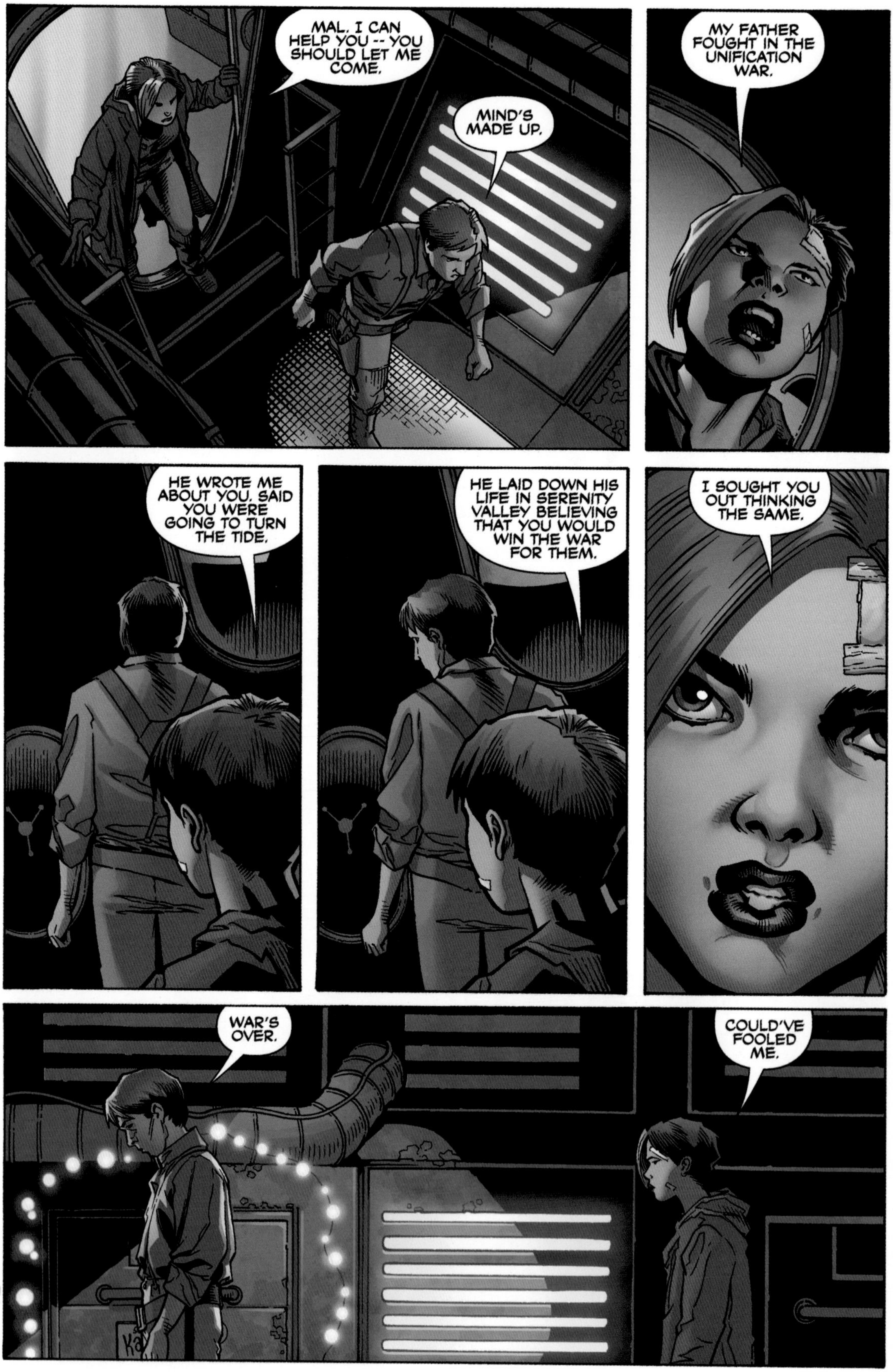
MAL, I CAN HELP YOU -- YOU SHOULD LET ME COME.
MIND'S MADE UP.
MY FATHER FOUGHT IN THE UNIFICATION WAR.
HE WROTE ME ABOUT YOU. SAID YOU WERE GOING TO TURN THE TIDE.
HE LAID DOWN HIS LIFE IN SERENITY VALLEY BELIEVING THAT YOU WOULD WIN THE WAR FOR THEM.
I SOUGHT YOU OUT THINKING THE SAME.
WAR'S OVER.
COULD'VE FOOLED ME.

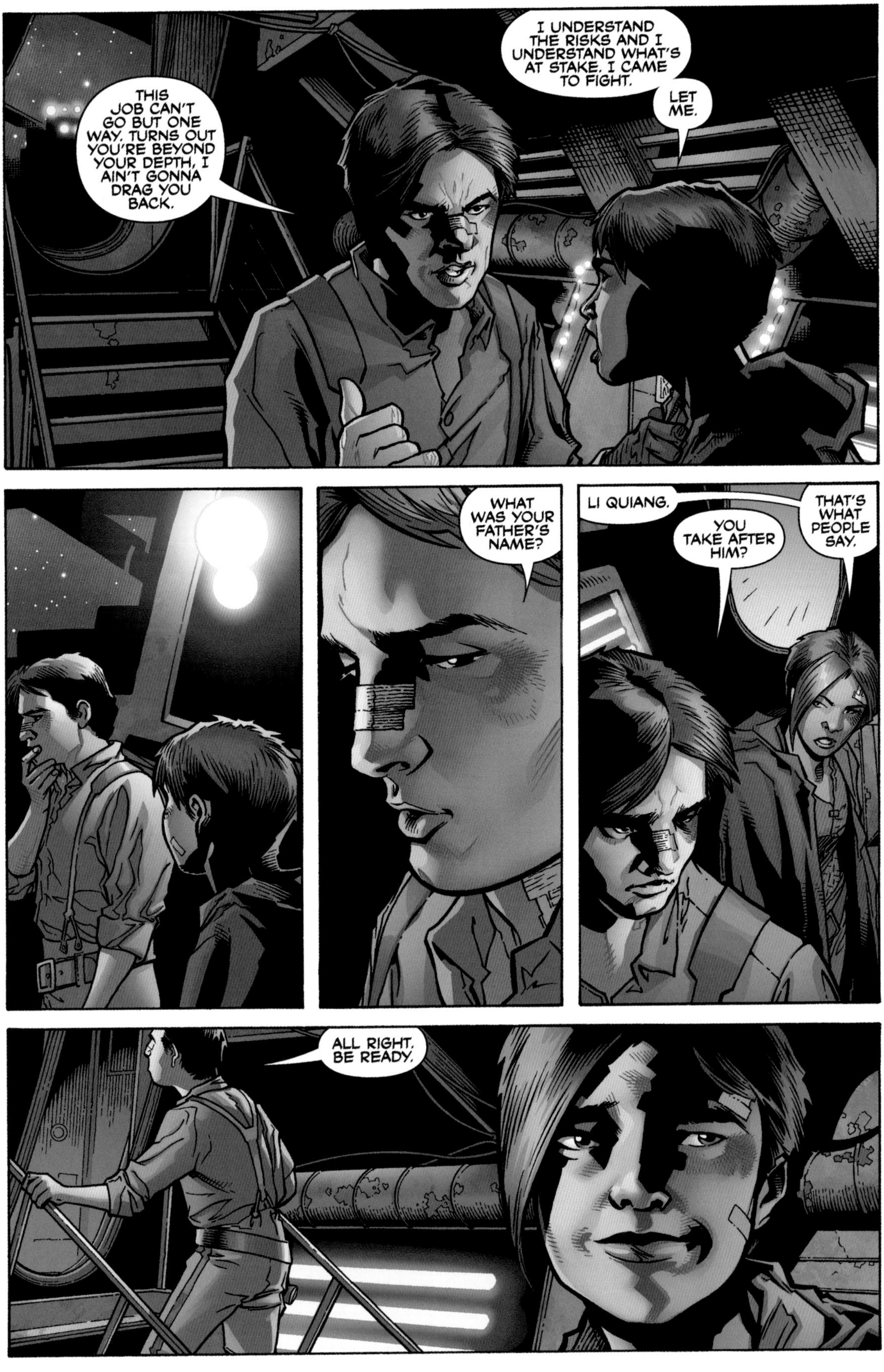
THIS JOB CAN'T GO BUT ONE WAY. TURNS OUT YOU'RE BEYOND YOUR DEPTH, I AIN'T GONNA DRAG YOU BACK.
I UNDERSTAND THE RISKS AND I UNDERSTAND WHAT'S AT STAKE. I CAME TO FIGHT.
LET ME.
WHAT WAS YOUR FATHER'S NAME?
LI QUIANG.
YOU TAKE AFTER HIM?
THAT'S WHAT PEOPLE SAY.
ALL RIGHT. BE READY.

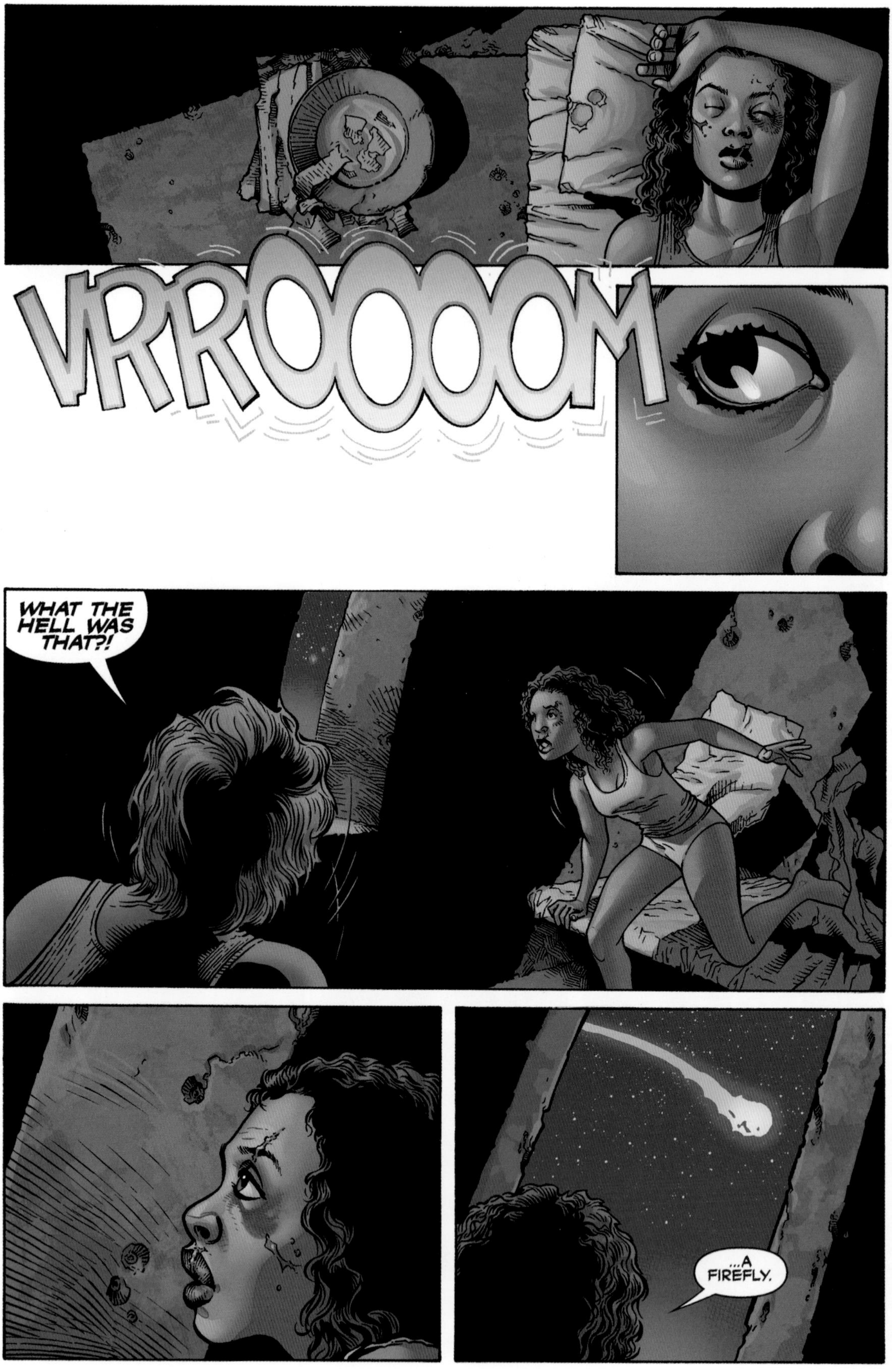
VRROOOOOM
WHAT THE HELL WAS THAT?!
...A FIREFLY.

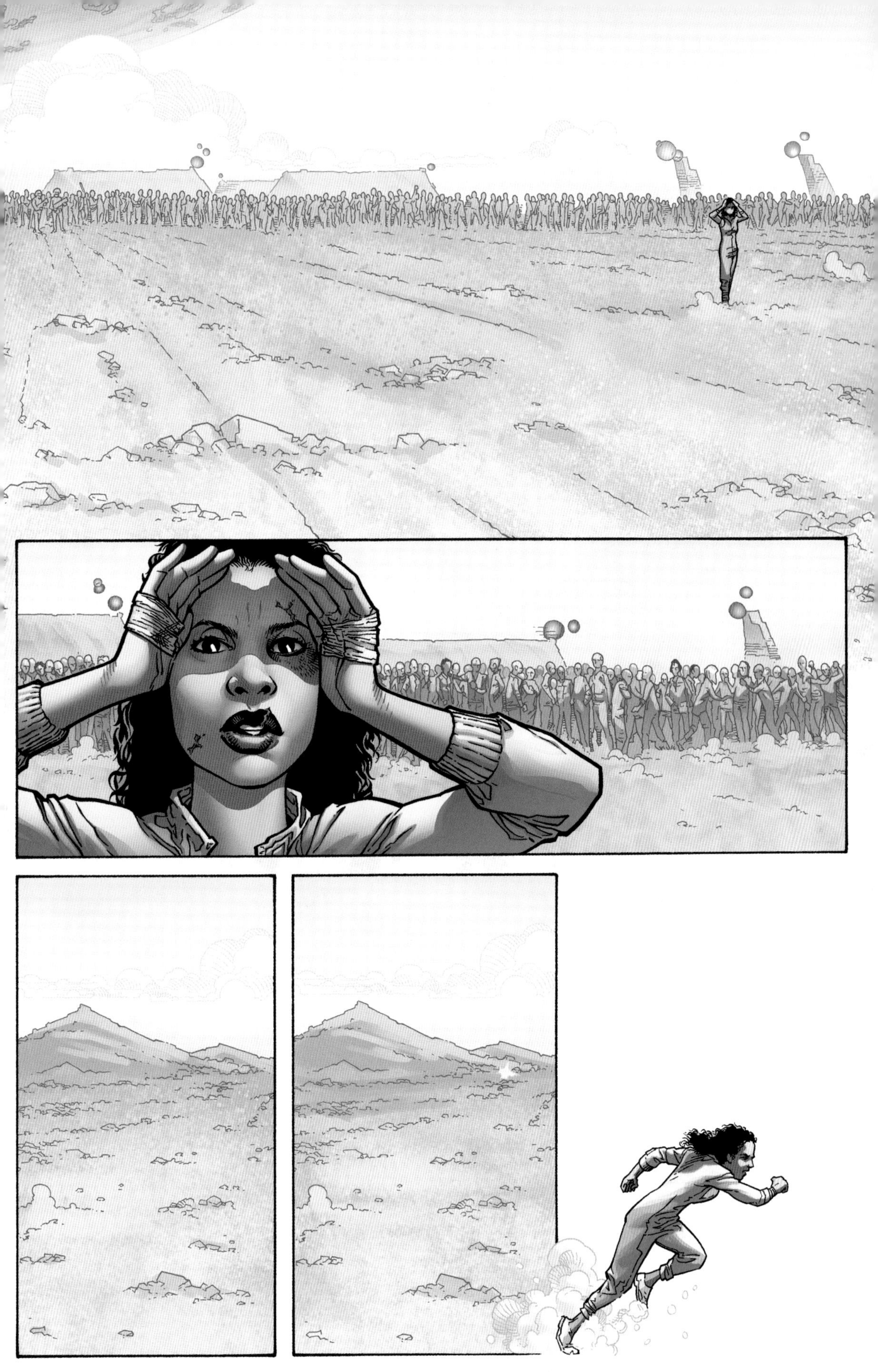

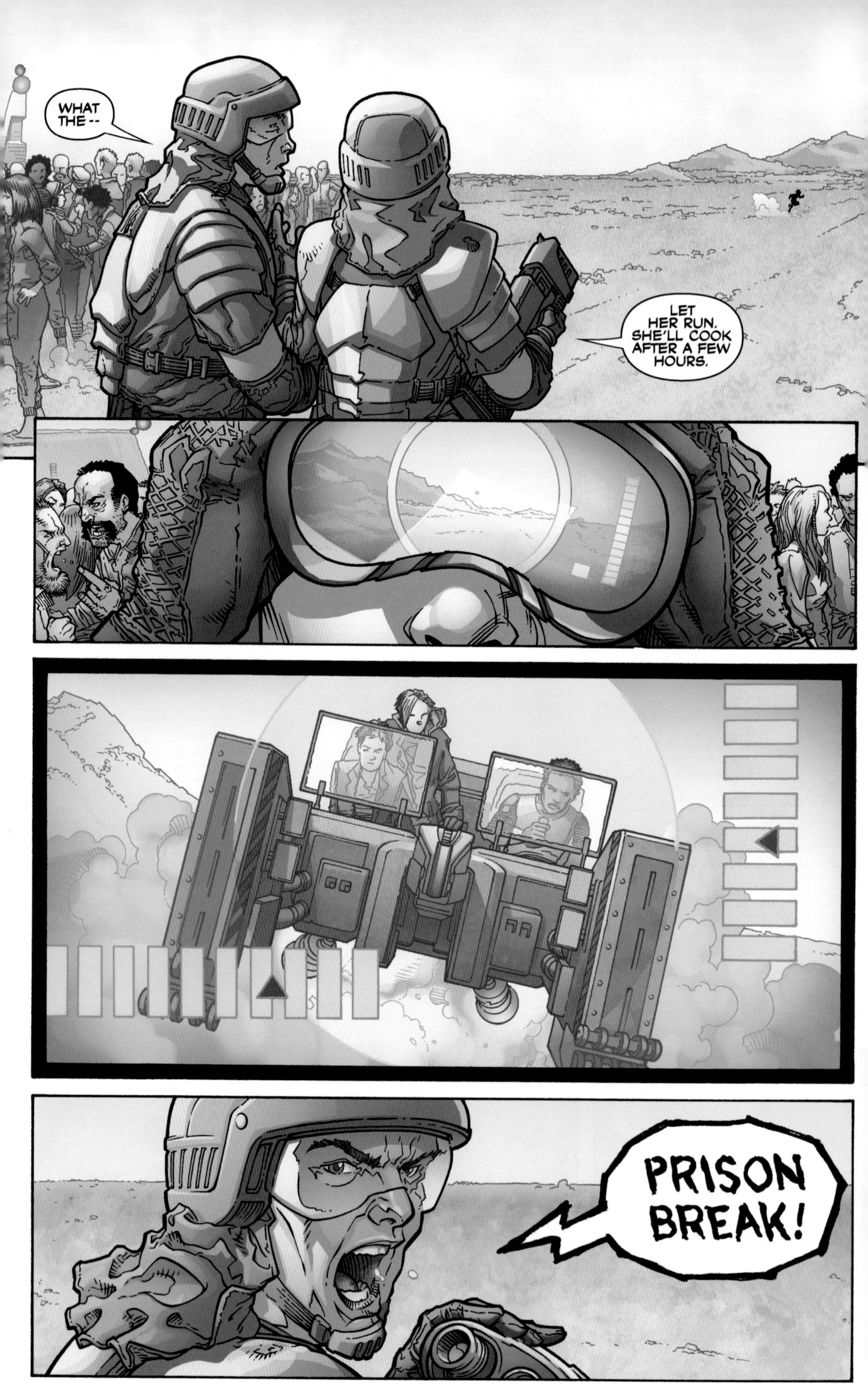
WHAT THE --
LET HER RUN. SHE'LL COOK AFTER A FEW HOURS.
PRISON BREAK!

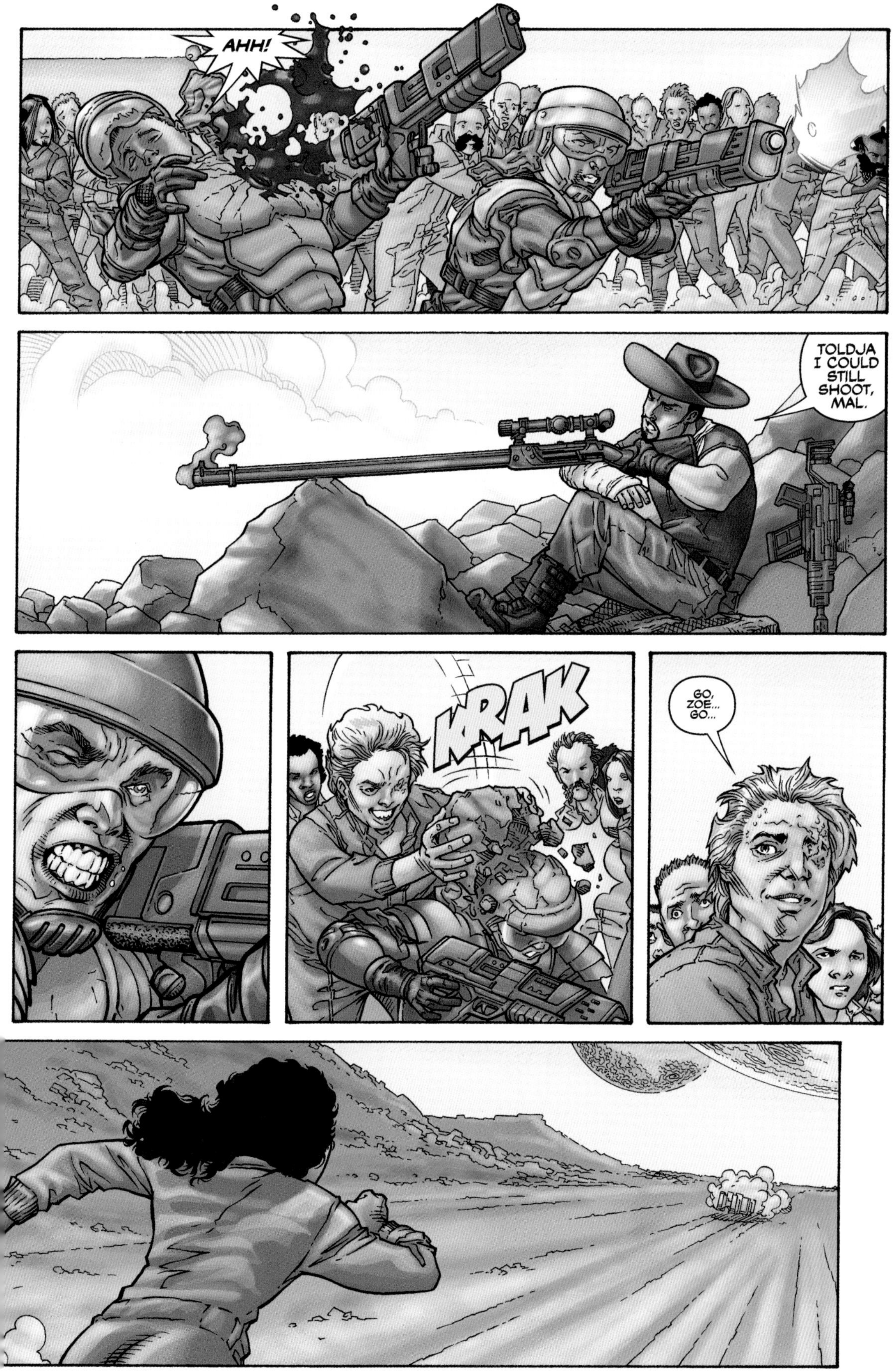
AHH!
TOLDJA I COULD STILL SHOOT, MAL.
KRAK
GO, ZOE... GO...

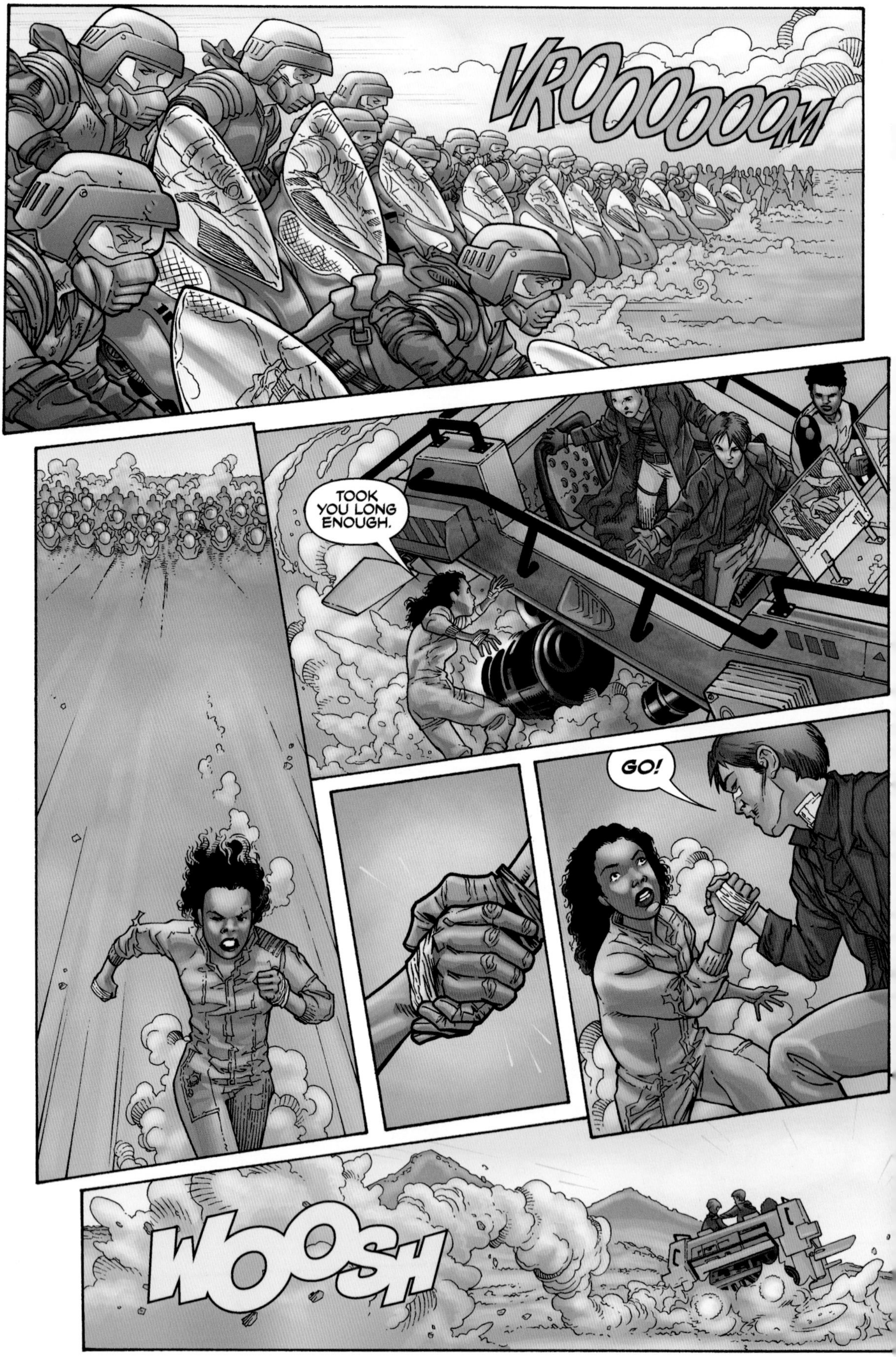
VROOOOOOM
TOOK YOU LONG ENOUGH.
GO!
WOOSH

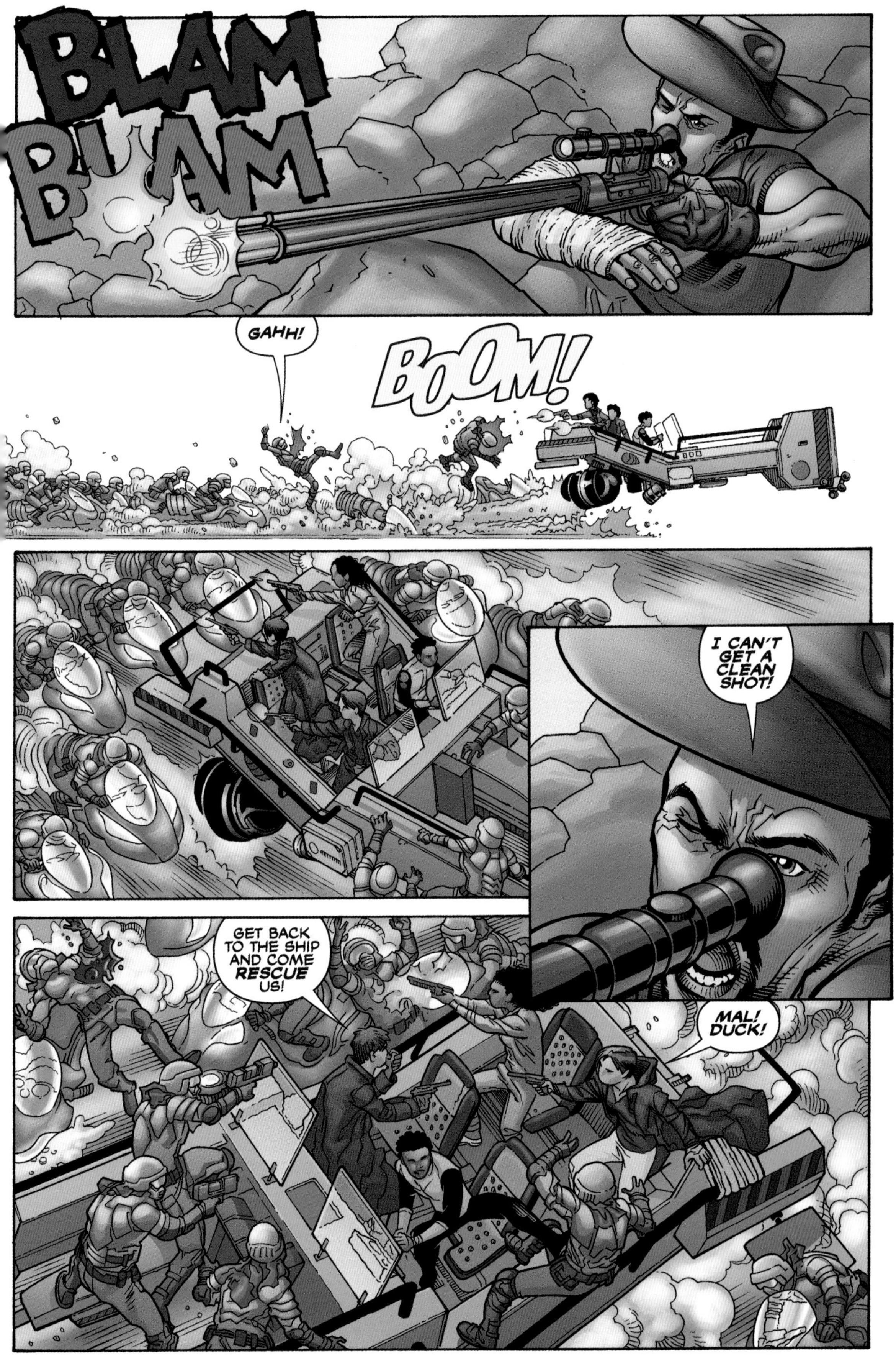
BLAM
BLAM
GAHH!
BOOM!
I CAN'T GET A CLEAN SHOT!
GET BACK TO THE SHIP AND COME RESCUE US!
MAL! DUCK!

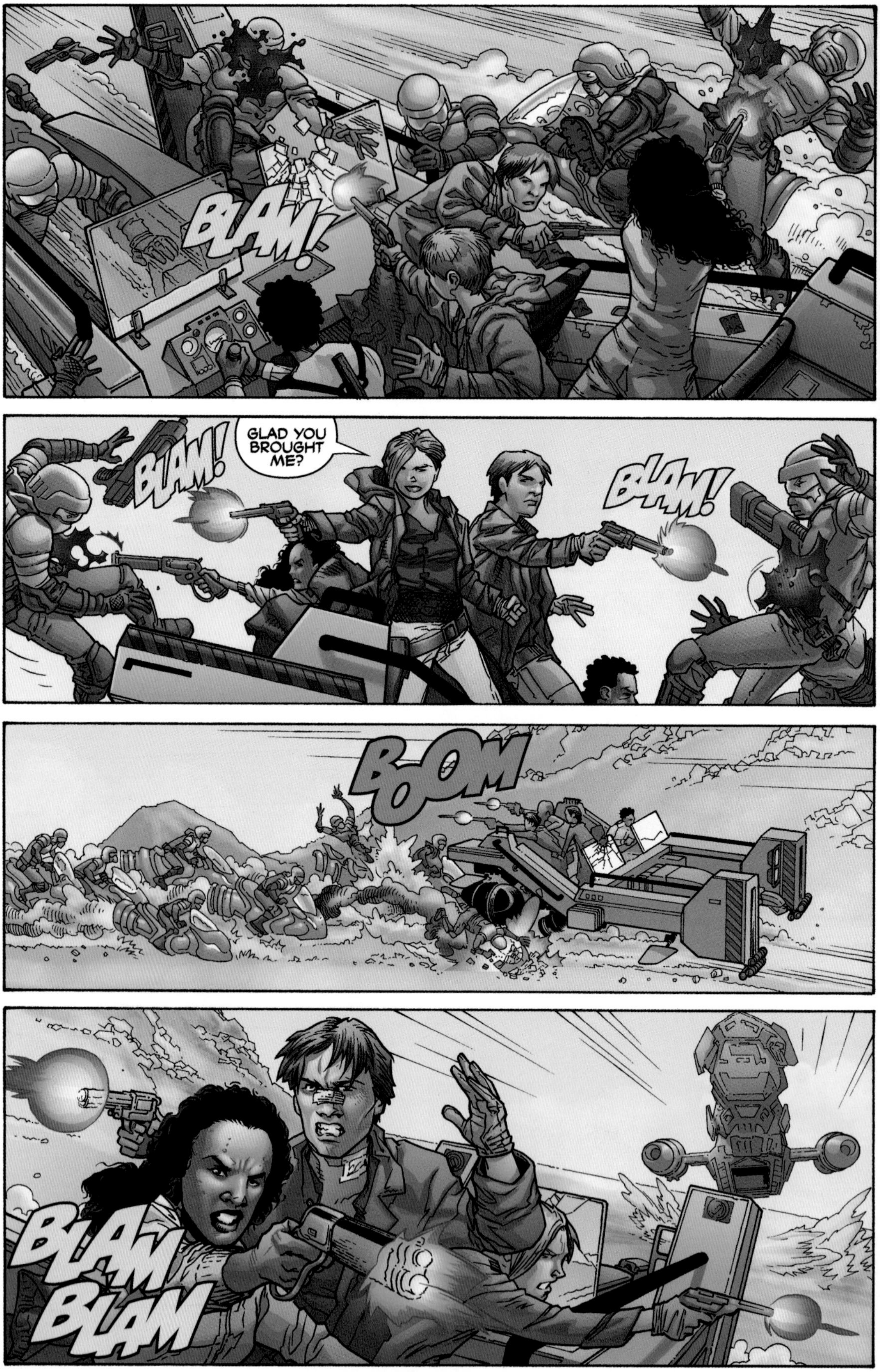
BLAM!
BLAM!
GLAD YOU BROUGHT ME?
BLAM!
BOOM
BLAM
BLAM

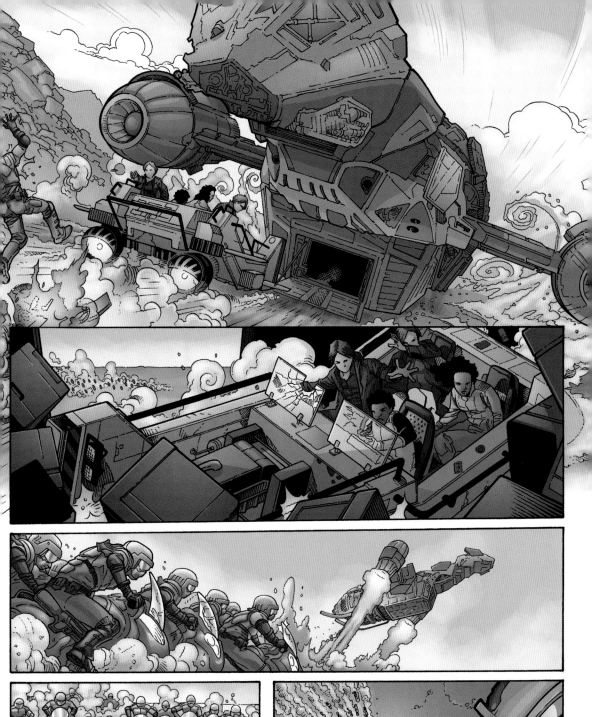

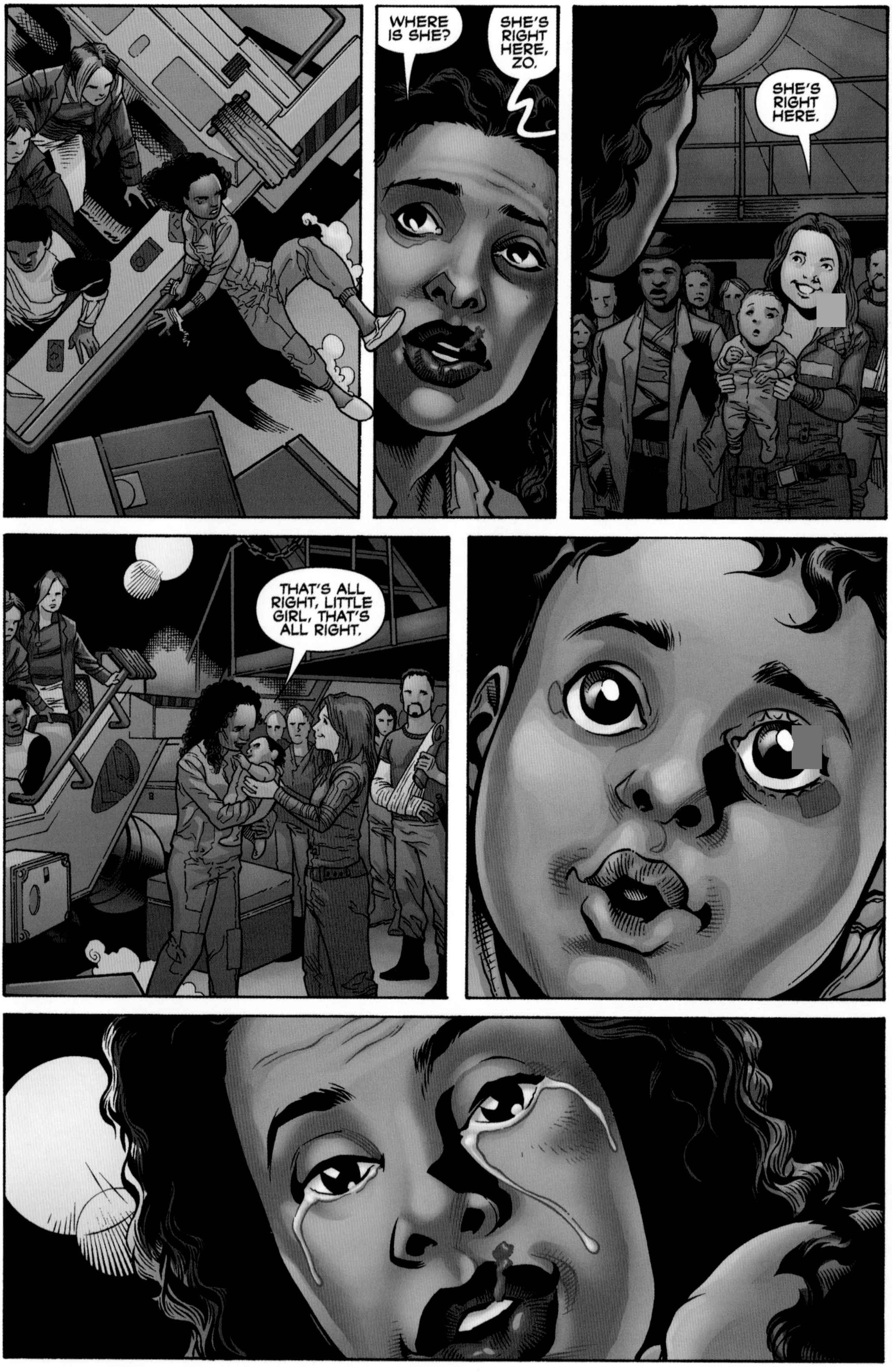
WHERE IS SHE?
SHE'S RIGHT HERE, ZO.
SHE'S RIGHT HERE.
THAT'S ALL RIGHT, LITTLE GIRL, THAT'S ALL RIGHT.

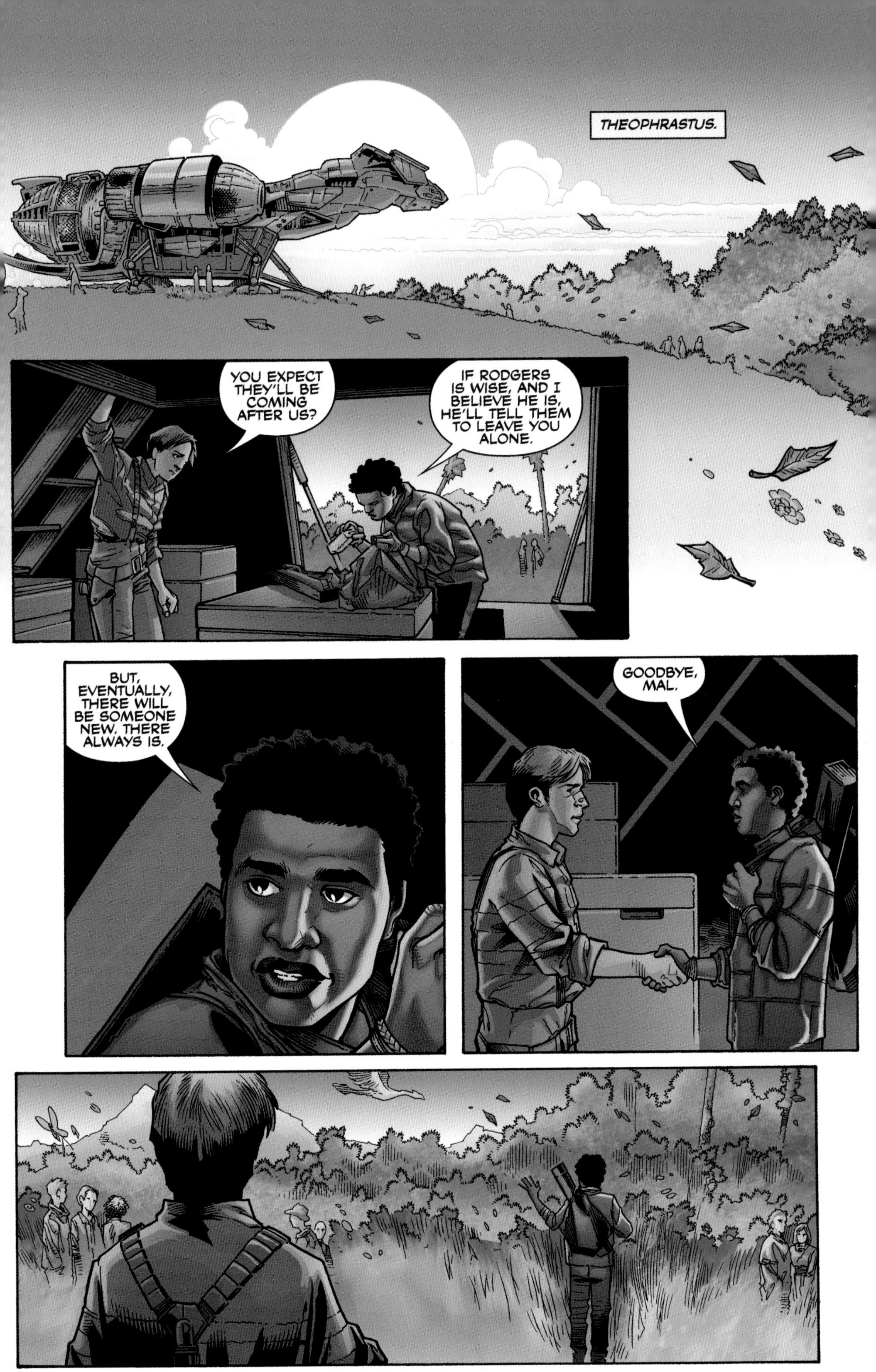
THEOPHRASTUS.
YOU EXPECT THEY'LL BE COMING AFTER US?
IF RODGERS IS WISE, AND I BELIEVE HE IS, HE'LL TELL THEM TO LEAVE YOU ALONE.
BUT, EVENTUALLY, THERE WILL BE SOMEONE NEW. THERE ALWAYS IS.
GOODBYE, MAL.

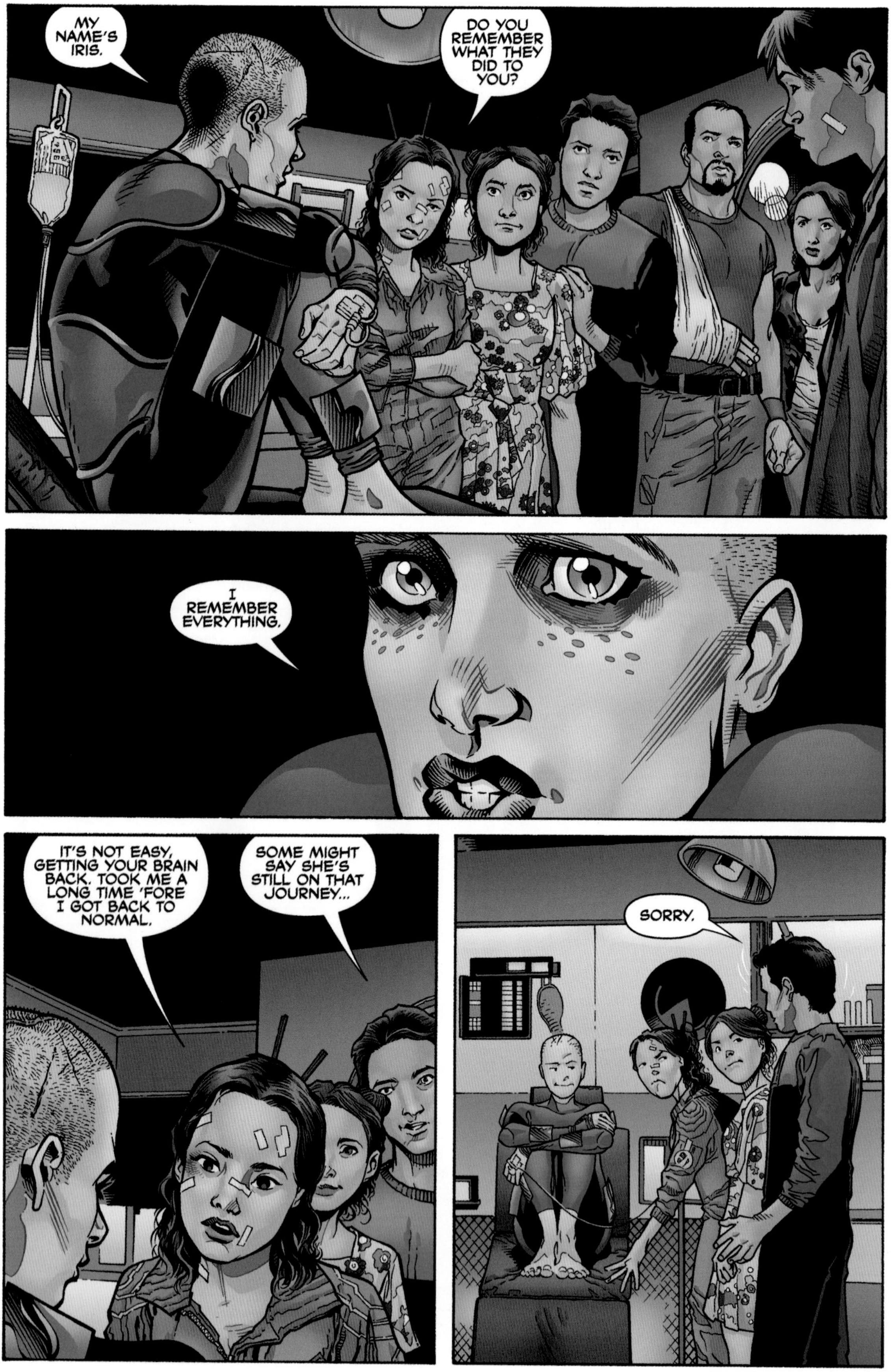
MY NAME'S IRIS.
DO YOU REMEMBER WHAT THEY DID TO YOU?
I REMEMBER EVERYTHING.
IT'S NOT EASY, GETTING YOUR BRAIN BACK. TOOK ME A LONG TIME 'FORE I GOT BACK TO NORMAL.
SOME MIGHT SAY SHE'S STILL ON THAT JOURNEY...
SORRY.

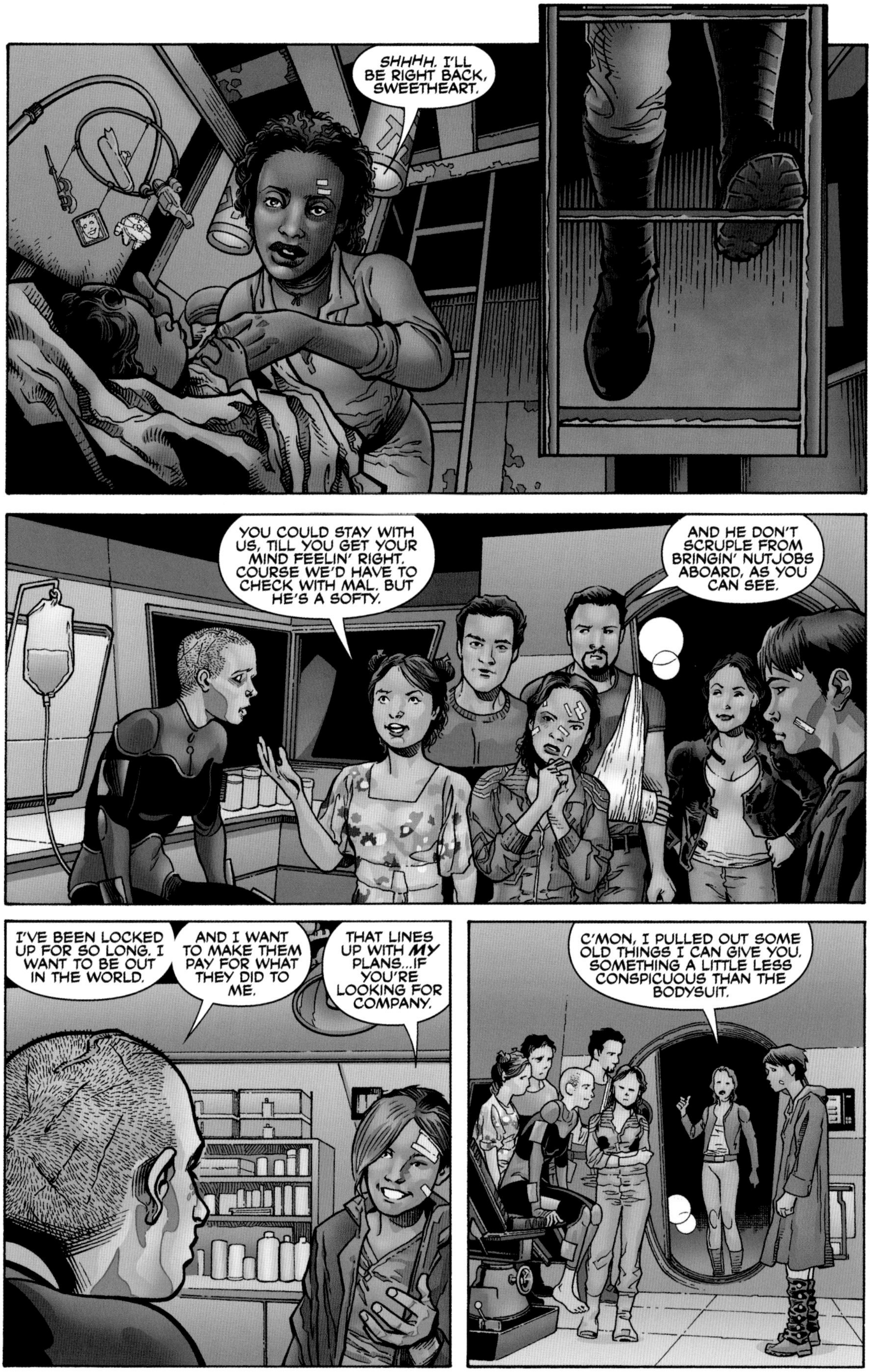
SHHHH. I'LL BE RIGHT BACK, SWEETHEART.
YOU COULD STAY WITH US, TILL YOU GET YOUR MIND FEELIN' RIGHT. COURSE WE'D HAVE TO CHECK WITH MAL. BUT HE'S A SOFTY.
AND HE DON'T SCRUPLE FROM BRINGIN' NUTJOBS ABOARD, AS YOU CAN SEE.
I'VE BEEN LOCKED UP FOR SO LONG. I WANT TO BE OUT IN THE WORLD.
AND I WANT TO MAKE THEM PAY FOR WHAT THEY DID TO ME.
THAT LINES UP WITH MY PLANS...IF YOU'RE LOOKING FOR COMPANY.
C'MON, I PULLED OUT SOME OLD THINGS I CAN GIVE YOU. SOMETHING A LITTLE LESS CONSPICUOUS THAN THE BODYSUIT.

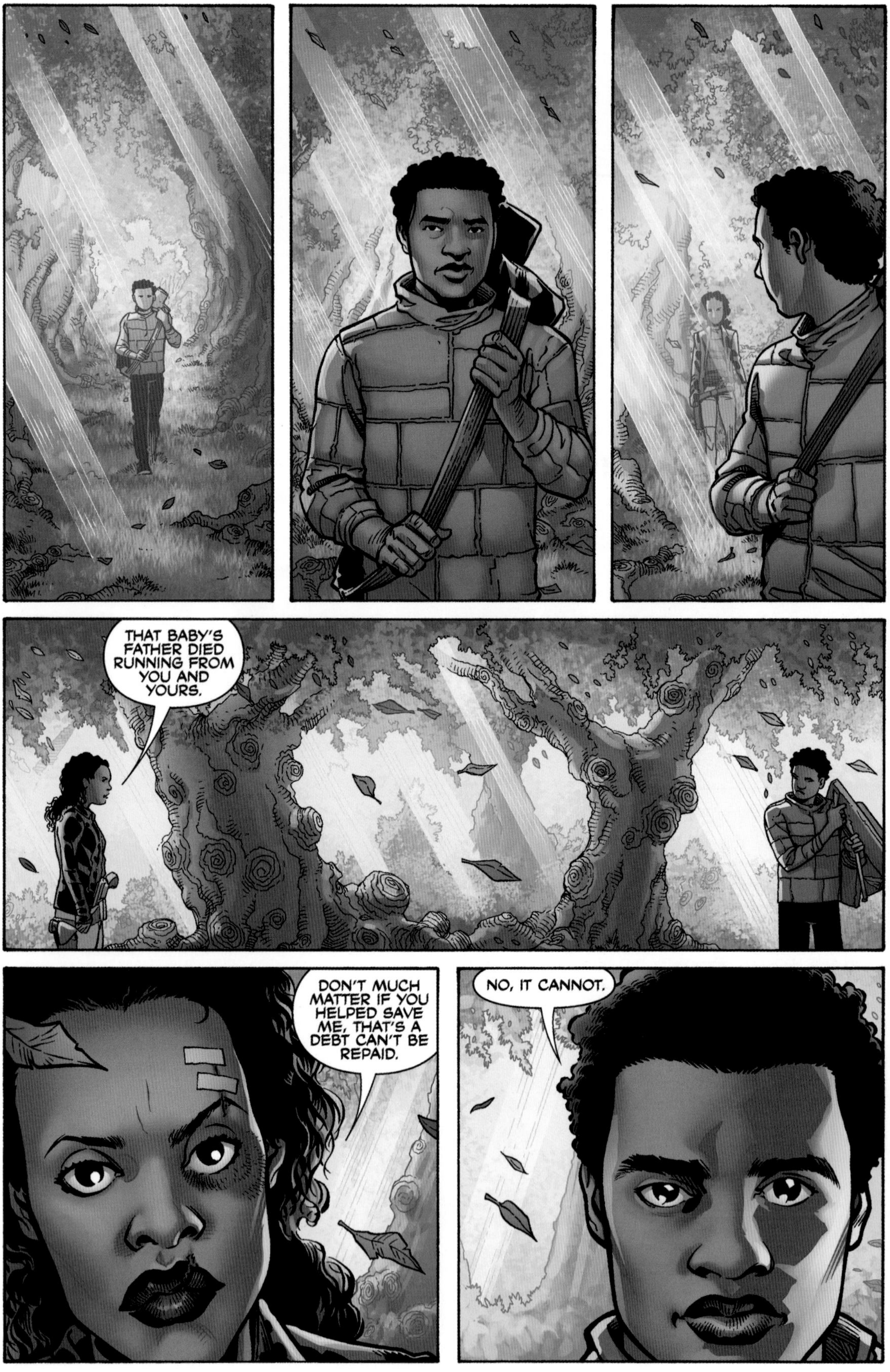
THAT BABY'S FATHER DIED RUNNING FROM YOU AND YOURS.
DON'T MUCH MATTER IF YOU HELPED SAVE ME, THAT'S A DEBT CAN'T BE REPAID.
NO, IT CANNOT.

THUD

I WILL DEFEND MYSELF.

I'M COUNTIN' ON IT.

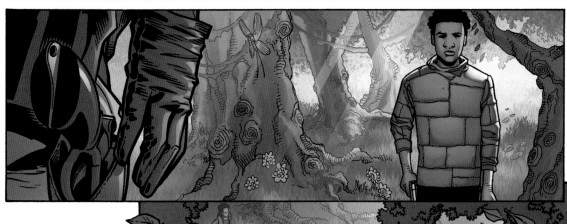

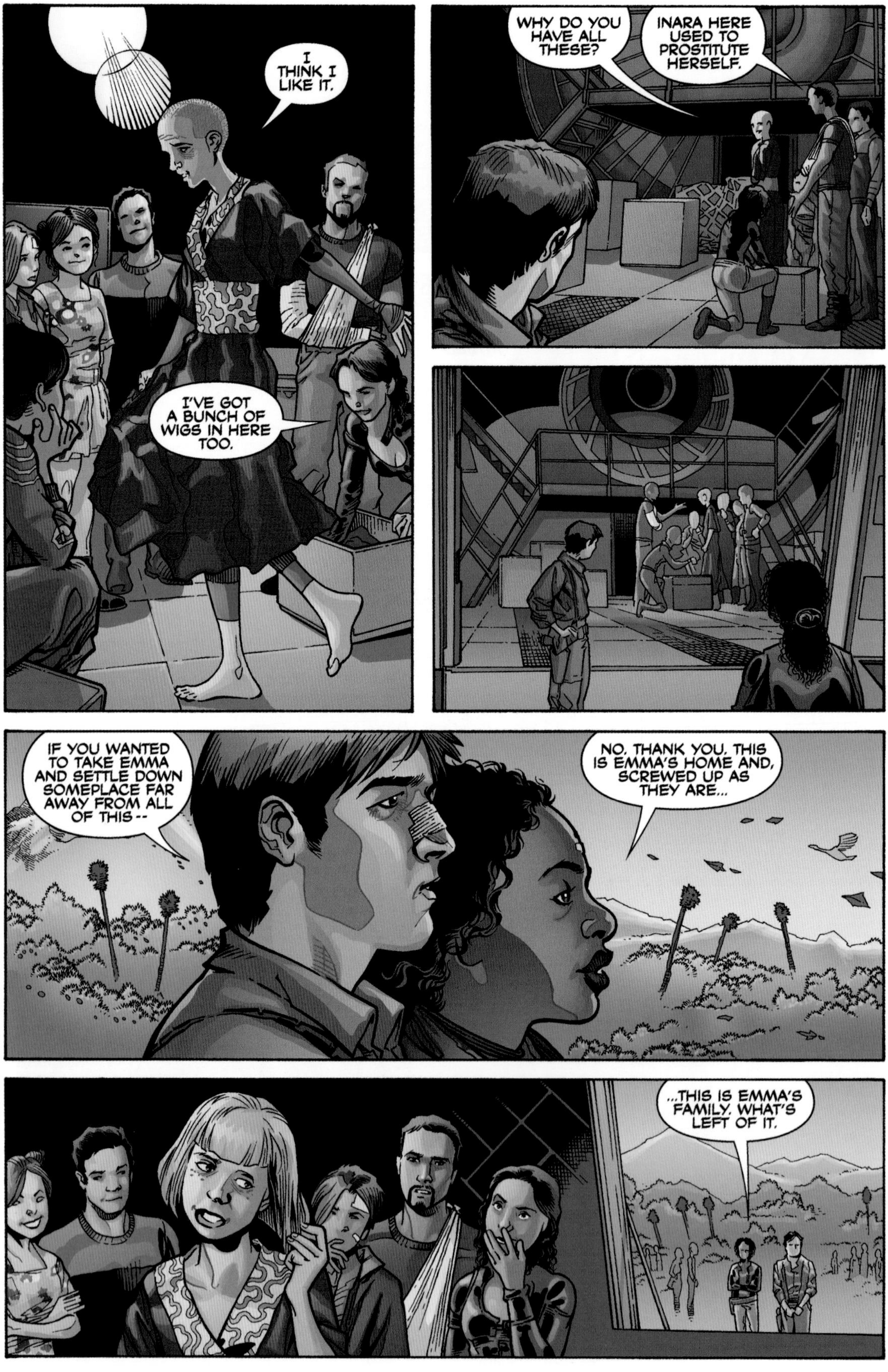
I THINK I LIKE IT.
I'VE GOT A BUNCH OF WIGS IN HERE TOO.
WHY DO YOU HAVE ALL THESE?
INARA HERE USED TO PROSTITUTE HERSELF.
IF YOU WANTED TO TAKE EMMA AND SETTLE DOWN SOMEPLACE FAR AWAY FROM ALL OF THIS --
NO, THANK YOU. THIS IS EMMA'S HOME AND, SCREWED UP AS THEY ARE...
...THIS IS EMMA'S FAMILY. WHAT'S LEFT OF IT.

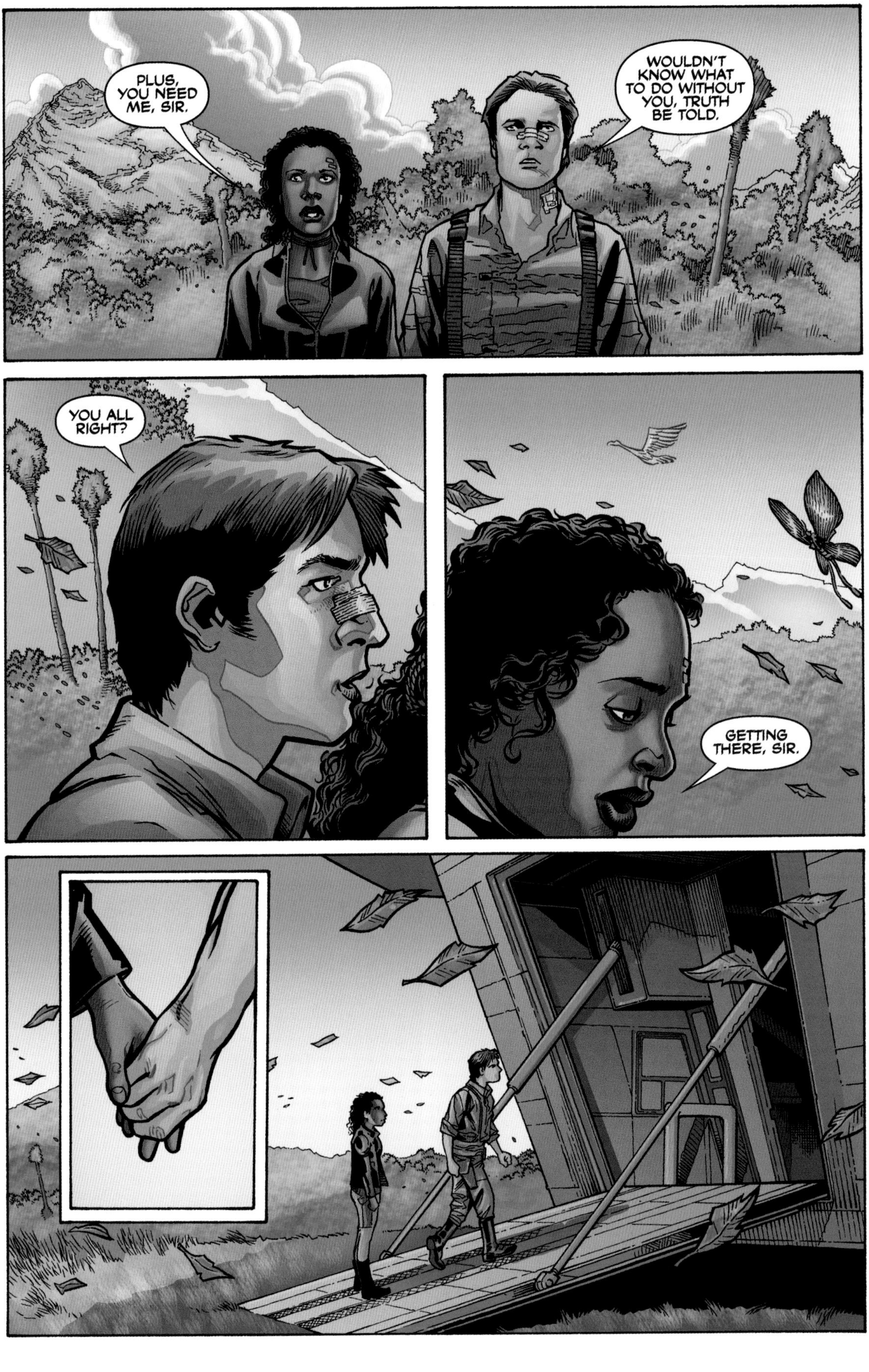
PLUS, YOU NEED ME, SIR.
WOULDN'T KNOW WHAT TO DO WITHOUT YOU, TRUTH BE TOLD.
YOU ALL RIGHT?
GETTING THERE, SIR.

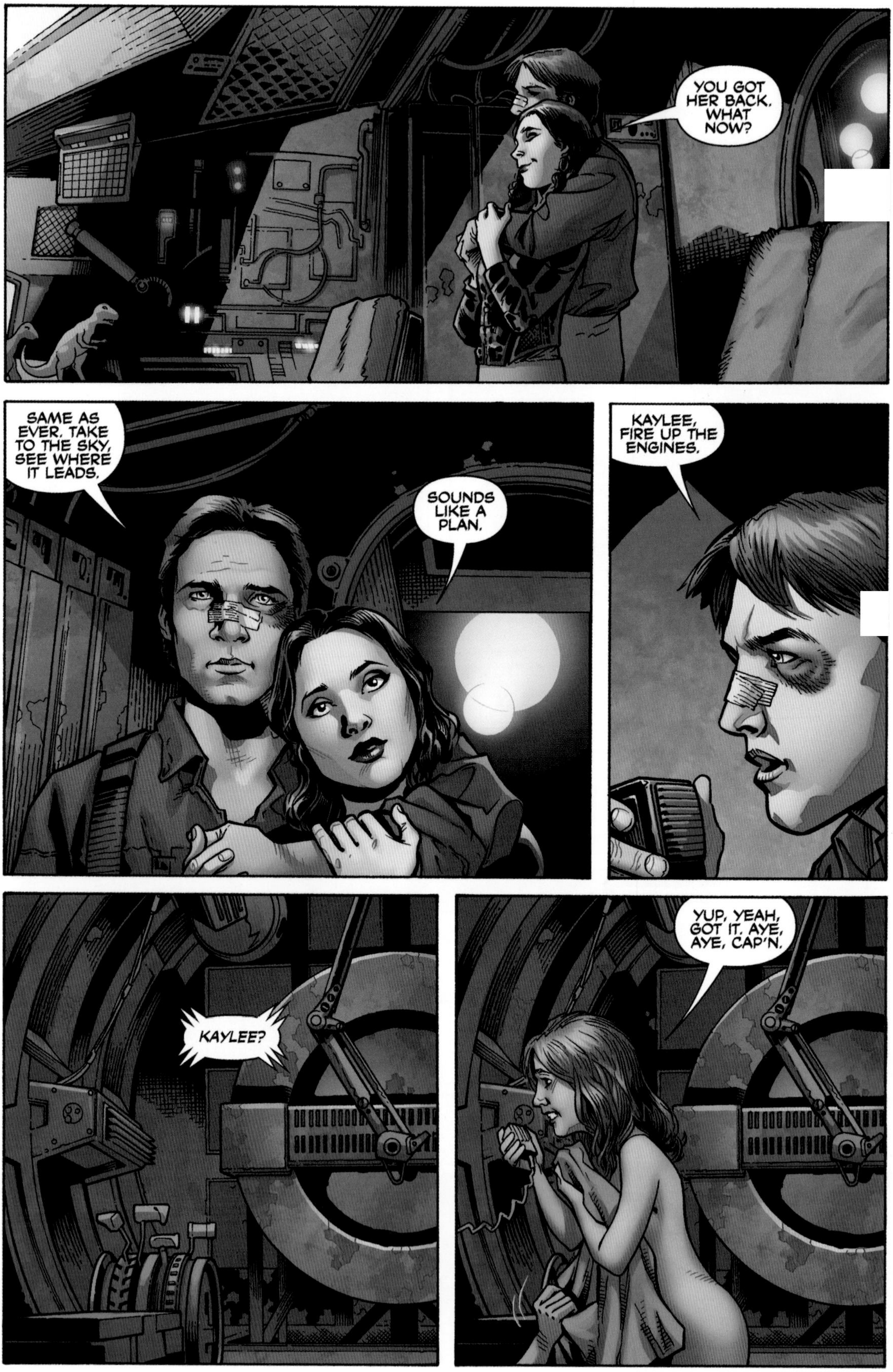
YOU GOT HER BACK. WHAT NOW?
SAME AS EVER. TAKE TO THE SKY, SEE WHERE IT LEADS.
SOUNDS LIKE A PLAN.
KAYLEE, FIRE UP THE ENGINES.
KAYLEE?
YUP, YEAH, GOT IT. AYE, AYE, CAP'N.

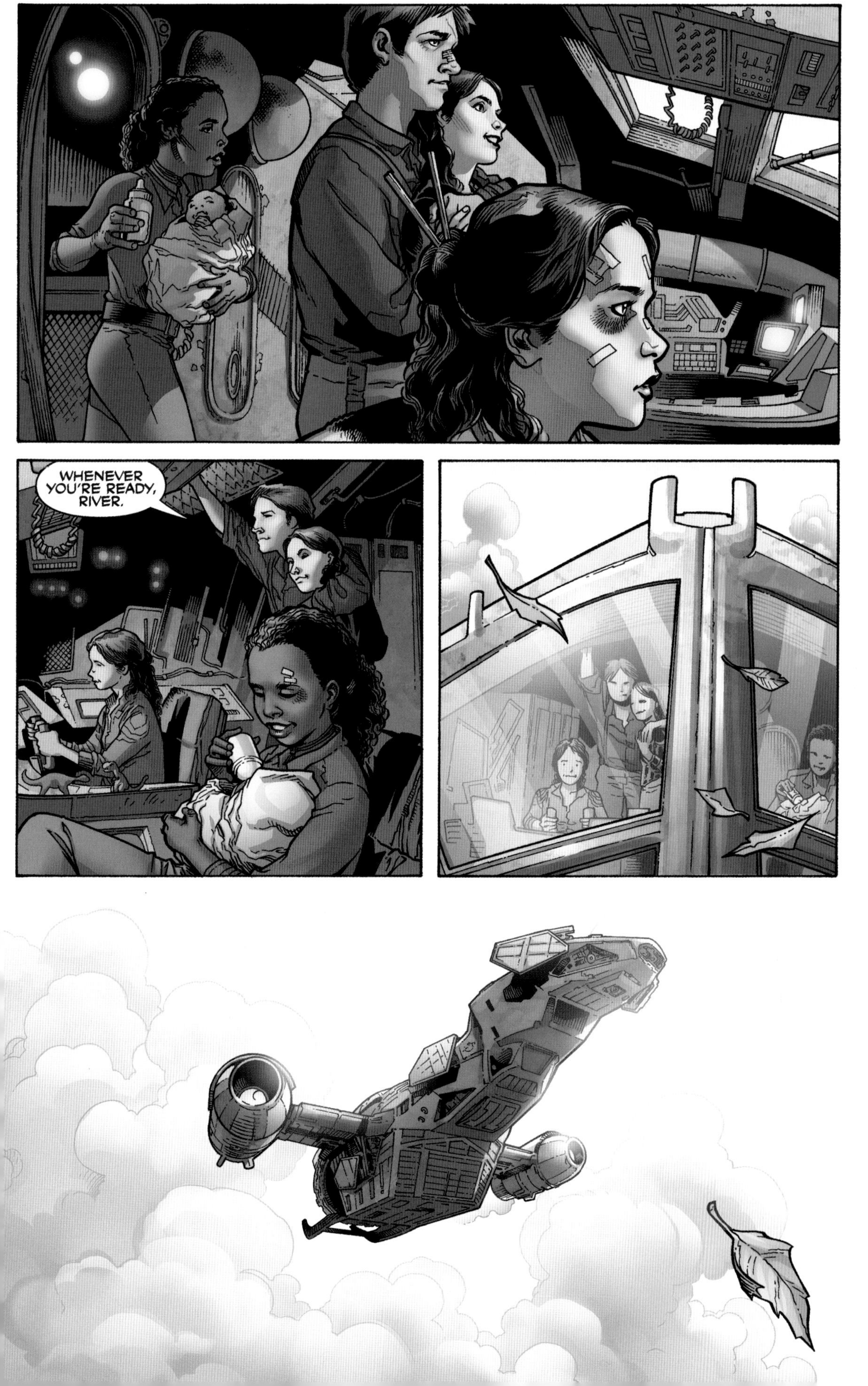
WHENEVER YOU'RE READY, RIVER.

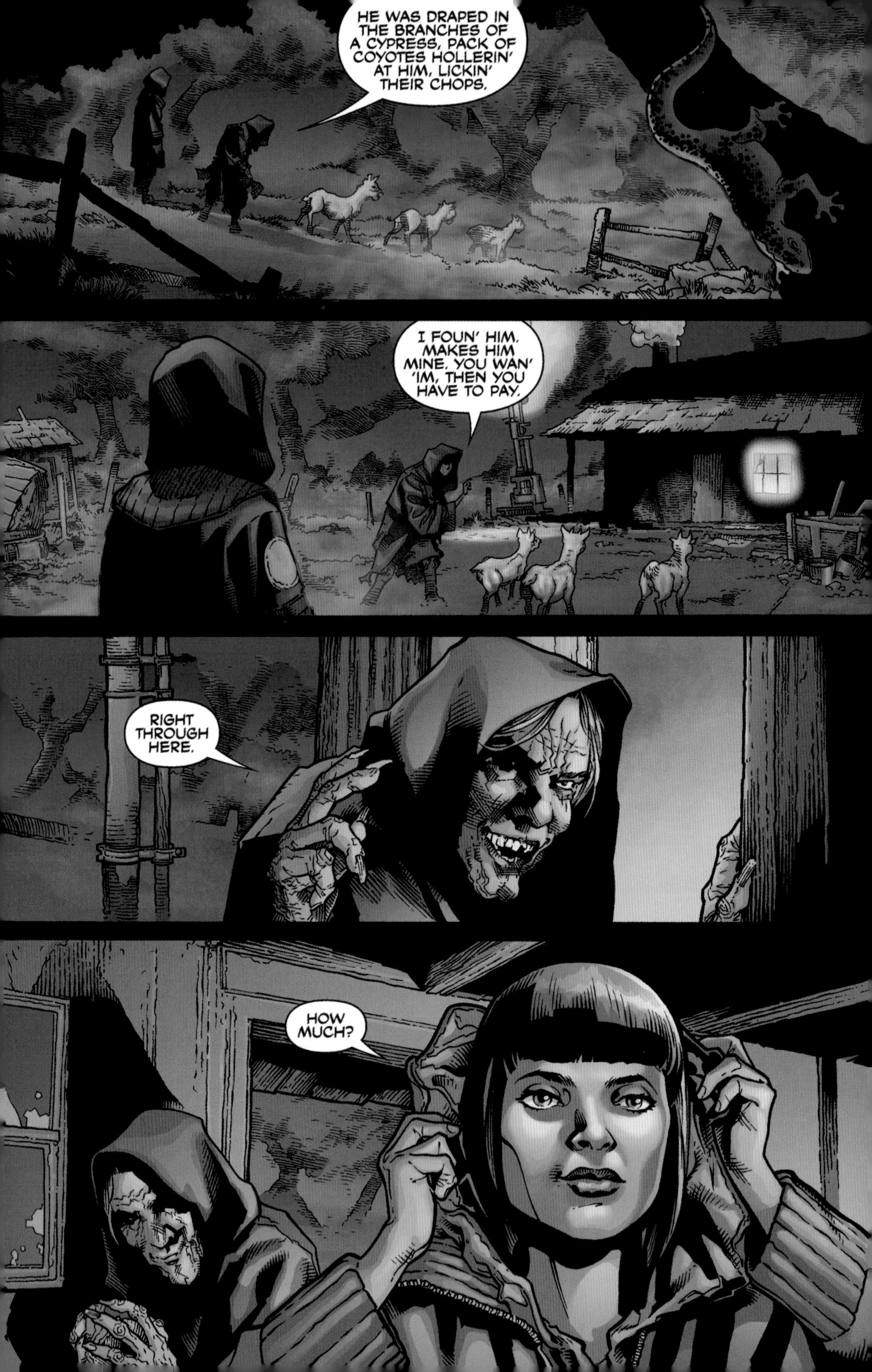
HE WAS DRAPED IN THE BRANCHES OF A CYPRESS, PACK OF COYOTES HOLLERIN' AT HIM, LICKIN' THEIR CHOPS.
I FOUN' HIM. MAKES HIM MINE. YOU WAN' 'IM, THEN YOU HAVE TO PAY.
RIGHT THROUGH HERE.
HOW MUCH?

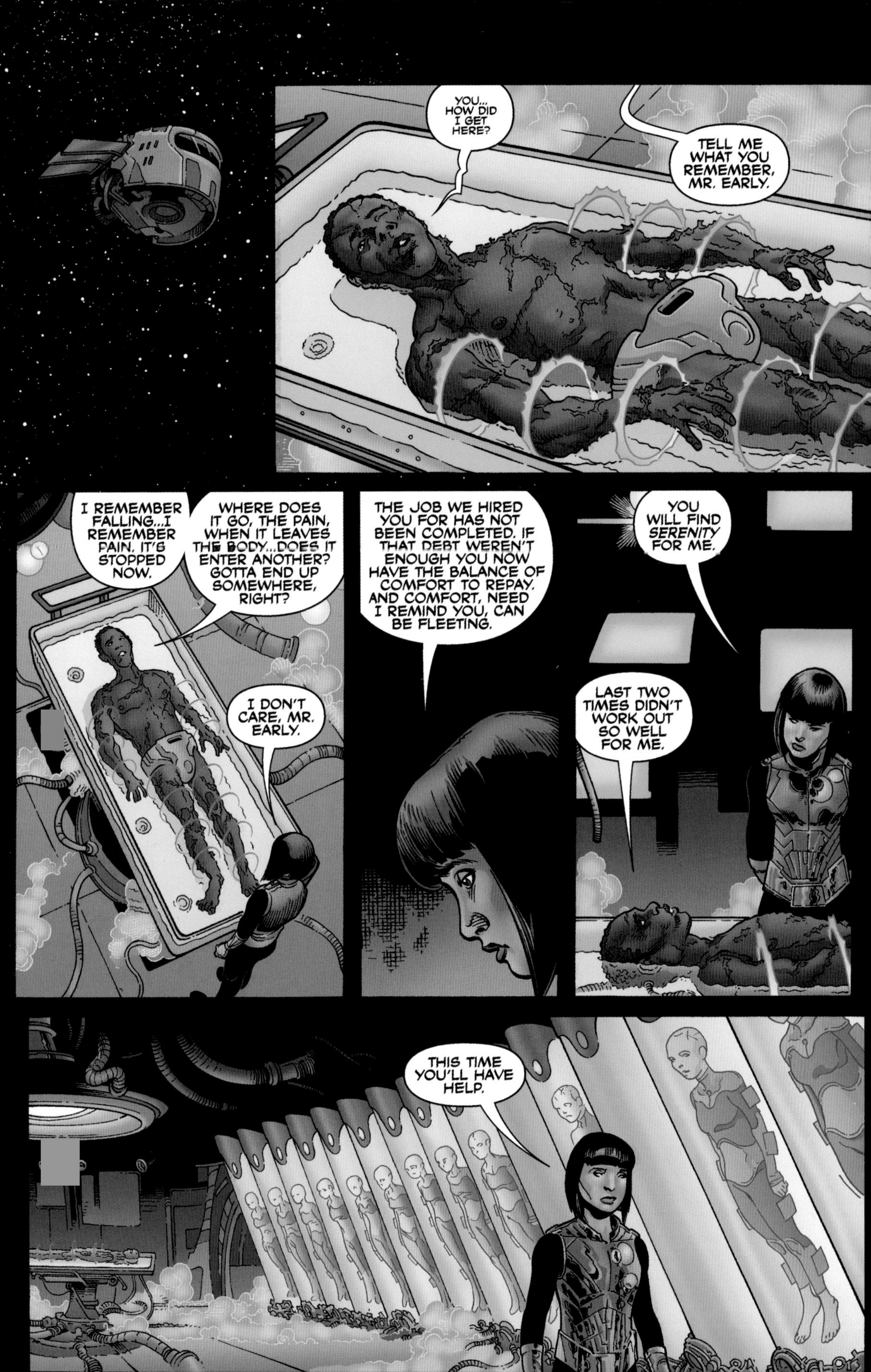
YOU... HOW DID I GET HERE?
TELL ME WHAT YOU REMEMBER, MR. EARLY.
I REMEMBER FALLING...I REMEMBER PAIN. IT'S STOPPED NOW.
WHERE DOES IT GO, THE PAIN, WHEN IT LEAVES THE BODY...DOES IT ENTER ANOTHER? GOTTA END UP SOMEWHERE, RIGHT?
I DON'T CARE, MR. EARLY.
THE JOB WE HIRED YOU FOR HAS NOT BEEN COMPLETED. IF THAT DEBT WEREN'T ENOUGH YOU NOW HAVE THE BALANCE OF COMFORT TO REPAY. AND COMFORT, NEED I REMIND YOU, CAN BE FLEETING.
YOU WILL FIND SERENITY FOR ME.
LAST TWO TIMES DIDN'T WORK OUT SO WELL FOR ME.
THIS TIME YOU'LL HAVE HELP.

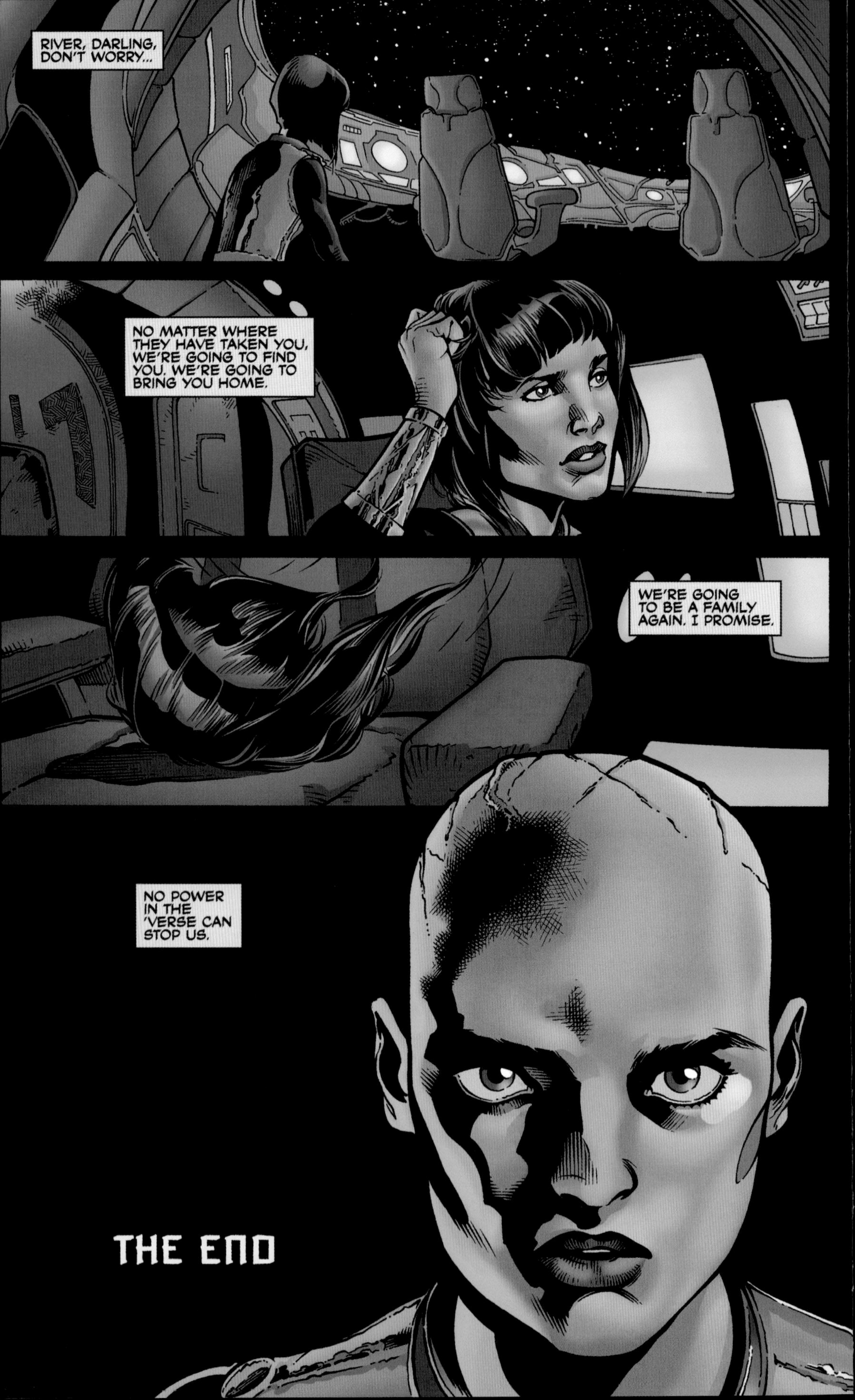

RIVER, DARLING, DON'T WORRY...
NO MATTER WHERE THEY HAVE TAKEN YOU, WE'RE GOING TO FIND YOU. WE'RE GOING TO BRING YOU HOME.
WE'RE GOING TO BE A FAMILY AGAIN. I PROMISE.
NO POWER IN THE 'VERSE CAN STOP US.
THE END

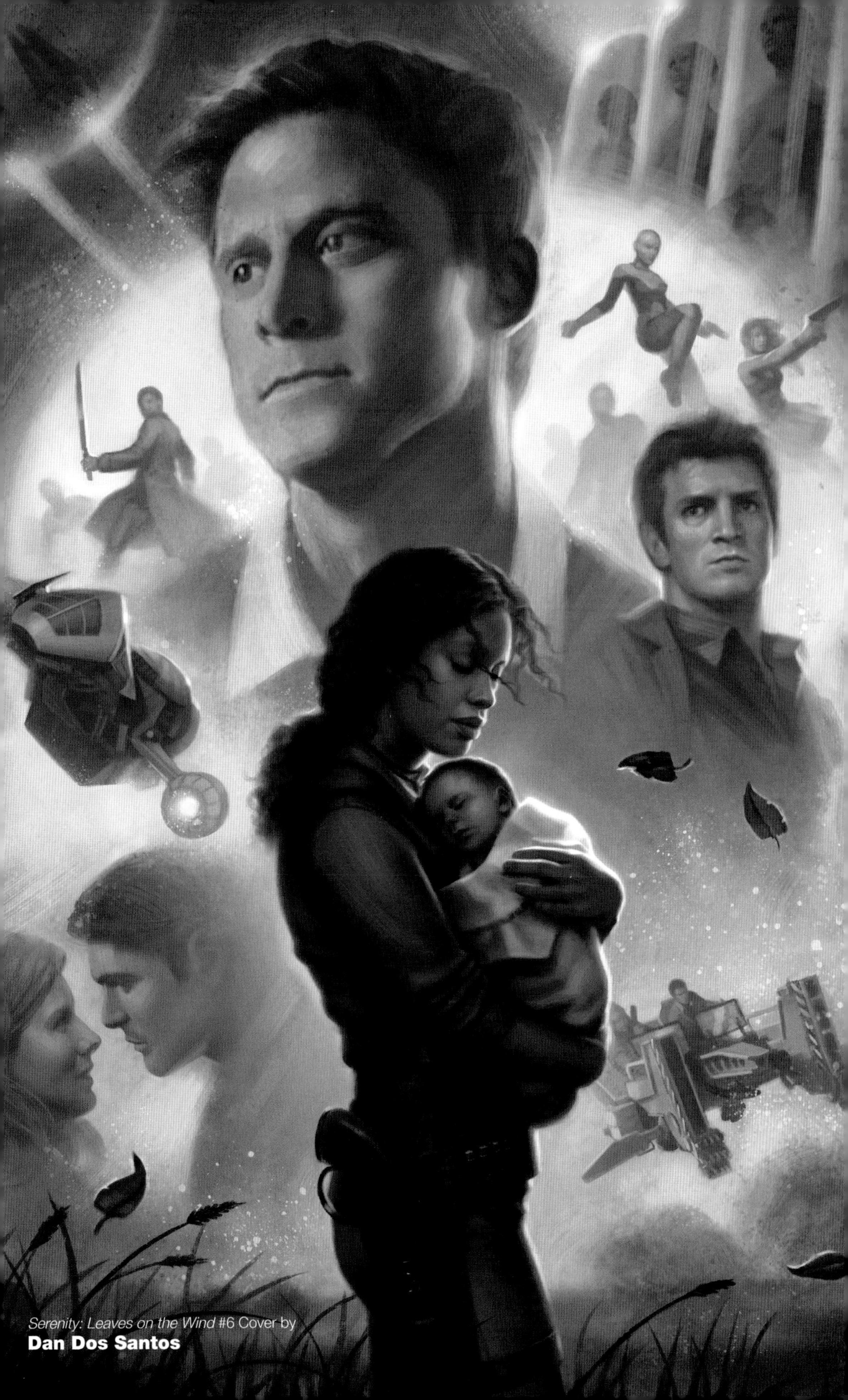

Serenity: Leaves on the Wind #6 Cover by
Dan Dos Santos

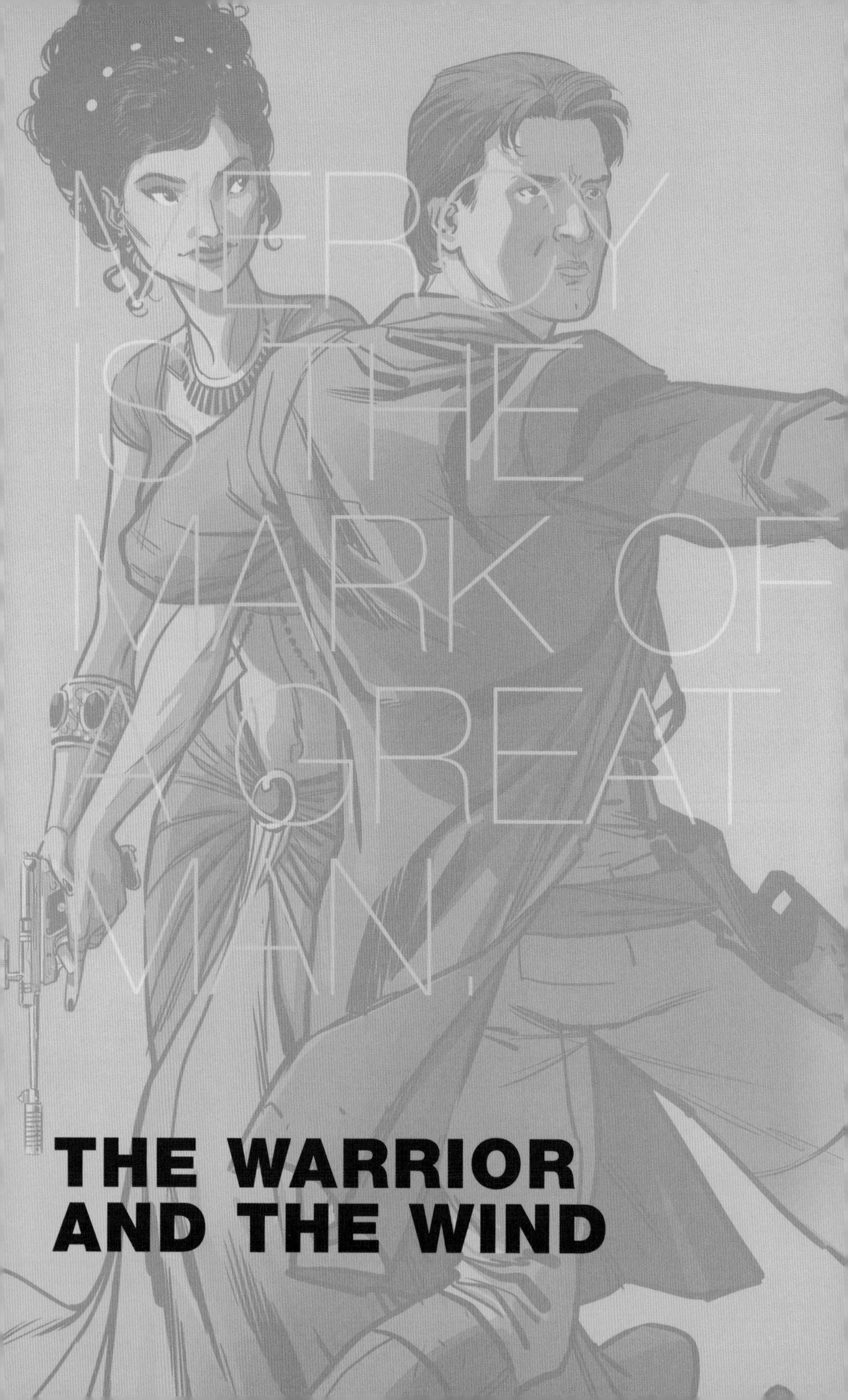
MERCY IS THE MARK OF A GREAT MAN.

THE WARRIOR AND THE WIND

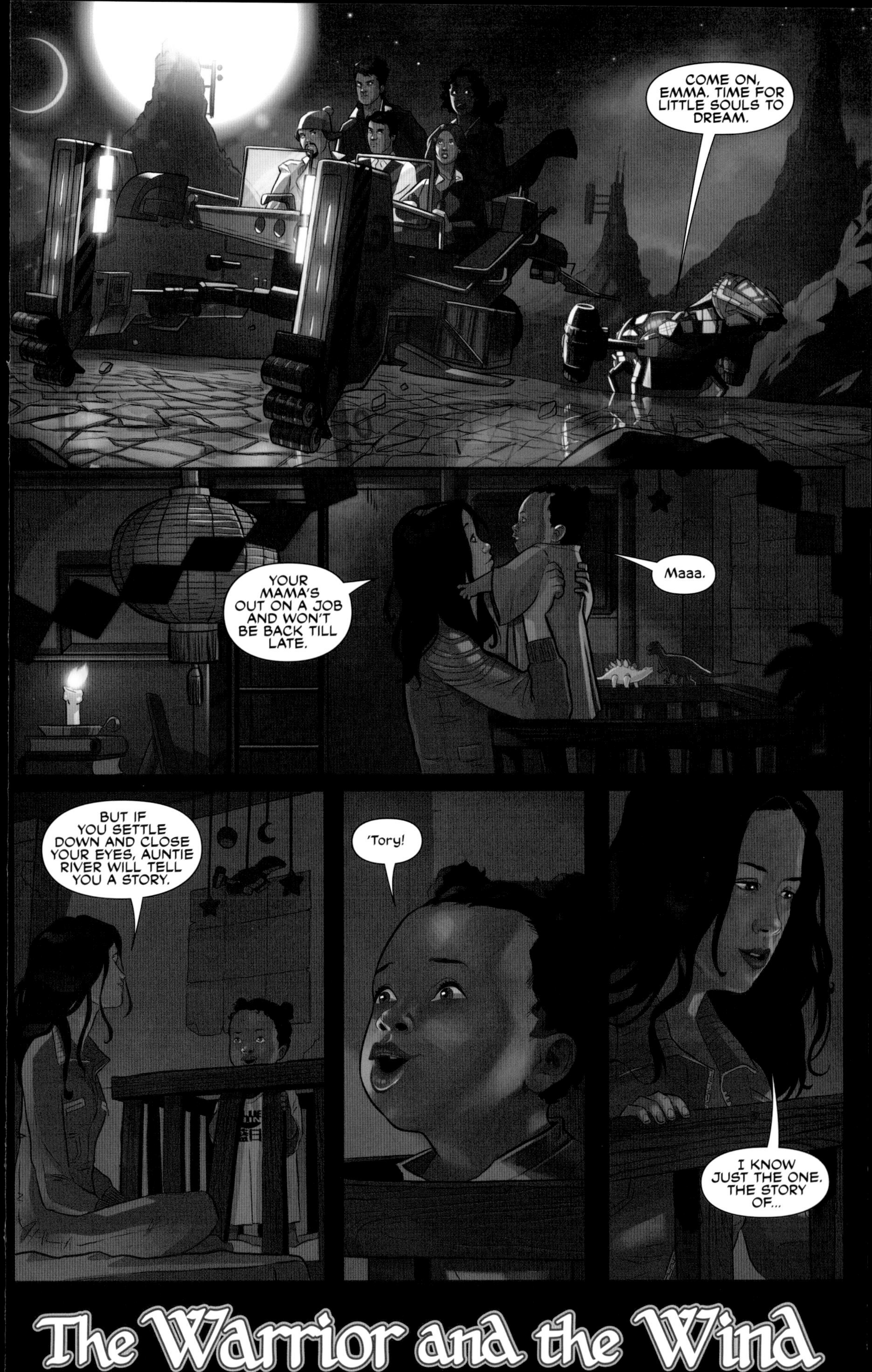
COME ON, EMMA. TIME FOR LITTLE SOULS TO DREAM.
YOUR MAMA'S OUT ON A JOB AND WON'T BE BACK TILL LATE.
Maaa.
BUT IF YOU SETTLE DOWN AND CLOSE YOUR EYES, AUNTIE RIVER WILL TELL YOU A STORY.
'Tory!
I KNOW JUST THE ONE. THE STORY OF...
The Warrior and the Wind

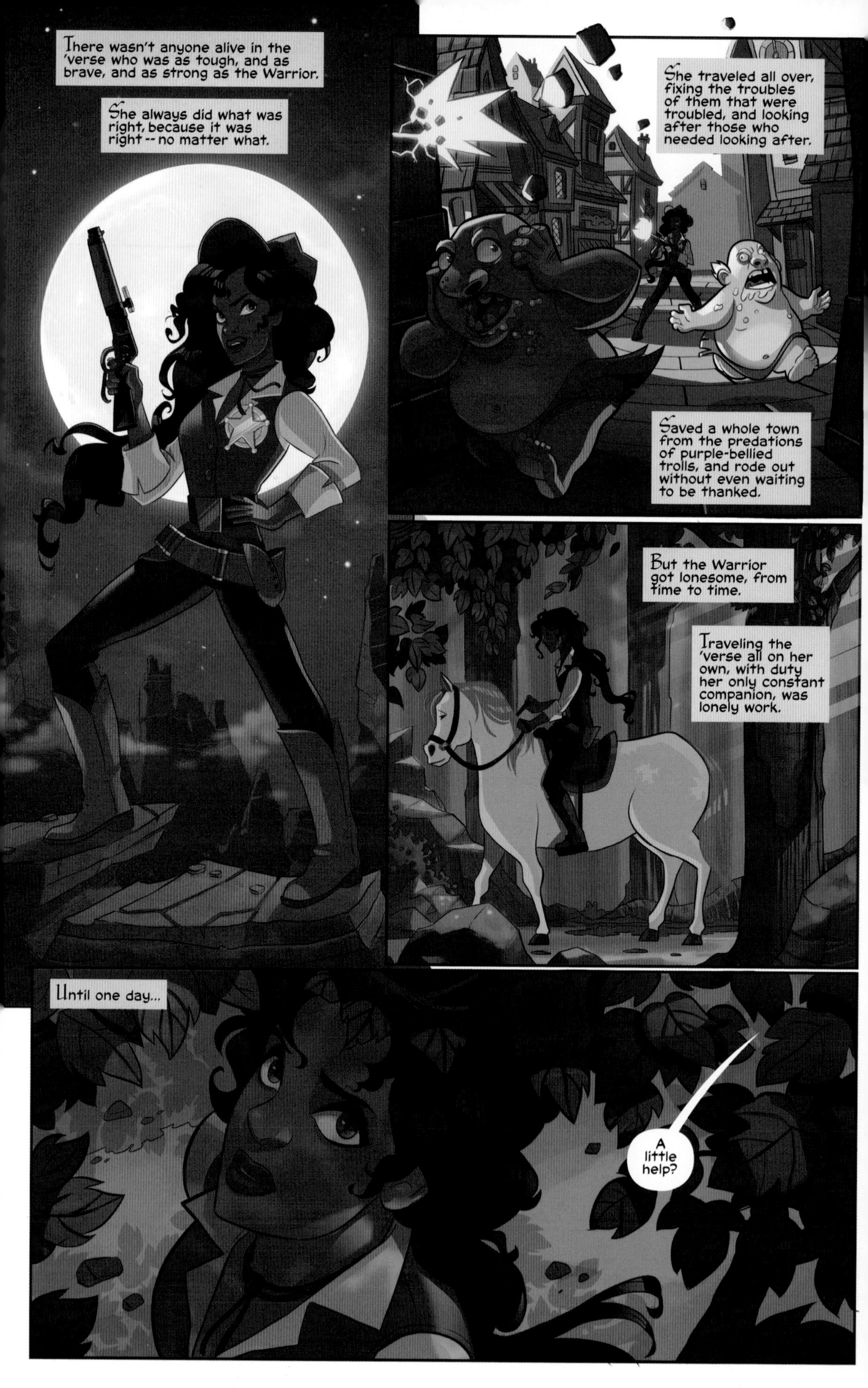
There wasn't anyone alive in the 'verse who was as tough, and as brave, and as strong as the Warrior.
She always did what was right, because it was right -- no matter what.
She traveled all over, fixing the troubles of them that were troubled, and looking after those who needed looking after.
Saved a whole town from the predations of purple-bellied trolls, and rode out without even waiting to be thanked.
But the Warrior got lonesome, from time to time.
Traveling the 'verse all on her own, with duty her only constant companion, was lonely work.
Until one day...
A little help?

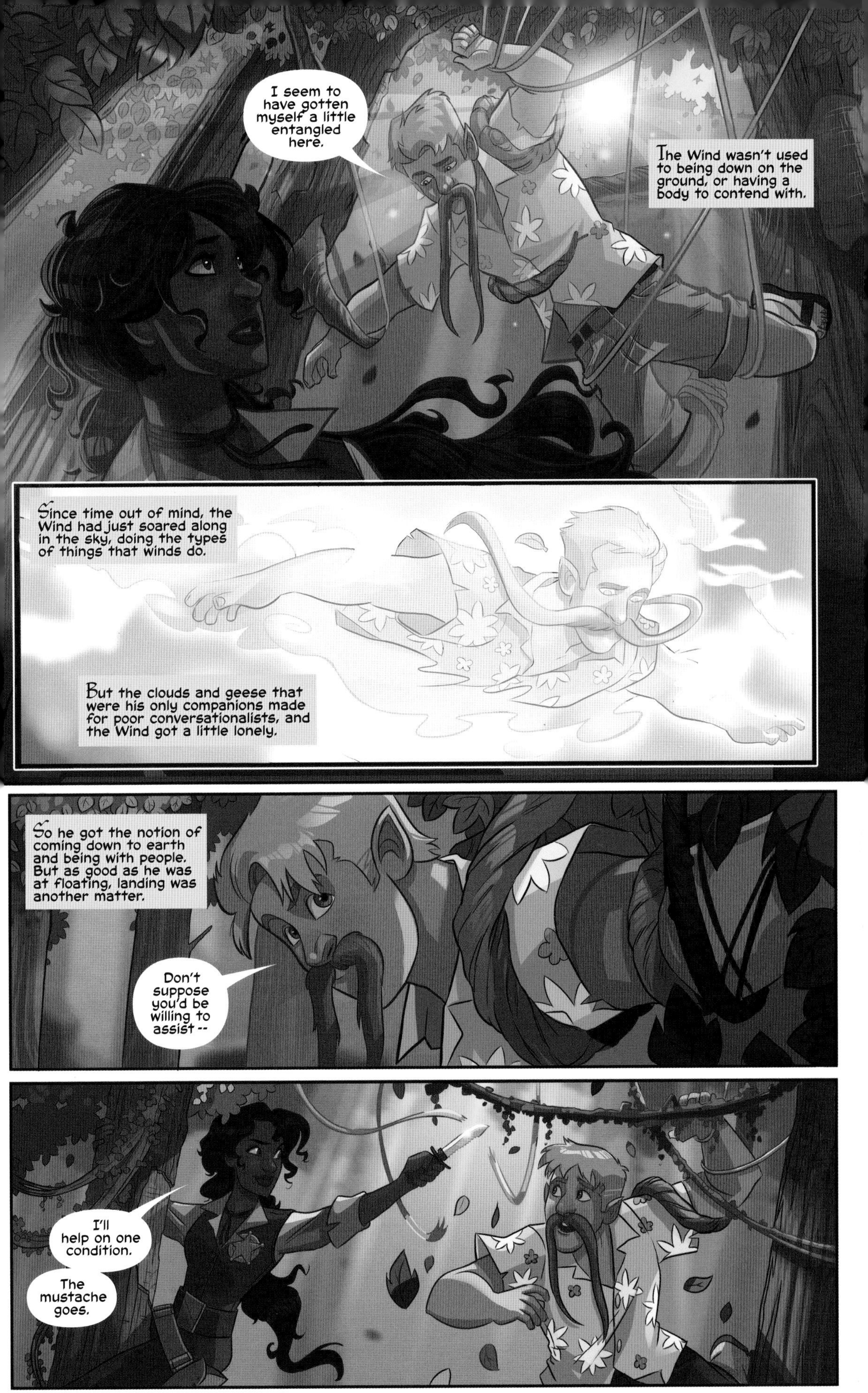
I seem to have gotten myself a little entangled here.
The Wind wasn't used to being down on the ground, or having a body to contend with.
Since time out of mind, the Wind had just soared along in the sky, doing the types of things that winds do.
But the clouds and geese that were his only companions made for poor conversationalists, and the Wind got a little lonely.
So he got the notion of coming down to earth and being with people. But as good as he was at floating, landing was another matter.
Don't suppose you'd be willing to assist --
I'll help on one condition.
The mustache goes.

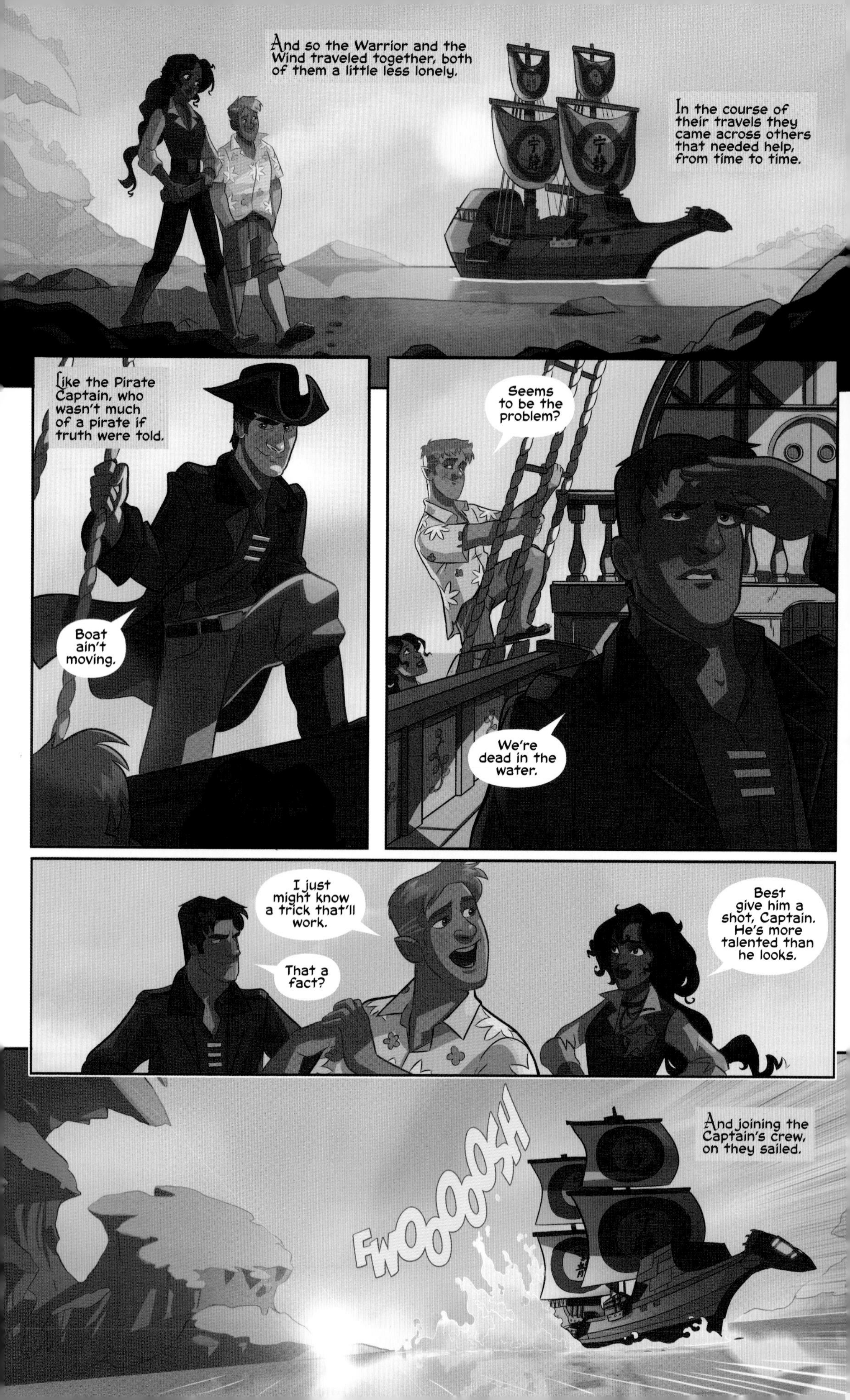
And so the Warrior and the Wind traveled together, both of them a little less lonely.
In the course of their travels they came across others that needed help, from time to time.
Like the Pirate Captain, who wasn't much of a pirate if truth were told.
Boat ain't moving.
Seems to be the problem?
We're dead in the water.
I just might know a trick that'll work.
That a fact?
Best give him a shot, Captain. He's more talented than he looks.
FWOOOOSH
And joining the Captain's crew, on they sailed.

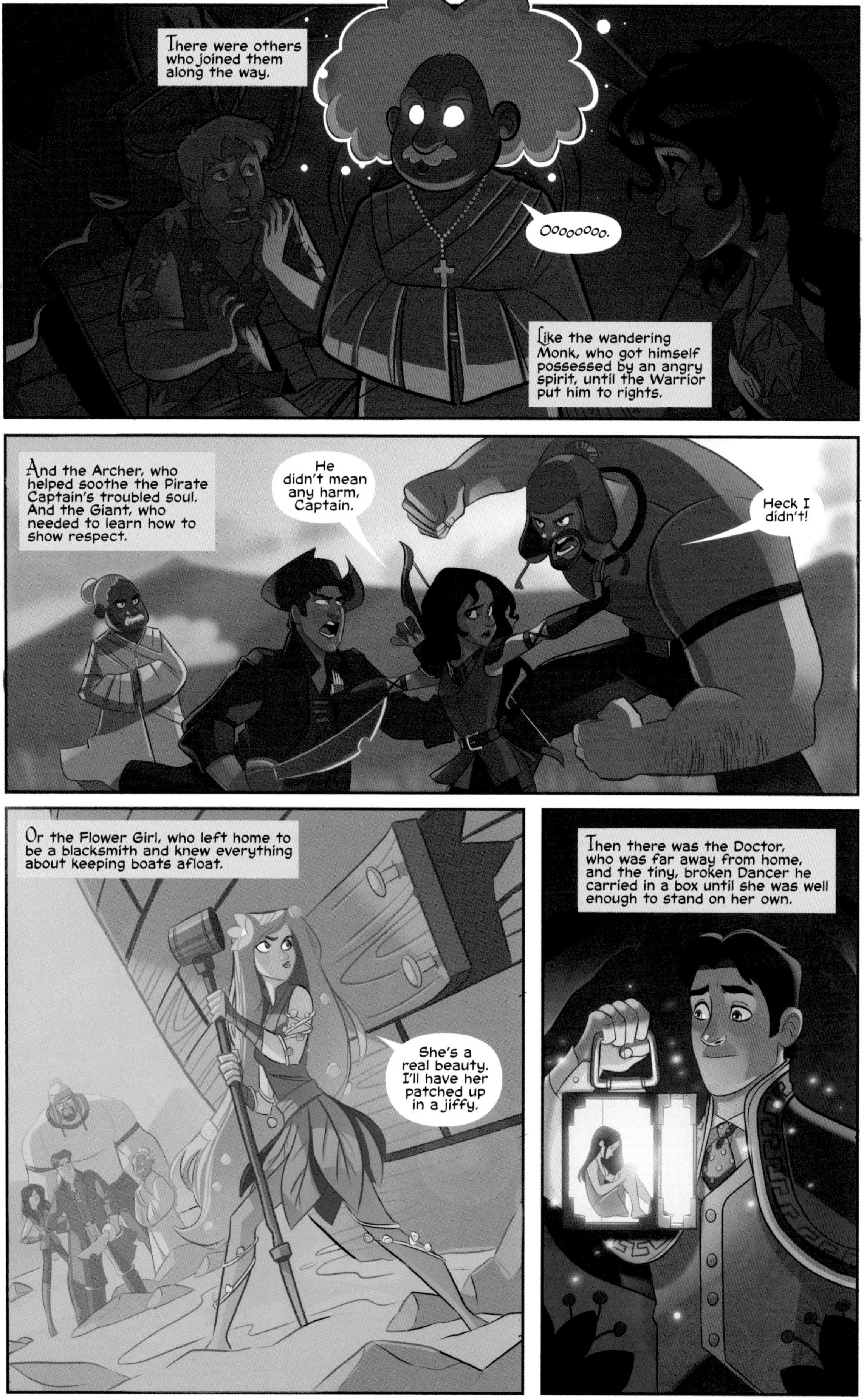
There were others who joined them along the way.
Ooooooo.
Like the wandering Monk, who got himself possessed by an angry spirit, until the Warrior put him to rights.
And the Archer, who helped soothe the Pirate Captain's troubled soul. And the Giant, who needed to learn how to show respect.
He didn't mean any harm, Captain.
Heck I didn't!
Or the Flower Girl, who left home to be a blacksmith and knew everything about keeping boats afloat.
She's a real beauty. I'll have her patched up in a jiffy.
Then there was the Doctor, who was far away from home, and the tiny, broken Dancer he carried in a box until she was well enough to stand on her own.

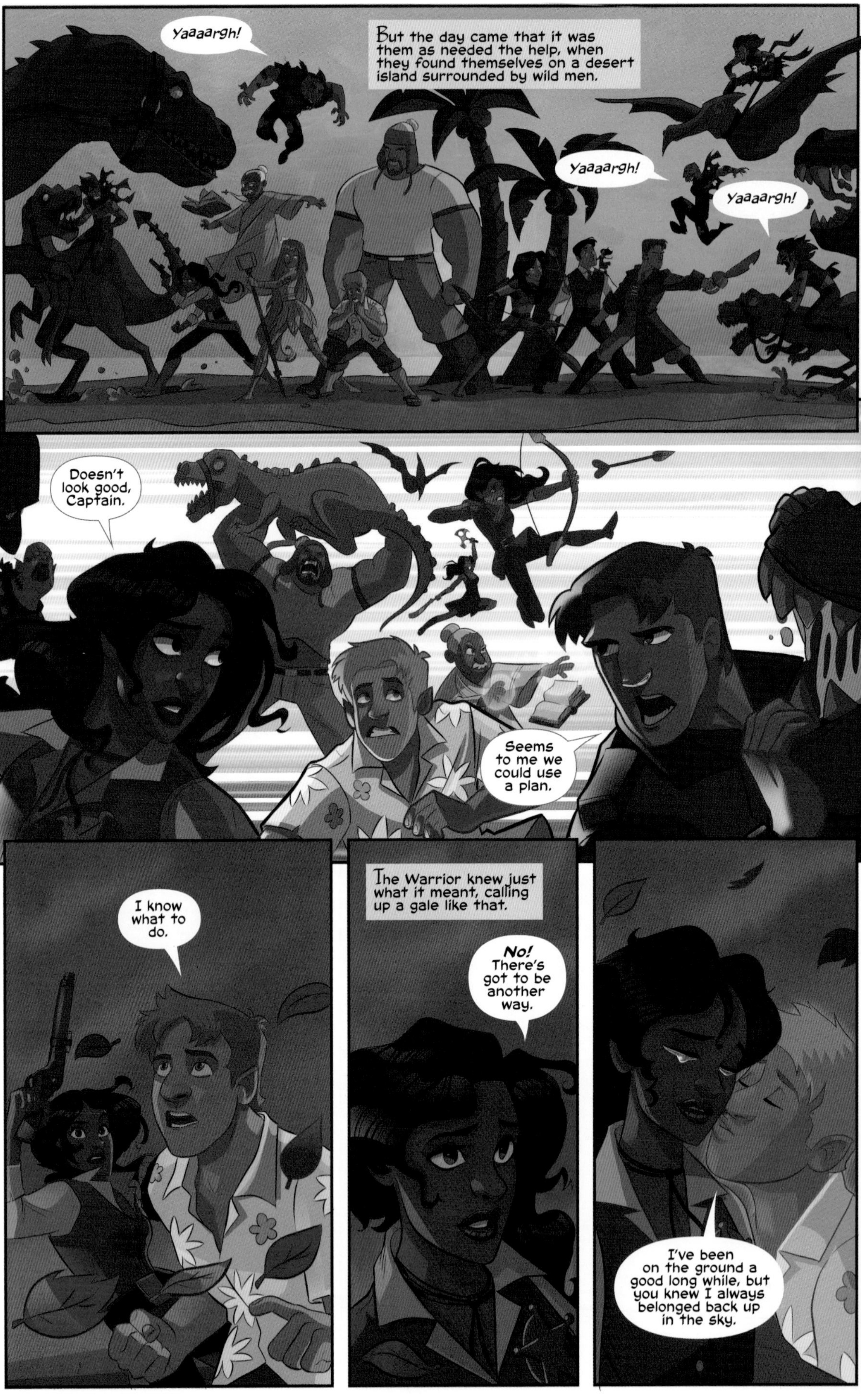
Yaaaargh!
But the day came that it was them as needed the help, when they found themselves on a desert island surrounded by wild men.
Yaaaargh!
Yaaaargh!
Doesn't look good, Captain.
Seems to me we could use a plan.
I know what to do.
The Warrior knew just what it meant, calling up a gale like that.
No! There's got to be another way.
I've been on the ground a good long while, but you knew I always belonged back up in the sky.

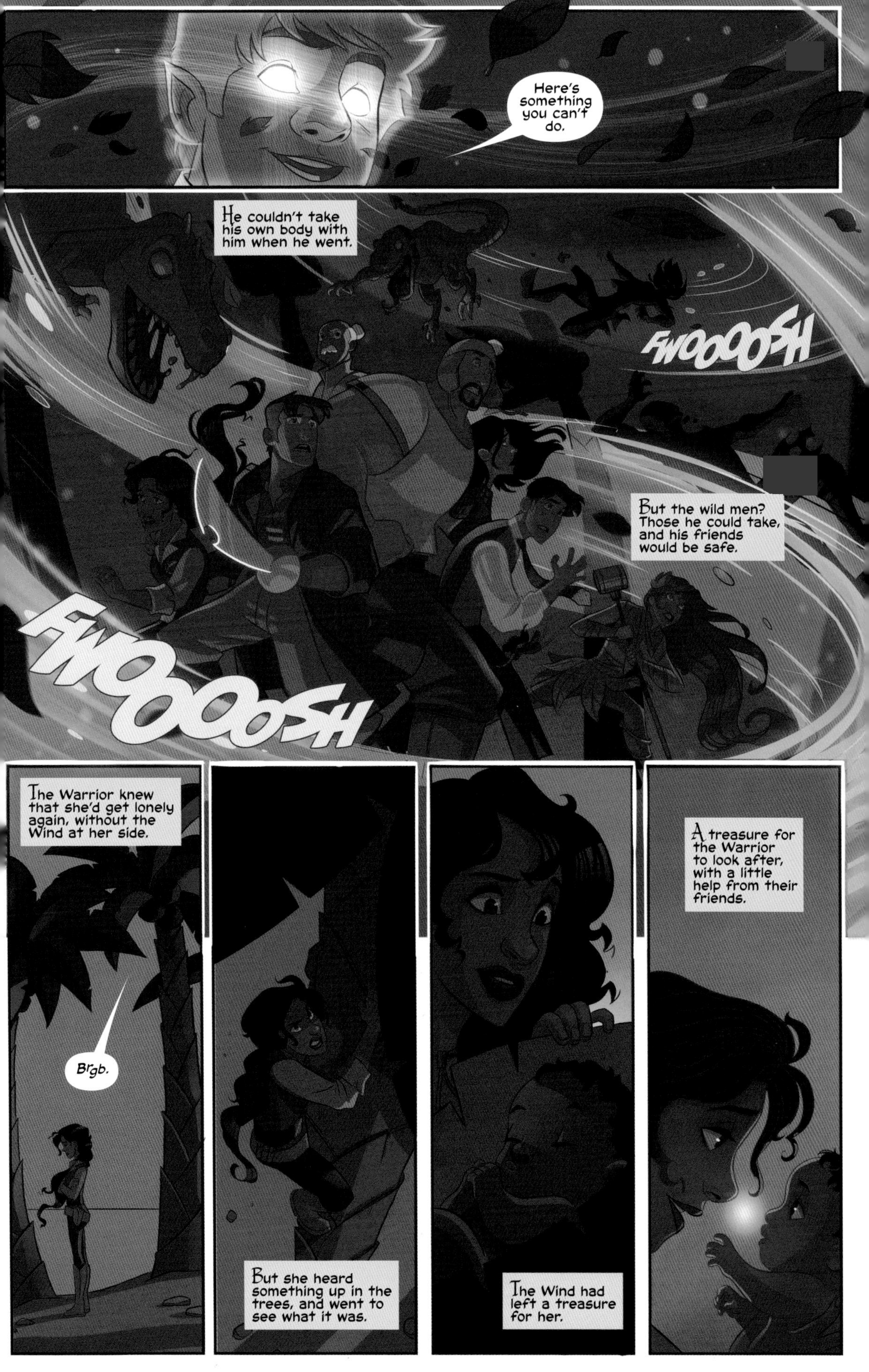
Here's something you can't do.
He couldn't take his own body with him when he went.
FWOOOOSH
But the wild men? Those he could take, and his friends would be safe.
FWOOOOSH
The Warrior knew that she'd get lonely again, without the Wind at her side.
Brgb.
But she heard something up in the trees, and went to see what it was.
The Wind had left a treasure for her.
A treasure for the Warrior to look after, with a little help from their friends.

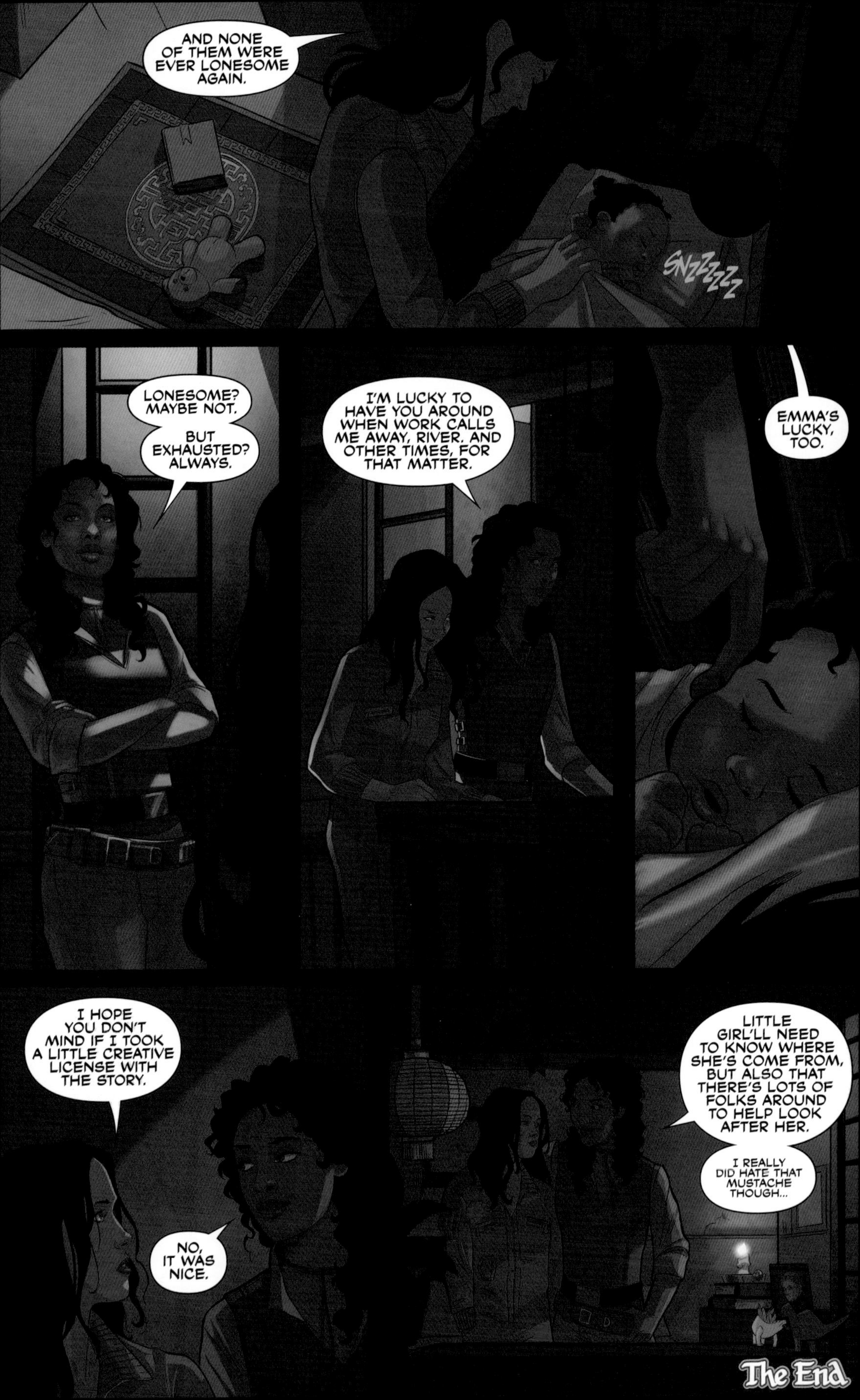
AND NONE OF THEM WERE EVER LONESOME AGAIN.
SNZZZZZZ
LONESOME? MAYBE NOT.
BUT EXHAUSTED? ALWAYS.
I'M LUCKY TO HAVE YOU AROUND WHEN WORK CALLS ME AWAY, RIVER. AND OTHER TIMES, FOR THAT MATTER.
EMMA'S LUCKY, TOO.
I HOPE YOU DON'T MIND IF I TOOK A LITTLE CREATIVE LICENSE WITH THE STORY.
NO, IT WAS NICE.
LITTLE GIRL'LL NEED TO KNOW WHERE SHE'S COME FROM, BUT ALSO THAT THERE'S LOTS OF FOLKS AROUND TO HELP LOOK AFTER HER.
I REALLY DID HATE THAT MUSTACHE THOUGH...
The End

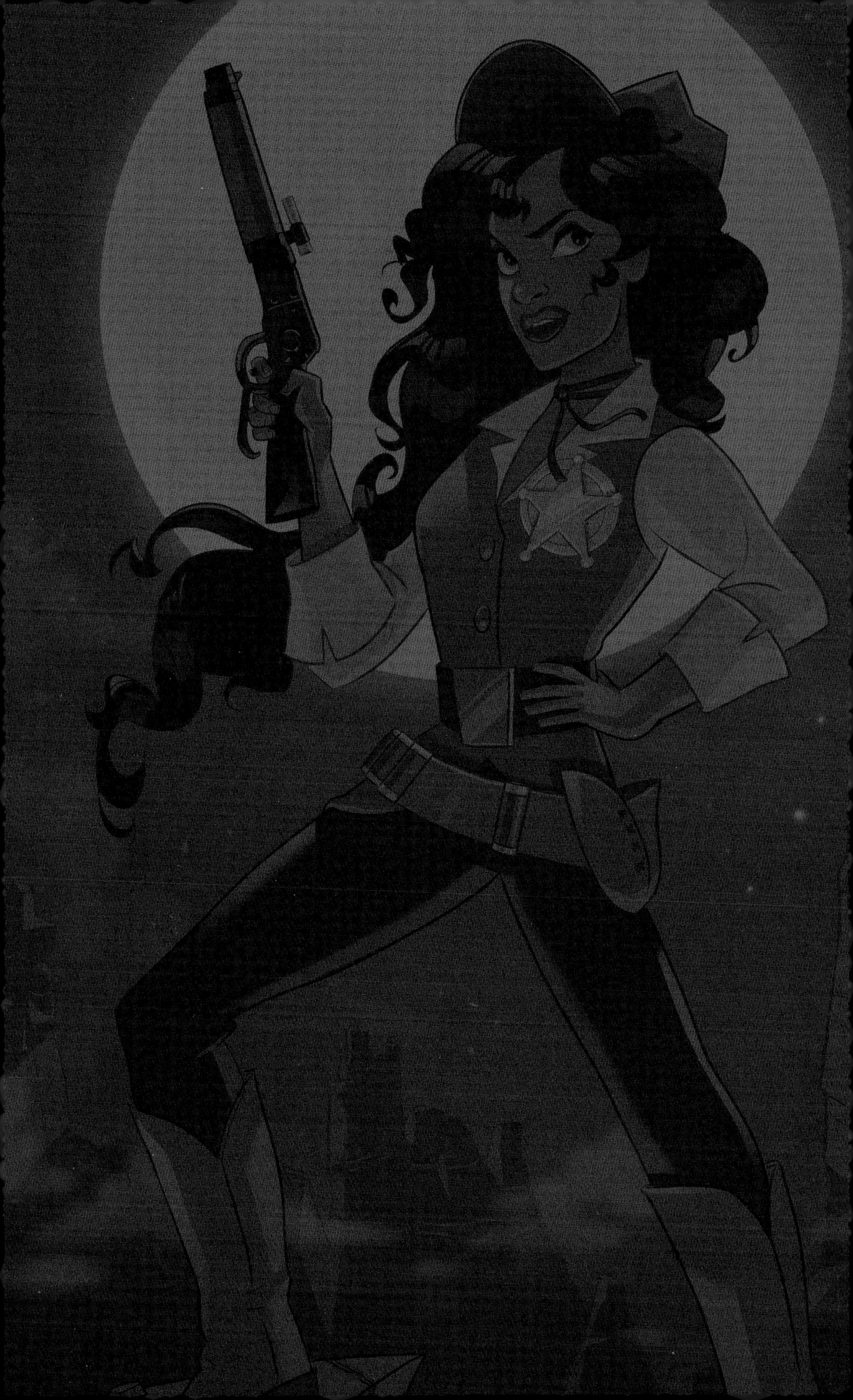

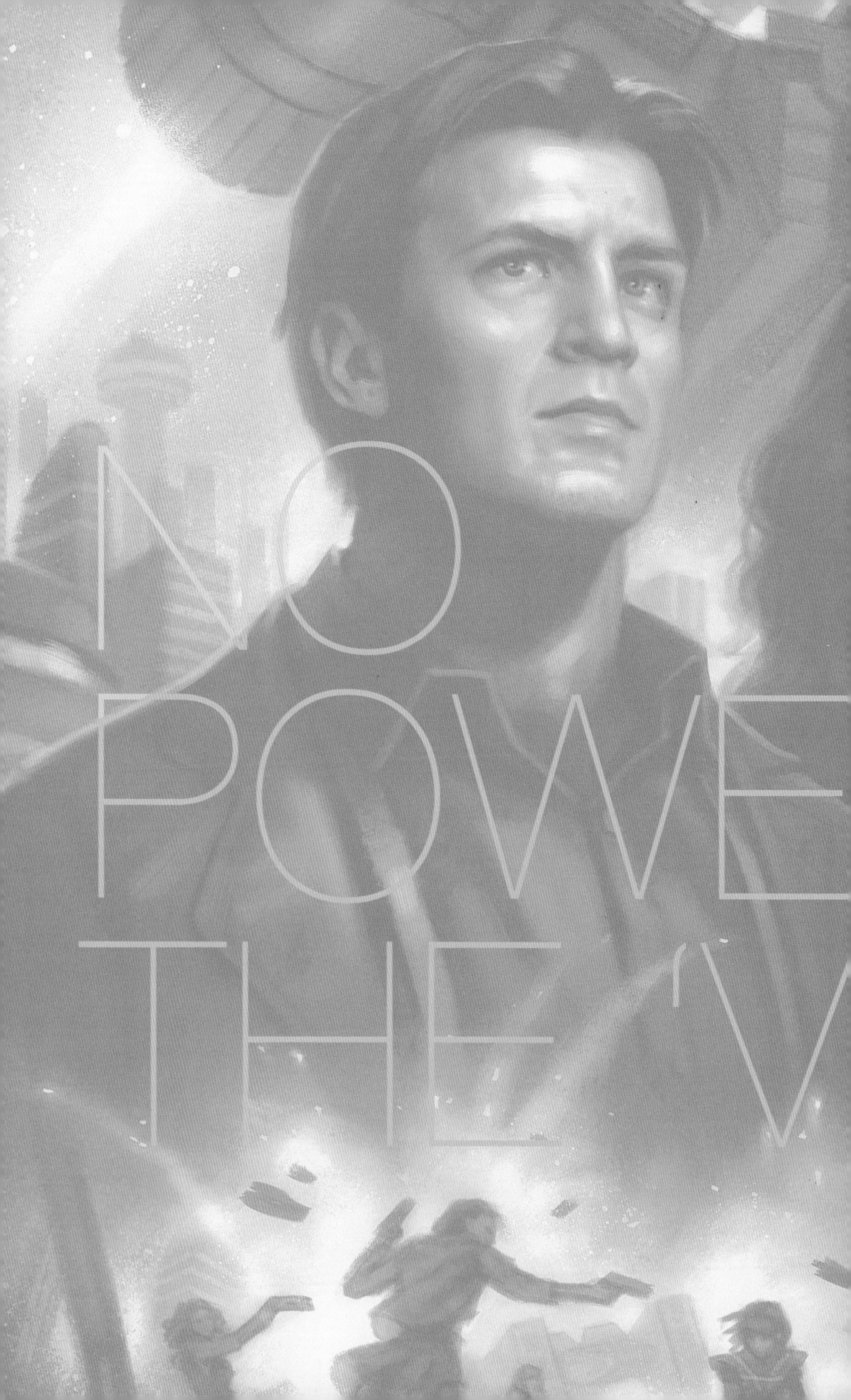
NO
POWE
THE

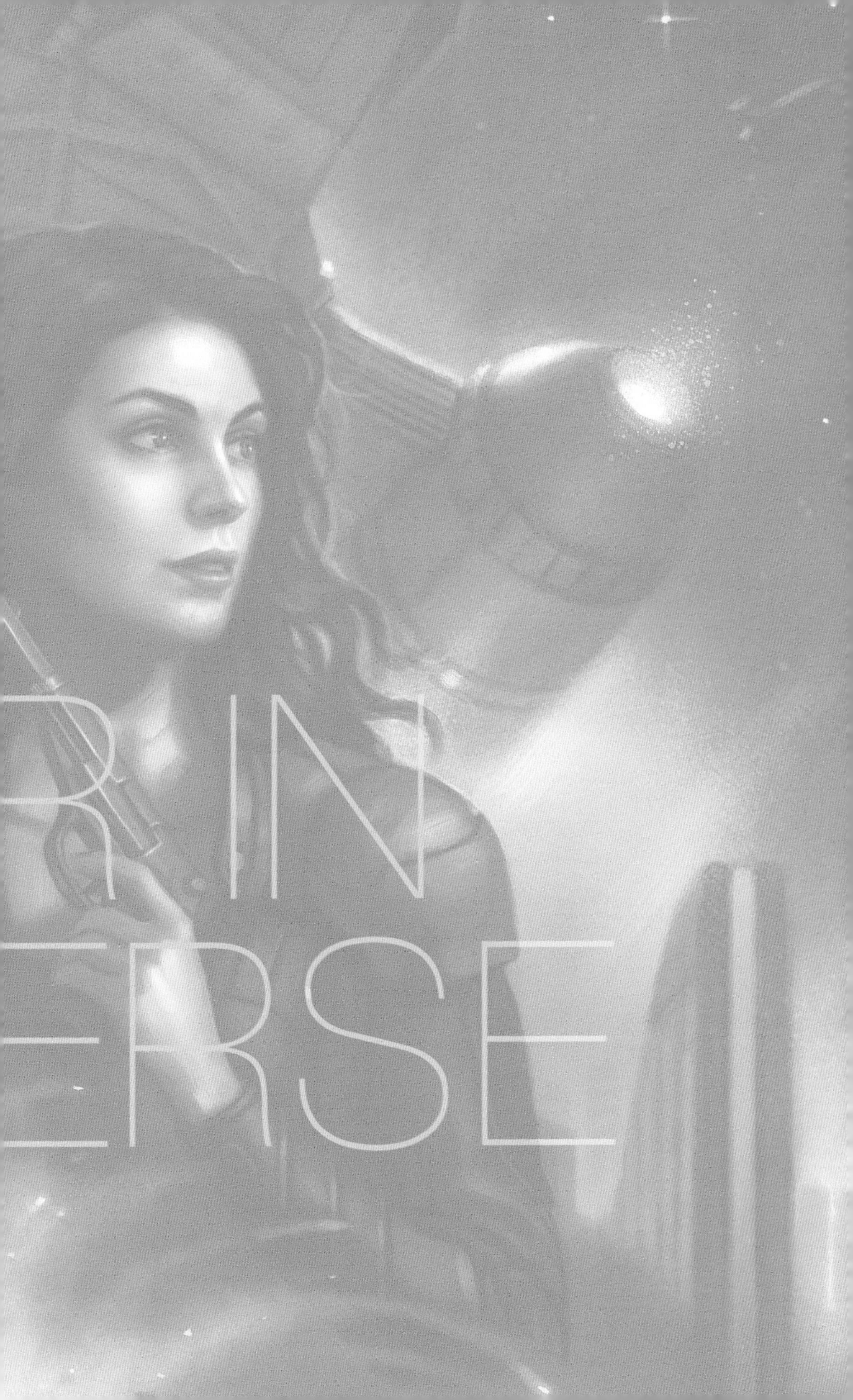
RIN
ERSE

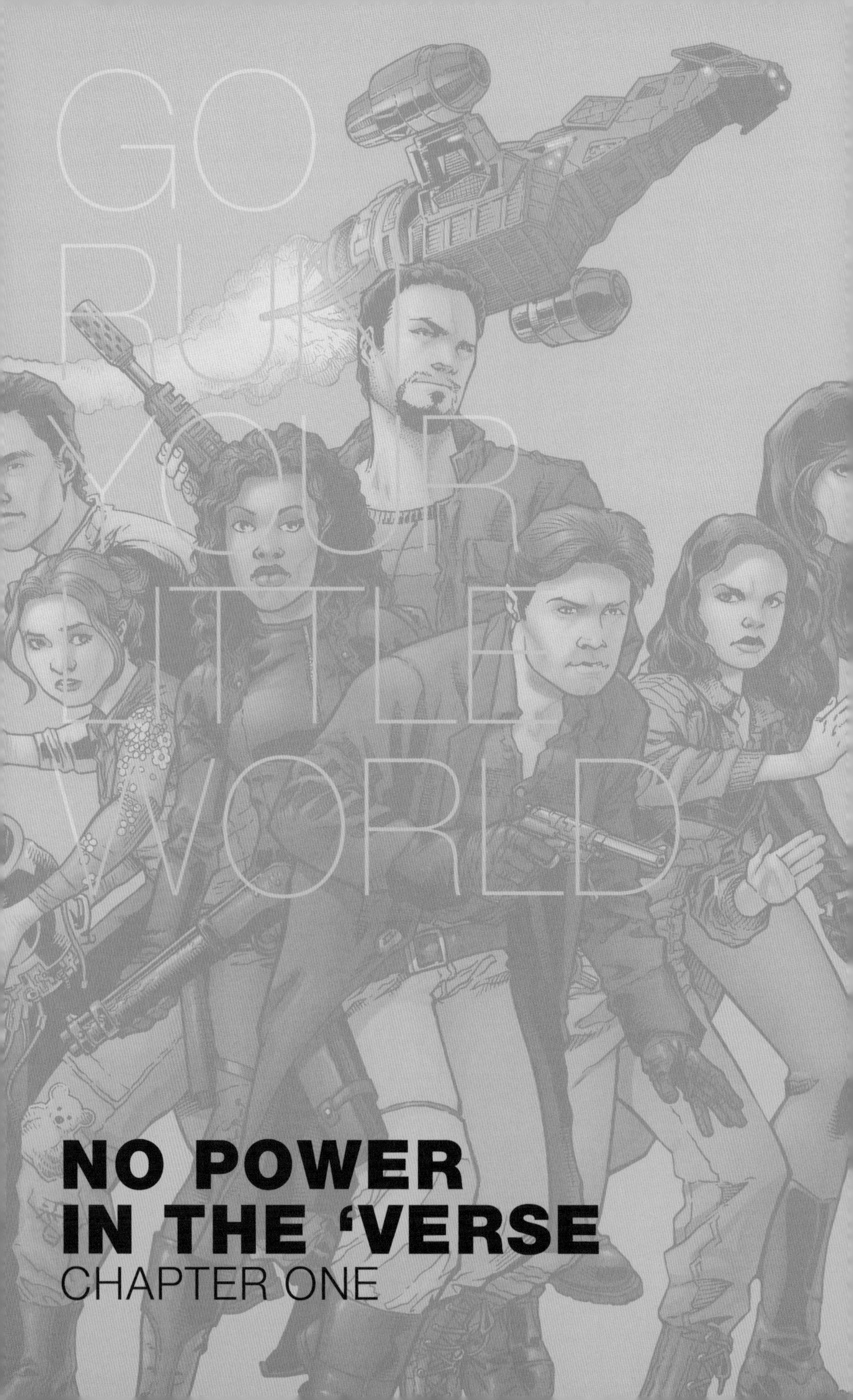

NO POWER IN THE 'VERSE

CHAPTER ONE

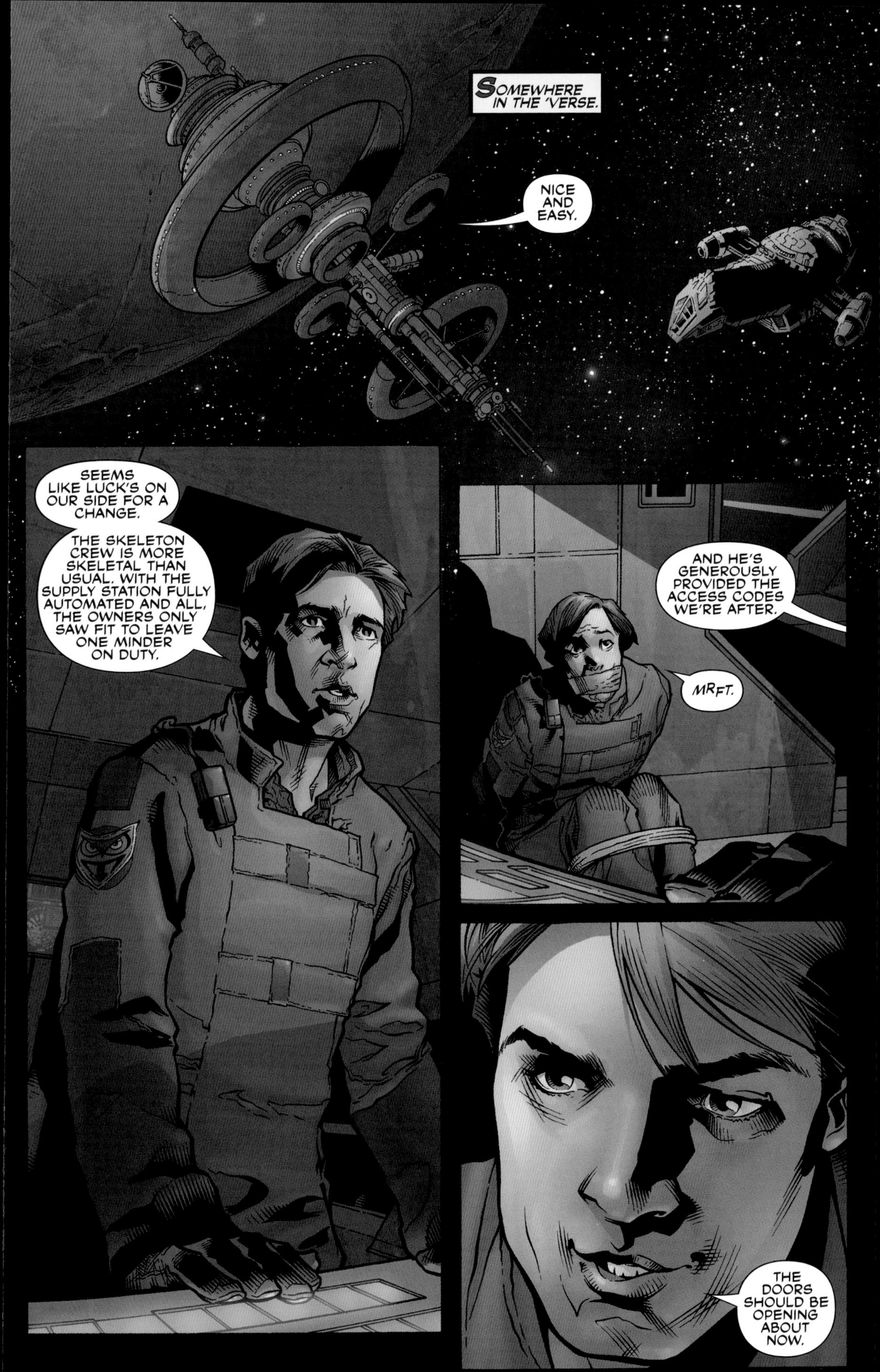
SOMEWHERE IN THE 'VERSE.
NICE AND EASY.
SEEMS LIKE LUCK'S ON OUR SIDE FOR A CHANGE.
THE SKELETON CREW IS MORE SKELETAL THAN USUAL. WITH THE SUPPLY STATION FULLY AUTOMATED AND ALL, THE OWNERS ONLY SAW FIT TO LEAVE ONE MINDER ON DUTY.
AND HE'S GENEROUSLY PROVIDED THE ACCESS CODES WE'RE AFTER.
MRFT.
THE DOORS SHOULD BE OPENING ABOUT NOW.

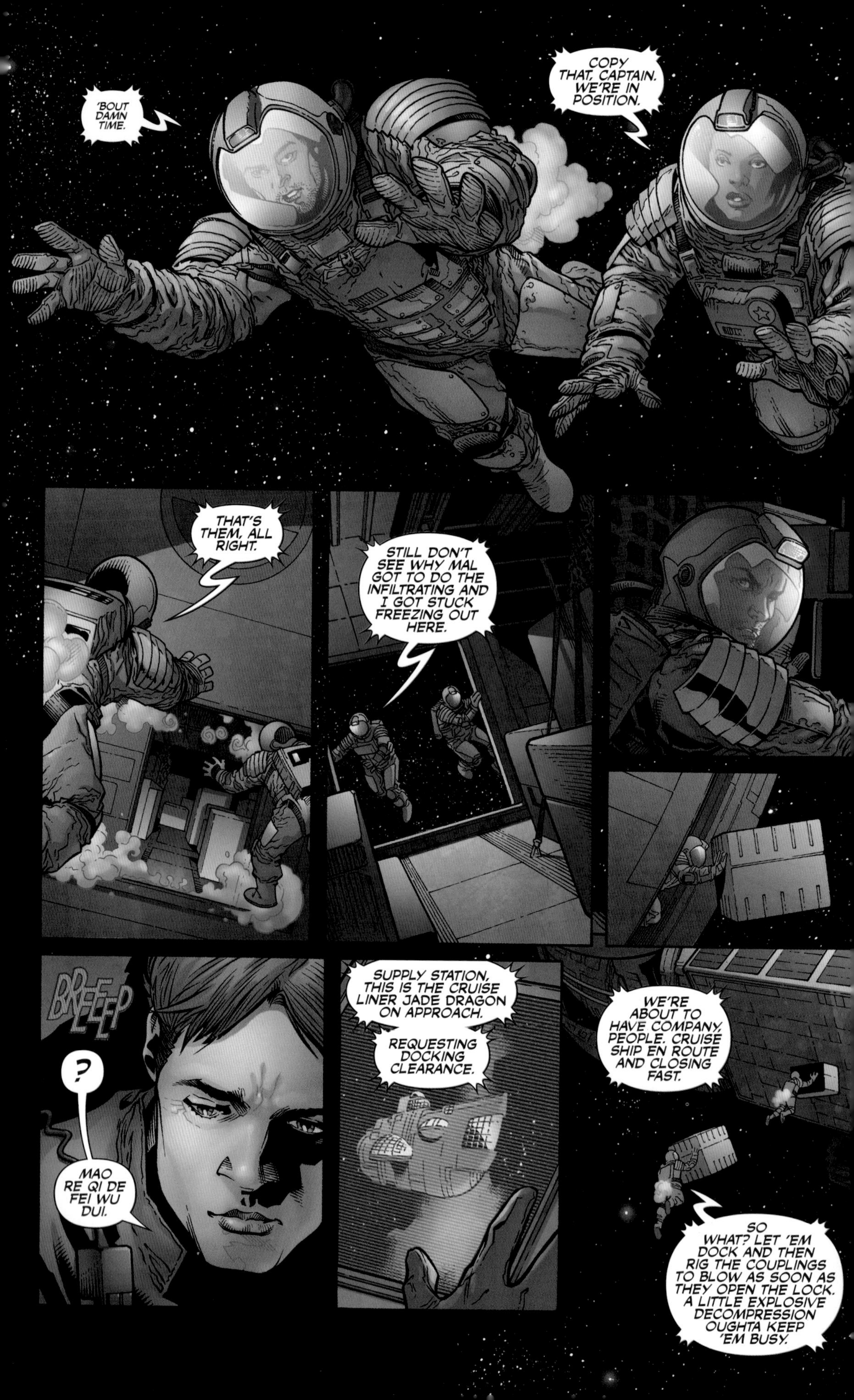
'BOUT DAMN TIME.
COPY THAT, CAPTAIN. WE'RE IN POSITION.
THAT'S THEM, ALL RIGHT.
STILL DON'T SEE WHY MAL GOT TO DO THE INFILTRATING AND I GOT STUCK FREEZING OUT HERE.
BREEEEP
?
MAO RE QI DE FEI WU DUI.
SUPPLY STATION, THIS IS THE CRUISE LINER JADE DRAGON ON APPROACH.
REQUESTING DOCKING CLEARANCE.
WE'RE ABOUT TO HAVE COMPANY, PEOPLE. CRUISE SHIP EN ROUTE AND CLOSING FAST.
SO WHAT? LET 'EM DOCK AND THEN RIG THE COUPLINGS TO BLOW AS SOON AS THEY OPEN THE LOCK. A LITTLE EXPLOSIVE DECOMPRESSION OUGHTA KEEP 'EM BUSY.

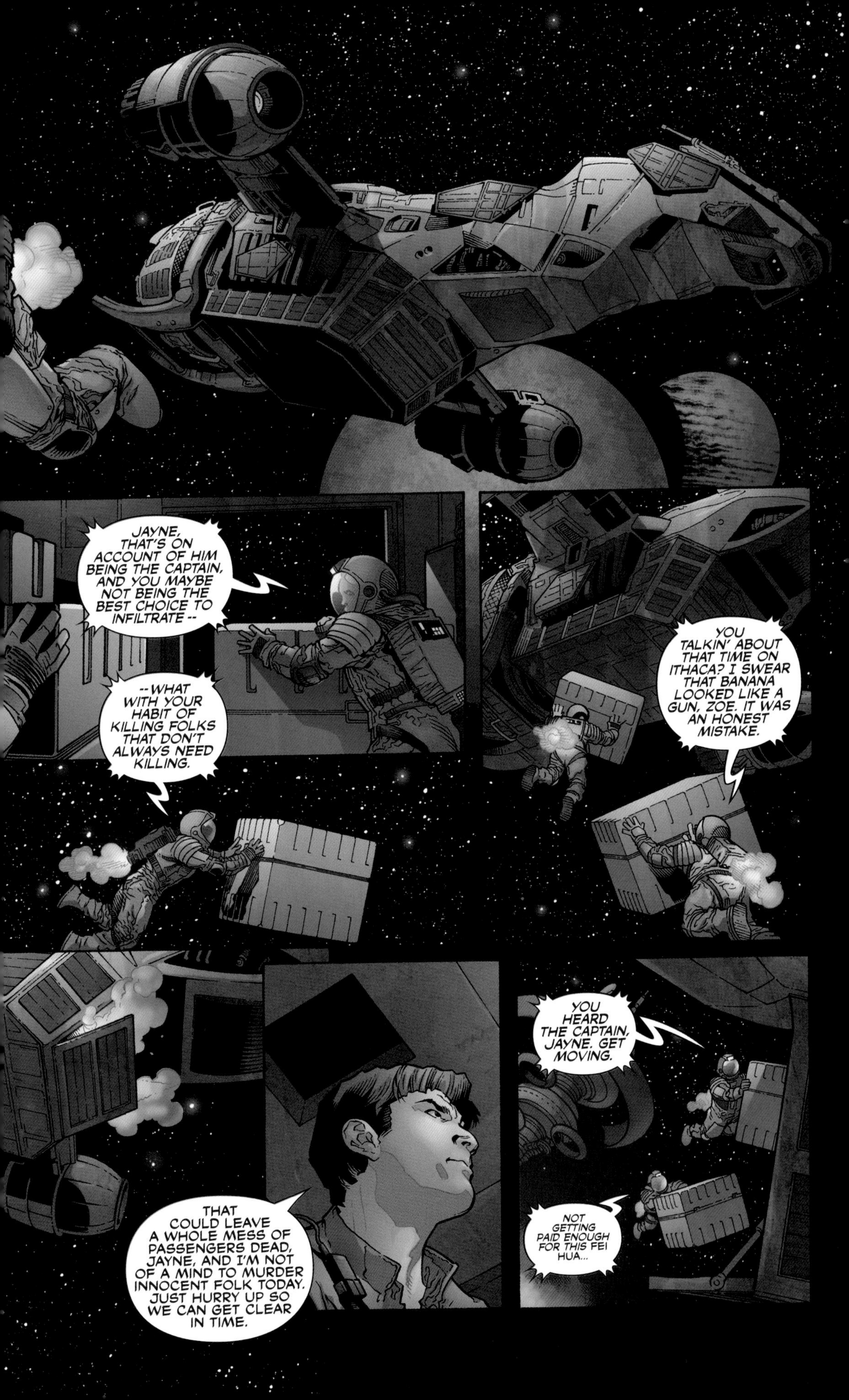

JAYNE, THAT'S ON ACCOUNT OF HIM BEING THE CAPTAIN, AND YOU MAYBE NOT BEING THE BEST CHOICE TO INFILTRATE --
--WHAT WITH YOUR HABIT OF KILLING FOLKS THAT DON'T ALWAYS NEED KILLING.
YOU TALKIN' ABOUT THAT TIME ON ITHACA? I SWEAR THAT BANANA LOOKED LIKE A GUN, ZOE. IT WAS AN HONEST MISTAKE.
THAT COULD LEAVE A WHOLE MESS OF PASSENGERS DEAD, JAYNE, AND I'M NOT OF A MIND TO MURDER INNOCENT FOLK TODAY. JUST HURRY UP SO WE CAN GET CLEAR IN TIME.
YOU HEARD THE CAPTAIN, JAYNE. GET MOVING.
NOT GETTING PAID ENOUGH FOR THIS FEI HUA...

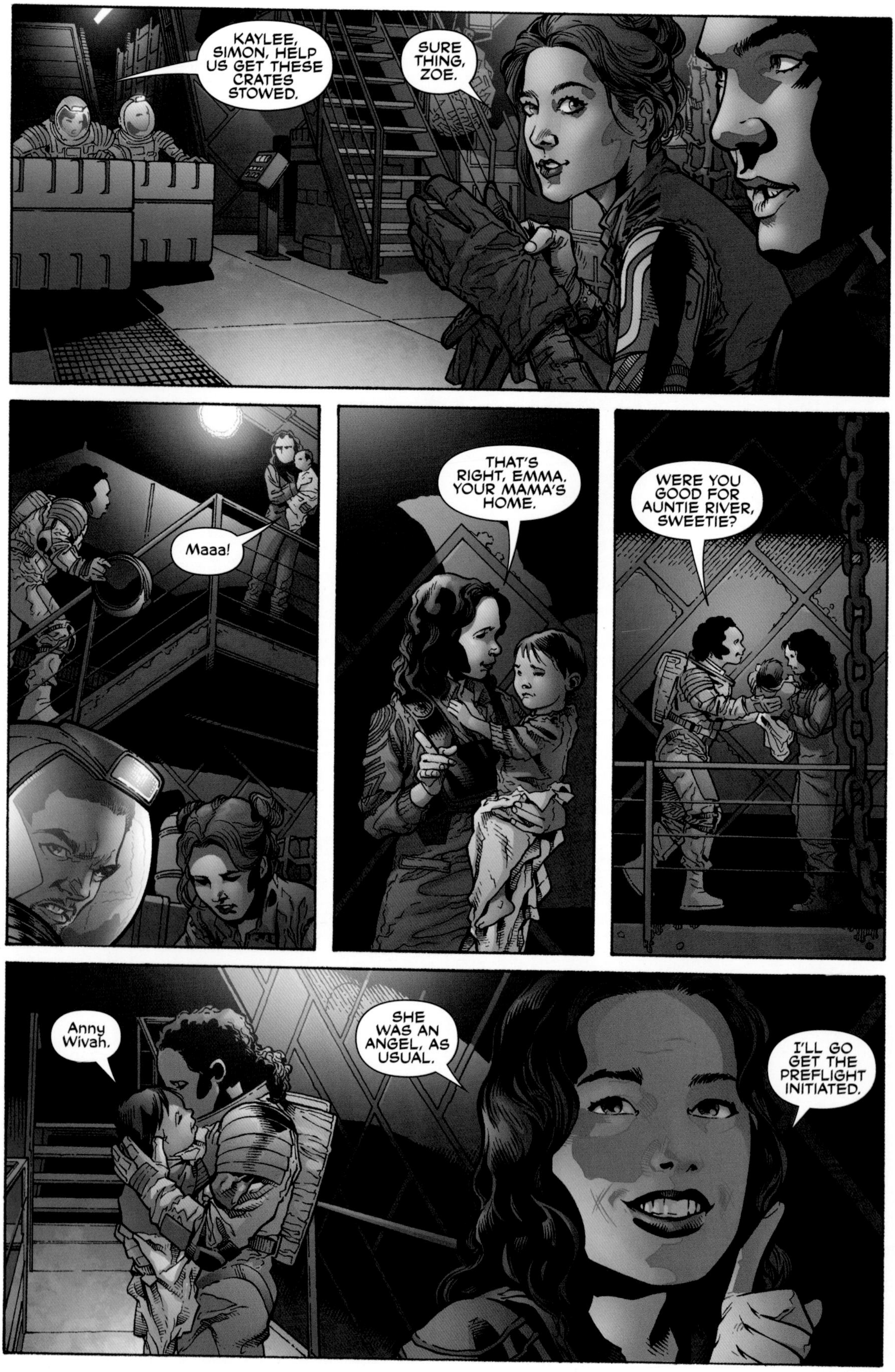
KAYLEE, SIMON, HELP US GET THESE CRATES STOWED.
SURE THING, ZOE.
Maaa!
THAT'S RIGHT, EMMA. YOUR MAMA'S HOME.
WERE YOU GOOD FOR AUNTIE RIVER, SWEETIE?
Anny Wivah.
SHE WAS AN ANGEL, AS USUAL.
I'LL GO GET THE PREFLIGHT INITIATED.

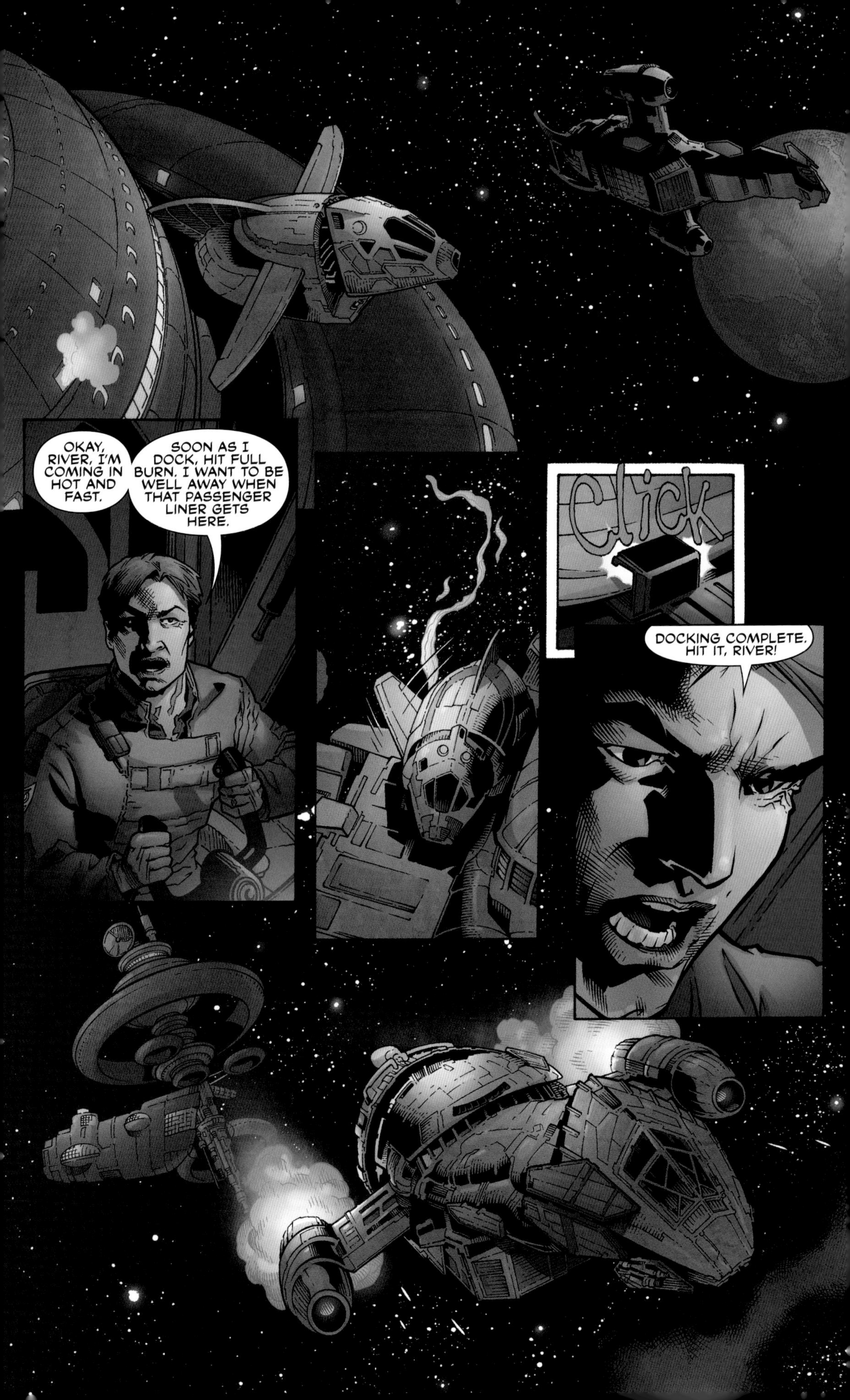
OKAY, RIVER, I'M COMING IN HOT AND FAST.
SOON AS I DOCK, HIT FULL BURN. I WANT TO BE WELL AWAY WHEN THAT PASSENGER LINER GETS HERE.
CLICK
DOCKING COMPLETE. HIT IT, RIVER!

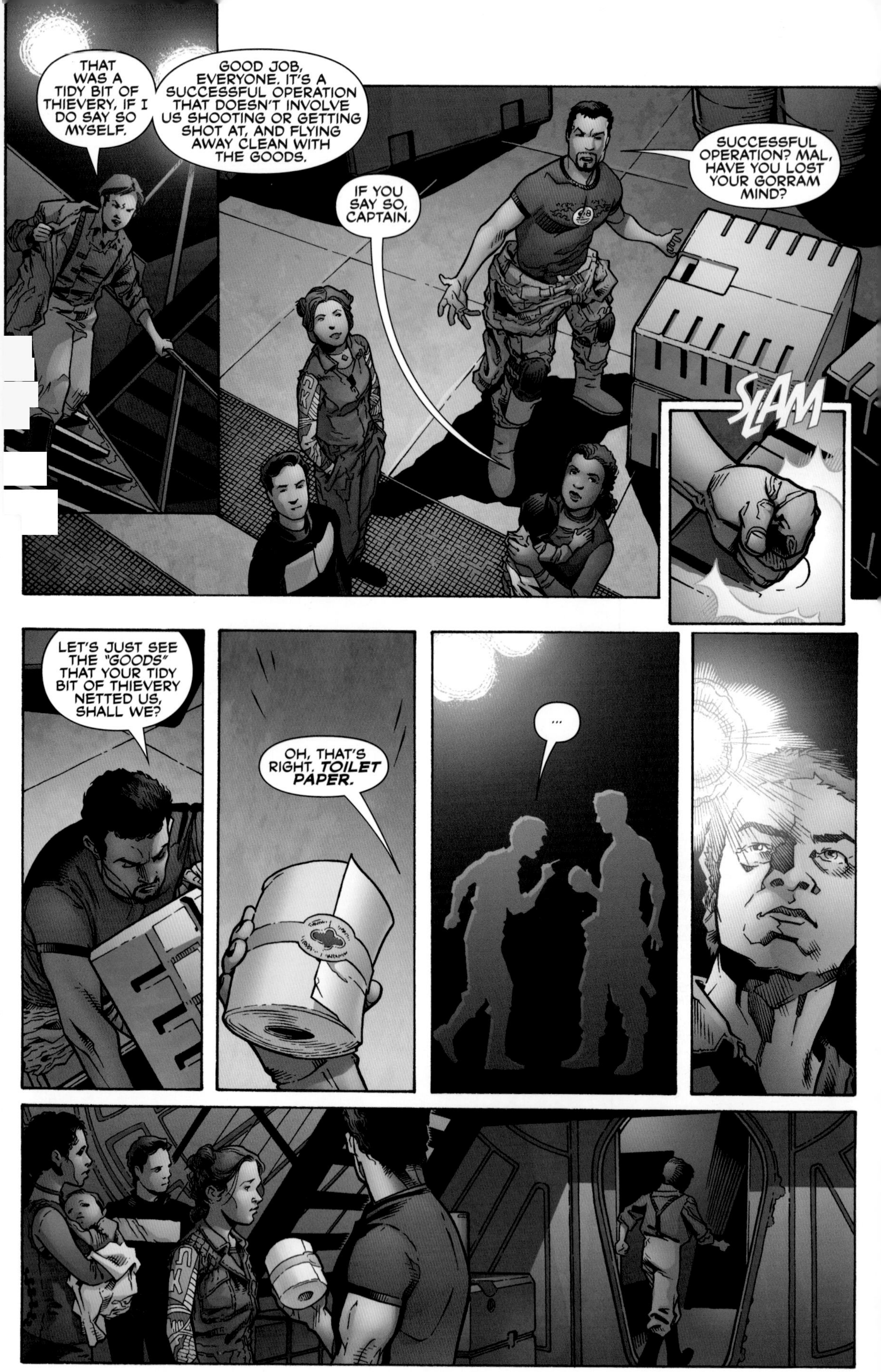

THAT WAS A TIDY BIT OF THIEVERY, IF I DO SAY SO MYSELF.
GOOD JOB, EVERYONE. IT'S A SUCCESSFUL OPERATION THAT DOESN'T INVOLVE US SHOOTING OR GETTING SHOT AT, AND FLYING AWAY CLEAN WITH THE GOODS.
IF YOU SAY SO, CAPTAIN.
SUCCESSFUL OPERATION? MAL, HAVE YOU LOST YOUR GORRAM MIND?
SLAM
LET'S JUST SEE THE "GOODS" THAT YOUR TIDY BIT OF THIEVERY NETTED US, SHALL WE?
OH, THAT'S RIGHT. TOILET PAPER.
...

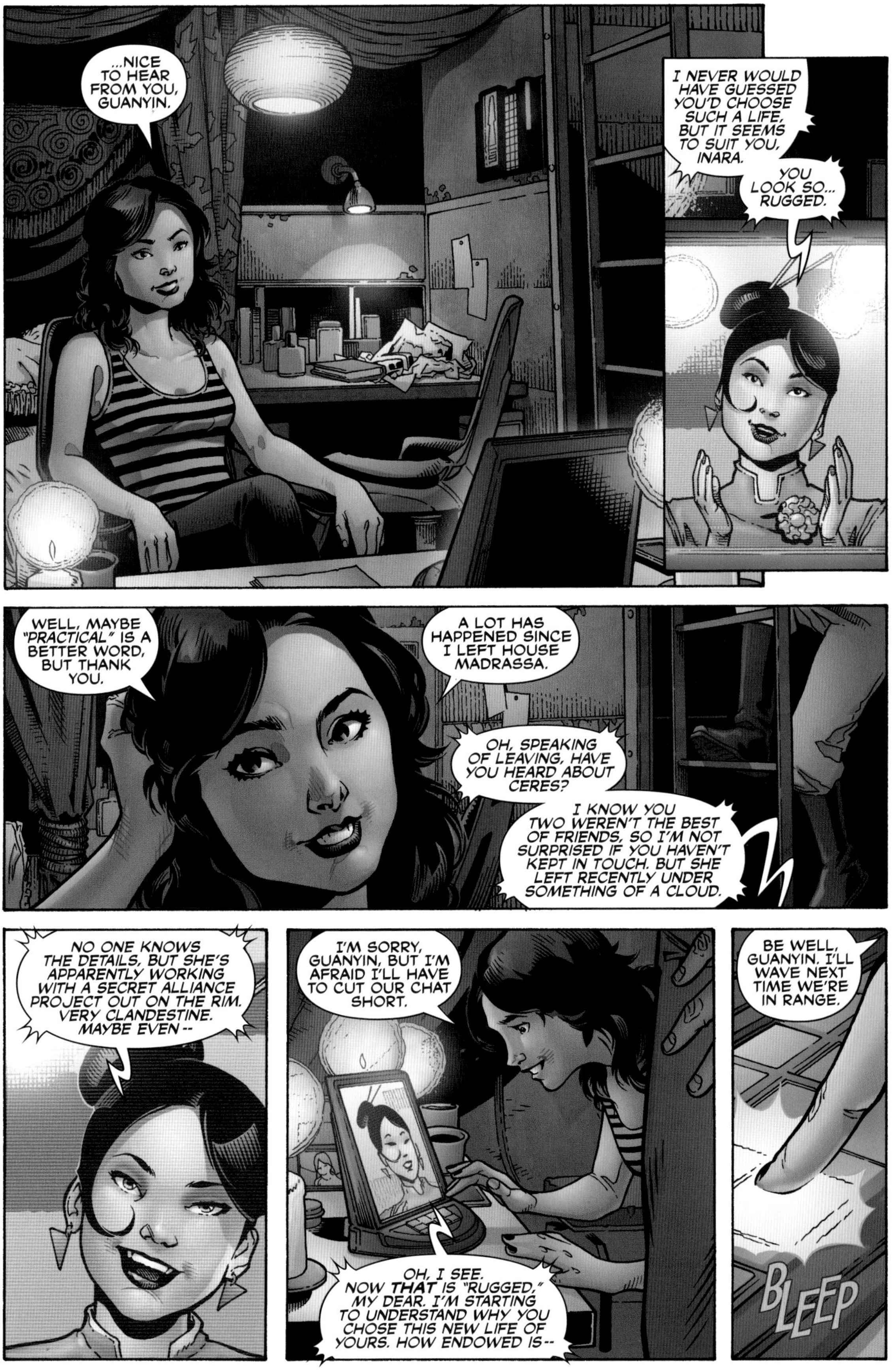

...NICE TO HEAR FROM YOU, GUANYIN.
I NEVER WOULD HAVE GUESSED YOU'D CHOOSE SUCH A LIFE, BUT IT SEEMS TO SUIT YOU, INARA.
YOU LOOK SO... RUGGED.
WELL, MAYBE "PRACTICAL" IS A BETTER WORD, BUT THANK YOU.
A LOT HAS HAPPENED SINCE I LEFT HOUSE MADRASSA.
OH, SPEAKING OF LEAVING, HAVE YOU HEARD ABOUT CERES?
I KNOW YOU TWO WEREN'T THE BEST OF FRIENDS, SO I'M NOT SURPRISED IF YOU HAVEN'T KEPT IN TOUCH. BUT SHE LEFT RECENTLY UNDER SOMETHING OF A CLOUD.
NO ONE KNOWS THE DETAILS, BUT SHE'S APPARENTLY WORKING WITH A SECRET ALLIANCE PROJECT OUT ON THE RIM. VERY CLANDESTINE. MAYBE EVEN --
I'M SORRY, GUANYIN, BUT I'M AFRAID I'LL HAVE TO CUT OUR CHAT SHORT.
OH, I SEE. NOW THAT IS "RUGGED," MY DEAR. I'M STARTING TO UNDERSTAND WHY YOU CHOSE THIS NEW LIFE OF YOURS. HOW ENDOWED IS --
BE WELL, GUANYIN. I'LL WAVE NEXT TIME WE'RE IN RANGE.
BLEEP

DIDN'T MEAN TO INTERRUPT. WHAT WAS THAT ABOUT "ENDOWED"?

OH, NOTHING. JUST TALKING TO AN OLD FRIEND BACK ON SIHNON.

HOW DID THE JOB GO?

A ROUSING SUCCESS. WE SHOULD BE ABLE TO UNLOAD THE GOODS WITHOUT TROUBLE NEXT RIM WORLD WE HIT.

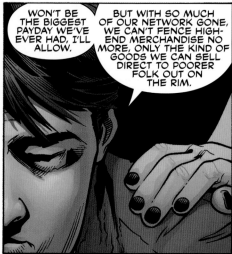

WON'T BE THE BIGGEST PAYDAY WE'VE EVER HAD, I'LL ALLOW.

BUT WITH SO MUCH OF OUR NETWORK GONE, WE CAN'T FENCE HIGH-END MERCHANDISE NO MORE, ONLY THE KIND OF GOODS WE CAN SELL DIRECT TO POORER FOLK OUT ON THE RIM.

LIKE TOILET PAPER?

EVERYBODY'S GOT TO WIPE, AND THERE'S MANY WHO'LL PAY FOR THE PRIVILEGE.

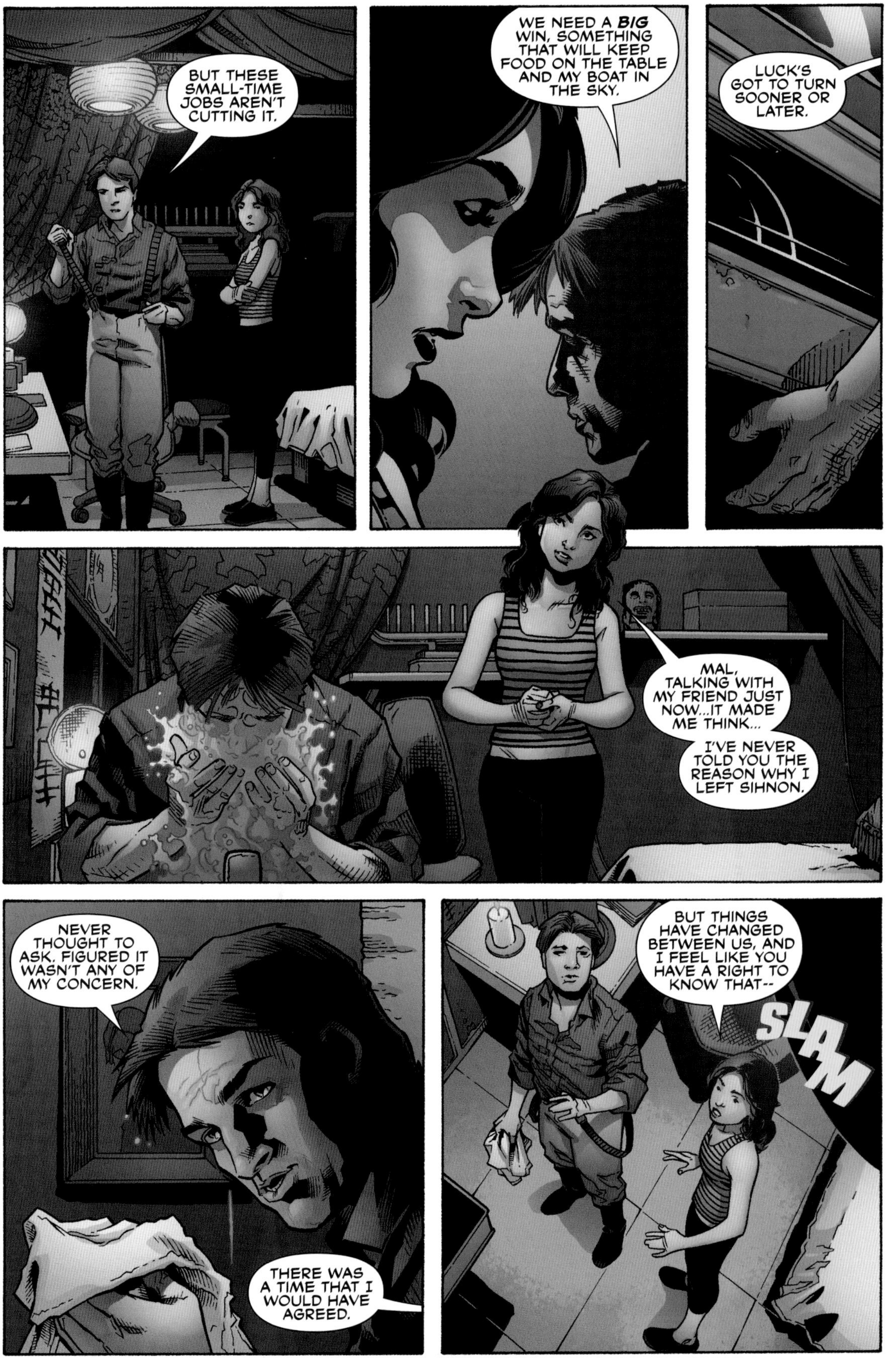
BUT THESE SMALL-TIME JOBS AREN'T CUTTING IT.
WE NEED A *BIG* WIN, SOMETHING THAT WILL KEEP FOOD ON THE TABLE AND MY BOAT IN THE SKY.
LUCK'S GOT TO TURN SOONER OR LATER.
MAL, TALKING WITH MY FRIEND JUST NOW...IT MADE ME THINK...
I'VE NEVER TOLD YOU THE REASON WHY I LEFT SIHNON.
NEVER THOUGHT TO ASK. FIGURED IT WASN'T ANY OF MY CONCERN.
THERE WAS A TIME THAT I WOULD HAVE AGREED.
BUT THINGS HAVE CHANGED BETWEEN US, AND I FEEL LIKE YOU HAVE A RIGHT TO KNOW THAT--
SLAM

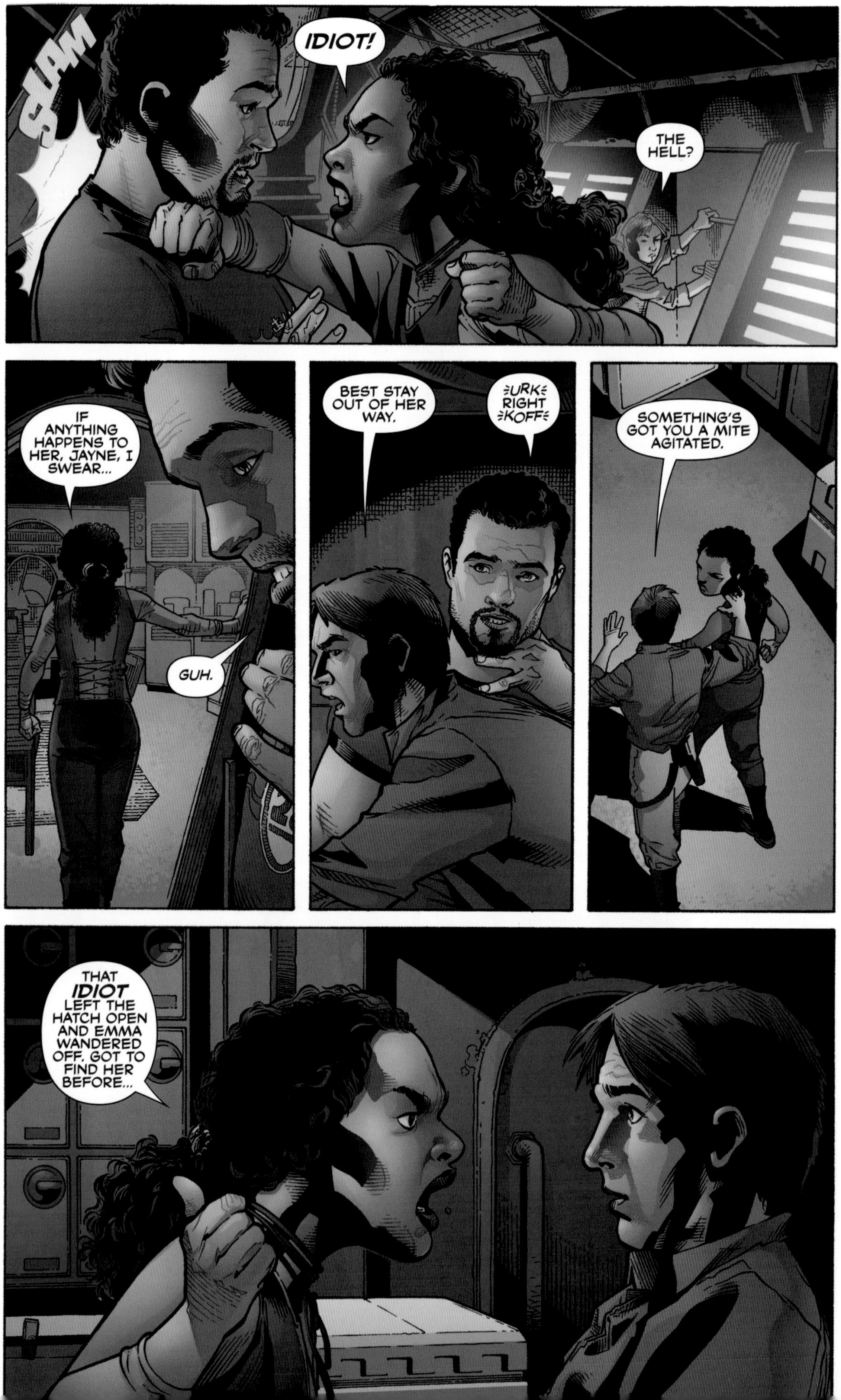
SLAM
IDIOT!
THE HELL?
IF ANYTHING HAPPENS TO HER, JAYNE, I SWEAR...
GUH.
BEST STAY OUT OF HER WAY.
URK RIGHT KOFF
SOMETHING'S GOT YOU A MITE AGITATED.
THAT IDIOT LEFT THE HATCH OPEN AND EMMA WANDERED OFF. GOT TO FIND HER BEFORE...

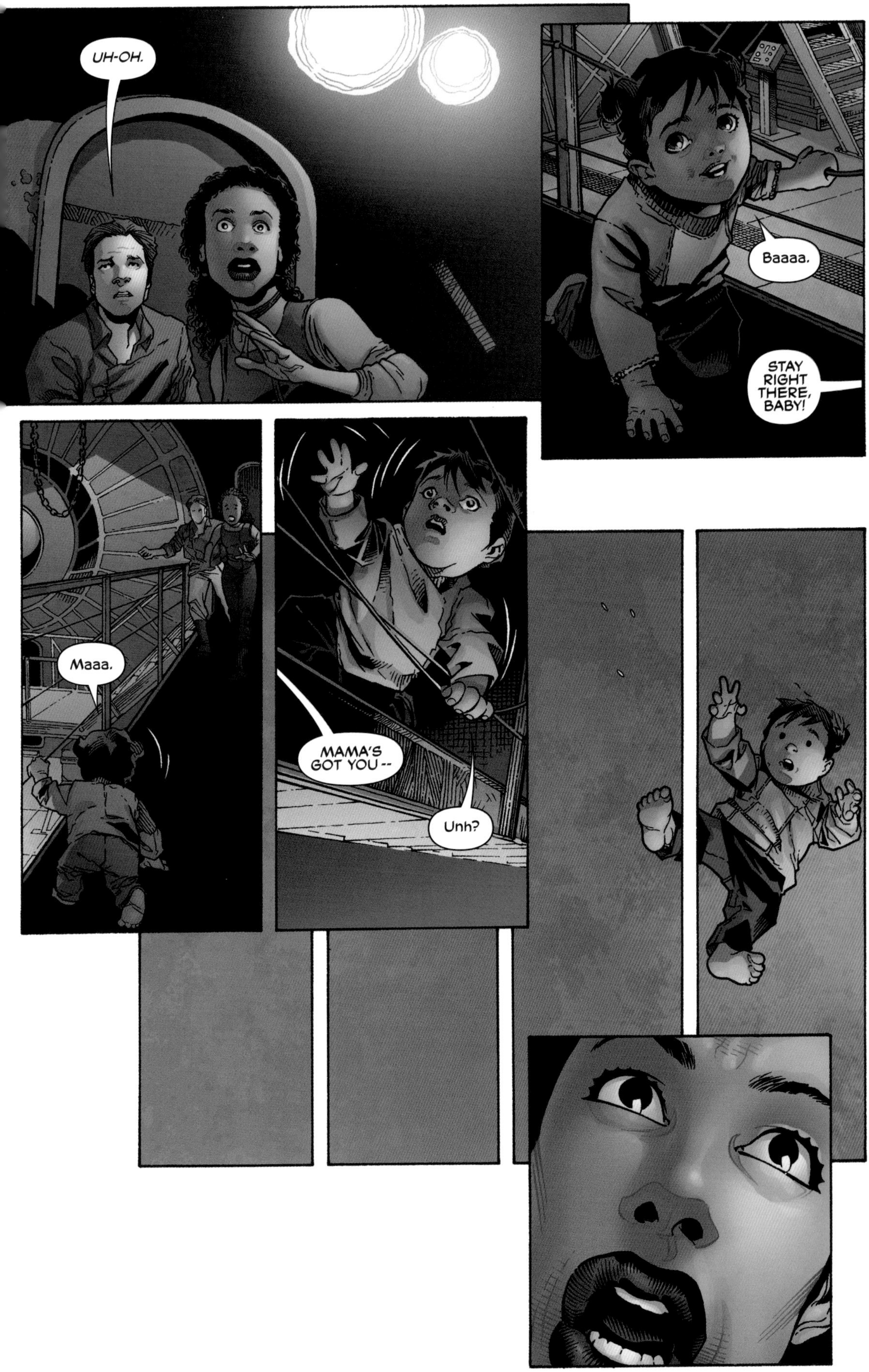
UH-OH.
Baaaa.
STAY RIGHT THERE, BABY!
Maaa.
MAMA'S GOT YOU --
Unh?

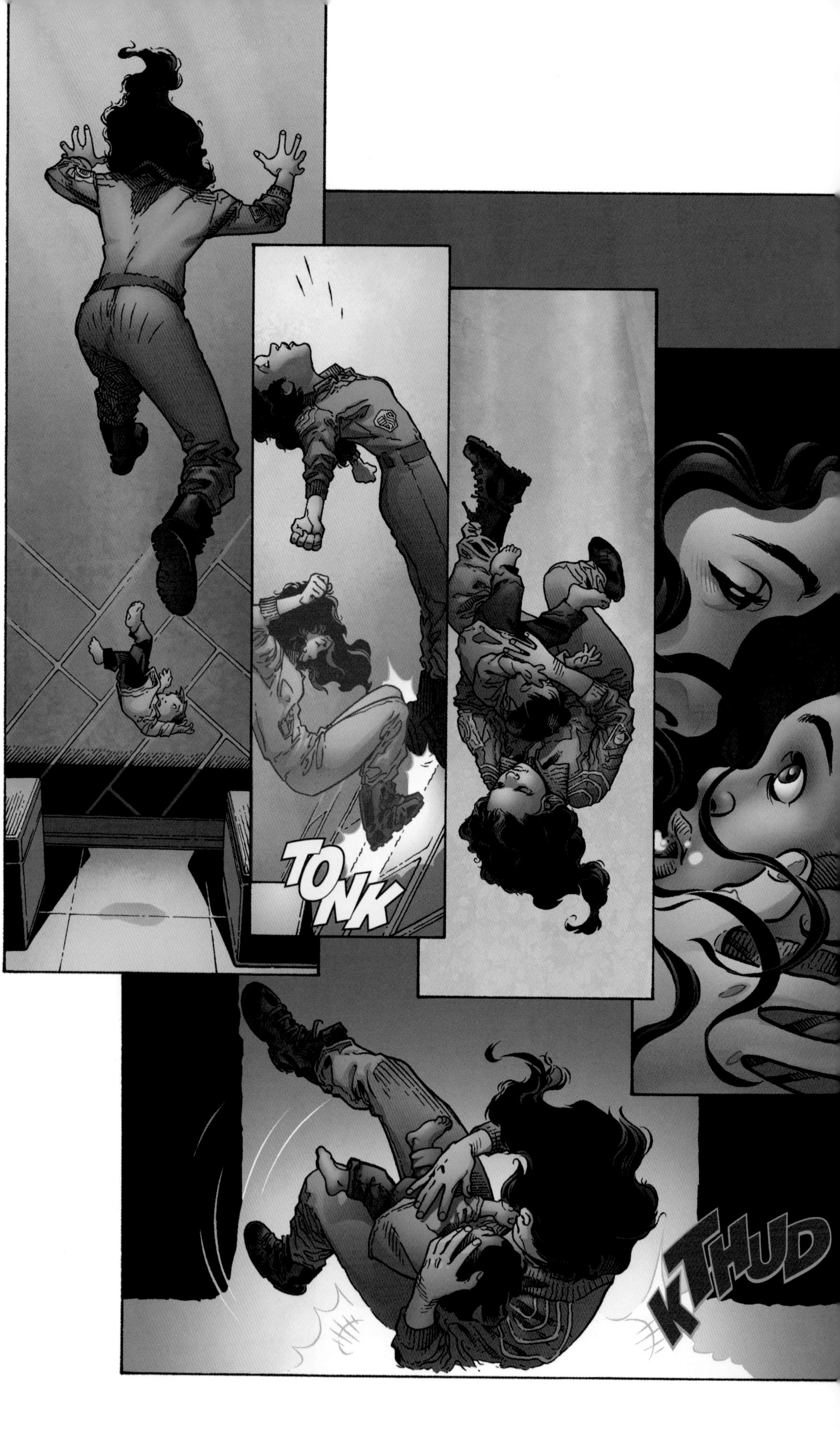
TONK
KTHUD

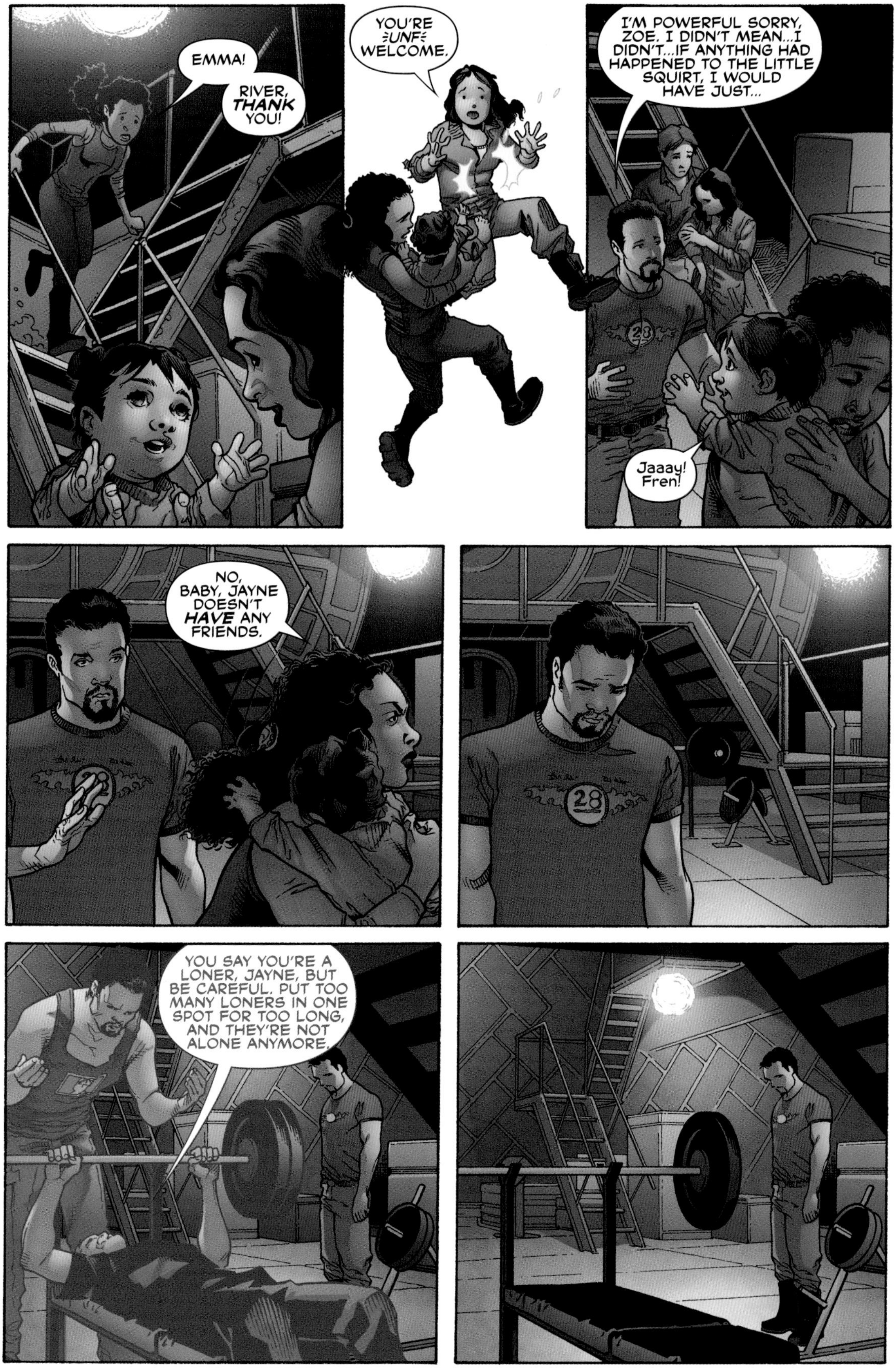

EMMA!
RIVER, THANK YOU!
YOU'RE UNF WELCOME.
I'M POWERFUL SORRY, ZOE. I DIDN'T MEAN...I DIDN'T...IF ANYTHING HAD HAPPENED TO THE LITTLE SQUIRT, I WOULD HAVE JUST...
Jaaay! Fren!
NO, BABY, JAYNE DOESN'T HAVE ANY FRIENDS.
YOU SAY YOU'RE A LONER, JAYNE, BUT BE CAREFUL. PUT TOO MANY LONERS IN ONE SPOT FOR TOO LONG, AND THEY'RE NOT ALONE ANYMORE.

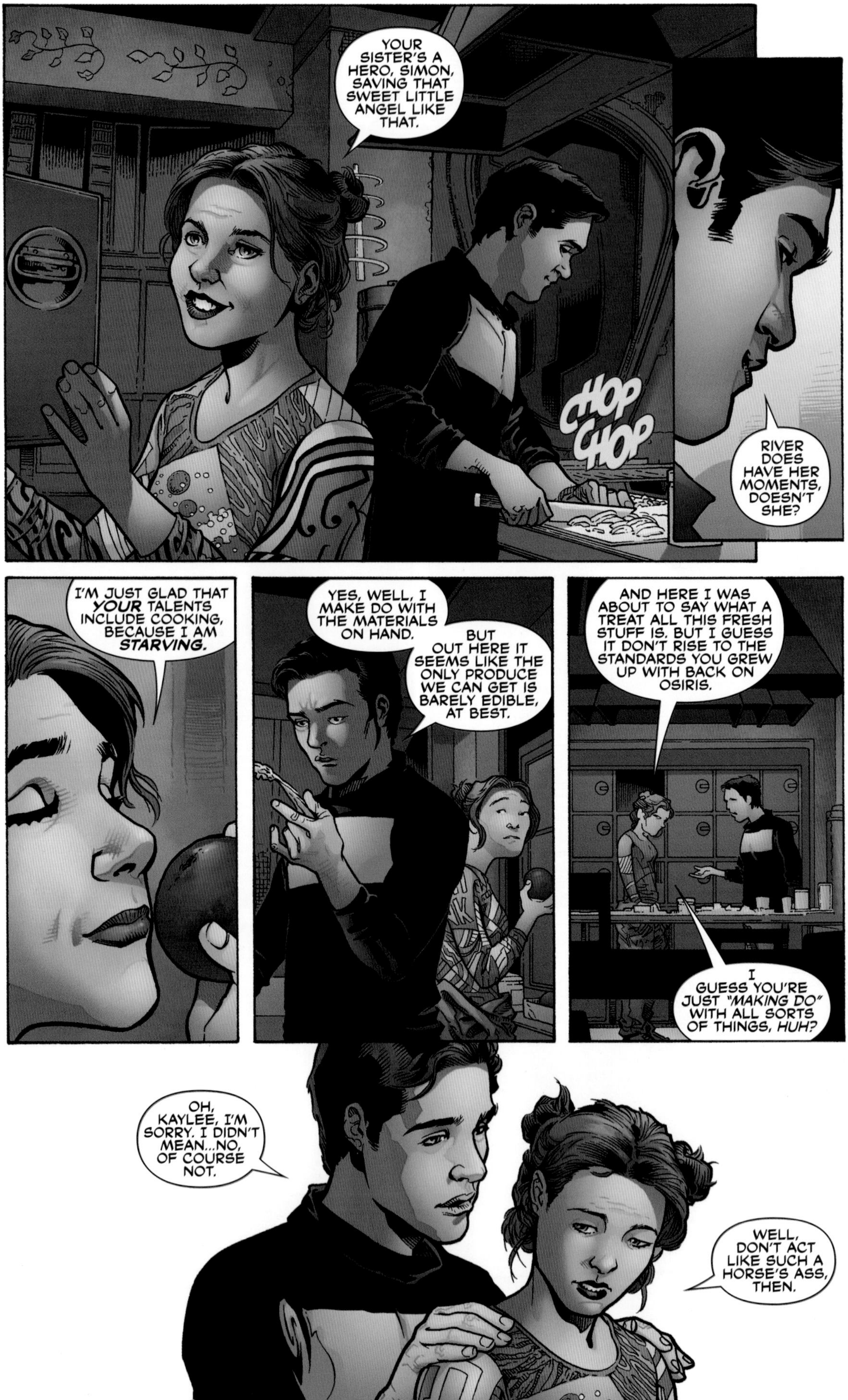
YOUR SISTER'S A HERO, SIMON, SAVING THAT SWEET LITTLE ANGEL LIKE THAT.
CHOP CHOP
RIVER DOES HAVE HER MOMENTS, DOESN'T SHE?
I'M JUST GLAD THAT YOUR TALENTS INCLUDE COOKING, BECAUSE I AM STARVING.
YES, WELL, I MAKE DO WITH THE MATERIALS ON HAND.
BUT OUT HERE IT SEEMS LIKE THE ONLY PRODUCE WE CAN GET IS BARELY EDIBLE, AT BEST.
AND HERE I WAS ABOUT TO SAY WHAT A TREAT ALL THIS FRESH STUFF IS. BUT I GUESS IT DON'T RISE TO THE STANDARDS YOU GREW UP WITH BACK ON OSIRIS.
I GUESS YOU'RE JUST "MAKING DO" WITH ALL SORTS OF THINGS, HUH?
OH, KAYLEE, I'M SORRY. I DIDN'T MEAN...NO, OF COURSE NOT.
WELL, DON'T ACT LIKE SUCH A HORSE'S ASS, THEN.

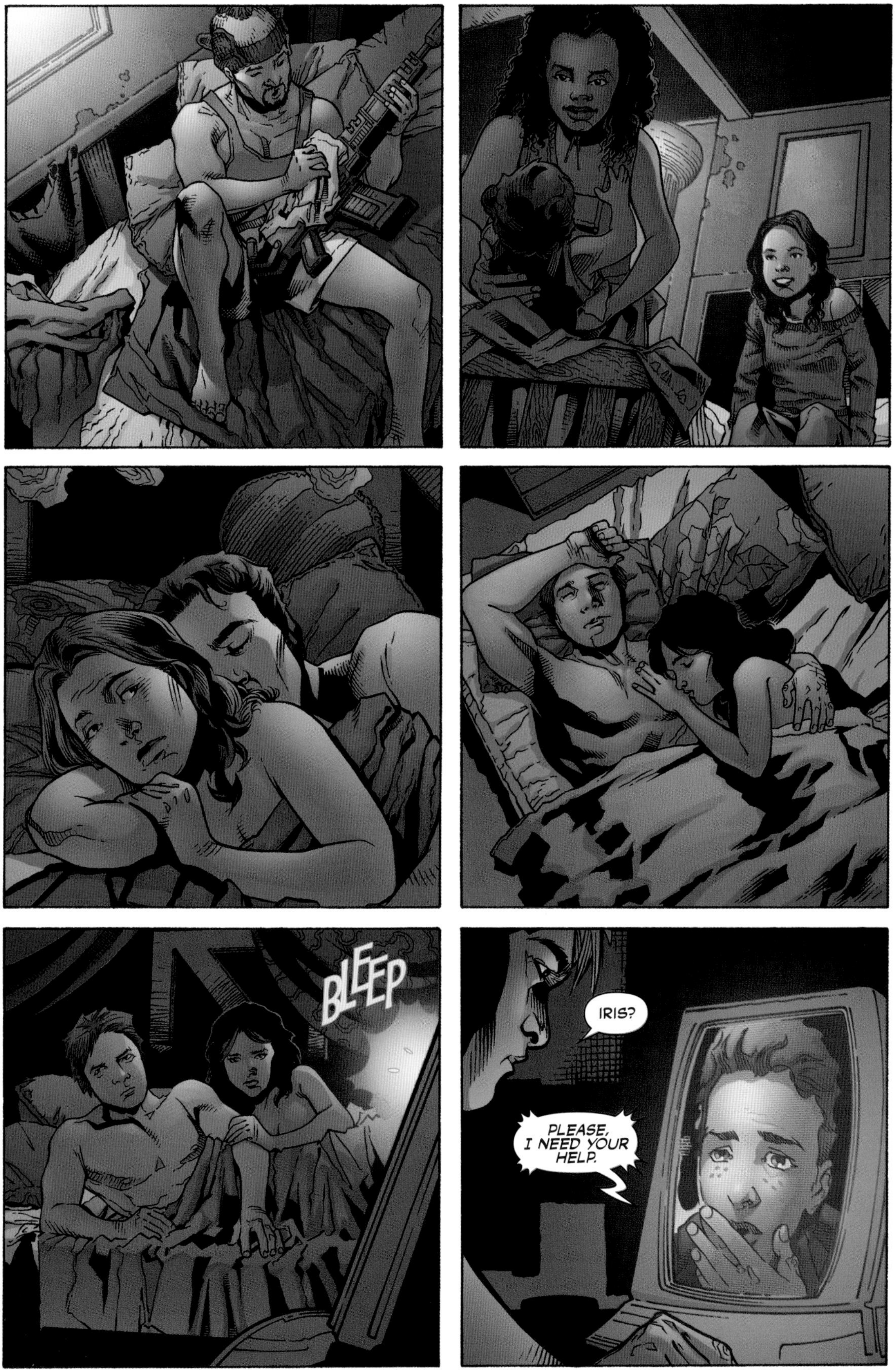
BLEEP
IRIS?
PLEASE, I NEED YOUR HELP.

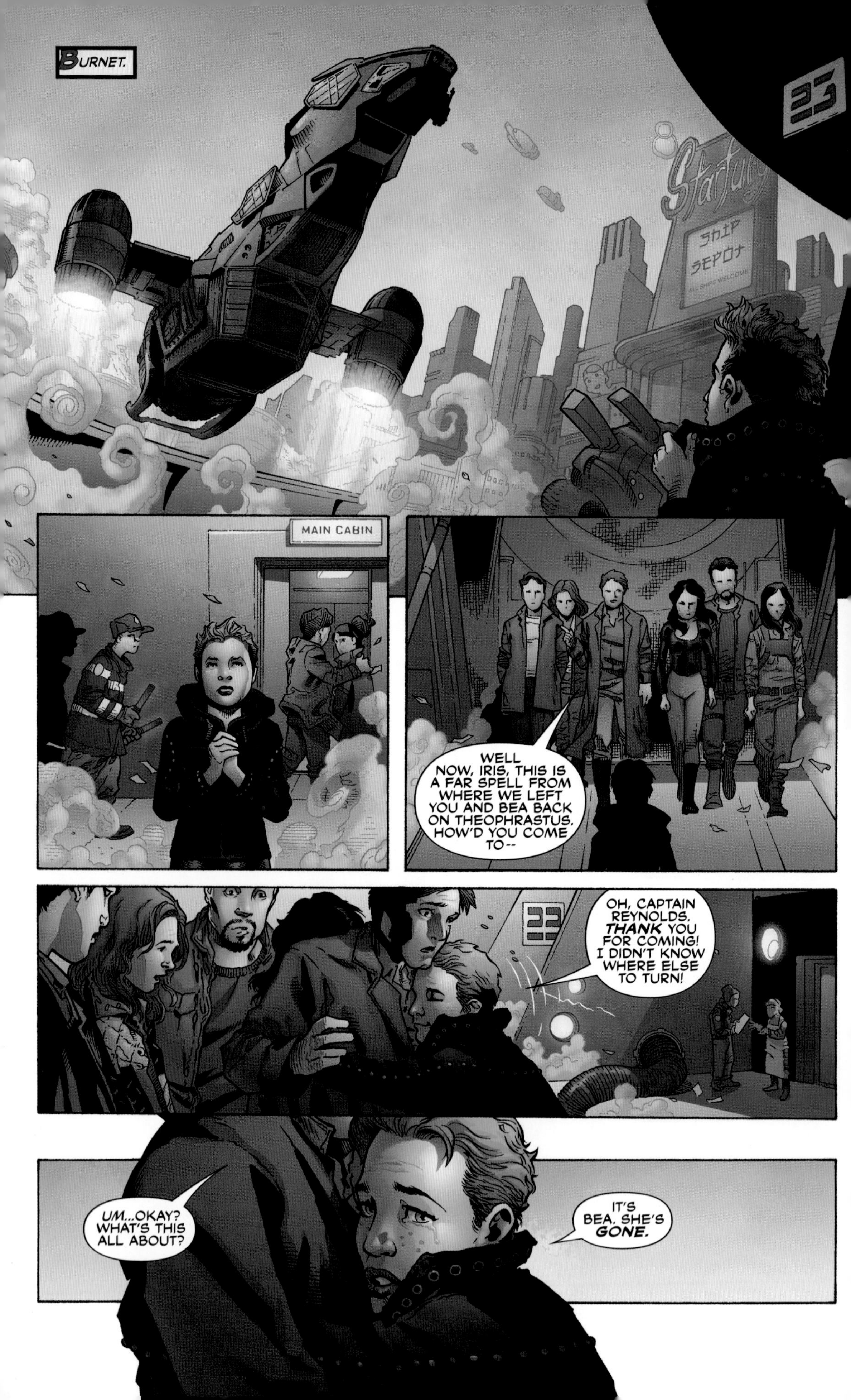

BURNET.
23
Starfly
SHIP DEPOT
ALL SHIPS WELCOME
MAIN CABIN
WELL NOW, IRIS, THIS IS A FAR SPELL FROM WHERE WE LEFT YOU AND BEA BACK ON THEOPHRASTUS. HOW'D YOU COME TO--
23
OH, CAPTAIN REYNOLDS. THANK YOU FOR COMING! I DIDN'T KNOW WHERE ELSE TO TURN!
UM...OKAY? WHAT'S THIS ALL ABOUT?
IT'S BEA. SHE'S GONE.

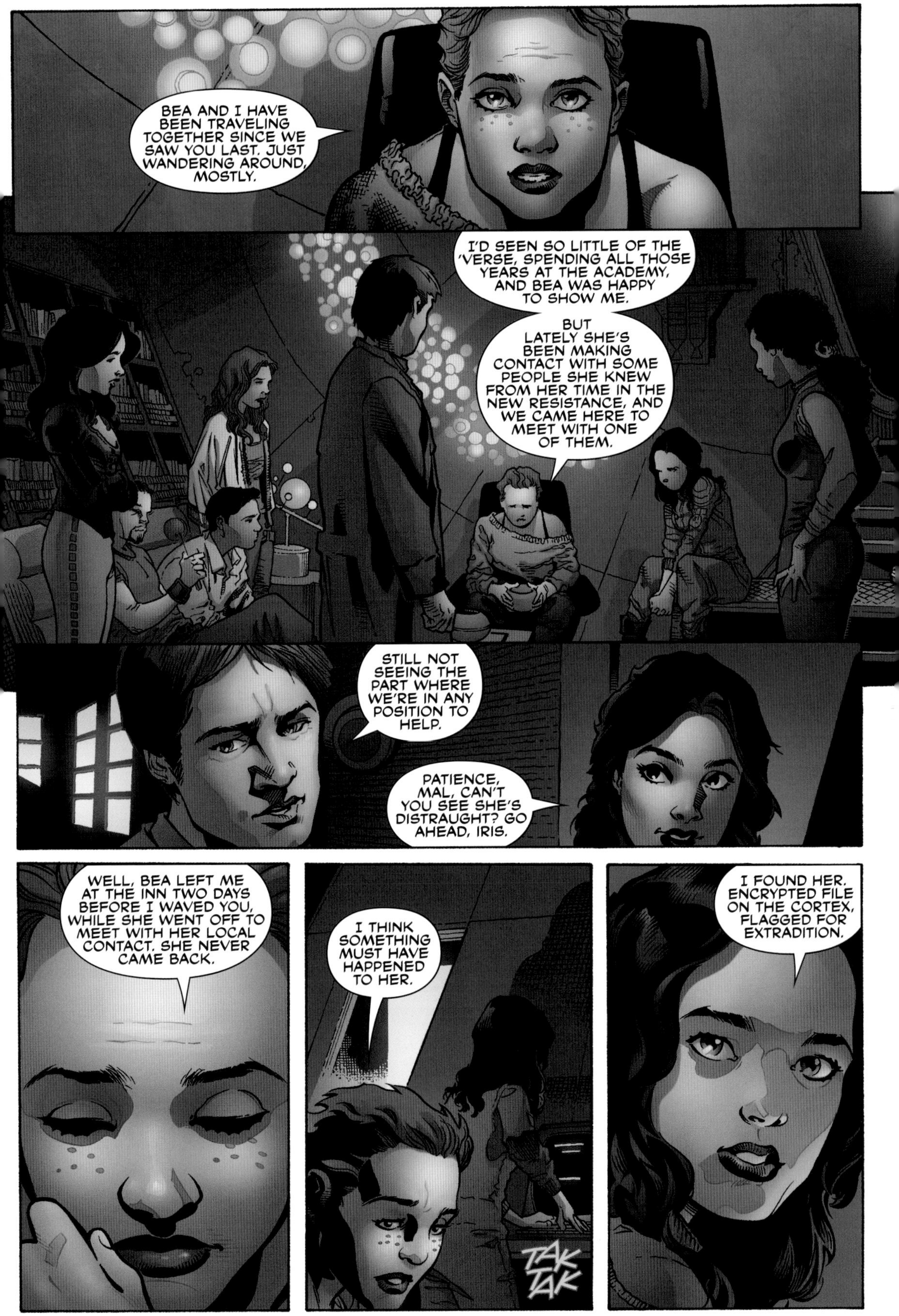
BEA AND I HAVE BEEN TRAVELING TOGETHER SINCE WE SAW YOU LAST. JUST WANDERING AROUND, MOSTLY.
I'D SEEN SO LITTLE OF THE 'VERSE, SPENDING ALL THOSE YEARS AT THE ACADEMY, AND BEA WAS HAPPY TO SHOW ME.
BUT LATELY SHE'S BEEN MAKING CONTACT WITH SOME PEOPLE SHE KNEW FROM HER TIME IN THE NEW RESISTANCE, AND WE CAME HERE TO MEET WITH ONE OF THEM.
STILL NOT SEEING THE PART WHERE WE'RE IN ANY POSITION TO HELP.
PATIENCE, MAL, CAN'T YOU SEE SHE'S DISTRAUGHT? GO AHEAD, IRIS.
WELL, BEA LEFT ME AT THE INN TWO DAYS BEFORE I WAVED YOU, WHILE SHE WENT OFF TO MEET WITH HER LOCAL CONTACT. SHE NEVER CAME BACK.
I THINK SOMETHING MUST HAVE HAPPENED TO HER.
TAK TAK
I FOUND HER. ENCRYPTED FILE ON THE CORTEX, FLAGGED FOR EXTRADITION.

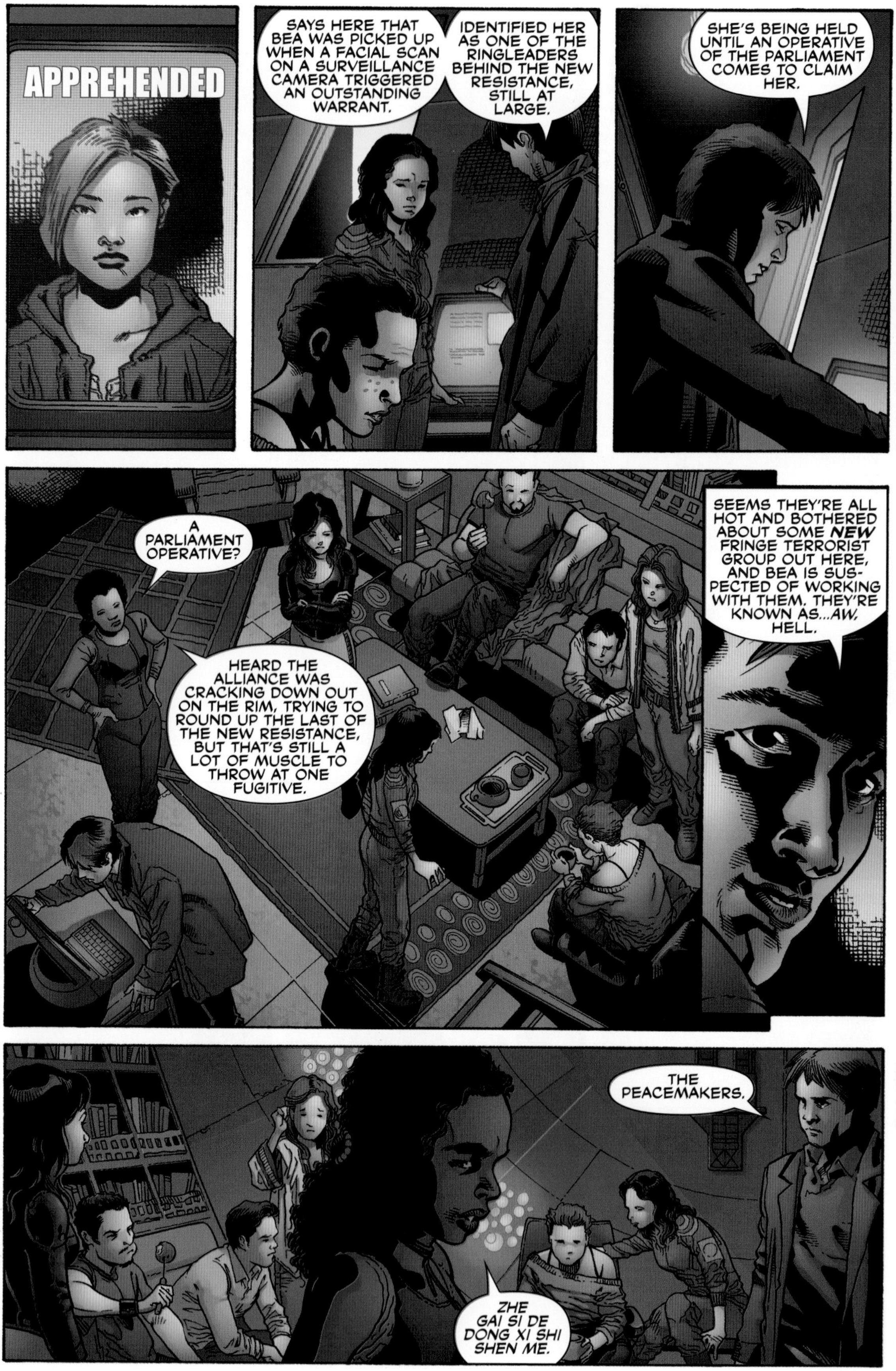
APPREHENDED
SAYS HERE THAT BEA WAS PICKED UP WHEN A FACIAL SCAN ON A SURVEILLANCE CAMERA TRIGGERED AN OUTSTANDING WARRANT.
IDENTIFIED HER AS ONE OF THE RINGLEADERS BEHIND THE NEW RESISTANCE, STILL AT LARGE.
SHE'S BEING HELD UNTIL AN OPERATIVE OF THE PARLIAMENT COMES TO CLAIM HER.
A PARLIAMENT OPERATIVE?
HEARD THE ALLIANCE WAS CRACKING DOWN OUT ON THE RIM, TRYING TO ROUND UP THE LAST OF THE NEW RESISTANCE, BUT THAT'S STILL A LOT OF MUSCLE TO THROW AT ONE FUGITIVE.
SEEMS THEY'RE ALL HOT AND BOTHERED ABOUT SOME *NEW* FRINGE TERRORIST GROUP OUT HERE, AND BEA IS SUSPECTED OF WORKING WITH THEM. THEY'RE KNOWN AS...*AW*, HELL.
THE PEACEMAKERS.
ZHE GAI SI DE DONG XI SHI SHEN ME.

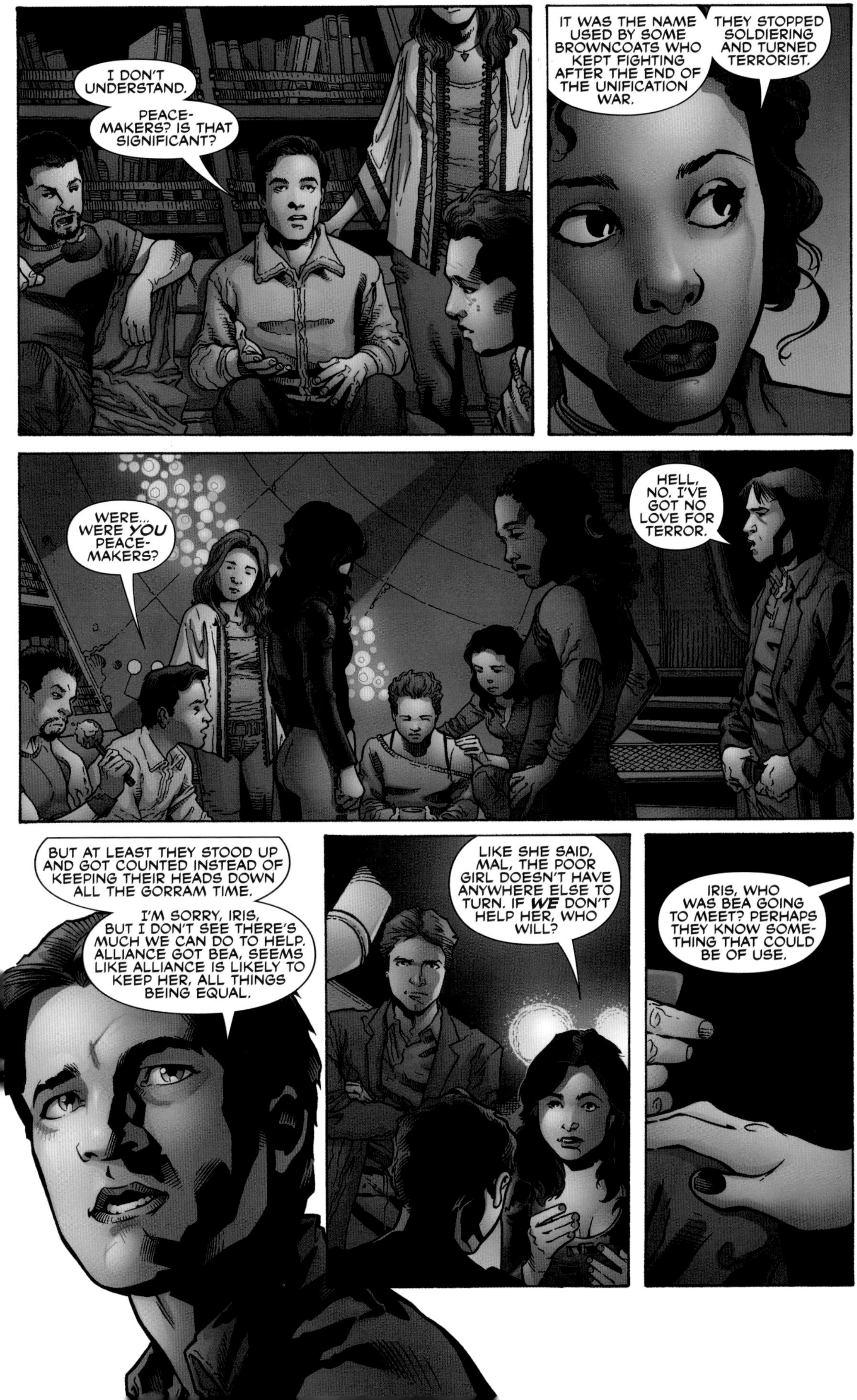

I DON'T UNDERSTAND.
PEACE-MAKERS? IS THAT SIGNIFICANT?
IT WAS THE NAME USED BY SOME BROWNCOATS WHO KEPT FIGHTING AFTER THE END OF THE UNIFICATION WAR.
THEY STOPPED SOLDIERING AND TURNED TERRORIST.
WERE... WERE *YOU* PEACE-MAKERS?
HELL, NO. I'VE GOT NO LOVE FOR TERROR.
BUT AT LEAST THEY STOOD UP AND GOT COUNTED INSTEAD OF KEEPING THEIR HEADS DOWN ALL THE GORRAM TIME.
I'M SORRY, IRIS, BUT I DON'T SEE THERE'S MUCH WE CAN DO TO HELP. ALLIANCE GOT BEA, SEEMS LIKE ALLIANCE IS LIKELY TO KEEP HER, ALL THINGS BEING EQUAL.
LIKE SHE SAID, MAL, THE POOR GIRL DOESN'T HAVE ANYWHERE ELSE TO TURN. IF *WE* DON'T HELP HER, WHO WILL?
IRIS, WHO WAS BEA GOING TO MEET? PERHAPS THEY KNOW SOME-THING THAT COULD BE OF USE.

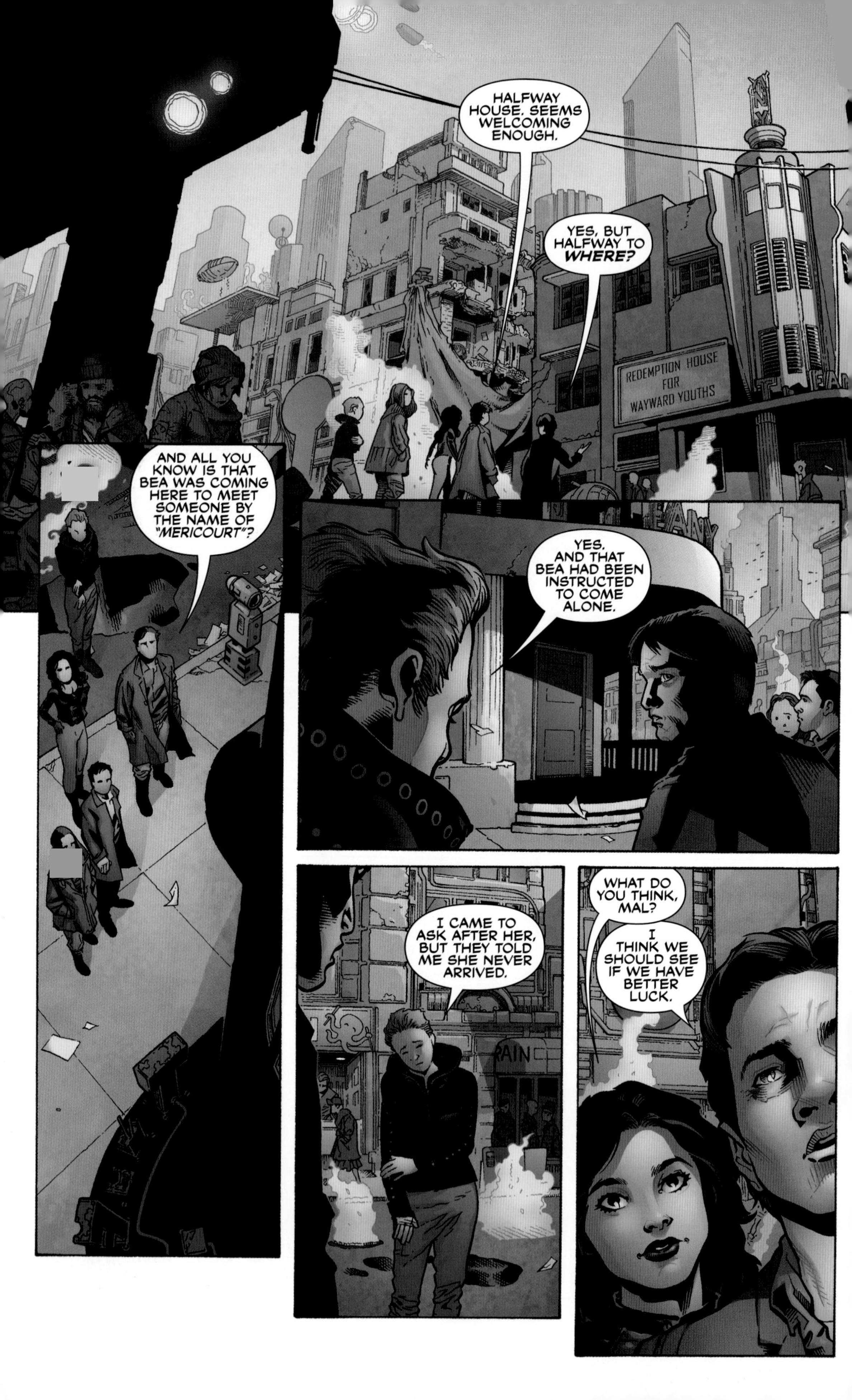
HALFWAY HOUSE. SEEMS WELCOMING ENOUGH.
YES, BUT HALFWAY TO ***WHERE?***
REDEMPTION HOUSE FOR WAYWARD YOUTHS
AND ALL YOU KNOW IS THAT BEA WAS COMING HERE TO MEET SOMEONE BY THE NAME OF *"MERICOURT"*?
YES. AND THAT BEA HAD BEEN INSTRUCTED TO COME ALONE.
I CAME TO ASK AFTER HER, BUT THEY TOLD ME SHE NEVER ARRIVED.
WHAT DO YOU THINK, MAL?
I THINK WE SHOULD SEE IF WE HAVE BETTER LUCK.

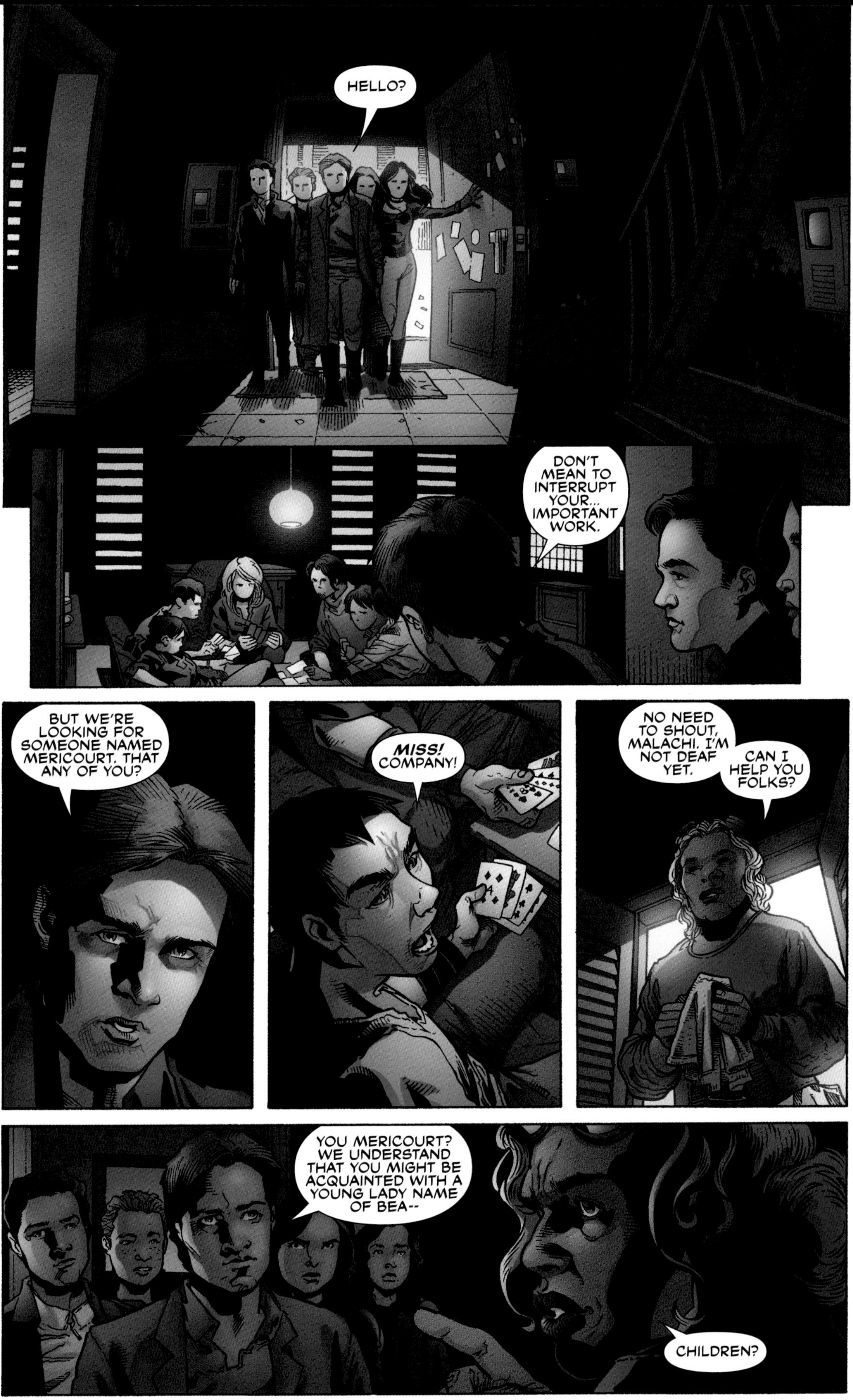
HELLO?
DON'T MEAN TO INTERRUPT YOUR... IMPORTANT WORK.
BUT WE'RE LOOKING FOR SOMEONE NAMED MERICOURT. THAT ANY OF YOU?
MISS! COMPANY!
NO NEED TO SHOUT, MALACHI. I'M NOT DEAF YET.
CAN I HELP YOU FOLKS?
YOU MERICOURT? WE UNDERSTAND THAT YOU MIGHT BE ACQUAINTED WITH A YOUNG LADY NAME OF BEA--
CHILDREN?

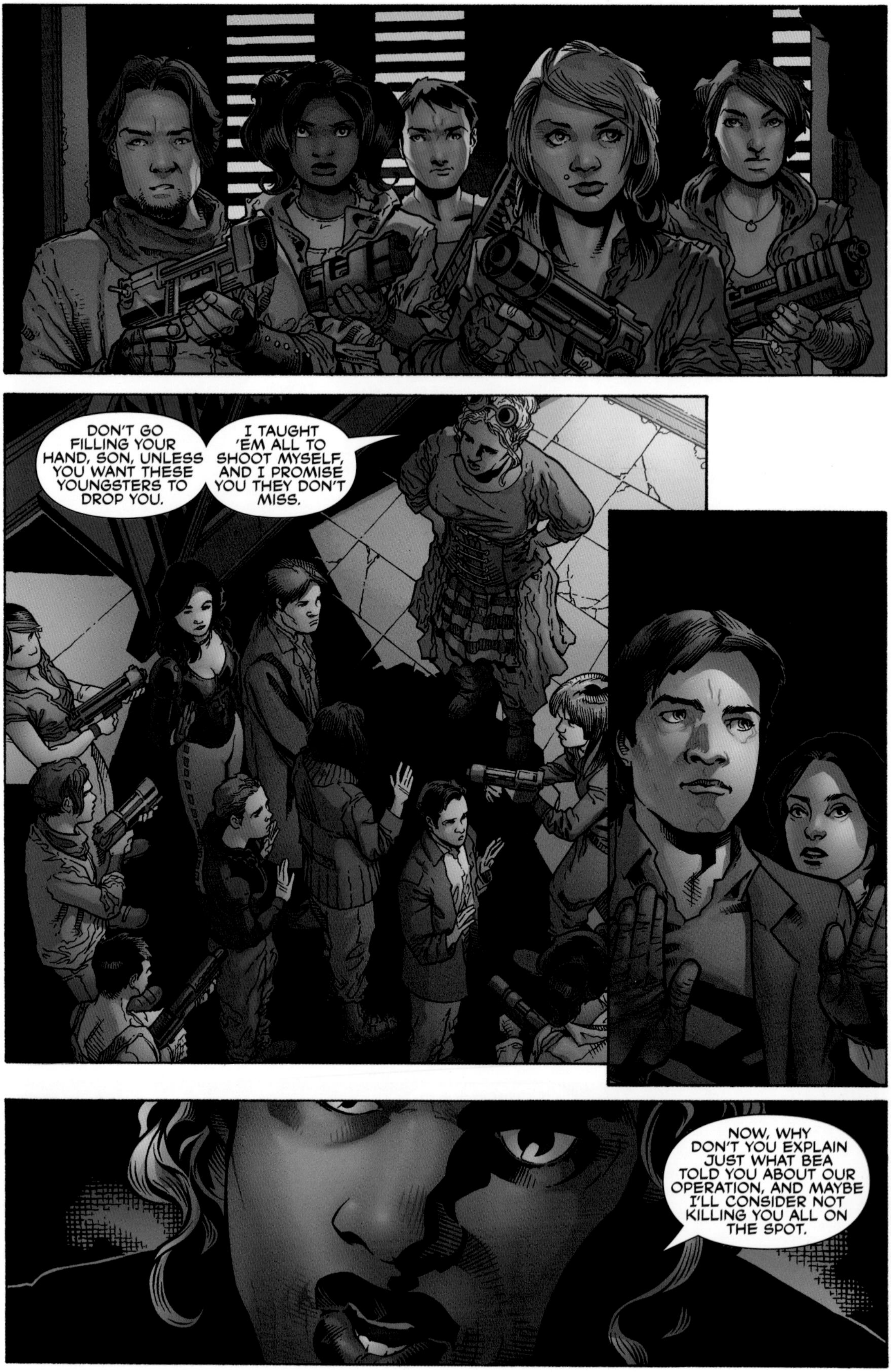

DON'T GO FILLING YOUR HAND, SON, UNLESS YOU WANT THESE YOUNGSTERS TO DROP YOU.
I TAUGHT 'EM ALL TO SHOOT MYSELF, AND I PROMISE YOU THEY DON'T MISS.
NOW, WHY DON'T YOU EXPLAIN JUST WHAT BEA TOLD YOU ABOUT OUR OPERATION, AND MAYBE I'LL CONSIDER NOT KILLING YOU ALL ON THE SPOT.

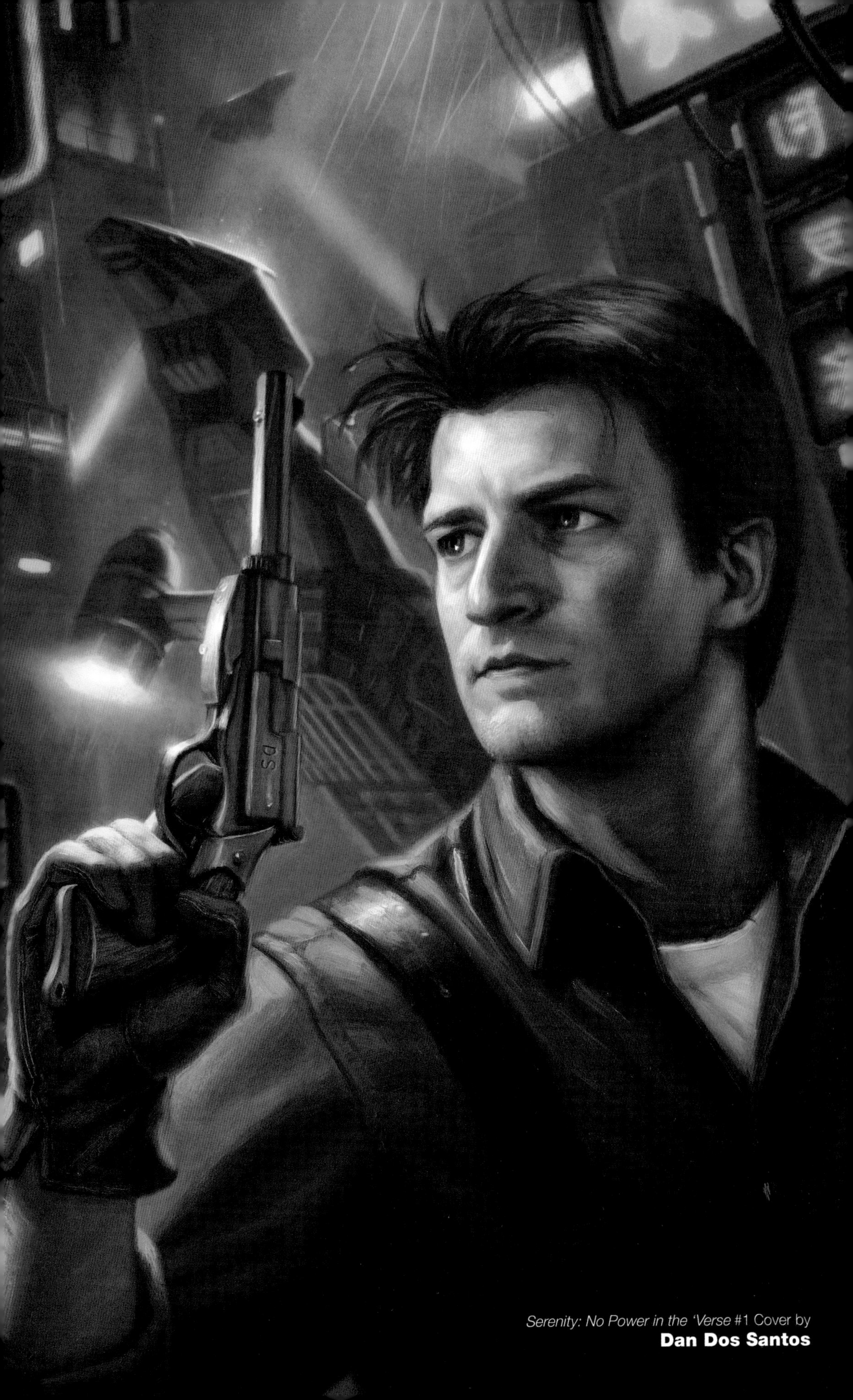
DS

Serenity: No Power in the 'Verse #1 Cover by
Dan Dos Santos

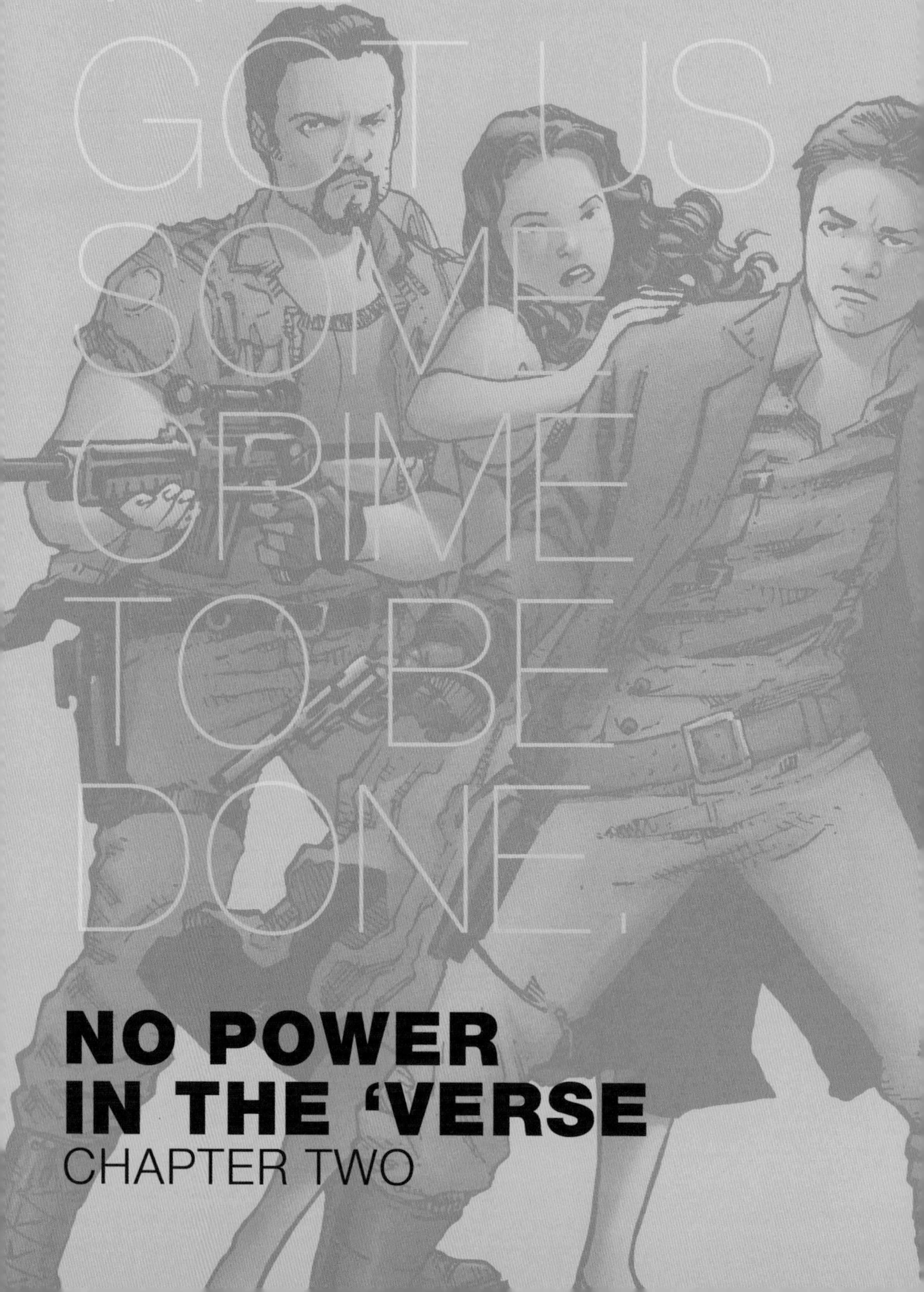

WE GOT US SOME CRIME TO BE DONE.

NO POWER IN THE ‘VERSE

CHAPTER TWO

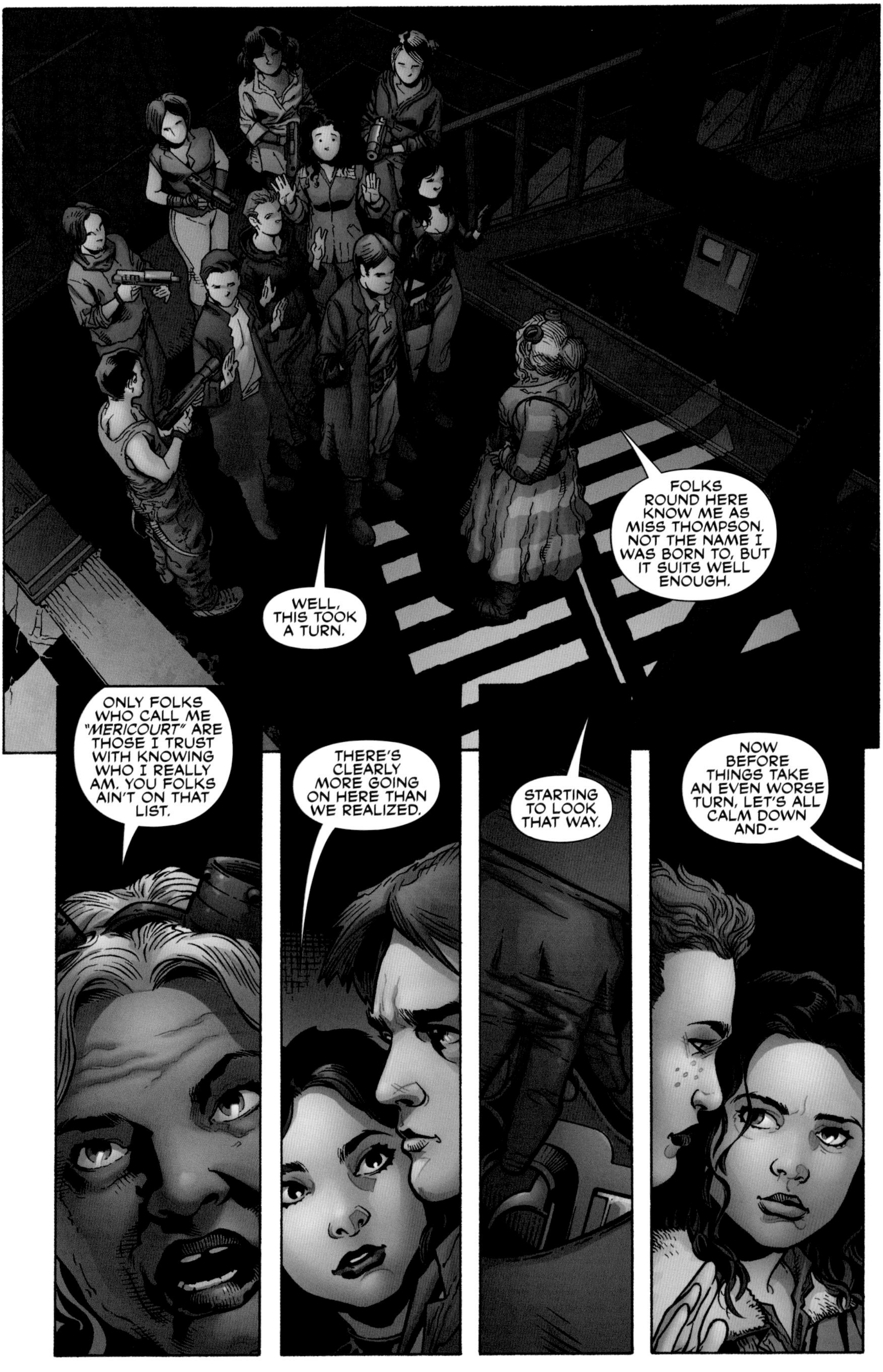
FOLKS ROUND HERE KNOW ME AS MISS THOMPSON. NOT THE NAME I WAS BORN TO, BUT IT SUITS WELL ENOUGH.
WELL, THIS TOOK A TURN.
ONLY FOLKS WHO CALL ME *"MERICOURT"* ARE THOSE I TRUST WITH KNOWING WHO I REALLY AM. YOU FOLKS AIN'T ON THAT LIST.
THERE'S CLEARLY MORE GOING ON HERE THAN WE REALIZED.
STARTING TO LOOK THAT WAY.
NOW BEFORE THINGS TAKE AN EVEN WORSE TURN, LET'S ALL CALM DOWN AND--

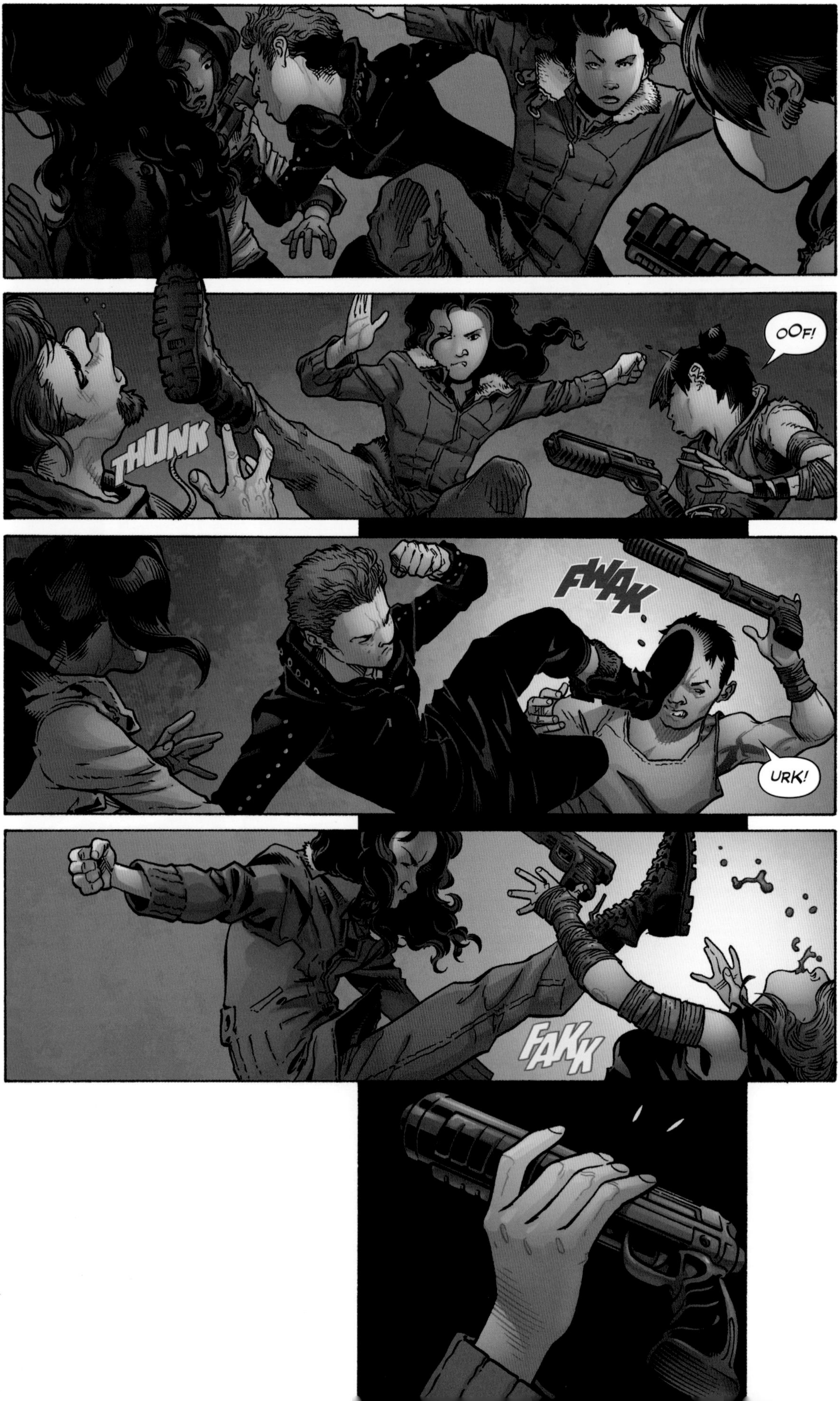
THUNK
OOF!
FWAK
URK!
FAKK

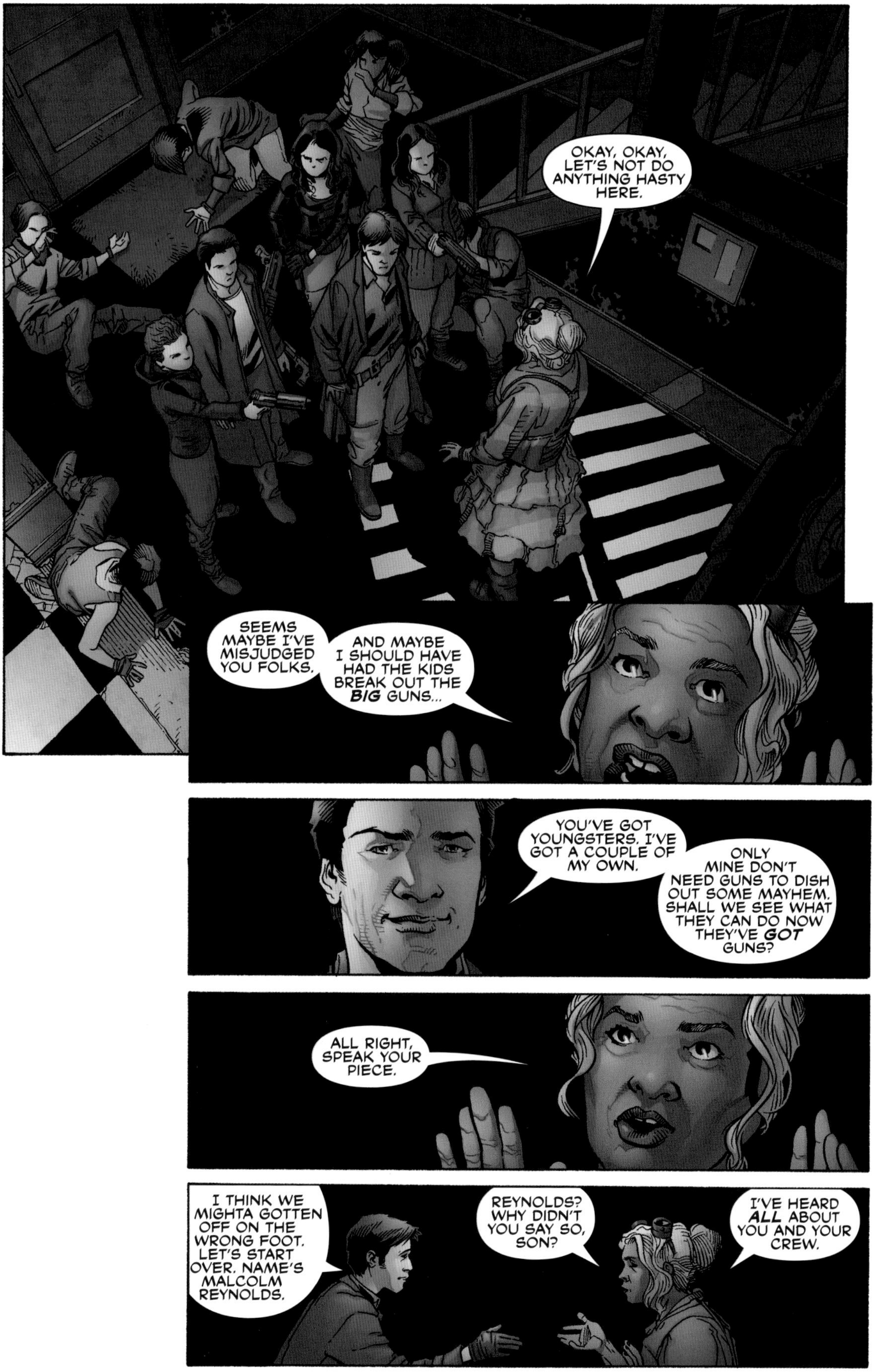
OKAY, OKAY, LET'S NOT DO ANYTHING HASTY HERE.
SEEMS MAYBE I'VE MISJUDGED YOU FOLKS.
AND MAYBE I SHOULD HAVE HAD THE KIDS BREAK OUT THE ***BIG*** GUNS...
YOU'VE GOT YOUNGSTERS. I'VE GOT A COUPLE OF MY OWN.
ONLY MINE DON'T NEED GUNS TO DISH OUT SOME MAYHEM. SHALL WE SEE WHAT THEY CAN DO NOW THEY'VE ***GOT*** GUNS?
ALL RIGHT, SPEAK YOUR PIECE.
I THINK WE MIGHTA GOTTEN OFF ON THE WRONG FOOT. LET'S START OVER. NAME'S MALCOLM REYNOLDS.
REYNOLDS? WHY DIDN'T YOU SAY SO, SON?
I'VE HEARD ***ALL*** ABOUT YOU AND YOUR CREW.

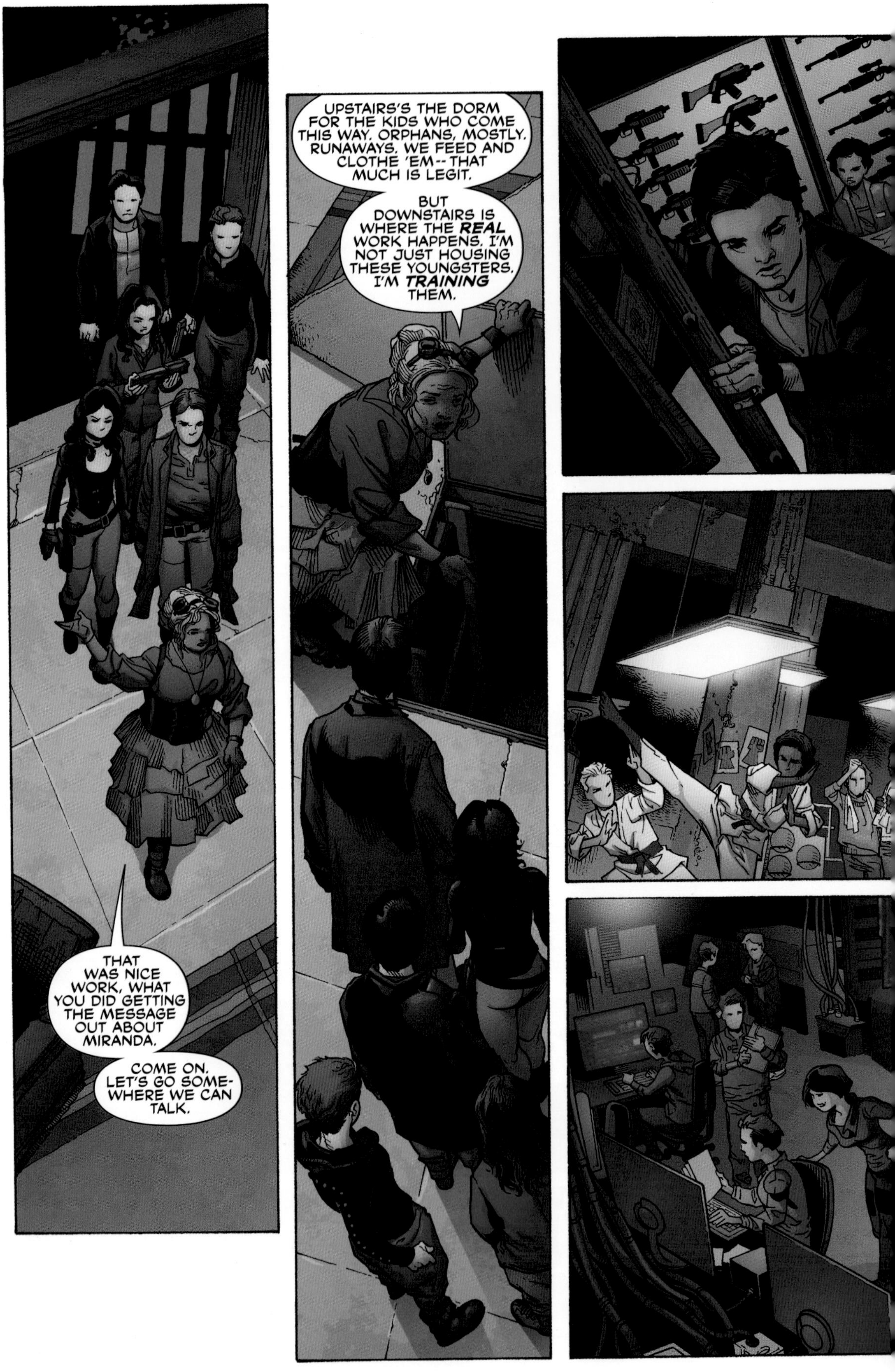
THAT WAS NICE WORK, WHAT YOU DID GETTING THE MESSAGE OUT ABOUT MIRANDA.
COME ON. LET'S GO SOMEWHERE WE CAN TALK.
UPSTAIRS'S THE DORM FOR THE KIDS WHO COME THIS WAY. ORPHANS, MOSTLY. RUNAWAYS. WE FEED AND CLOTHE 'EM-- THAT MUCH IS LEGIT.
BUT DOWNSTAIRS IS WHERE THE ***REAL*** WORK HAPPENS. I'M NOT JUST HOUSING THESE YOUNGSTERS, I'M ***TRAINING*** THEM.

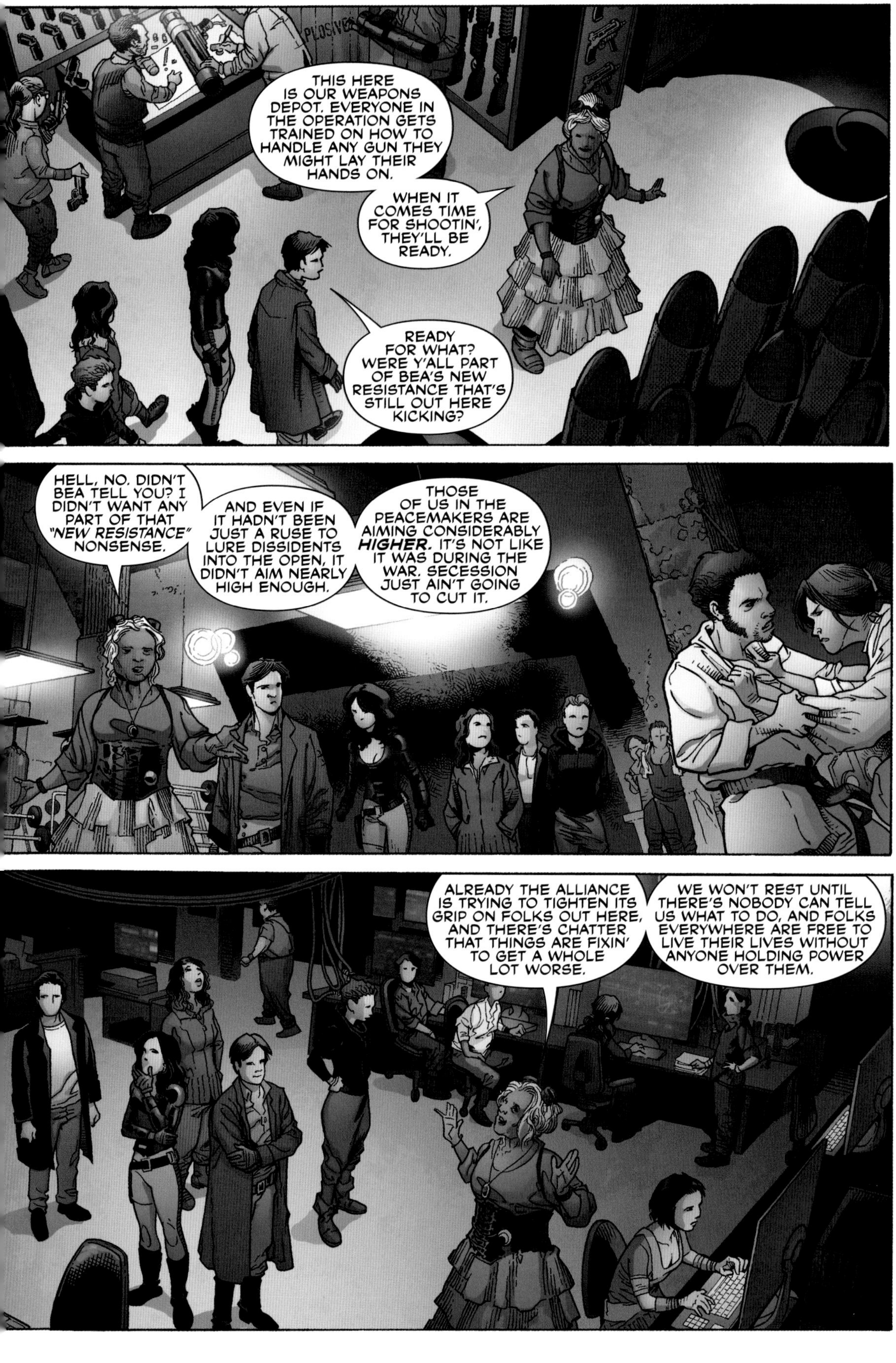
THIS HERE IS OUR WEAPONS DEPOT. EVERYONE IN THE OPERATION GETS TRAINED ON HOW TO HANDLE ANY GUN THEY MIGHT LAY THEIR HANDS ON.
WHEN IT COMES TIME FOR SHOOTIN', THEY'LL BE READY.
READY FOR WHAT? WERE Y'ALL PART OF BEA'S NEW RESISTANCE THAT'S STILL OUT HERE KICKING?
HELL, NO. DIDN'T BEA TELL YOU? I DIDN'T WANT ANY PART OF THAT *"NEW RESISTANCE"* NONSENSE.
AND EVEN IF IT HADN'T BEEN JUST A RUSE TO LURE DISSIDENTS INTO THE OPEN, IT DIDN'T AIM NEARLY HIGH ENOUGH.
THOSE OF US IN THE PEACEMAKERS ARE AIMING CONSIDERABLY ***HIGHER.*** IT'S NOT LIKE IT WAS DURING THE WAR. SECESSION JUST AIN'T GOING TO CUT IT.
ALREADY THE ALLIANCE IS TRYING TO TIGHTEN ITS GRIP ON FOLKS OUT HERE, AND THERE'S CHATTER THAT THINGS ARE FIXIN' TO GET A WHOLE LOT WORSE.
WE WON'T REST UNTIL THERE'S NOBODY CAN TELL US WHAT TO DO, AND FOLKS EVERYWHERE ARE FREE TO LIVE THEIR LIVES WITHOUT ANYONE HOLDING POWER OVER THEM.

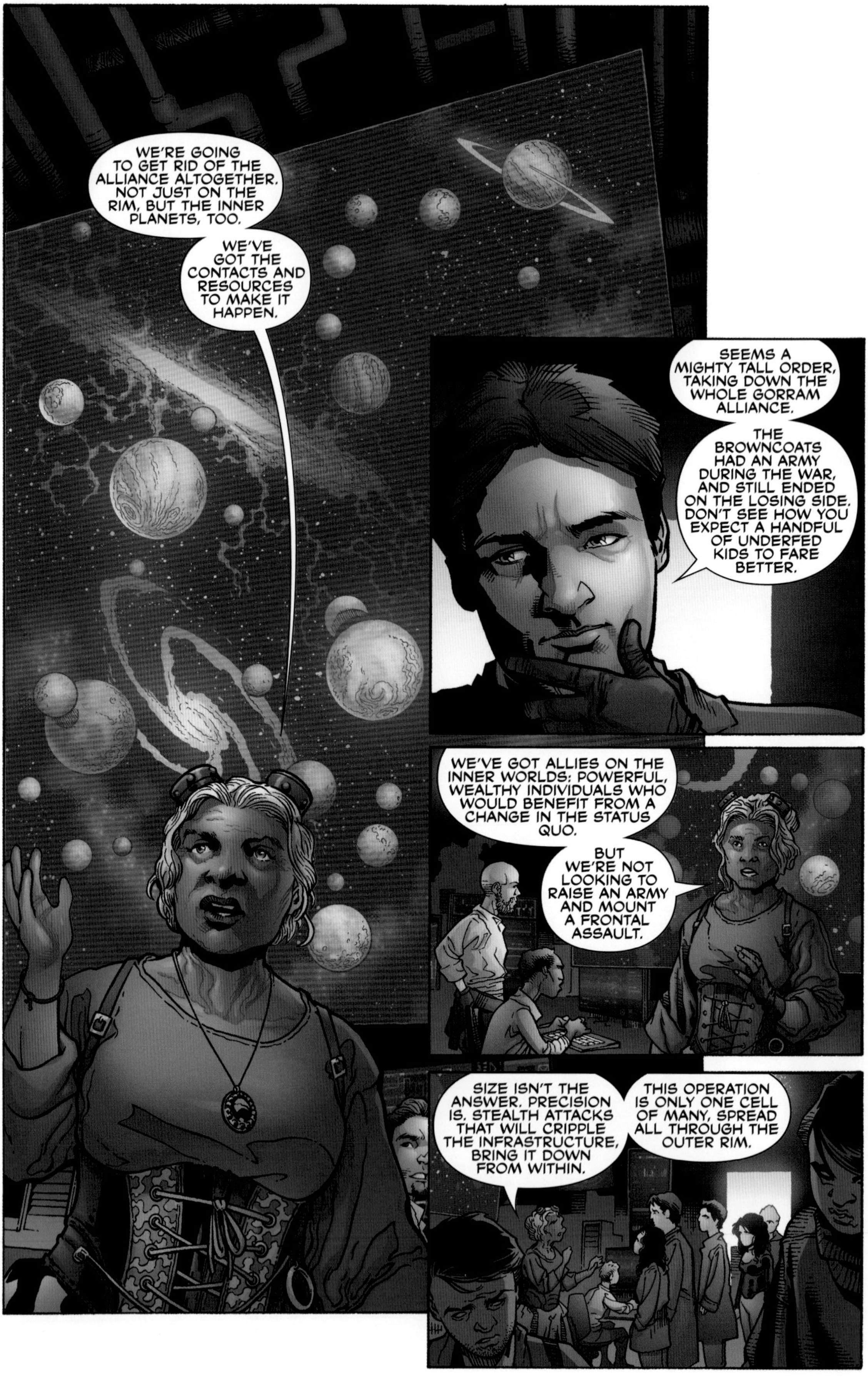
WE'RE GOING TO GET RID OF THE ALLIANCE ALTOGETHER. NOT JUST ON THE RIM, BUT THE INNER PLANETS, TOO.
WE'VE GOT THE CONTACTS AND RESOURCES TO MAKE IT HAPPEN.
SEEMS A MIGHTY TALL ORDER, TAKING DOWN THE WHOLE GORRAM ALLIANCE.
THE BROWNCOATS HAD AN ARMY DURING THE WAR, AND STILL ENDED ON THE LOSING SIDE. DON'T SEE HOW YOU EXPECT A HANDFUL OF UNDERFED KIDS TO FARE BETTER.
WE'VE GOT ALLIES ON THE INNER WORLDS: POWERFUL, WEALTHY INDIVIDUALS WHO WOULD BENEFIT FROM A CHANGE IN THE STATUS QUO.
BUT WE'RE NOT LOOKING TO RAISE AN ARMY AND MOUNT A FRONTAL ASSAULT.
SIZE ISN'T THE ANSWER. PRECISION IS. STEALTH ATTACKS THAT WILL CRIPPLE THE INFRASTRUCTURE, BRING IT DOWN FROM WITHIN.
THIS OPERATION IS ONLY ONE CELL OF MANY, SPREAD ALL THROUGH THE OUTER RIM.

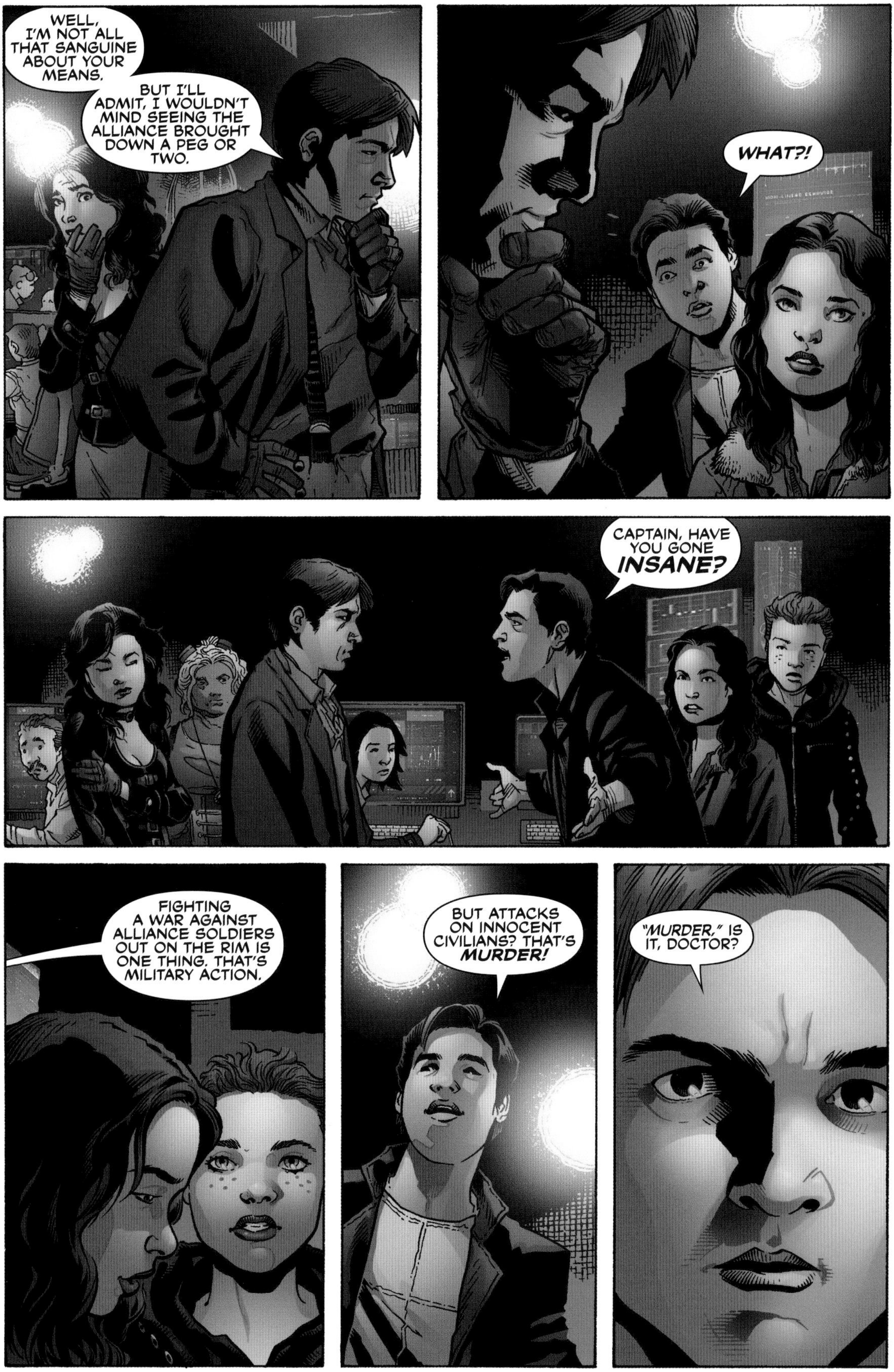

WELL, I'M NOT ALL THAT SANGUINE ABOUT YOUR MEANS.
BUT I'LL ADMIT, I WOULDN'T MIND SEEING THE ALLIANCE BROUGHT DOWN A PEG OR TWO.
WHAT?!
CAPTAIN, HAVE YOU GONE *INSANE?*
FIGHTING A WAR AGAINST ALLIANCE SOLDIERS OUT ON THE RIM IS ONE THING. THAT'S MILITARY ACTION.
BUT ATTACKS ON INNOCENT CIVILIANS? THAT'S *MURDER!*
"MURDER," IS IT, DOCTOR?

LET ME TELL YOU A LITTLE SOMETHING ABOUT *"MILITARY ACTION"* AND *"MURDER."*

MY OWN HOME WORLD GOT DESTROYED DURING THE WAR, AND WEREN'T THERE PLENTY OF *"INNOCENT CIVILIANS"* ON SHADOW WHEN IT GOT BLOWN TO ASHES?

AND SURE, IT MIGHT HAVE BEEN FIGHTING FOLK WHO WILLINGLY LAID DOWN THEIR LIVES IN SERENITY VALLEY.

BUT WHAT ABOUT THE REFUGEES AND CAMP FOLLOWERS WHO WERE ON FIDDLER'S GREEN WHEN THE ALLIANCE CAME CALLING?

OR WEREN'T THEY INNOCENT ENOUGH FOR YOUR LIKING?

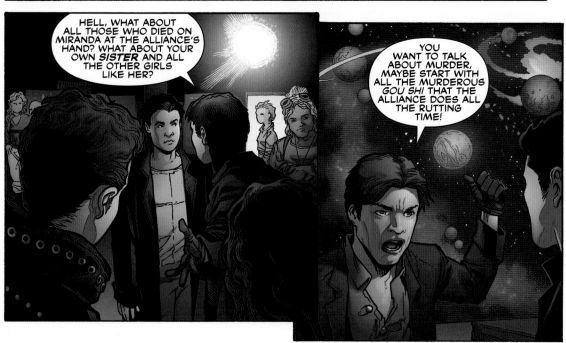

HELL, WHAT ABOUT ALL THOSE WHO DIED ON MIRANDA AT THE ALLIANCE'S HAND? WHAT ABOUT YOUR OWN *SISTER* AND ALL THE OTHER GIRLS LIKE HER?

YOU WANT TO TALK ABOUT MURDER, MAYBE START WITH ALL THE MURDEROUS *GOU SHI* THAT THE ALLIANCE DOES ALL THE RUTTING TIME!

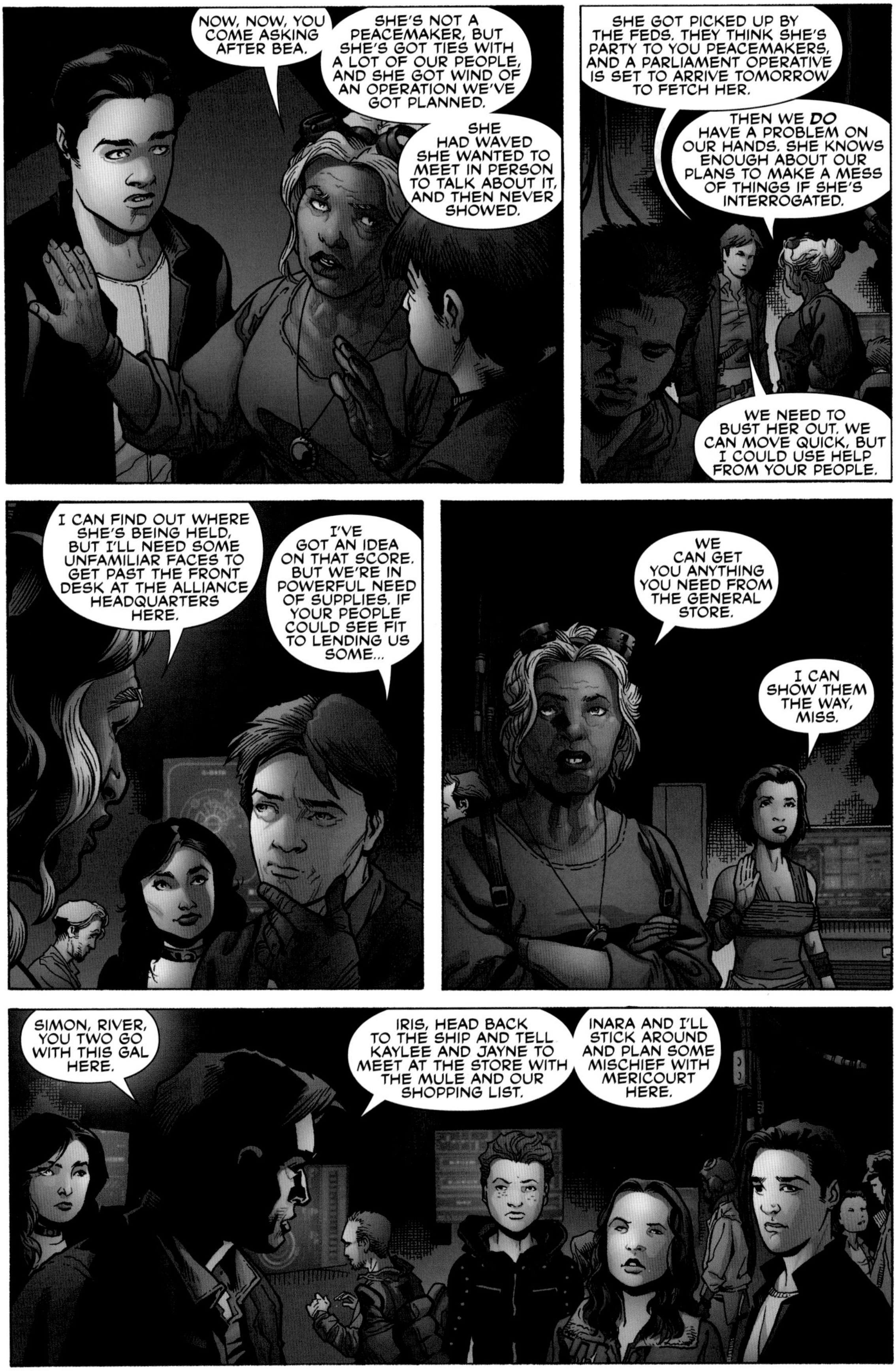
NOW, NOW, YOU COME ASKING AFTER BEA.
SHE'S NOT A PEACEMAKER, BUT SHE'S GOT TIES WITH A LOT OF OUR PEOPLE, AND SHE GOT WIND OF AN OPERATION WE'VE GOT PLANNED.
SHE HAD WAVED SHE WANTED TO MEET IN PERSON TO TALK ABOUT IT, AND THEN NEVER SHOWED.
SHE GOT PICKED UP BY THE FEDS. THEY THINK SHE'S PARTY TO YOU PEACEMAKERS, AND A PARLIAMENT OPERATIVE IS SET TO ARRIVE TOMORROW TO FETCH HER.
THEN WE *DO* HAVE A PROBLEM ON OUR HANDS. SHE KNOWS ENOUGH ABOUT OUR PLANS TO MAKE A MESS OF THINGS IF SHE'S INTERROGATED.
WE NEED TO BUST HER OUT. WE CAN MOVE QUICK, BUT I COULD USE HELP FROM YOUR PEOPLE.
I CAN FIND OUT WHERE SHE'S BEING HELD, BUT I'LL NEED SOME UNFAMILIAR FACES TO GET PAST THE FRONT DESK AT THE ALLIANCE HEADQUARTERS HERE.
I'VE GOT AN IDEA ON THAT SCORE. BUT WE'RE IN POWERFUL NEED OF SUPPLIES. IF YOUR PEOPLE COULD SEE FIT TO LENDING US SOME...
WE CAN GET YOU ANYTHING YOU NEED FROM THE GENERAL STORE.
I CAN SHOW THEM THE WAY, MISS.
SIMON, RIVER, YOU TWO GO WITH THIS GAL HERE.
IRIS, HEAD BACK TO THE SHIP AND TELL KAYLEE AND JAYNE TO MEET AT THE STORE WITH THE MULE AND OUR SHOPPING LIST.
INARA AND I'LL STICK AROUND AND PLAN SOME MISCHIEF WITH MERICOURT HERE.

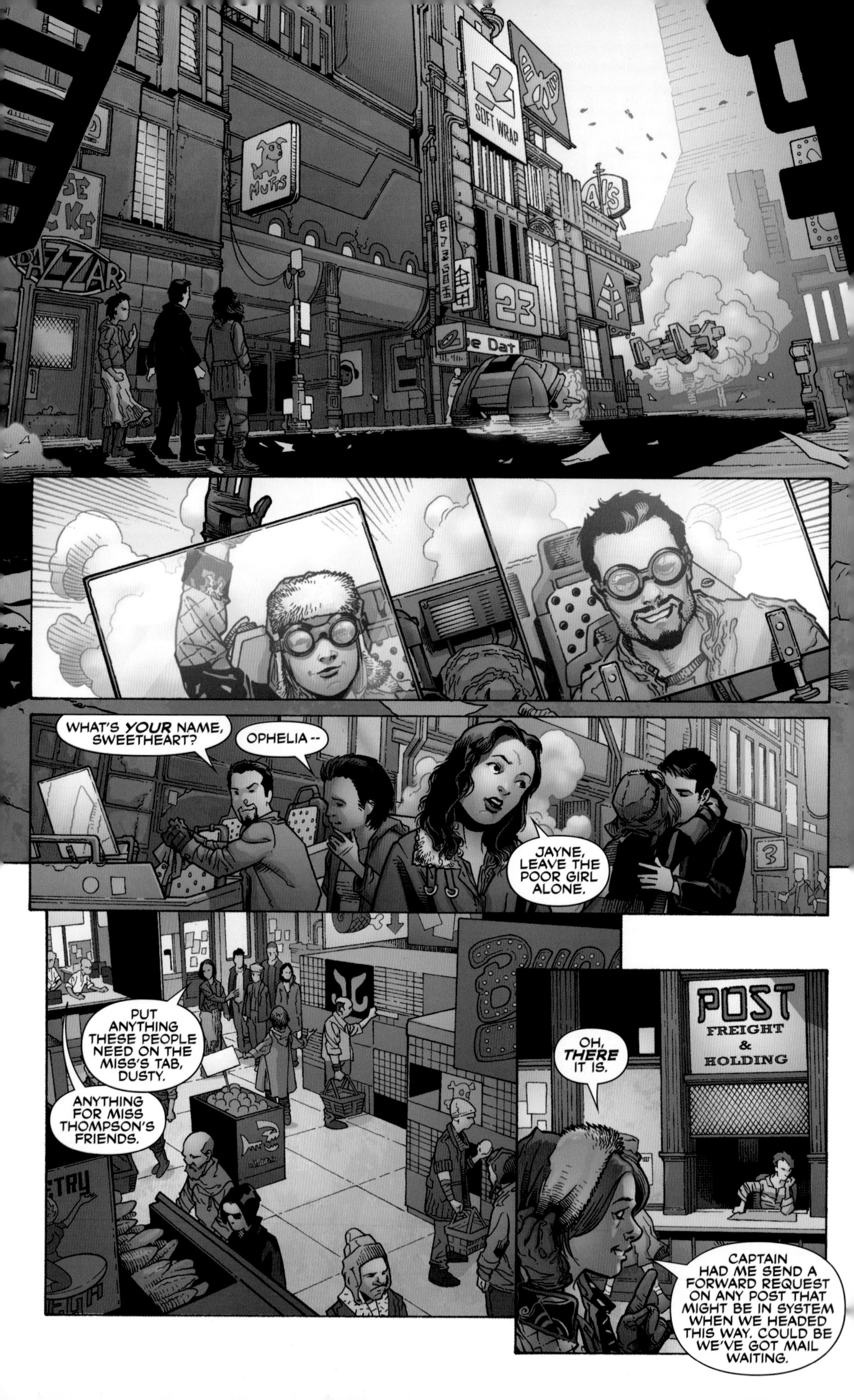
SOFT WRAP
MUTTS
23
POST
FREIGHT
&
HOLDING
WHAT'S *YOUR* NAME, SWEETHEART?
OPHELIA --
JAYNE, LEAVE THE POOR GIRL ALONE.
PUT ANYTHING THESE PEOPLE NEED ON THE MISS'S TAB, DUSTY.
ANYTHING FOR MISS THOMPSON'S FRIENDS.
OH, *THERE* IT IS.
CAPTAIN HAD ME SEND A FORWARD REQUEST ON ANY POST THAT MIGHT BE IN SYSTEM WHEN WE HEADED THIS WAY. COULD BE WE'VE GOT MAIL WAITING.

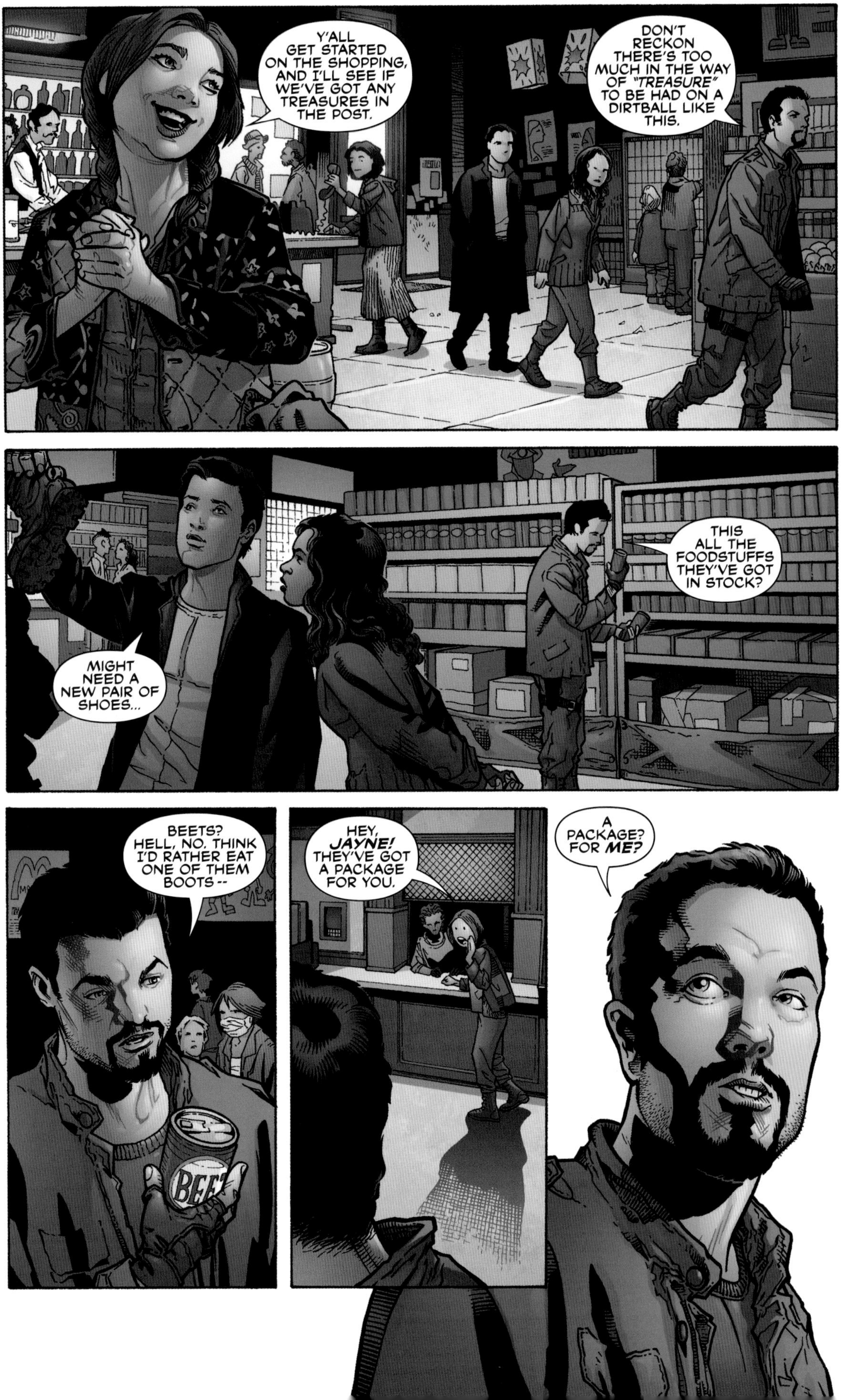
Y'ALL GET STARTED ON THE SHOPPING, AND I'LL SEE IF WE'VE GOT ANY TREASURES IN THE POST.
DON'T RECKON THERE'S TOO MUCH IN THE WAY OF "TREASURE" TO BE HAD ON A DIRTBALL LIKE THIS.
MIGHT NEED A NEW PAIR OF SHOES...
THIS ALL THE FOODSTUFFS THEY'VE GOT IN STOCK?
BEETS? HELL, NO. THINK I'D RATHER EAT ONE OF THEM BOOTS --
BEE
HEY, JAYNE! THEY'VE GOT A PACKAGE FOR YOU.
A PACKAGE? FOR ME?

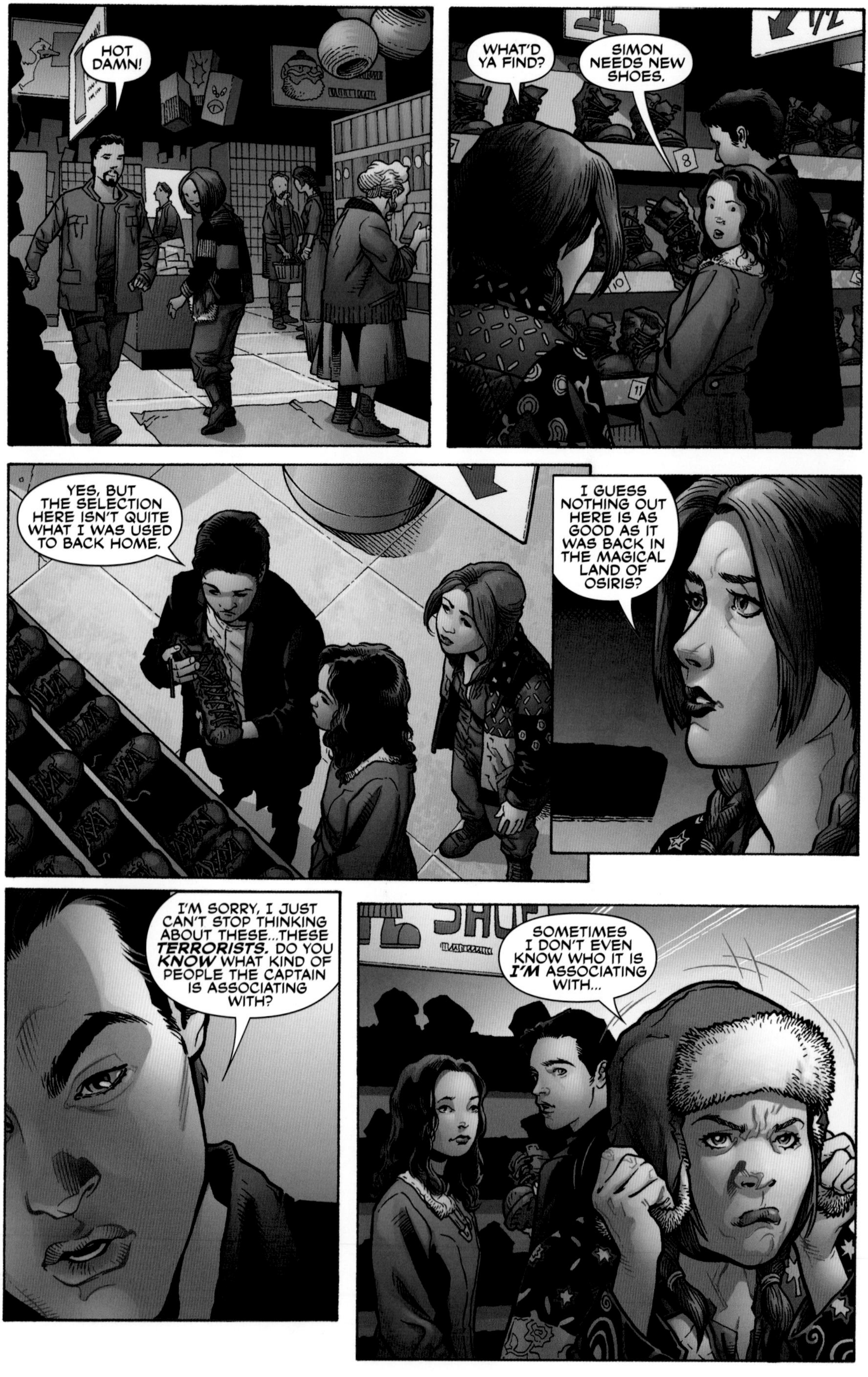
HOT DAMN!
WHAT'D YA FIND?
SIMON NEEDS NEW SHOES.
YES, BUT THE SELECTION HERE ISN'T QUITE WHAT I WAS USED TO BACK HOME.
I GUESS NOTHING OUT HERE IS AS GOOD AS IT WAS BACK IN THE MAGICAL LAND OF OSIRIS?
I'M SORRY, I JUST CAN'T STOP THINKING ABOUT THESE...THESE TERRORISTS. DO YOU KNOW WHAT KIND OF PEOPLE THE CAPTAIN IS ASSOCIATING WITH?
SOMETIMES I DON'T EVEN KNOW WHO IT IS I'M ASSOCIATING WITH...

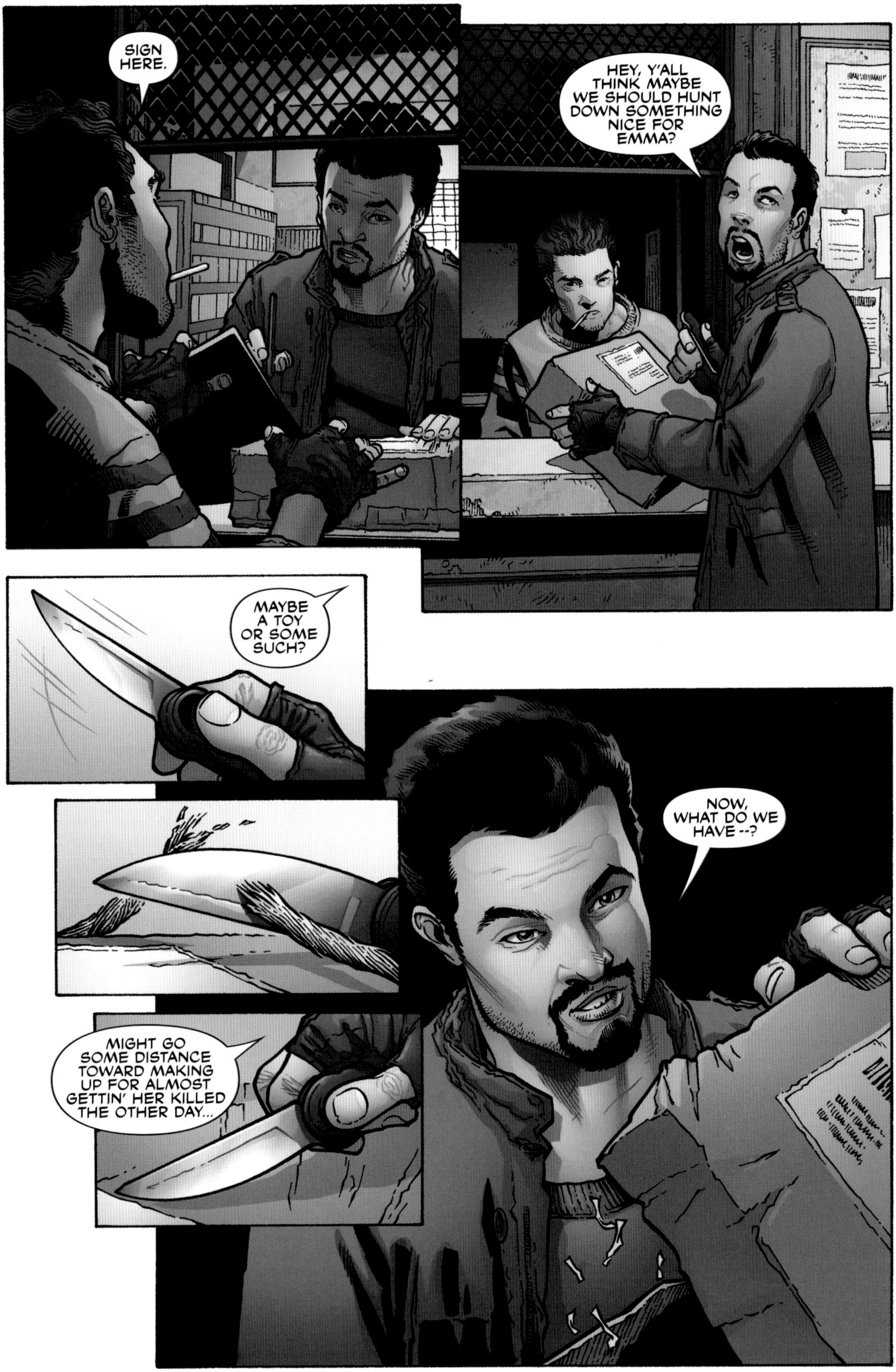
SIGN HERE.
HEY, Y'ALL THINK MAYBE WE SHOULD HUNT DOWN SOMETHING NICE FOR EMMA?
MAYBE A TOY OR SOME SUCH?
NOW, WHAT DO WE HAVE --?
MIGHT GO SOME DISTANCE TOWARD MAKING UP FOR ALMOST GETTIN' HER KILLED THE OTHER DAY...

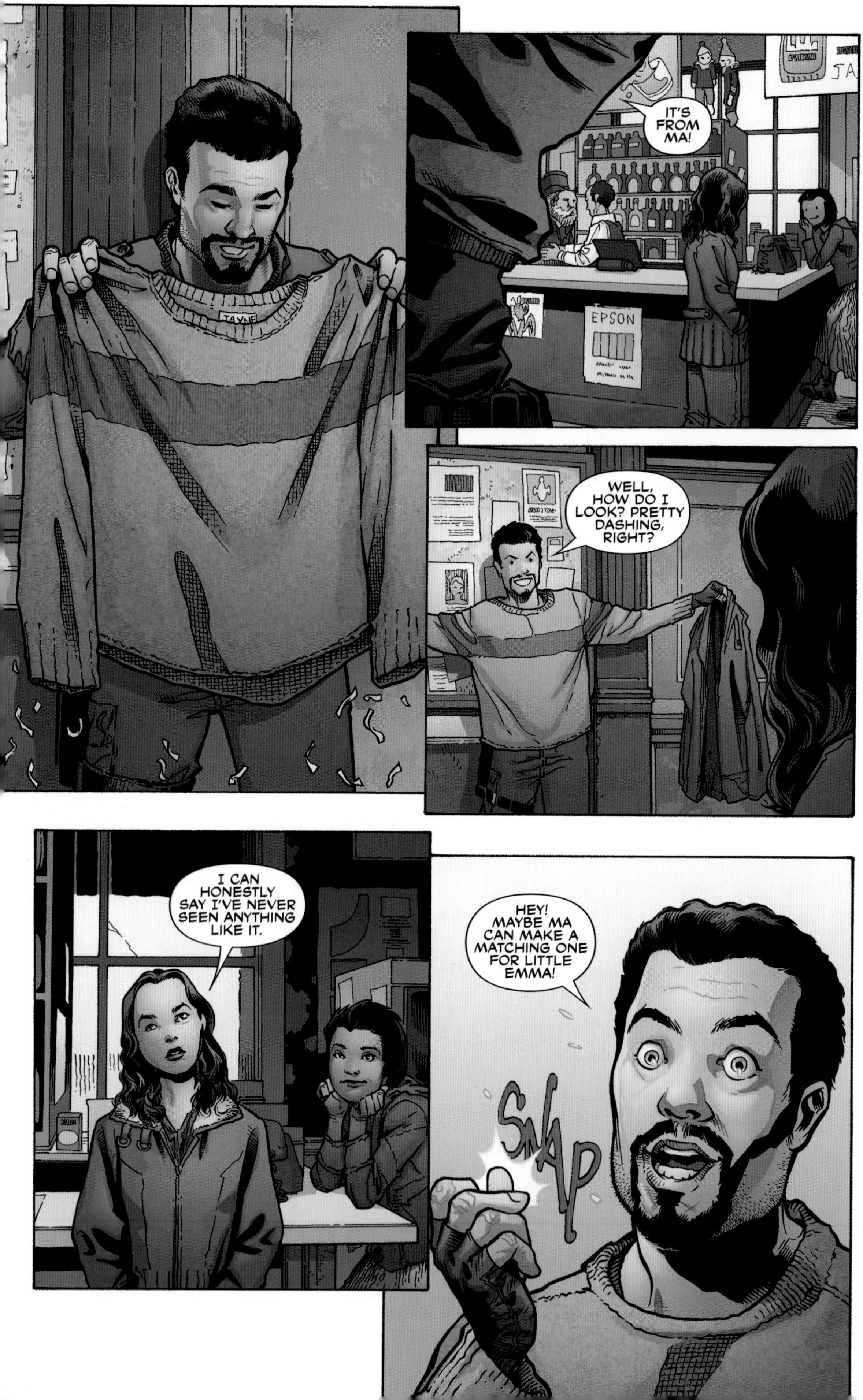
TAYNE
IT'S FROM MA!
EPSON
WELL, HOW DO I LOOK? PRETTY DASHING, RIGHT?
I CAN HONESTLY SAY I'VE NEVER SEEN ANYTHING LIKE IT.
HEY! MAYBE MA CAN MAKE A MATCHING ONE FOR LITTLE EMMA!
SNAP

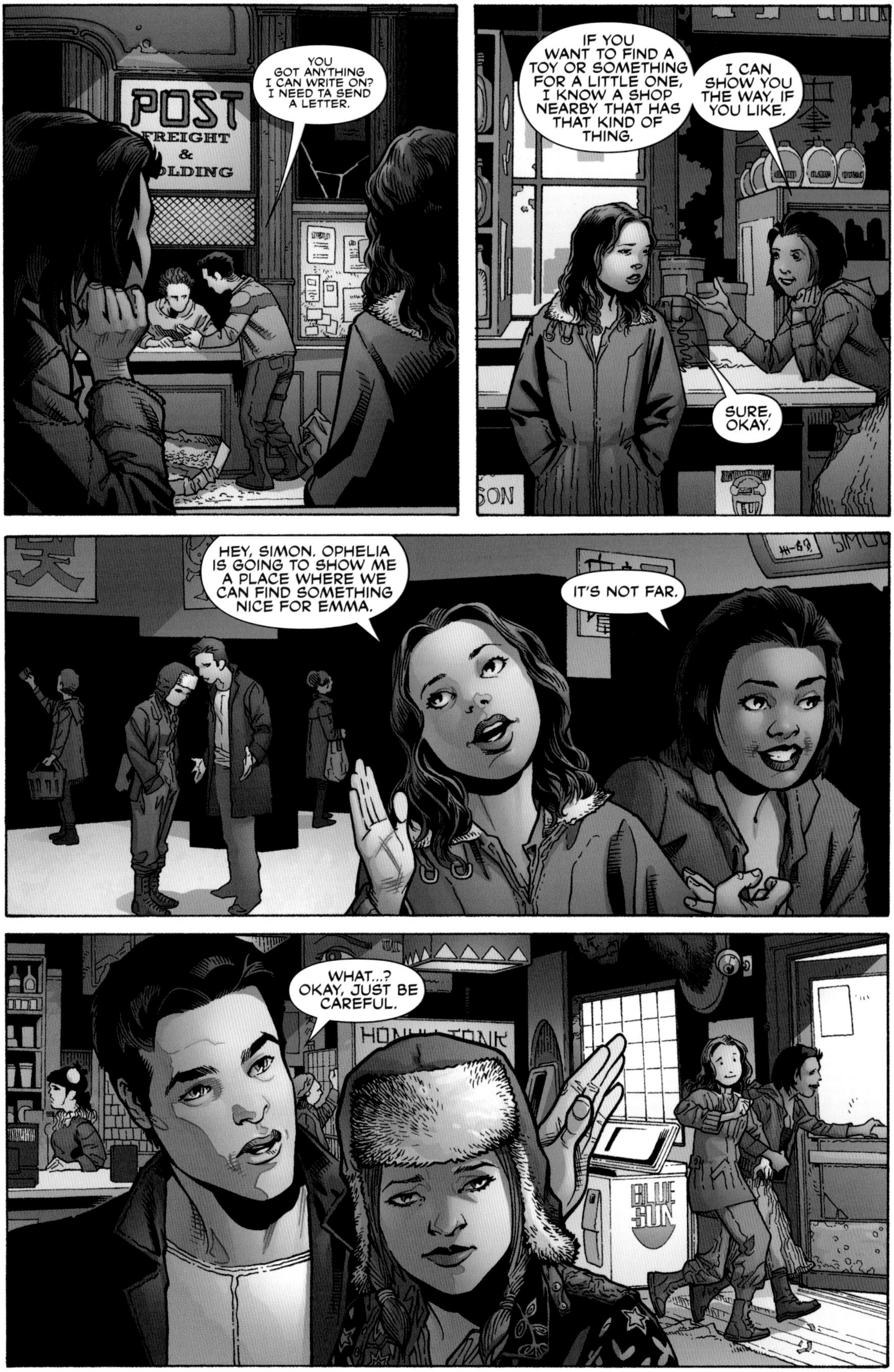
POST
FREIGHT
&
OLDING
YOU GOT ANYTHING I CAN WRITE ON? I NEED TA SEND A LETTER.
IF YOU WANT TO FIND A TOY OR SOMETHING FOR A LITTLE ONE, I KNOW A SHOP NEARBY THAT HAS THAT KIND OF THING.
I CAN SHOW YOU THE WAY, IF YOU LIKE.
SURE, OKAY.
HEY, SIMON. OPHELIA IS GOING TO SHOW ME A PLACE WHERE WE CAN FIND SOMETHING NICE FOR EMMA.
IT'S NOT FAR.
WHAT...? OKAY, JUST BE CAREFUL.
BLUE SUN

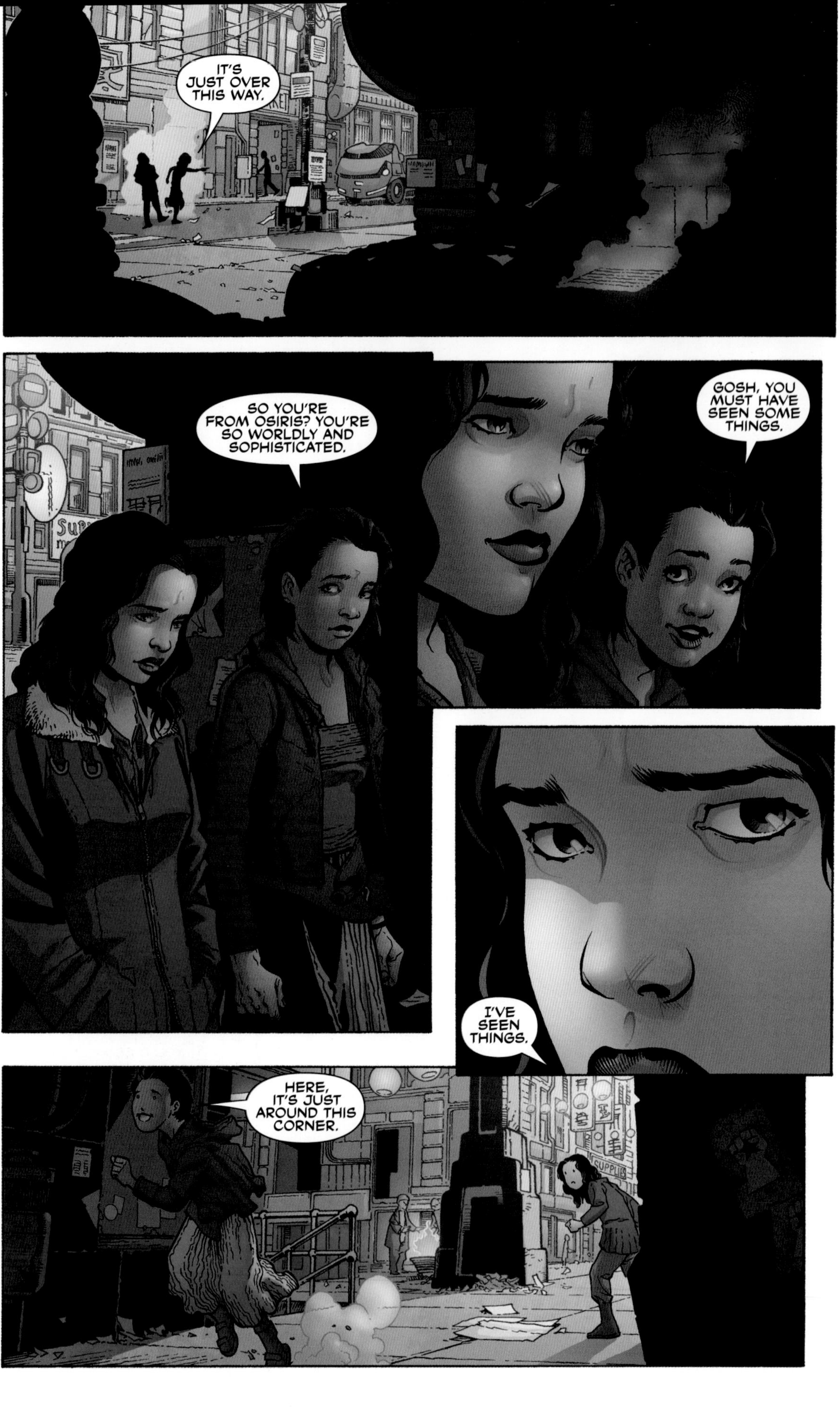
IT'S JUST OVER THIS WAY.
SO YOU'RE FROM OSIRIS? YOU'RE SO WORLDLY AND SOPHISTICATED.
GOSH, YOU MUST HAVE SEEN SOME THINGS.
I'VE SEEN THINGS.
HERE, IT'S JUST AROUND THIS CORNER.

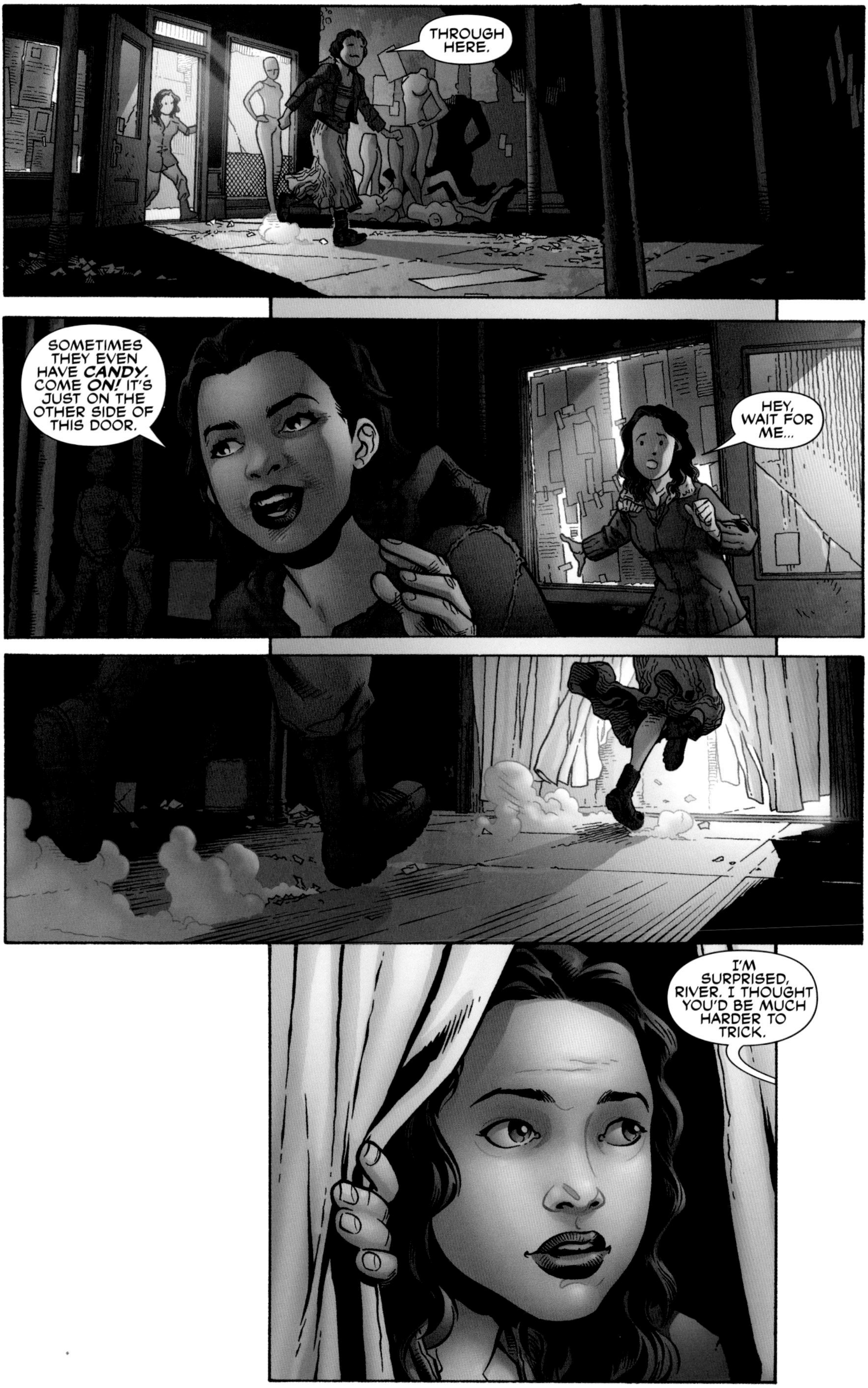
THROUGH HERE.
SOMETIMES THEY EVEN HAVE *CANDY.* COME *ON!* IT'S JUST ON THE OTHER SIDE OF THIS DOOR.
HEY, WAIT FOR ME...
I'M SURPRISED, RIVER. I THOUGHT YOU'D BE MUCH HARDER TO TRICK.

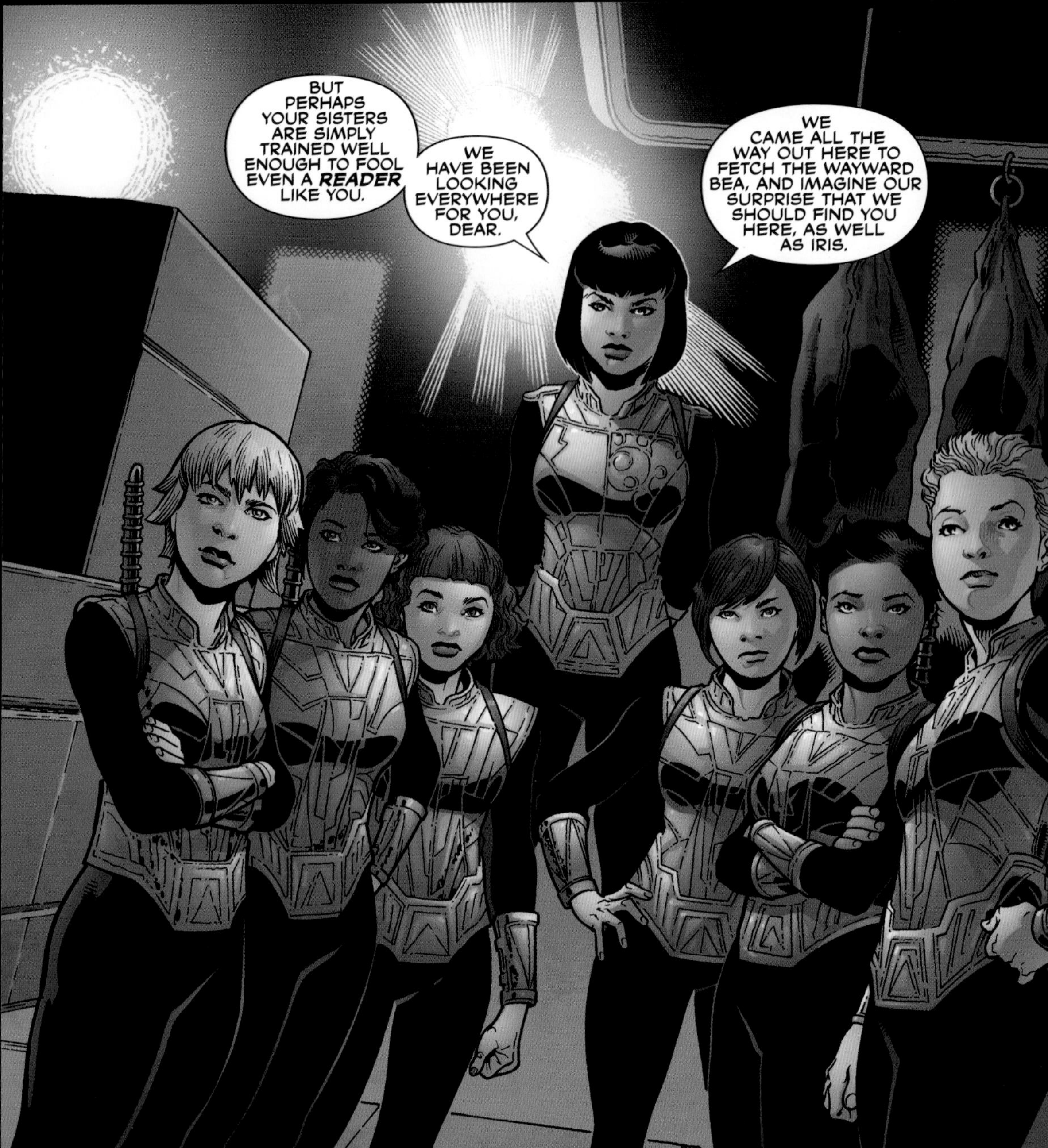
BUT PERHAPS YOUR SISTERS ARE SIMPLY TRAINED WELL ENOUGH TO FOOL EVEN A **READER** LIKE YOU.
WE HAVE BEEN LOOKING EVERYWHERE FOR YOU, DEAR.
WE CAME ALL THE WAY OUT HERE TO FETCH THE WAYWARD BEA, AND IMAGINE OUR SURPRISE THAT WE SHOULD FIND YOU HERE, AS WELL AS IRIS.

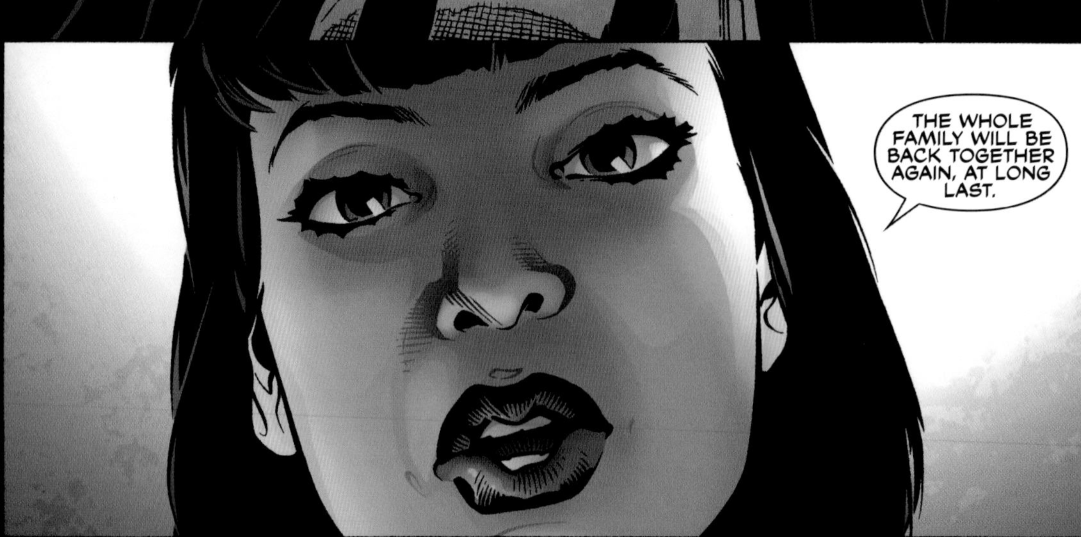
THE WHOLE FAMILY WILL BE BACK TOGETHER AGAIN, AT LONG LAST.

I'LL SKIP THE REUNION IF IT'S ALL THE SAME TO YOU, KALISTA.

YOU'RE CONFUSED. YOU WERE TAKEN FROM THE ACADEMY BEFORE YOUR TRAINING WAS COMPLETE. BUT COME WITH ME AND I CAN MAKE IT ALL BETTER.

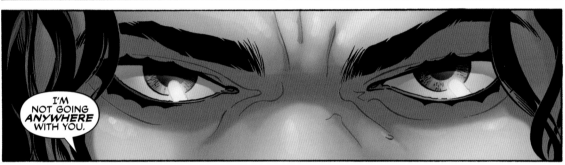

I'M NOT GOING *ANYWHERE* WITH YOU.

PITY. BUT I EXPECTED AS MUCH.

NO BLADES, DISCIPLES. I DON'T WANT RIVER TO SUFFER FROM ANY INJURIES THAT WON'T HEAL IN TIME.

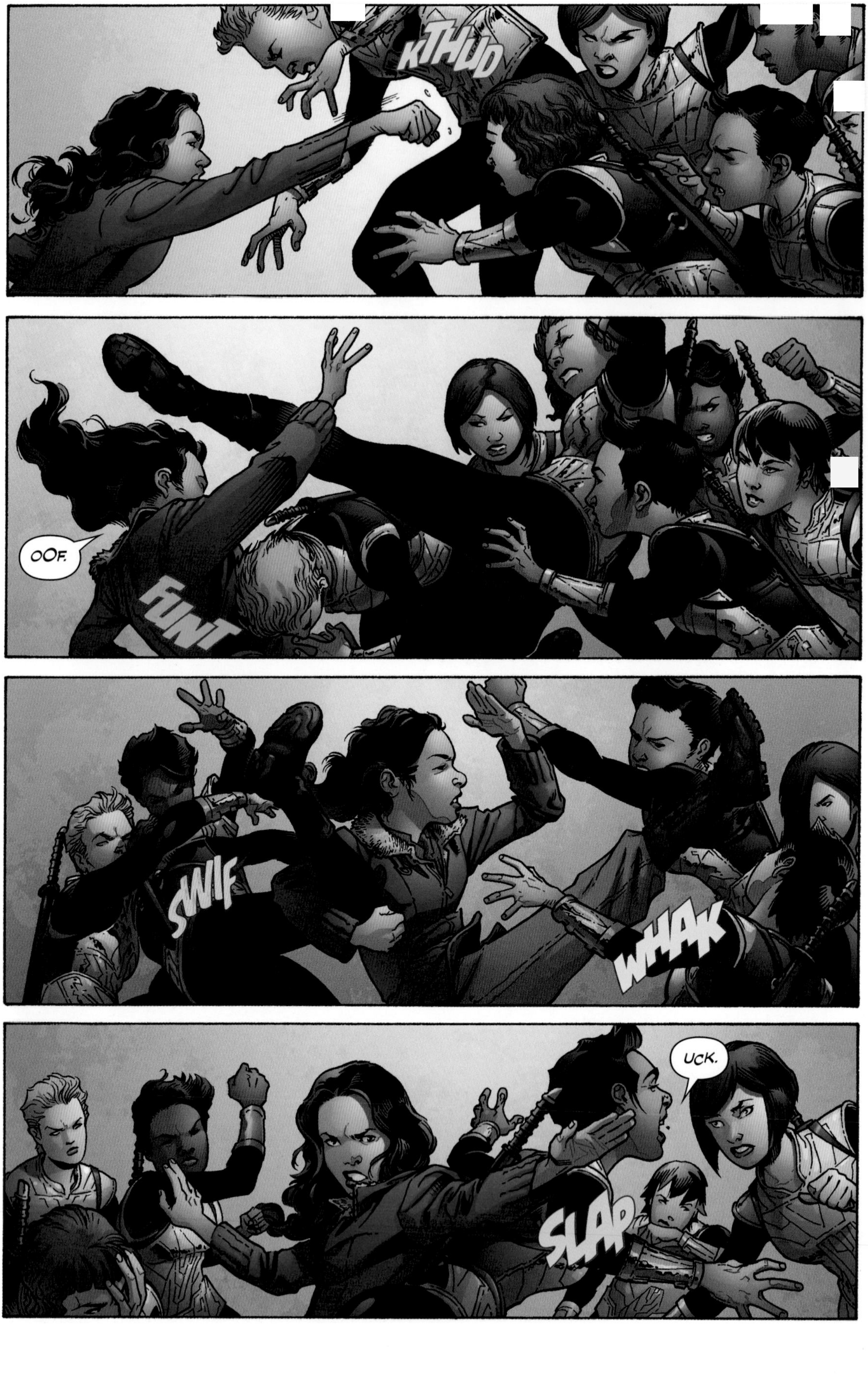
KTHUD
OOF.
FUNT
SWIF
WHAK
UCK.
SLAP

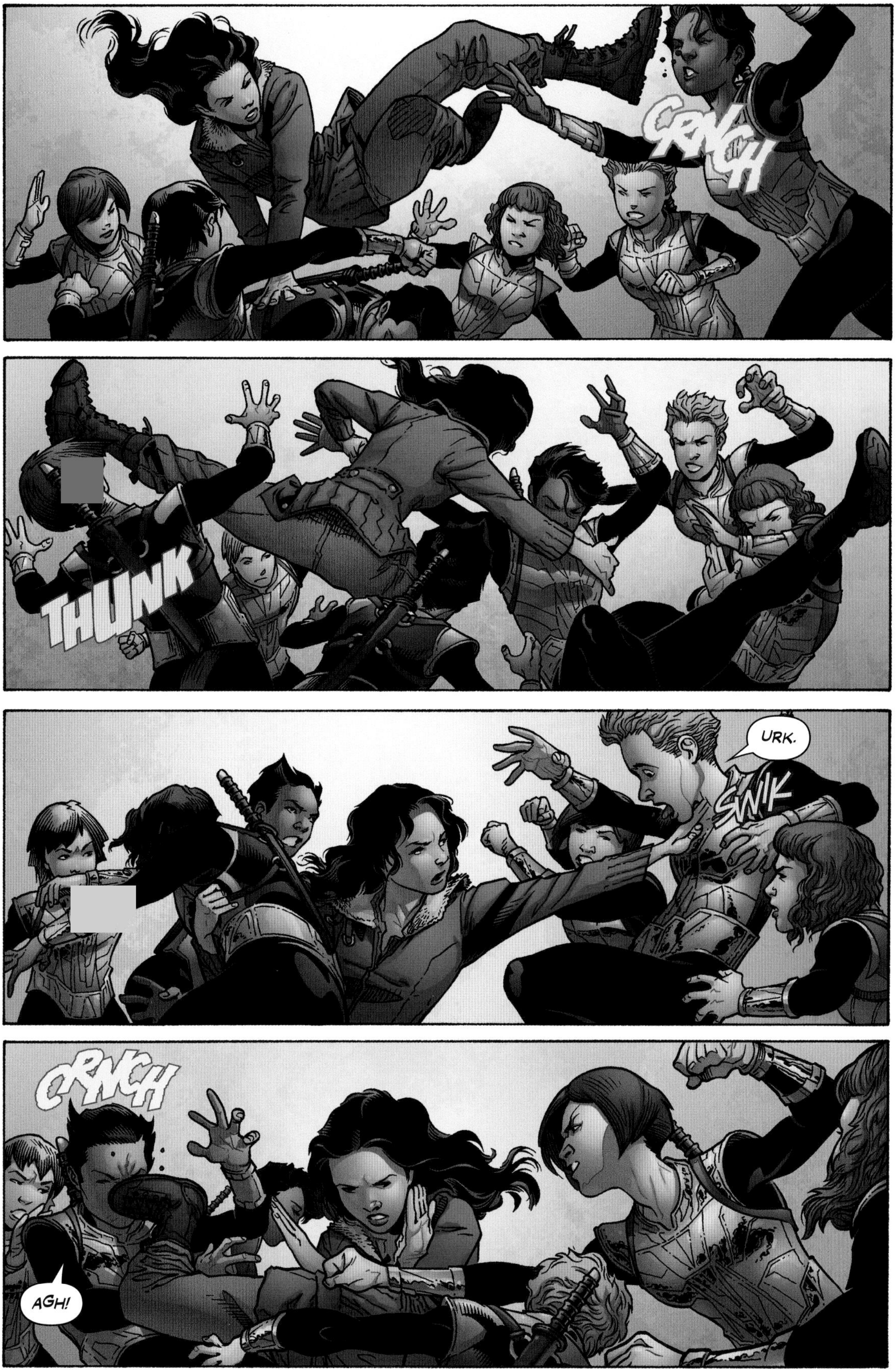
CRNCH
THUNK
URK.
SNIK
CRNCH
AGH!

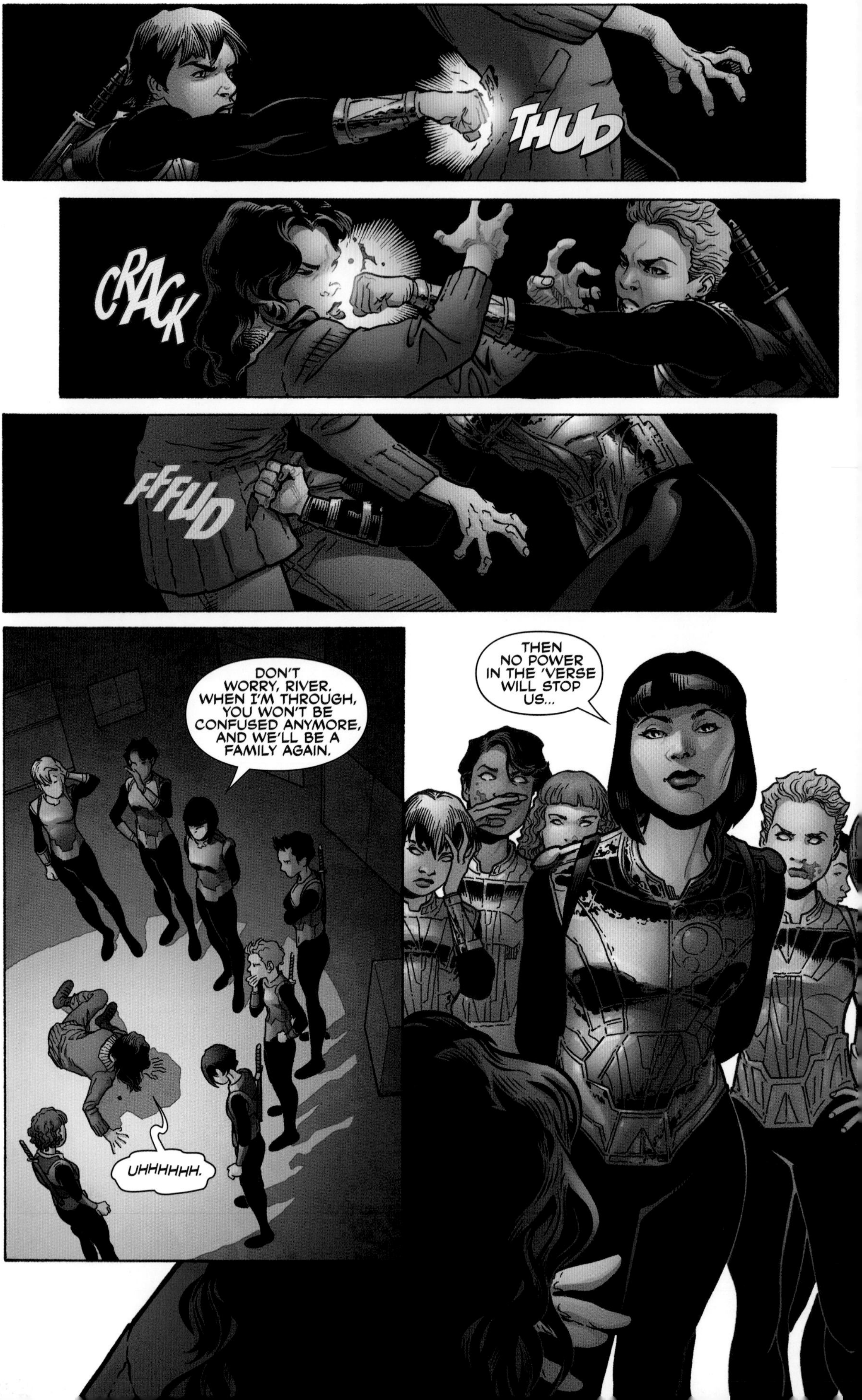
THUD
CRACK
FFFUD
DON'T WORRY, RIVER. WHEN I'M THROUGH, YOU WON'T BE CONFUSED ANYMORE, AND WE'LL BE A FAMILY AGAIN.
UHHHHHH.
THEN NO POWER IN THE 'VERSE WILL STOP US...

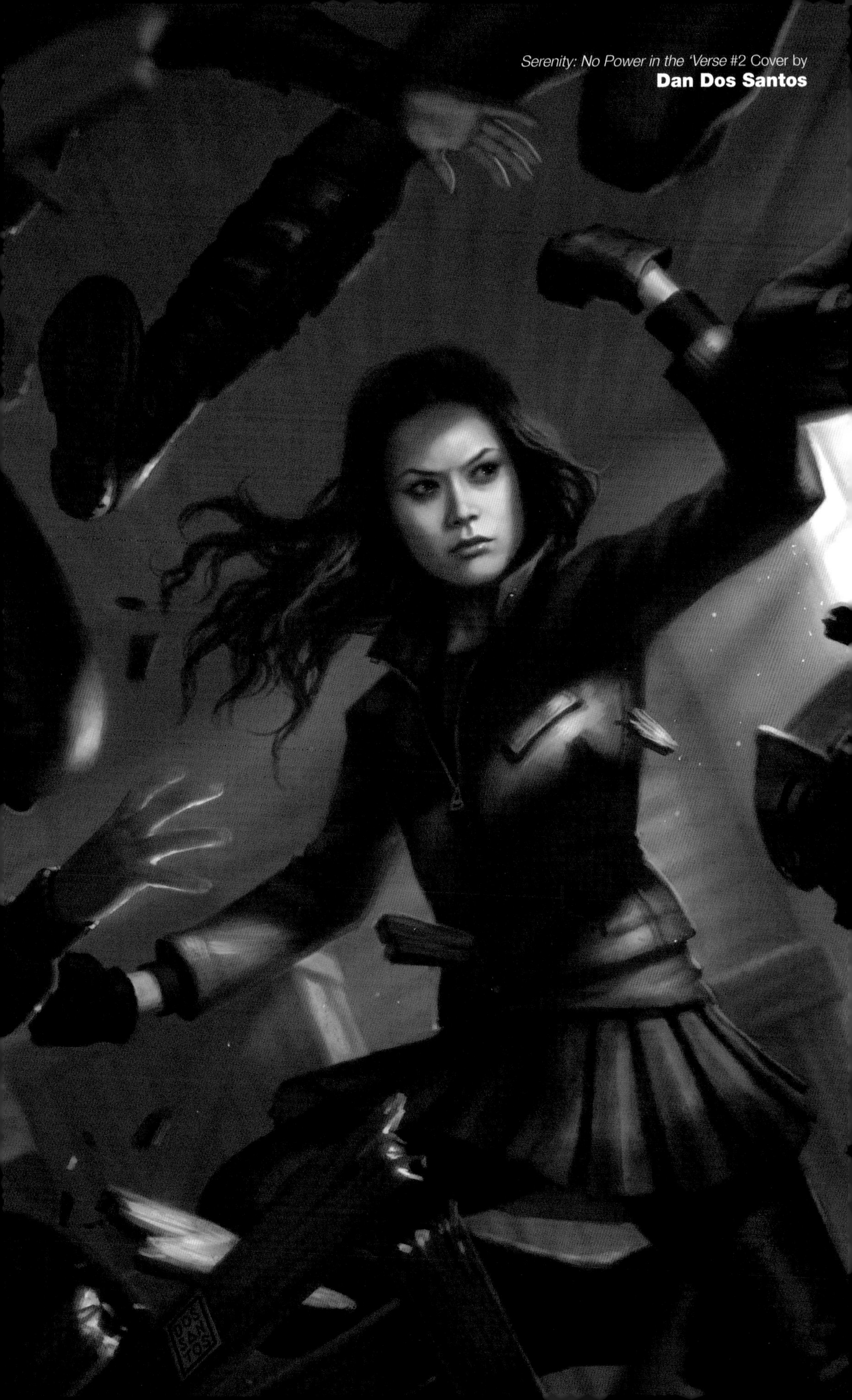

Serenity: No Power in the 'Verse #2 Cover by
Dan Dos Santos

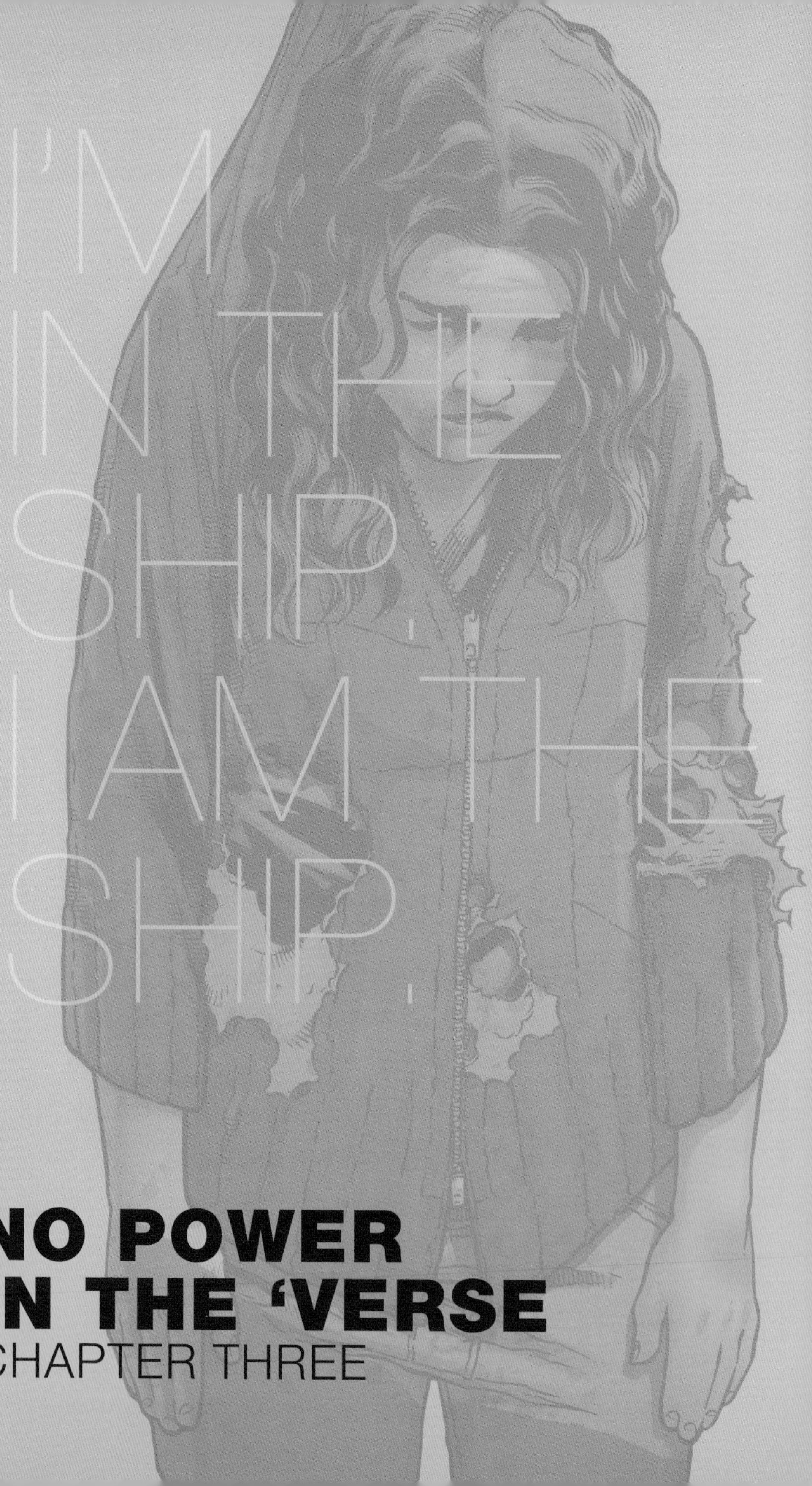
I'M IN THE SHIP. I AM THE SHIP.

NO POWER IN THE 'VERSE

CHAPTER THREE

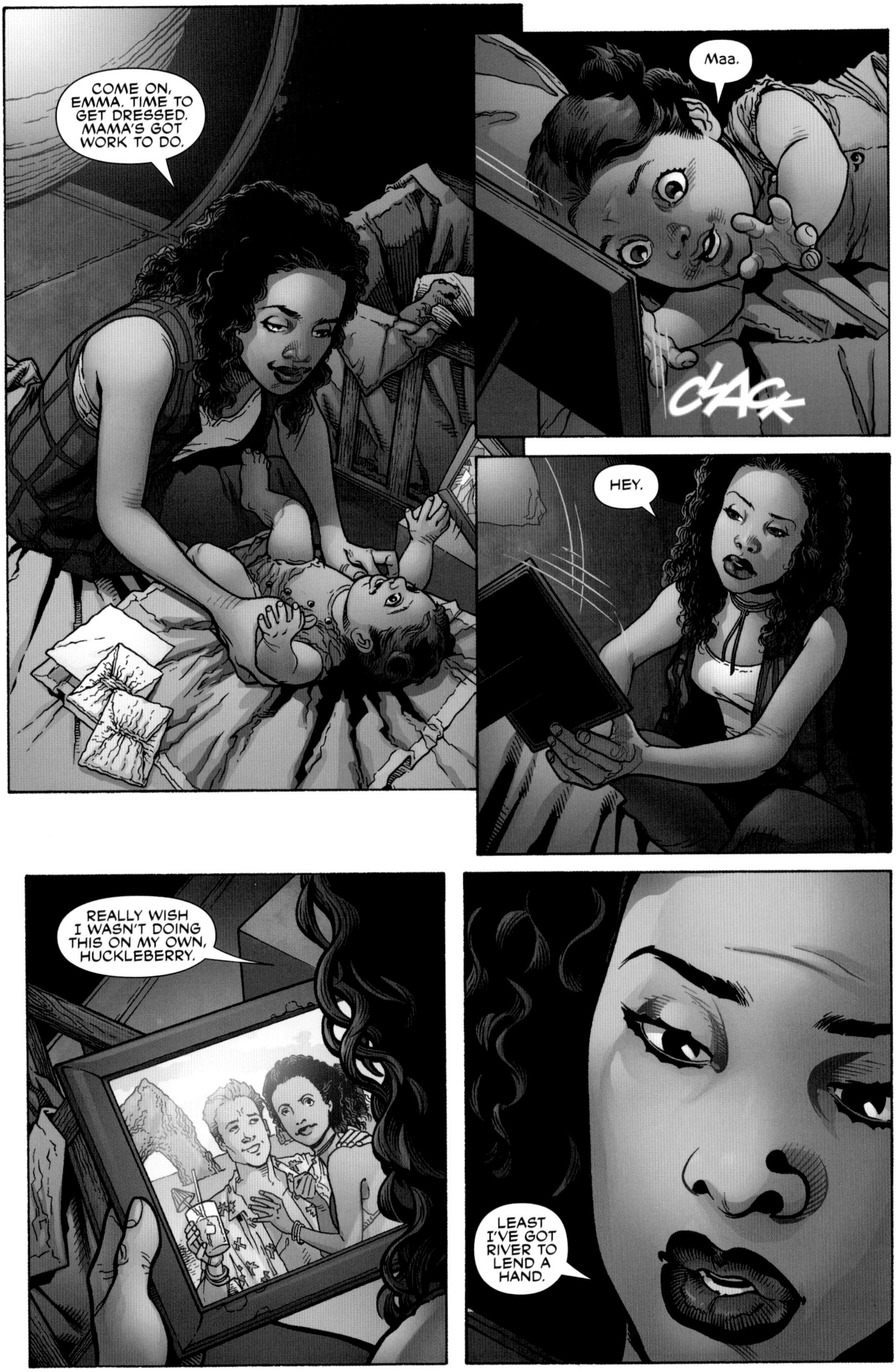
COME ON, EMMA. TIME TO GET DRESSED. MAMA'S GOT WORK TO DO.
Maa.
CLACK
HEY.
REALLY WISH I WASN'T DOING THIS ON MY OWN, HUCKLEBERRY.
LEAST I'VE GOT RIVER TO LEND A HAND.

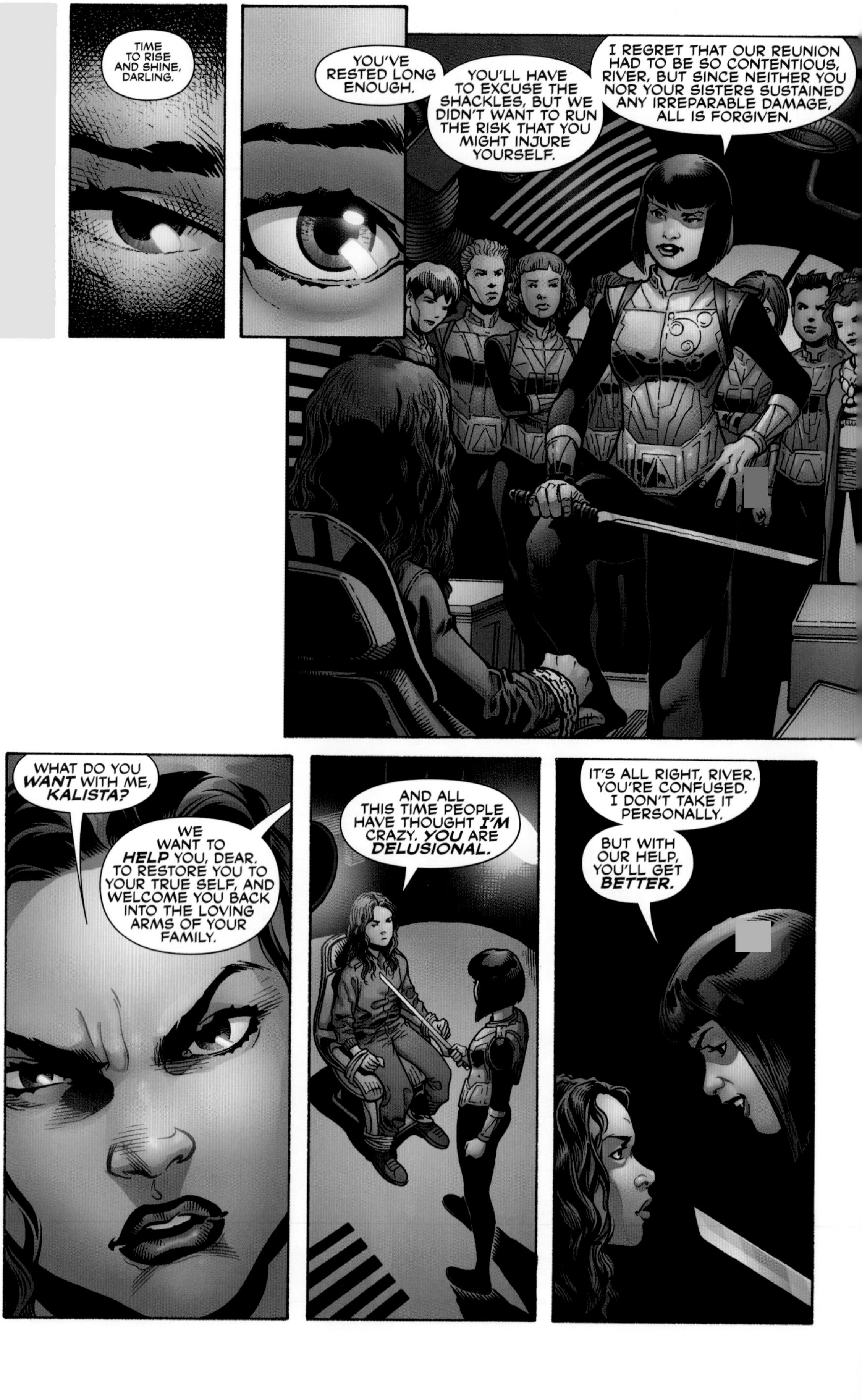
TIME TO RISE AND SHINE, DARLING.
YOU'VE RESTED LONG ENOUGH.
YOU'LL HAVE TO EXCUSE THE SHACKLES, BUT WE DIDN'T WANT TO RUN THE RISK THAT YOU MIGHT INJURE YOURSELF.
I REGRET THAT OUR REUNION HAD TO BE SO CONTENTIOUS, RIVER, BUT SINCE NEITHER YOU NOR YOUR SISTERS SUSTAINED ANY IRREPARABLE DAMAGE, ALL IS FORGIVEN.
WHAT DO YOU **WANT** WITH ME, **KALISTA?**
WE WANT TO **HELP** YOU, DEAR. TO RESTORE YOU TO YOUR TRUE SELF, AND WELCOME YOU BACK INTO THE LOVING ARMS OF YOUR FAMILY.
AND ALL THIS TIME PEOPLE HAVE THOUGHT ***I'M*** CRAZY. ***YOU*** ARE ***DELUSIONAL.***
IT'S ALL RIGHT, RIVER. YOU'RE CONFUSED. I DON'T TAKE IT PERSONALLY.
BUT WITH OUR HELP, YOU'LL GET ***BETTER.***

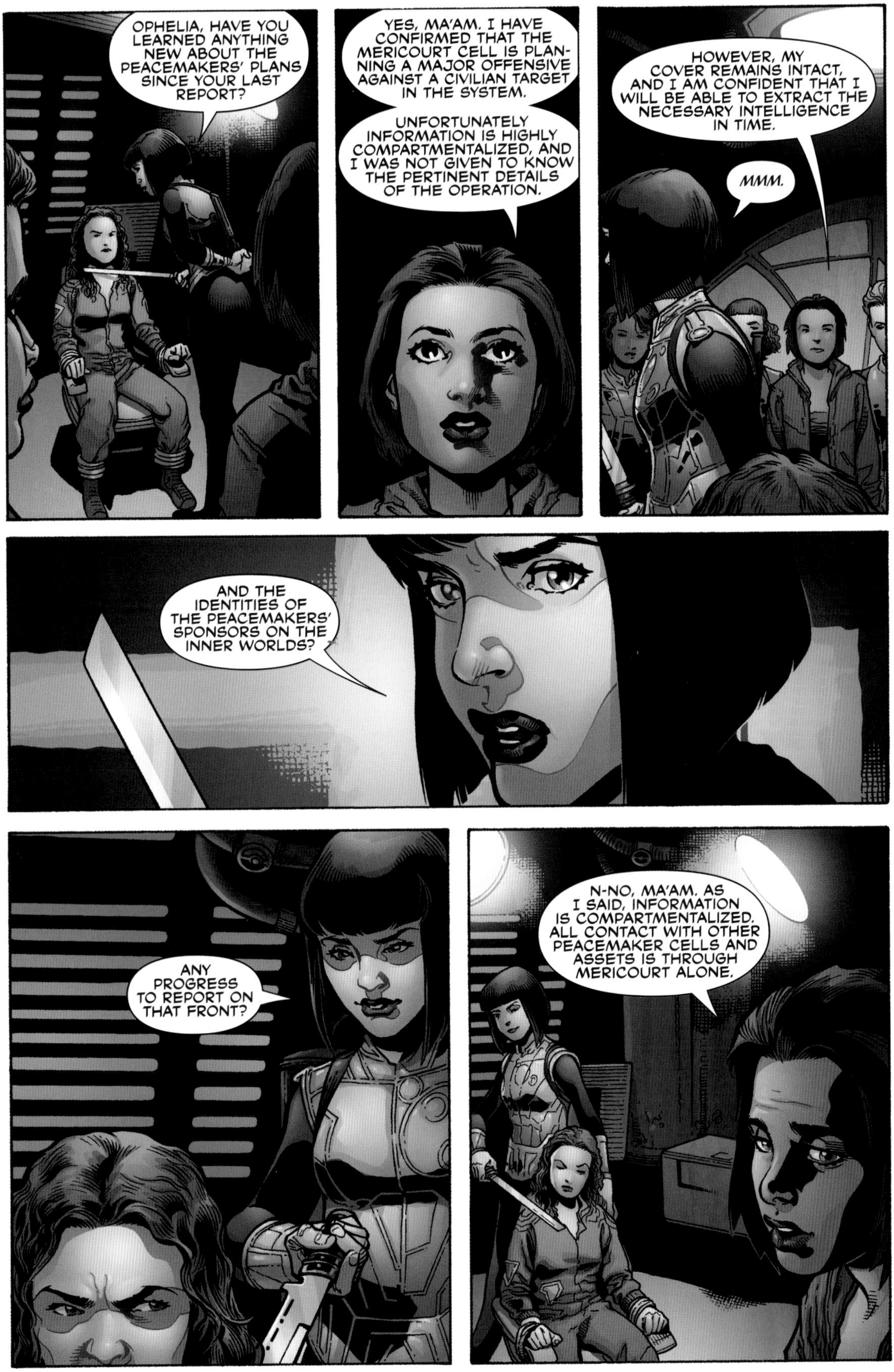
OPHELIA, HAVE YOU LEARNED ANYTHING NEW ABOUT THE PEACEMAKERS' PLANS SINCE YOUR LAST REPORT?
YES, MA'AM. I HAVE CONFIRMED THAT THE MERICOURT CELL IS PLANNING A MAJOR OFFENSIVE AGAINST A CIVILIAN TARGET IN THE SYSTEM.
UNFORTUNATELY INFORMATION IS HIGHLY COMPARTMENTALIZED, AND I WAS NOT GIVEN TO KNOW THE PERTINENT DETAILS OF THE OPERATION.
HOWEVER, MY COVER REMAINS INTACT, AND I AM CONFIDENT THAT I WILL BE ABLE TO EXTRACT THE NECESSARY INTELLIGENCE IN TIME.
MMM.
AND THE IDENTITIES OF THE PEACEMAKERS' SPONSORS ON THE INNER WORLDS?
ANY PROGRESS TO REPORT ON THAT FRONT?
N-NO, MA'AM. AS I SAID, INFORMATION IS COMPARTMENTALIZED. ALL CONTACT WITH OTHER PEACEMAKER CELLS AND ASSETS IS THROUGH MERICOURT ALONE.

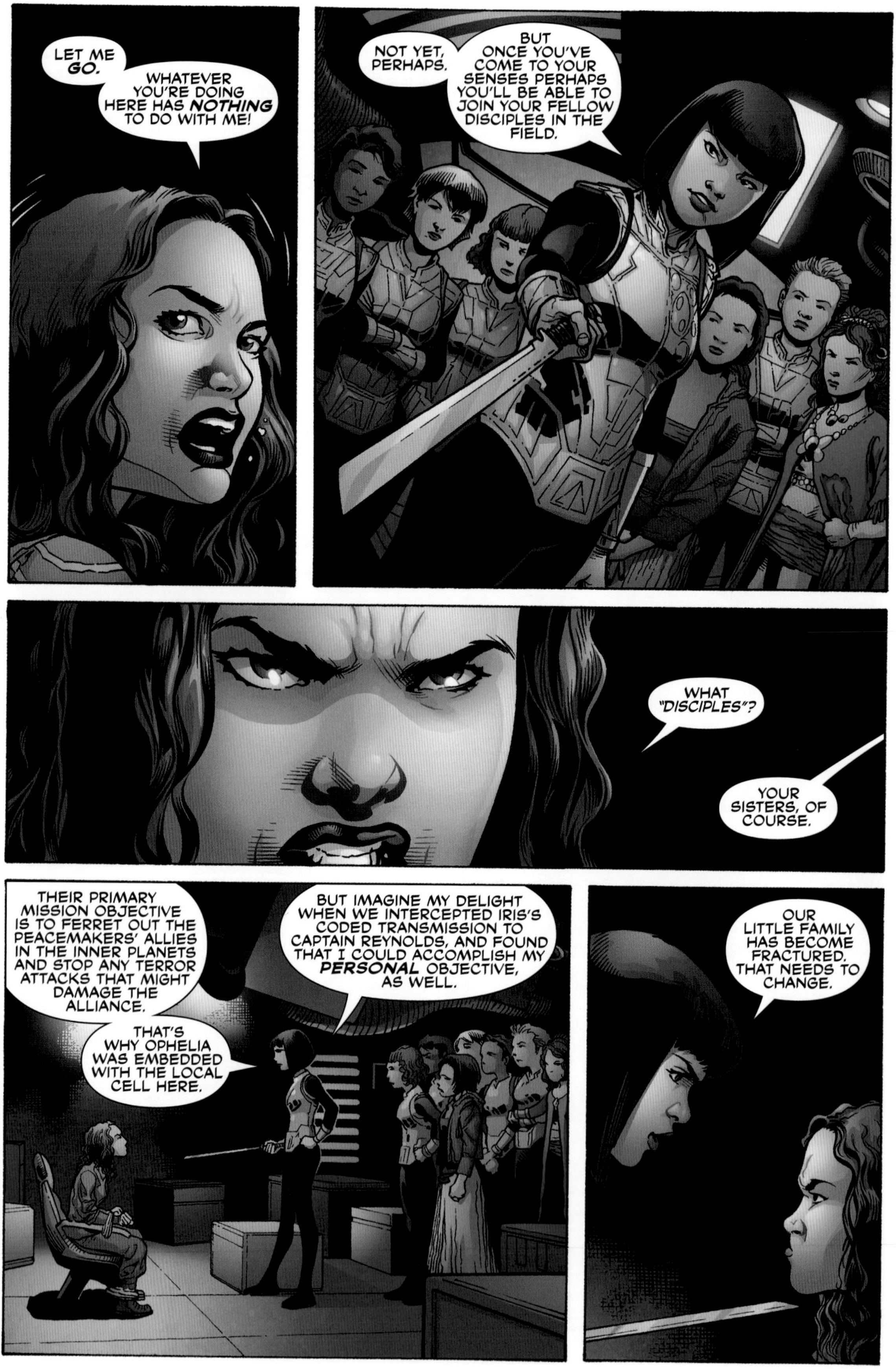
LET ME GO.
WHATEVER YOU'RE DOING HERE HAS NOTHING TO DO WITH ME!
NOT YET, PERHAPS.
BUT ONCE YOU'VE COME TO YOUR SENSES PERHAPS YOU'LL BE ABLE TO JOIN YOUR FELLOW DISCIPLES IN THE FIELD.
WHAT "DISCIPLES"?
YOUR SISTERS, OF COURSE.
THEIR PRIMARY MISSION OBJECTIVE IS TO FERRET OUT THE PEACEMAKERS' ALLIES IN THE INNER PLANETS AND STOP ANY TERROR ATTACKS THAT MIGHT DAMAGE THE ALLIANCE.
THAT'S WHY OPHELIA WAS EMBEDDED WITH THE LOCAL CELL HERE.
BUT IMAGINE MY DELIGHT WHEN WE INTERCEPTED IRIS'S CODED TRANSMISSION TO CAPTAIN REYNOLDS, AND FOUND THAT I COULD ACCOMPLISH MY PERSONAL OBJECTIVE, AS WELL.
OUR LITTLE FAMILY HAS BECOME FRACTURED. THAT NEEDS TO CHANGE.

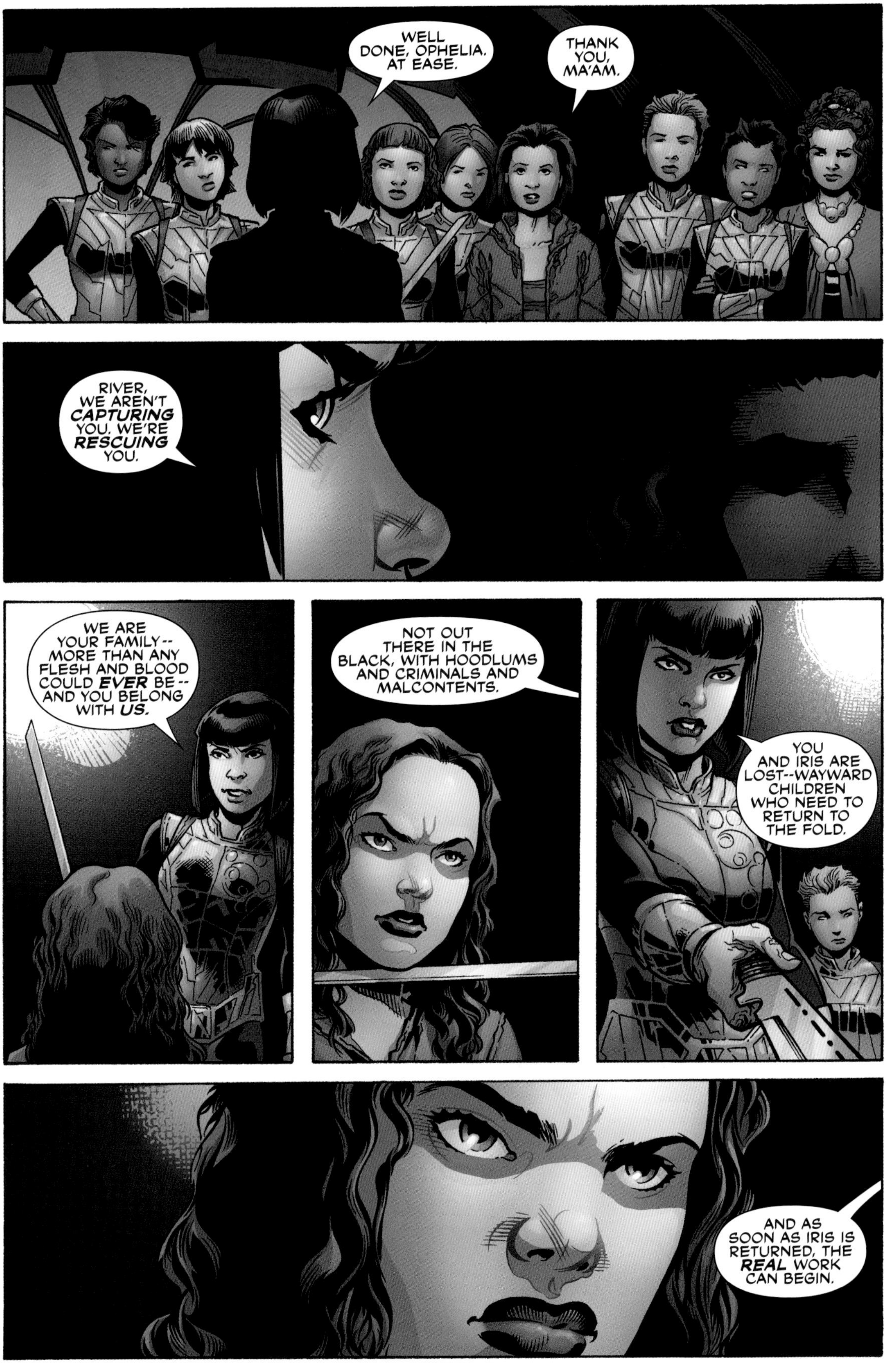
WELL DONE, OPHELIA. AT EASE.
THANK YOU, MA'AM.
RIVER, WE AREN'T **CAPTURING** YOU. WE'RE **RESCUING** YOU.
WE ARE YOUR FAMILY-- MORE THAN ANY FLESH AND BLOOD COULD **EVER** BE-- AND YOU BELONG WITH **US.**
NOT OUT THERE IN THE BLACK, WITH HOODLUMS AND CRIMINALS AND MALCONTENTS.
YOU AND IRIS ARE LOST--WAYWARD CHILDREN WHO NEED TO RETURN TO THE FOLD.
AND AS SOON AS IRIS IS RETURNED, THE **REAL** WORK CAN BEGIN.

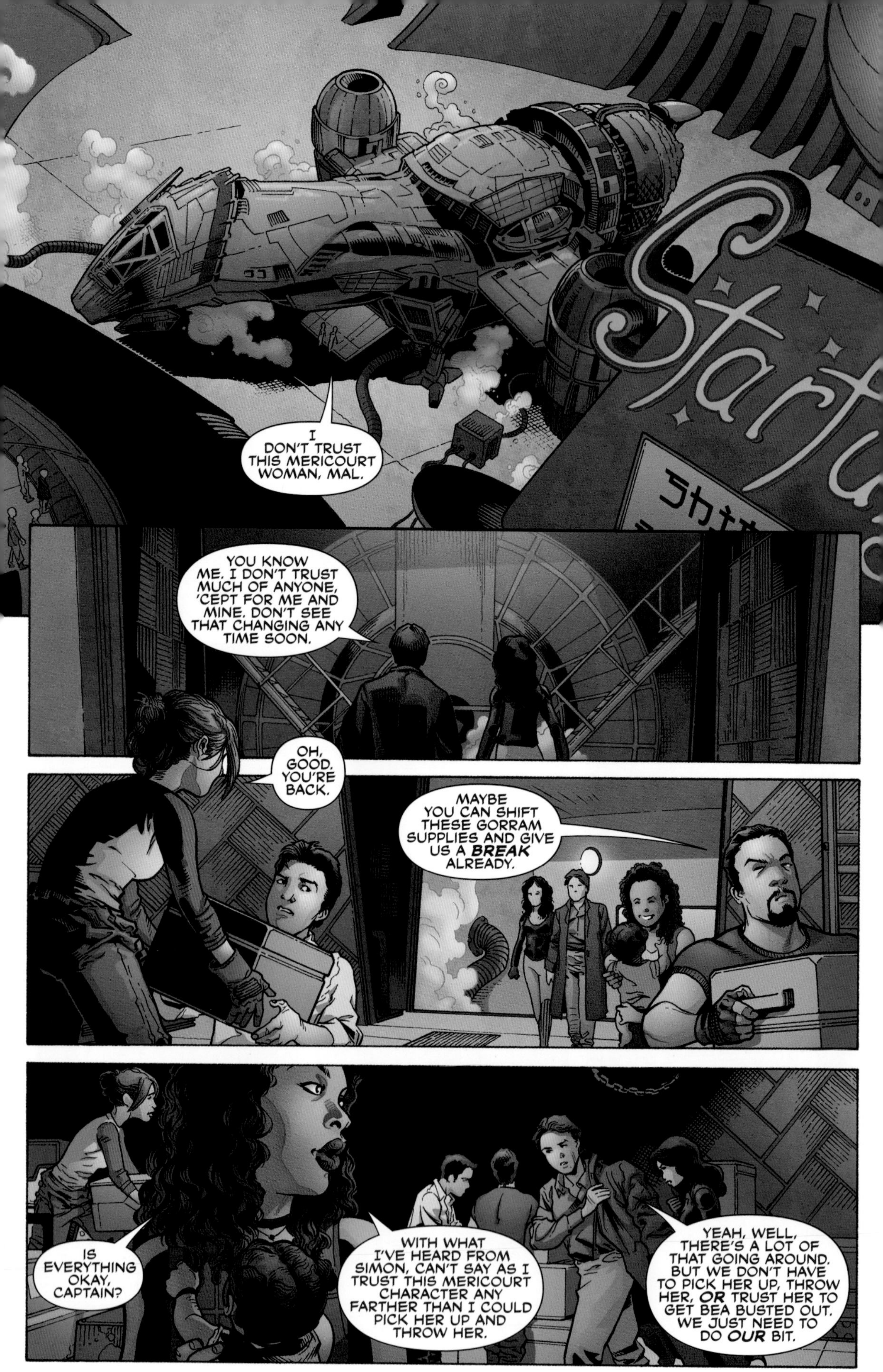
Starfu
I DON'T TRUST THIS MERICOURT WOMAN, MAL.
YOU KNOW ME. I DON'T TRUST MUCH OF ANYONE, 'CEPT FOR ME AND MINE. DON'T SEE THAT CHANGING ANY TIME SOON.
OH, GOOD. YOU'RE BACK.
MAYBE YOU CAN SHIFT THESE GORRAM SUPPLIES AND GIVE US A ***BREAK*** ALREADY.
IS EVERYTHING OKAY, CAPTAIN?
WITH WHAT I'VE HEARD FROM SIMON, CAN'T SAY AS I TRUST THIS MERICOURT CHARACTER ANY FARTHER THAN I COULD PICK HER UP AND THROW HER.
YEAH, WELL, THERE'S A LOT OF THAT GOING AROUND. BUT WE DON'T HAVE TO PICK HER UP, THROW HER, ***OR*** TRUST HER TO GET BEA BUSTED OUT. WE JUST NEED TO DO ***OUR*** BIT.

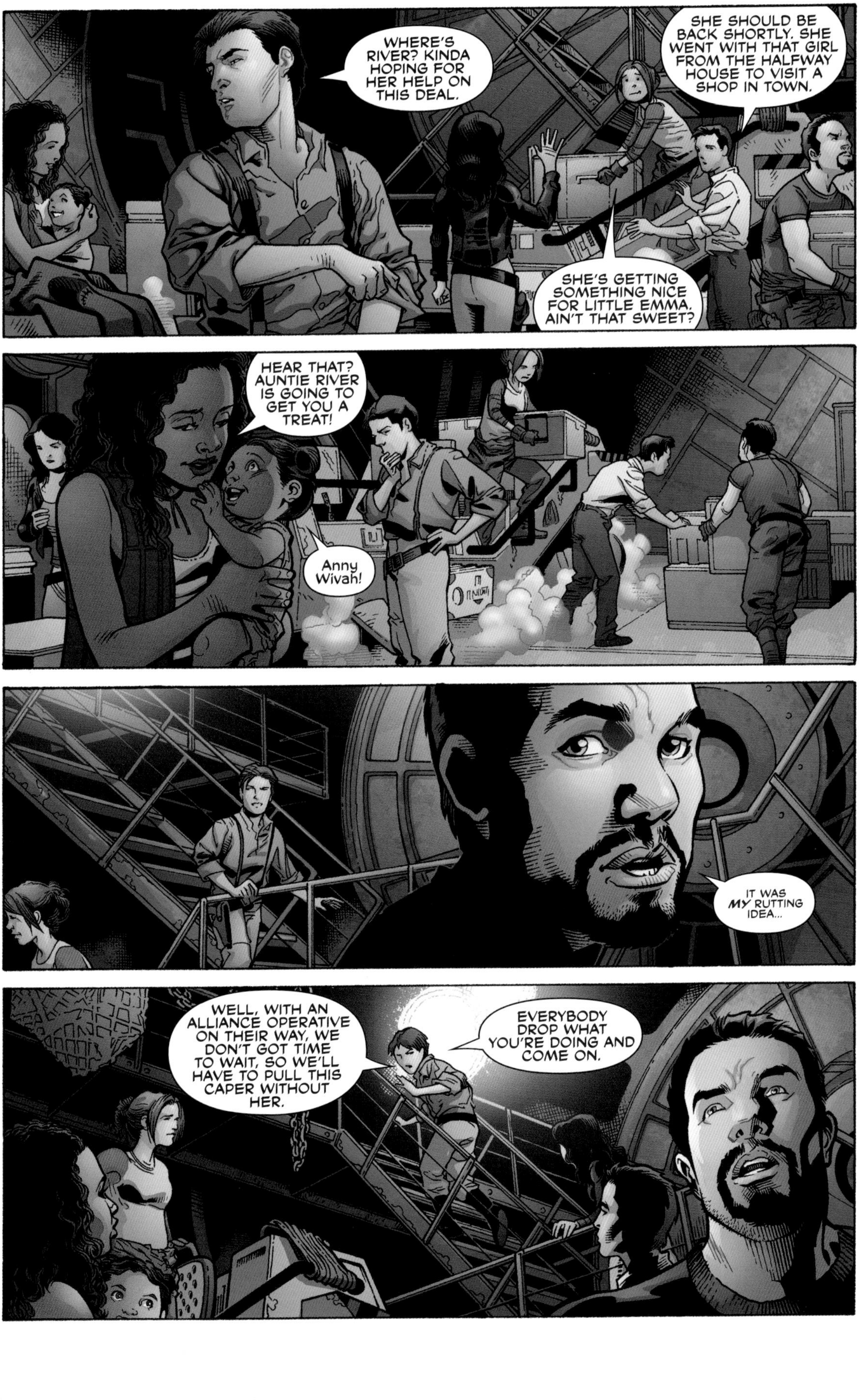
WHERE'S RIVER? KINDA HOPING FOR HER HELP ON THIS DEAL.
SHE SHOULD BE BACK SHORTLY. SHE WENT WITH THAT GIRL FROM THE HALFWAY HOUSE TO VISIT A SHOP IN TOWN.
SHE'S GETTING SOMETHING NICE FOR LITTLE EMMA. AIN'T THAT SWEET?
HEAR THAT? AUNTIE RIVER IS GOING TO GET YOU A TREAT!
Anny Wivah!
IT WAS *MY* RUTTING IDEA...
WELL, WITH AN ALLIANCE OPERATIVE ON THEIR WAY, WE DON'T GOT TIME TO WAIT, SO WE'LL HAVE TO PULL THIS CAPER WITHOUT HER.
EVERYBODY DROP WHAT YOU'RE DOING AND COME ON.

NOW BEFORE ANYONE ELSE CHIMES IN, *NO*, I DON'T TRUST MERICOURT.

SHE'S HIDING THINGS FROM US, I CAN TELL.

I'M NOT AIMING TO WED HER. WE JUST GOT COMMON CAUSE FOR A SPELL, THAT'S ALL.

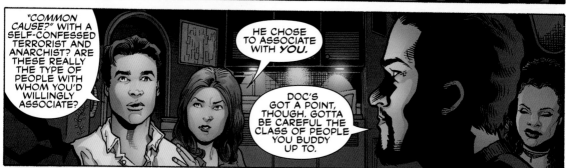

"COMMON CAUSE?" WITH A SELF-CONFESSED TERRORIST AND ANARCHIST? ARE THESE REALLY THE TYPE OF PEOPLE WITH WHOM YOU'D WILLINGLY ASSOCIATE?

HE CHOSE TO ASSOCIATE WITH *YOU*.

DOC'S GOT A POINT, THOUGH. GOTTA BE CAREFUL THE CLASS OF PEOPLE YOU BUDDY UP TO.

JAYNE, NOBODY MUCH CARES ABOUT YOUR VIEWS ON WHO WE SHOULD OR SHOULDN'T *"BUDDY UP TO."*

GOSH, ZOE, I WAS JUST --

ENOUGH ALREADY. THIS AIN'T A DEMOCRACY.

MERICOURT'S RELATIVE MERITS DON'T MAKE A DAMNED BIT OF DIFFERENCE. IT'S *OUR* FRIEND BEA THAT'S LOCKED UP IN ALLIANCE HANDS.

IF IT SUITS MERICOURT'S INTERESTS TO GET BEA BUSTED OUT, THEN WE'LL GLADLY ACCEPT HER HELP.

NOW WE'VE GOT A PLAN, AND WE'RE GONNA STICK TO IT. THAT'S THE END OF DISCUSSION.

INARA, SINCE YOU'RE HAVING TO GET ALL GUSSIED UP, I HOPE YOU STILL GOT SOME OF YOUR FRILLY FINERY SOCKED AWAY SOMEWHERE?

JUST BECAUSE I ADDED A FEW *PRAGMATIC* OPTIONS TO MY WARDROBE DOESN'T MEAN I LOST MY *MIND*, MAL.

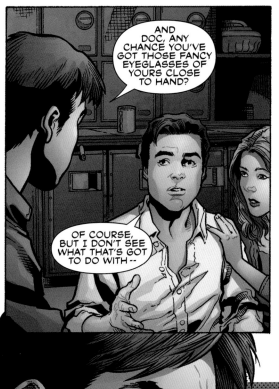

AND DOC, ANY CHANCE YOU'VE GOT THOSE FANCY EYEGLASSES OF YOURS CLOSE TO HAND?

OF COURSE, BUT I DON'T SEE WHAT THAT'S GOT TO DO WITH --

IF YOU'RE PLANNING WHAT I THINK YOU'RE PLANNING, CAPTAIN, I RESPECTFULLY INQUIRE WHETHER YOU'RE SURE THAT'S A GOOD IDEA.

ASK AGAIN WHEN WE FIND OUT IF IT WORKS OR NOT.

SO HERE'S WHAT WE'RE GOING TO DO...

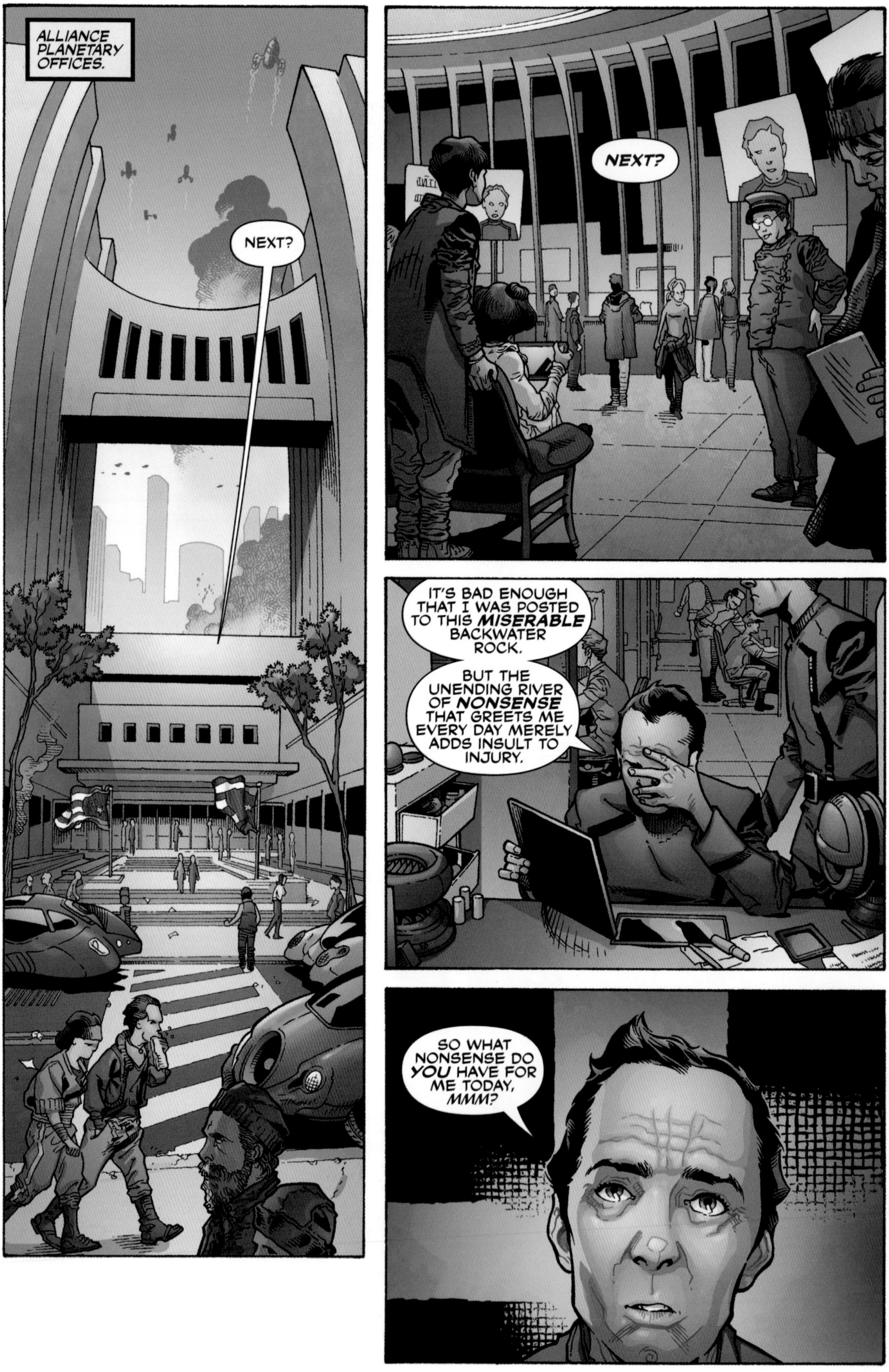
ALLIANCE PLANETARY OFFICES.
NEXT?
NEXT?
IT'S BAD ENOUGH THAT I WAS POSTED TO THIS *MISERABLE* BACKWATER ROCK.
BUT THE UNENDING RIVER OF *NONSENSE* THAT GREETS ME EVERY DAY MERELY ADDS INSULT TO INJURY.
SO WHAT NONSENSE DO *YOU* HAVE FOR ME TODAY, *MMM?*

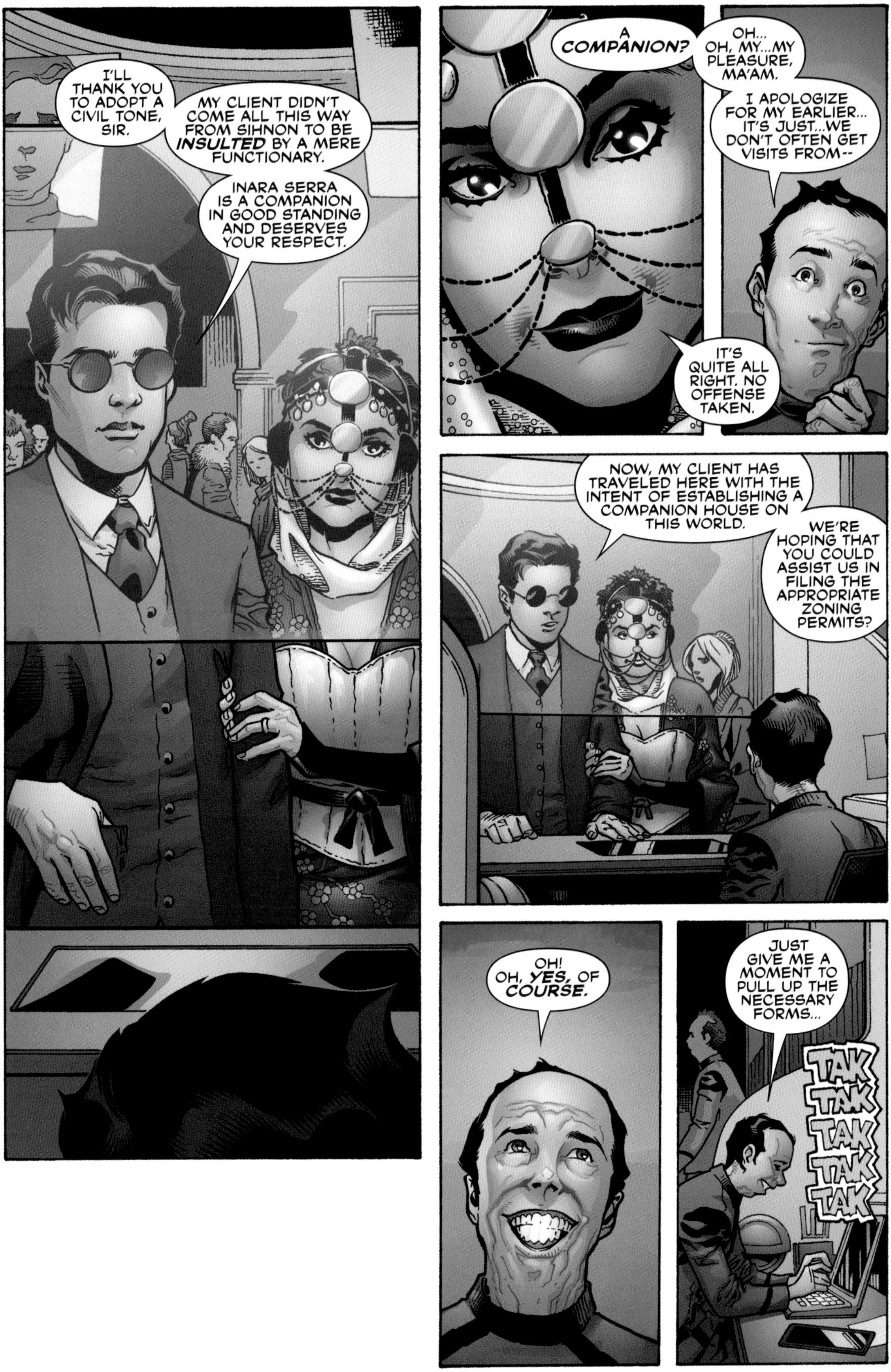
I'LL THANK YOU TO ADOPT A CIVIL TONE, SIR.
MY CLIENT DIDN'T COME ALL THIS WAY FROM SIHNON TO BE *INSULTED* BY A MERE FUNCTIONARY.
INARA SERRA IS A COMPANION IN GOOD STANDING AND DESERVES YOUR RESPECT.
A *COMPANION?*
OH... OH, MY...MY PLEASURE, MA'AM.
I APOLOGIZE FOR MY EARLIER... IT'S JUST...WE DON'T OFTEN GET VISITS FROM--
IT'S QUITE ALL RIGHT. NO OFFENSE TAKEN.
NOW, MY CLIENT HAS TRAVELED HERE WITH THE INTENT OF ESTABLISHING A COMPANION HOUSE ON THIS WORLD.
WE'RE HOPING THAT YOU COULD ASSIST US IN FILING THE APPROPRIATE ZONING PERMITS?
OH! OH, *YES,* OF *COURSE.*
JUST GIVE ME A MOMENT TO PULL UP THE NECESSARY FORMS...
TAK TAK TAK TAK TAK

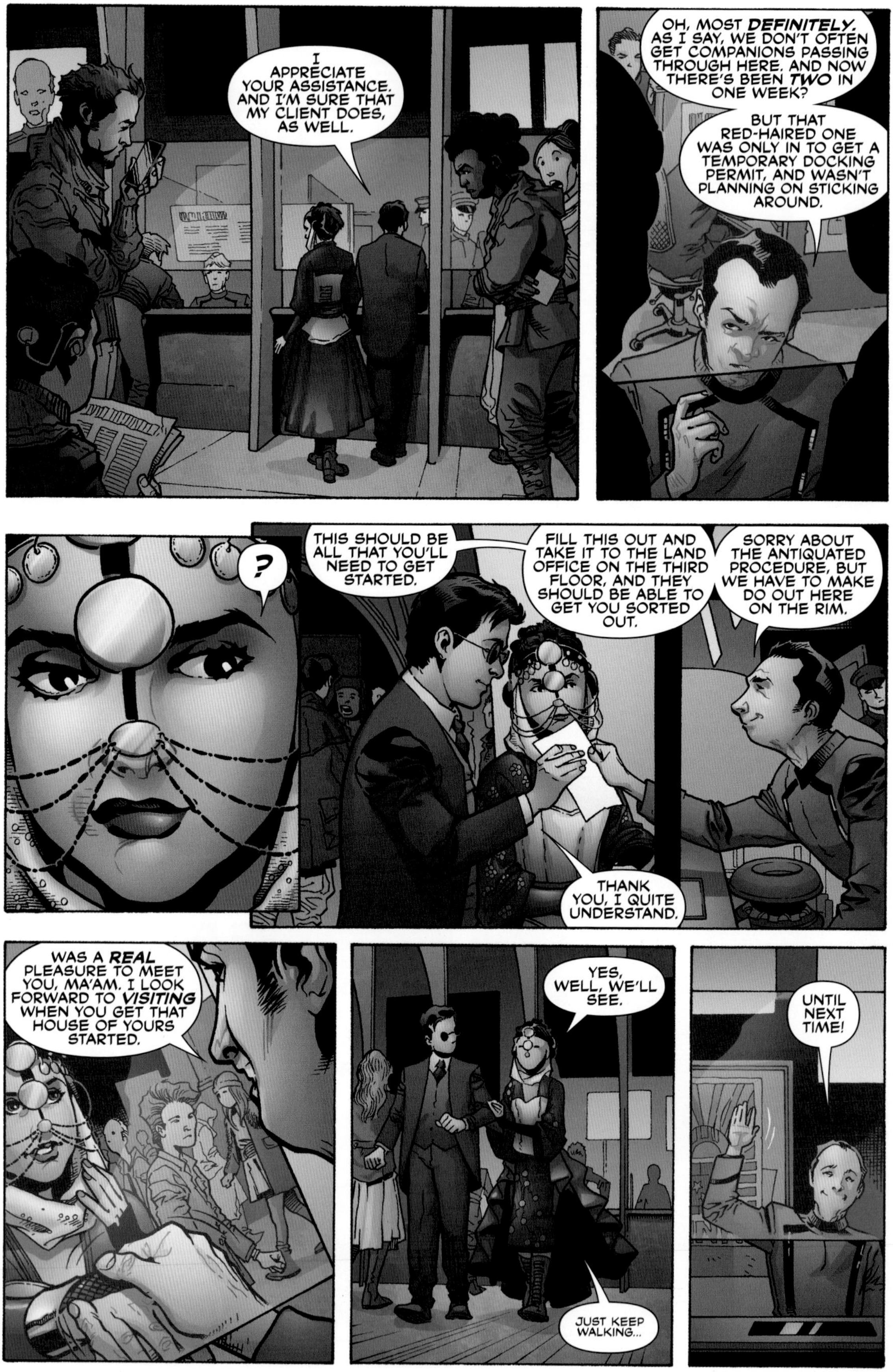

I APPRECIATE YOUR ASSISTANCE. AND I'M SURE THAT MY CLIENT DOES, AS WELL.
OH, MOST DEFINITELY. AS I SAY, WE DON'T OFTEN GET COMPANIONS PASSING THROUGH HERE. AND NOW THERE'S BEEN TWO IN ONE WEEK?
BUT THAT RED-HAIRED ONE WAS ONLY IN TO GET A TEMPORARY DOCKING PERMIT, AND WASN'T PLANNING ON STICKING AROUND.
?
THIS SHOULD BE ALL THAT YOU'LL NEED TO GET STARTED.
FILL THIS OUT AND TAKE IT TO THE LAND OFFICE ON THE THIRD FLOOR, AND THEY SHOULD BE ABLE TO GET YOU SORTED OUT.
SORRY ABOUT THE ANTIQUATED PROCEDURE, BUT WE HAVE TO MAKE DO OUT HERE ON THE RIM.
THANK YOU, I QUITE UNDERSTAND.
WAS A REAL PLEASURE TO MEET YOU, MA'AM. I LOOK FORWARD TO VISITING WHEN YOU GET THAT HOUSE OF YOURS STARTED.
YES, WELL, WE'LL SEE.
JUST KEEP WALKING...
UNTIL NEXT TIME!

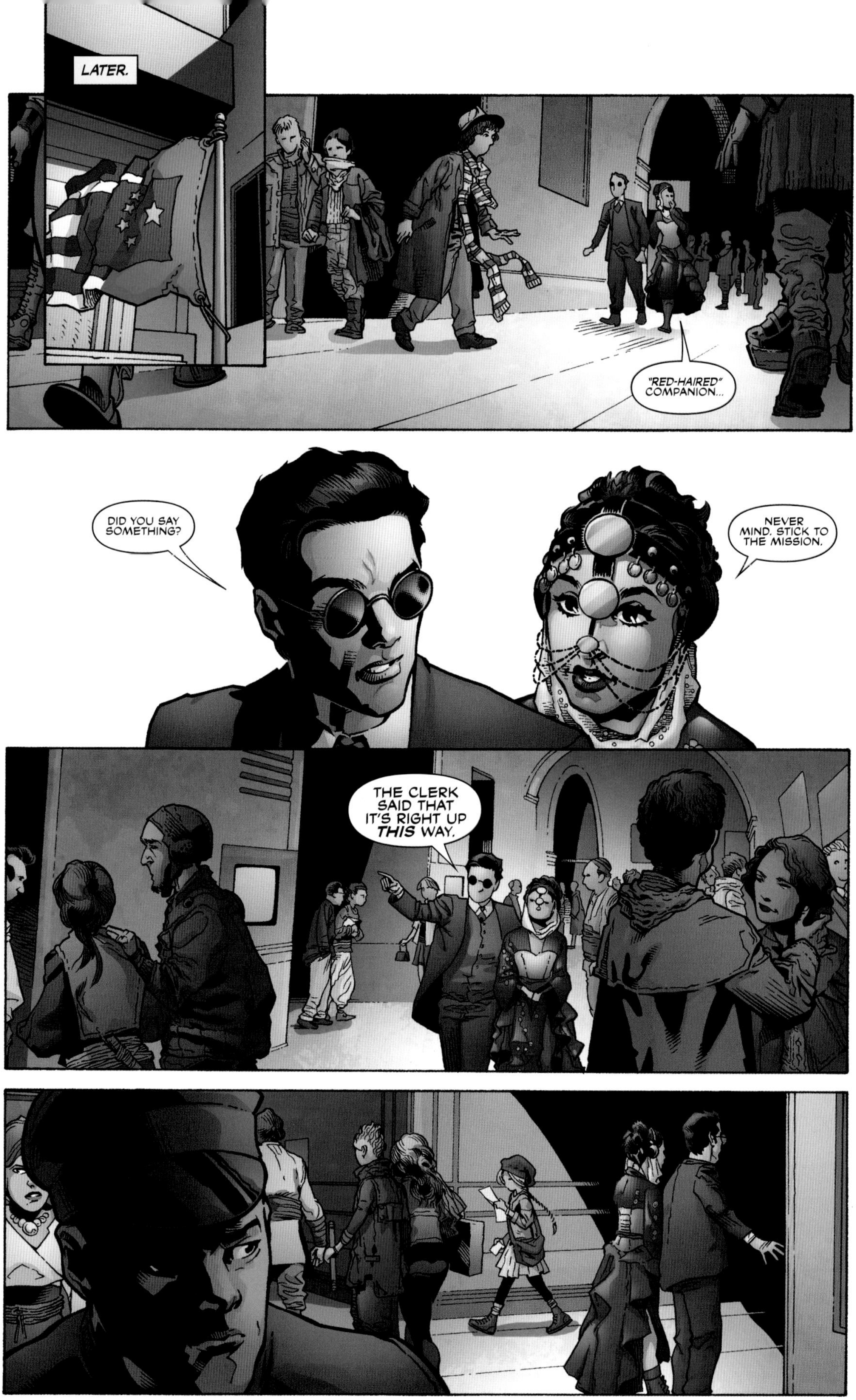
LATER.
"RED-HAIRED" COMPANION...
DID YOU SAY SOMETHING?
NEVER MIND. STICK TO THE MISSION.
THE CLERK SAID THAT IT'S RIGHT UP THIS WAY.

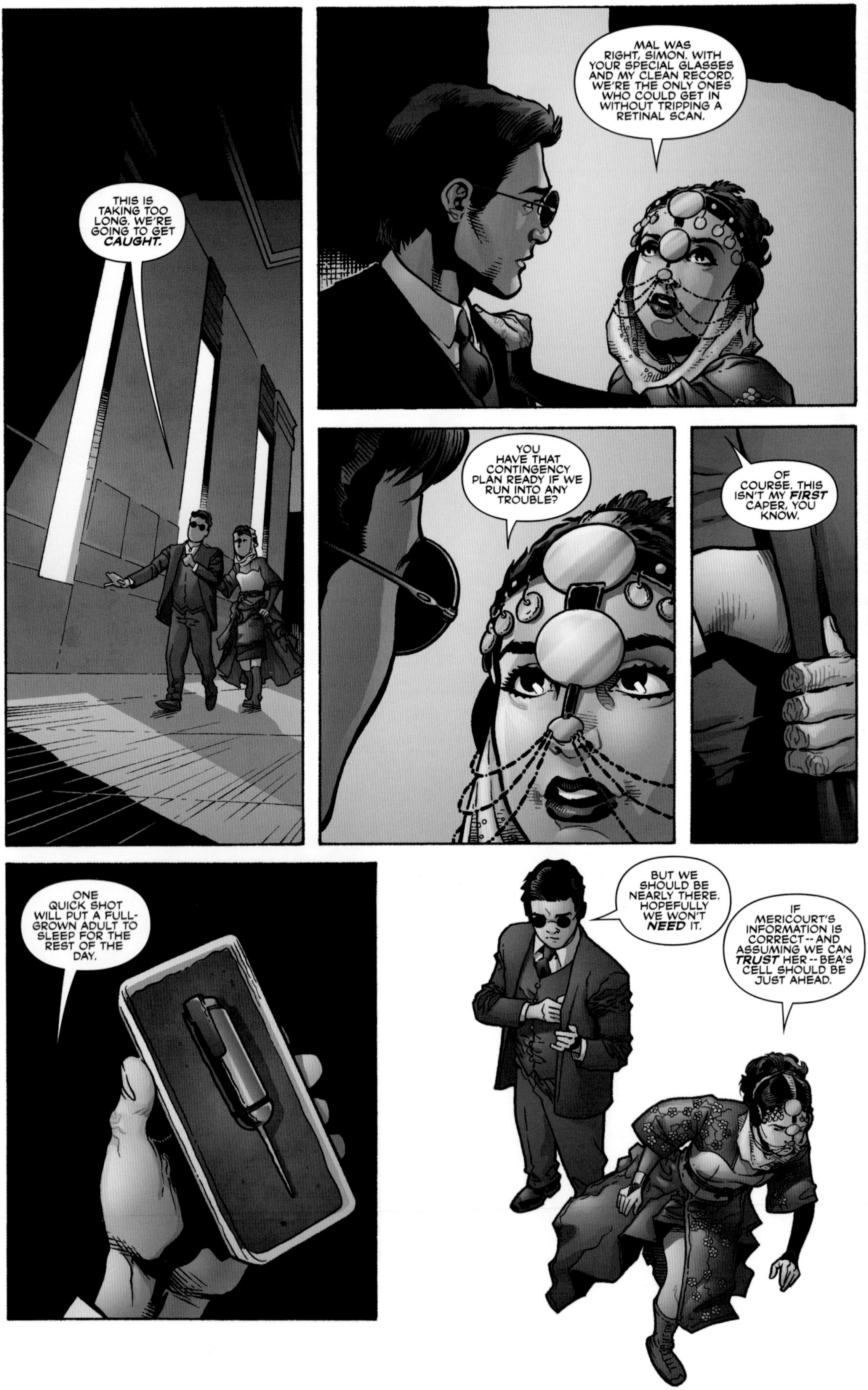
THIS IS TAKING TOO LONG. WE'RE GOING TO GET *CAUGHT.*
MAL WAS RIGHT, SIMON. WITH YOUR SPECIAL GLASSES AND MY CLEAN RECORD, WE'RE THE ONLY ONES WHO COULD GET IN WITHOUT TRIPPING A RETINAL SCAN.
YOU HAVE THAT CONTINGENCY PLAN READY IF WE RUN INTO ANY TROUBLE?
OF COURSE. THIS ISN'T MY *FIRST* CAPER, YOU KNOW.
ONE QUICK SHOT WILL PUT A FULL-GROWN ADULT TO SLEEP FOR THE REST OF THE DAY.
BUT WE SHOULD BE NEARLY THERE. HOPEFULLY WE WON'T *NEED* IT.
IF MERICOURT'S INFORMATION IS CORRECT -- AND ASSUMING WE CAN *TRUST* HER -- BEA'S CELL SHOULD BE JUST AHEAD.

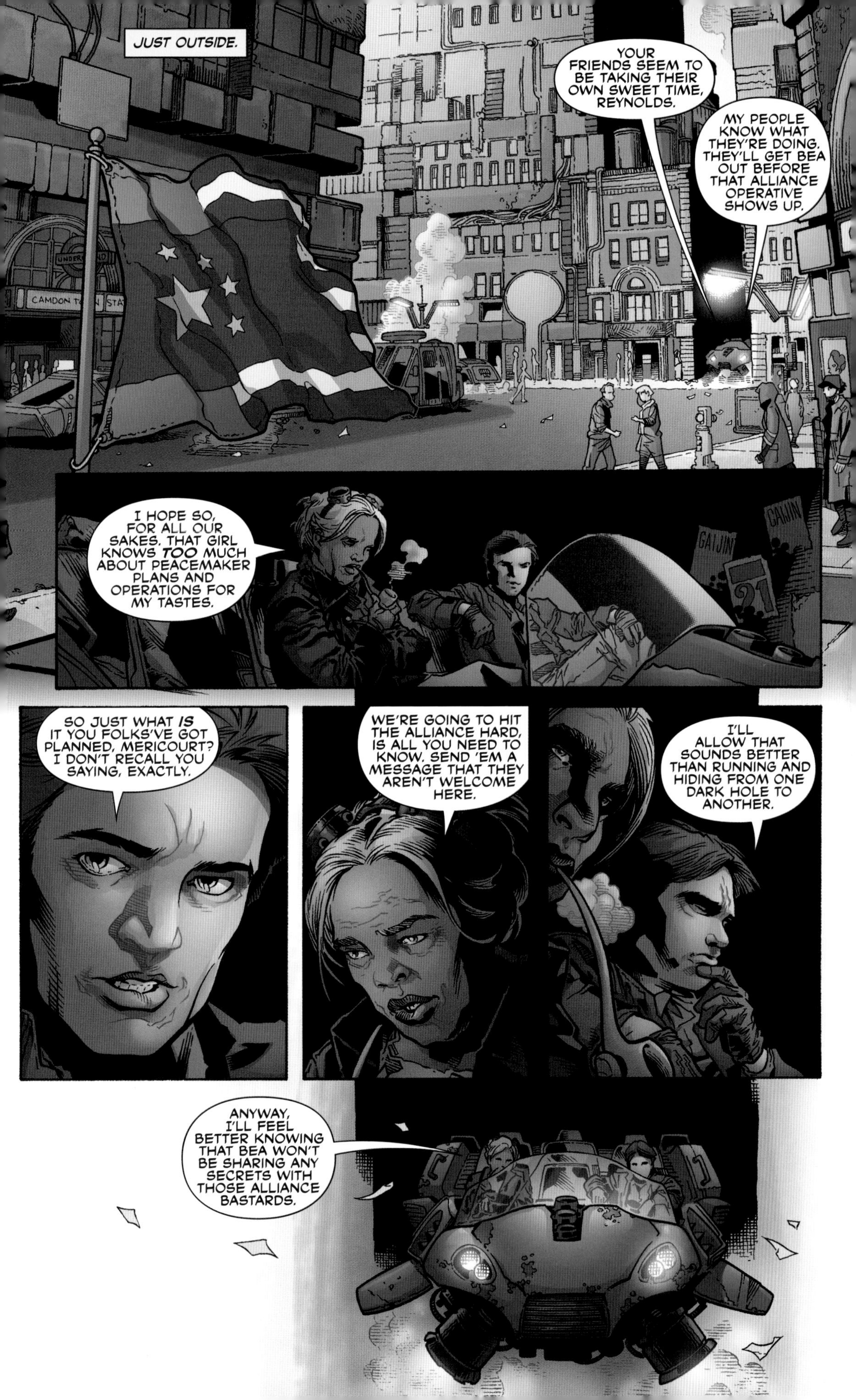
JUST OUTSIDE.
YOUR FRIENDS SEEM TO BE TAKING THEIR OWN SWEET TIME, REYNOLDS.
MY PEOPLE KNOW WHAT THEY'RE DOING. THEY'LL GET BEA OUT BEFORE THAT ALLIANCE OPERATIVE SHOWS UP.
I HOPE SO, FOR ALL OUR SAKES. THAT GIRL KNOWS TOO MUCH ABOUT PEACEMAKER PLANS AND OPERATIONS FOR MY TASTES.
GAIJIN
GAIJIN
SO JUST WHAT IS IT YOU FOLKS'VE GOT PLANNED, MERICOURT? I DON'T RECALL YOU SAYING, EXACTLY.
WE'RE GOING TO HIT THE ALLIANCE HARD, IS ALL YOU NEED TO KNOW. SEND 'EM A MESSAGE THAT THEY AREN'T WELCOME HERE.
I'LL ALLOW THAT SOUNDS BETTER THAN RUNNING AND HIDING FROM ONE DARK HOLE TO ANOTHER.
ANYWAY, I'LL FEEL BETTER KNOWING THAT BEA WON'T BE SHARING ANY SECRETS WITH THOSE ALLIANCE BASTARDS.

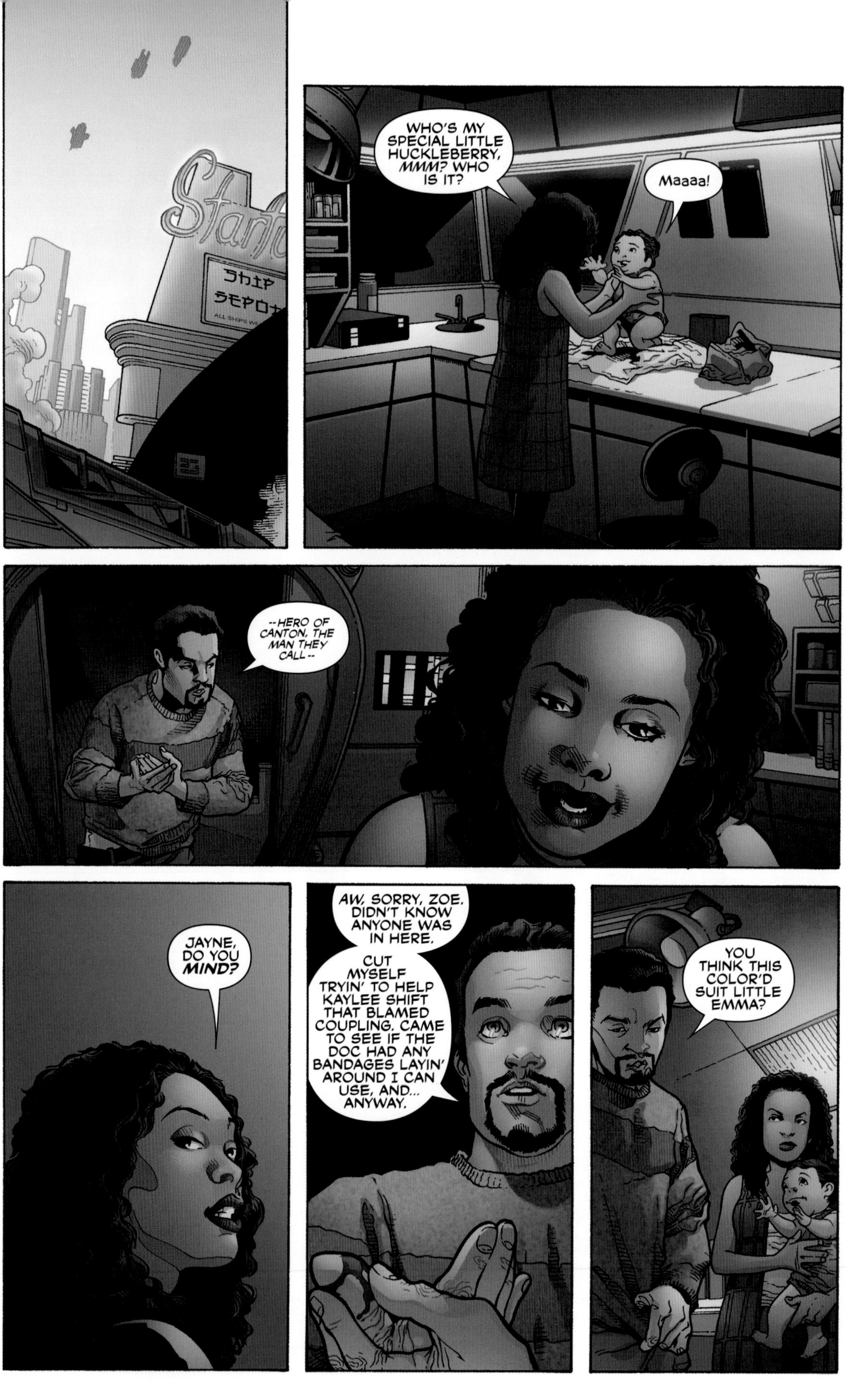

Starfi
SHIP
DEPOT
WHO'S MY SPECIAL LITTLE HUCKLEBERRY, MMM? WHO IS IT?
Maaaa!
--HERO OF CANTON, THE MAN THEY CALL--
JAYNE, DO YOU MIND?
AW, SORRY, ZOE. DIDN'T KNOW ANYONE WAS IN HERE.
CUT MYSELF TRYIN' TO HELP KAYLEE SHIFT THAT BLAMED COUPLING. CAME TO SEE IF THE DOC HAD ANY BANDAGES LAYIN' AROUND I CAN USE, AND... ANYWAY.
YOU THINK THIS COLOR'D SUIT LITTLE EMMA?

CLANG CLANG

LOT OF HELP *HE* IS. "I CUT MYSELF, KAYLEE. I'M *BLEEDIN'*, KAYLEE."

JAYNE WOULDN'T LAST FIVE MINUTES, HE HAD TO DO *MY* JOB.

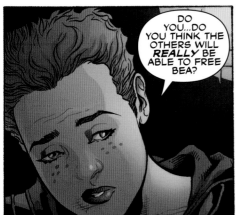

DO YOU...DO YOU THINK THE OTHERS WILL *REALLY* BE ABLE TO FREE BEA?

AW, YOU'RE WORRIED ABOUT YOUR FRIEND, AIN'T YA? POOR THING.

NOW DON'T YOU WORRY FOR A SEC, IRIS. SIMON AND INARA WILL HAVE HER OUT IN *NO* TIME.

AND SOON AS THEY DO, YOU TWO WILL BE FREE TO ROAM THE 'VERSE AGAIN, HAVING ADVENTURES AND THE LIKE.

I HOPE SO. BUT MAYBE NEXT TIME --

BREEP

SIMMER DOWN, GIRL, IT'S JUST THE DOORBELL. YOU STAY HERE AND I'LL CHECK IT OUT.

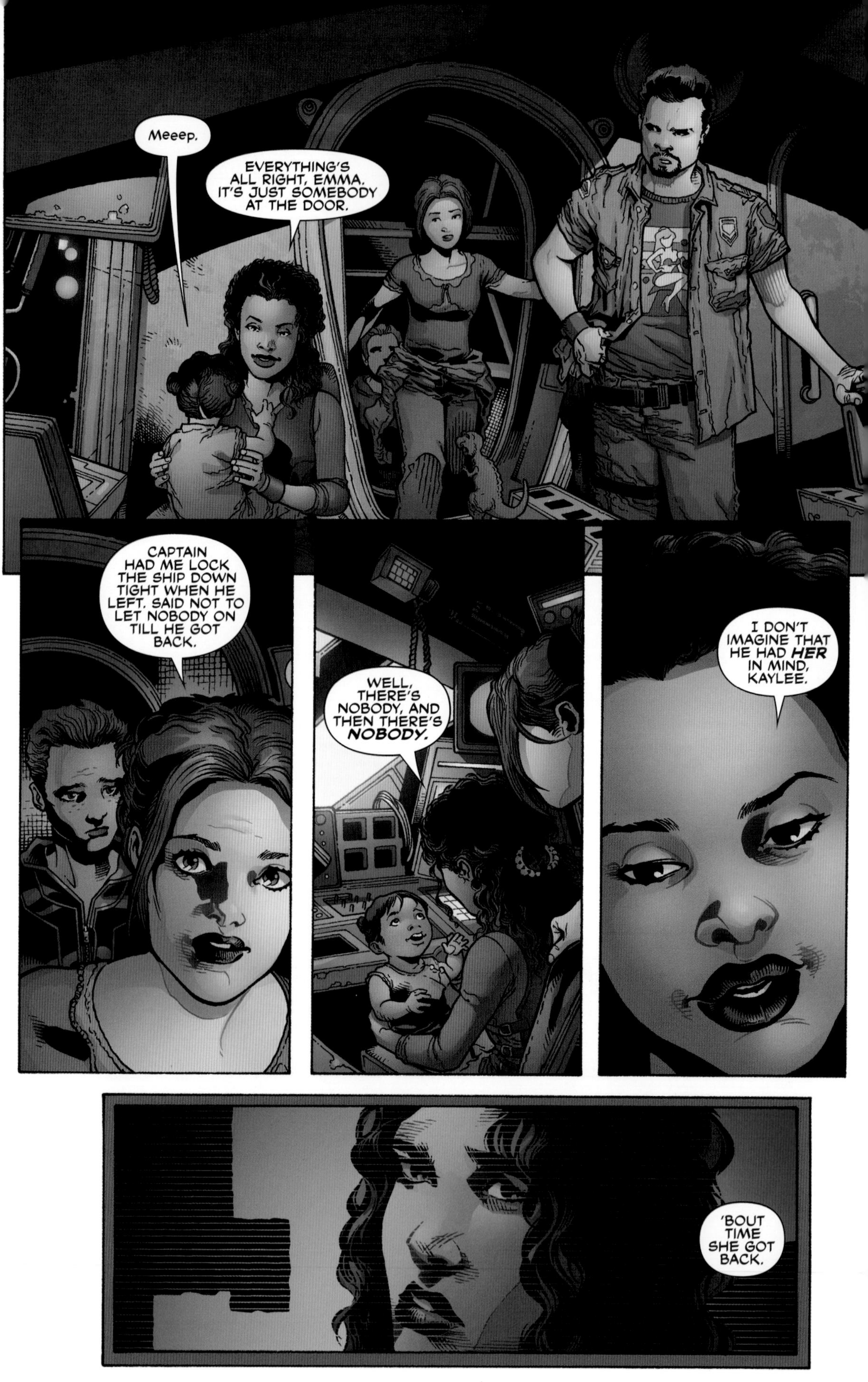
Meeep.
EVERYTHING'S ALL RIGHT, EMMA. IT'S JUST SOMEBODY AT THE DOOR.
CAPTAIN HAD ME LOCK THE SHIP DOWN TIGHT WHEN HE LEFT. SAID NOT TO LET NOBODY ON TILL HE GOT BACK.
WELL, THERE'S NOBODY, AND THEN THERE'S NOBODY.
I DON'T IMAGINE THAT HE HAD HER IN MIND, KAYLEE.
'BOUT TIME SHE GOT BACK.

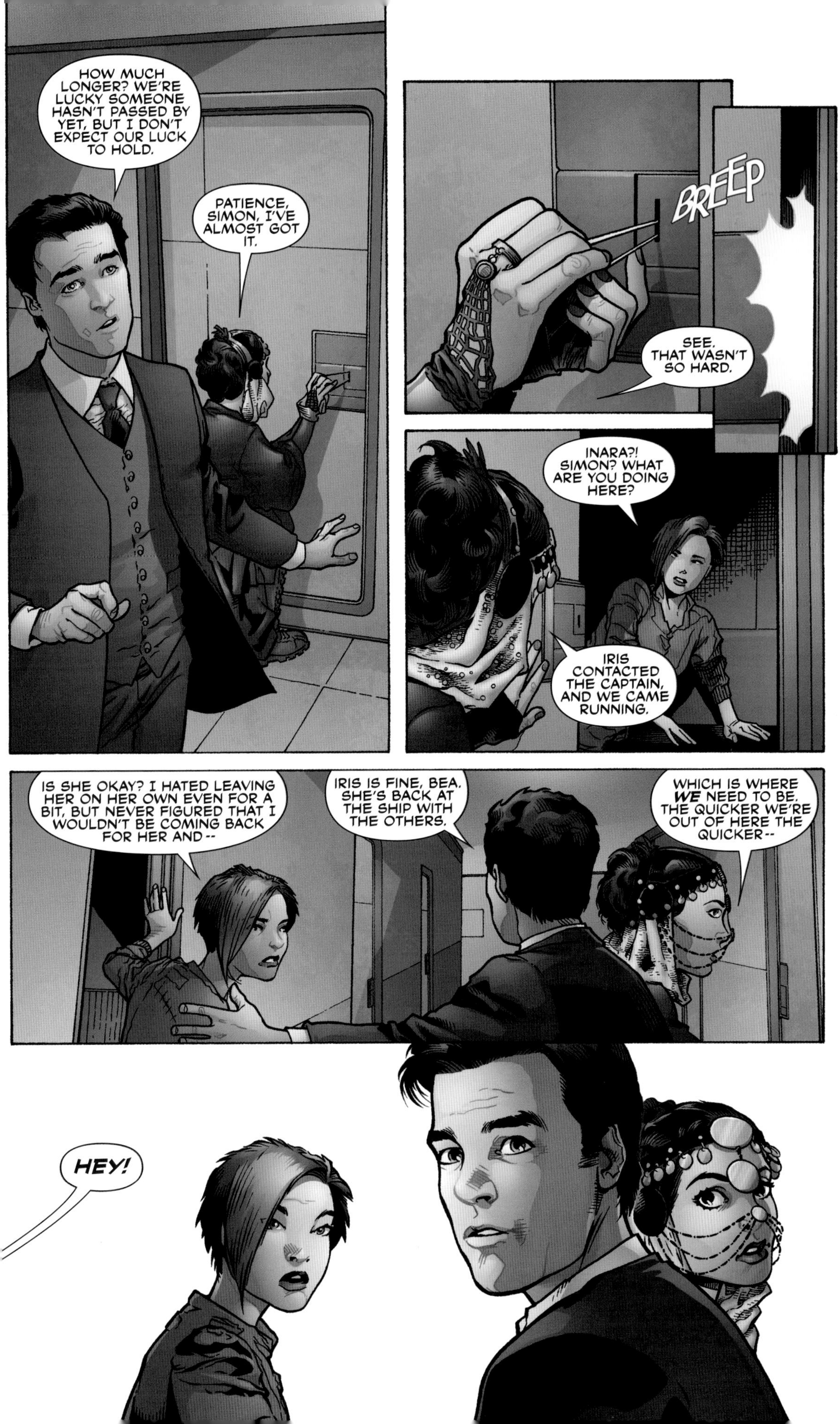
HOW MUCH LONGER? WE'RE LUCKY SOMEONE HASN'T PASSED BY YET, BUT I DON'T EXPECT OUR LUCK TO HOLD.
PATIENCE, SIMON, I'VE ALMOST GOT IT.
BREEP
SEE. THAT WASN'T SO HARD.
INARA?! SIMON? WHAT ARE YOU DOING HERE?
IRIS CONTACTED THE CAPTAIN, AND WE CAME RUNNING.
IS SHE OKAY? I HATED LEAVING HER ON HER OWN EVEN FOR A BIT, BUT NEVER FIGURED THAT I WOULDN'T BE COMING BACK FOR HER AND--
IRIS IS FINE, BEA. SHE'S BACK AT THE SHIP WITH THE OTHERS.
WHICH IS WHERE WE NEED TO BE. THE QUICKER WE'RE OUT OF HERE THE QUICKER--
HEY!

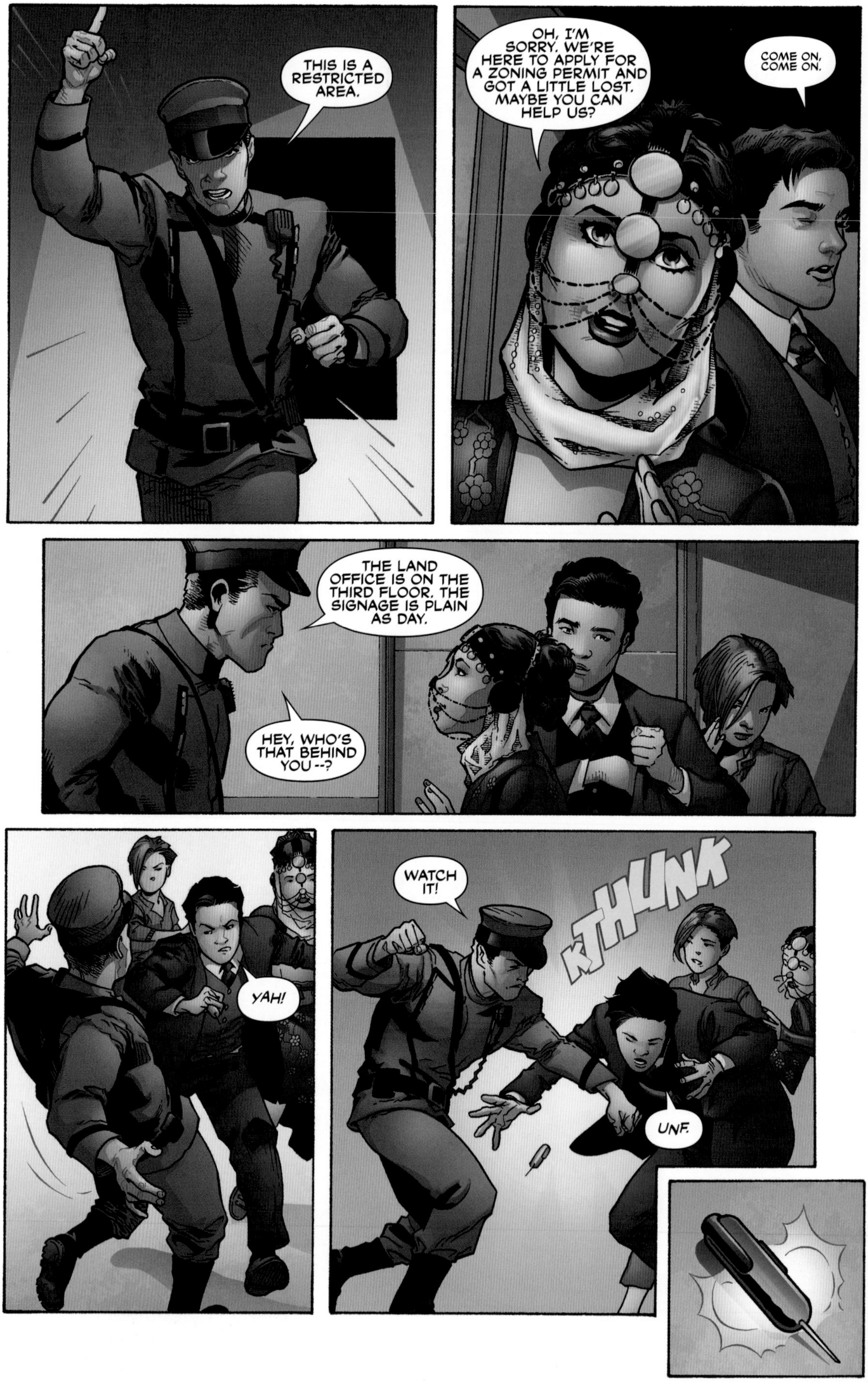
THIS IS A RESTRICTED AREA.
OH, I'M SORRY. WE'RE HERE TO APPLY FOR A ZONING PERMIT AND GOT A LITTLE LOST. MAYBE YOU CAN HELP US?
COME ON, COME ON.
THE LAND OFFICE IS ON THE THIRD FLOOR. THE SIGNAGE IS PLAIN AS DAY.
HEY, WHO'S THAT BEHIND YOU --?
YAH!
WATCH IT!
KTHUNK
UNF.

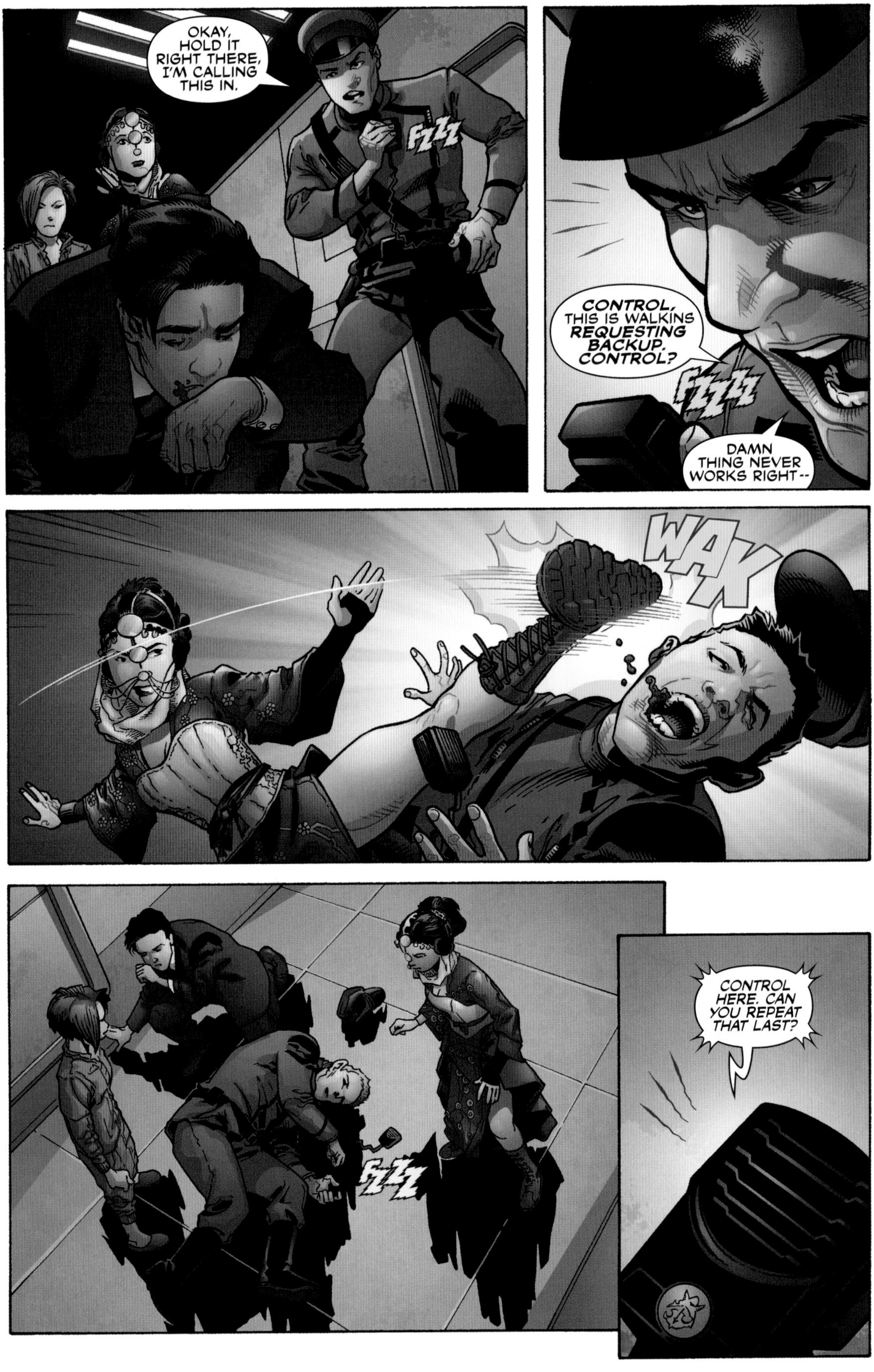
OKAY, HOLD IT RIGHT THERE, I'M CALLING THIS IN.
FZZZ
CONTROL, THIS IS WALKINS REQUESTING BACKUP. CONTROL?
FZZZZ
DAMN THING NEVER WORKS RIGHT--
WAK
CONTROL HERE. CAN YOU REPEAT THAT LAST?
FZZZ

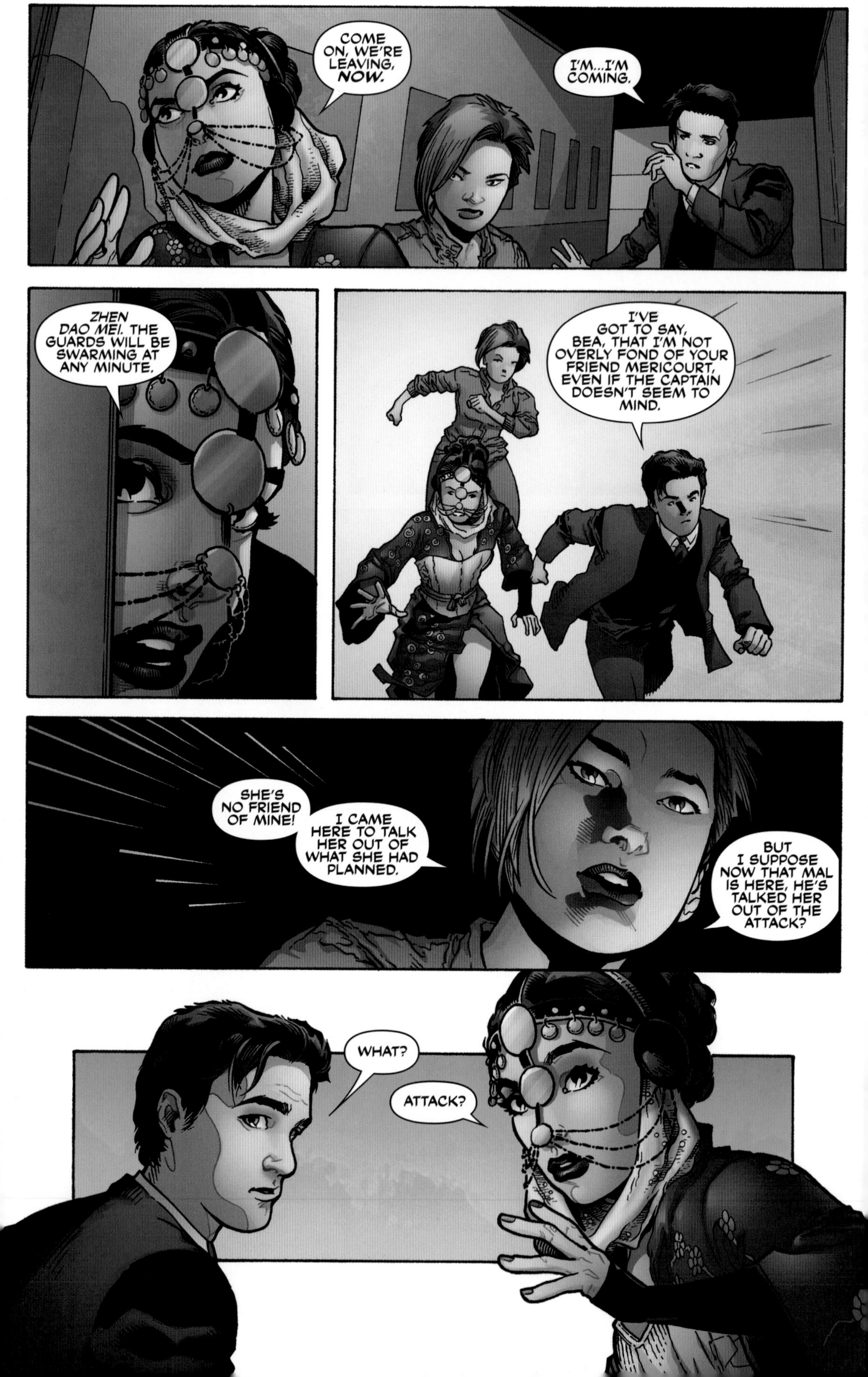
COME ON, WE'RE LEAVING, *NOW.*
I'M...I'M COMING.
ZHEN DAO MEI! THE GUARDS WILL BE SWARMING AT ANY MINUTE.
I'VE GOT TO SAY, BEA, THAT I'M NOT OVERLY FOND OF YOUR FRIEND MERICOURT, EVEN IF THE CAPTAIN DOESN'T SEEM TO MIND.
SHE'S NO FRIEND OF MINE!
I CAME HERE TO TALK HER OUT OF WHAT SHE HAD PLANNED.
BUT I SUPPOSE NOW THAT MAL IS HERE, HE'S TALKED HER OUT OF THE ATTACK?
WHAT?
ATTACK?

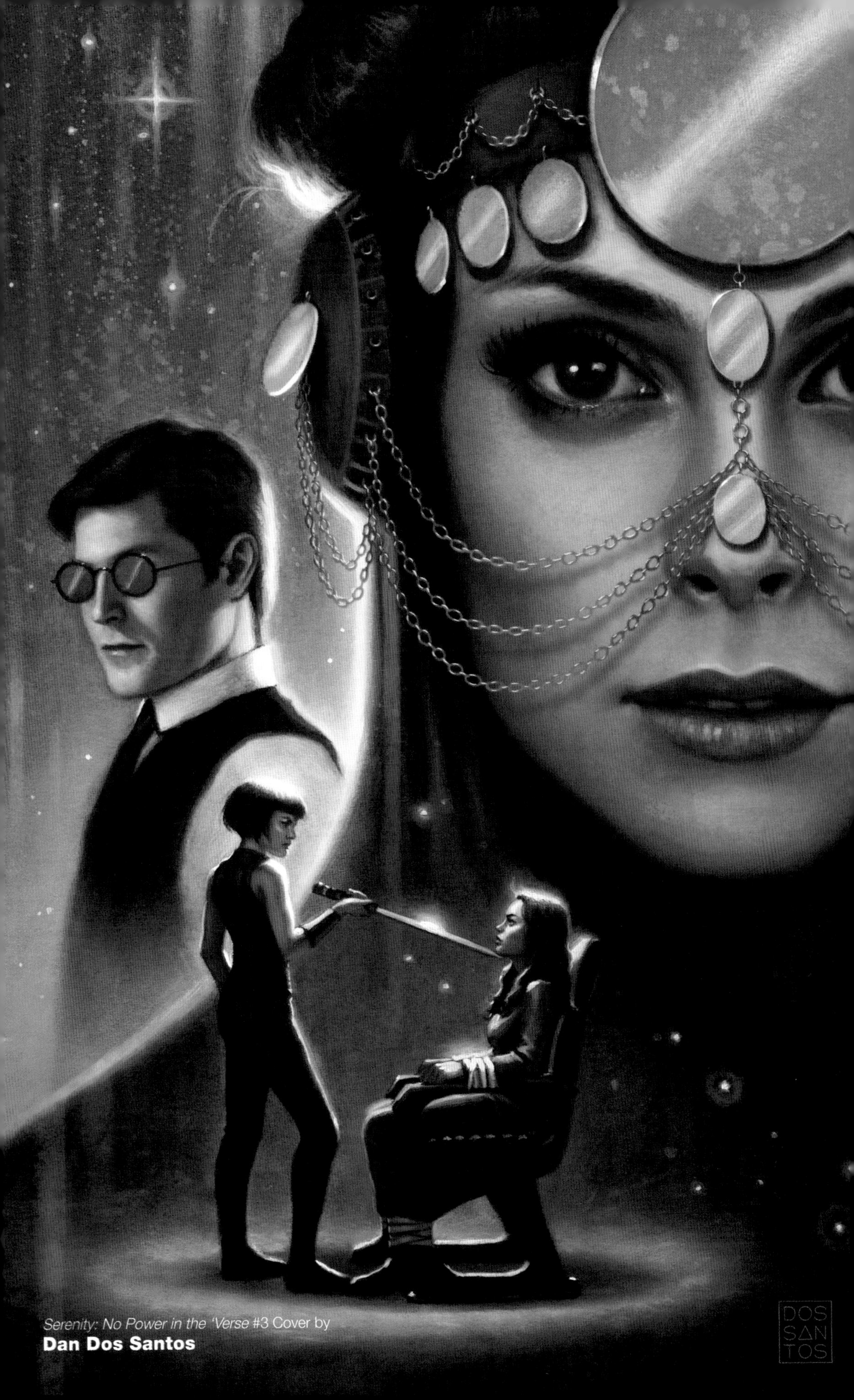
DOS
SANTOS

Serenity: No Power in the 'Verse #3 Cover by
Dan Dos Santos

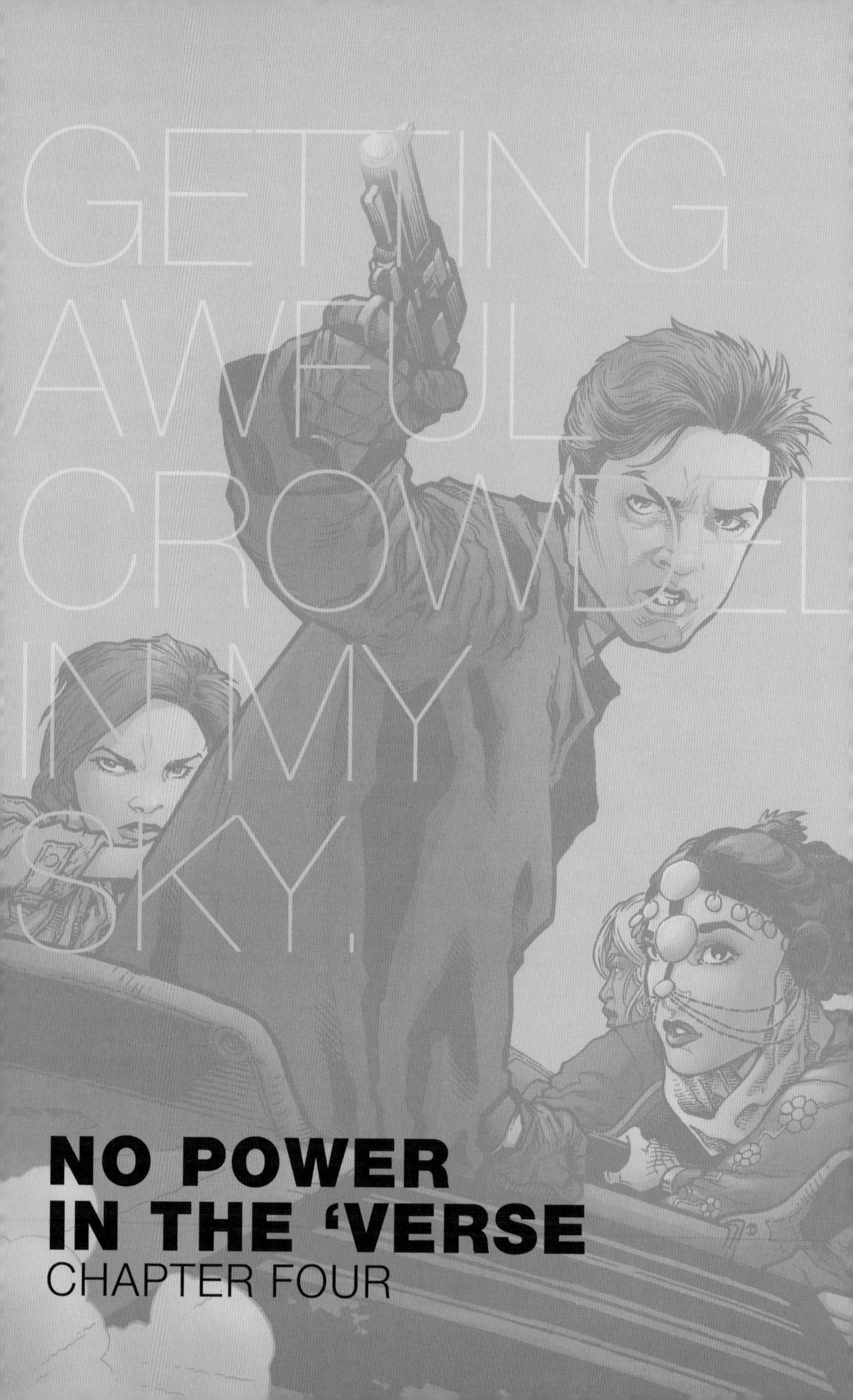
GETTING AWFUL CROWDED IN MY SKY.

NO POWER IN THE 'VERSE

CHAPTER FOUR

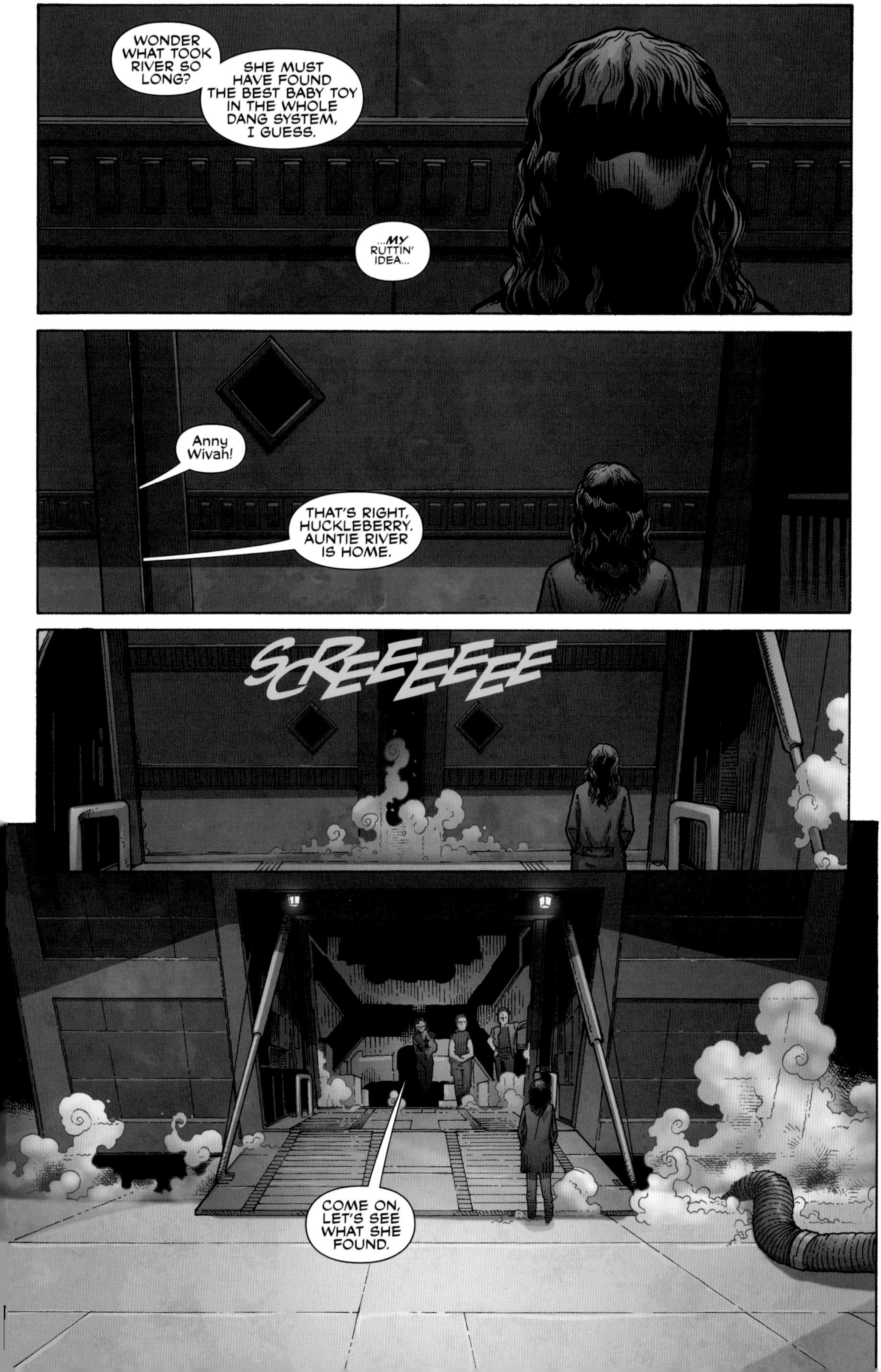
WONDER WHAT TOOK RIVER SO LONG?
SHE MUST HAVE FOUND THE BEST BABY TOY IN THE WHOLE DANG SYSTEM, I GUESS.
...MY RUTTIN' IDEA...
Anny Wivah!
THAT'S RIGHT, HUCKLEBERRY. AUNTIE RIVER IS HOME.
SCREEEEEEE
COME ON, LET'S SEE WHAT SHE FOUND.

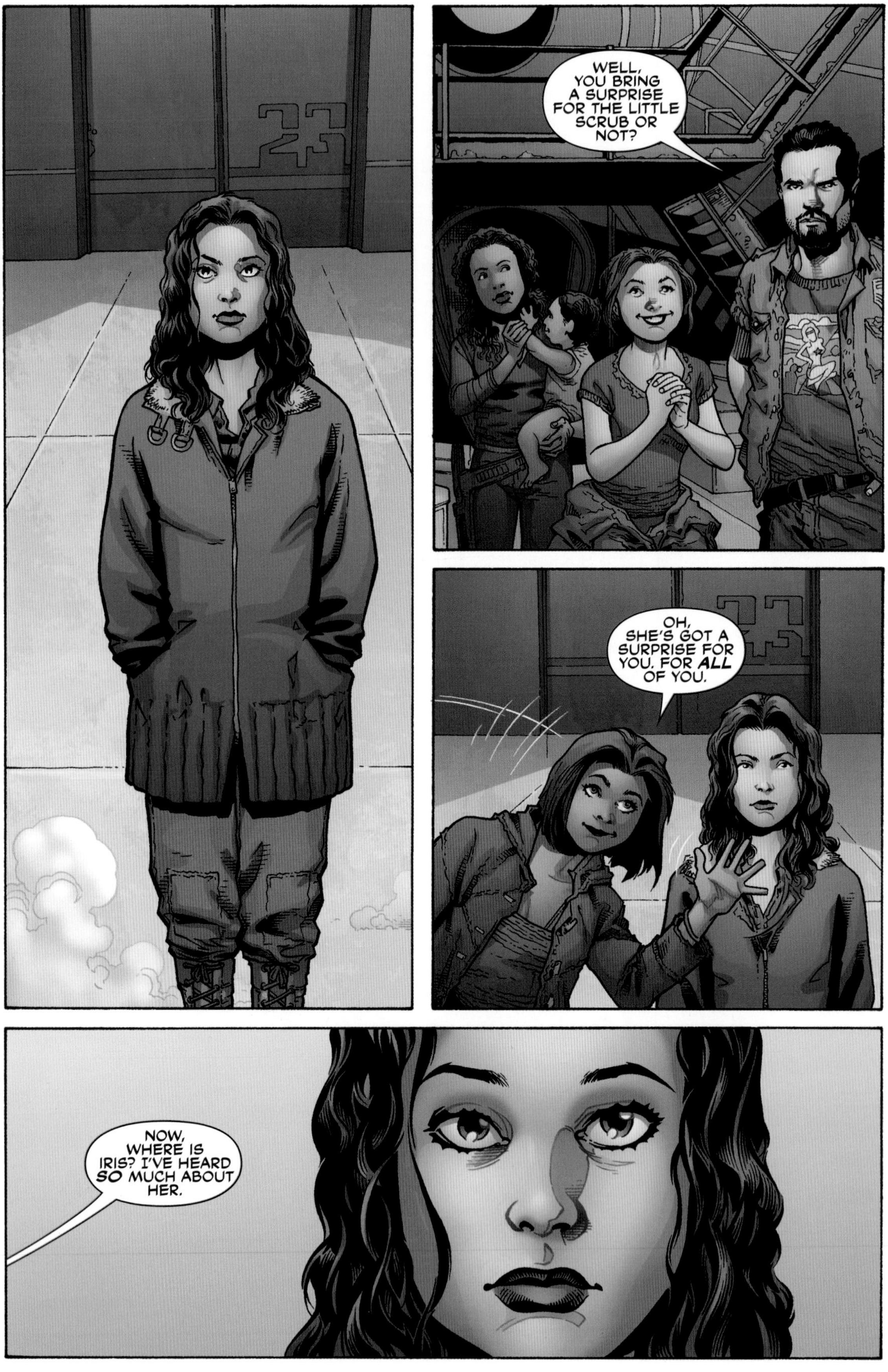
WELL, YOU BRING A SURPRISE FOR THE LITTLE SCRUB OR NOT?
OH, SHE'S GOT A SURPRISE FOR YOU. FOR *ALL* OF YOU.
NOW, WHERE IS IRIS? I'VE HEARD *SO* MUCH ABOUT HER.

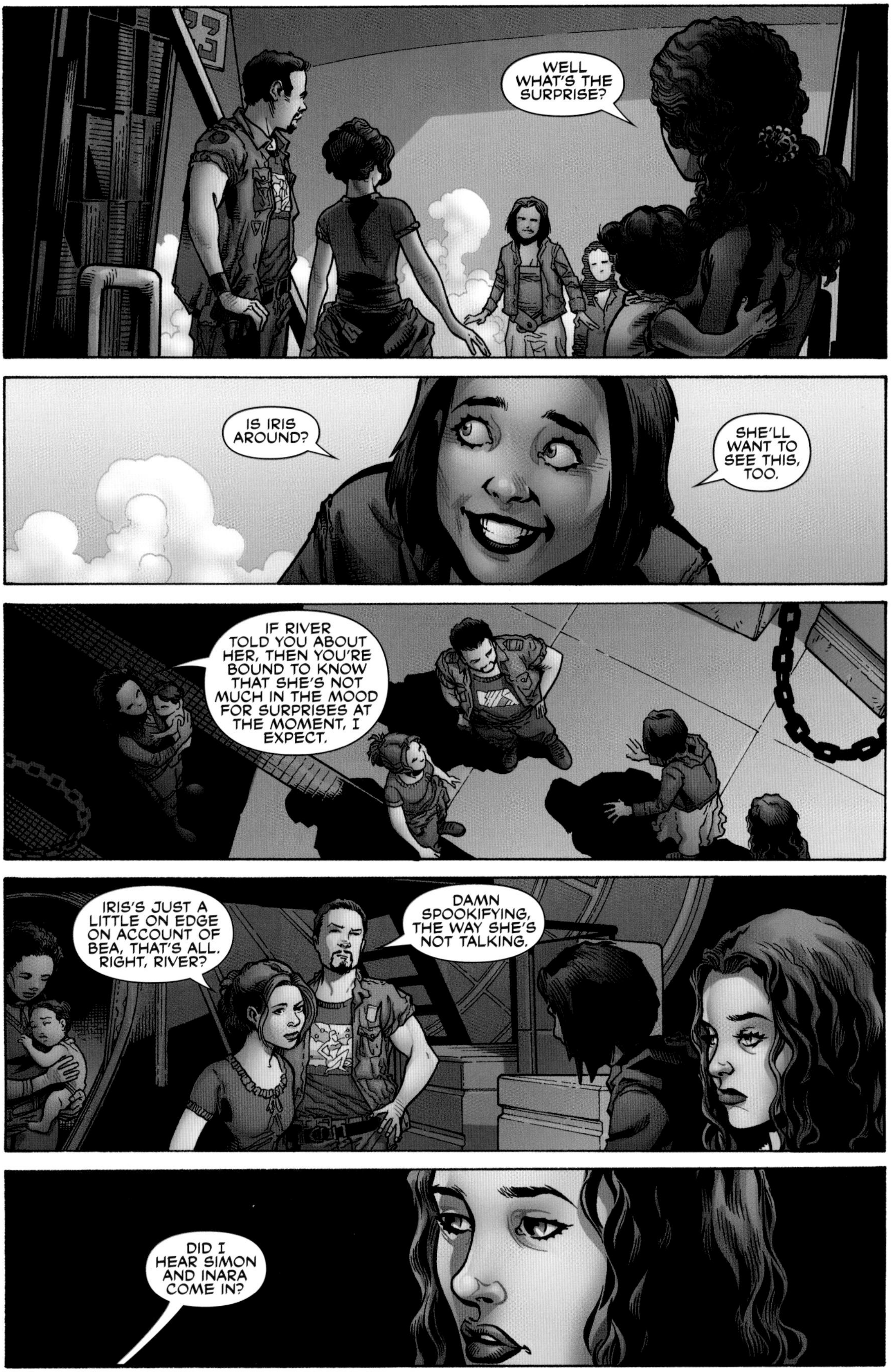
WELL WHAT'S THE SURPRISE?
IS IRIS AROUND?
SHE'LL WANT TO SEE THIS, TOO.
IF RIVER TOLD YOU ABOUT HER, THEN YOU'RE BOUND TO KNOW THAT SHE'S NOT MUCH IN THE MOOD FOR SURPRISES AT THE MOMENT, I EXPECT.
IRIS'S JUST A LITTLE ON EDGE ON ACCOUNT OF BEA, THAT'S ALL. RIGHT, RIVER?
DAMN SPOOKIFYING, THE WAY SHE'S NOT TALKING.
DID I HEAR SIMON AND INARA COME IN?

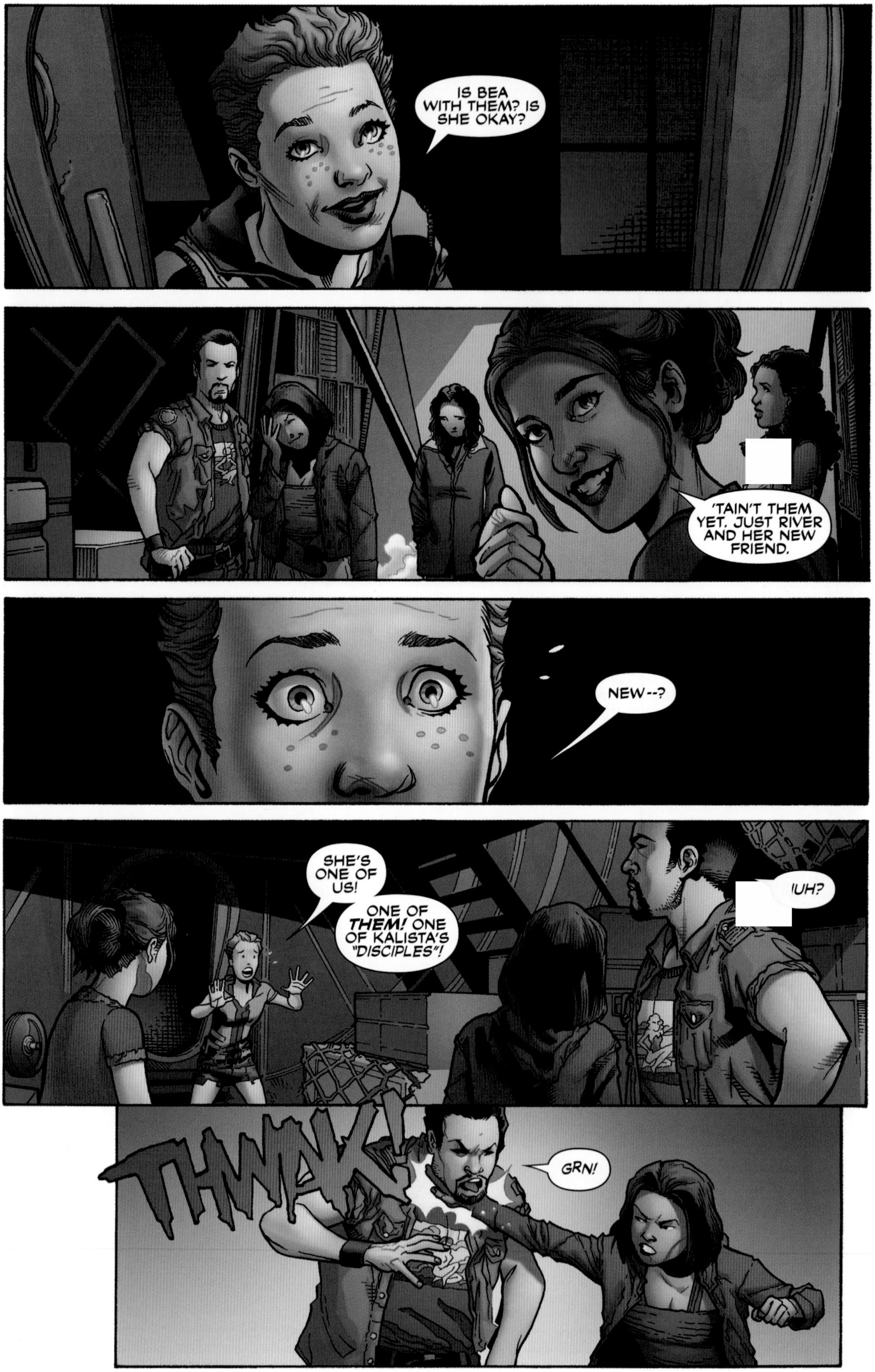

IS BEA WITH THEM? IS SHE OKAY?
'TAIN'T THEM YET. JUST RIVER AND HER NEW FRIEND.
NEW--?
SHE'S ONE OF US!
ONE OF *THEM!* ONE OF KALISTA'S *"DISCIPLES"!*
UH?
THWAK!
GRN!

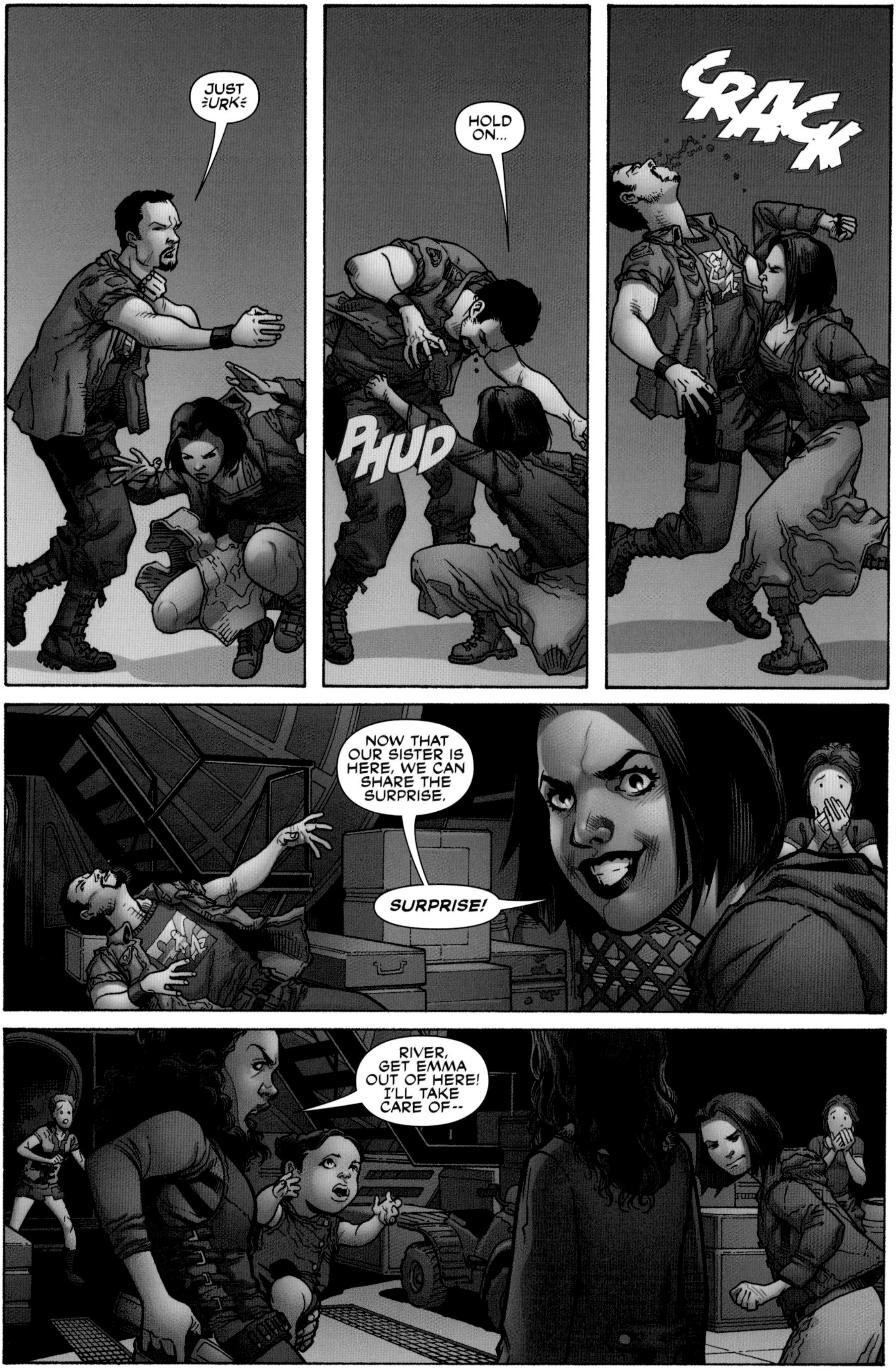
JUST
URK
HOLD ON...
PHUD
CRACK
NOW THAT OUR SISTER IS HERE, WE CAN SHARE THE SURPRISE.
SURPRISE!
RIVER, GET EMMA OUT OF HERE! I'LL TAKE CARE OF--

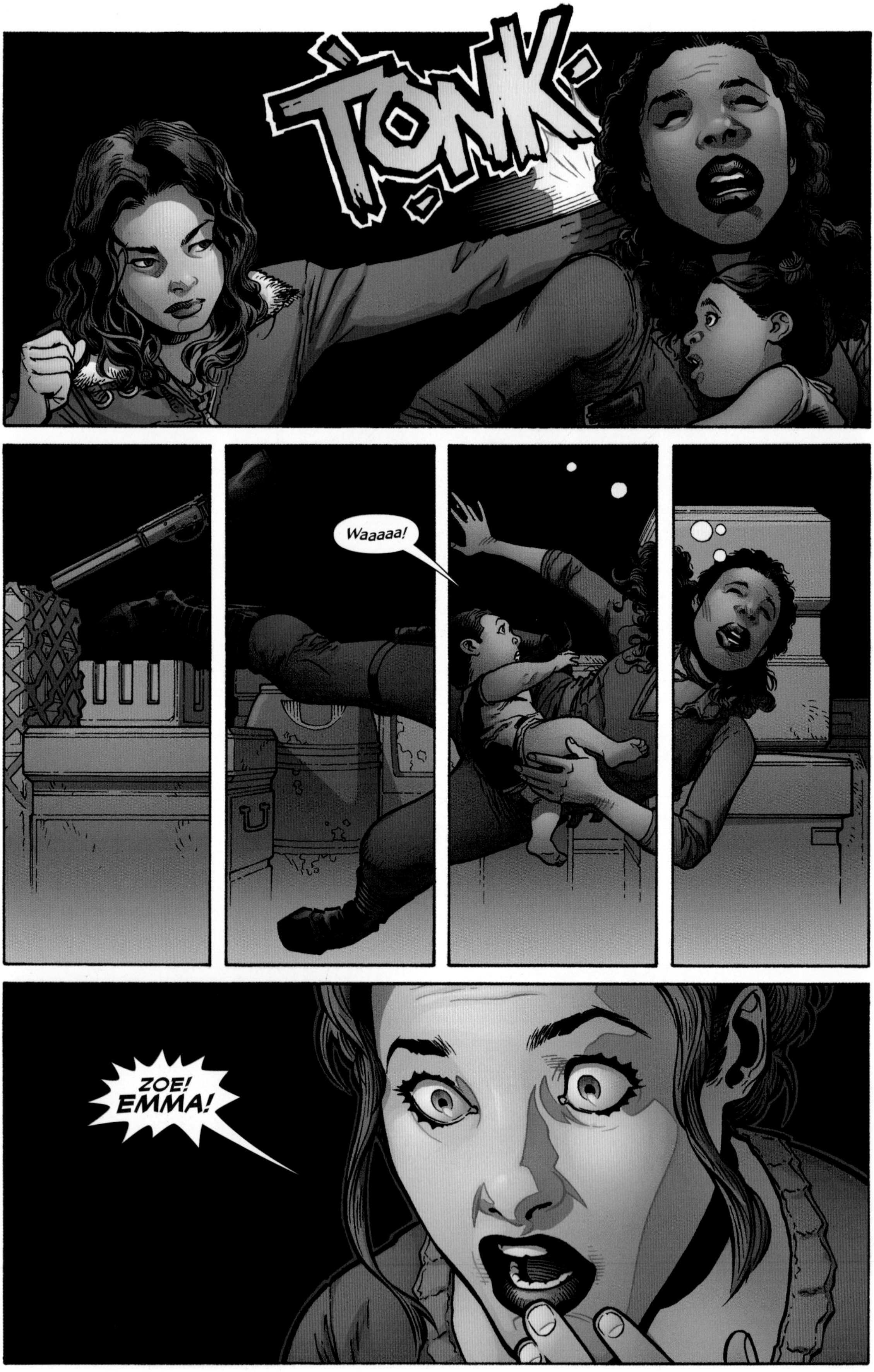
TONK!
Waaaaa!
ZOE! EMMA!

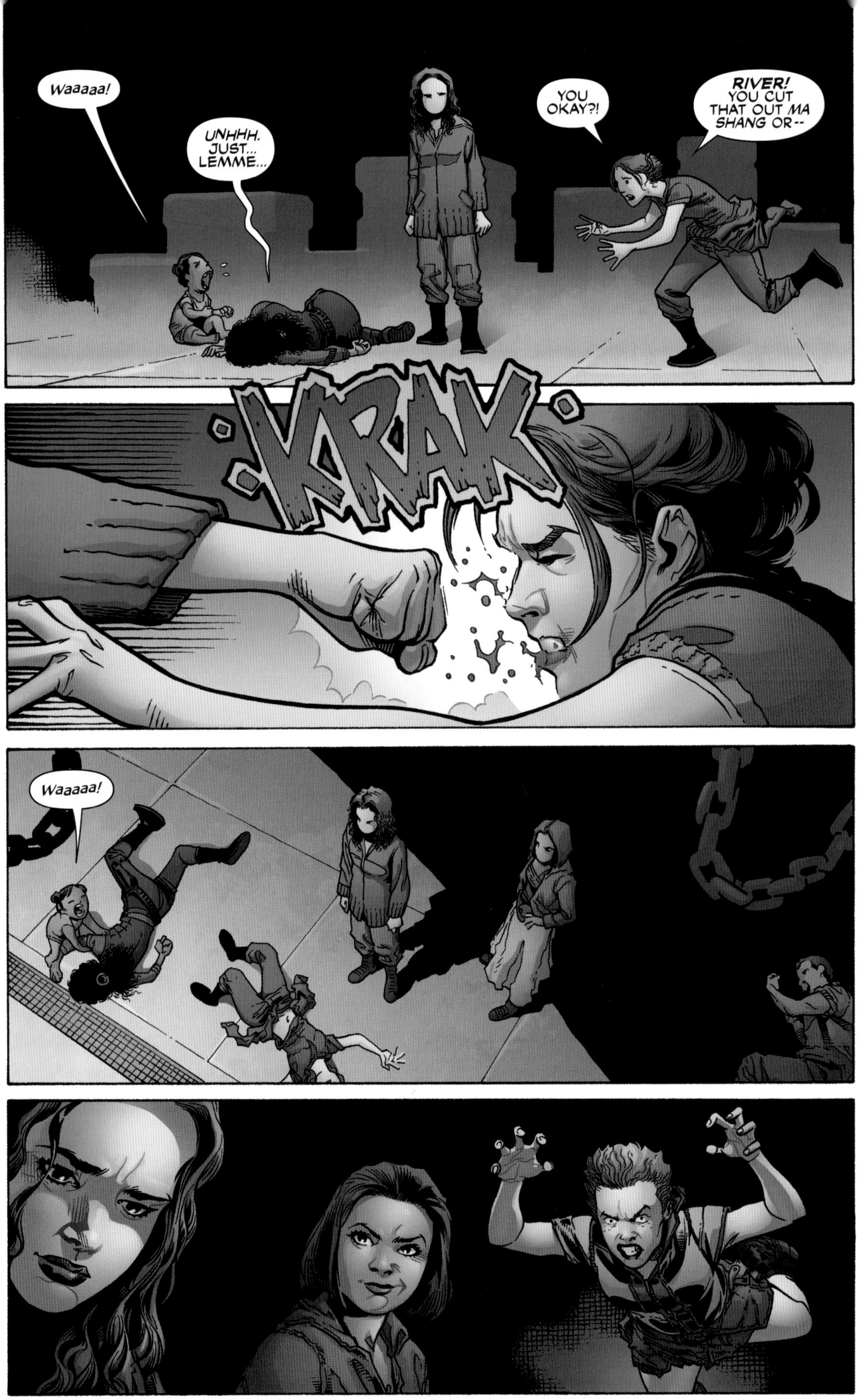
Waaaaa!
UNHHH. JUST... LEMME...
YOU OKAY?!
RIVER! YOU CUT THAT OUT MA SHANG OR--
KRAK
Waaaaa!

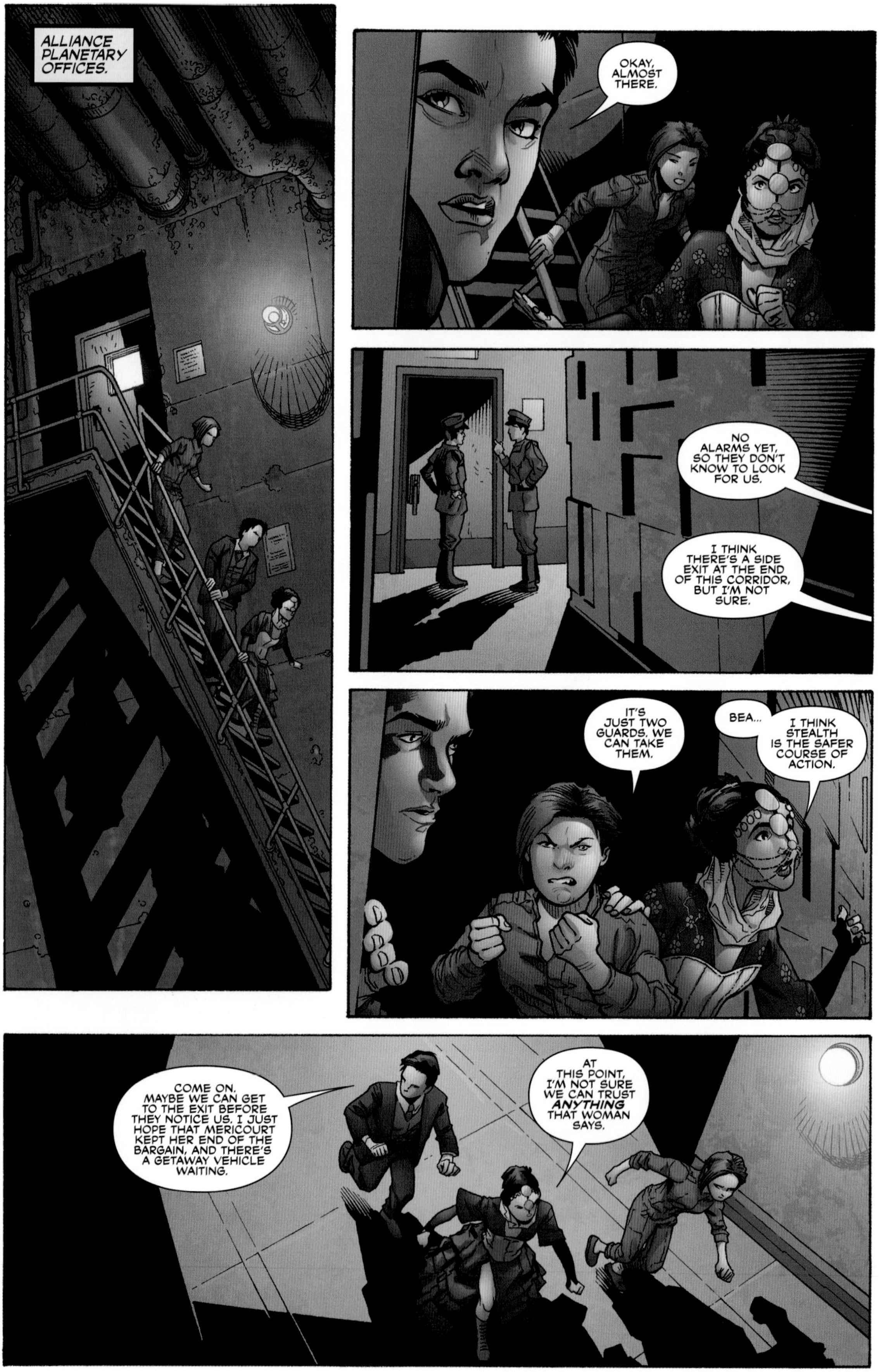
ALLIANCE PLANETARY OFFICES.
OKAY, ALMOST THERE.
NO ALARMS YET, SO THEY DON'T KNOW TO LOOK FOR US.
I THINK THERE'S A SIDE EXIT AT THE END OF THIS CORRIDOR, BUT I'M NOT SURE.
IT'S JUST TWO GUARDS. WE CAN TAKE THEM.
BEA...
I THINK STEALTH IS THE SAFER COURSE OF ACTION.
COME ON. MAYBE WE CAN GET TO THE EXIT BEFORE THEY NOTICE US. I JUST HOPE THAT MERICOURT KEPT HER END OF THE BARGAIN, AND THERE'S A GETAWAY VEHICLE WAITING.
AT THIS POINT, I'M NOT SURE WE CAN TRUST ANYTHING THAT WOMAN SAYS.

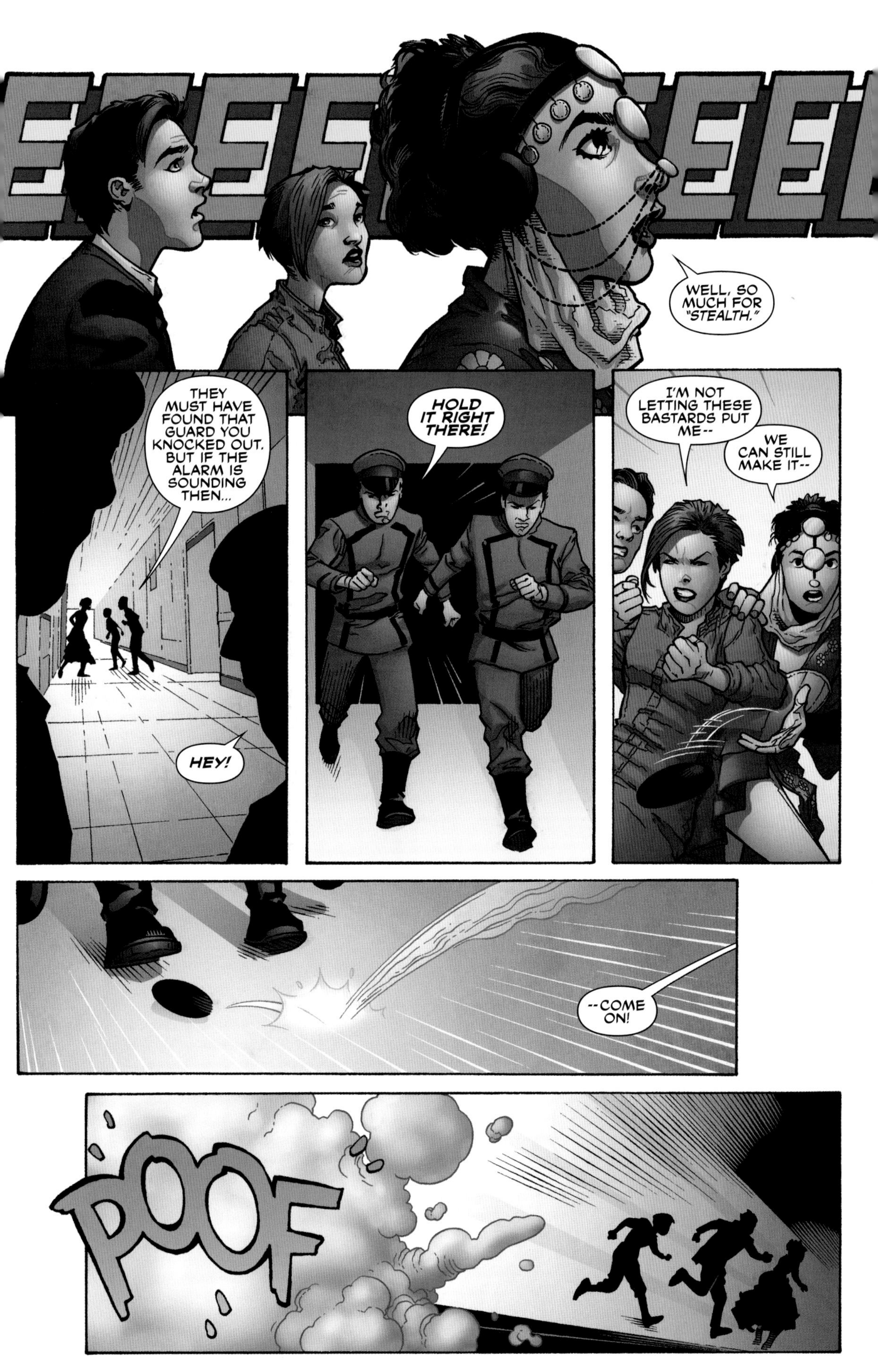
EEEEEEEEEEE
WELL, SO MUCH FOR "STEALTH."
THEY MUST HAVE FOUND THAT GUARD YOU KNOCKED OUT. BUT IF THE ALARM IS SOUNDING THEN...
HEY!
HOLD IT RIGHT THERE!
I'M NOT LETTING THESE BASTARDS PUT ME--
WE CAN STILL MAKE IT--
--COME ON!
POOF

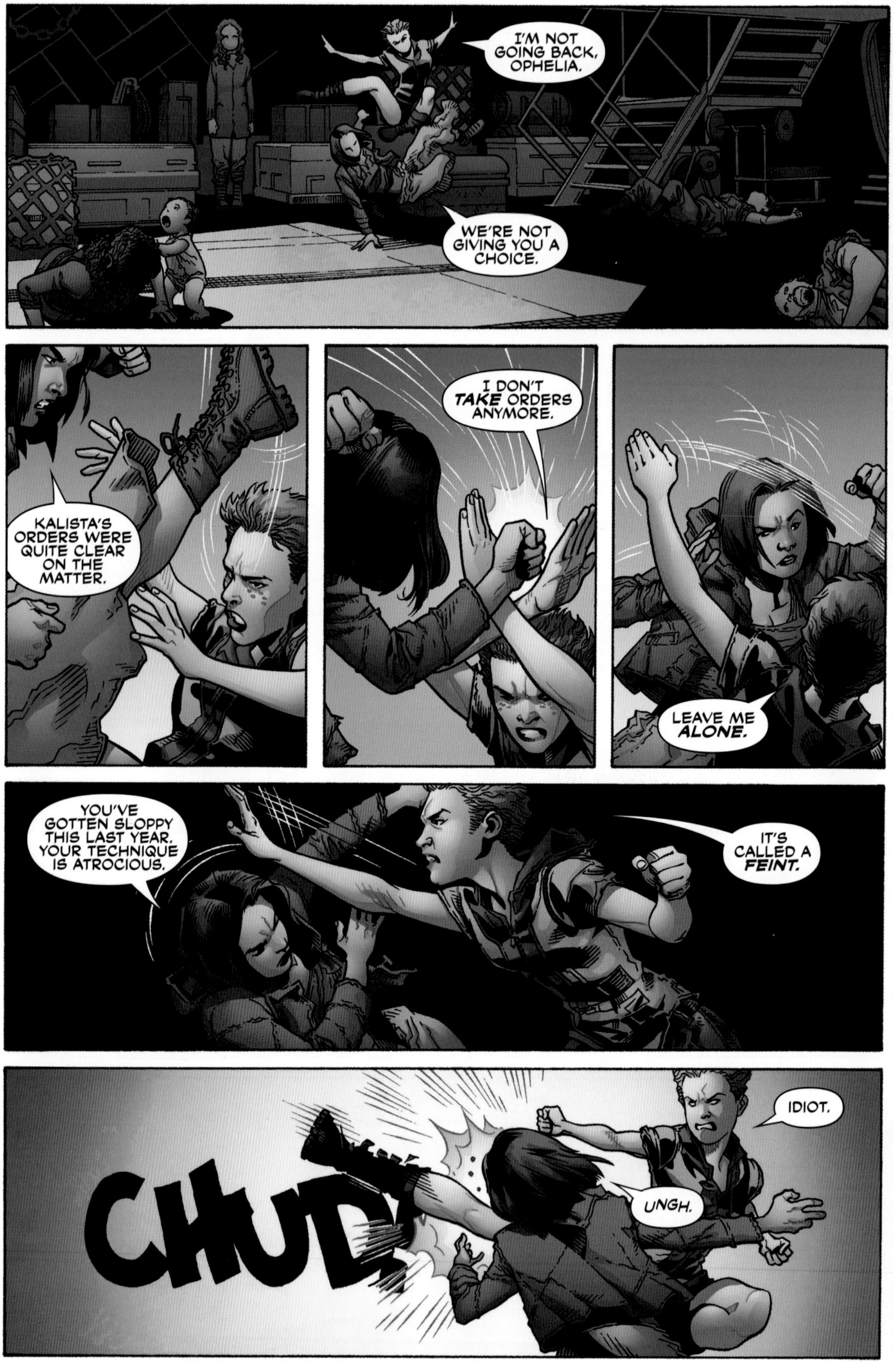
I'M NOT GOING BACK, OPHELIA.
WE'RE NOT GIVING YOU A CHOICE.
KALISTA'S ORDERS WERE QUITE CLEAR ON THE MATTER.
I DON'T *TAKE* ORDERS ANYMORE.
LEAVE ME *ALONE.*
YOU'VE GOTTEN SLOPPY THIS LAST YEAR. YOUR TECHNIQUE IS ATROCIOUS.
IT'S CALLED A *FEINT.*
IDIOT.
CHUD
UNGH.

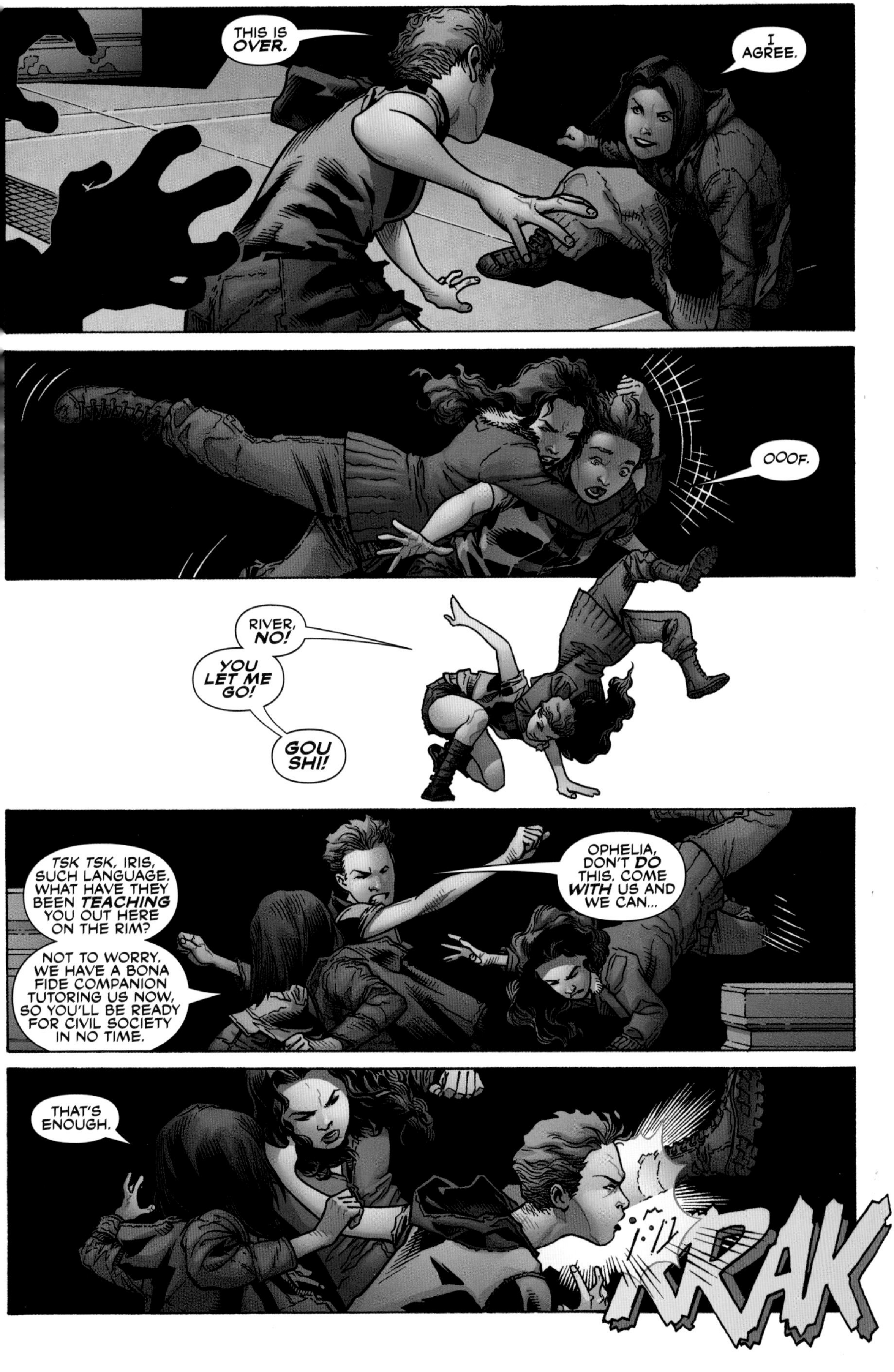
THIS IS OVER.
I AGREE.
OOOF.
RIVER, NO!
YOU LET ME GO!
GOU SHI!
TSK TSK, IRIS, SUCH LANGUAGE. WHAT HAVE THEY BEEN TEACHING YOU OUT HERE ON THE RIM?
NOT TO WORRY. WE HAVE A BONA FIDE COMPANION TUTORING US NOW, SO YOU'LL BE READY FOR CIVIL SOCIETY IN NO TIME.
OPHELIA, DON'T DO THIS. COME WITH US AND WE CAN...
THAT'S ENOUGH.
KRAK

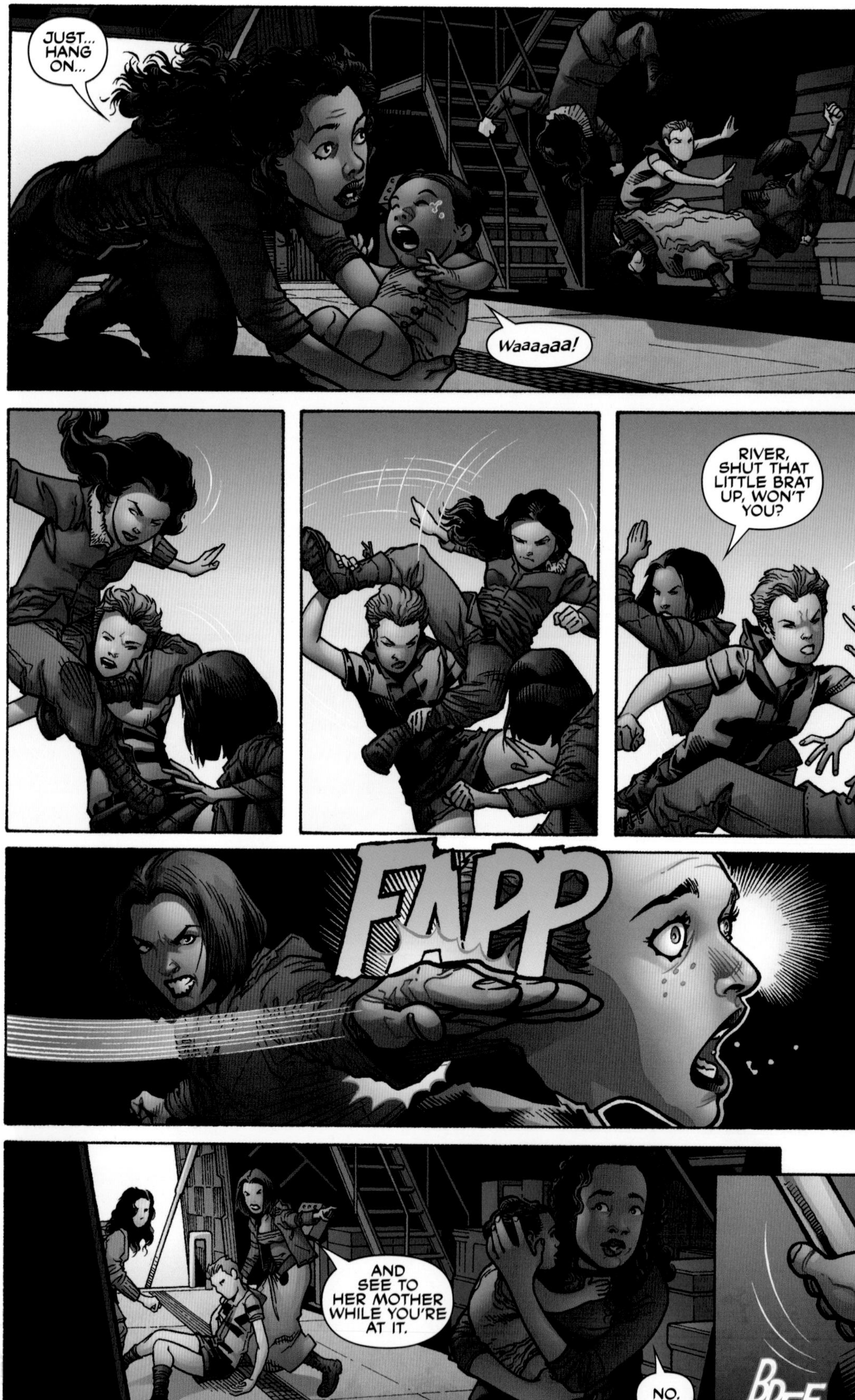
JUST... HANG ON...
Waaaaaa!
RIVER, SHUT THAT LITTLE BRAT UP, WON'T YOU?
FAPP
AND SEE TO HER MOTHER WHILE YOU'RE AT IT.
NO.
BREEEEP

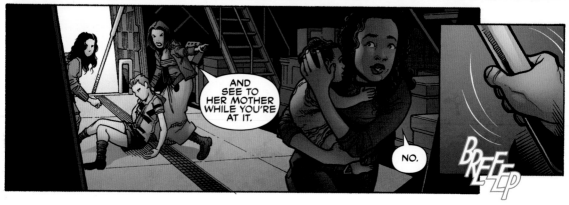

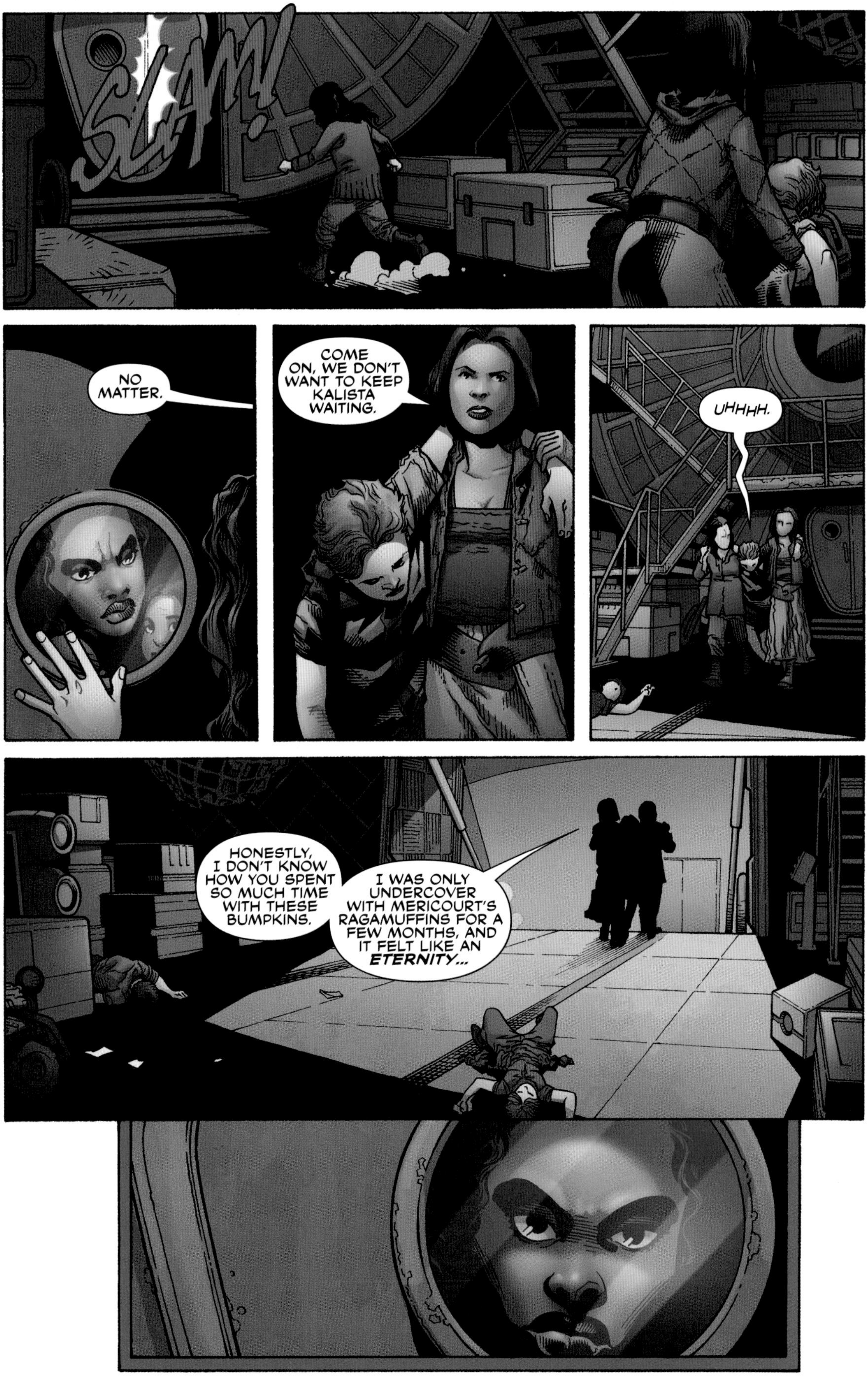
SLAM!
NO MATTER.
COME ON, WE DON'T WANT TO KEEP KALISTA WAITING.
UHHHH.
HONESTLY, I DON'T KNOW HOW YOU SPENT SO MUCH TIME WITH THESE BUMPKINS.
I WAS ONLY UNDERCOVER WITH MERICOURT'S RAGAMUFFINS FOR A FEW MONTHS, AND IT FELT LIKE AN *ETERNITY...*

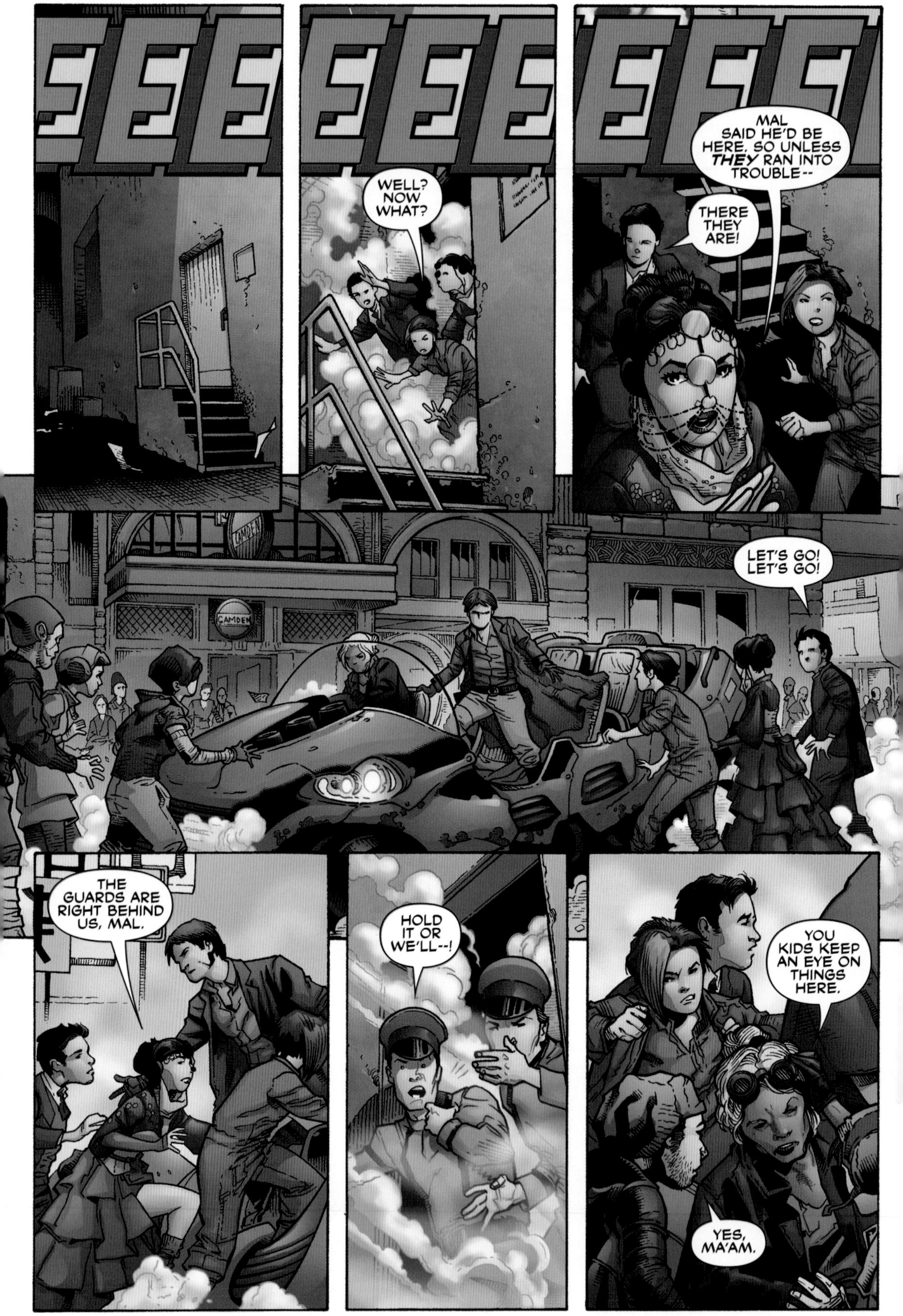
EEEEEEEEEEE
WELL? NOW WHAT?
MAL SAID HE'D BE HERE, SO UNLESS *THEY* RAN INTO TROUBLE--
THERE THEY ARE!
LET'S GO! LET'S GO!
THE GUARDS ARE RIGHT BEHIND US, MAL.
HOLD IT OR WE'LL--!
YOU KIDS KEEP AN EYE ON THINGS HERE.
YES, MA'AM.

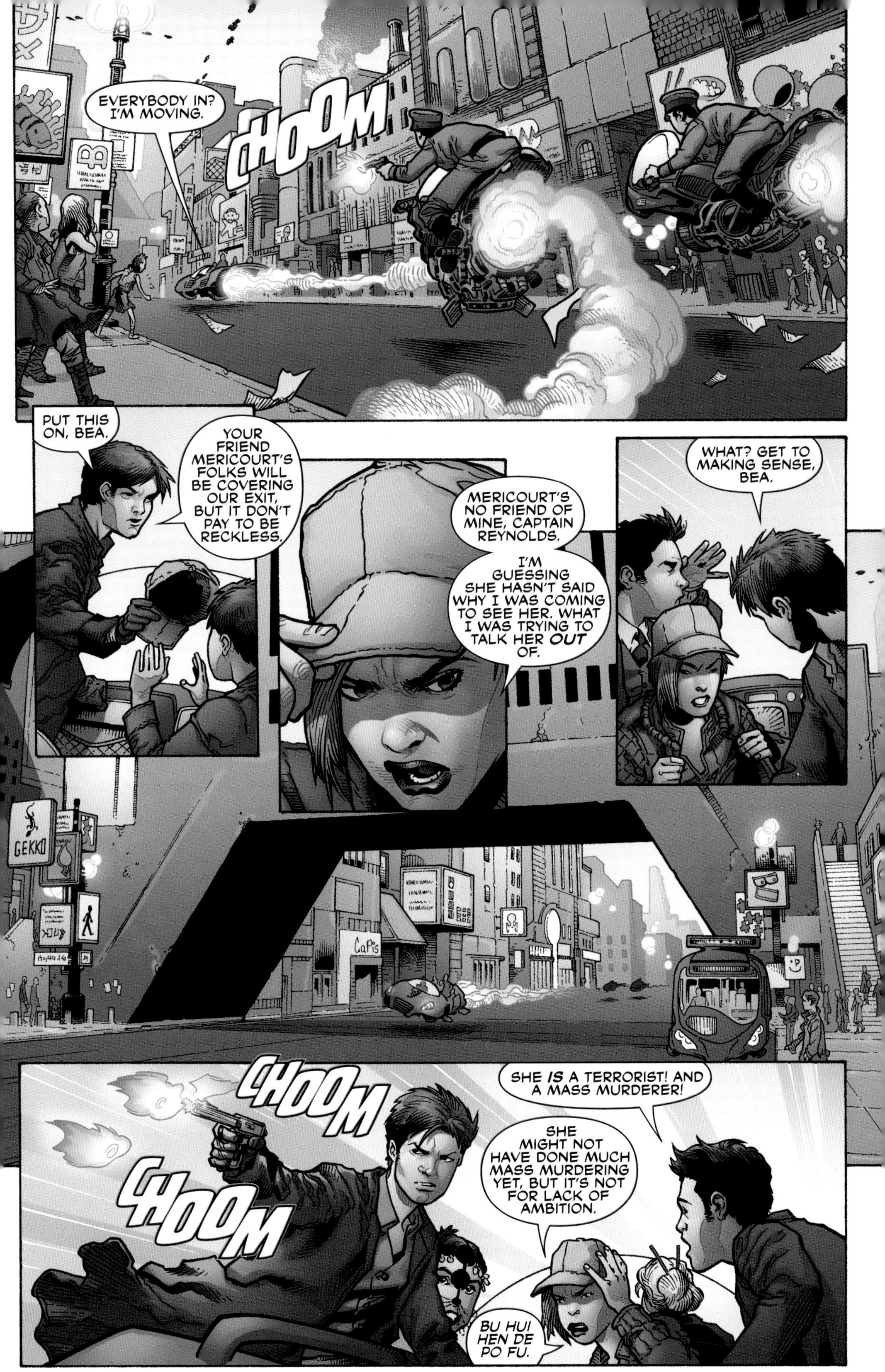
EVERYBODY IN? I'M MOVING.
CHOOM
PUT THIS ON, BEA.
YOUR FRIEND MERICOURT'S FOLKS WILL BE COVERING OUR EXIT, BUT IT DON'T PAY TO BE RECKLESS.
MERICOURT'S NO FRIEND OF MINE, CAPTAIN REYNOLDS.
I'M GUESSING SHE HASN'T SAID WHY I WAS COMING TO SEE HER. WHAT I WAS TRYING TO TALK HER *OUT* OF.
WHAT? GET TO MAKING SENSE, BEA.
GEKKO
CaPis
CHOOM
CHOOM
SHE *IS* A TERRORIST! AND A MASS MURDERER!
SHE MIGHT NOT HAVE DONE MUCH MASS MURDERING YET, BUT IT'S NOT FOR LACK OF AMBITION.
BU HUI HEN DE PO FU.

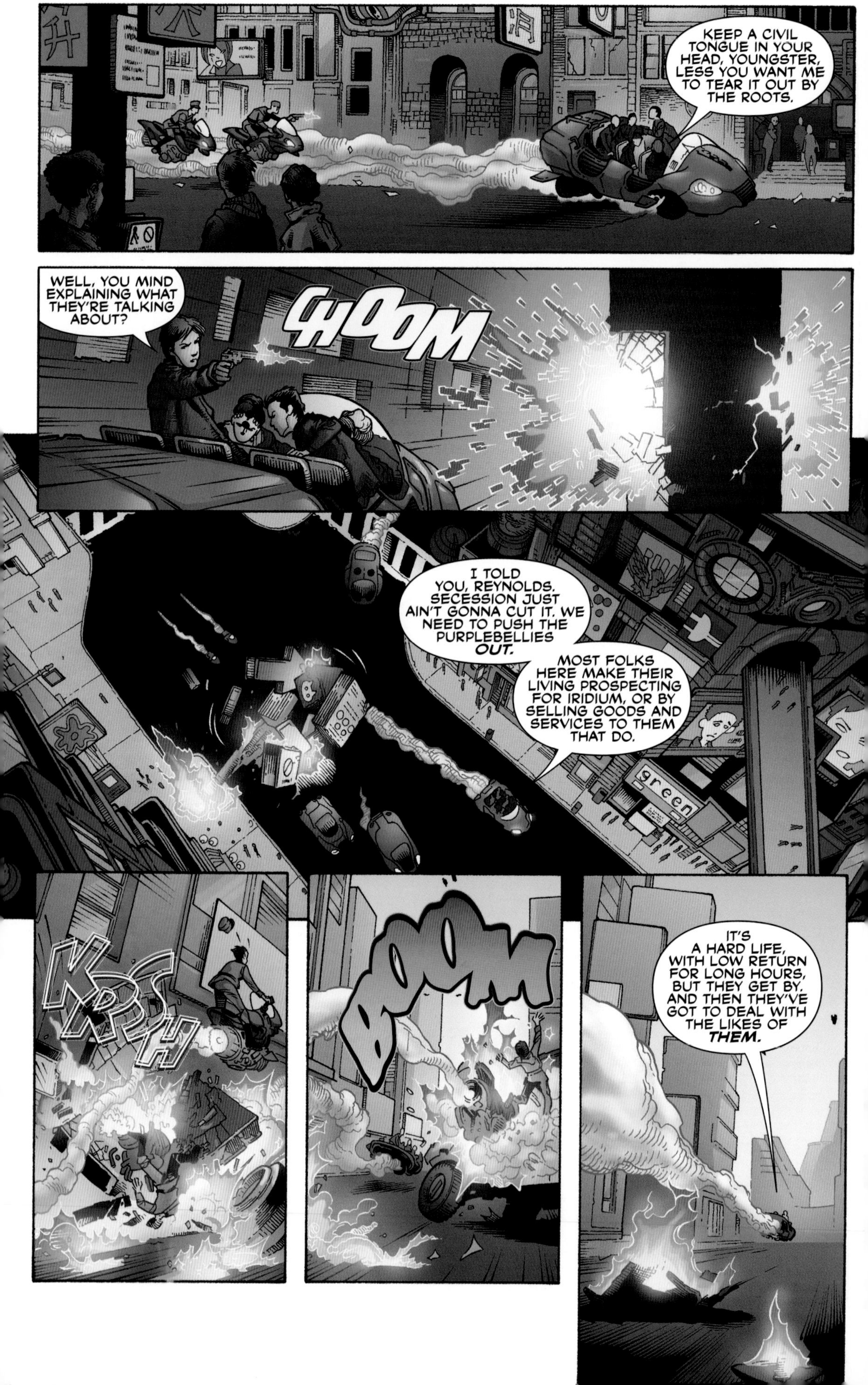
KEEP A CIVIL TONGUE IN YOUR HEAD, YOUNGSTER, LESS YOU WANT ME TO TEAR IT OUT BY THE ROOTS.
WELL, YOU MIND EXPLAINING WHAT THEY'RE TALKING ABOUT?
CHOOM
I TOLD YOU, REYNOLDS. SECESSION JUST AIN'T GONNA CUT IT. WE NEED TO PUSH THE PURPLEBELLIES OUT.
MOST FOLKS HERE MAKE THEIR LIVING PROSPECTING FOR IRIDIUM, OR BY SELLING GOODS AND SERVICES TO THEM THAT DO.
green
KRSH
BOOM
IT'S A HARD LIFE, WITH LOW RETURN FOR LONG HOURS, BUT THEY GET BY. AND THEN THEY'VE GOT TO DEAL WITH THE LIKES OF THEM.

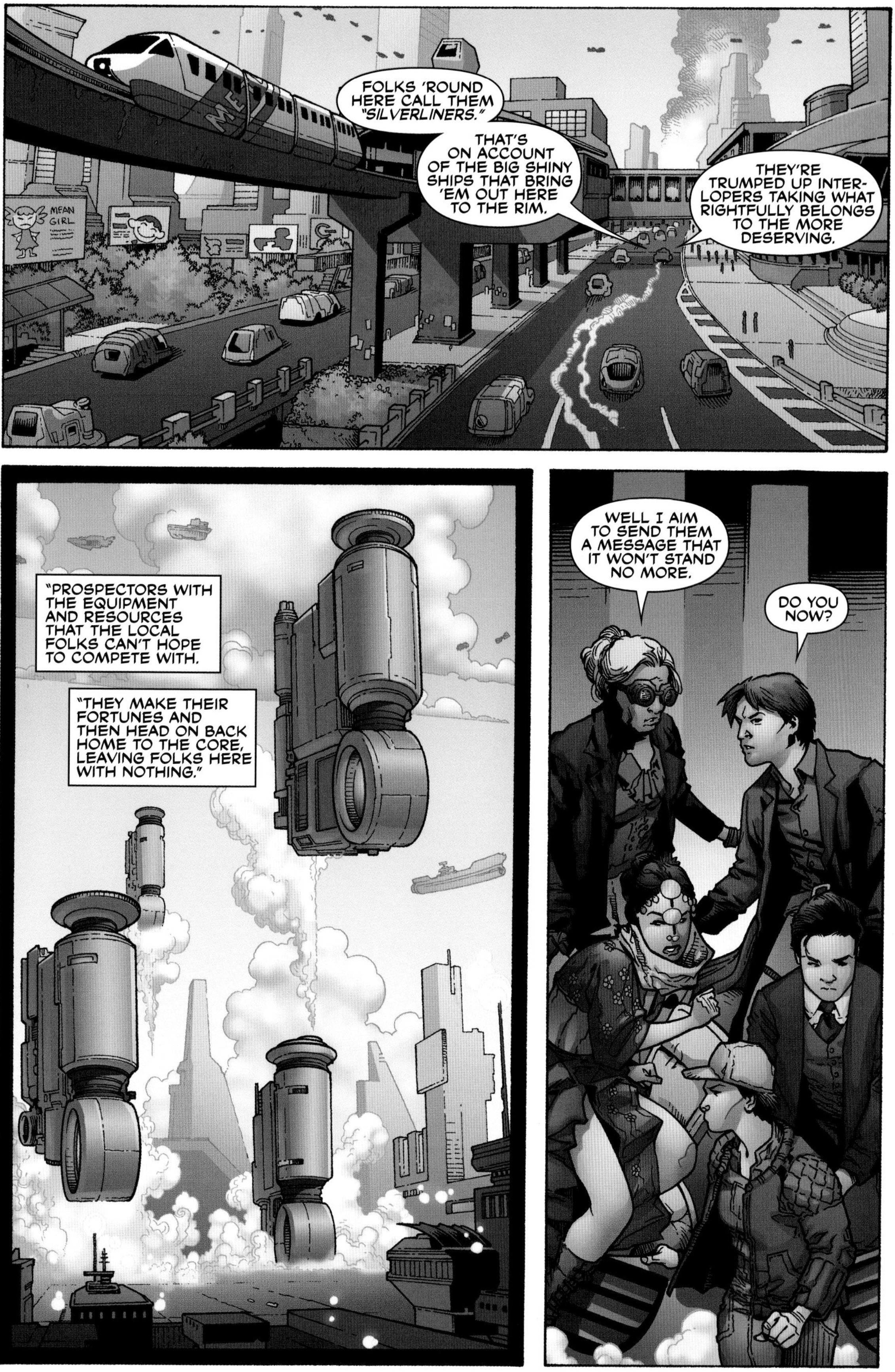
FOLKS 'ROUND HERE CALL THEM "SILVERLINERS."
THAT'S ON ACCOUNT OF THE BIG SHINY SHIPS THAT BRING 'EM OUT HERE TO THE RIM.
MEAN GIRL
THEY'RE TRUMPED UP INTER-LOPERS TAKING WHAT RIGHTFULLY BELONGS TO THE MORE DESERVING.
"PROSPECTORS WITH THE EQUIPMENT AND RESOURCES THAT THE LOCAL FOLKS CAN'T HOPE TO COMPETE WITH.
"THEY MAKE THEIR FORTUNES AND THEN HEAD ON BACK HOME TO THE CORE, LEAVING FOLKS HERE WITH NOTHING."
WELL I AIM TO SEND THEM A MESSAGE THAT IT WON'T STAND NO MORE.
DO YOU NOW?

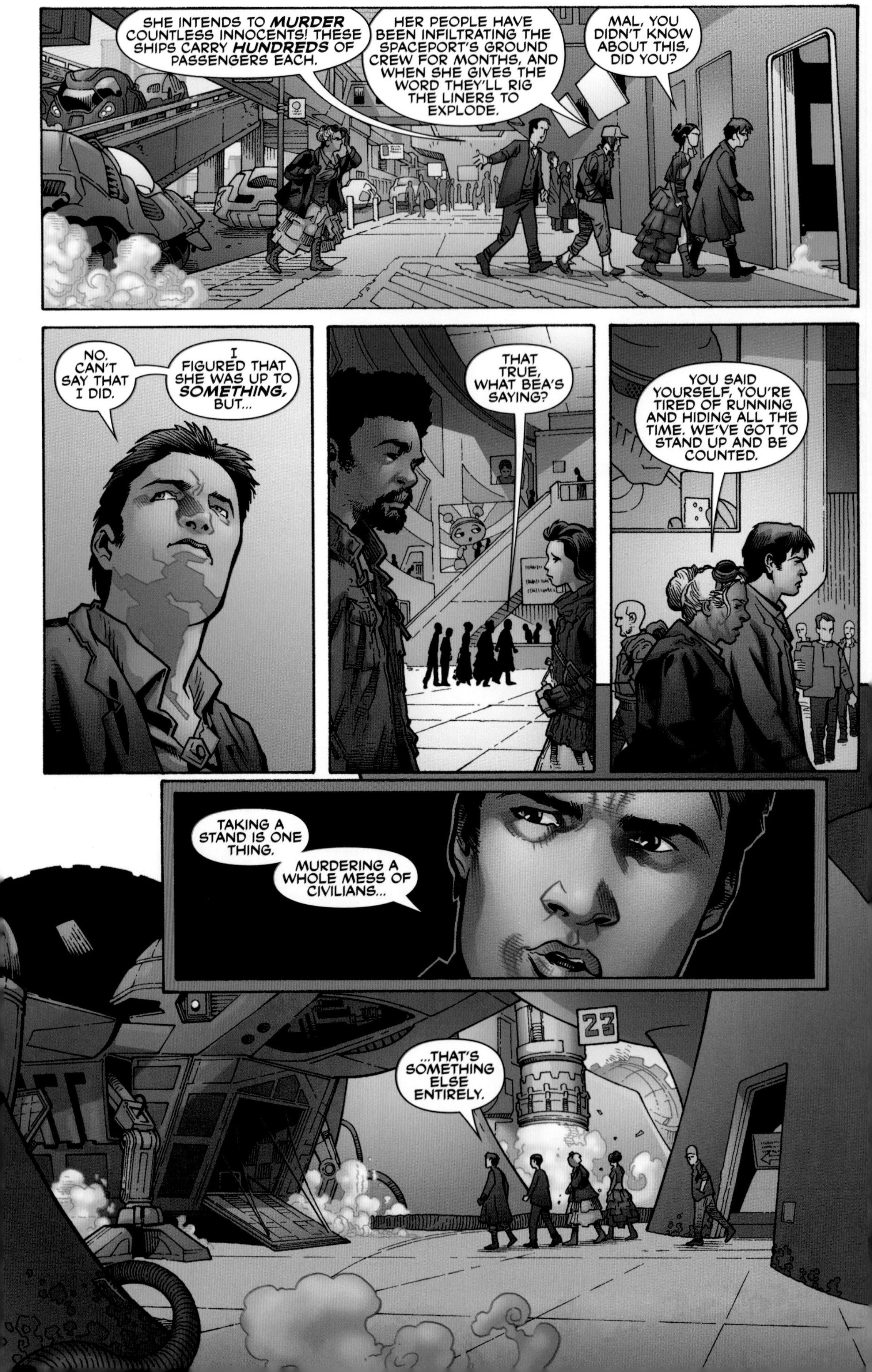
SHE INTENDS TO MURDER COUNTLESS INNOCENTS! THESE SHIPS CARRY HUNDREDS OF PASSENGERS EACH.
HER PEOPLE HAVE BEEN INFILTRATING THE SPACEPORT'S GROUND CREW FOR MONTHS, AND WHEN SHE GIVES THE WORD THEY'LL RIG THE LINERS TO EXPLODE.
MAL, YOU DIDN'T KNOW ABOUT THIS, DID YOU?
NO. CAN'T SAY THAT I DID.
I FIGURED THAT SHE WAS UP TO SOMETHING, BUT...
THAT TRUE, WHAT BEA'S SAYING?
YOU SAID YOURSELF, YOU'RE TIRED OF RUNNING AND HIDING ALL THE TIME. WE'VE GOT TO STAND UP AND BE COUNTED.
TAKING A STAND IS ONE THING.
MURDERING A WHOLE MESS OF CIVILIANS...
...THAT'S SOMETHING ELSE ENTIRELY.
23

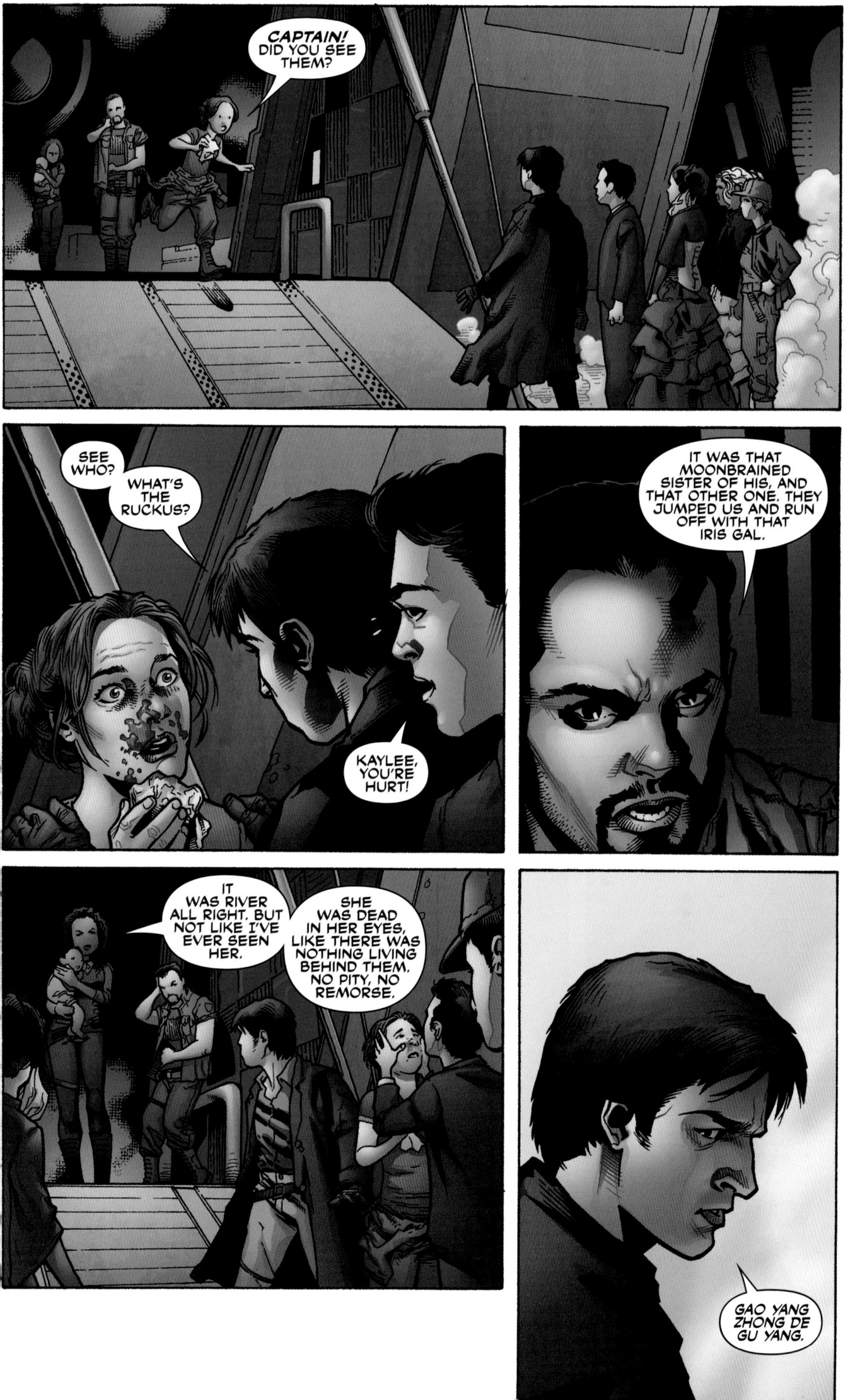
CAPTAIN! DID YOU SEE THEM?
SEE WHO?
WHAT'S THE RUCKUS?
KAYLEE, YOU'RE HURT!
IT WAS THAT MOONBRAINED SISTER OF HIS, AND THAT OTHER ONE. THEY JUMPED US AND RUN OFF WITH THAT IRIS GAL.
IT WAS RIVER ALL RIGHT. BUT NOT LIKE I'VE EVER SEEN HER.
SHE WAS DEAD IN HER EYES, LIKE THERE WAS NOTHING LIVING BEHIND THEM. NO PITY, NO REMORSE.
GAO YANG ZHONG DE GU YANG.

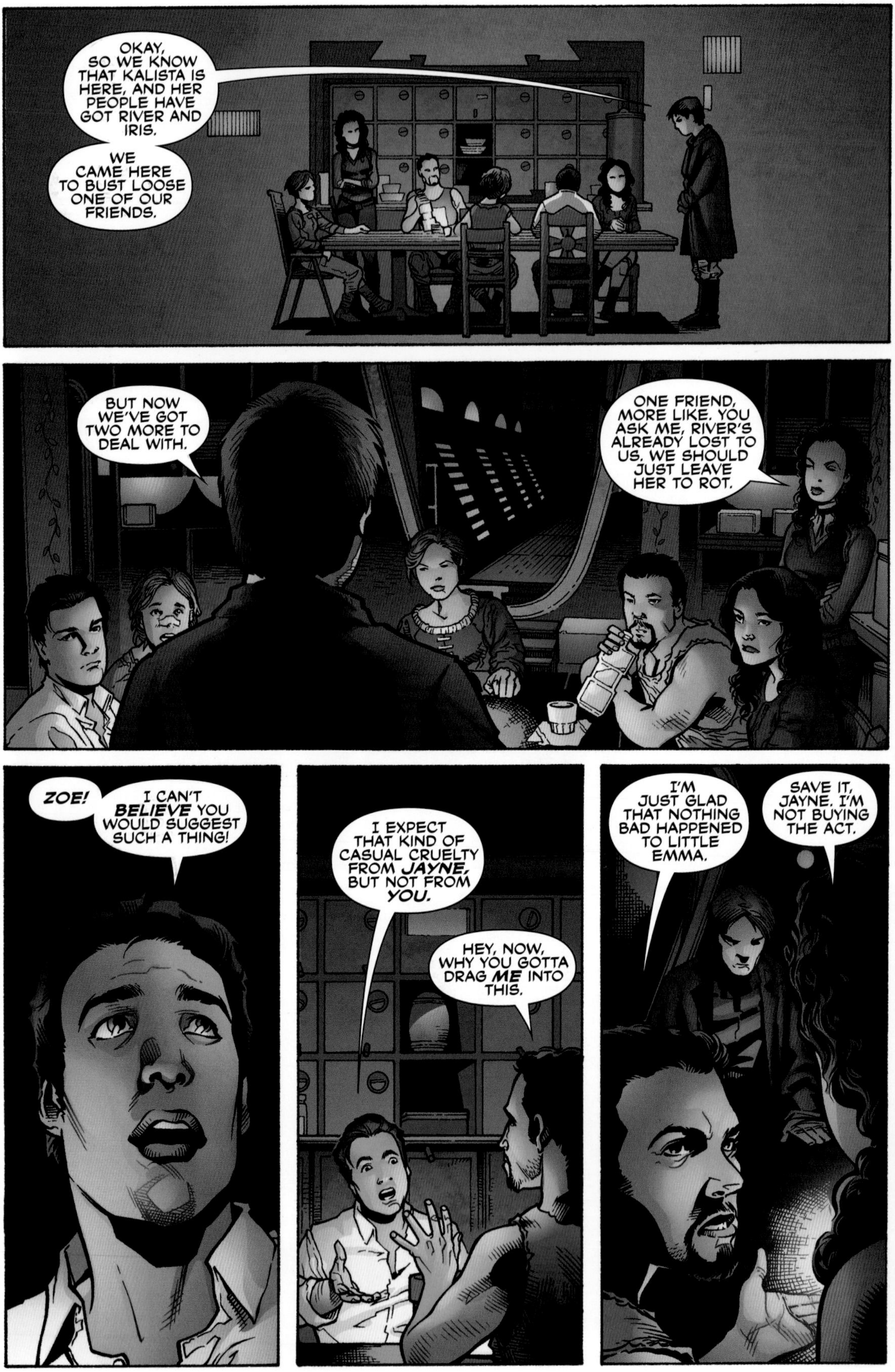

OKAY, SO WE KNOW THAT KALISTA IS HERE, AND HER PEOPLE HAVE GOT RIVER AND IRIS.
WE CAME HERE TO BUST LOOSE ONE OF OUR FRIENDS.
BUT NOW WE'VE GOT TWO MORE TO DEAL WITH.
ONE FRIEND, MORE LIKE. YOU ASK ME, RIVER'S ALREADY LOST TO US. WE SHOULD JUST LEAVE HER TO ROT.
ZOE!
I CAN'T BELIEVE YOU WOULD SUGGEST SUCH A THING!
I EXPECT THAT KIND OF CASUAL CRUELTY FROM JAYNE, BUT NOT FROM YOU.
HEY, NOW, WHY YOU GOTTA DRAG ME INTO THIS.
I'M JUST GLAD THAT NOTHING BAD HAPPENED TO LITTLE EMMA.
SAVE IT, JAYNE. I'M NOT BUYING THE ACT.

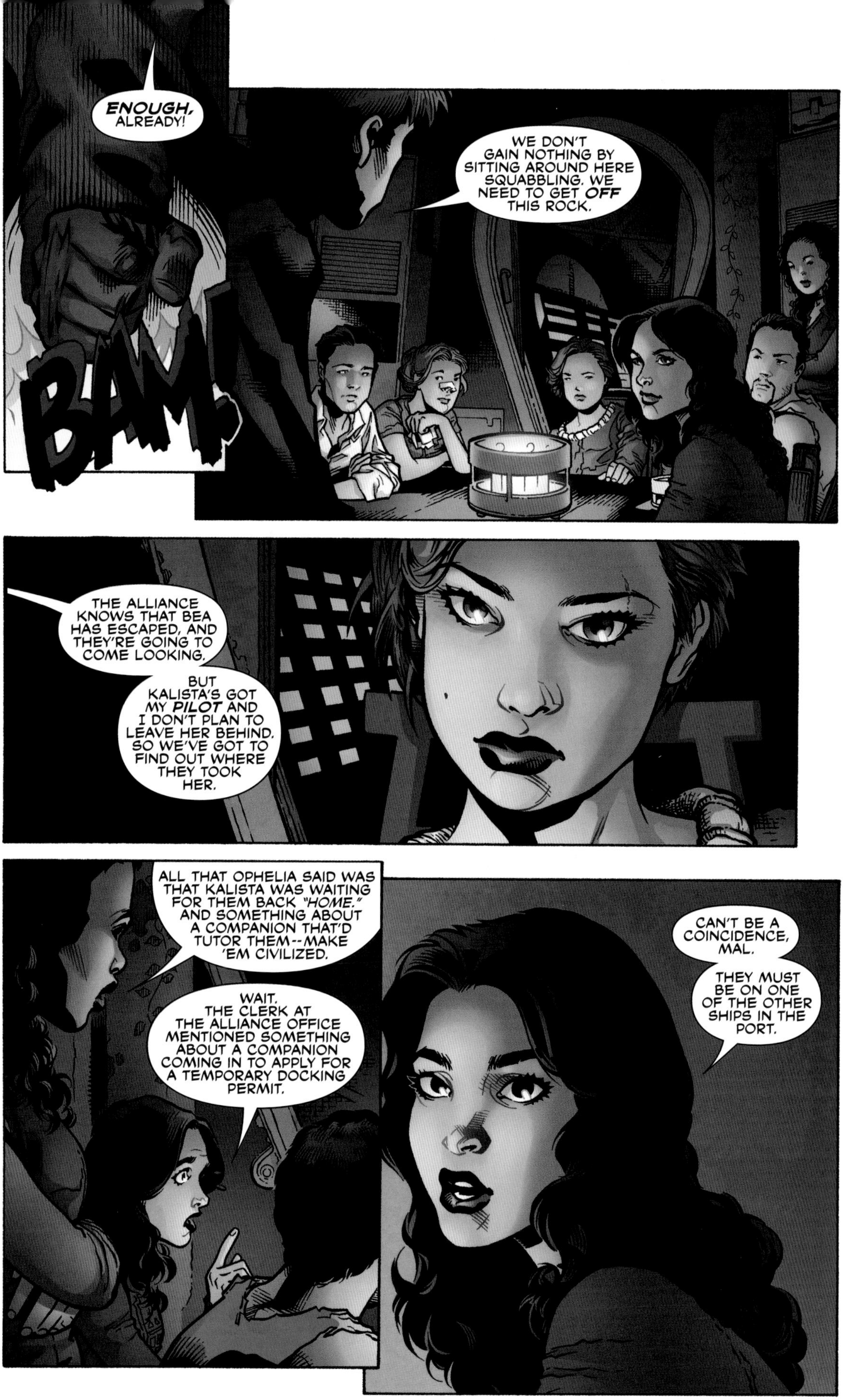
ENOUGH, ALREADY!
BAM!
WE DON'T GAIN NOTHING BY SITTING AROUND HERE SQUABBLING. WE NEED TO GET OFF THIS ROCK.
THE ALLIANCE KNOWS THAT BEA HAS ESCAPED, AND THEY'RE GOING TO COME LOOKING.
BUT KALISTA'S GOT MY PILOT AND I DON'T PLAN TO LEAVE HER BEHIND, SO WE'VE GOT TO FIND OUT WHERE THEY TOOK HER.
ALL THAT OPHELIA SAID WAS THAT KALISTA WAS WAITING FOR THEM BACK "HOME." AND SOMETHING ABOUT A COMPANION THAT'D TUTOR THEM--MAKE 'EM CIVILIZED.
WAIT. THE CLERK AT THE ALLIANCE OFFICE MENTIONED SOMETHING ABOUT A COMPANION COMING IN TO APPLY FOR A TEMPORARY DOCKING PERMIT.
CAN'T BE A COINCIDENCE, MAL.
THEY MUST BE ON ONE OF THE OTHER SHIPS IN THE PORT.

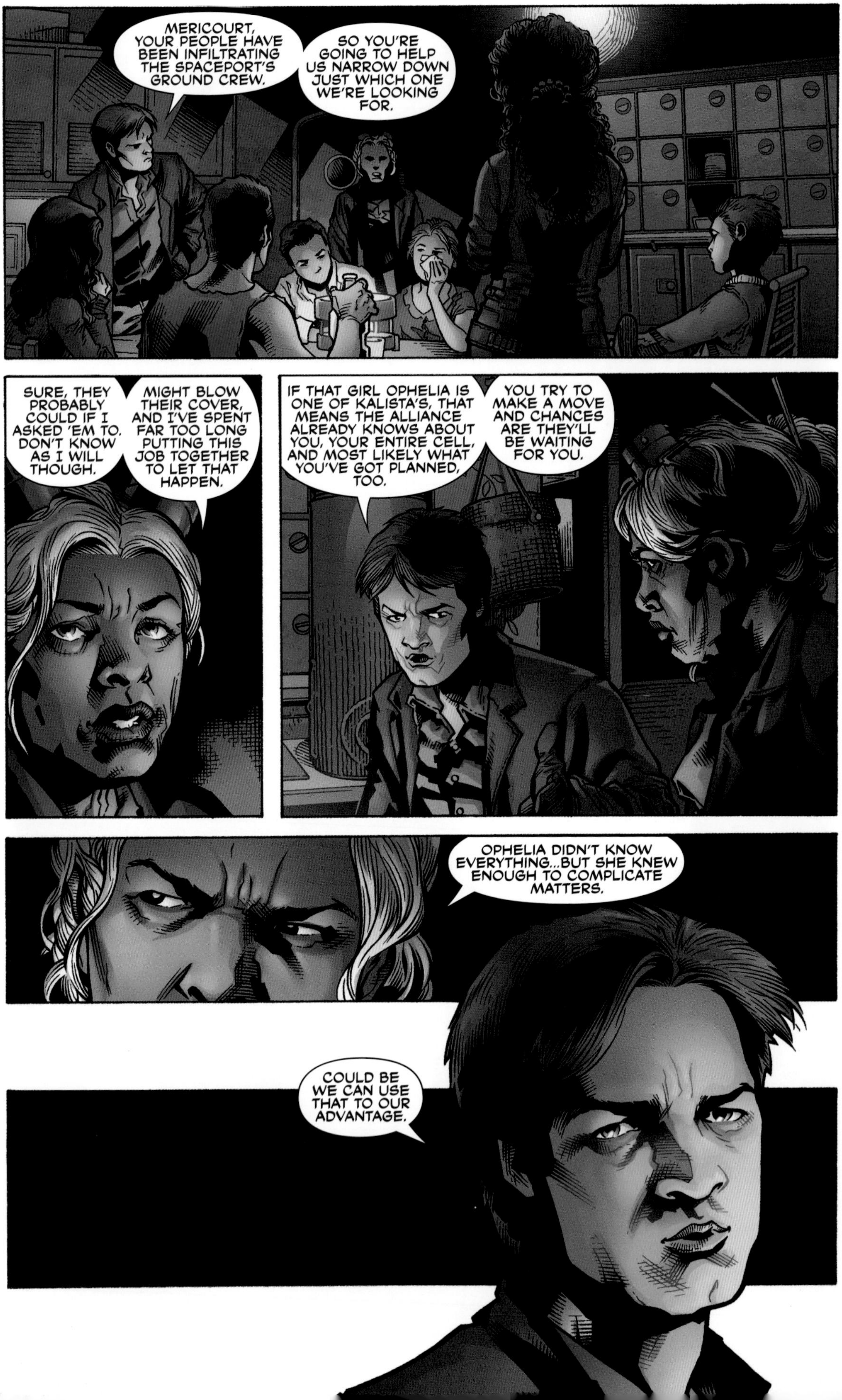
MERICOURT, YOUR PEOPLE HAVE BEEN INFILTRATING THE SPACEPORT'S GROUND CREW.
SO YOU'RE GOING TO HELP US NARROW DOWN JUST WHICH ONE WE'RE LOOKING FOR.
SURE, THEY PROBABLY COULD IF I ASKED 'EM TO. DON'T KNOW AS I WILL THOUGH.
MIGHT BLOW THEIR COVER, AND I'VE SPENT FAR TOO LONG PUTTING THIS JOB TOGETHER TO LET THAT HAPPEN.
IF THAT GIRL OPHELIA IS ONE OF KALISTA'S, THAT MEANS THE ALLIANCE ALREADY KNOWS ABOUT YOU, YOUR ENTIRE CELL, AND MOST LIKELY WHAT YOU'VE GOT PLANNED, TOO.
YOU TRY TO MAKE A MOVE AND CHANCES ARE THEY'LL BE WAITING FOR YOU.
OPHELIA DIDN'T KNOW EVERYTHING...BUT SHE KNEW ENOUGH TO COMPLICATE MATTERS.
COULD BE WE CAN USE THAT TO OUR ADVANTAGE.

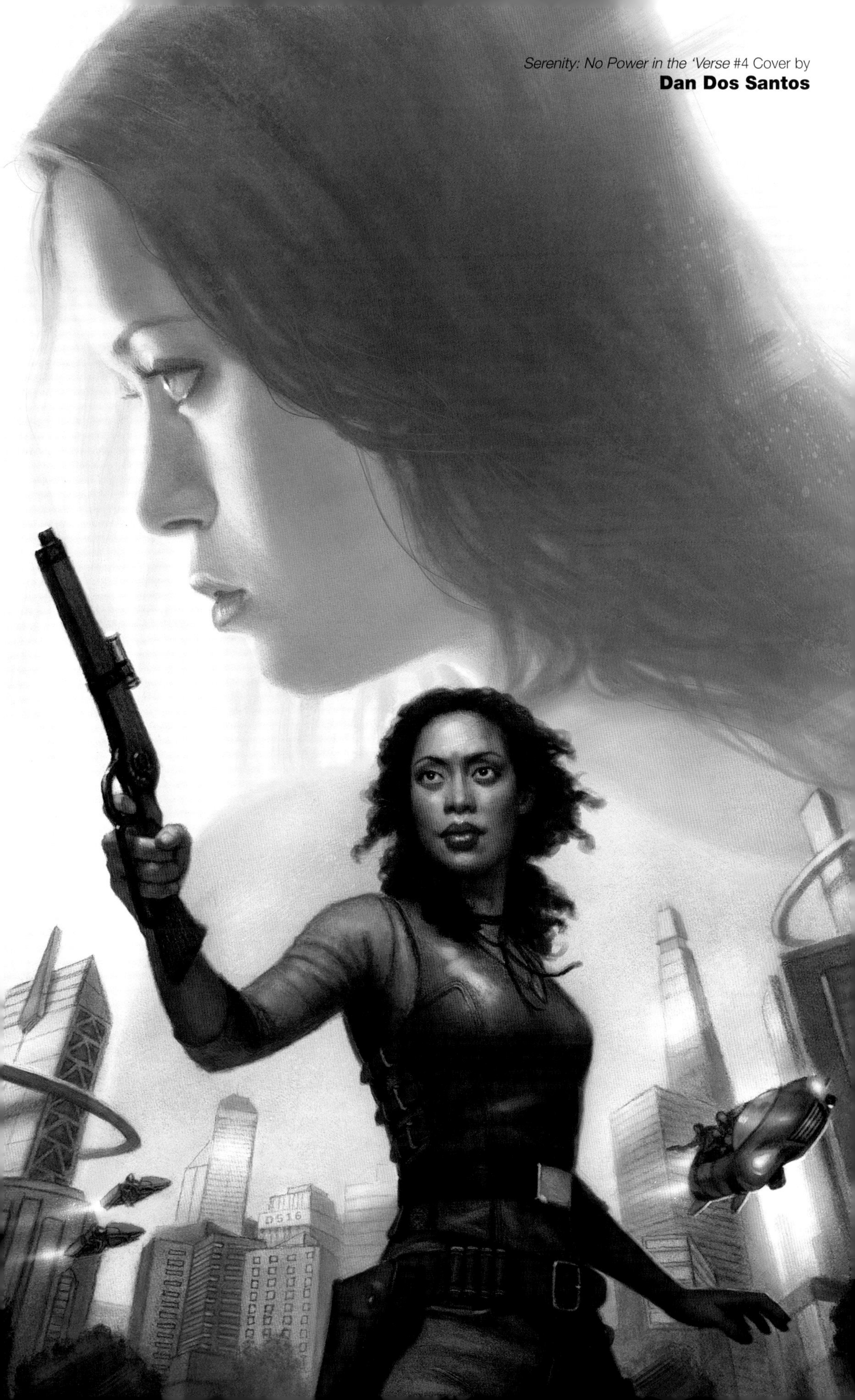

Serenity: No Power in the 'Verse #4 Cover by
Dan Dos Santos

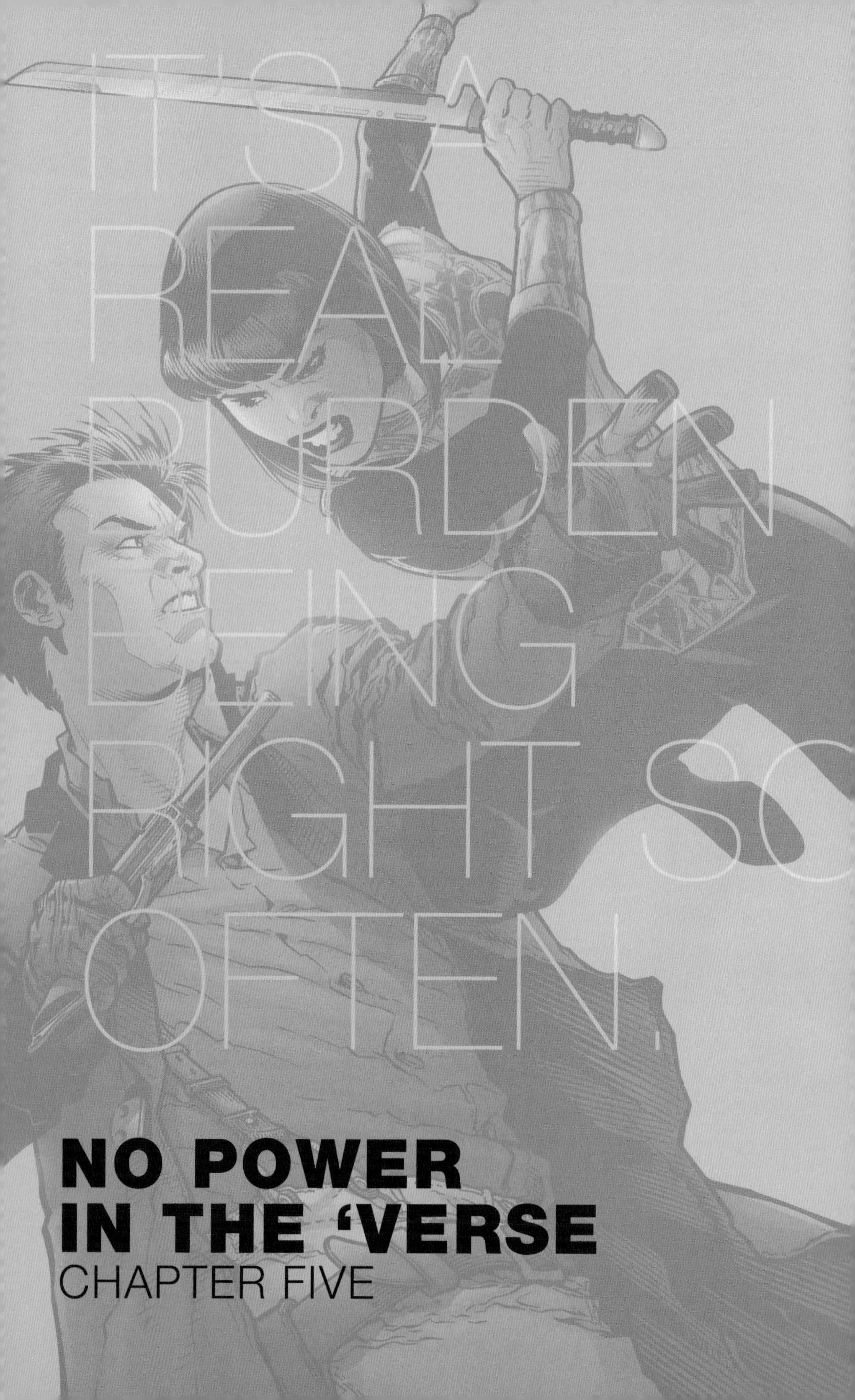
IT'S A REAL BURDEN BEING RIGHT SO OFTEN.

NO POWER IN THE 'VERSE

CHAPTER FIVE

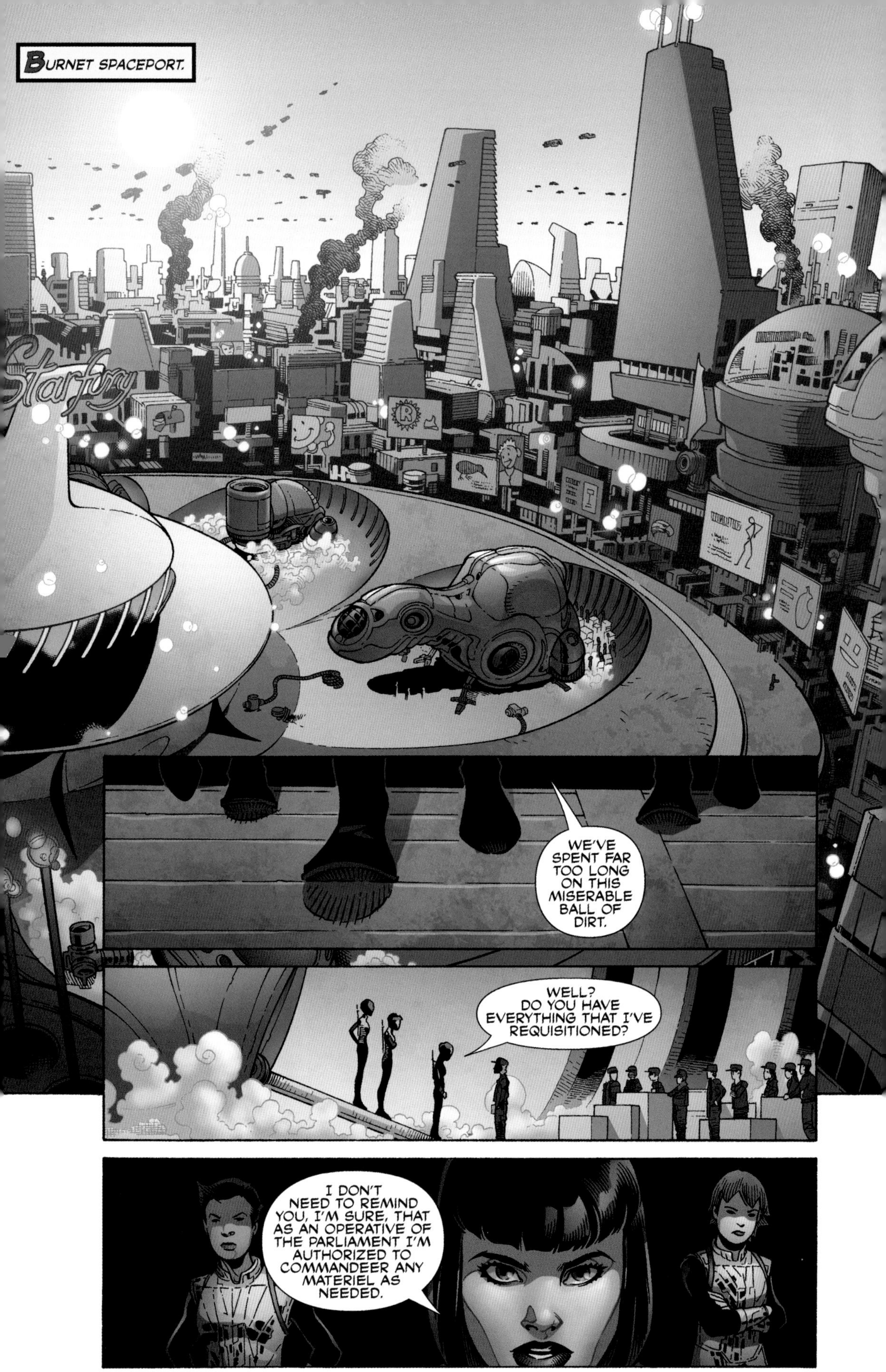
BURNET SPACEPORT.
Starfury
WE'VE SPENT FAR TOO LONG ON THIS MISERABLE BALL OF DIRT.
WELL? DO YOU HAVE EVERYTHING THAT I'VE REQUISITIONED?
I DON'T NEED TO REMIND YOU, I'M SURE, THAT AS AN OPERATIVE OF THE PARLIAMENT I'M AUTHORIZED TO COMMANDEER ANY MATERIEL AS NEEDED.

THERE'S NO CALL TO GET ALL HIGH HAT WITH ME, MA'AM.

I'VE GOT ALL THE SUPPLIES YOU ASKED FOR. NO FUSS, NO MUSS.

MY CREW WILL GET YOUR BOAT FUELED AND LOADED WITH TIME TO SPARE.

YOU'LL MAKE YOUR LAUNCH WINDOW, I GUARANTEE.

I JUST NEED YOUR AUTHORIZATION TO GET THINGS MOVING.

GET TO WORK.

WELL IT'S A PLEASURE DOING BUSINESS WITH YOU, MIZ KALISTA, I'M SURE.

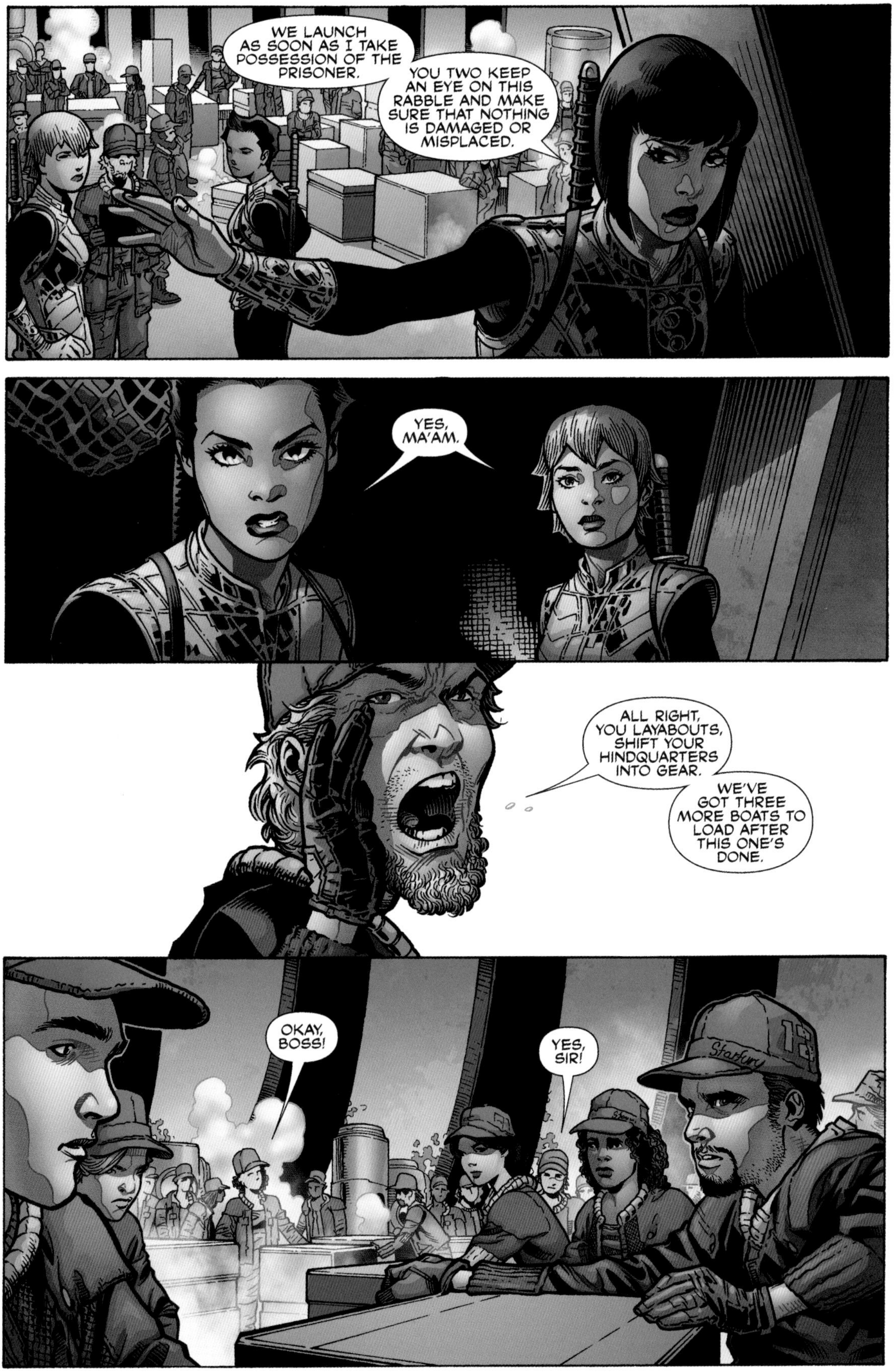
WE LAUNCH AS SOON AS I TAKE POSSESSION OF THE PRISONER.
YOU TWO KEEP AN EYE ON THIS RABBLE AND MAKE SURE THAT NOTHING IS DAMAGED OR MISPLACED.
YES, MA'AM.
ALL RIGHT, YOU LAYABOUTS, SHIFT YOUR HINDQUARTERS INTO GEAR.
WE'VE GOT THREE MORE BOATS TO LOAD AFTER THIS ONE'S DONE.
OKAY, BOSS!
YES, SIR!

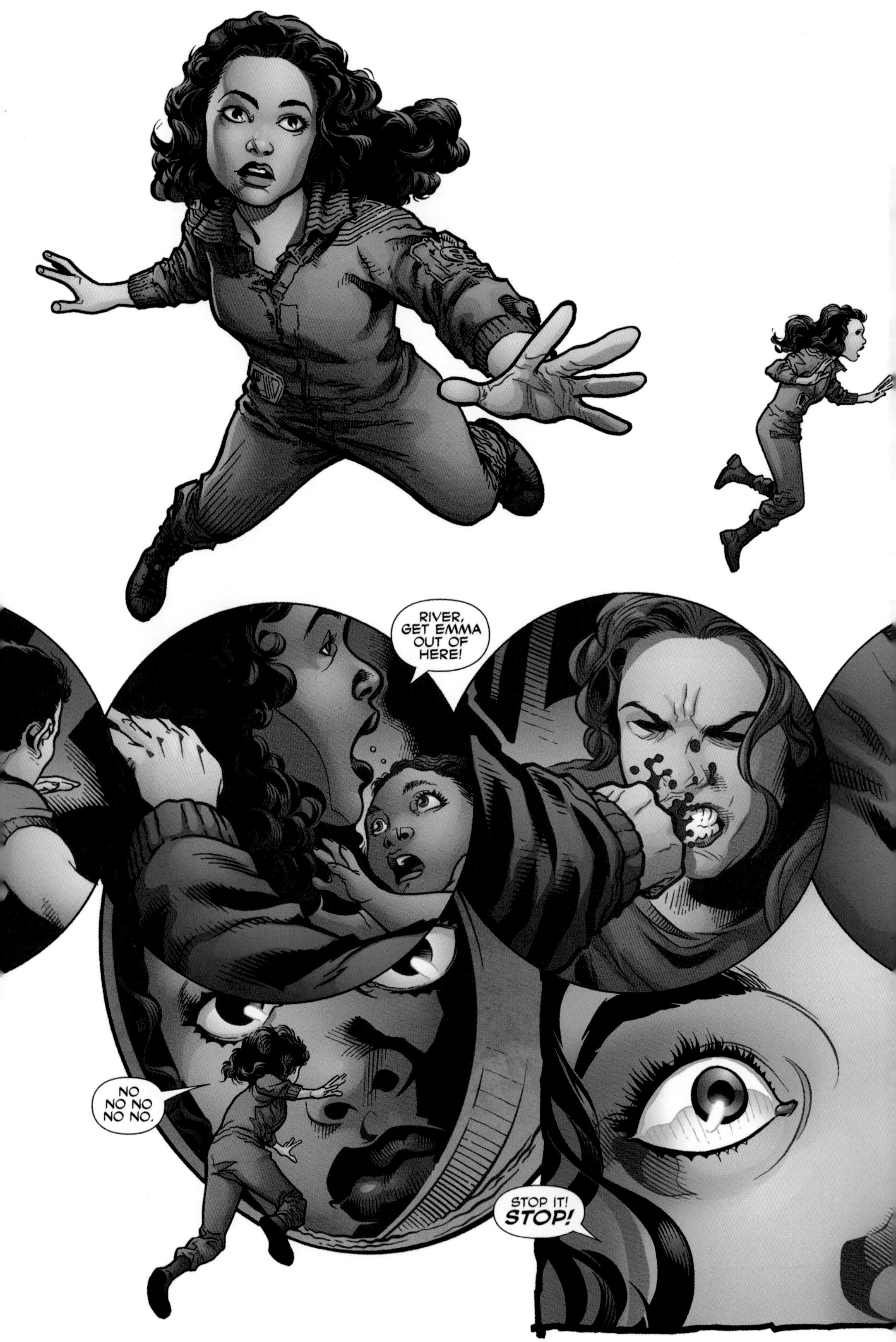
RIVER, GET EMMA OUT OF HERE!
NO NO NO NO NO.
STOP IT! STOP!

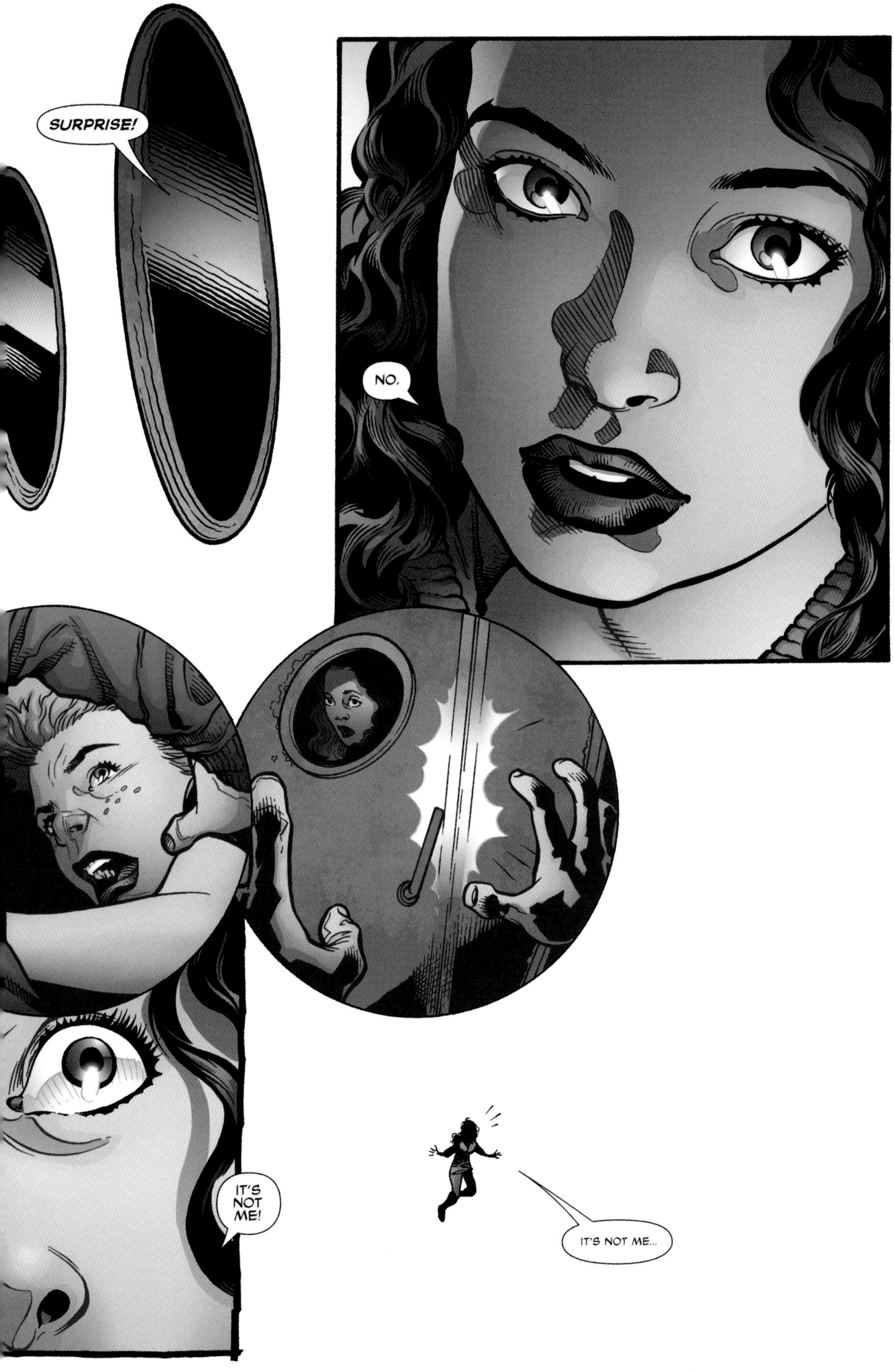
SURPRISE!
NO.
IT'S NOT ME!
IT'S NOT ME...

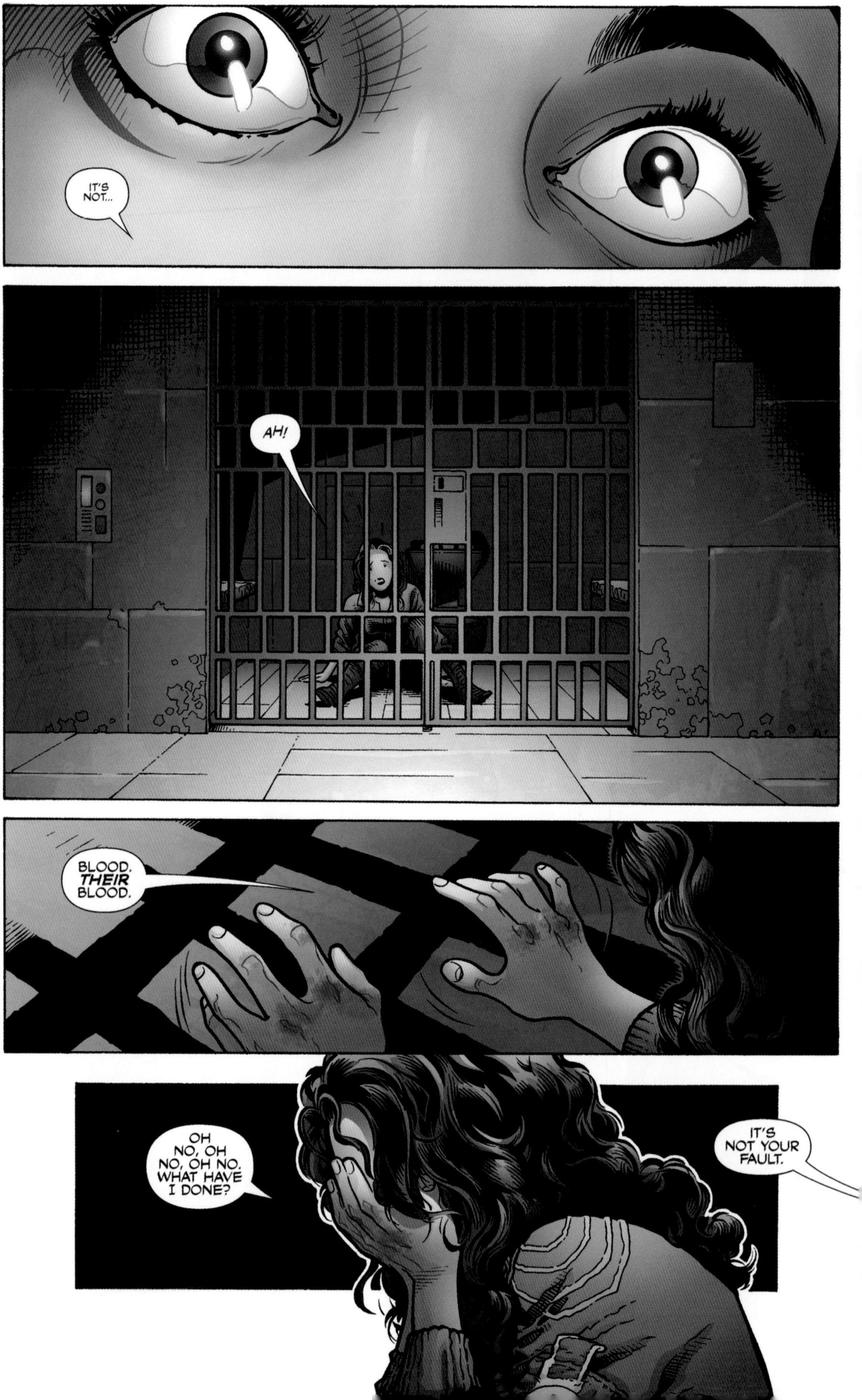
IT'S NOT...
AH!
BLOOD. THEIR BLOOD.
OH NO, OH NO, OH NO. WHAT HAVE I DONE?
IT'S NOT YOUR FAULT.

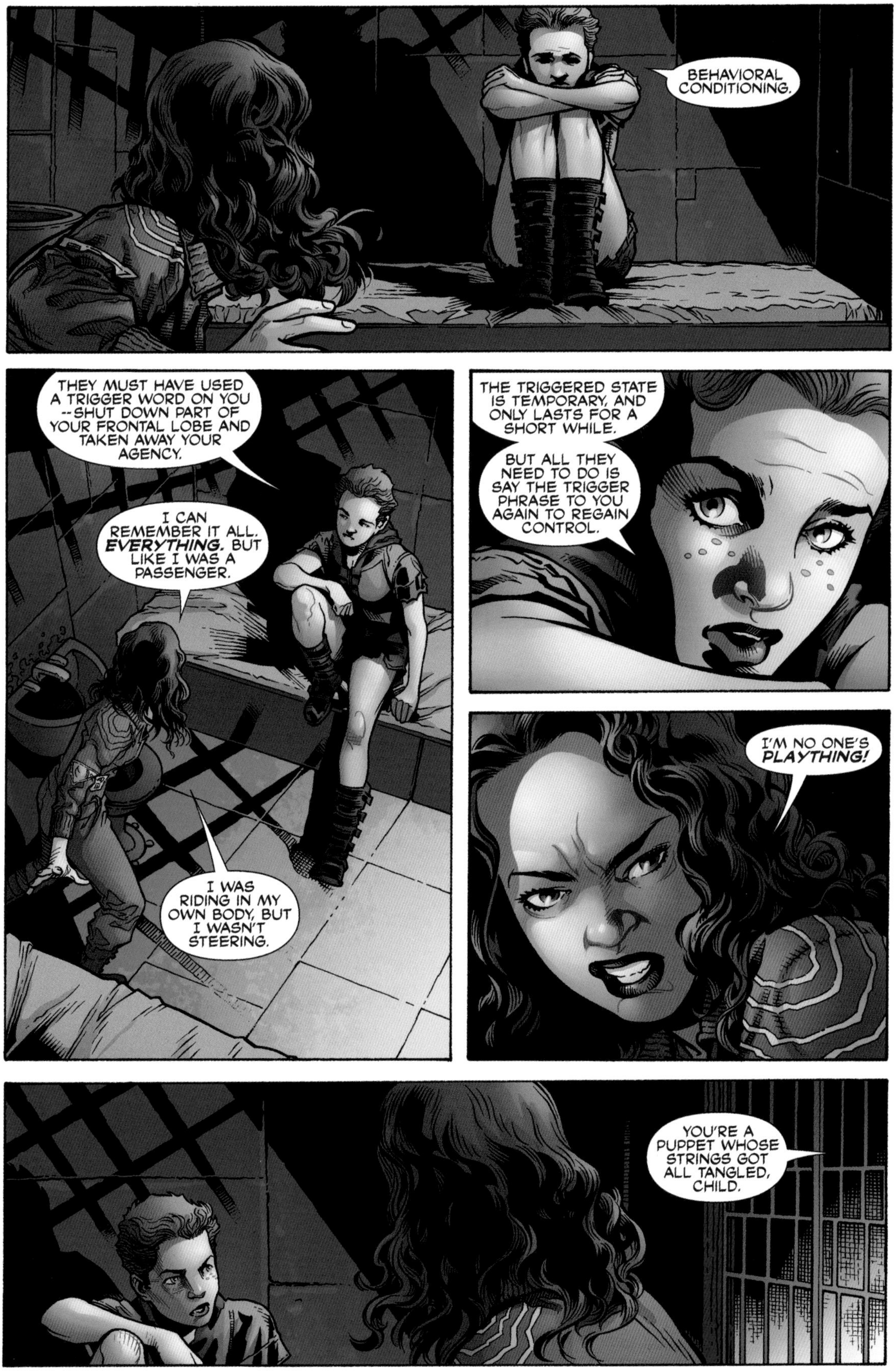
BEHAVIORAL CONDITIONING.
THEY MUST HAVE USED A TRIGGER WORD ON YOU --SHUT DOWN PART OF YOUR FRONTAL LOBE AND TAKEN AWAY YOUR AGENCY.
I CAN REMEMBER IT ALL. EVERYTHING. BUT LIKE I WAS A PASSENGER.
I WAS RIDING IN MY OWN BODY, BUT I WASN'T STEERING.
THE TRIGGERED STATE IS TEMPORARY, AND ONLY LASTS FOR A SHORT WHILE.
BUT ALL THEY NEED TO DO IS SAY THE TRIGGER PHRASE TO YOU AGAIN TO REGAIN CONTROL.
I'M NO ONE'S PLAYTHING!
YOU'RE A PUPPET WHOSE STRINGS GOT ALL TANGLED, CHILD.

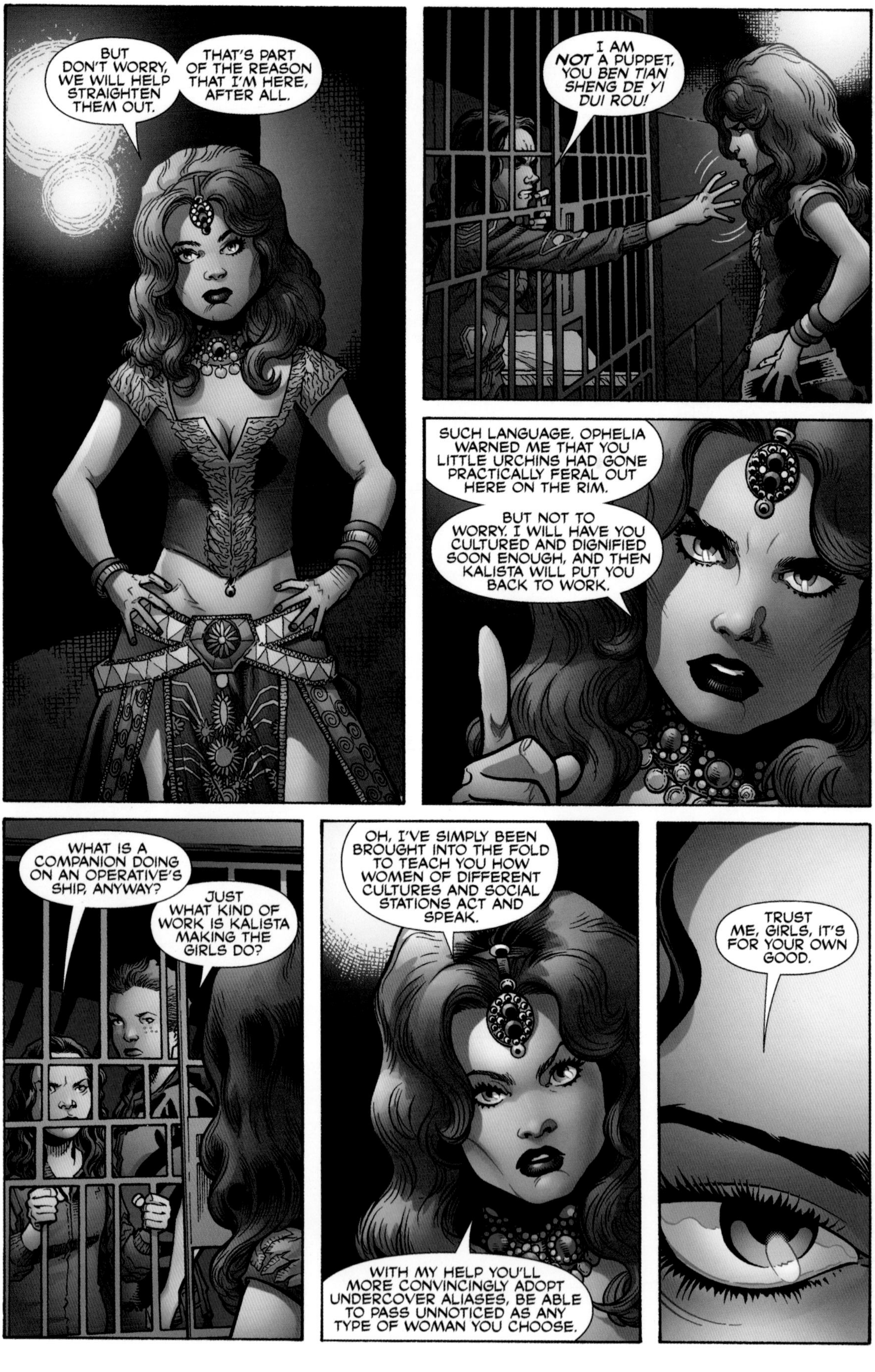
BUT DON'T WORRY, WE WILL HELP STRAIGHTEN THEM OUT.
THAT'S PART OF THE REASON THAT I'M HERE, AFTER ALL.
I AM *NOT* A PUPPET, YOU *BEN TIAN SHENG DE YI DUI ROU!*
SUCH LANGUAGE. OPHELIA WARNED ME THAT YOU LITTLE URCHINS HAD GONE PRACTICALLY FERAL OUT HERE ON THE RIM.
BUT NOT TO WORRY. I WILL HAVE YOU CULTURED AND DIGNIFIED SOON ENOUGH, AND THEN KALISTA WILL PUT YOU BACK TO WORK.
WHAT IS A COMPANION DOING ON AN OPERATIVE'S SHIP, ANYWAY?
JUST WHAT KIND OF WORK IS KALISTA MAKING THE GIRLS DO?
OH, I'VE SIMPLY BEEN BROUGHT INTO THE FOLD TO TEACH YOU HOW WOMEN OF DIFFERENT CULTURES AND SOCIAL STATIONS ACT AND SPEAK.
WITH MY HELP YOU'LL MORE CONVINCINGLY ADOPT UNDERCOVER ALIASES, BE ABLE TO PASS UNNOTICED AS ANY TYPE OF WOMAN YOU CHOOSE.
TRUST ME, GIRLS, IT'S FOR YOUR OWN GOOD.

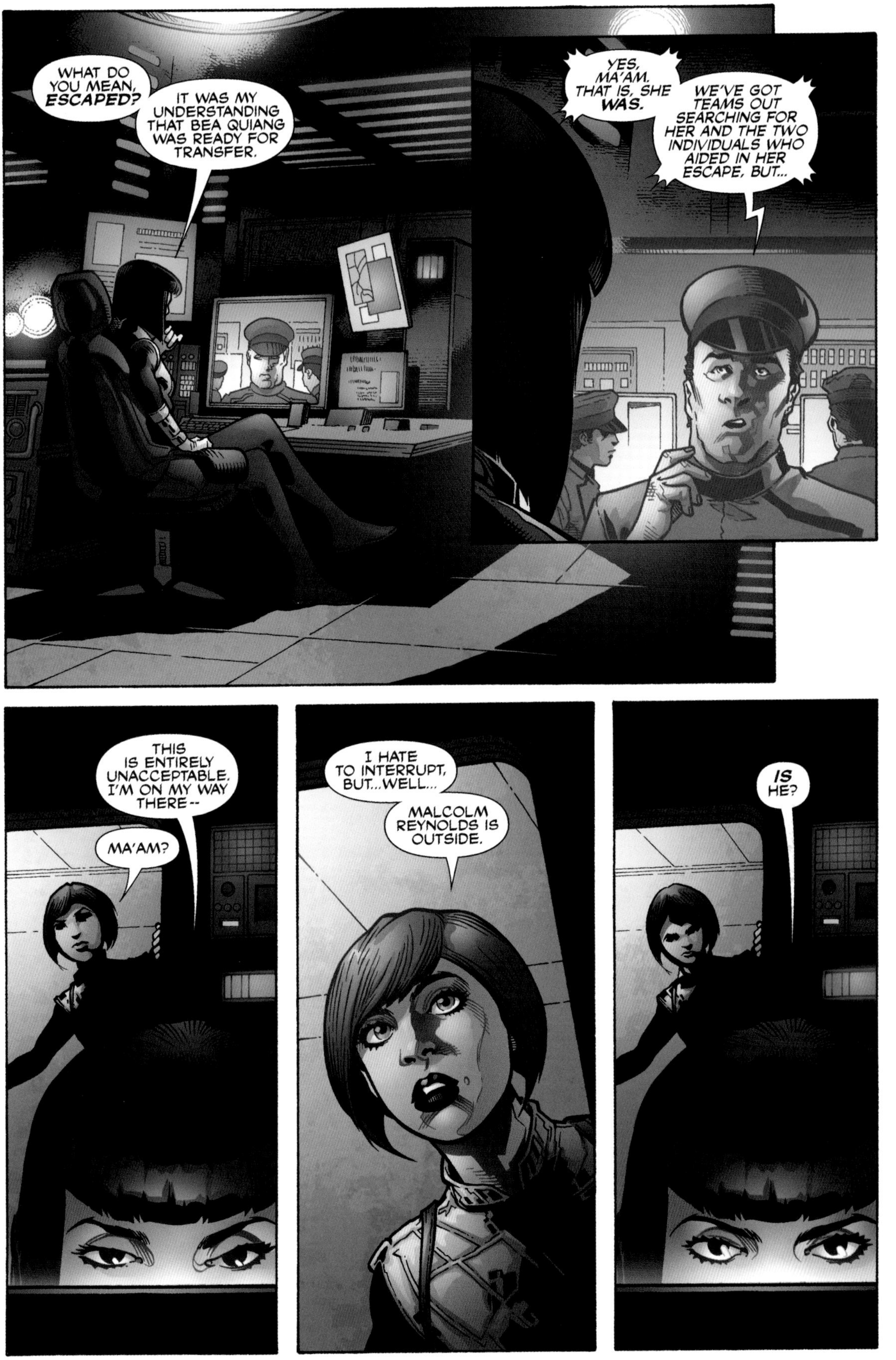
WHAT DO YOU MEAN, ***ESCAPED?***
IT WAS MY UNDERSTANDING THAT BEA QUIANG WAS READY FOR TRANSFER.
YES, MA'AM. THAT IS, SHE ***WAS.***
WE'VE GOT TEAMS OUT SEARCHING FOR HER AND THE TWO INDIVIDUALS WHO AIDED IN HER ESCAPE, BUT...
THIS IS ENTIRELY UNACCEPTABLE. I'M ON MY WAY THERE--
MA'AM?
I HATE TO INTERRUPT, BUT...WELL...
MALCOLM REYNOLDS IS OUTSIDE.
IS HE?

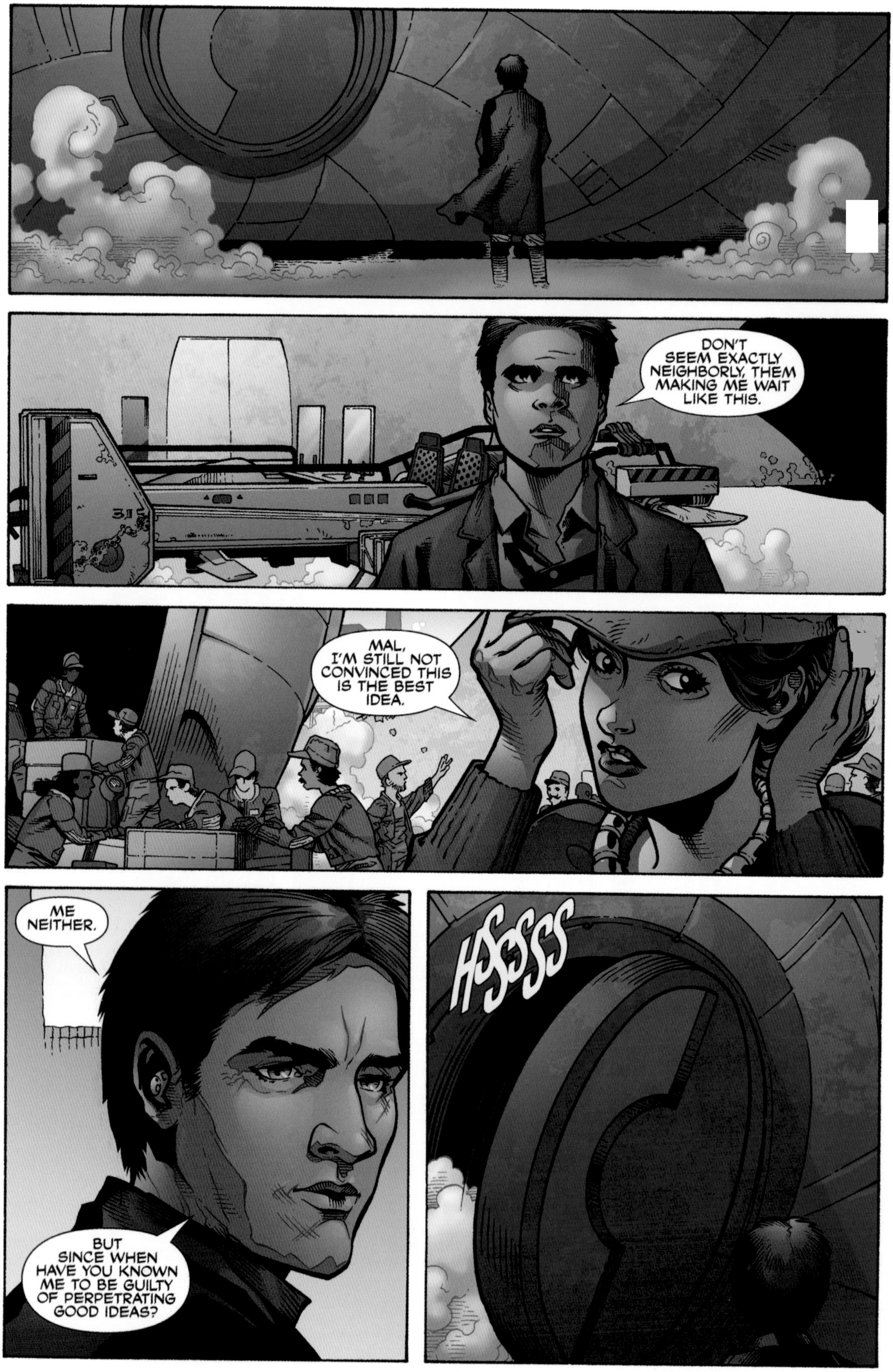
DON'T SEEM EXACTLY NEIGHBORLY, THEM MAKING ME WAIT LIKE THIS.
MAL, I'M STILL NOT CONVINCED THIS IS THE BEST IDEA.
ME NEITHER.
BUT SINCE WHEN HAVE YOU KNOWN ME TO BE GUILTY OF PERPETRATING GOOD IDEAS?
HSSSSS

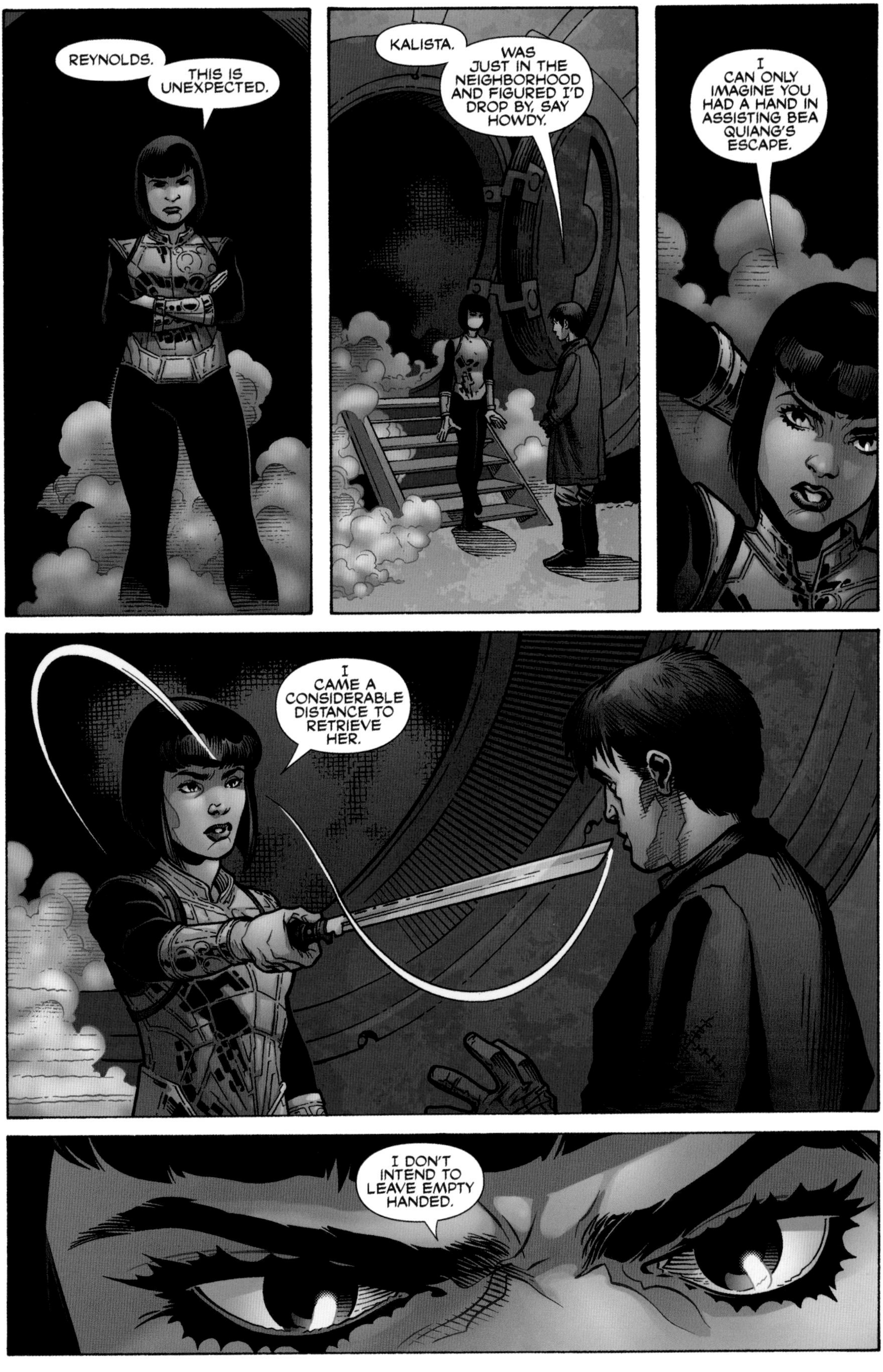

REYNOLDS.
THIS IS UNEXPECTED.
KALISTA.
WAS JUST IN THE NEIGHBORHOOD AND FIGURED I'D DROP BY, SAY HOWDY.
I CAN ONLY IMAGINE YOU HAD A HAND IN ASSISTING BEA QUIANG'S ESCAPE.
I CAME A CONSIDERABLE DISTANCE TO RETRIEVE HER.
I DON'T INTEND TO LEAVE EMPTY HANDED.

CAREFUL WITH THOSE CRATES.

KALISTA WILL HAVE YOUR HIDE IF YOU DAMAGE ANY OF THAT EQUIPMENT.

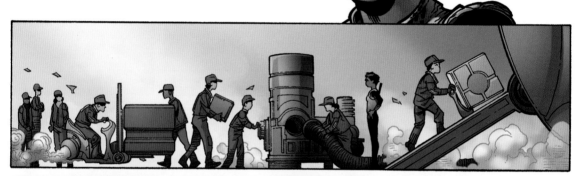

I HOPE SO, BEA.

DO YOU THINK IRIS AND YOUR SISTER ARE OKAY?

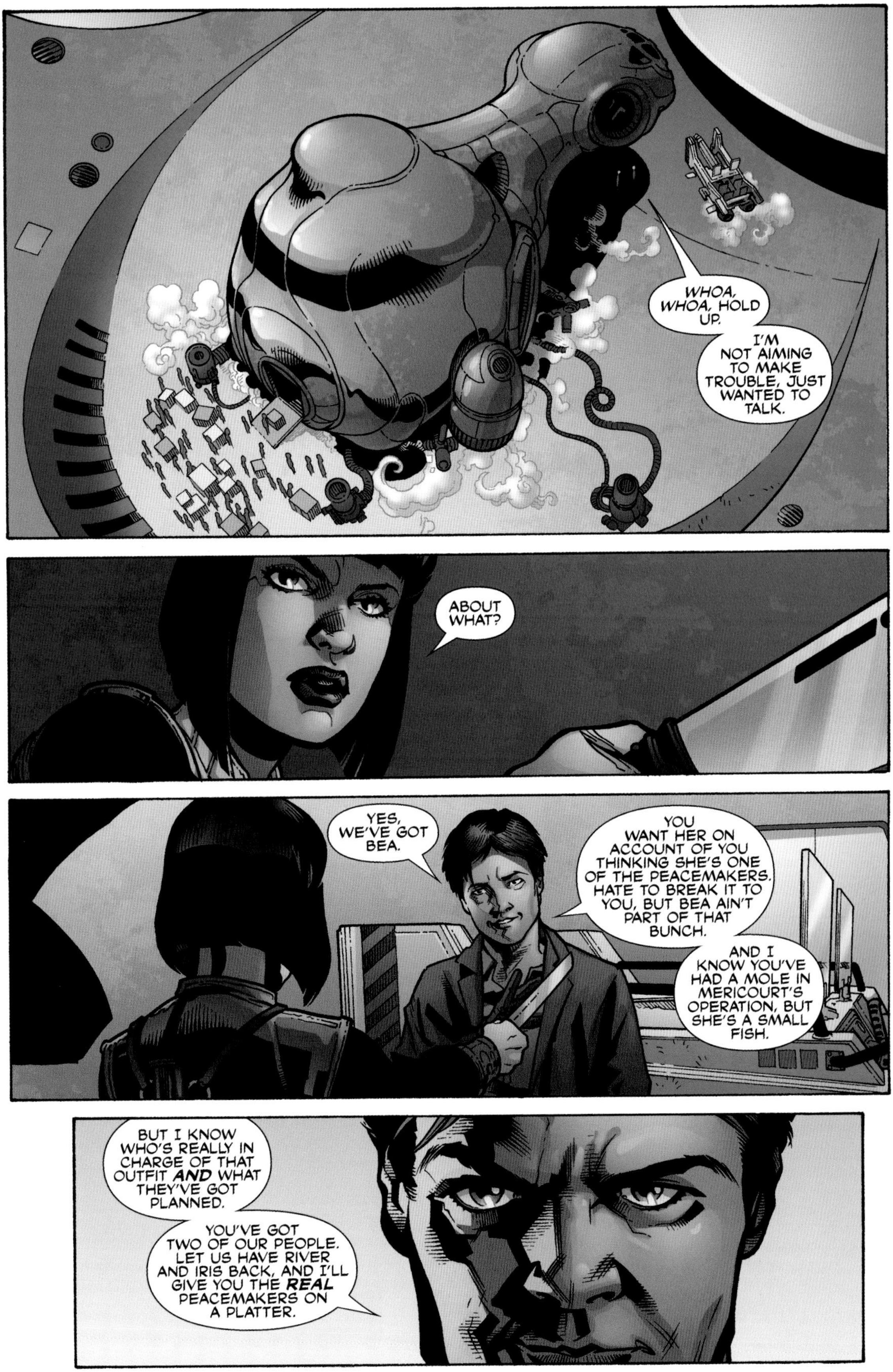
WHOA, WHOA, HOLD UP.
I'M NOT AIMING TO MAKE TROUBLE, JUST WANTED TO TALK.
ABOUT WHAT?
YES, WE'VE GOT BEA.
YOU WANT HER ON ACCOUNT OF YOU THINKING SHE'S ONE OF THE PEACEMAKERS. HATE TO BREAK IT TO YOU, BUT BEA AIN'T PART OF THAT BUNCH.
AND I KNOW YOU'VE HAD A MOLE IN MERICOURT'S OPERATION, BUT SHE'S A SMALL FISH.
BUT I KNOW WHO'S REALLY IN CHARGE OF THAT OUTFIT AND WHAT THEY'VE GOT PLANNED.
YOU'VE GOT TWO OF OUR PEOPLE. LET US HAVE RIVER AND IRIS BACK, AND I'LL GIVE YOU THE REAL PEACEMAKERS ON A PLATTER.

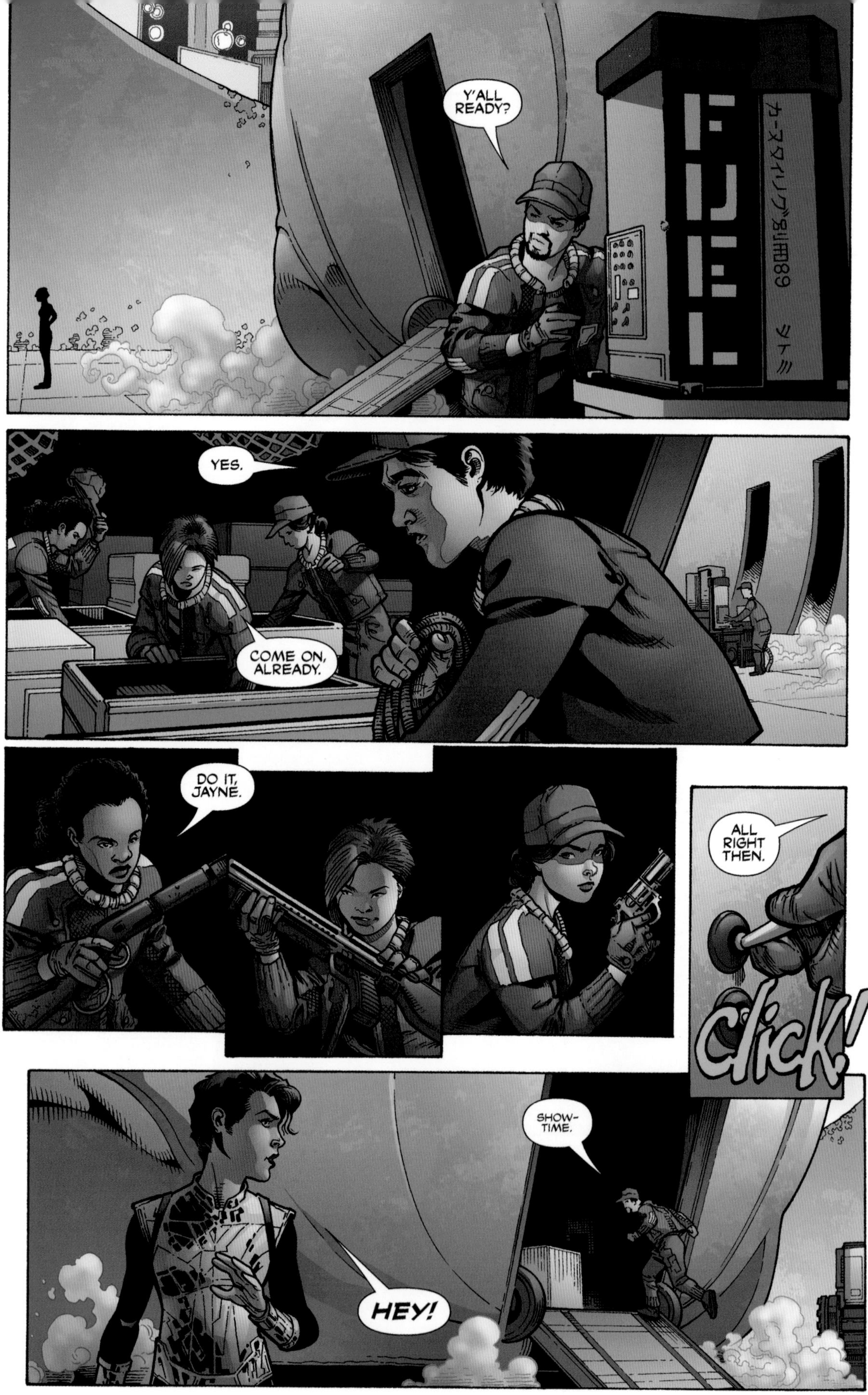
Y'ALL READY?
YES.
COME ON, ALREADY.
DO IT, JAYNE.
ALL RIGHT THEN.
CLICK!
SHOW-TIME.
HEY!

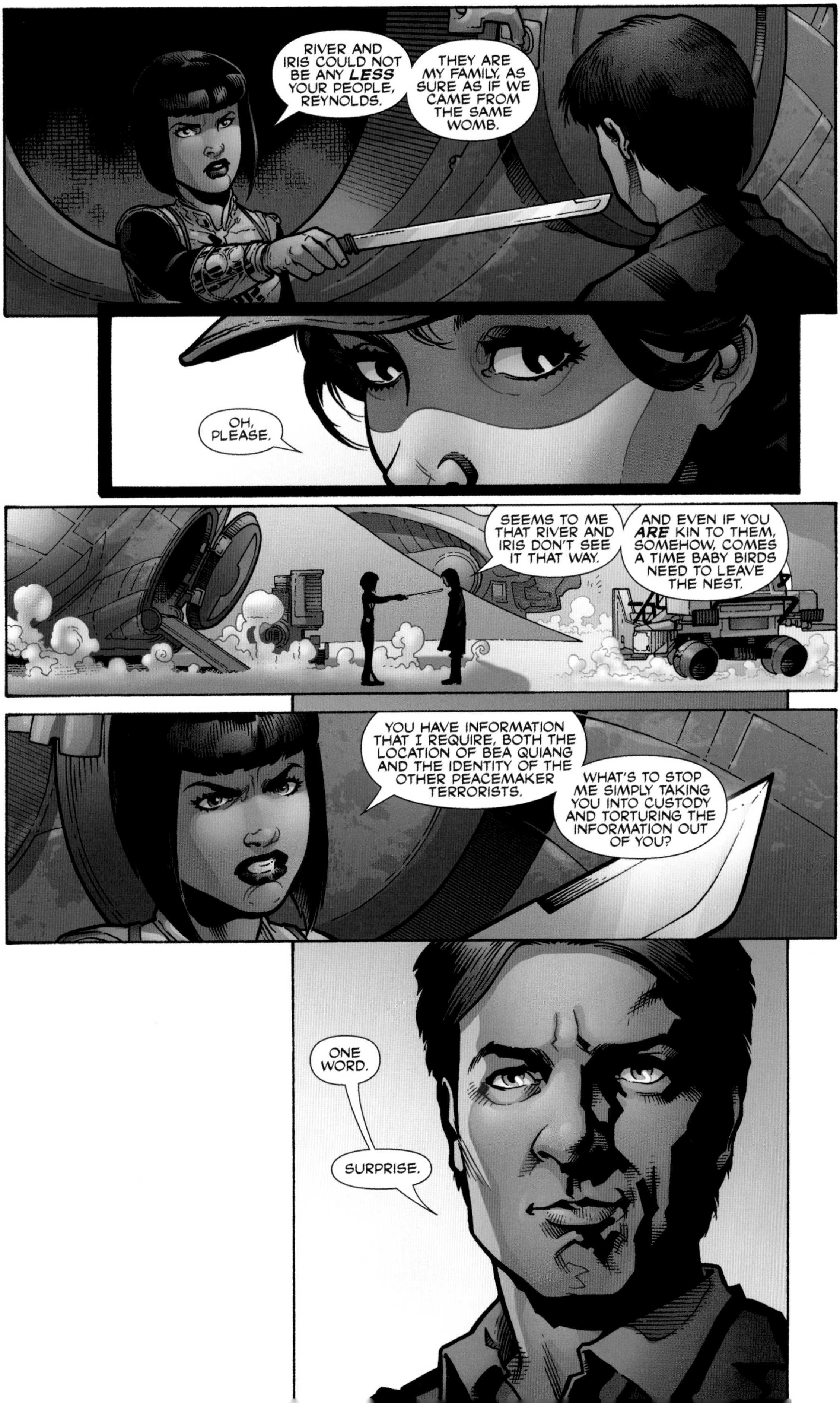
RIVER AND IRIS COULD NOT BE ANY LESS YOUR PEOPLE, REYNOLDS.
THEY ARE MY FAMILY, AS SURE AS IF WE CAME FROM THE SAME WOMB.
OH, PLEASE.
SEEMS TO ME THAT RIVER AND IRIS DON'T SEE IT THAT WAY.
AND EVEN IF YOU ARE KIN TO THEM, SOMEHOW, COMES A TIME BABY BIRDS NEED TO LEAVE THE NEST.
YOU HAVE INFORMATION THAT I REQUIRE, BOTH THE LOCATION OF BEA QUIANG AND THE IDENTITY OF THE OTHER PEACEMAKER TERRORISTS.
WHAT'S TO STOP ME SIMPLY TAKING YOU INTO CUSTODY AND TORTURING THE INFORMATION OUT OF YOU?
ONE WORD.
SURPRISE.

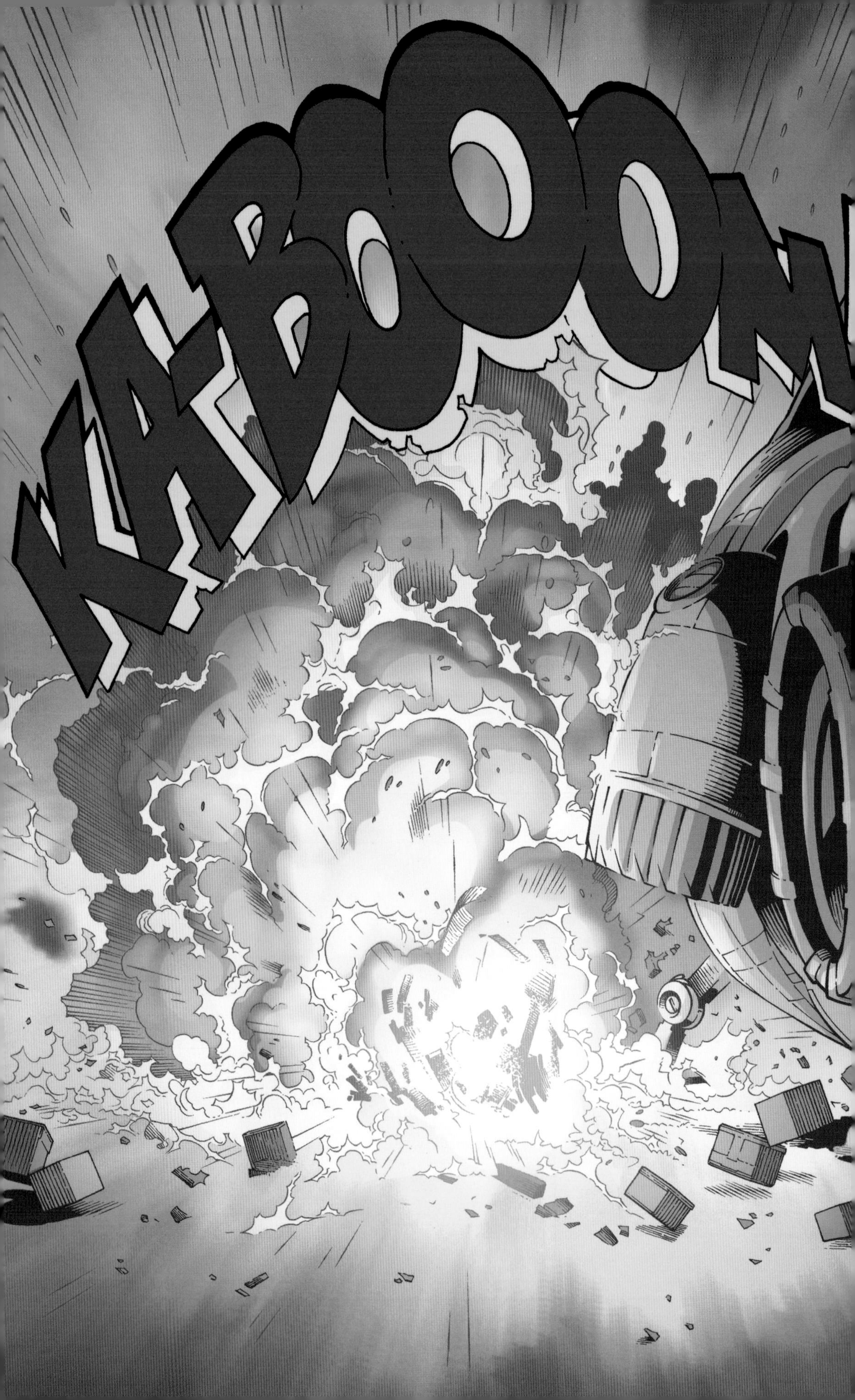
KA-BOOOM

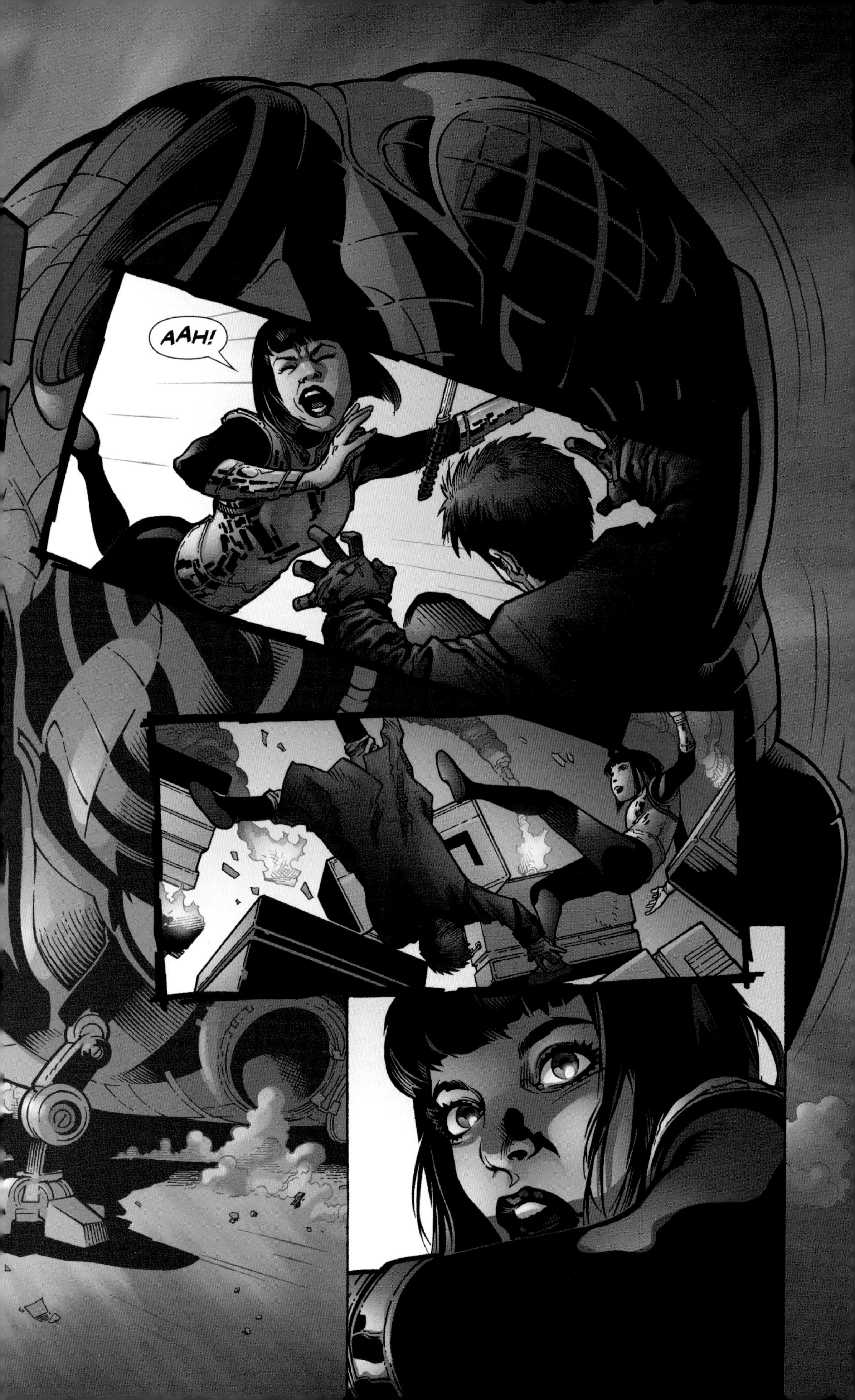
AAH!

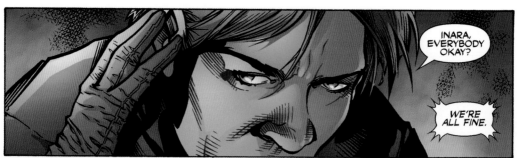

INARA, EVERYBODY OKAY?

WE'RE ALL FINE.

STICK TO THE PLAN. I'VE GOT THINGS COVERED OVER HERE.

GRN.

UNGF.

THOK

MAL IS KEEPING KALISTA OCCUPIED. WE SHOULD SPLIT UP, AND FIND THE GIRLS AS QUICKLY AS WE CAN.

OKAY, RIVER, WHERE ARE THEY KEEPING YOU...?

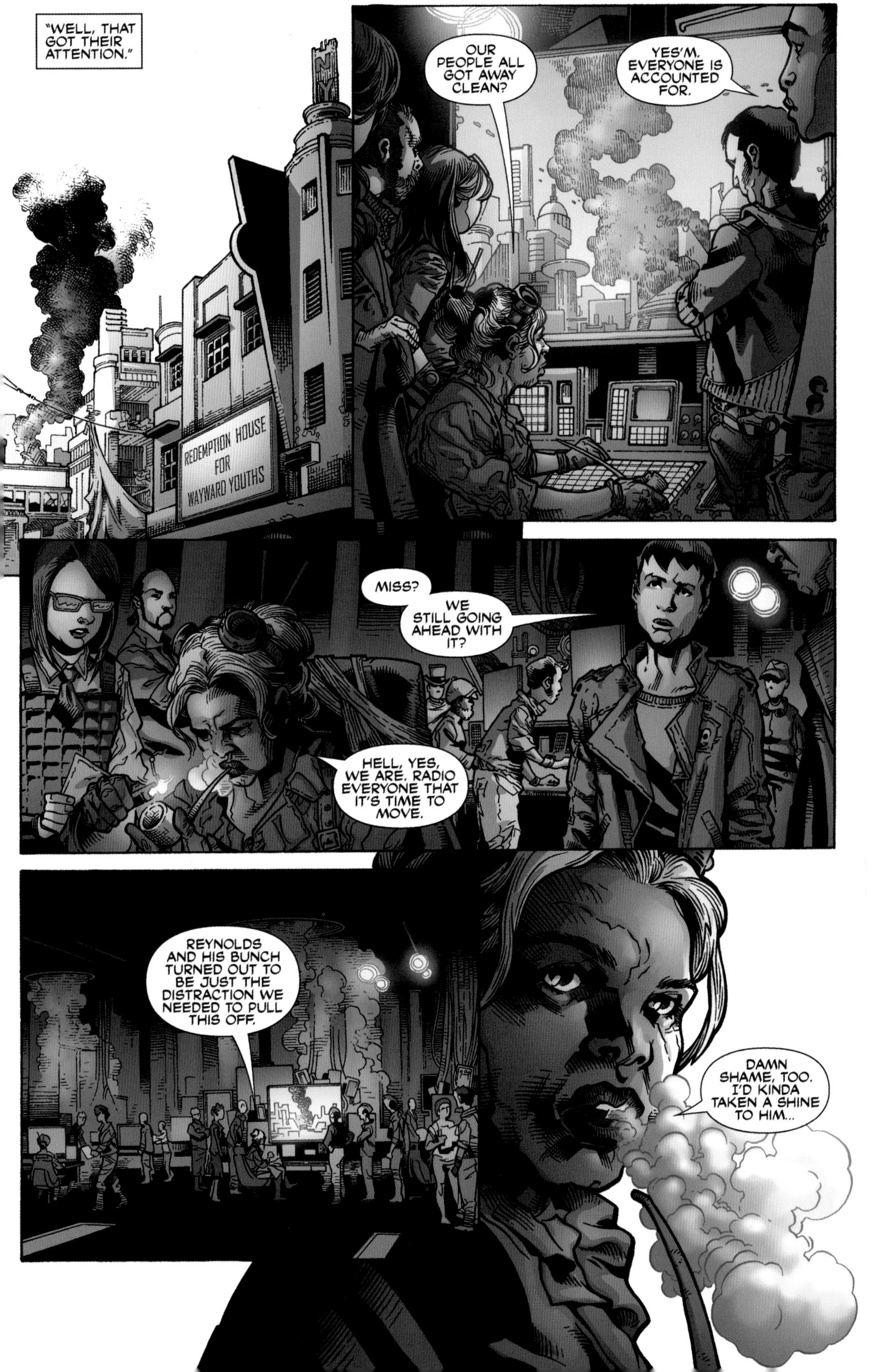
"WELL, THAT GOT THEIR ATTENTION."
NY
REDEMPTION HOUSE FOR WAYWARD YOUTHS
OUR PEOPLE ALL GOT AWAY CLEAN?
YES'M. EVERYONE IS ACCOUNTED FOR.
MISS?
WE STILL GOING AHEAD WITH IT?
HELL, YES, WE ARE. RADIO EVERYONE THAT IT'S TIME TO MOVE.
REYNOLDS AND HIS BUNCH TURNED OUT TO BE JUST THE DISTRACTION WE NEEDED TO PULL THIS OFF.
DAMN SHAME, TOO. I'D KINDA TAKEN A SHINE TO HIM...

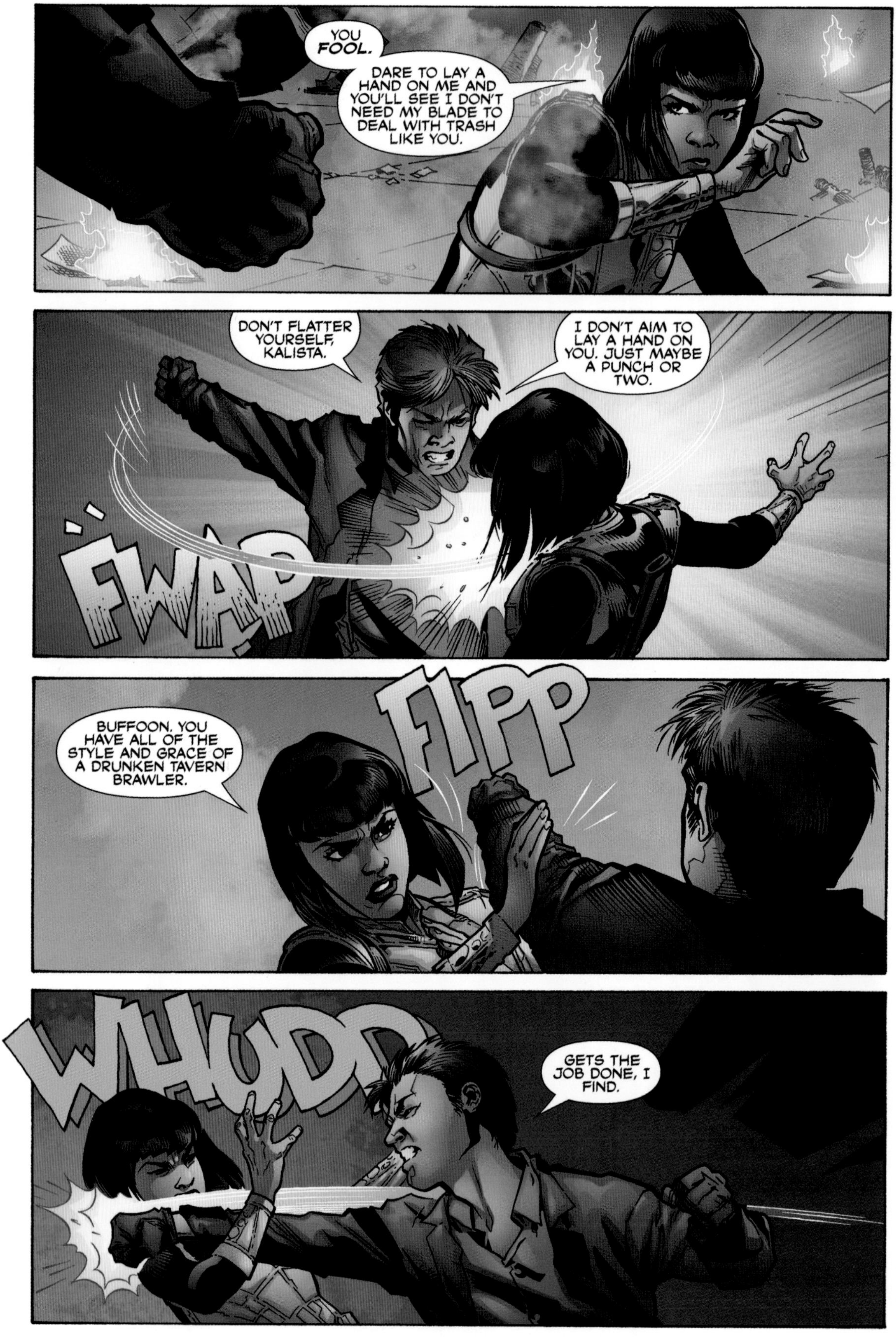
YOU FOOL.
DARE TO LAY A HAND ON ME AND YOU'LL SEE I DON'T NEED MY BLADE TO DEAL WITH TRASH LIKE YOU.
DON'T FLATTER YOURSELF, KALISTA.
I DON'T AIM TO LAY A HAND ON YOU. JUST MAYBE A PUNCH OR TWO.
FWAP
FIPP
BUFFOON. YOU HAVE ALL OF THE STYLE AND GRACE OF A DRUNKEN TAVERN BRAWLER.
WHUDD
GETS THE JOB DONE, I FIND.

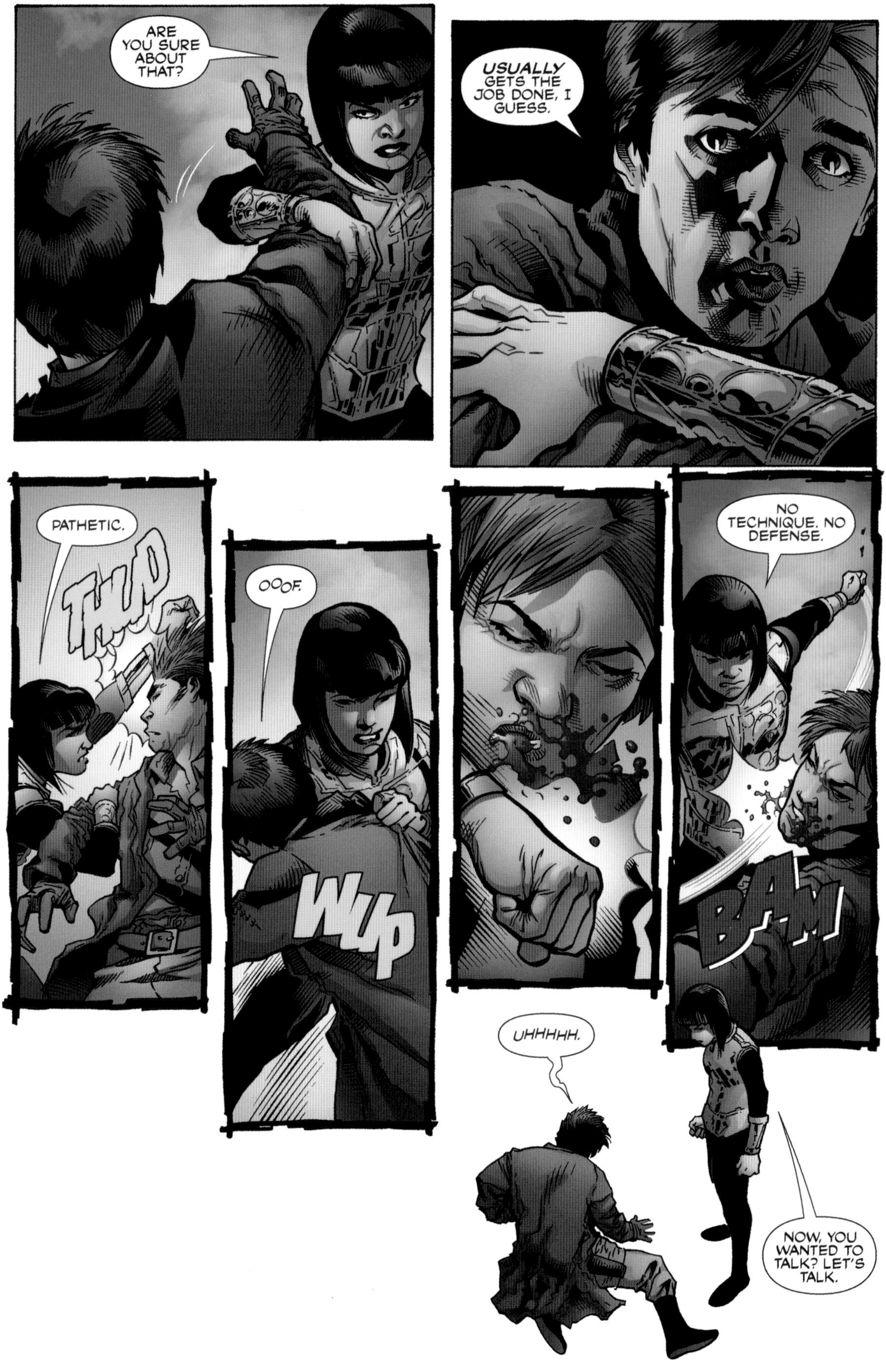
ARE YOU SURE ABOUT THAT?
USUALLY GETS THE JOB DONE, I GUESS.
PATHETIC.
THUD
OOOF.
WUP
NO TECHNIQUE. NO DEFENSE.
BAM
UHHHHH.
NOW, YOU WANTED TO TALK? LET'S TALK.

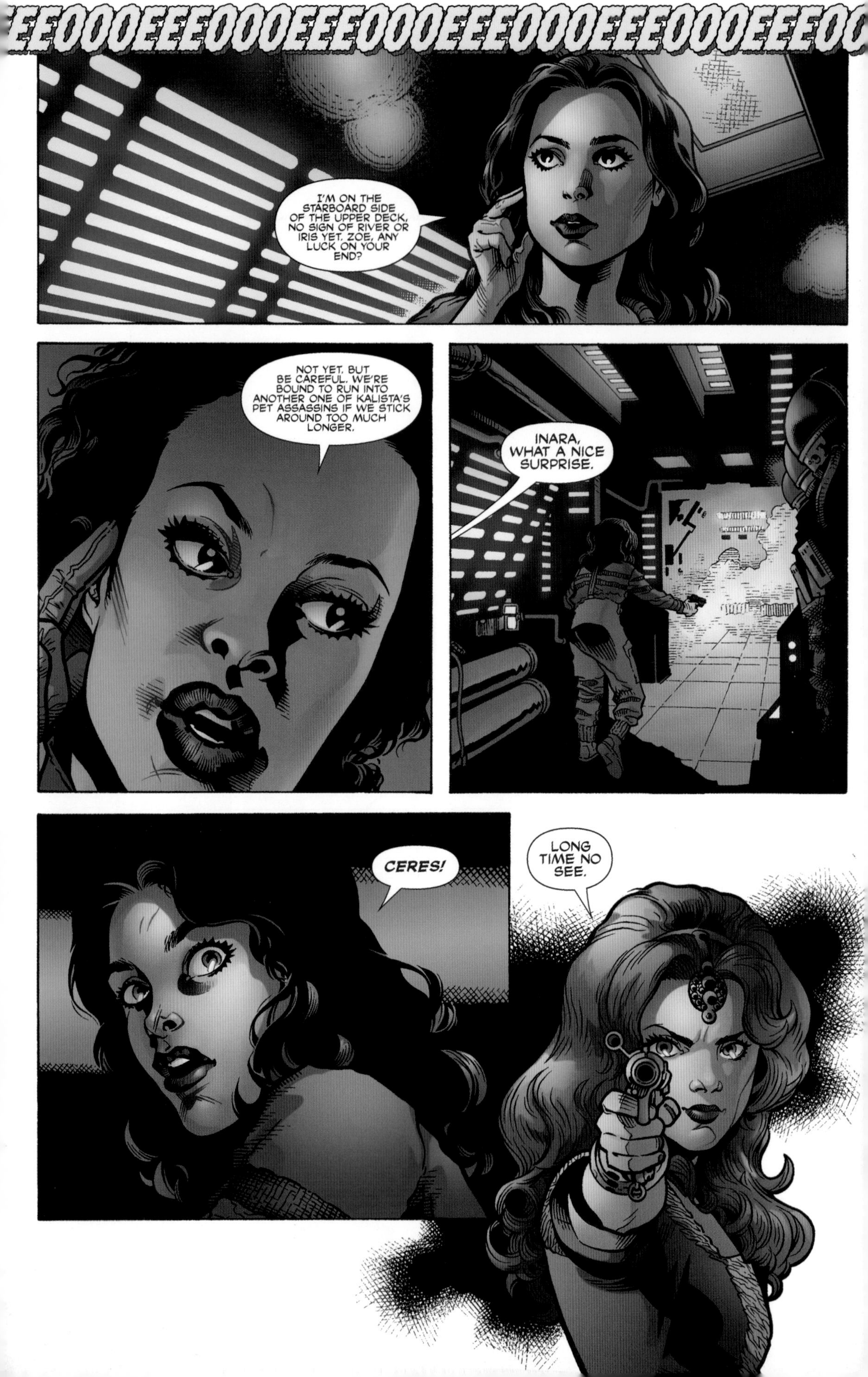
EEOOOEEEOOOEEEOOOEEEOOOEEEOOOEEEOOOEEEOO
I'M ON THE STARBOARD SIDE OF THE UPPER DECK, NO SIGN OF RIVER OR IRIS YET. ZOE, ANY LUCK ON YOUR END?
NOT YET. BUT BE CAREFUL. WE'RE BOUND TO RUN INTO ANOTHER ONE OF KALISTA'S PET ASSASSINS IF WE STICK AROUND TOO MUCH LONGER.
INARA, WHAT A NICE SURPRISE.
CERES!
LONG TIME NO SEE.

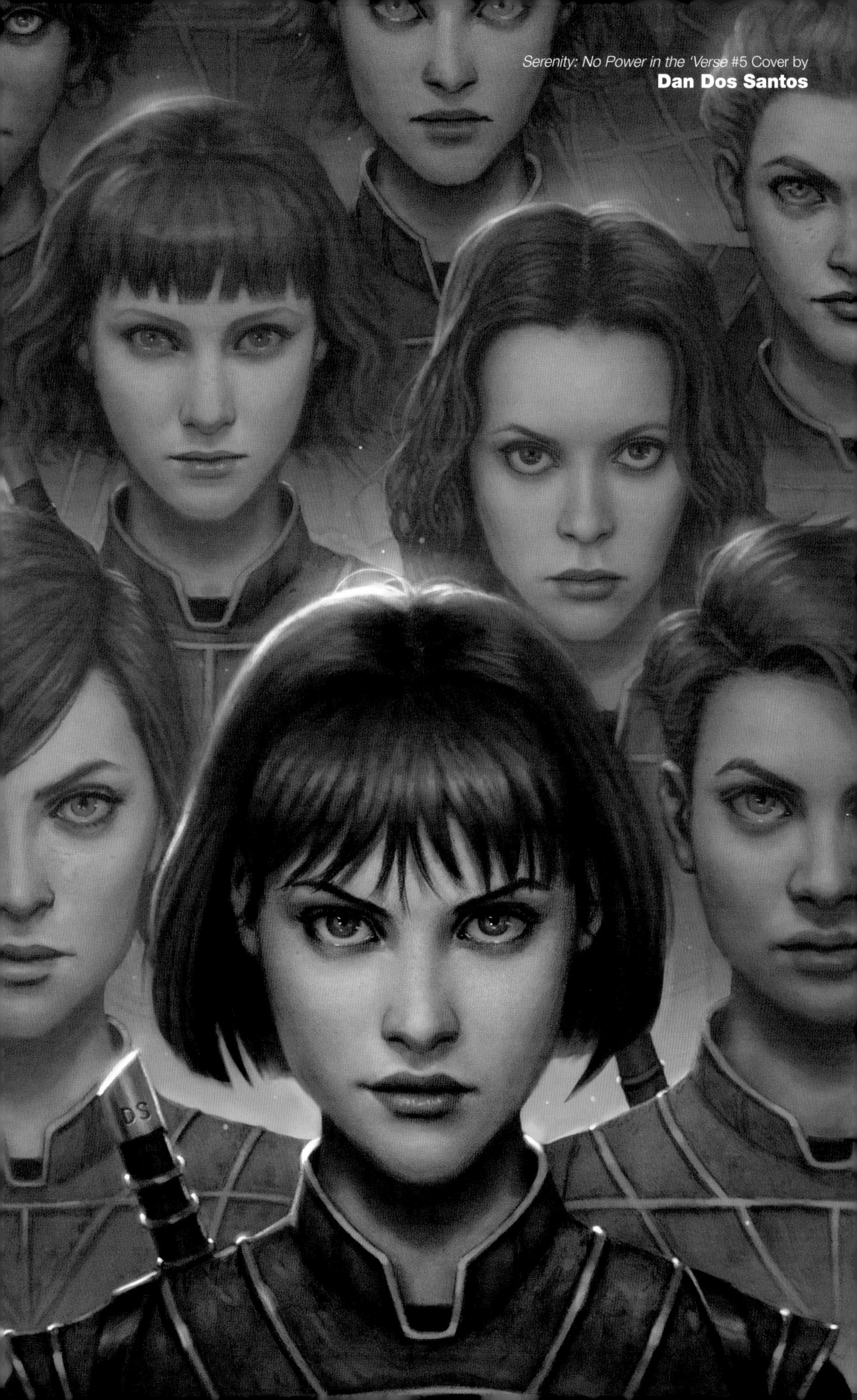

Serenity: No Power in the 'Verse #5 Cover by
Dan Dos Santos

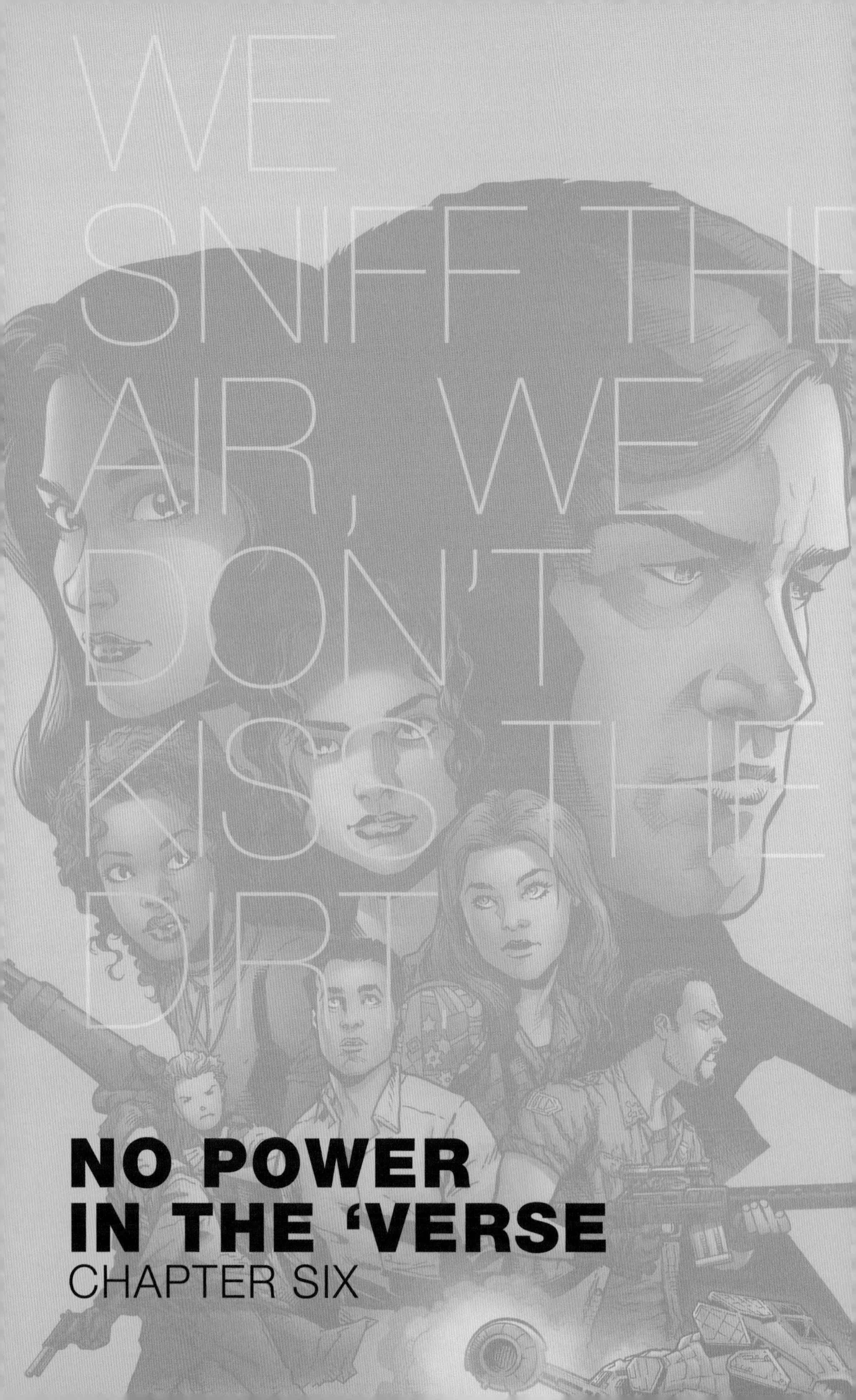
WE SNIFF THE AIR, WE DON'T KISS THE DIRT

NO POWER IN THE 'VERSE

CHAPTER SIX

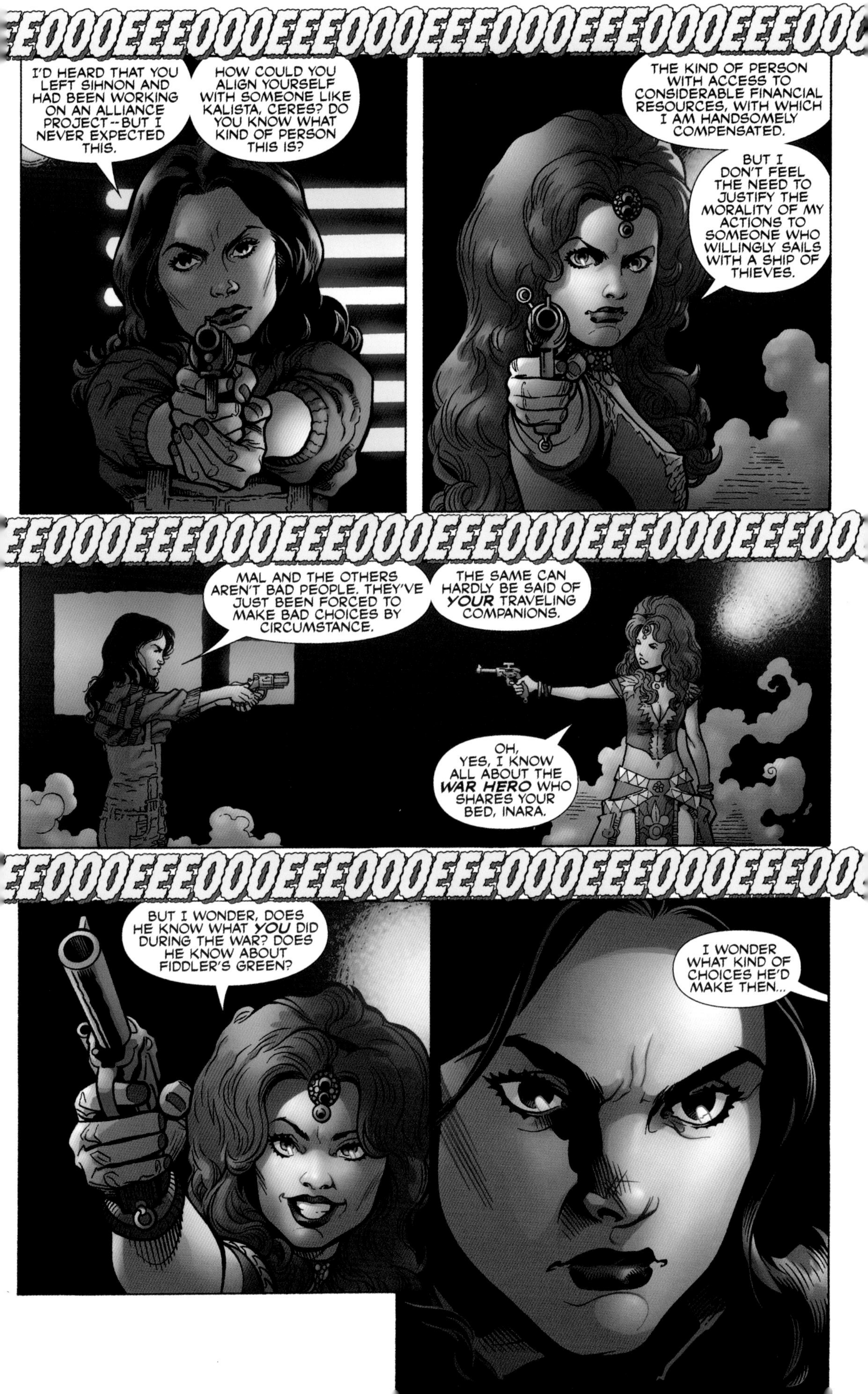
EEOOOEEEOOOEEEOOOEEEOOOEEEOOOEEEOOO
I'D HEARD THAT YOU LEFT SIHNON AND HAD BEEN WORKING ON AN ALLIANCE PROJECT--BUT I NEVER EXPECTED THIS.
HOW COULD YOU ALIGN YOURSELF WITH SOMEONE LIKE KALISTA, CERES? DO YOU KNOW WHAT KIND OF PERSON THIS IS?
THE KIND OF PERSON WITH ACCESS TO CONSIDERABLE FINANCIAL RESOURCES, WITH WHICH I AM HANDSOMELY COMPENSATED.
BUT I DON'T FEEL THE NEED TO JUSTIFY THE MORALITY OF MY ACTIONS TO SOMEONE WHO WILLINGLY SAILS WITH A SHIP OF THIEVES.
EEOOOEEEOOOEEEOOOEEEOOOEEEOOOEEEOO
MAL AND THE OTHERS AREN'T BAD PEOPLE. THEY'VE JUST BEEN FORCED TO MAKE BAD CHOICES BY CIRCUMSTANCE.
THE SAME CAN HARDLY BE SAID OF *YOUR* TRAVELING COMPANIONS.
OH, YES, I KNOW ALL ABOUT THE ***WAR HERO*** WHO SHARES YOUR BED, INARA.
EEOOOEEEOOOEEEOOOEEEOOOEEEOOOEEEOO
BUT I WONDER, DOES HE KNOW WHAT *YOU* DID DURING THE WAR? DOES HE KNOW ABOUT FIDDLER'S GREEN?
I WONDER WHAT KIND OF CHOICES HE'D MAKE THEN...

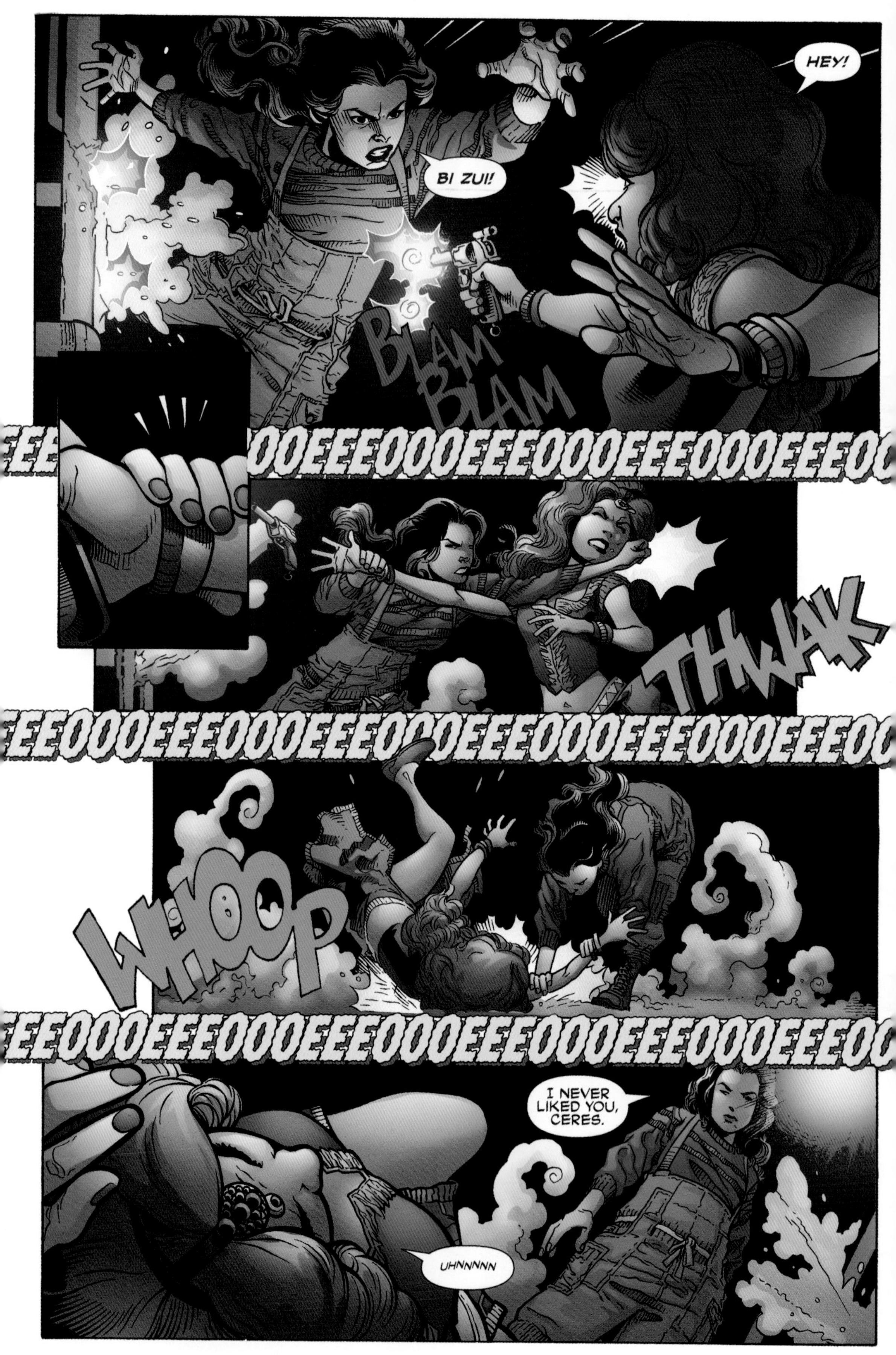
HEY!
BI ZUI!
BLAM BLAM
EEOOOEEEOOOEEEOOOEEEOOOEEEOO
THWAK
EEOOOEEEOOOEEEOOOEEEOOOEEEOOOEEEOO
WHOOP
EEOOOEEEOOOEEEOOOEEEOOOEEEOOOEEEOO
I NEVER LIKED YOU, CERES.
UHNNNNN

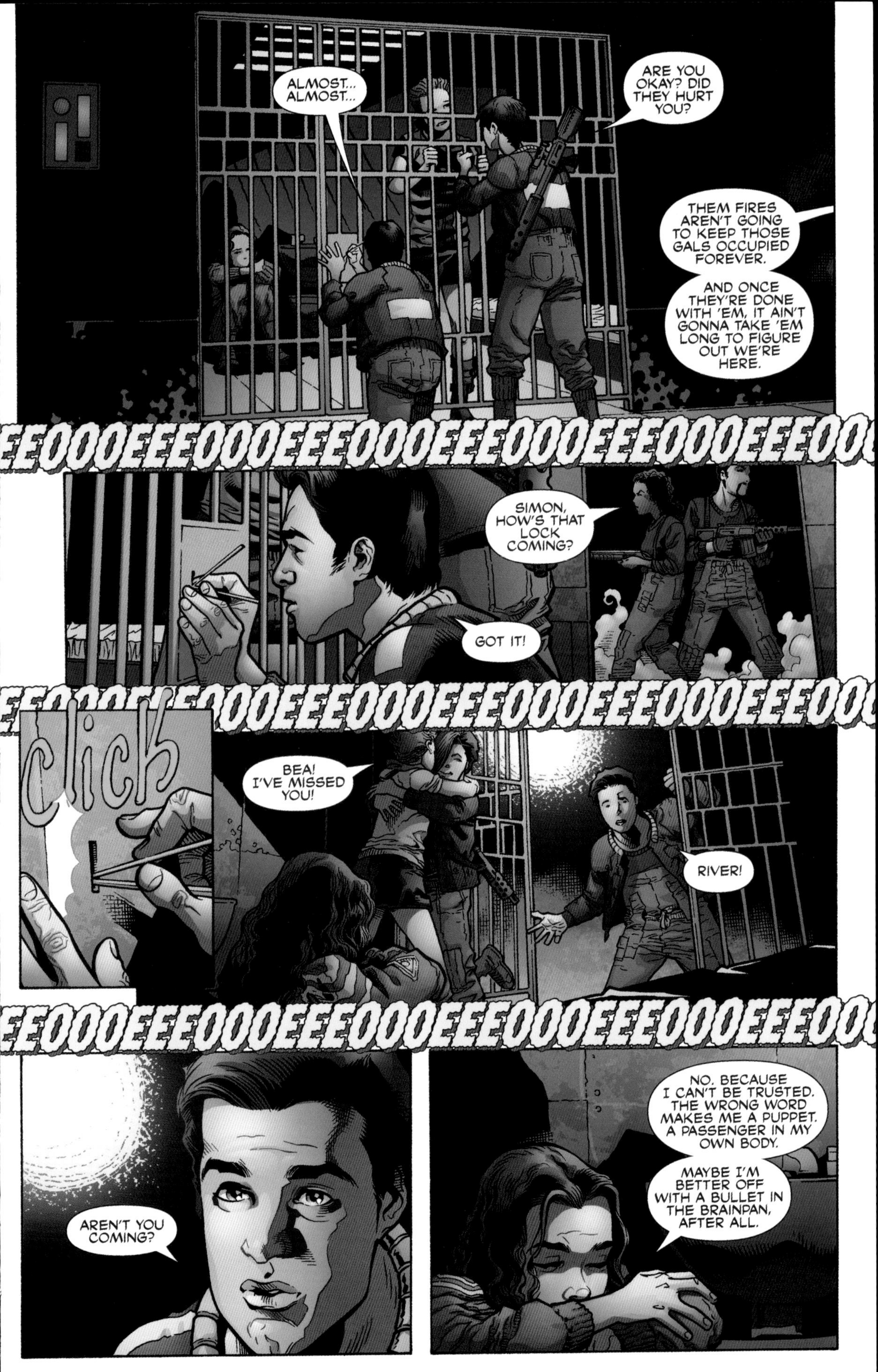
ALMOST... ALMOST...
ARE YOU OKAY? DID THEY HURT YOU?
THEM FIRES AREN'T GOING TO KEEP THOSE GALS OCCUPIED FOREVER.
AND ONCE THEY'RE DONE WITH 'EM, IT AIN'T GONNA TAKE 'EM LONG TO FIGURE OUT WE'RE HERE.
EEOOOEEEOOOEEEOOOEEEOOOEEEOOOEEEOO
SIMON, HOW'S THAT LOCK COMING?
GOT IT!
EEOOOEEEOOOEEEOOOEEEOOOEEEOO
click
BEA! I'VE MISSED YOU!
RIVER!
EEOOOEEEOOOEEEOOOEEEOOOEEEOOOEEEOO
AREN'T YOU COMING?
NO. BECAUSE I CAN'T BE TRUSTED. THE WRONG WORD MAKES ME A PUPPET. A PASSENGER IN MY OWN BODY.
MAYBE I'M BETTER OFF WITH A BULLET IN THE BRAINPAN, AFTER ALL.

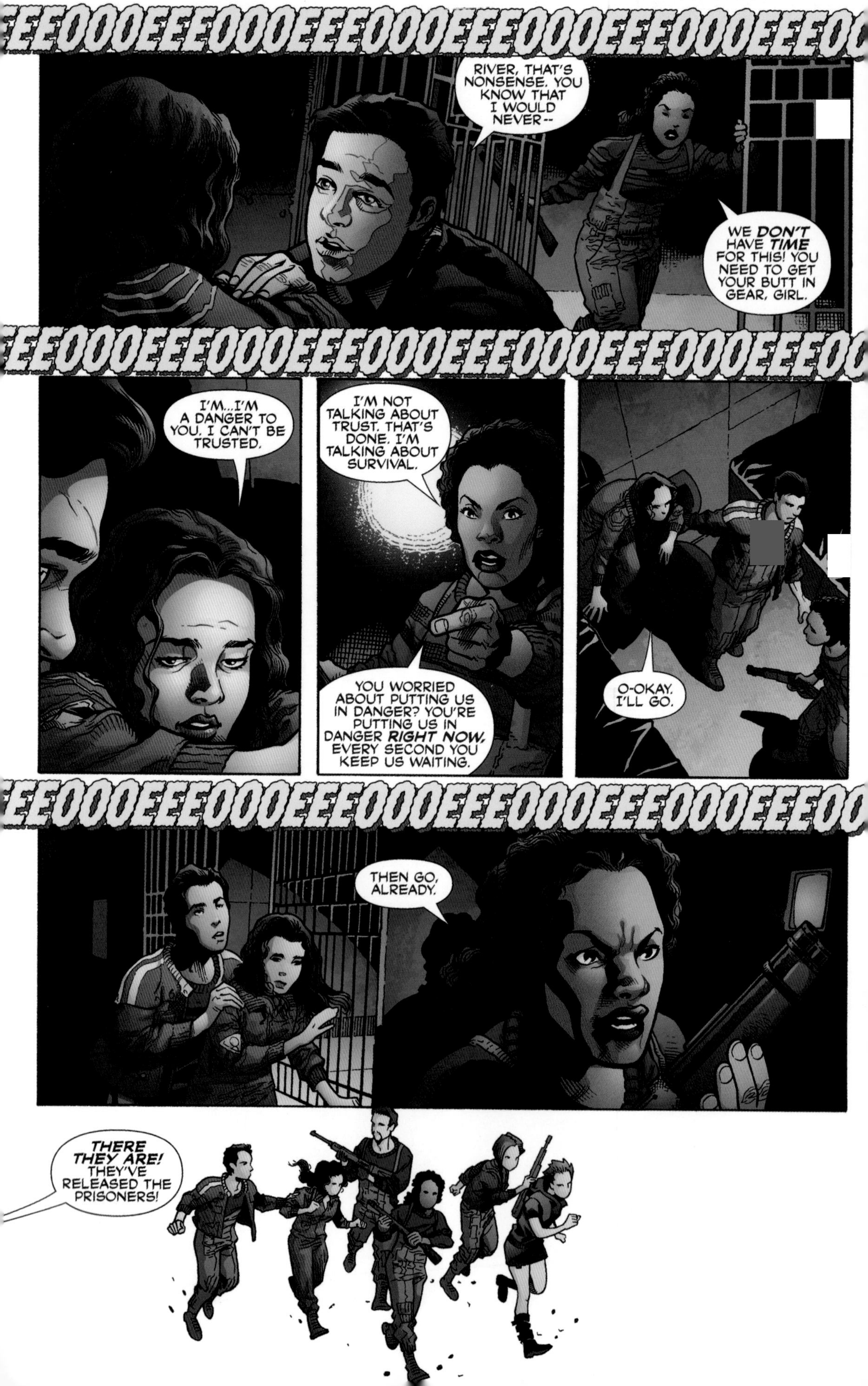
EEOOOEEEOOOEEEOOOEEEOOOEEEOOOEEEOO
RIVER, THAT'S NONSENSE. YOU KNOW THAT I WOULD NEVER--
WE DON'T HAVE TIME FOR THIS! YOU NEED TO GET YOUR BUTT IN GEAR, GIRL.
EEOOOEEEOOOEEEOOOEEEOOOEEEOOOEEEOO
I'M...I'M A DANGER TO YOU. I CAN'T BE TRUSTED.
I'M NOT TALKING ABOUT TRUST. THAT'S DONE. I'M TALKING ABOUT SURVIVAL.
YOU WORRIED ABOUT PUTTING US IN DANGER? YOU'RE PUTTING US IN DANGER RIGHT NOW. EVERY SECOND YOU KEEP US WAITING.
O-OKAY. I'LL GO.
EEOOOEEEOOOEEEOOOEEEOOOEEEOOOEEEOO
THEN GO, ALREADY.
THERE THEY ARE! THEY'VE RELEASED THE PRISONERS!

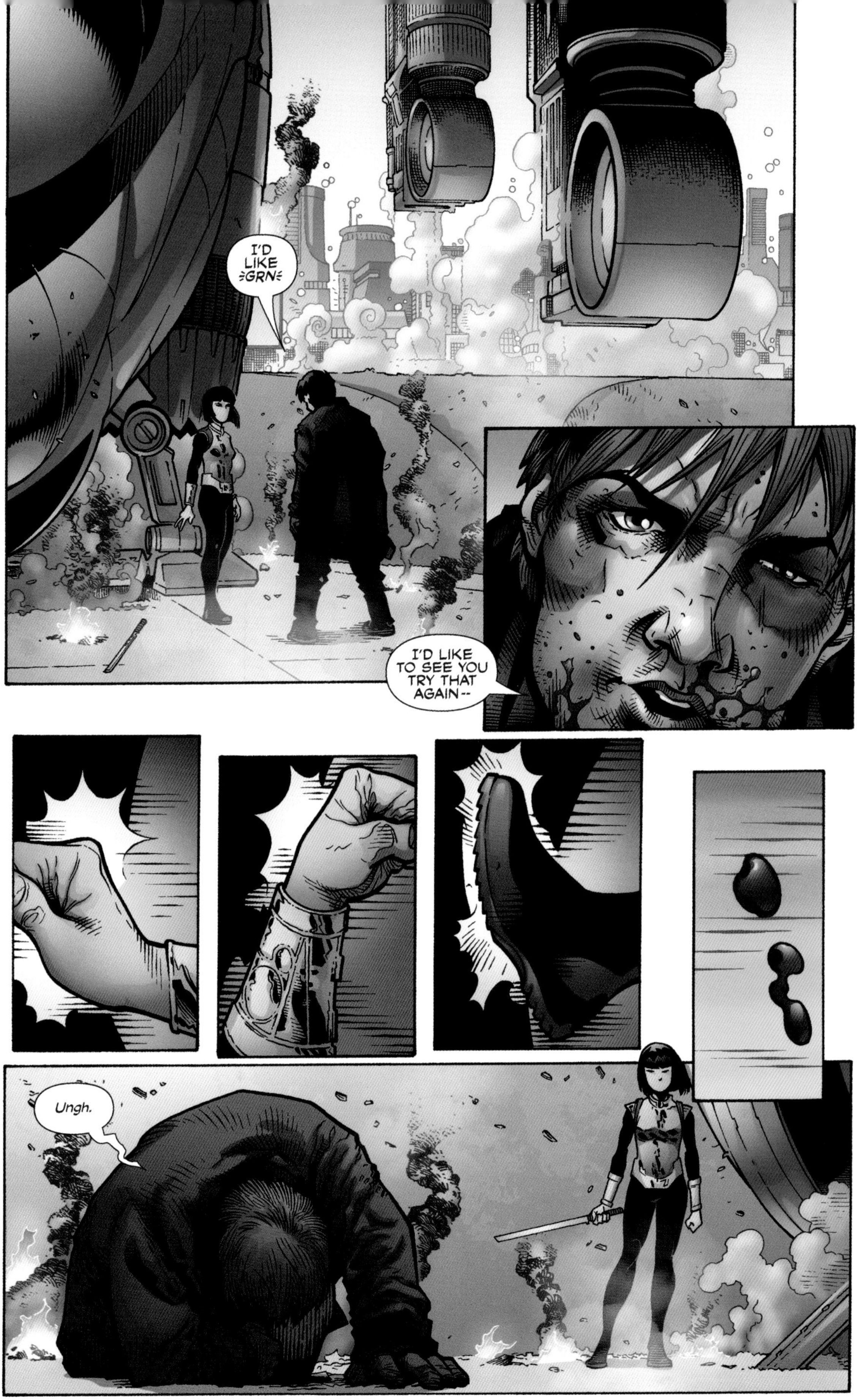
I'D LIKE GRN
I'D LIKE TO SEE YOU TRY THAT AGAIN--
Ungh.

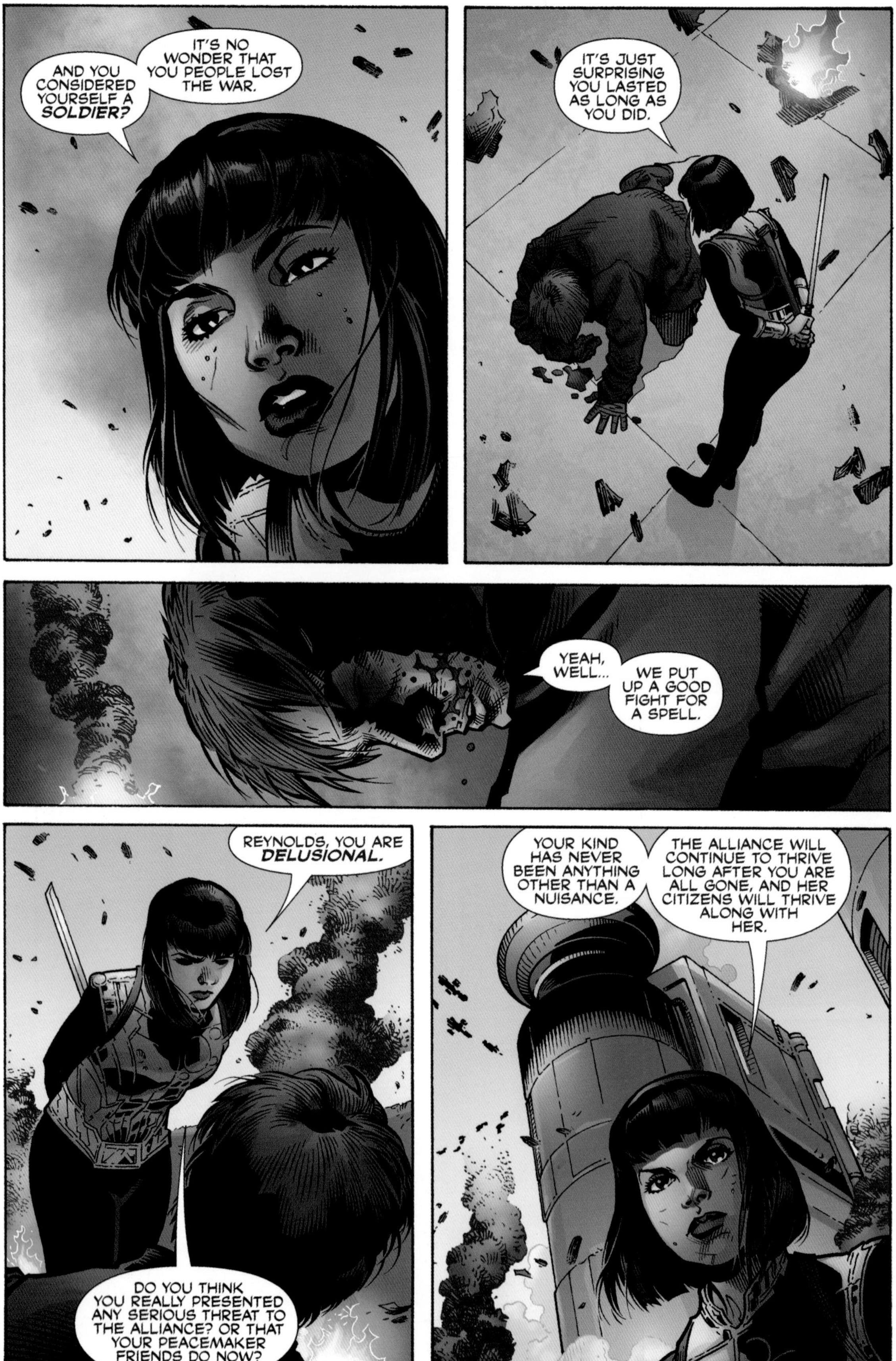
IT'S NO WONDER THAT YOU PEOPLE LOST THE WAR.
AND YOU CONSIDERED YOURSELF A SOLDIER?
IT'S JUST SURPRISING YOU LASTED AS LONG AS YOU DID.
YEAH, WELL...
WE PUT UP A GOOD FIGHT FOR A SPELL.
REYNOLDS, YOU ARE DELUSIONAL.
DO YOU THINK YOU REALLY PRESENTED ANY SERIOUS THREAT TO THE ALLIANCE? OR THAT YOUR PEACEMAKER FRIENDS DO NOW?
YOUR KIND HAS NEVER BEEN ANYTHING OTHER THAN A NUISANCE.
THE ALLIANCE WILL CONTINUE TO THRIVE LONG AFTER YOU ARE ALL GONE, AND HER CITIZENS WILL THRIVE ALONG WITH HER.

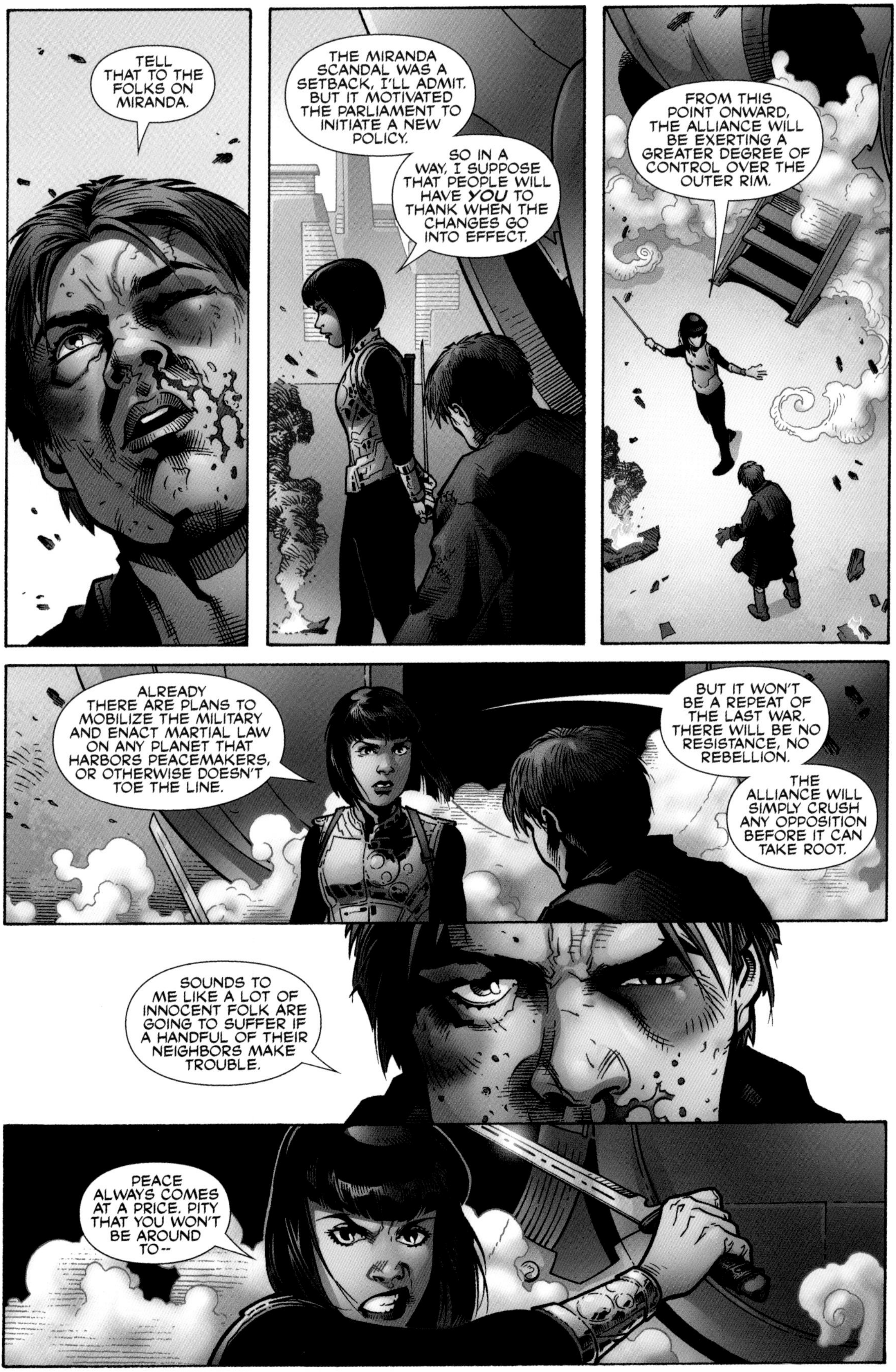
TELL THAT TO THE FOLKS ON MIRANDA.
THE MIRANDA SCANDAL WAS A SETBACK, I'LL ADMIT. BUT IT MOTIVATED THE PARLIAMENT TO INITIATE A NEW POLICY.
SO IN A WAY, I SUPPOSE THAT PEOPLE WILL HAVE *YOU* TO THANK WHEN THE CHANGES GO INTO EFFECT.
FROM THIS POINT ONWARD, THE ALLIANCE WILL BE EXERTING A GREATER DEGREE OF CONTROL OVER THE OUTER RIM.
ALREADY THERE ARE PLANS TO MOBILIZE THE MILITARY AND ENACT MARTIAL LAW ON ANY PLANET THAT HARBORS PEACEMAKERS, OR OTHERWISE DOESN'T TOE THE LINE.
BUT IT WON'T BE A REPEAT OF THE LAST WAR. THERE WILL BE NO RESISTANCE, NO REBELLION.
THE ALLIANCE WILL SIMPLY CRUSH ANY OPPOSITION BEFORE IT CAN TAKE ROOT.
SOUNDS TO ME LIKE A LOT OF INNOCENT FOLK ARE GOING TO SUFFER IF A HANDFUL OF THEIR NEIGHBORS MAKE TROUBLE.
PEACE ALWAYS COMES AT A PRICE. PITY THAT YOU WON'T BE AROUND TO--

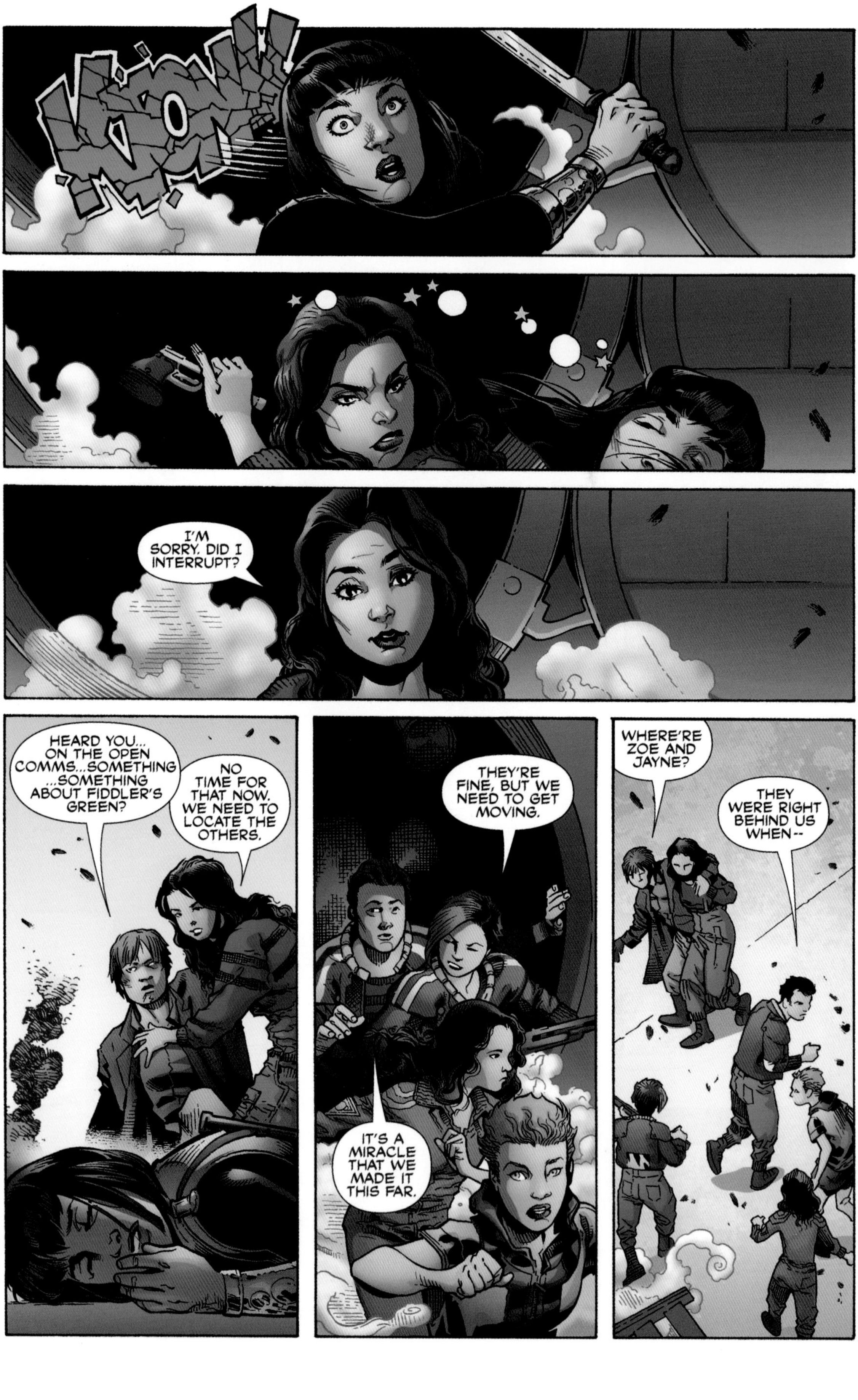
KRONK!
I'M SORRY. DID I INTERRUPT?
HEARD YOU... ON THE OPEN COMMS...SOMETHING ...SOMETHING ABOUT FIDDLER'S GREEN?
NO TIME FOR THAT NOW. WE NEED TO LOCATE THE OTHERS.
THEY'RE FINE, BUT WE NEED TO GET MOVING.
IT'S A MIRACLE THAT WE MADE IT THIS FAR.
WHERE'RE ZOE AND JAYNE?
THEY WERE RIGHT BEHIND US WHEN--

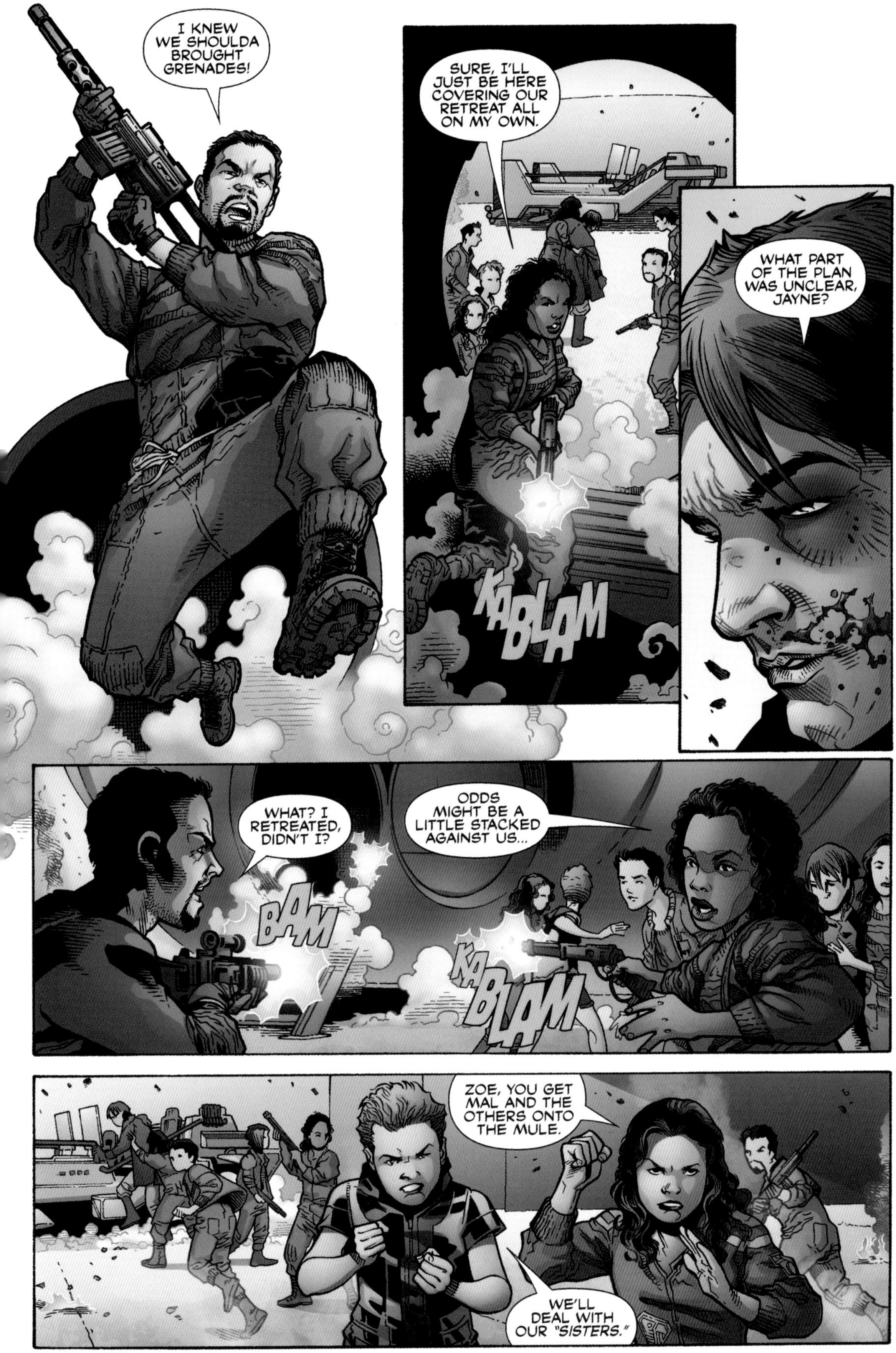
I KNEW WE SHOULDA BROUGHT GRENADES!
SURE, I'LL JUST BE HERE COVERING OUR RETREAT ALL ON MY OWN.
KABLAM
WHAT PART OF THE PLAN WAS UNCLEAR, JAYNE?
WHAT? I RETREATED, DIDN'T I?
ODDS MIGHT BE A LITTLE STACKED AGAINST US...
BAM
KABLAM
ZOE, YOU GET MAL AND THE OTHERS ONTO THE MULE.
WE'LL DEAL WITH OUR "SISTERS."

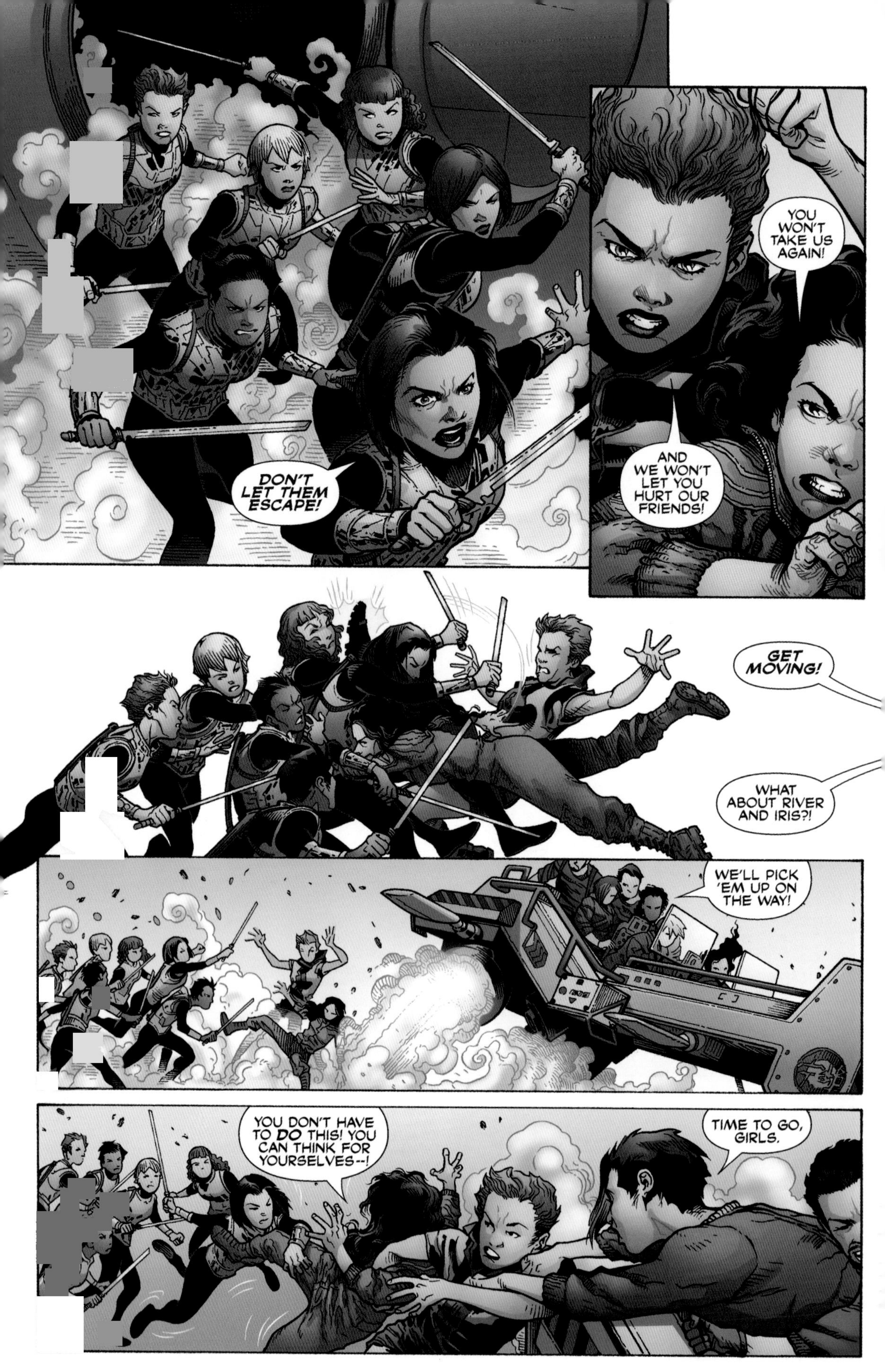
DON'T LET THEM ESCAPE!
YOU WON'T TAKE US AGAIN!
AND WE WON'T LET YOU HURT OUR FRIENDS!
GET MOVING!
WHAT ABOUT RIVER AND IRIS?!
WE'LL PICK 'EM UP ON THE WAY!
YOU DON'T HAVE TO DO THIS! YOU CAN THINK FOR YOURSELVES--!
TIME TO GO, GIRLS.

WHAP

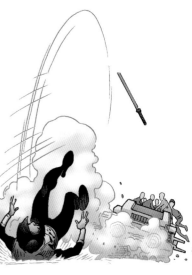

WAIT...?

AIN'T THAT SOME OF MERICOURT'S KIDS...?

THEY GOT NO BUSINESS BEING BY THAT SILVERLINER...

OH, NO.

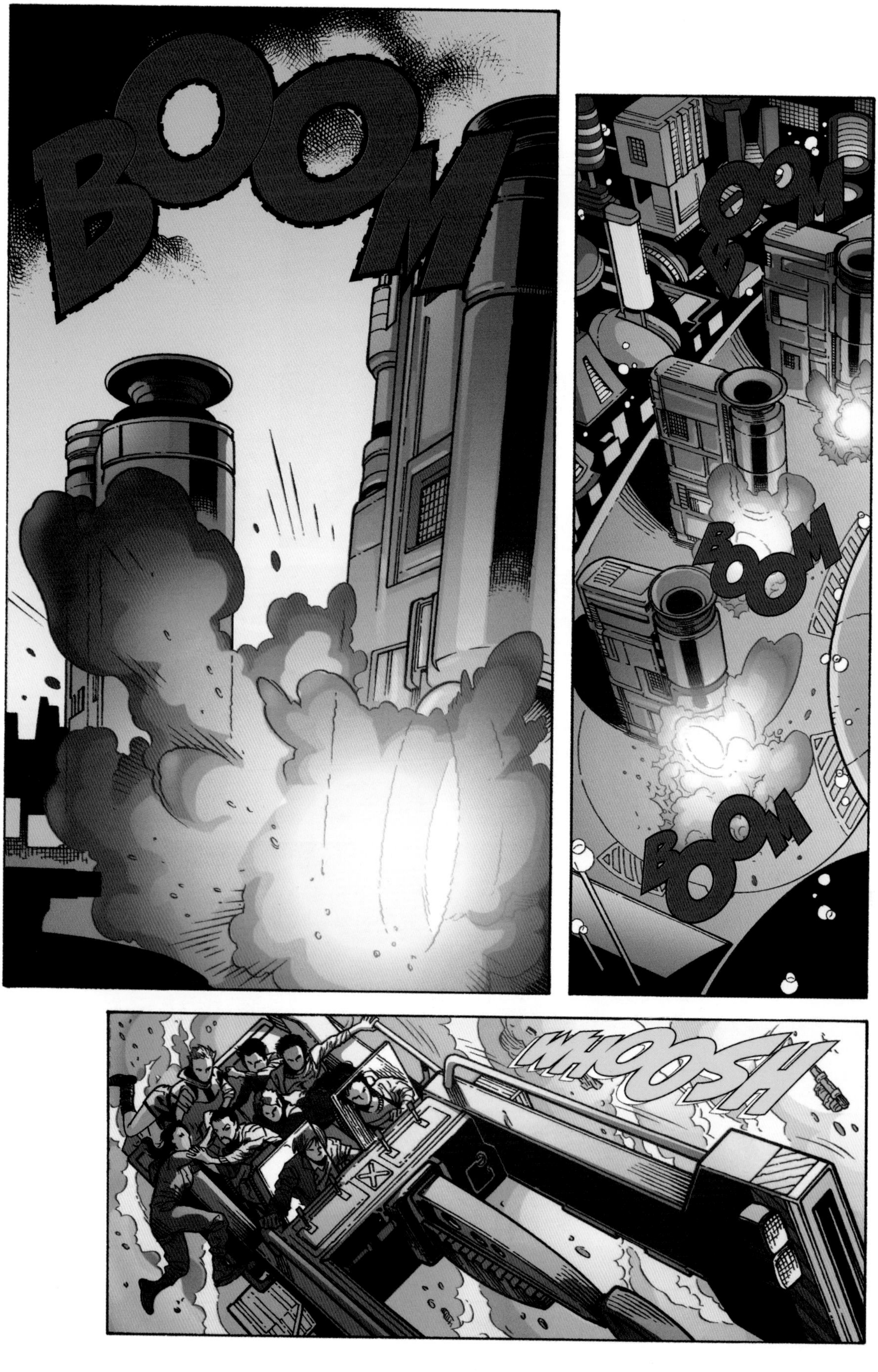
BOOM
BOOM
BOOM
BOOM
WHOOSH

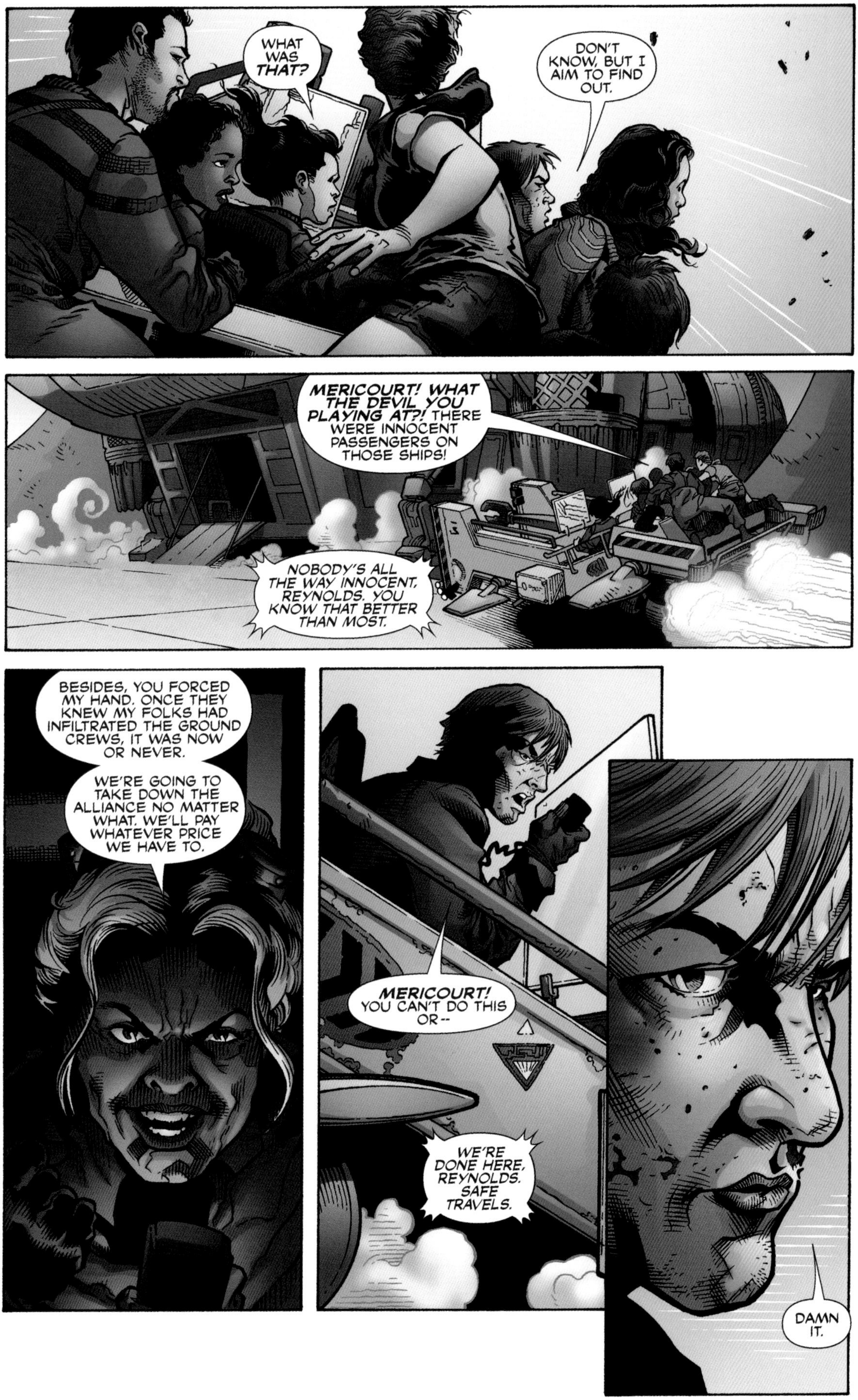
WHAT WAS *THAT?*
DON'T KNOW, BUT I AIM TO FIND OUT.
MERICOURT! WHAT THE DEVIL YOU PLAYING AT?! THERE WERE INNOCENT PASSENGERS ON THOSE SHIPS!
NOBODY'S ALL THE WAY INNOCENT, REYNOLDS. YOU KNOW THAT BETTER THAN MOST.
BESIDES, YOU FORCED MY HAND. ONCE THEY KNEW MY FOLKS HAD INFILTRATED THE GROUND CREWS, IT WAS NOW OR NEVER.
WE'RE GOING TO TAKE DOWN THE ALLIANCE NO MATTER WHAT. WE'LL PAY WHATEVER PRICE WE HAVE TO.
MERICOURT! YOU CAN'T DO THIS OR--
WE'RE DONE HERE, REYNOLDS. SAFE TRAVELS.
DAMN IT.

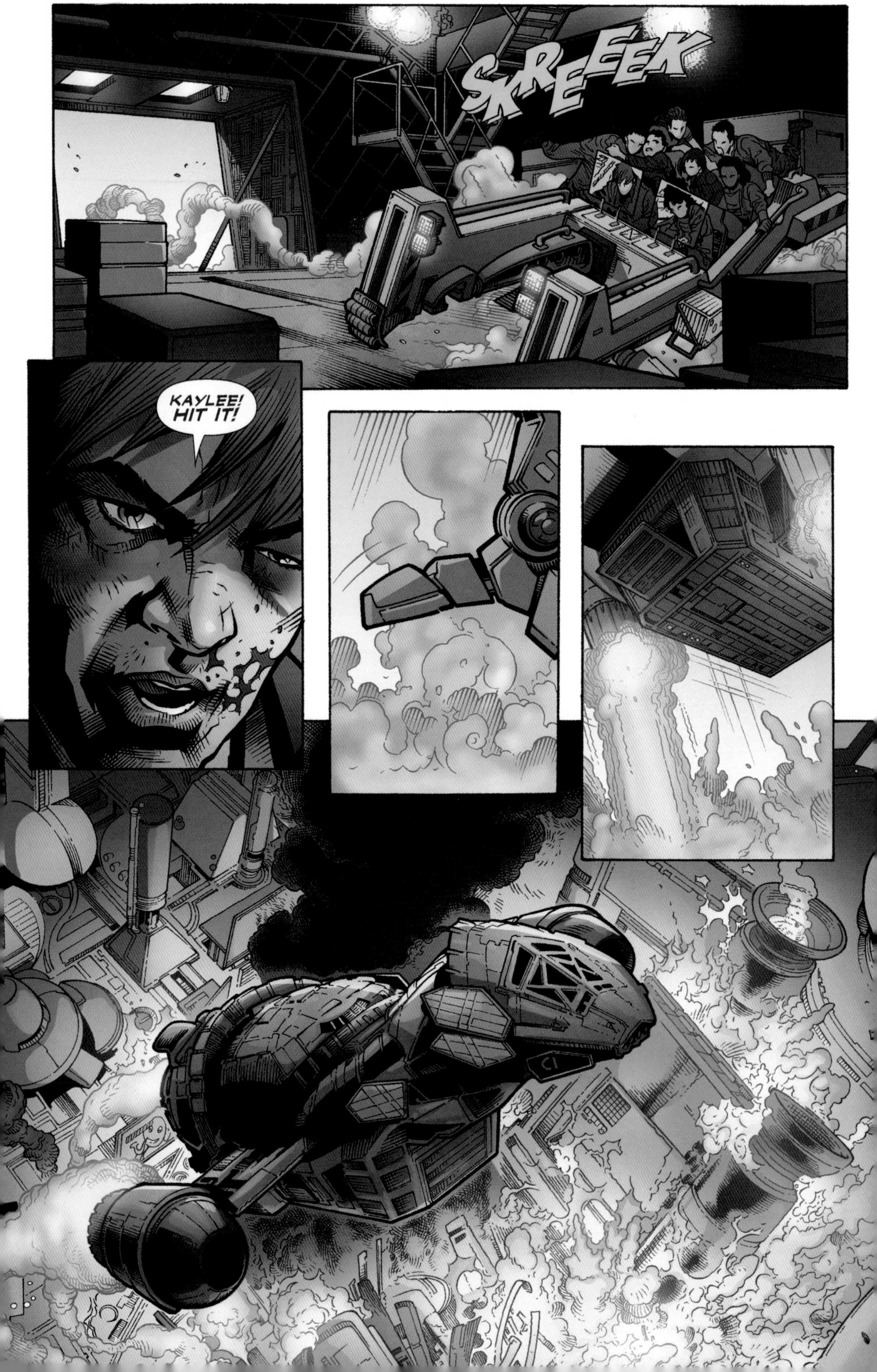
SKREEEK
KAYLEE! HIT IT!

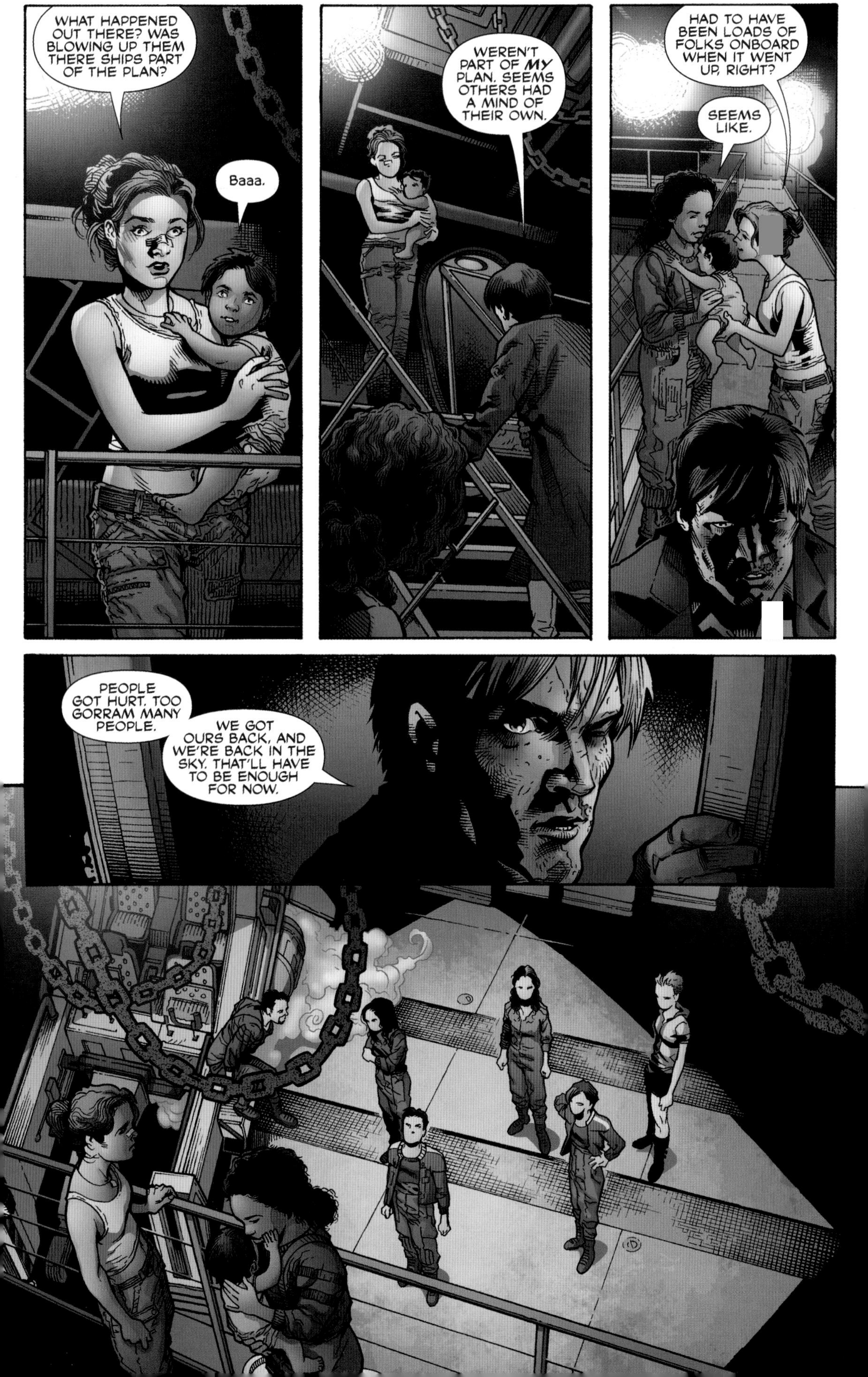
WHAT HAPPENED OUT THERE? WAS BLOWING UP THEM THERE SHIPS PART OF THE PLAN?
Baaa.
WEREN'T PART OF MY PLAN. SEEMS OTHERS HAD A MIND OF THEIR OWN.
HAD TO HAVE BEEN LOADS OF FOLKS ONBOARD WHEN IT WENT UP, RIGHT?
SEEMS LIKE.
PEOPLE GOT HURT. TOO GORRAM MANY PEOPLE.
WE GOT OURS BACK, AND WE'RE BACK IN THE SKY. THAT'LL HAVE TO BE ENOUGH FOR NOW.

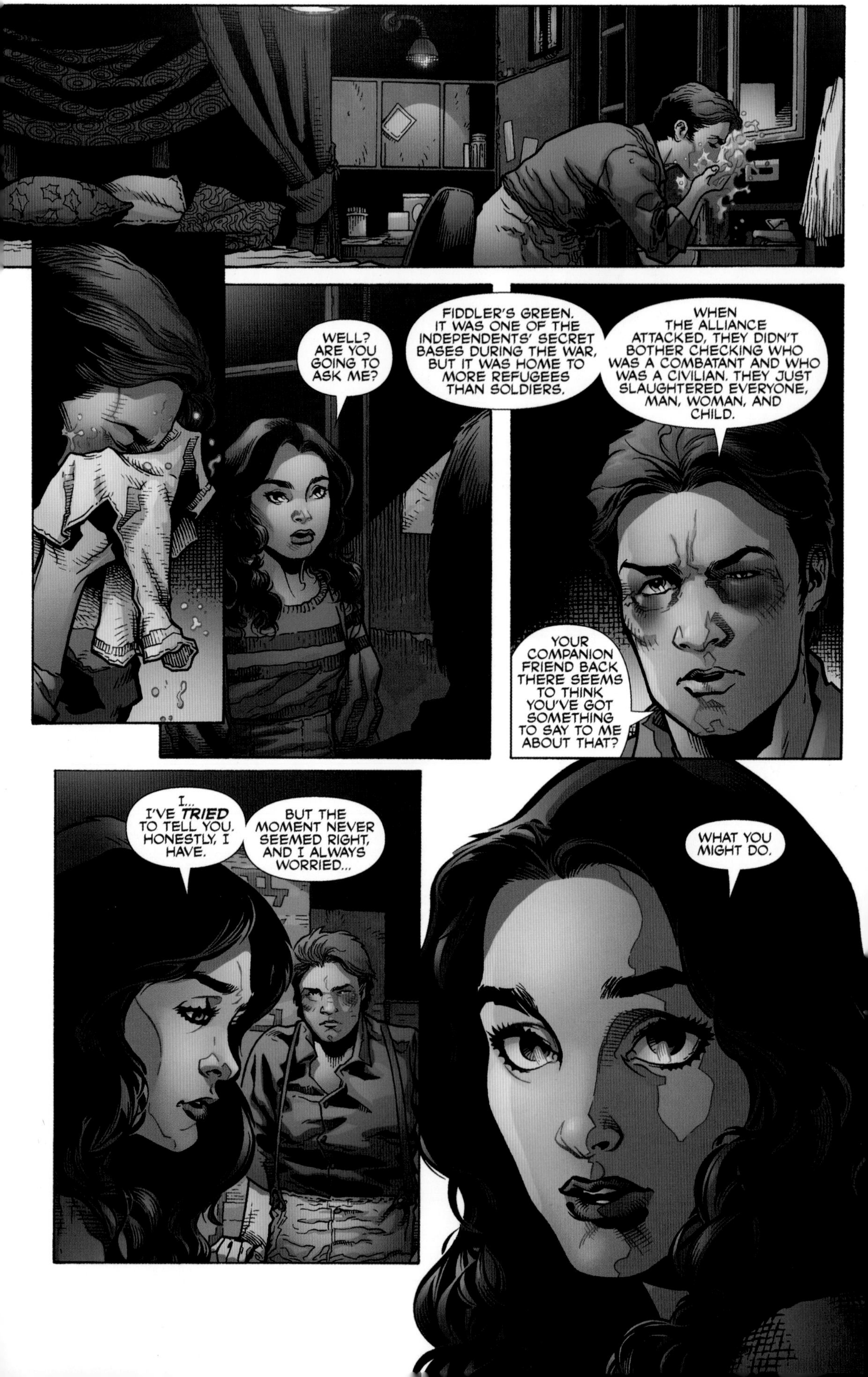
WELL? ARE YOU GOING TO ASK ME?
FIDDLER'S GREEN. IT WAS ONE OF THE INDEPENDENTS' SECRET BASES DURING THE WAR, BUT IT WAS HOME TO MORE REFUGEES THAN SOLDIERS.
WHEN THE ALLIANCE ATTACKED, THEY DIDN'T BOTHER CHECKING WHO WAS A COMBATANT AND WHO WAS A CIVILIAN. THEY JUST SLAUGHTERED EVERYONE, MAN, WOMAN, AND CHILD.
YOUR COMPANION FRIEND BACK THERE SEEMS TO THINK YOU'VE GOT SOMETHING TO SAY TO ME ABOUT THAT?
I... I'VE *TRIED* TO TELL YOU. HONESTLY, I HAVE.
BUT THE MOMENT NEVER SEEMED RIGHT, AND I ALWAYS WORRIED...
WHAT YOU MIGHT DO.

THE REASON I LEFT SIHNON IS THAT I BROKE THE CONFIDENTIALITY RULES OF HOUSE MADRASSA. COMPANIONS ARE SWORN NEVER TO REVEAL THINGS SPOKEN TO THEM IN CONFIDENCE.

ONE OF MY CLIENTS WAS A SECRET SUPPLIER TO THE INDEPENDENTS, AND DURING ONE OF OUR SESSIONS HE LET SLIP SOME DETAILS ABOUT A MAJOR OFFENSIVE THEY HAD PLANNED.

I...I ALERTED THE AUTHORITIES, AND LET THEM KNOW THE LOCATION OF THE BASE THAT HE WAS SUPPLYING.

YOU'VE GOT TO UNDERSTAND THAT MY HOPE WAS TO PREVENT NEEDLESS DEATHS, ON *BOTH* SIDES. BUT...

HONESTLY, MAL, IF I'D EVEN SUSPECTED...

IT WAS A HUGE SCANDAL IN HOUSE MADRASSA.

NOT BECAUSE THEY WERE SYMPATHETIC TO THE INDEPENDENTS, BUT BECAUSE THE CONFIDENTIALITY VOWS ARE SACROSANCT.

I WAS ASKED TO LEAVE AND NEVER RETURN. I WOULD REMAIN A COMPANION, BUT I COULD NEVER GO HOME.

I CAN'T BEGIN TO EXPRESS THE GUILT THAT I'VE FELT OVER THOSE DEATHS ALL THESE YEARS.

I JUST HOPED THAT SOMEHOW... WELL...

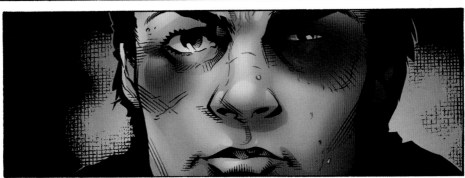

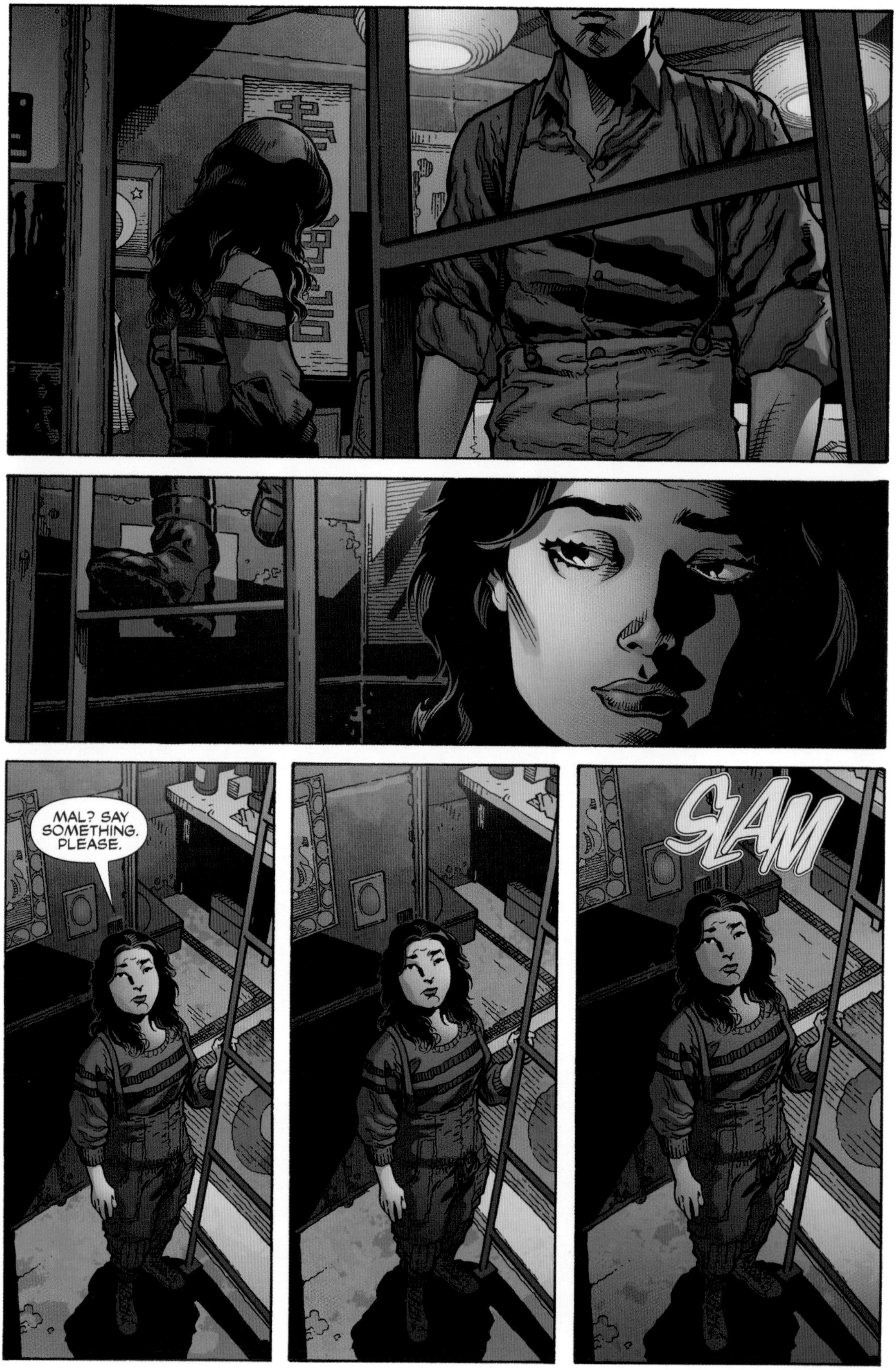
MAL? SAY SOMETHING. PLEASE.
SLAM

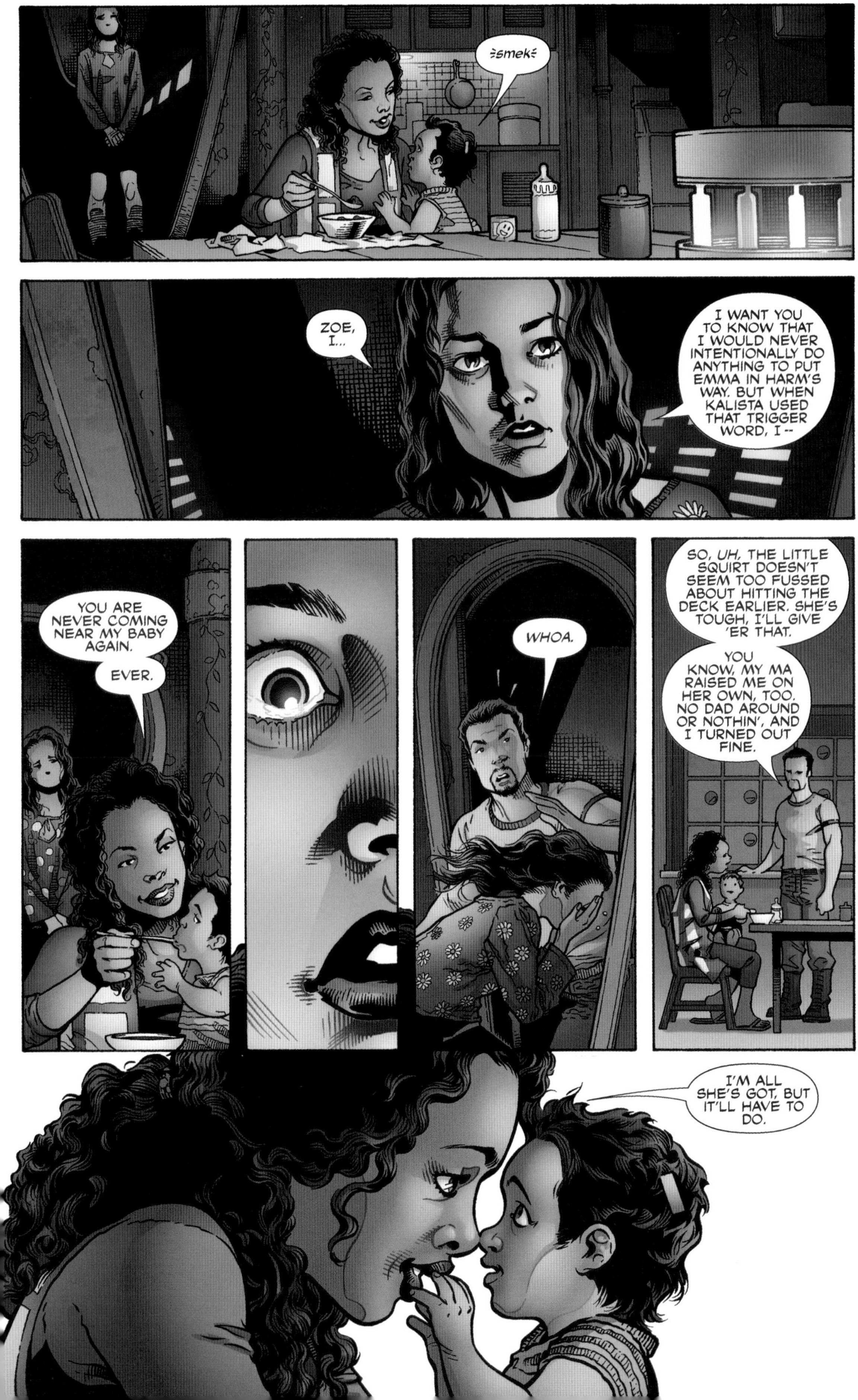

smek
ZOE, I...
I WANT YOU TO KNOW THAT I WOULD NEVER INTENTIONALLY DO ANYTHING TO PUT EMMA IN HARM'S WAY. BUT WHEN KALISTA USED THAT TRIGGER WORD, I --
YOU ARE NEVER COMING NEAR MY BABY AGAIN.
EVER.
WHOA.
SO, UH, THE LITTLE SQUIRT DOESN'T SEEM TOO FUSSED ABOUT HITTING THE DECK EARLIER. SHE'S TOUGH, I'LL GIVE 'ER THAT.
YOU KNOW, MY MA RAISED ME ON HER OWN, TOO. NO DAD AROUND OR NOTHIN', AND I TURNED OUT FINE.
I'M ALL SHE'S GOT, BUT IT'LL HAVE TO DO.

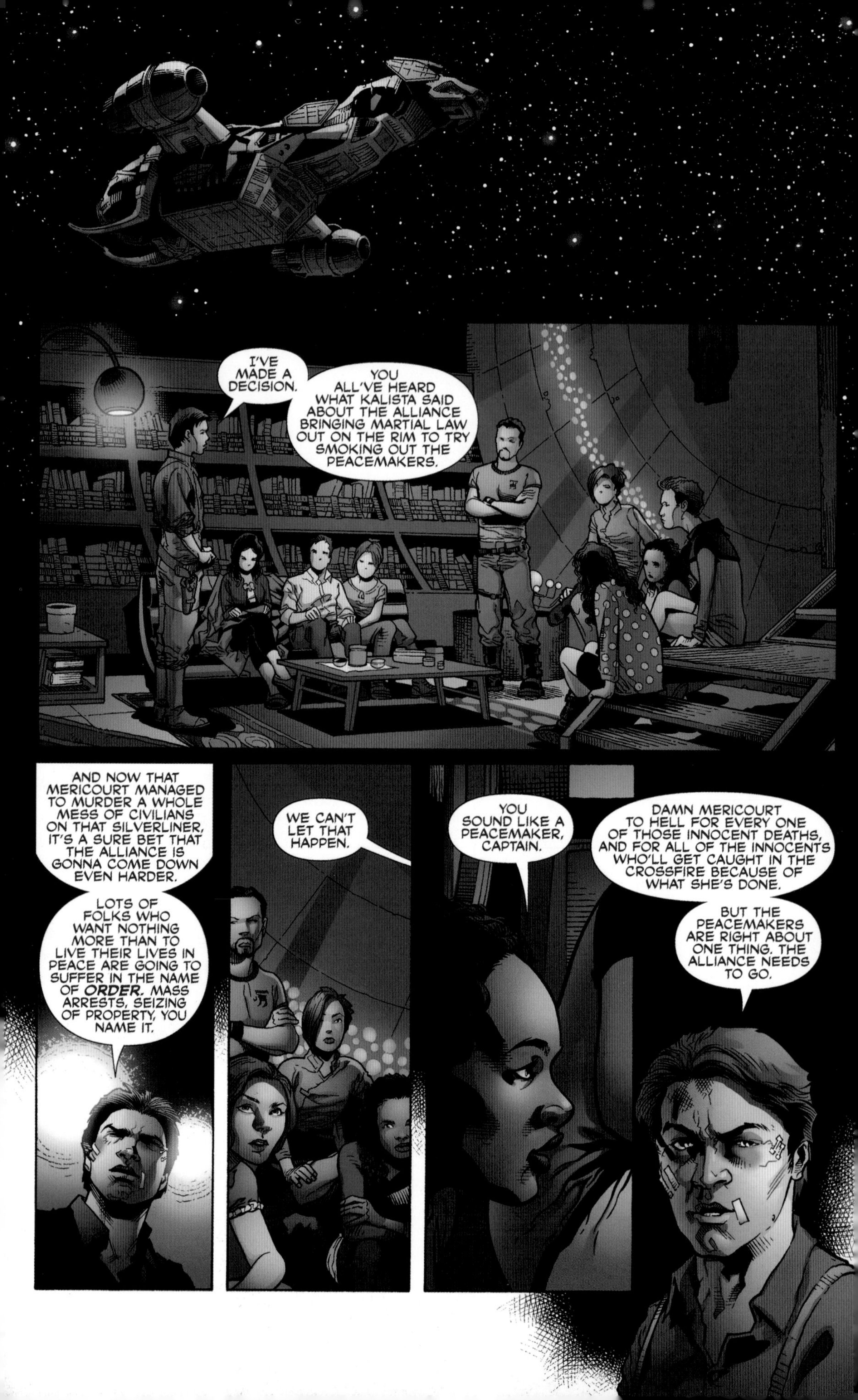
I'VE MADE A DECISION.
YOU ALL'VE HEARD WHAT KALISTA SAID ABOUT THE ALLIANCE BRINGING MARTIAL LAW OUT ON THE RIM TO TRY SMOKING OUT THE PEACEMAKERS.
AND NOW THAT MERICOURT MANAGED TO MURDER A WHOLE MESS OF CIVILIANS ON THAT SILVERLINER, IT'S A SURE BET THAT THE ALLIANCE IS GONNA COME DOWN EVEN HARDER.
LOTS OF FOLKS WHO WANT NOTHING MORE THAN TO LIVE THEIR LIVES IN PEACE ARE GOING TO SUFFER IN THE NAME OF *ORDER.* MASS ARRESTS, SEIZING OF PROPERTY, YOU NAME IT.
WE CAN'T LET THAT HAPPEN.
YOU SOUND LIKE A PEACEMAKER, CAPTAIN.
DAMN MERICOURT TO HELL FOR EVERY ONE OF THOSE INNOCENT DEATHS, AND FOR ALL OF THE INNOCENTS WHO'LL GET CAUGHT IN THE CROSSFIRE BECAUSE OF WHAT SHE'S DONE.
BUT THE PEACEMAKERS ARE RIGHT ABOUT ONE THING. THE ALLIANCE NEEDS TO GO.

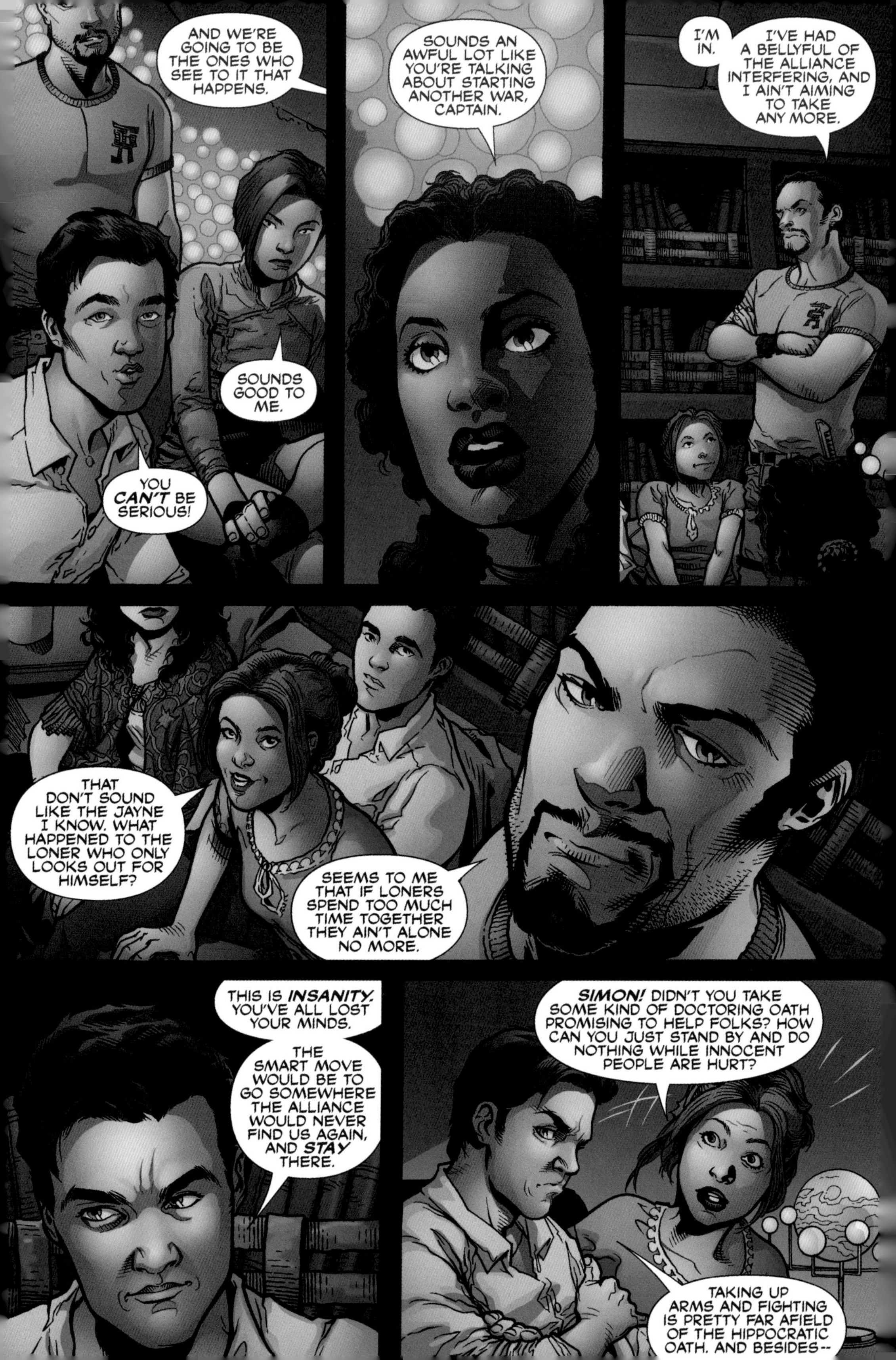

AND WE'RE GOING TO BE THE ONES WHO SEE TO IT THAT HAPPENS.
SOUNDS GOOD TO ME.
YOU *CAN'T* BE SERIOUS!
SOUNDS AN AWFUL LOT LIKE YOU'RE TALKING ABOUT STARTING ANOTHER WAR, CAPTAIN.
I'M IN.
I'VE HAD A BELLYFUL OF THE ALLIANCE INTERFERING, AND I AIN'T AIMING TO TAKE ANY MORE.
THAT DON'T SOUND LIKE THE JAYNE I KNOW. WHAT HAPPENED TO THE LONER WHO ONLY LOOKS OUT FOR HIMSELF?
SEEMS TO ME THAT IF LONERS SPEND TOO MUCH TIME TOGETHER THEY AIN'T ALONE NO MORE.
THIS IS *INSANITY.* YOU'VE ALL LOST YOUR MINDS.
THE SMART MOVE WOULD BE TO GO SOMEWHERE THE ALLIANCE WOULD NEVER FIND US AGAIN, AND *STAY* THERE.
SIMON! DIDN'T YOU TAKE SOME KIND OF DOCTORING OATH PROMISING TO HELP FOLKS? HOW CAN YOU JUST STAND BY AND DO NOTHING WHILE INNOCENT PEOPLE ARE HURT?
TAKING UP ARMS AND FIGHTING IS PRETTY FAR AFIELD OF THE HIPPOCRATIC OATH. AND BESIDES--

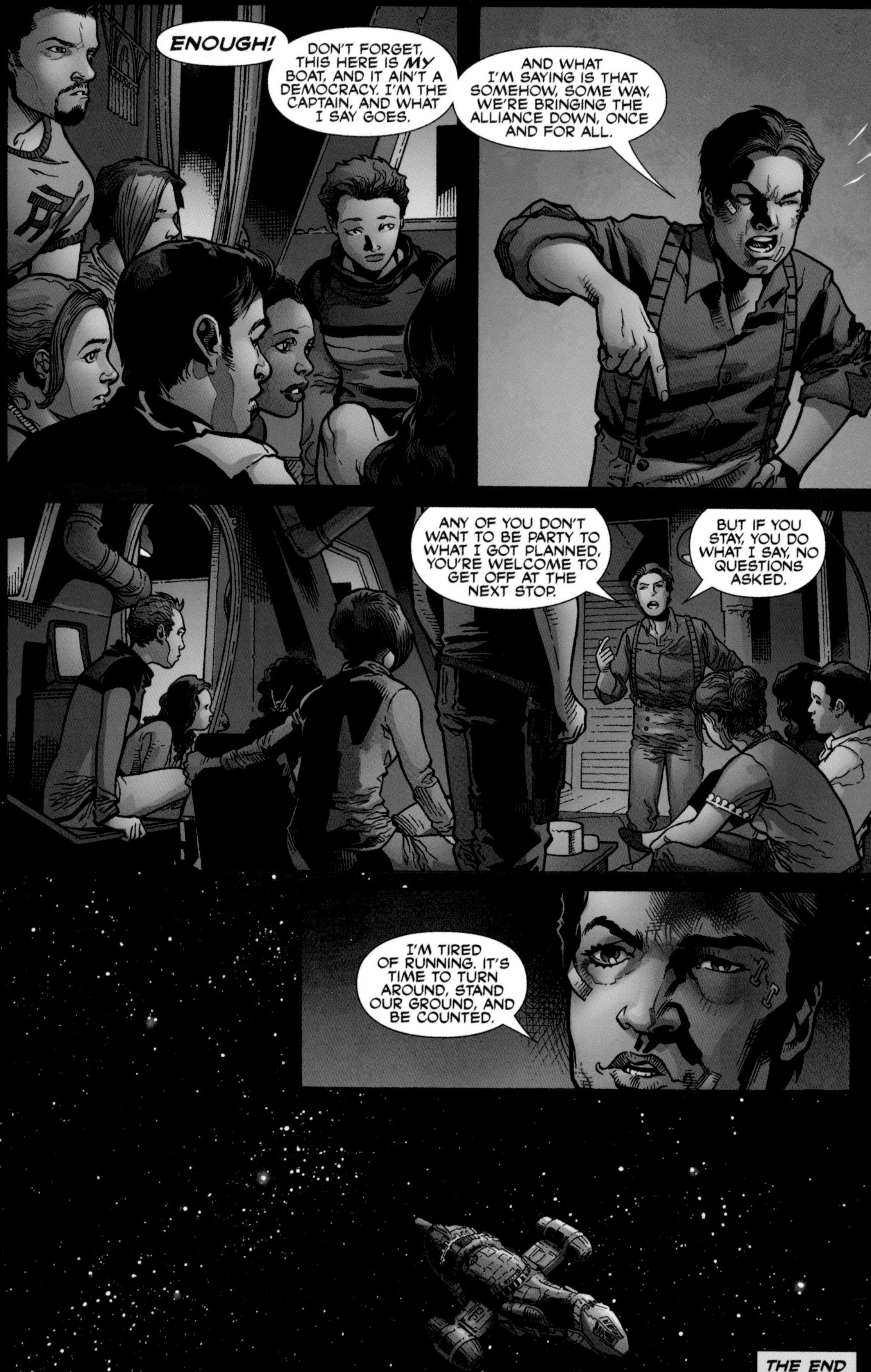
ENOUGH!
DON'T FORGET, THIS HERE IS MY BOAT, AND IT AIN'T A DEMOCRACY. I'M THE CAPTAIN, AND WHAT I SAY GOES.
AND WHAT I'M SAYING IS THAT SOMEHOW, SOME WAY, WE'RE BRINGING THE ALLIANCE DOWN, ONCE AND FOR ALL.
ANY OF YOU DON'T WANT TO BE PARTY TO WHAT I GOT PLANNED, YOU'RE WELCOME TO GET OFF AT THE NEXT STOP.
BUT IF YOU STAY, YOU DO WHAT I SAY, NO QUESTIONS ASKED.
I'M TIRED OF RUNNING. IT'S TIME TO TURN AROUND, STAND OUR GROUND, AND BE COUNTED.
THE END

Serenity: No Power in the 'Verse #6 Cover by
Dan Dos Santos

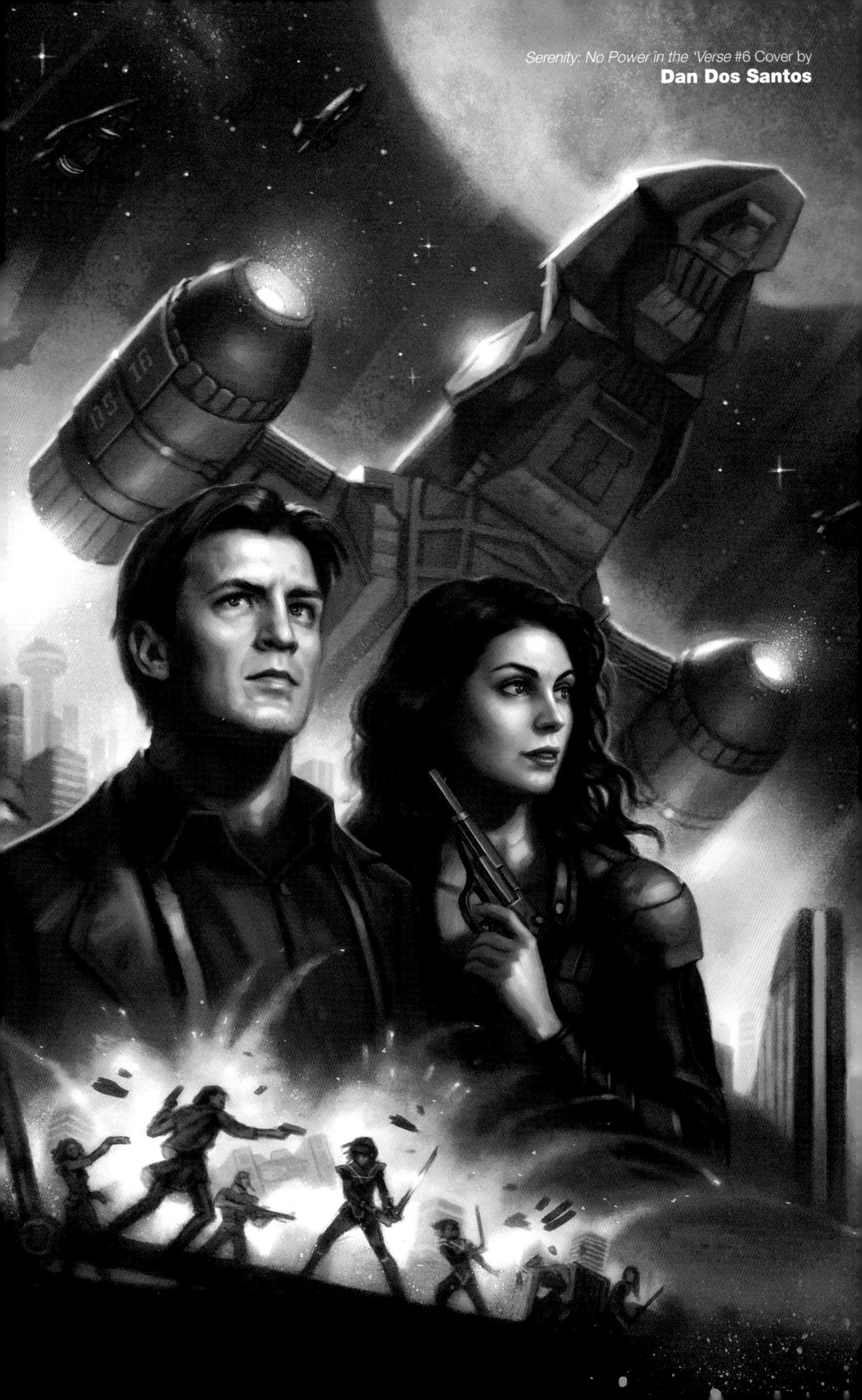

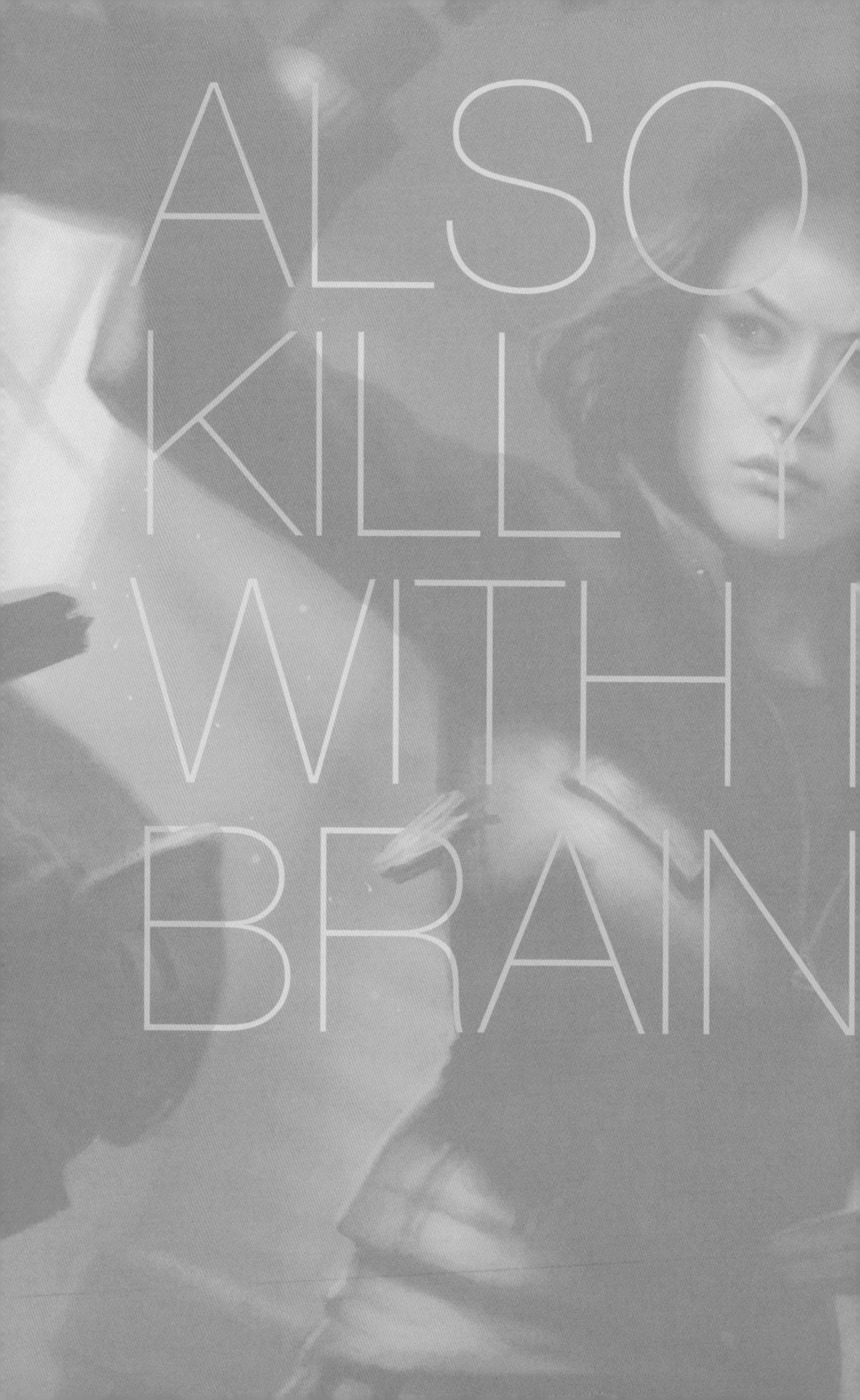
ALSO
KILL
WITH
BRAIN

CAN
OU
MY

COVER GALLERY

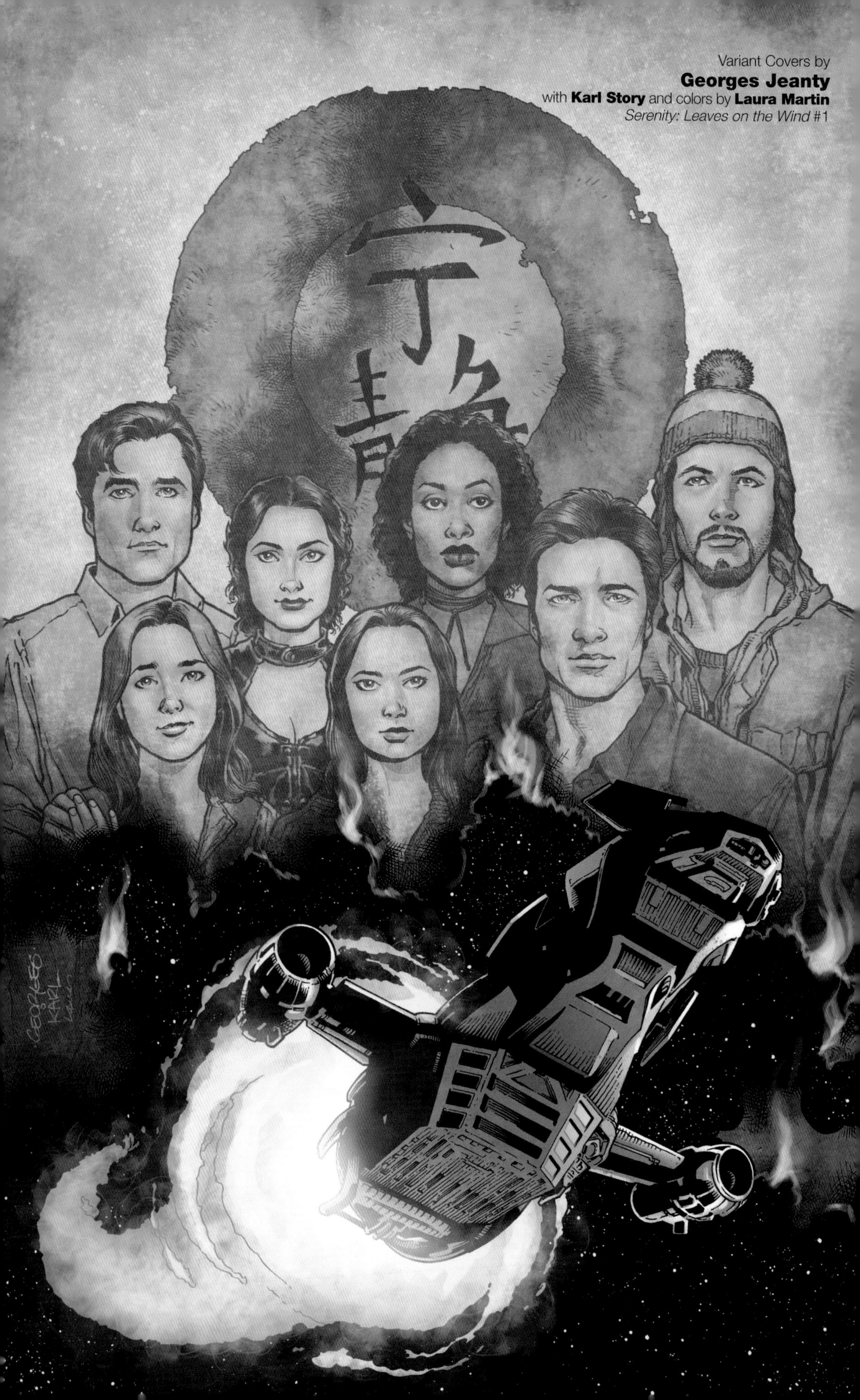

Variant Covers by
Georges Jeanty
with **Karl Story** and colors by **Laura Martin**
Serenity: Leaves on the Wind #1

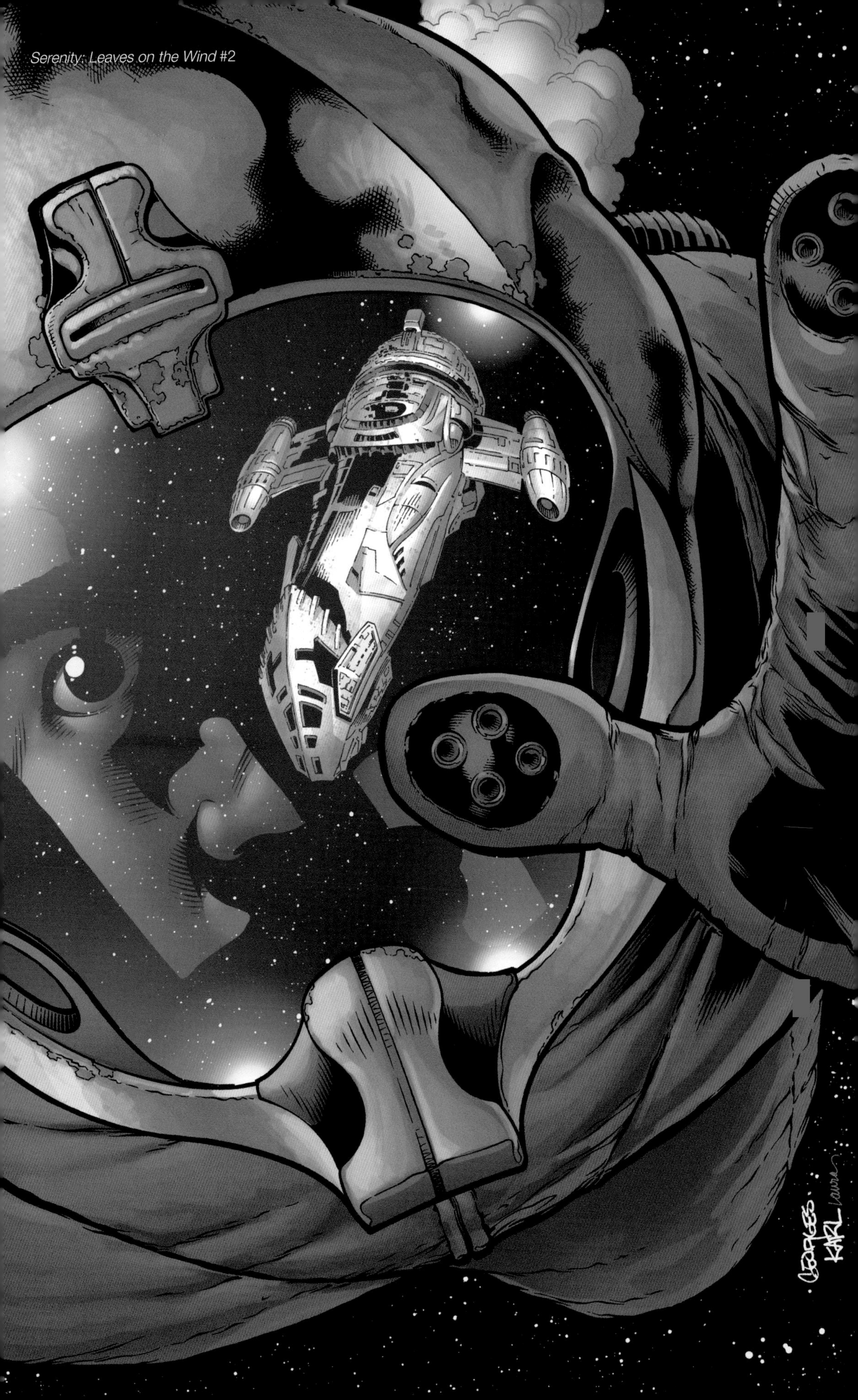
Serenity: Leaves on the Wind #2

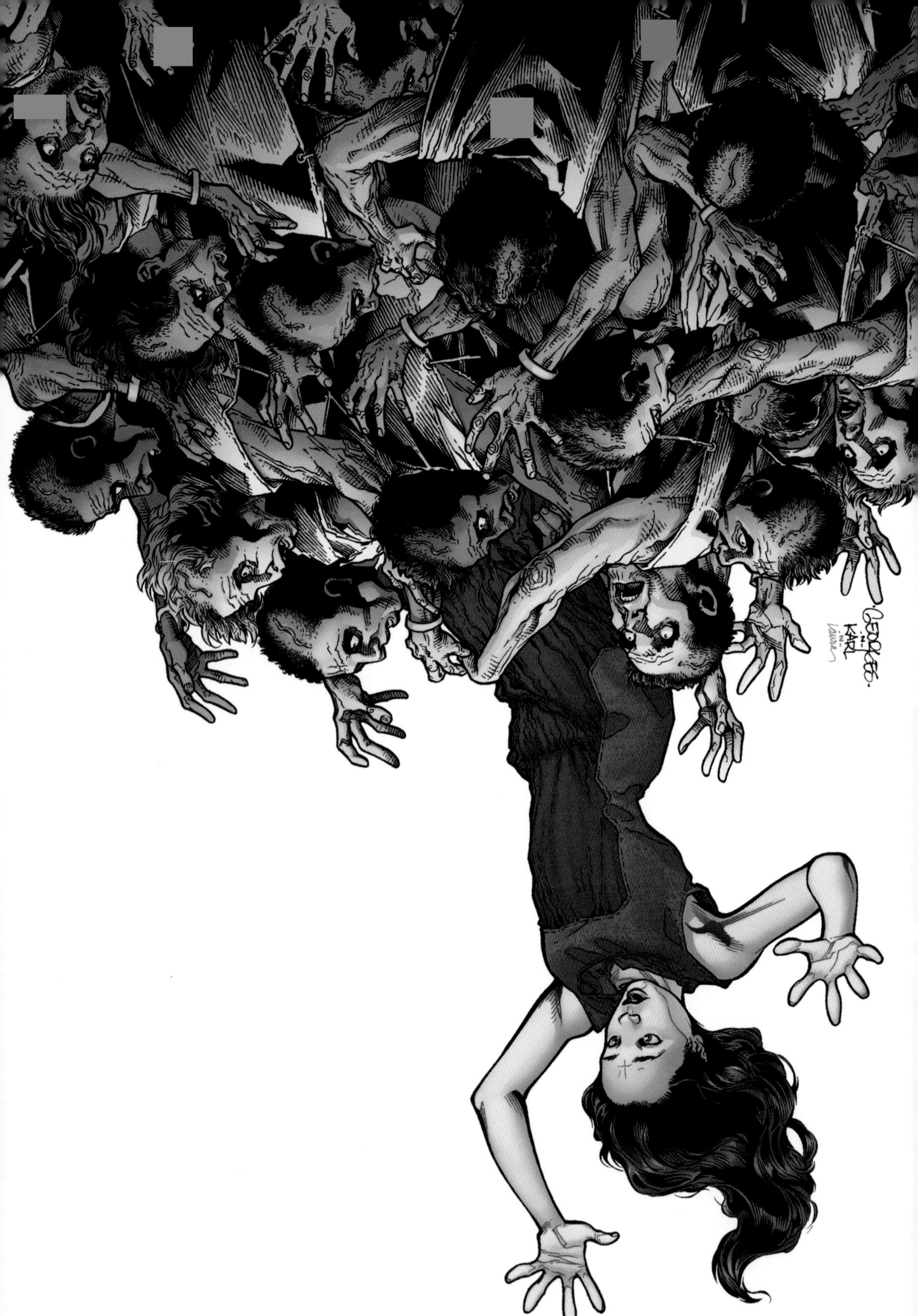

Serenity: Leaves on the Wind #3

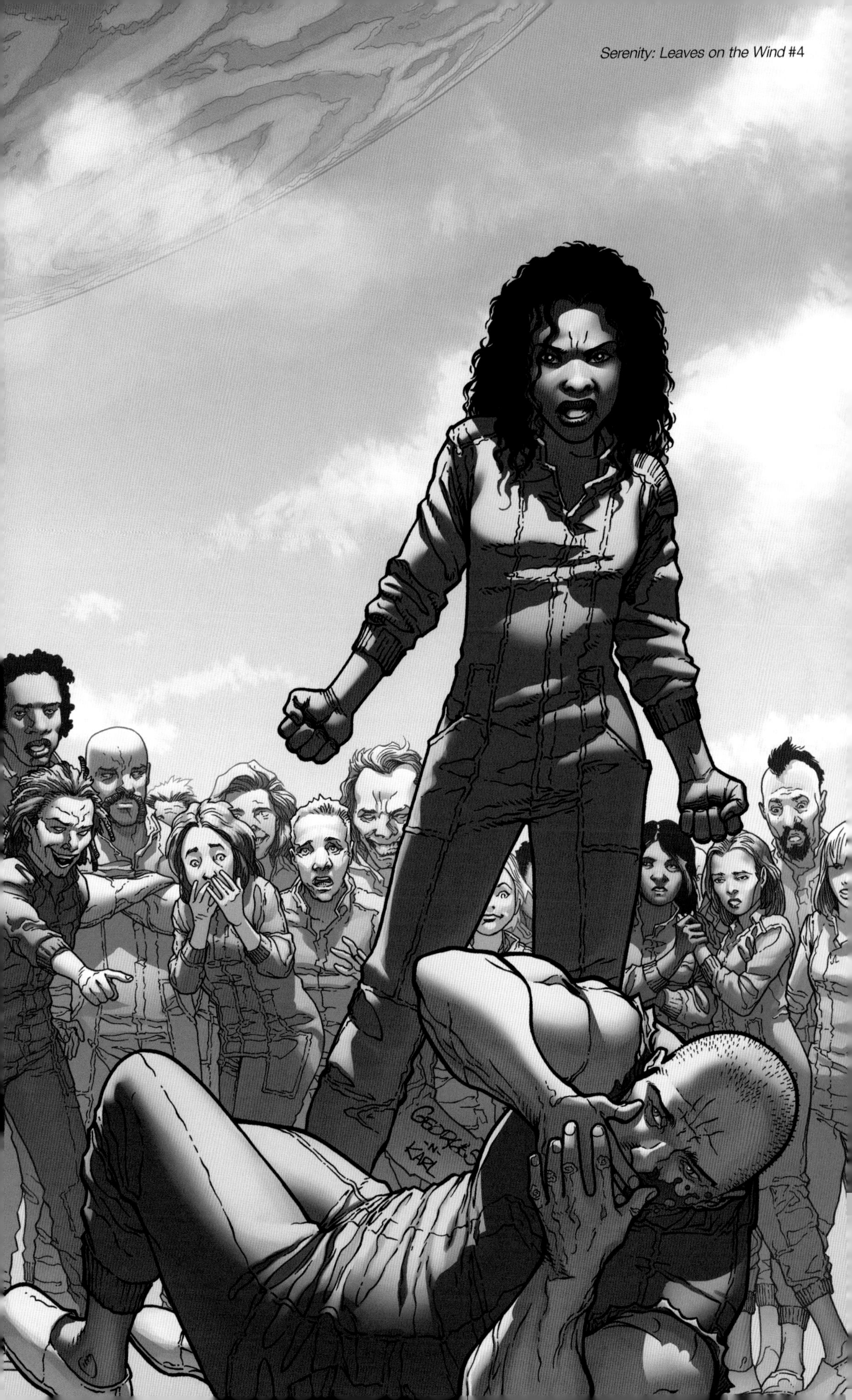
GEORGES
'N'
KARL

Serenity: Leaves on the Wind #4

Serenity: Leaves on the Wind #5

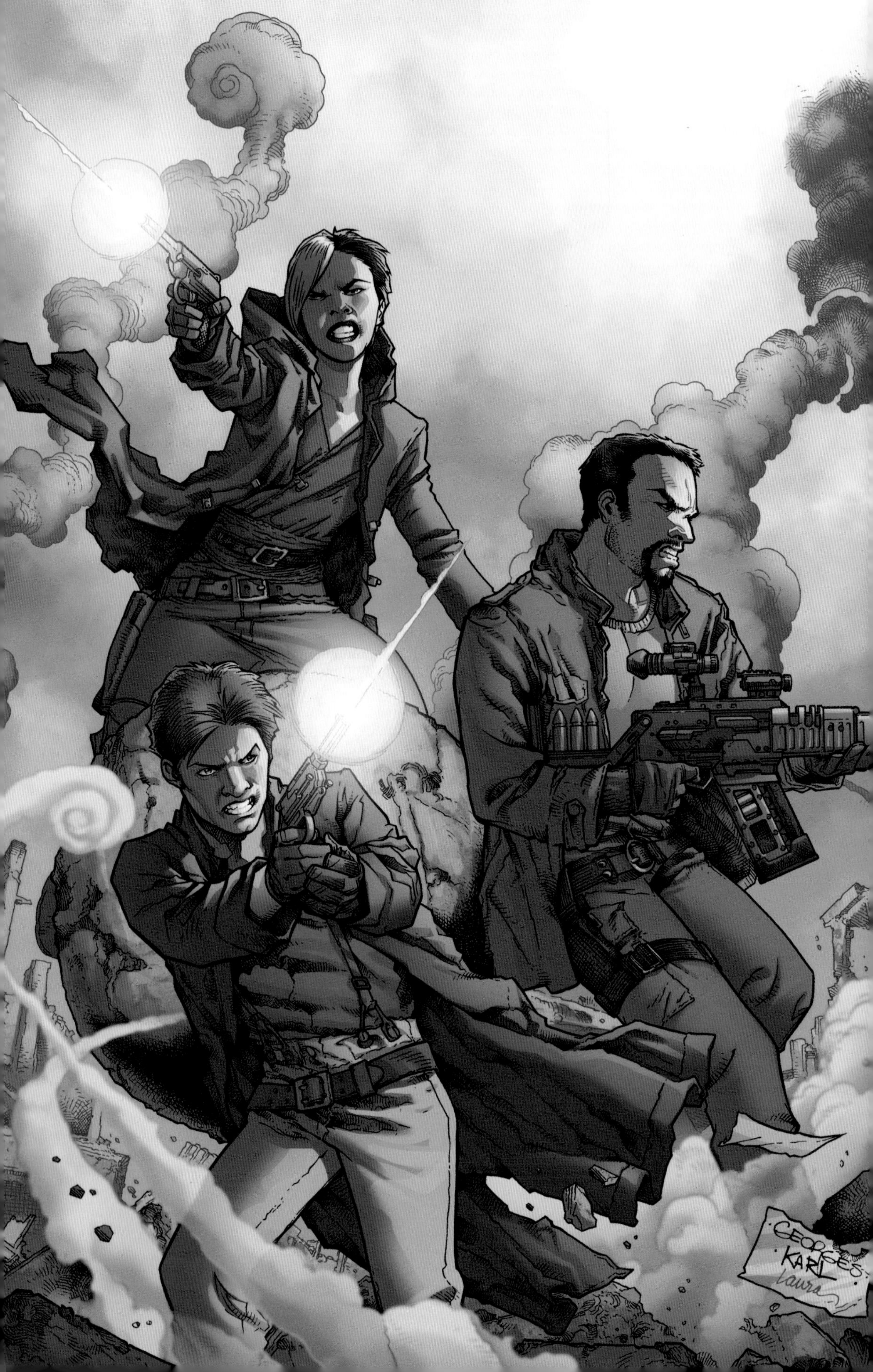
GEORGES
KARL
Laura

Serenity: Leaves on the Wind #6

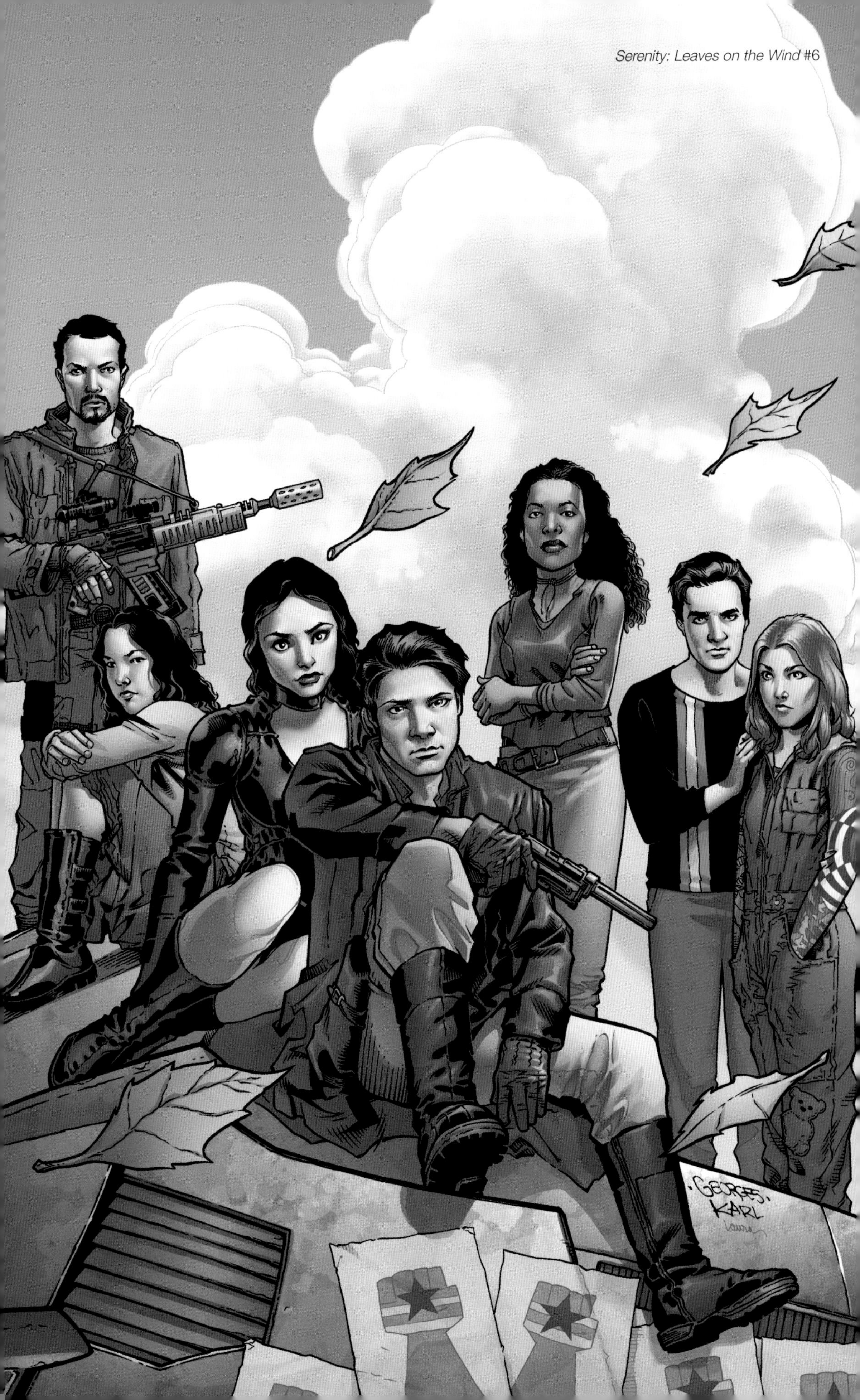
GEORGES.
KARL

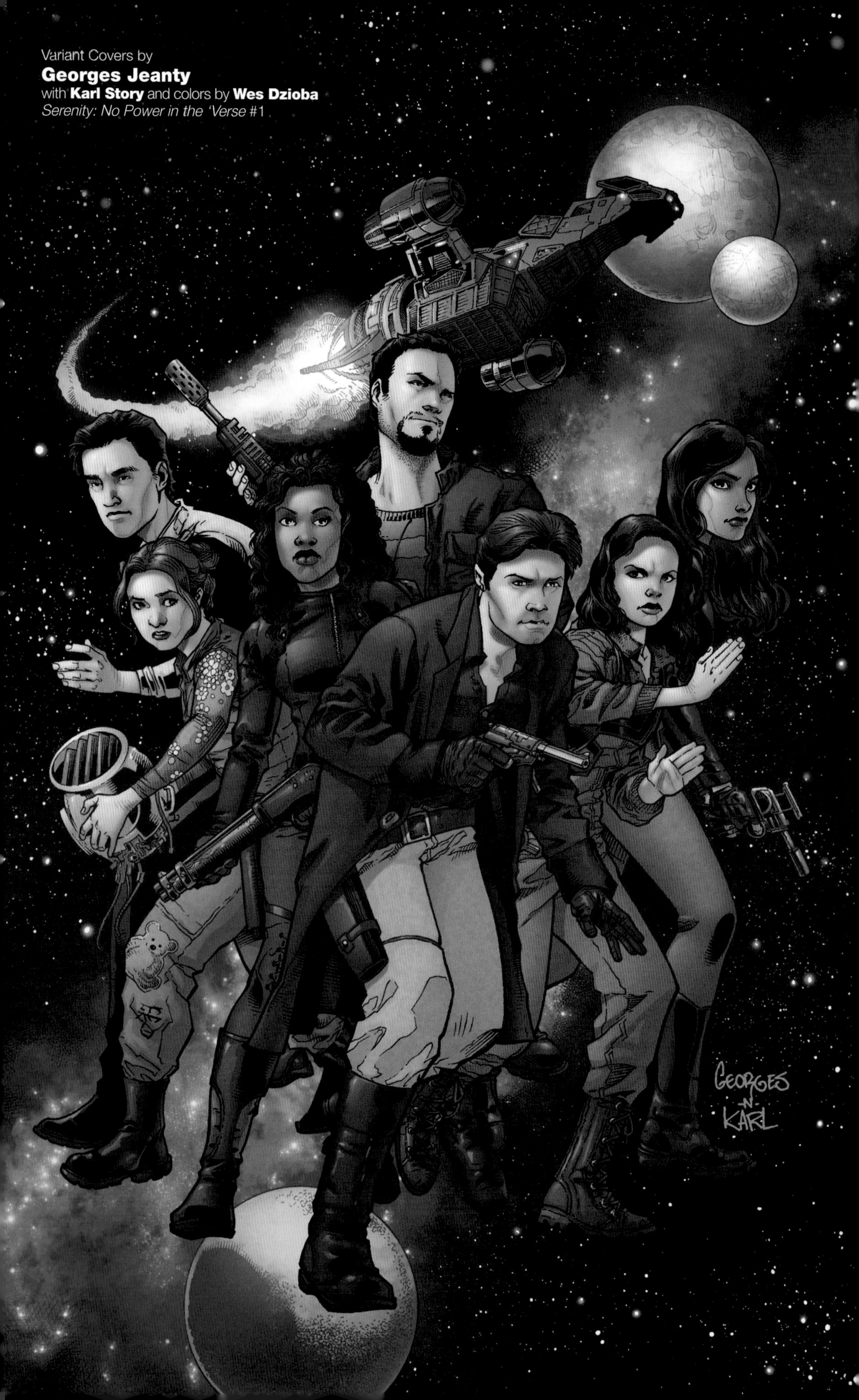
GEORGES
-N-
KARL

Variant Covers by

Georges Jeanty

with **Karl Story** and colors by **Wes Dzioba**

Serenity: No Power in the 'Verse #1

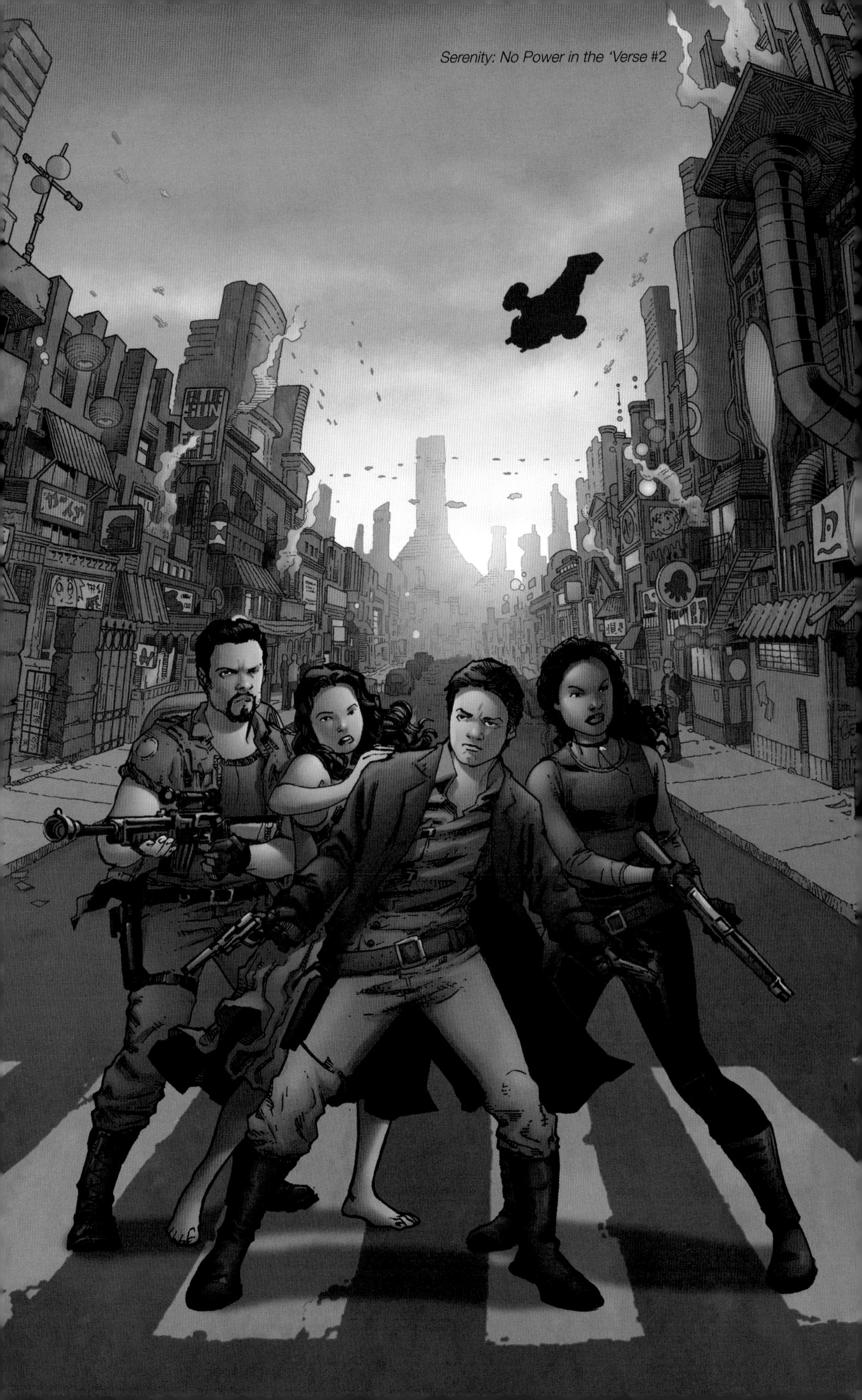
BLUE SUN

Serenity: No Power in the 'Verse #2

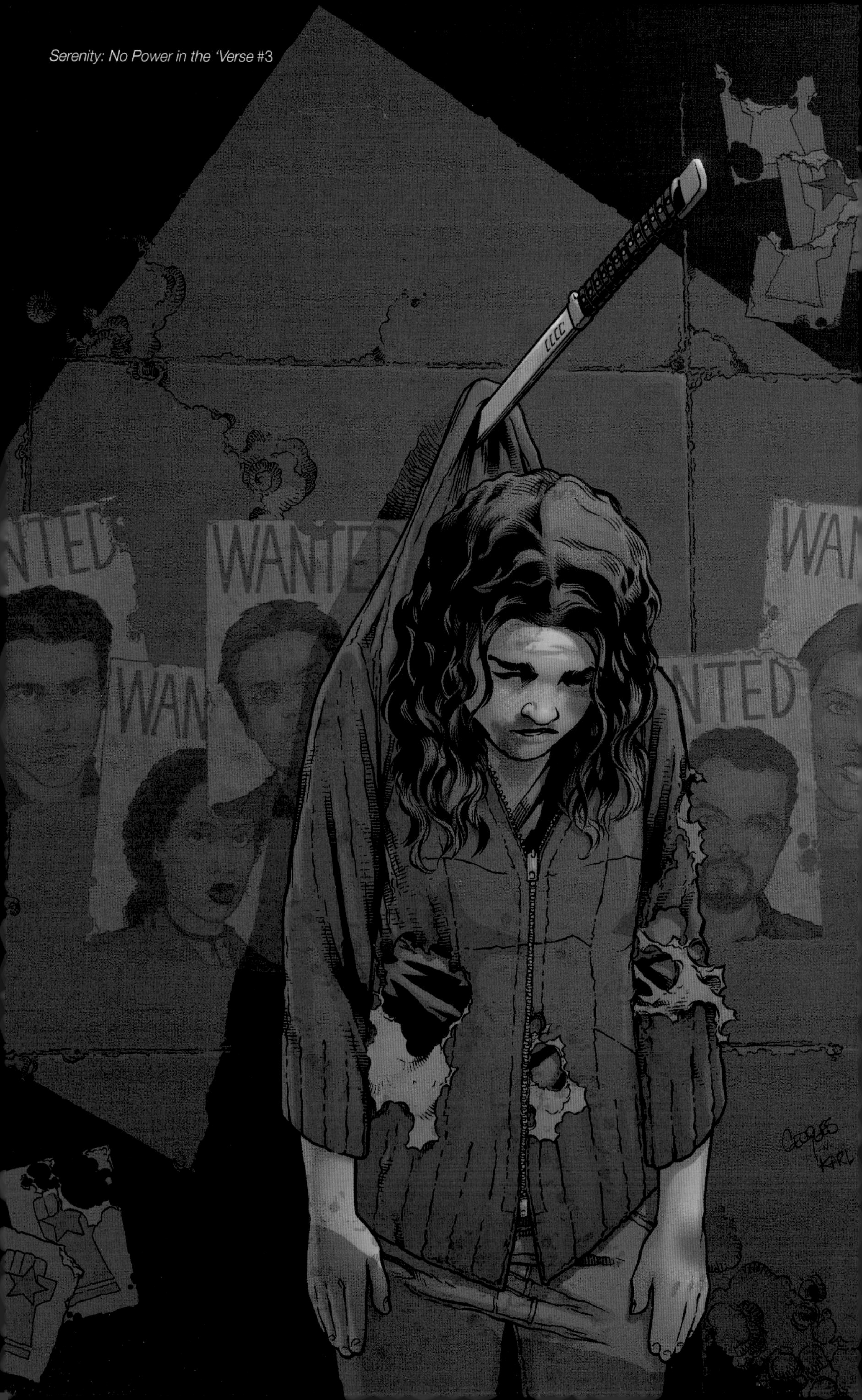
NTED
WANTE
WAN
NTED
WAN

Serenity: No Power in the 'Verse #3

Serenity: No Power in the 'Verse #4

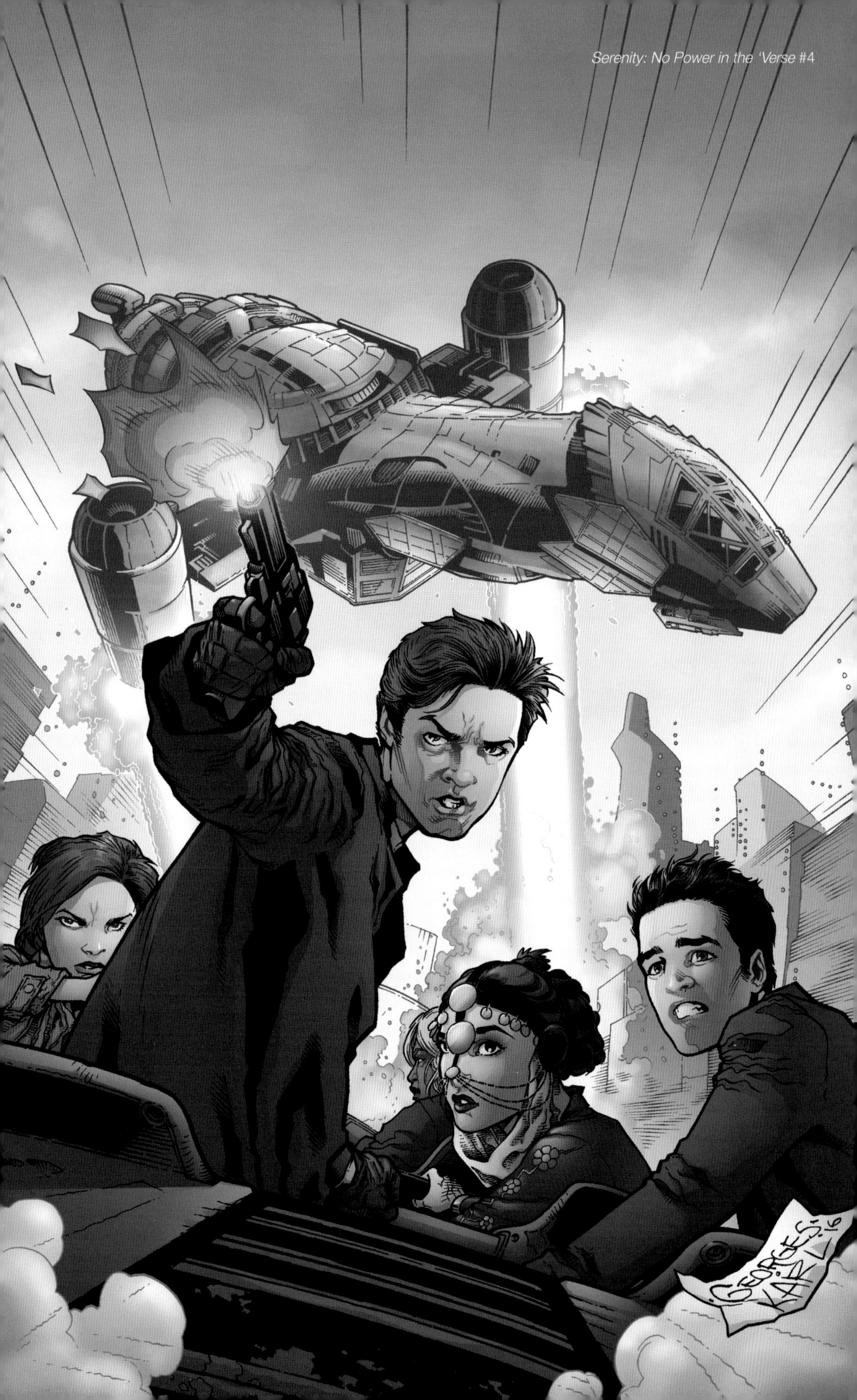
GEORGES. KARL '16

Serenity: No Power in the 'Verse #5

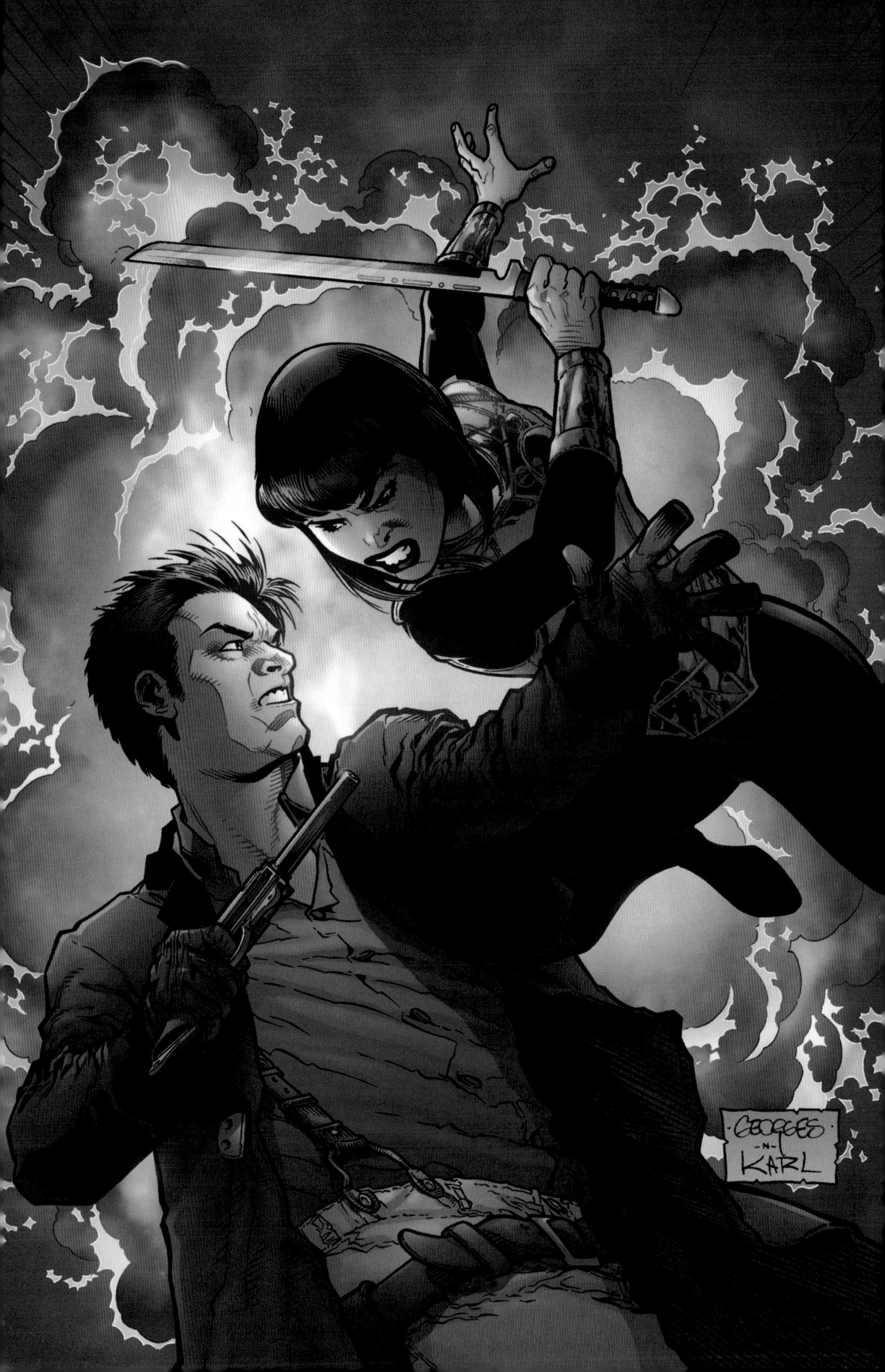

GEORGES
-N-
KARL

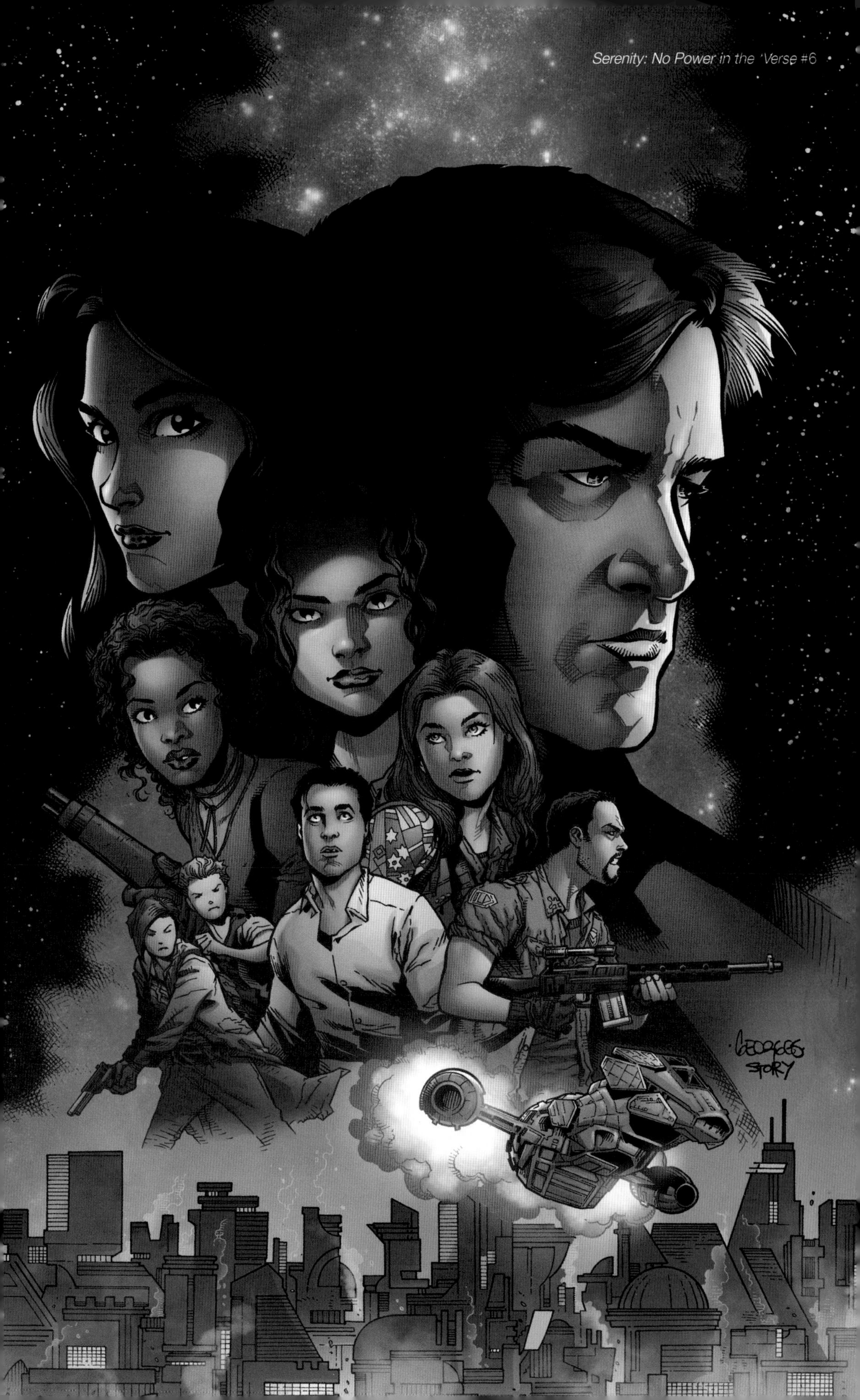
Serenity: No Power in the 'Verse #6
GEORGES STORY

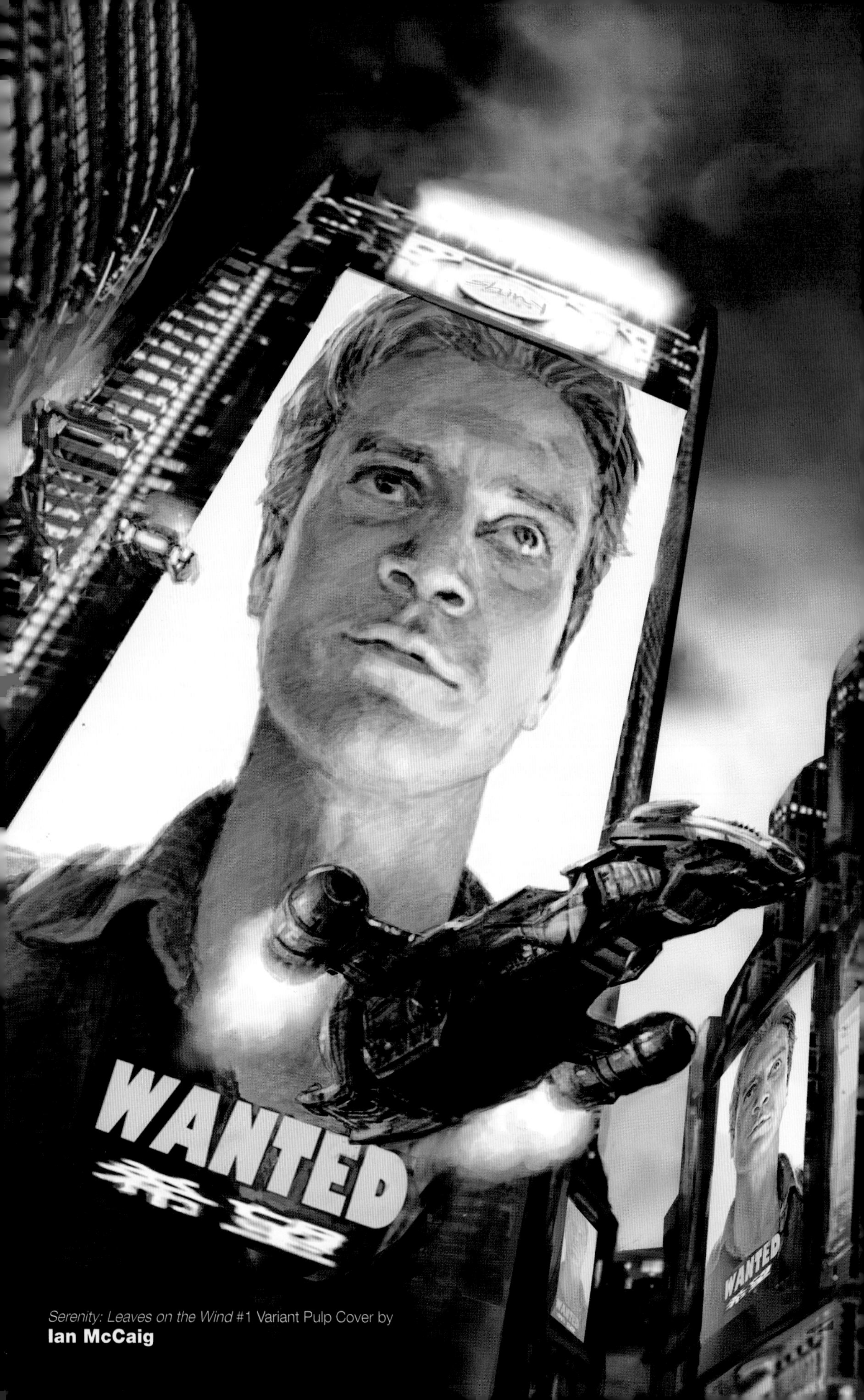
WANTED
WANTED

Serenity: Leaves on the Wind #1 Variant Pulp Cover by
Ian McCaig

Serenity: Leaves on the Wind #1 Variant Cover by
Jenny Frisson

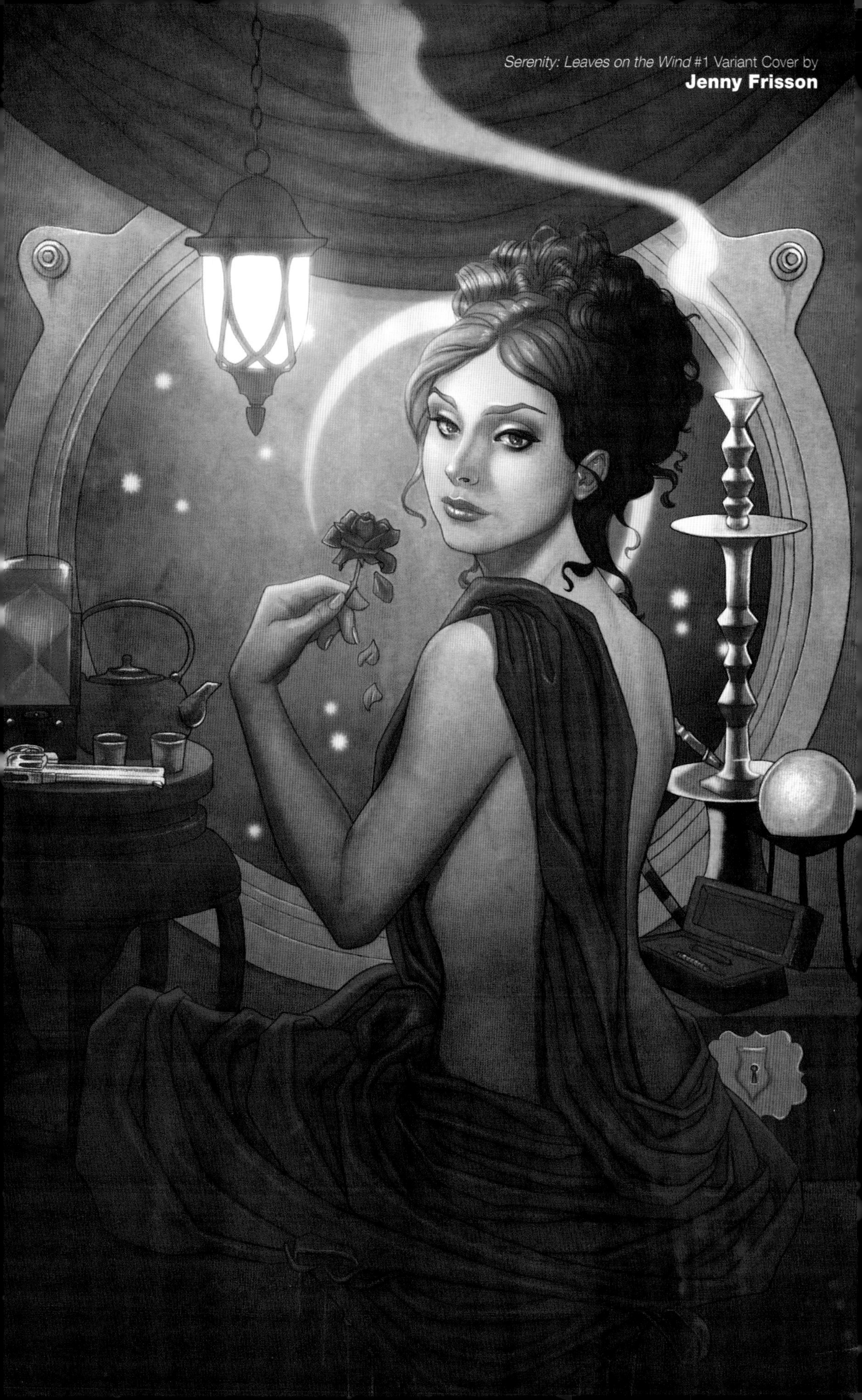

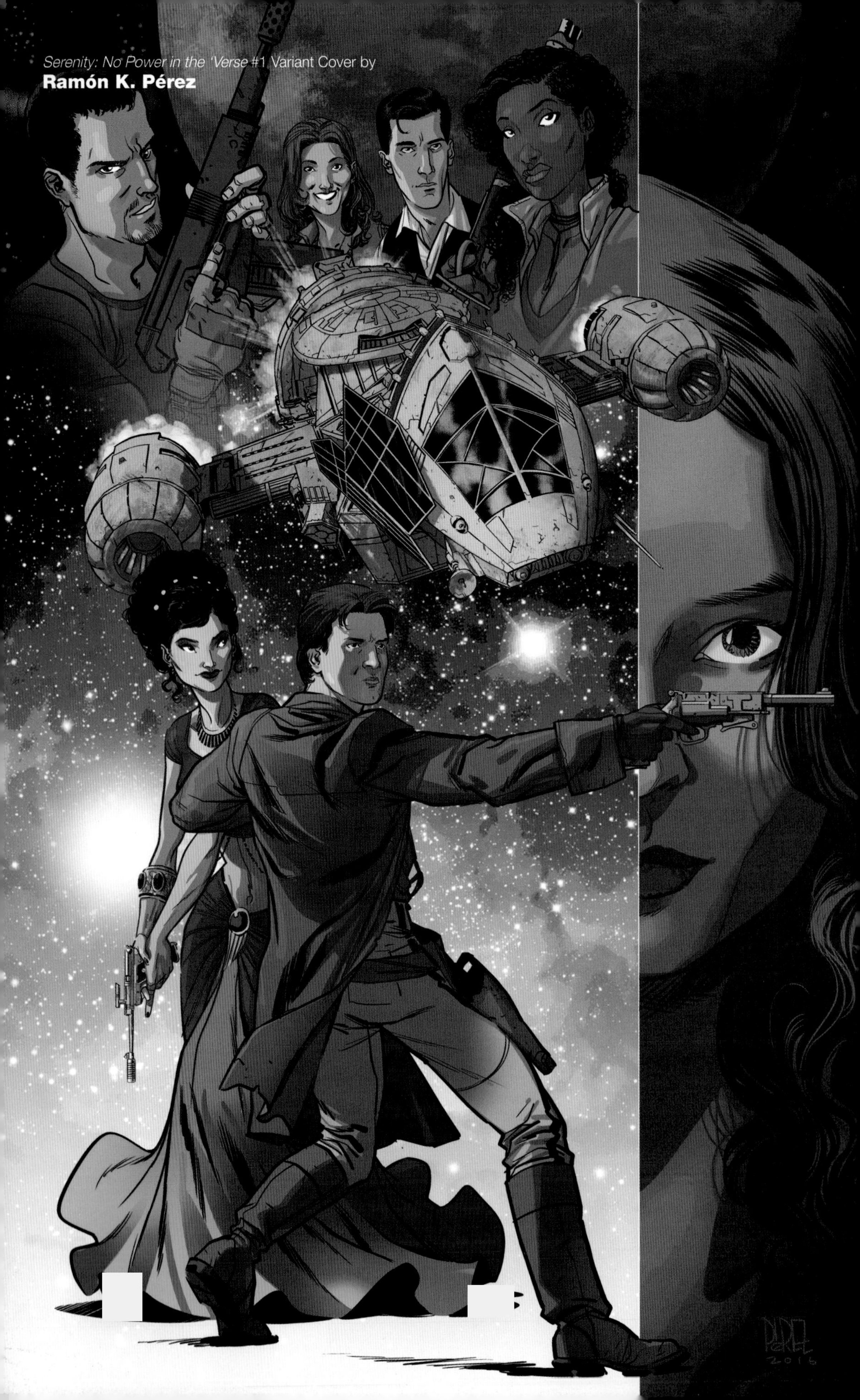

Serenity: No Power in the 'Verse #1 Variant Cover by
Ramón K. Pérez

Serenity: No Power in the 'Verse #1 Variant Cover by

Francesco Francavilla

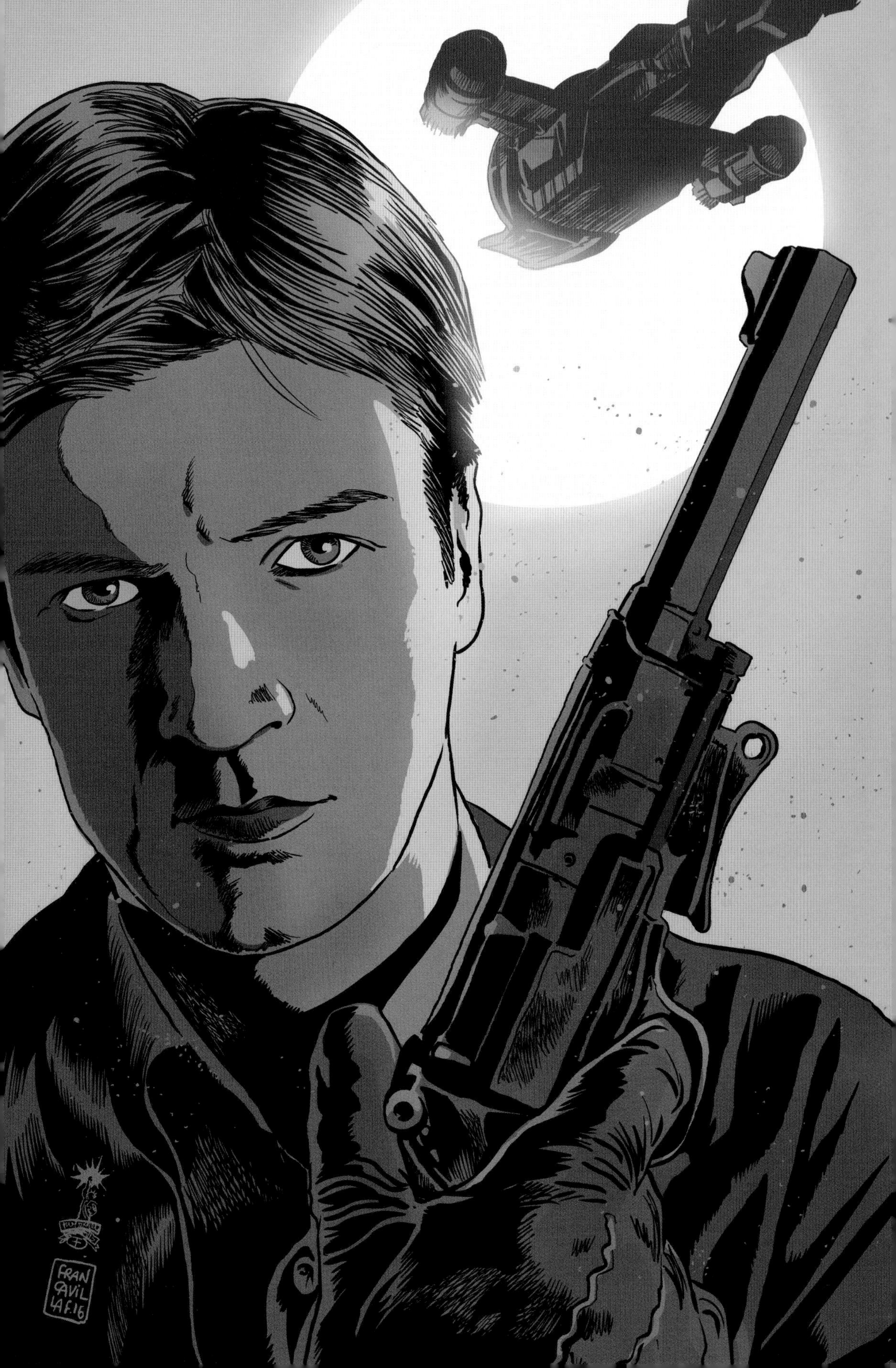

Serenity: No Power in the 'Verse #1 Variant Cover by
Yuko Shimizu

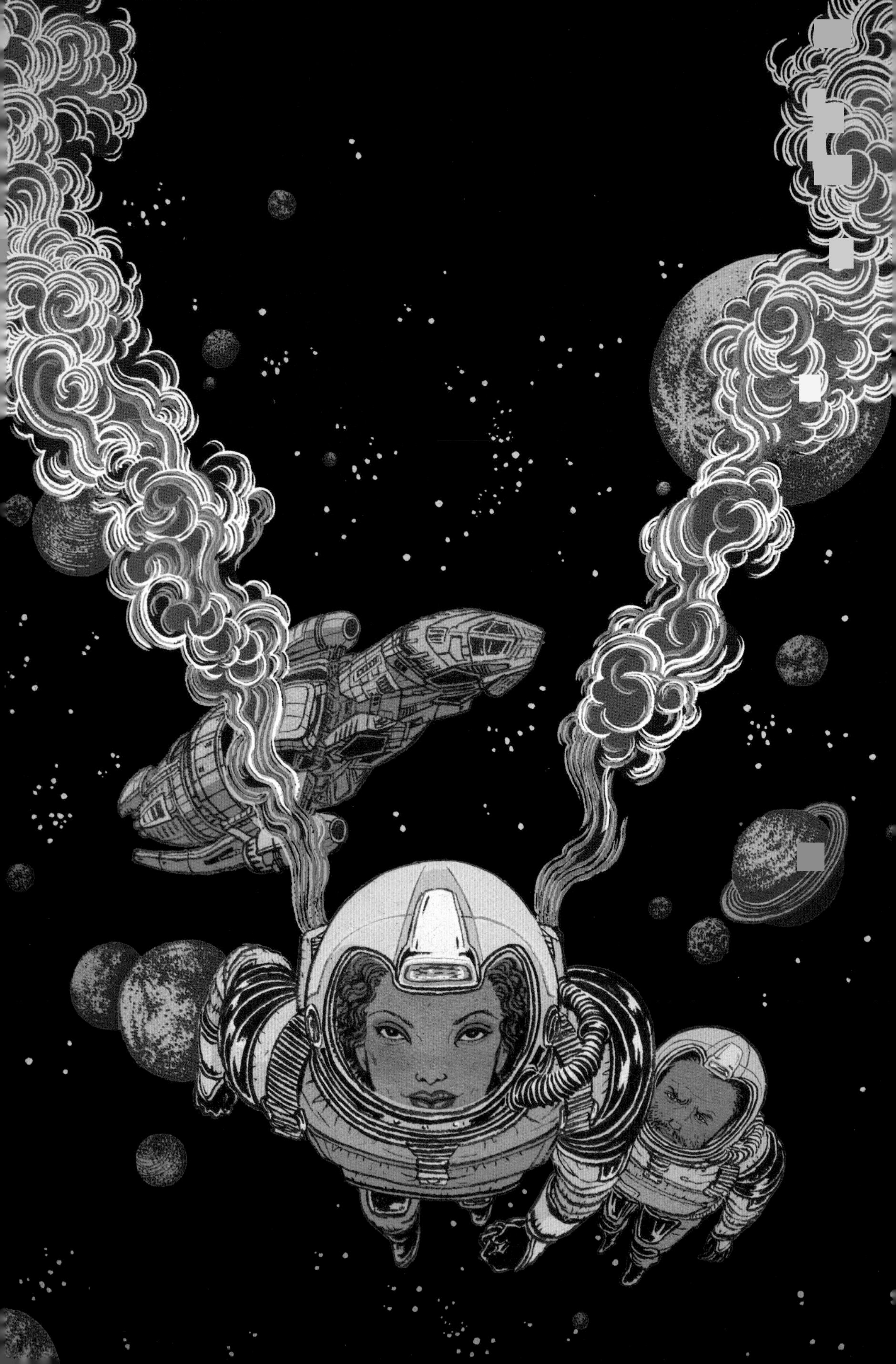

Serenity: No Power in the 'Verse #1 Variant Cover by
Adam Hughes

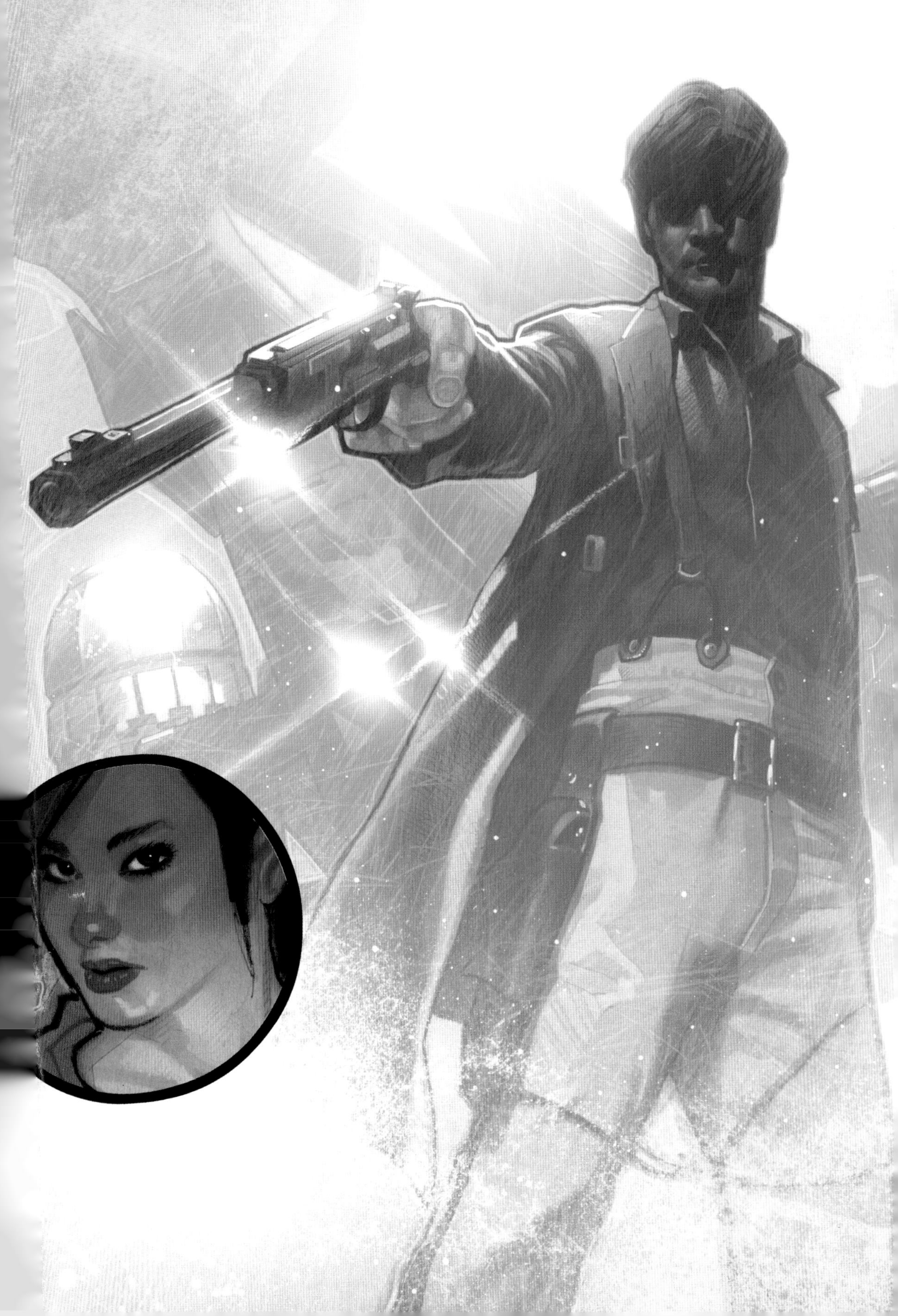

DISCOVER
VISIONARY CREATORS

THE WOODS
JAMES TYNION IV • MICHAEL DIALYNAS
VOL 1
THE ARROW

"The Spire is fantastic! My kind of genre free-for-all."
—BRIAN K. VAUGHAN (Saga)
THE SPIRE
SIMON SPURRIER
JEFF STOKELY
ANDRÉ MAY

MARK WAID • PETER KRAUSE
IRREDEEMABLE
AFTERWORD BY GRANT MORRISON

MARK WAID • JEAN DIAZ
INCORRUPTIBLE

MICHAEL ALAN NELSON
DAN MORA
GABRIEL CASSATA
HEXED
THE HARLOT & THE THIEF VOLUME ONE

ABNETT & CULBARD
WILD'S END
FIRST LIGHT
IT'S REALLY GREAT!
JEFF LEMIRE

BOOM! STUDIOS

AVAILABLE AT YOUR LOCAL COMICS SHOP AND BOOKSTORE

To find a comics shop in your area, visit www.comicshoplocator.com

WWW.**BOOM-STUDIOS**.COM

James Tynion IV
The Woods
Volume 1
ISBN: 978-1-60886-454-6 | $9.99 US
Volume 2
ISBN: 978-1-60886-495-9 | $14.99 US
Volume 3
ISBN: 978-1-60886-773-8 | $14.99 US

The Backstagers
Volume 1
ISBN: 978-1-60886-993-0 | $14.99 US

Simon Spurrier
Six-Gun Gorilla
ISBN: 978-1-60886-390-7 | $19.99 US

The Spire
ISBN: 978-1-60886-913-8 | $29.99 US

Weavers
ISBN: 978-1-60886-963-3 | $19.99 US

Mark Waid
Irredeemable
Volume 1
ISBN: 978-1-93450-690-5 | $16.99 US
Volume 2
ISBN: 978-1-60886-000-5 | $16.99 US

Incorruptible
Volume 1
ISBN: 978-1-60886-015-9 | $16.99 US
Volume 2
ISBN: 978-1-60886-028-9 | $16.99 US

Michael Alan Nelson
Hexed The Harlot & The Thief
Volume 1
ISBN: 978-1-60886-718-9 | $14.99 US
Volume 2
ISBN: 978-1-60886-816-2 | $14.99 US

Day Men
Volume 1
ISBN: 978-1-60886-393-8 | $9.99 US
Volume 2
ISBN: 978-1-60886-852-0 | $9.99 US

Dan Abnett
Wild's End
Volume 1: First Light
ISBN: 978-1-60886-735-6 | $19.99 US
Volume 2: The Enemy Within
ISBN: 978-1-60886-877-3 | $19.99 US

Hypernaturals
Volume 1
ISBN: 978-1-60886-298-6 | $16.99 US
Volume 2
ISBN: 978-1-60886-319-8 | $19.99 US